Cradle of the Union

know your
history —

Also by Erik Schlimmer

Thru Hiker's Guide to America

Blue Line to Blue Line

History Inside the Blue Line

My Adirondacks

Among the Cloud Splitters

Cradle of the Union

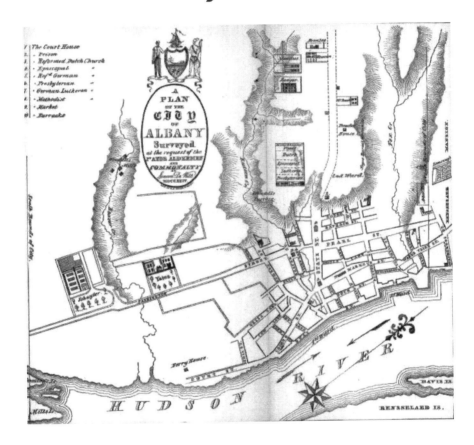

A Street by Street History of New York's Capital City

Erik Schlimmer

Foreword by John J. McEneny

ISBN 978-0-9891996-4-3

 Published by Beechwood Books of Rensselaer, New York, as an imprint under the protection of Friends of the Trans Adirondack Route, LLC.

 The tree colophon of Beechwood Books represents our world as well as the American beech (*Fagus grandifolia*) itself, a hardwood species native to the Northeast.

If you have corrections or additions to suggest, please contact the author directly: transadk@gmail.com.

Edited by Elizabeth Romero. Layout, design, and typesetting by Terry Bradshaw.

Cover image: "View in Albany, House of the First Dutch Governors" by Jacques Gérard Milbert (1766–1840) from 1819. This image portrays the home of Teunis Vanderpoel, which was built in 1682 and stood until 1832 at the northeast corner of State and North Pearl streets, once known as Elm Tree Corner. Milbert commented that "noteworthy is the palace of the former Dutch governors, whose odd, characteristic architecture aroused my curiosity to such an extent I decided to draw it." Digitized image courtesy SP Lohia Collection.

Title page image: "A Plan of the City of Albany" by Simeon DeWitt, 1794.

Author photo by Craig Carlson.

All other images are in the public domain and can be found within three sources:

New York Public Library Digital Collections:

https://digitalcollections.nypl.org

Library of Congress Prints and Photographs Online Catalog:

http://www.loc.gov/pictures/

New York Heritage Digital Collections of Albany Public Library (identified "courtesy APL"):

https://nyheritage.org/contributors/albany-public-library

For all the underdogs

"A sense of history is an antidote to self-pity and self-importance, of which there is much too much in our time." ~ David McCullough

CONTENTS

ACKNOWLEDGMENTS

As was the case when I was writing my two other history books, I relied on a combination of perceptive individuals and good old-fashioned research. Historians, researchers, authors, and salt-of-the-earth Capital Region residents provided invaluable support and research clues during the years it took to produce *Cradle of the Union*. I have great appreciation for Bernice Aviza; Walter Ayres, Sacred Heart Church parish life coordinator; Hank Bankhead, Albany Heritage Area Visitor Center tour guide; Laura Barber, New York State Unified Court System principal law librarian; Stefan Bielinski, retired New York State Department of Education historian; Michael F. Conners II, Albany County comptroller; Lelia Danker; Joel Davis, University at Albany student financial services director; Louie Fasciolo, SP Lohia Collection; Kevin Franklin, Town of Colonie historian; Stephen Frankoski, Benevolent and Protective Order of Elks Albany secretary; Scott Gallup, Capital Hills at Albany Golf Course superintendent; Bradley Glass, City of Albany principal planner; Paul Grondahl, *Times Union* reporter; Dianne Hansen, Manning Boulevard Neighborhood Association president; Peter Hess, author of the *People of Albany* series; David Hochfelder, University at Albany history professor; and William Hummel, Albany Fire Department battalion chief.

Equally appreciated are Susan Leath, Town of Bethlehem historian; Gerald Ladouceur; Roy McDonald, former senator from New York; Sean McLaughlin, City of Albany confidential assistant to the director of planning and development; Mary Millus, City of Albany geographic information systems manager; Kathleen Naughter; Mike Nolan, University at Albany communications specialist; Tony Opalka, City of Albany historian; William B. Picotte, Picotte Companies senior vice president; John Pipkin, University at Albany geography and planning professor; Rosemary E. Redmond; Lyle Renodin; Melissa Samuels, University at Albany alumni programs director; Charles L. Touhey, Touhey Associates; and Cheryle Webber and Ellen Zunon, Dutch Settlers Society of Albany.

The staff at the University at Albany's University Library were most helpful, especially when it came to letting me borrow in-house-only research material and facilitating interlibrary loan items. Albany Public Library's local history room that contains the Pruyn Collection of Albany History and this room's staff proved priceless. A treasure of information was unearthed at the Albany County Hall of Records, and their staff were most helpful sorting through the gems and rubies of their archival collection. Sean Krause and Liz Romero helped build the indexes, a tedious process at best, and Liz served as editor as well, buffing a final sheen onto my work. Adam Etringer, Pat Parks, Christy Ralston, Glenn Read, John Sasso, and Lucille S. Uhlman served as proofreaders. Terry Bradshaw skillfully designed and typeset the manuscript.

Two men deserve special recognition, and they are Jack McEneny and Jason Privler. They dedicated many hours of their personal time to review and expand the *Cradle of the Union* manuscript, sharing the depth and breadth of their expertise and asking for nothing in return. As the author of *Albany*, Jack is a wellspring of wisdom. Even when he fell seriously ill, he demanded he assist me in any way he could. Encouraging him to recover from his unexpected illness first, I told him, "You really don't have to worry about my project. Just take care of yourself." Without hesitation he replied, "No, no, no. I promised to help you. If I have trouble reading the manuscript, I'll just have my wife read the entire thing to me out loud and dictate my responses." Sticking with my research project right to its end, Jack was kind enough to contribute the foreword.

The meeting of Jason was serendipitous. A year or two into my research, I arranged to meet Jack for the first time. We chose to rendezvous at a local research facility to discuss street name history. Initially unbeknown to us, Jason just happened to be in that facility at the exact same moment, by mere chance standing close enough to overhear our conversation. The timing proved priceless when he offered to help me in my project. Few men know more about Albany history than Jason does.

APPRECIATION

It is with great sorrow and honor that I am able to share with my readers a little about my grandfather, Richard Ward, who died at the age of 92 the day I finished writing *Cradle of the Union*. The timing of his death, as it relates to my career as a writer, is peculiar. My grandmother, Nancy Ward, died at the age of 87 in August 2014, just three weeks after my book *My Adirondacks* was published. It's frightening that while I mature as a writer, the people I love continue to disappear. I suppose I'm learning that such is life, though. My grandfather was born in Poughkeepsie, New York, on July 17, 1925, to Charles C. Ward and Georgianna Veach Ward as the oldest of five boys. To put that era into perspective, the day after my grandfather was born was the day Adolf Hitler had the first volume of his *Mein Kampf* published. This dictator's rise to power would define the prime years of my grandfather's life. But more on that later.

Richard Ward and Nancy Way,
G.I. Town, circa 1950

When my grandfather was a kid, he worked as a berry picker and newspaper boy. He then worked for an iron works and was later employed at the Bacu Ice Company, which was founded in Poughkeepsie when he was ten days old. A *Poughkeepsie Eagle News* article from that year, 1925, stated that the Bacu Ice Company was operating out of a brand-new "big brick building" that had an "advanced water system" to make ice. The building and equipment set this company back a lot of money, but investors were optimistic: "Because of the fact that pure ice can be obtained to meet the strictest standard, the firm is confident that it will succeed." By 1941, Bacu was defending its trenches from a frontal assault of Freon-powered refrigerators. Despite this company reminding customers that old-time iceboxes were "the least expensive of all ways to keep food at a cool enough temperature to prevent spoilage," Americans were ready for something new. But Bacu wasn't. They thought it silly that newfangled refrigerators were "incorporating gadgets" into their construction. Bacu faded during the World War II era despite diversifying their services and offering "fur storage for local furriers." This original Bacu Ice Company building still stands at 35 High Street.

My grandfather attended Poughkeepsie High School for three years, obtained his general equivalency diploma, and then entered the Army in October 1943 as a field lineman, for, as his contract stipulated, "the duration of the War or other emergency, plus six months, subject to the discretion of the President or otherwise according to law." On June 6, 1944, he took part in the assault of Omaha Beach in German-occupied France, wading through bloody salt water and staggering past the bodies of fellow soldiers towards the relative protection of the coast's chalk cliffs. He fought throughout the European Theater and later survived the Battle of the Bulge in France, Belgium, and Luxembourg. During this five-week battle the Germans sustained somewhere between 70,000 and 125,000 casualties, while the Americans saw approximately 10,000 killed, 50,000 wounded, and 25,000 captured or missing in action. Between the two sides, equipment loss was stunning: 2,000 tanks and heavy guns blown to scrap and 2,000 aircraft destroyed. My grandfather operated in combat zones with the 29th Infantry Division for two years and was awarded the American Defense Service Ribbon, American Campaign Ribbon, Army Good Conduct Ribbon, European-African-Middle Eastern Campaign Ribbon (with four campaign stars), and French Croix De Guerre Ribbon (with arrowhead device for his amphibious assault on D Day).

On a few occasions I asked my grandfather about his war experiences, but he didn't want to talk about them. He told me only one brief story, sharing it just a few years before he died. This was shortly after the death of my grandmother, and I felt an urgency to learn all I could about my grandfather before he died, too. We were eating a dinner of ham, mashed potatoes, and corn that I had made for us in his home when I asked a question I already knew the answer to. I figured it was an innocuous conversation-starter. "Gramps, how did you get to Europe to fight in the war? You were on a ship, right?" Being a man of few words, he looked up from his meal and said, "Yeah. We took a ship." Yet the ship brought back other, more vivid memories, and he decided to share one of them with me.

He told me how his unit was clearing an evacuated French town and stumbled upon a dead Army paratrooper, who had parachuted behind the front lines, hanging off a power pole by his parachute and harness. His parachute had gotten caught on the pole, perhaps during a nighttime jump, and he hadn't been able to release himself from his harness before being killed by Nazi soldiers. By the time my grandfather's unit came across this young American, passing Nazis had used his body for target practice, shooting it dozens of times. Being a former Army paratrooper myself, I hastily thought I could relate to the doomed soldier and imagine what it would be like to be stuck there in my harness, unable to reach my rifle strapped to my leg. But I had no idea what it was like to be in World War II, let alone what it was like to have been in that paratrooper's or my grandfather's boots in that little French town. After telling me this story, my grandfather aimlessly played with his mashed potatoes with his fork for a moment. Then he looked back up and asked me how school was.

After being discharged in January 1946, my grandfather returned to Poughkeepsie and lived on Bellevue Avenue near the train station. This street used to connect Harris Avenue with South Clover Street, but Harris Avenue is long-gone, today's Route 9 running over its grave. The brownstone house my grandfather lived in is also gone. No homes are on Bellevue Avenue today—it's a 100-foot dead-end street. In 1951, he moved to a little community in the city known as G.I. Town, which was located on the corner of Hooker Avenue and South Grand Avenue. This neighborhood of little white cottages earned its name due to so many World War II veterans living there. It was there that he met his future wife, my future grandmother, Nancy Way. She had moved into the community three years earlier as a single mother with her two young daughters, Velvet and Lee. Today an apartment complex built during the 1970s stands on the grave of G.I. Town. My grandfather, grandmother, mother, and aunt then moved to Cannon Street in 1952. Richard and Nancy married in 1954, and this family of four then moved to Lincoln Avenue. They moved to Franklin Street the following year. By the time my grandparents moved to their final home, on Beechwood Park, in 1969, my mother and aunt had started families of their own. They purchased this final home—a three-bedroom, two-story brick house at the end of this dead-end street—for $22,000. It's now appraised at a quarter-million dollars.

In the 1950s, my grandfather, despite being a high school dropout, became a civil engineer for the State of New York after running his own auto garage on the other side of the river in Newburgh. The engineering project he was most proud of during his career was the Hudson Valley section of Interstate 84, which he helped build during his first decade on the job. During the 1970s and 1980s my grandfather survived two terrible accidents while working in the field. In the 1970s, he was run over by a massive six-wheeled motor grader at a road project. What saved his life was that it had rained heavily before the accident and the other five wheels supported the machine. He spent a few days in the hospital after being smashed facedown in the mud. In the 1980s he wasn't so lucky. While working on a paving project, a steamroller was backing up, its driver wasn't paying attention, and a young workman next to the steamroller wasn't paying attention. My grandfather shoved the young workman out of the way to save his life but then my grandfather was pinned between the steamroller and a blacktop spreader. The lower half of his left leg was sheared off just below the knee, and his other leg, which the doctors saved, was broken in seven places. During the 1990s, more than a decade after he retired from the state due to the steamroller accident, his snowblower gnawed two of his fingers off. My grandmother, who had a keen sense of humor, warned him with a tsk-tsk tone, "Dick, if you keep this up they're going to bury you in a shoebox."

My grandmother lived at their Beechwood Park home for 45 years. She died one night in August 2014 while climbing the stairs with my grandfather. They were on their way to bed. My grandfather lived in this home, by himself, for another three years until he went downstairs one morning in March 2018, entered the kitchen for breakfast, and dropped dead on the floor. Our family plumber, who had known my grandparents for more than forty years, found him a few hours later.

What I know my grandfather experienced in old-time Poughkeepsie is only what he told me, and he didn't tell me much. I know that when he was a kid no one locked their doors, residents would grab their pillows and blankets on especially steamy nights and go sleep in Eastman Park, the port on the Hudson River was busy shipping local beer south to New York City, and everyone knew all their neighbors but pretty much minded their business. The death of my grandfather is the end of an era for my family. We now know no one who witnessed the Great Depression, voted during the Truman election, was born at home, or lived in Poughkeepsie since the day they were born.

As each of us age, we wonder what history will say of us, what our children and grandchildren will remember best about us. What I remember best about my grandfather, Richard Ward, is that he was a great man from the Greatest Generation. He was someone who worked long days but found time to raise a family, was never rich but always paid for things in cash, and was handsome but remained faithful to his wife of sixty years. He was the type of man who never took for granted the sacrifices Americans made before his time, just like I never took for granted the sacrifices he made for today's Americans. Therefore, Gramps, this history book's for you.

FOREWORD

The people of Albany love their history. They read their favorite local authors, visit the city's museums, search archives in libraries, and challenge lively history bloggers. They especially enjoy searching for those odd facts and undiscovered mysteries that give this city its individual character. Yet, somehow, one obvious underappreciated resource stares them in the face from every view and thoroughfare, guiding them through every neighborhood where they carry out their daily lives. These are Albany's street signs. Leave it to Erik Schlimmer, a writer who's as at home relating the tales of the Adirondacks as he is when searching for the origins of urban roadways. More than just a compiler of names, Erik restores a new appreciation for the commonplace among these integral parts of our home environment.

Albany was never one of those communities that was content to let the logical succession of numerical names satisfy the hopes of taxi and pizza delivery drivers who try to navigate the city. We maxed out with Fourth Avenue and Third and North Third streets. (Nineteenth Street was a notable exception, but mercifully renamed before anyone got too attached to it.)

After all, the selection of street names immortalizes the leaders who established Albany in its days of infancy. How many families living in the homes of Pine Hills realize they live in a neighborhood whose names were designated to immortalize Dutch colonists like Bancker, Ryckman or De Peyster, the long forgotten mayors of Albany? National and state leaders, not to mention great military heroes, receive their well-deserved gratitude from citizens whenever they say their names on the signs and give directions to addresses.

But it's not just the great and near-great who have been christened with each street sign. Amid the logical and often attractive or woodsy names of most developments' new street names, there often lingers the name of a farm that once existed, which tells the story of a family that once tilled the soil or raised the livestock within that now-unrecognizable land. Names like Weis, Ramsey, and Van Schoick seem incongruent with neighboring compatible street names of trees and birds. These old surnames, if only surviving in street names, remind us of the very continuity and change that make a city unique from generation to generation.

As far back as the break-up of Philip Schuyler's South End estate, the naming of adjoining streets still remind us of the close relationship of the celebrated Hamilton and Schuyler family members who once lived in their mansion. Later on, streets carved out of the lawns of Whitehall came to memorialize Ten Eyck family members. Developments covering the former uptown farms immortalize members of the Besch and Picotte families and scores of others whose labors still make their mark on the city through architecture and street names.

Many names give allusions to antiquity, colleges, industries, and Mother Nature. Their origins are common and need little explanation. But then again, *Cradle of the Union* shows us that, in Albany, there are always exceptions to the predictable. Easily overlooked is the name of a prominent West Albany railroad personality named Buchanan whose street sign is located in sequence to that of several presidents. Guess whose memory, without this discovery, would be eclipsed in favor of the national personality? Historians have helped name streets after long-forgotten mansions like Greyledge. The names of folk heroes were chosen by their contemporary fans at that time. Their names once all had clear origins, yet many other origins were subsequently unknown. Some seem to have no relationship to our area at all, such as Tampa, Orlando, Hopi, and Zuni.

Erik's book has brought back many fond memories. His extensive research has drawn on innumerable publications, newspapers, and irreplaceable oral history. His result has accomplished what has been wished for on many occasions over at least the last fifty years in my memory. While the book restores much missing information, the author has left us with more than a few mysteries still unsolved. May this effort encourage future historians to keep searching for new information and no doubt argue with enthusiasm as we continue to embrace and explore our beloved city.

JOHN J. MCENENY
NEW YORK ASSEMBLYMAN (RET.)
FORMER ALBANY COUNTY HISTORIAN

INTRODUCTION

Why

The quest for knowledge centers on age-old questions, and one of them is, *Why is that thing over there called that?* We all possess instinctive interest in finding the meaning behind what's communicated to us, and we experience delightful Sherlock Holmes-esque moments when we decode something cryptic, especially something others have not bothered to think much about. Every term that's communicated to us—a logo, a brand name, a saying, the names of New York communities (and of course the names of streets)—usually has a sophisticated and entertaining story behind it.

For example, the original logo of Sirius Satellite Radio (now known as Sirius/XM) was a dog. A dog was chosen because Sirius, the brightest star in our night sky, is nicknamed the Dog Star (look closely at this broadcast company's logo and you'll notice the dog's eye is a star). Sirius is found in the constellation Canis Major, Latin for "Greater Dog." The brand name Häagen-Dazs was invented by the founder of this company, Reuben Mattus, a Jewish man from Poland, who immigrated to the U.S. He wanted to honor Denmark, the country that saved incalculable Jewish lives during World War II. So he created the name Häagen-Dazs, which sounds Danish but actually means nothing. The saying "a cakewalk" stems from a style of intricate dance performed within black communities in the U.S. during the 1800s and was coined in 1874. Competitions using this style of dance were held, and the prize was a fancy cake (we also get the saying "that takes the cake" from these competitions). In New York you can visit communities named Cairo, Horseheads, Oswegatchie, Alabama, Ephratah, Hannibal, Redhouse, Swastika, and Sempronius. How could there not be good stories behind each of these names? Just as there are hidden curious stories behind logos, brand names, sayings, and settlements, there are equally veiled and entertaining tales behind street names.

Street name history is a fresh endeavor for me. My background is in decoding features far from the hustle and bustle of city streets. I decode names in the mountains. The Adirondack Mountains of Upstate New York, my traditional area of study, hold thousands of natural features with names, such names dubbed "toponyms." The range holds nearly 2,000 named mountains alone. I took the time to decode hundreds of toponyms in two books, *History Inside the Blue Line* and *Among the Cloud Splitters*. Within these volumes I revealed stories of Civil War politicians, hardy settlers, natural disasters, and men of science, for examples, who are memorialized through the features Seymour

Mountain, Alford Mountain, Avalanche Lake, and Mount Redfield, respectively. I decoded simple names like Moose Pond and Cold River and was left scratching my head regarding obscure features such as Chicken Coop Brook and Latham Pond. I fell in love with decoding toponyms, and my readers fell in love with me doing all the work, which was a labor of love. As I worked through more than 200 research sources for these two books, one name kept popping up: Verplanck Colvin. If there even is such a thing, Colvin was a famous 1800s surveyor. His name is legend in the Adirondack Mountains. Ascending peaks, paddling lakes and rivers, camping on high summits, and stamping his feet in the cold, he became first to map the Adirondack region. A man must be important to have not one but two features named for him. Verplanck Colvin is immortalized through Colvin Brook and Mount Colvin.

Carrying a curiosity with me for how New York features got their names, one sunny day during the summer of 2014 I found myself driving down Washington Avenue in the City of Albany. I had recently moved to the Capital Region for work and to begin a graduate degree program. As I was driving west, an adjacent street sign caught my eye: Colvin Avenue. I guessed it was named for Verplanck Colvin, and I stored that guess away for later contemplation. A week later I was driving down Western Avenue and noticed a historical marker on this street between Cortland Place and Quail Street. Being one of those people who actually stops to read such markers, I pulled over, walked up to it, and read it: "The Elms. Home of Verplanck Colvin, surveyor of the Adirondack Wilderness and state lands from 1872 to 1900. Champion of the N.Y. forest preserve." This sign intensified my interest in Colvin's connection to Colvin Avenue. Research revealed this street is actually named for his father, Senator Andrew Colvin, though during the late 1800s the younger Colvin owned property where the namesake street now is. I then said something to myself that began four years of rigorous research: *I wonder how all these other streets got their names.*

How

To begin my investigation I needed to find or compose a list containing every street within the City of Albany. Being unaware of the extent of the city, I figured there were maybe 200 streets to decode. I assumed I would make quick work of these streets, finding official city documents that listed when, why, and for whom each street was named. I predicted it would be less a research project and more a task of transcribing orderly information that already existed. I could not have been more wrong.

I contacted the City of Albany and made a connection with a geographic information systems specialist, who indeed had the city's official list of streets. I received this Excel file the same day of my inquiry and happily opened this alphabetically-arranged document. Yet much confusion arose from the very list that would get my project started. The 6,107-line file includes sections of pavement that are not true streets, such as the 678 on- and off-ramps of interstates and highways and the 103 driveways identified. The file also habitually repeats street names, is comprised partly of streets that fall outside City of Albany boundaries, and includes streets that no longer exist. With much editing I pruned this sprawling list by eliminating faux streets and ensuring each street is within the city's limits. This latter task was completed by consulting two geographic information systems resources: the city's Parcel Viewer and its Ward Boundaries interactive programs. Eventually, that initial 6,107-line file was pared down to a succinct alphabetical list of Albany's 785 formal streets.

Ninety percent of the streets on my new list I had never even heard of, let alone visited. Academy Road, Access Road, Adirondack Street . . . Bancker Street, Bancroft Street, Barclay Street . . . Caldwell Street, Cambridge Road, Campus Access Road . . . Daisy Lane, Dale Street, Dallius Street . . . On and on the names cascaded. By the time I got to street number 200 I still wasn't even out of the D's! I finally panned to the end of my eighteen-page list to meet Zuni Street. There were nearly 600 more streets within Albany than I had thought.

Not one to give up easily, I maintained course to decode every single street within New York's capital city. I started poking around the Internet for street name information and found a few valuable sources, notably Stefan Bielinski's outstanding Colonial Albany Social History Project. Then I took my first walking history tour of downtown Albany and got a feel for who did what in Albany when. I noticed street naming patterns and was handed a few answers during the tour. I took a second walking tour, this journey a personal one with none other than Bielinski himself. The retired historian was patient with me, a guy who had only recently become aware of North Pearl Street, where we met, and had no clue as to why it would be named after those valuable commodities, if that was in fact what it was named after. We strolled down James Street, Broadway, Van Tromp Street, Chapel Street, Columbia Street, and Steuben Street, among others, the proud tour guide figuratively leading me among Dutch sloops, Indians, Civil War heroes, politicians, and long-dead merchants. At Steuben Street, Bielinski asked, "You must know why Steuben Street's named so, right?" I shook my head. "It's named for the Prussian . . . you know . . . von Steuben." The historian's tone was trivial, as if to communicate, "Erik, everyone in this city knows Steuben Street is named for Baron Friedrich Wilhelm August Heinrich Ferdinand von Steuben, the Prussian who fought in the War of the Austrian Succession and the French and Indian War before joining the American Revolution after meeting Benjamin Franklin in Paris in 1777 only to arrive with his dog, Azor, and then write the first training manual for the Continental Army!" All I could offer was, "Oh. I see."

I think Bielinski had his doubts about me reaching my research goal, especially because other scholars had promised to tackle such a project, and yet they had each faded into the mist. One historian, Virginia Bowers, had made decent progress decoding street names before dying during her research. I could not have blamed Bielinski for possible reservations about me. I was feeling overwhelmed by the end of our hour-long walk, though I did manage to fill three pages of notes while trying to keep up with his expert narration. Bielinski made something clear at the end of our stroll: There is no single source that tells when, why, or for whom each street was named. I would be exploring uncharted territory, and I would be alone a lot of the time for few people are closely familiar with Albany history, and only a few of those few know street name history. As one man wrote to me when I was just beginning this project, "I think the general knowledge of Albany history is that the Dutch and later English arrived at Albany, stole all the land, traded for valuable furs with beads and useless trinkets, and killed all the Indians with foreign diseases and drove them into extinction. Some of the more successful Dutch and English may have had streets named for them." I would have to dig to get a lead, then dig somewhere else to get a lead on that lead. By the end of this research project my shovel would be worn out, its handle splintered and oily, the head rusted and bent. The theme of my assignment would be "Little gold, lots of dirt."

After my walking tours and consultation with Bielinski, it was time to hit the books. Books are generally shunned by researchers half my age, bound material deemed fuddy-duddy, paper products christened holdovers. Nonsense. However, I had no sound method for chasing specific street names. I figured I could read books cover to cover and keep a sharp lookout for personal names that coincided with street names. For example, if I were to stumble across notable Albany figures named Bancker, Maguire, or Ten Eyck, perhaps they had connections to Bancker Street, Maguire Avenue, or Ten Eyck Avenue, respectively. I read classics first, a sample of them being Hislop's *Albany*, McEneny's *Albany*, Van Laer's *Settlers of Rensselaerswyck 1630–1658*, and Venema's *Beverwijck*. Old-time books were read, too, a few of them being Clark's *The Heroes of Albany* from 1867, Munsell's *The Annals of Albany* from 1859, Weise's *The History of the City of Albany* from 1884, and Ashley's *New York State Men* from 1918. I reviewed past books I had read, at the time of initial readings having no idea they would tie into a future street name project. Catton's *The Civil War*, Bolton's *Coronado*, McCullough's *1776*, and Wissler's *Indians of the United States* were worth revisiting. Beyond these hefty publications I read newspapers ranging from the *Times Union* to the long-gone *The Knickerbocker News* and examined trustworthy websites extending from those managed by the Albany Housing Authority to the United States Geological Survey.

Once I gained leads on why some streets may be named so, I examined unusually obscure books to shed light on characters and access additional history. The more esoteric sources included Albany County's *Index to the Public Records of the County of Albany, State of New York, 1630–1894*, Fletcher's *Leicestershire Pedigrees and Royal Descents*, the city's *Laws and Ordinances of the Common Council of the City of Albany*, and *The American Whig Review, Volume Six*, a 650-page behemoth from 1847 that was written anonymously and could be classified as a nonnarcotic sleep aid. These in turn led me back to modern books that had nothing to do with street names yet enriched biographies and clarified narratives. These included Elder's *What's Race Got to Do with It*, Sowell's *Wealth, Poverty, and Politics*, Isenberg's *Sex and Citizenship in Antebellum America*, and Shapiro's *Project President*.

I read street name books dedicated to Philadelphia, Brooklyn, Chicago, St. Paul, Baltimore, the Bronx, and Manhattan to see if those locales' streets had historical overlap with Albany's city streets, and I wanted to learn these authors' approaches to decoding and writing. I figuratively left the smog and crowds and headed back to the mountains for a short time by reading place name books about Vermont's Long Trail, the South's Smoky Mountains, and New Hampshire's White Mountains. I examined place name documents about New Jersey, Ohio, Pennsylvania, Missouri, Massachusetts, and the American West's and Midwest's railroad stops and one-horse towns because street name clues may turn up where one least expects them. Nearly every historical Albany map and atlas was perused, surnames were explored through *A Dictionary of Surnames* and *Encyclopedia of American Family Names*, and genealogies were deconstructed.

I trusted Bielinski's comment on how there was no expansive source that told the history of Albany street names. Nonetheless, I chased rumors of illuminating engineer reports and other official documents. I came up empty-handed despite visiting a host of city and county offices in which I believe I eventually started annoying staff with my mysterious and persistent inquiries. The *Times Union* ran a story about my research project in which they were kind enough to invite readers to assist me, and I created a Facebook community where visitors could lend street name historical hints. Through this social media source a few definite answers were offered to me, yet there were many more wild goose chases. Not giving up on the locals, I interviewed historians, public servants, authors, developers, and residents. They offered answers and support that inspired me not to quit. Upon examining early drafts of my manuscript they offered feedback: "You nailed that one—nice work," "Oh, that one's easy. It's named for so-and-so," and "I don't know why that street is named so, but it's definitely not named for *that*." Throw in analysis of more than 700 print and online sources from every conceivable corner of my local interlibrary loan office and the Internet, and research concluded after four years of full-time work, yet only after a handful of proofreaders and historians studied the 560-page manuscript prior to publication. It really was as simple as that!

What

During my research I scrutinized histories that were authenticated, biographies that were written, timelines that were assembled, and stories that were told, and this brings us to a discussion regarding what *Cradle of the Union* is and what it means to readers. As with the conversation Bielinski and I had before my research had even begun, during this project I was exploring new land where I had to use deduction, intellect, and good old-fashioned hunches to reach points at which I could conclude, This street is named for so-and-so. Such confidence is rare in street name research for there is little science to interpreting absent or unclear history. A goal of obtaining absolute historical confirmation for 785 street names is impossible.

Additionally, when one examines nearly 1,000 sources produced across a period of 500 years, with many of these sources initially written in foreign languages, conflicting information will be encountered. One source would give birth and death dates of such-and-such while another source would offer conflicting dates. Supposed matching names were spelled in myriad ways (a local historian commented that "there was no correct spelling for any word" in distant history, and that "any combination of letters caused a reader to say the word was okay"), persons were confirmed to be relatives and then proved not to be relatives, the sizes of families waxed and waned, and a few times the math just didn't add up (like when I calculated that a Supreme Court judge began that position when he was 12 years old). Sources confidently explained why a street may be named so, and I would discover a source that theorized otherwise. As I learned years ago, there can never be a final edition of a place name book. So, every place name author at some point needs to say to himself, to quote a publisher I work with, To hell with it! If such authors were to interminably work on manuscripts, there would be no place name books.

Cradle of the Union is not merely a book about Albany. Broader and deeper than this capital city itself, this publication conveys national and world history told through one American city. Compared to other street name books, this one dives deep enough to make your ears pop. Between the covers of *Cradle of the Union* you can travel to every corner of this 332-year-old city from the historic and confining downtown district to the breezy and rolling suburbs on streets named for Revolutionary War heroes, mathematicians, presidents, abolitionists, and explorers, among others. Among those street names are sprinkled the names of flowers, communities, trees, universities, rivers, and other odds and ends. From the first entry that discusses an Albany educational institution that opened in 1817 to the last entry that describes an American Indian tribe discovered by conquistadors in 1540, I write for the pleasure of gritty detective work and the thrill of the hunt. I write to answer the age-old question, *Why is that thing over there called that?*

A

Academy Road

Formerly called Highland Avenue, Academy Road is now named so because the Albany Academy was relocated there. Don Rittner reported in his *Times Union* article "Another Removal of Albany History Hits the Road" that today's Academy Road area during the 1920s was home to "some of the first suburban tracts to go up in Albany as the city moved off the flood plain and up the hill." Highland Avenue was built in 1929, and construction of the new Albany Academy was finished in 1931. The cornerstone had been laid by Governor Franklin D. Roosevelt on November 21, 1929. A row of ninety-year-old eastern white pines mark the northern property line of Albany Academy from Academy Road to Forest Avenue, these trees having been planted when the land was developed.

The original Albany Academy building stands in downtown's Academy Park. Construction of this Federal style brownstone structure, the oldest civic building in the city, began in 1815, and the school opened during September 1817. The earliest classes at Albany Academy, those held prior to its official opening, took place in a building that was rented from Killiaen K. Van Rensselaer and stood between State Street and Elk Street. By the 1920s the student population and mission of Albany Academy outgrew their space and moved to what was Highland Avenue. In 1929 the city purchased the original downtown building for $450,000 and hired architect Marcus Reynolds to oversee renovation of the interior. Originally designed by Philip Hooker, this building was added to the National Register of Historic Places in 1971. It's now home to the City School District of Albany. Notable Albany Academy alumni include Herman Melville, Andy Rooney, Verplanck Colvin, Marcus Reynolds, and Theodore Roosevelt Jr.

To be labeled a "road," the thoroughfare in question is usually long, at least a half-mile in length, though this length rule is rarely followed today. Use of the word road to label a thoroughfare connecting points A and B appeared during the 1300s and comes from the Old English *rad* and *ridan*, meaning "riding expedition." Within Albany there are more than sixty roads.

Access Road

A utilitarian name, Access Road provides access to the back of Crossgates Commons, a strip mall that opened in 1994 and contains Walmart, Panera Bread, Planet Fitness, and Home Depot, among other businesses. The two-story, 260,000-square-foot Walmart Supercenter of Crossgates Commons is reputed to be the largest Walmart store in the United States.

Adirondack Street

Besides this one, four other Albany streets carry the names of mountain ranges. These include Helderberg Avenue, Catskill Street, Berkshire Boulevard, and South Berkshire Boulevard. Adirondack Street was built prior to 1922. The word Adirondack is an Anglicized Indian term meaning "bark eater," an insulting proverb used by Mohawks to communicate adversaries' inferior hunting abilities. Instead of eating wild game, their enemies were allegedly reduced to eating the inner layer of bark, the cork cambium layer. Other Indian words are perhaps tied to the origin of the word Adirondack. These include the Huron's *Attiwandaronk* ("those who speak a slightly different language") and *Arendahronon* ("rock clan") as well as the Mohawk's *Aderon-dackx* ("Frenchmen" and "Englishmen") and *Rondaxe* ("Hurons"). The term Adirondack was given to this range between September 1837 and February 1838 by Ebenezer Emmons, leader of an Adirondack geological survey. He first used this term to label the highest of the High Peaks bunched around New York's high point, 5,344-foot Mount Marcy. The term soon spread across the entire range. Before the Adirondacks were called the Adirondacks, they hosted names that have since fallen by the wayside. Outdated names include the Ancient Couchsachraga (pronounced "kook-suh-krah-guh," an Indian term meaning "beaver hunting grounds" and "dismal wilderness"), the North Mountains, the Peruvian Mountains, Brown's Mountains, and the Corlear Mountains, among others.

Some administrators reserve the title "street" for thoroughfares that run in a certain direction, such as north-south, yet the City of Albany does not employ this rule. The word street we use today comes from the Old English *stret* and the West Saxon *stræt*, meaning "high road," which comes from the Late Latin *strata*, meaning "paved road." This is related to the Latin *sternere*, which means "lay down" and "pave." This Latin term stems from the Proto-Indo-European *streto* and *stere*. Germanic, Spanish, Old French, and Italian languages had their own words that sounded like the word street, which defined lanes of travel.

Albany Plan of Union Avenue

Washington Park Road opened in 1959, the same year nearby Lancaster Street and State Street were made one-way streets in an attempt to ease traffic congestion. In 1988, Washington Park Road was renamed Albany Plan of Union

Avenue, though this street still encircles Washington Park itself. A plan of union was put forth by Benjamin Franklin, this union to be an accord of force by having the Thirteen Colonies join against the French when the French and Indian War was foreseen. The conference in which Franklin proposed his idea was the Colonial Congress Albany Convention, held July 10, 1754. This conference produced the most famous political image in American history: Franklin's "Join, or Die" illustration of a snake chopped into eight pieces and thus being powerless to fight. Mike Lee, senator from Utah, summarized in *Written Out of History* that Franklin

> was more convinced than ever that the squabbling colonies needed to unite, especially now that they faced a war with France, one that could rage along the entire western frontier. Unification had been a pet project of Franklin's for years—an idea met with equal scorn by both London and the colonial legislatures . . . In light of that suspicion, Franklin knew that any unification effort would have to unfold incrementally in a series of small steps.

Franklin's plan was detailed in his "Short Hints Towards a Scheme for Uniting the Northern Colonies" and made perfect sense to him. Yet the colonies liked their independence and were apprehensive of any national, powerful control like Franklin was proposing. Lee wrote that on July 10 in Albany, "Franklin's plan was soundly defeated." The United Kingdom wouldn't even consider it. This superpower was "especially leery of any plot to unite the colonies" when rebellion was possible. The founding father kept his proposal close to his heart for another twenty years until March 1775 when he represented Pennsylvania as a delegate to the Second Continental Congress. That following July he presented his "Articles of Confederation and Perpetual Union," a near replica of his "Short Hints Towards a Scheme for Uniting the Northern Colonies." His proposal was not accepted verbatim, yet sections of it and the document's general theme were chosen to form our nation's 1777 Articles of Confederation. Because Franklin's push for a union took place in Albany, this city is nicknamed "Cradle of the Union." A historical marker at the intersection of Broadway and State Street memorializes Franklin's plan and what it led to: "Birthplace of American union. Near this site, Benjamin Franklin presented the 1st formal plan of national union; Congress of 1754." There are 30 official historical makers within the City of Albany. The county has nearly 200, the entire state nearly 3,000.

A sprawling mural of the Albany Convention can be found inside the Dewey Graduate Library, which is housed in the Hawley Building at the University at Albany's downtown graduate campus. This mural is but one corner of the 4,500 square feet worth of murals in this library. They were painted by William Van Ingen during 1937 and 1938 while he was working under the Works Progress Administration. These paintings were completed in his New York City studio, transferred to Albany, and plastered into place. Van Ingen murals can be found in the Library of Congress, Panama Canal Administration Building, and Pennsylvania State Capitol.

Codman Hislop, in *Albany*, takes us back to more innocent times inside Washington Park: "'A turn around the park' was a phrase more common among the ladies and gentlemen of Victorian Albany than it is among their children and their grandchildren. The graceful carriages, the clatter of horse hoofs, the lace-fringed parasols and the 'elegant' gentlemen escorts made Washington Park of yesterday a gay, colorful 'pleasure-ground' for the city." Hislop reported that during the first decade of the 1800s there wasn't much more than "a powder-house and a few farms" at the future site of Washington Park. The only prominent feature was the public cemetery, which opened in 1800 and accepted interments until the 1860s. In 1806 land was set aside for Middle Public Square, later named Washington Square and then Washington Parade Ground. The 81-acre park as we know it today was constructed in 1870. Park construction was gruesome business. About 12,000 bodies were exhumed from the public cemetery and reinterred in Albany Rural Cemetery in 1868. The park opened in 1871; Washington Park Lake, formed by damming Beaver Kill, was constructed in 1873; and the first lake house, made of wood, was built in 1875. That year a list of park rules was released. Among other rules, no one within the park was to "discharge firearms, throw stones or other missiles, or play at ball or marbles," "handle or appropriate the trees," "use indecent or profane language, or do any indecent or obscene act whatever," "travel or drive on any carriage roads of the Park at a rate faster than six miles per hour," and "pass through the Park with bundles of sticks, boards, ladders, wheelbarrows, or any other unsightly objects." A new lake house, opened in 1929, stands today, this Spanish Revival structure designed by J. Russell White. Albany's Townsend Park, named for former mayor John Townsend, was to be named Washington Park for George Washington. The Washington Park title was preserved by changing Washington Parade Grounds to Washington Park.

The word *avenue* is French. Circa 1600 it was used as a military term to define an approach. This word came from the Latin *advenire*, meaning "to arrive at." Avenue then came to mean "tree-bordered approach to a country house" and was first used in our nation's capital. In *Names on the Land*, George Stewart reported, "No American had Avenue as his address until after the founding of Washington [D.C.]. Even the later popularity of Avenue may be partially credited to New York [City]." In some cities, avenues are laid out in certain directions, such as east-west, yet this is not the case within the City of Albany.

Albany Street

The name Albany honors the Scottish title of Britain's King James II, who was also King James VII and Duke of York and Albany. Massachusetts's Dukes County and Maine's Town of York and York County are named for this man, who was born October 14, 1633, in London and died September 16, 1701, at Saint-Germain-en-Laye in France. The peerage title Duke of Albany was bestowed to sons in Scottish and British royal families, usually among the Stuart House and Windsor House. This title was initially granted to Robert Stewart by his brother, King Robert III of Scotland, in 1398. Albany-named communities in Illinois, New Hampshire, Pennsylvania, Wyoming, Indiana, Oregon, and Georgia are named after Albany, New York (these last three state's cities were settled by Albanians). Chicago's Albany Avenue and Albany Drive are named after this capital city, as is Boston's Albany Street.

Albany Street was first named Albany Avenue. Name change occurred February 13, 1871, the same year this street was declared a public street. It was officially opened by the Common Council on January 15, 1872. In 1890, Albany Street was paved for the first time. Granite blocks were used. Very few granite block streets survive (sections of Jay Street and Broad Street are probably the only ones left), yet many streets have old sections of pavement missing in which one can see the granite blocks that were hidden underneath. These blocks were also called Belgian blocks and Belgian setts. Historic Pavement describes them as

> a form of quarried stone pavement, typically rectangular in shape, six to twelve inches in length and half that dimension wide. A Belgian block is defined by its shape, rather than its material, which is most often granite, but could also be limestone or sandstone. They also vary in terms of the smoothness of their surface, ranging from very slick and almost glassy to very rough. Making their appearance in North American cities during the second half of the 19th century, Belgian blocks were used on streets bearing traffic with the heaviest loads.

For those who wonder what old-time Albany looked like, a fine portrayal of pre-1700 Albany can be found in David Lithgow's painting entitled "Albany as a Trading Post About 1695," from circa 1939, which can be found on the University at Albany's downtown graduate campus in their Theodore Fossieck Milne Alumni Room. Lithgow painted fourteen murals for this room between 1933 and 1945 and charged students $300 for each one. Dances and tea parties were organized by students to raise funds to obtain Lithgow's work. Beyond University at Albany, Lithgow painted scenes for the 1939 World's Fair in New York City, as well as the New York State Museum and State Bank of Albany. Another fine work portraying old-time Albany is Len Tantillo's gorgeous "Fort Orange and the Patroon's House" from 2009. This painting can be viewed at the New York State Library, which is on the seventh floor of Albany's New York State Museum.

Regarding the place name history of Albany, this capital city had eight names during its past 400 years: Fort Nassau, Fort Orange, Rensselaerswyck, the Fuyck, Beverwyck, New Albany, Albany, and Willemstadt, and some of these names vanished only to reappear.

The first Dutch settlement in North America and at Albany was Fort Nassau. It carried the name of the ruling House of Orange-Nassau, which was established in Europe in 1515. This fort was likely specifically named for Maurice, Prince of Orange-Nassau (1567–1625). Circa 1614 Adriaen Block (1567–1627, the man who named Long Island and for whom Block Island, Rhode Island, is named) and Hendrick Christiaensen (unknown-1616) finished construction of Fort Nassau on Castle Island, today's Westerlo Island. The fort, which was surrounded by a palisade and a moat and manned by a dozen sailors who traded with Indians, was built on the remains of a French trading post, also called a "castle," from 1540. This post is most interesting because it was built not even fifty years after Christopher Columbus first reached the New World. In *The Mapping of New York State*, David Allen wrote of the legacy of this ancient post:

> There are some indications of a French presence along the Hudson River in the first decades of the seventeenth century. One of the most intriguing is an annotation on the Block Chart, which has been translated as follows: "But as far as one can understand by what the Mohawk say and show, the French come with sloops as high up as their country to trade with them." This notation, which Block placed on his chart near present day Albany, lends itself to more than one interpretation. It seems to refer to French ships actually sailing up the Hudson River, but it might also be a confused reference to French goods being transported by Indians from the Saint Lawrence River via the Lake Champlain route.

As told in *Albany Architecture* by Diana Waite, Fort Nassau was "a square redoubt armed with cannons and smaller guns, with walls fifty-eight feet in length surrounded by a moat eighteen feet wide; inside the fort was a building measuring thirty-six by twenty-six feet in plan." Despite its seeming impenetrability, in 1618 a flood destroyed Fort Nassau. A new Fort Nassau was then built at the mouth of Normans Kill, yet that building was destroyed by a flood only a year later.

In 1624, the Dutch built Fort Orange to replace what was left of Fort Nassau. This is when permanent settlement took hold, which makes Albany the oldest continuously-occupied European settlement within the Thirteen Colonies (Jamestown, Virginia, was settled in 1607, abandoned in 1699, and is an archaeological site today). Fort Orange was settled by thirty Protestant Walloon families, who first came from today's Belgium after escaping the Spanish Inquisition. Within three years of arriving, these settlers were called to New Amsterdam, and it was deemed too expensive to send additional Europeans back up the river. The Walloons were happy to leave because Mohawks and Mohicans were fighting each other near the fort. Settlers were caught in the middle of flying arrows and tomahawks, and things got seriously out of hand when, in 1626, Mohawks killed four Dutchmen where today's Lincoln Park is.

They roasted and ate one of the dead and lugged an arm and a leg back home to show they were victorious.

On June 1, 1630, the name Rensselaerswyck was assigned to the land around Fort Orange because it belonged to Kiliaen Van Rensselaer, a Dutch merchant who owned nearly 700,000 acres in today's Capital Region. He bought the land from Mohawk Indians through his assistant, Sebastiaen Jansen Crol. In 1633 Van Rensselaer's nephew and associate, Wouter Van Twiller, came to America with Van Rensselaer's New World settlers, who were ready to tame the wilderness. They huddled around Fort Orange, a building that was not impressive. In 1643 Isaac Jogues, a French Jesuit missionary, visited the fort and described it with two adjectives: "little" and "wretched." This is probably because a flood ripped through the fort in 1640. This flood was so violent that residents ran up the hills, hunkered in tents and warmed themselves by bonfires until the wrath subsided. When Jogues visited Fort Orange there were 100 residents beating back the encroaching forest.

During the mid-1600s two other names were used for the communities around Fort Orange. One name was the Fuyck, *fuyck* being Dutch for "bow net for catching fish." Jack McEneny shared an entry from the April 1680 journal of Jasper Danckaerts, a Dutch missionary who visited Albany at that time. Danckaerts wrote that the area "was formerly named the Fuyck by the Hollanders, who first settled there, on account of two rows of houses standing there, opposite to each other, which being wide enough apart in the beginning, finally ran quite together like a 'fuyck,' and, therefore, they gave it this name . . . " Another name was Beverwyck. Beginning April 1, 1652, the one-legged governor of New Netherland, Pieter Stuyvesant, disregarded the name Fort Orange and called the area Beverwyck, meaning "place of the beaver." In *Seventeenth Century Albany*, Charlotte Wilcoxen reported that this name was given by Stuyvesant when he "organized [the community] into a legal entity . . . with its own court system, independent of [Kiliaen Van Rensselaer's] colonie." These were confusing times concerning who owned what. Van Rensselaer and associates maintained that Fort Orange stood on Van Rensselaer's land while Stuyvesant and his representatives maintained that the fort was built before Van Rensselaer owned any of the land. By this time, 100 houses stood in what would become Albany.

In 1664, the Dutch globally surrendered to the British without a battle. King Charles II granted territory including New Netherland, New England, Long Island, and Delaware to his royal brother, who held three titles: King James II, King James VII, and Duke of York and Albany. Dutchman Pieter Stuyvesant thus relinquished control of the area to Englishman Richard Nicolls, representative of King James. On September 24, 1664, the Fuyck and Beverwyck became Albany, though Nicolls first used the Latin name *Albania*. Fort Orange became Fort Albany, and New Amsterdam became New York City. These name changes were, in Stewart's words, "necessary as a symbol of the English rule." The loss of Dutch identity must have been stinging to the settlers because, as far as Stewart was concerned, King James was "bigoted and stupid, and as a libertine was even more unblushing, at the same time less witty, than his brother Charles II."

During 1673 and 1674, the Dutch regained control of the fort and surrounding community, got rid of the name Albany, and reinstated the name Fort Nassau. New York City became New Orange. This time the Dutch called the community surrounding the fort Willemstadt. This name honored the Prince of Orange, William II (1626–1650). Willemstadt was "Willem's city."

Finally, the English secured control of this area on February 19, 1674, via the Treaty of Westminster. They called the fort and community Albany, the name which has been in use ever since (they also used the term New Albany, but that label didn't last long). The old fort was abandoned, and a new fort, Fort Frederick, was built in 1676 at today's intersection of State Street and Lodge Street. It was named for Frederick Lewis, Prince of Wales (1707–1751), who was son of King George II and Caroline of Ansbach, and father of King George III. This fort was dismantled during the 1780s.

Albion Avenue

Albion Avenue, built prior to 1918, is next to Arcadia Avenue, built prior to 1914. These streets are connected through definition. Today the word albion is used to describe historic English poetry and refers to tranquil, pastoral places. It's an Old English word stemming from the Latin *albionis*, which is related to *albus*, meaning "white." This white referred to the bleached chalk cliffs of England's south coast and was an old-time name for England itself. The word arcadia also refers to tranquil, pastoral locales. The U.S. has communities named Albion in New York, Maine, Michigan, Nebraska, Washington, and Wisconsin as well as Albion toponyms—names of natural features such as lakes, mountains, and streams—in Alaska, Arkansas, and California.

Alden Avenue

John Alden has his Alden Avenue, this name designated in 1912 when this street was built. He was born circa 1599 as the son of Joseph Alden, a cooper and shipwright. The younger Alden was a member of the voyage of the *Mayflower*, a 100-foot-long, 180-ton Dutch cargo ship, which set sail from Plymouth, England, in early September 1620. The crew and passengers spotted the New World, in the form of Cape Cod, on November 9. It had been a miserable two months at sea in which two people died. Squeezed in the *Mayflower* with 130 others, Alden served as the ship's cooper. Upon landing, Alden inhabited Plymouth Colony, where he fulfilled political roles including assistant governor, commissioner to Yarmouth, Duxbury deputy to the General Court of Plymouth, member of the Council of War, and treasurer of Plymouth Colony. He was also a signer of the Mayflower Compact.

Alden's daughter, Elizabeth, one of his eleven children, was the first white female born in New England. John Alden died September 12, 1687, and was buried next to his wife, Priscilla Mullins Alden, in Myles Standish Burial Ground in Duxbury, Massachusetts. Also named for this man are the communities of Alden in Illinois and Iowa as well as Philadelphia's Alden Street. The name Alden comes from the Middle English name Aldine, which stems from the Old English name Ealdwine, which combines *eald* and *wine*, meaning "old friend."

Alexander Street
(and Hamilton Street)

Sections of Hamilton Street were formerly known as Kilby Street, Kilby Lane, and New Street. The current name was made official October 1, 1805. Hamilton Street was unpaved as late as 1900. That year its section from Quail Street to Partridge Street was paved with vitrified bricks. These bricks became, as told by Historic Pavement, "the most common type of street pavement" in America by 1900 and "were first used for paving in the United States in Charleston, West Virginia, in 1870." Vitrified bricks were suitable for streets because they were "fired at a higher temperature and for a longer period of time than a conventional brick . . . making it harder and impervious to the absorption of water." Few vitrified brick streets survive in Albany and are limited to sections of Kent Street, Lincoln Avenue, Orange Street, Park Avenue, Schuyler Street, West Lawrence Street, and West Street.

Alexander Street and Hamilton Street memorialize Alexander Hamilton, whose connection to Albany is precious. He married Elizabeth Schuyler, daughter of Philip Schuyler and Catherine Van Rensselaer Schuyler, at the Schuyler Mansion on December 14, 1780. David Lithgow's delightful circa 1939 painting "The Courtship" records the love of Hamilton and Schuyler. This work can be found on the University at Albany's downtown graduate campus in their Theodore Fossieck Milne Alumni Room. There are six "Schuyler streets" near this mansion: Alexander Street, Catherine Street, Elizabeth Street, Morton Avenue, Philip Street, and Schuyler Street (Hamilton Street is a half-mile from the mansion).

Few men were more active in politics during the Revolutionary War than Hamilton was. He was a founding father, chief staff aide to George Washington, founder of the United States Coast Guard, first secretary of the treasury, member of the Congress of the Confederation from New York, New York assemblyman, signer of the Constitution, and leader of the Federalist Party. He founded the Bank of New York in 1784 and the *New York Evening Post* in 1801 and is credited with establishing America's financial system and the U.S. Mint. With John Jay and James Madison Jr., he coauthored the Federalist Papers, a series of 85 essays that pressed New Yorkers to ratify the U.S. Constitution. These essays ran in New York newspapers during 1787 and 1788 and were said to be authored by Publius, the pseudonym of the three real authors.

Hamilton was born January 11, 1755, in the West Indies, of all places. The son of James A. Hamilton and Rachel Faucette Hamilton, he grew up in Charlestown, which is the capital of the island of Nevis, which is part of the Leeward Islands, which at the time was a British colony. He and his mother then moved to the Virgin Islands, which was a colony of Denmark. Hamilton's mother died February 19, 1768. As an orphan Hamilton was raised by two different men, who were not relatives of his. Being recognized as a bright child (he spoke English and French fluently and was an excellent writer), Hamilton's community pooled their resources and sent him to North America to be educated at Elizabethtown Academy in New Jersey and King's College, today's Columbia University, in New York City. After the battles of Lexington and Concord, Hamilton joined the revolution as a rebel, seeing combat in New York and New Jersey. After proving himself worthy on the battlefield, he was promoted to lieutenant colonel and served as General George Washington's aide. He held this position for four years. Missing the whine of whizzing bullets and the grumbling of artillery, Hamilton resigned from his position in 1781 to return to battle. He led a New York infantry battalion and fought in the last major battle between the Americans and the British, which took place in Yorktown, Virginia, during October 1781.

Hamilton died in a way that, unfortunately, not enough politicians die these days: in a duel. Aaron Burr Jr., already sore from not being elected president of the United States, was personally insulted by Hamilton. Burr demanded an apology, and Hamilton told him to bug off. The duel was accepted June 27, 1804. The morning of July 11, two shots were fired in Weehawken, New Jersey. Hamilton's round snapped a tree branch above Burr's head, and Burr's round nailed Hamilton, smashed his organs, and wedged in the man's spine. A paralyzed Hamilton died the next day in Greenwich Village, New York. (Strangely enough, Hamilton's oldest son, Philip, had been killed in a duel in 1801 with George Eacker after insulting him in a Manhattan theater.) Alexander Hamilton was buried in Trinity Church Cemetery in Manhattan. New York's Hamilton County and Hamilton College, among many other political and geographical features, are named for this man.

The name Alexander comes from the Greek name Alexandros, meaning "defender of men." This name became popular due to the fame of Alexander the Great (356–323 B.C.), the Macedonian conqueror. The name Hamilton is a Norman family name and an Irish and Scottish place name. It began as a combination of *hamel* and *dun*, meaning "scarred hill."

Alfred Street

When a man has the last name of Street, street naming becomes so clever, so fun. Alfred Billings Street, for whom this lane may be named, was New York's state librarian, editor of *Northern Light*, and author of *The Burning of Schenectady*, *Drawings and Tintings*, *Fugitive Poems*, *Frontenac*, *Woods and Waters*, *Lake and Mountain*, and *Eagle Pine*. Street was born December 18, 1811, in

Poughkeepsie, New York. His father was Randall Street, an Army officer, politician, and lawyer, and his mother was Cornelia Street.

Your author is familiar with Street because the man wrote *The Indian Pass*, an Adirondack classic written in 1868. Highly entertaining, *The Indian Pass* describes the writer's hike through this gorge and his ascent of Mount Marcy, the highest peak in New York. Street's writing is unashamed joy, like zooming down a playground slide when no one's looking. At one point he warned readers of a rare disease among the mountains that struck down weaklings on their way up Mount Marcy, this peak occasionally known as Tahawus at the time:

> The ascent of Tahawus is by no means an easy performance, an airy promenade. No! It is stern, persistent work; work that calls upon your mightiest energies! In attempting its ascent, strong, hardy trampers have given out, and lain down helpless in an attack of wood-sickness. And here is a new disease! I first heard of it in the Adirondacks! Wood-sickness! A sea-sickness on land! Brought on by excessive fatigue, or by being buried, day after day, in the greenness of the woods, these tremendous, tangled, sun-concealing, weltering woods! The symptoms are the same as its sister of the sea; as disheartening and enfeebling.

Street fought off dreaded wood-sickness and reached the summit, declaring, "Well here I am at last!" The humble poet didn't pound his chest though. "To tell the truth, I never thought I should ever reach the spot." Alfred Billings Street died June 2, 1881, at his home on the corner of Washington Avenue and Dove Street. He was buried in Albany Rural Cemetery. Surveyor Verplanck Colvin named Street Mountain, 24th highest peak in the Adirondacks, for this writer in 1872.

Identifying the oldest building on a particular street located beyond downtown, "old," Albany can help determine when someone first lived in that area. Likewise, there's no sense in doing this in downtown Albany because we already know that section of the city was well-settled before 1800. In the case of Alfred Street, the home at 7 Alfred Street, built circa 1850, is the oldest building along it. This house predates street construction by at least fifty years (that is, this house was out in the boonies, and then the street was built in front of it).

Alumni Drive
Located on University at Albany's main campus, Alumni Drive is the first of more than twenty streets on this campus and within the City of Albany. It runs near the college's Alumni House, which is home to the Alumni Association, and is the first true "drive" within *Cradle of the Union*. This title is usually reserved for curvilinear roadways at least a quarter-mile in length, though this rule is disregarded in most cases. There are nearly seventy drives in Albany.

Founded in 1844, University at Albany has had at least eight names during its existence. These include New York State Normal School (created 1884), New York State Normal College (1890), New York State College for Teachers (1914), State University College of Education at Albany (1959), State University College at Albany (1961), State University of New York at Albany (1962), and University at Albany State University of New York (1986). University at Albany, often contracted to U Albany, is the name in current fashion. The main, uptown campus was first occupied in 1964 and was designed by Edward Stone, who later designed the Kennedy Center in Washington, D.C. The first main campus building was part of Dutch Quad, back when students temporarily lived in motels. Since 1965, more than 100,000 bachelor's degrees had been conferred, and 65,000 graduate degrees were conferred within the school's three most popular programs: Master of Science, Master of Art, and Master of Social Work.

Because people often use the word alumni and related terms incorrectly, here is a short course. Alumna is a female graduate or former student of an educational institution, this word stemming from the feminine version of the Latin *alumnus*. The plural is alumnae (pronounced "alum-nee"). Alumnus is a male graduate or former student of an educational institution, this word stemming from the Latin word for "foster son" and "pupil," which came from the Latin *alere*, meaning "to nourish." The plural is alumni (pronounced "alum-nie"). People carelessly use the word alum to reference a former student, yet this is incorrect. According to the trusty 1,622-page eleventh edition of *Merriam-Webster's Collegiate Dictionary*, alum is: "a potassium aluminum sulfate $KA1(SO4)2$ $12H2O$ or an ammonium aluminum sulfate $NH4A1(SO4)2$ $12H20$ used especially as an emetic and as an astringent and styptic" and "any of various double salts isomorphous with potassium aluminum sulfate." No one wants to be called such things. Yet this carelessness is made even in professional circles. For example, the March 2017 issue of *Money* included a sentence that read: "The 45th President has also tapped several Goldman alums to run key posts . . . " (the word president is unnecessarily capitalized, too, so double shame on *Money* writer Taylor Tepper).

Amherst Avenue

Built prior to 1931, Amherst Avenue is named for Lord Jeffery Amherst. Amherst College takes its name from the Massachusetts community that carries his name. Amherst Avenue is one of six streets in Albany that memorializes a prominent member of the British military from the Revolutionary War era. The five others are Gage Avenue, named for Thomas Gage; Glynn Street, named for John Glynn; and Tryon Court, Tryon Place, and Tryon Street, named for William Tryon.

Amherst was born January 29, 1717, in England as the son of Jeffrey Amherst and Elizabeth Kerrill Amherst. Two of his siblings were military men. One of them, John, became an admiral. Another, William, became a lieutenant general. Jeffery Amherst first became a page of the Duke of Dorset and then joined the Grenadier Guards as an ensign. In the War of the Austrian Succession during the 1740s, he was at the battles of Dettingen, Fontenoy, Rocoux, and Lauffeld. During the French and Indian War, known to Europeans as the Seven Years' War, he was promoted to colonel. In 1758 he was promoted to commander in chief of the British Army in North America and colonel in chief of the 60th Royal Regiment. Amherst led troops and saw combat along the St. Lawrence River, Montreal, the Great Lakes, and the northeast Colonies until the French and Indian War ended in 1763 (meanwhile, he served as crown governor of Virginia from 1759 to 1768 and governor of the Province of Quebec from 1760 to 1763).

Citing his leadership and coolness, Amherst was made governor general of British North America and was promoted to major general. After fighting in Europe and America, he led expeditions to Cuba, Dominica, and Martinique, and then led soldiers in Pontiac's War, this conflict named for Chief Pontiac, leader of the Ottawa in today's Illinois and Ohio. Amherst was also militarily active in the American and French revolutions. Lord Jeffery Amherst was finally promoted to the rank of field marshal in 1796 and then retired, settling at his home in Montreal Park. He died August 3, 1797, and was buried at the Parish Church in Sevenoaks, England, the settlement in which he was born. The name Amherst dates to 1250 with Hemhurst Hill—now Amherst Hill—in County Kent, England. That name combined the Old English *hem* and *hyrst*, meaning "boundary" and "wooded hill."

Anchor Street
(and Boat Street, Port Street, Raft Street, South Port Road)

The Port of Albany gives Anchor Street, Boat Street, Port Street, Raft Street, and South Port Road their names. There is a reason why Albany is where it is. This capital city is at the uppermost navigable part of the Hudson River, and it's near the Mohawk River, which may be used to access central New York. Since the early 1600s, Indians, Europeans, Albanians, and ships' captains, both local and foreign, have been using the west shore of the Hudson River at present-day Albany to export and import goods ranging from beaver pelts to petroleum products, cement to produce, salt to steel. Yet it was not until 1766 that a formal port was created by the City of Albany. That year three docks and a sea wall were built. Two wharfs and an extended dock followed. In 1825, major construction took place with a 4,300-foot-long, 80-foot-wide pier being built. It wasn't until 100 years later that the Albany Port District was created. In 1932, Governor Franklin D. Roosevelt led construction of a 200-acre port on the Albany side of the river and a 34-acre port on the Rensselaer side at a cost of $32 million. In 2000, the Port of Albany was deemed a container port. It is overseen by the Albany Port District Commission of the City of Albany.

Anderson Drive

Set on the north side of the Albany rail yard, Anderson Drive likely memorializes someone who worked there, helped develop the yard, or owned property where this street now is. It is not known who this Mr. Anderson was, and more than 230 Andersons are buried in Albany Rural Cemetery. The ancient name Anderson comes from northern Europe and means "son of Anders or Andrew."

Arbor Drive

An estate gives this little street its name. Located in a northeast section of the city, the Arbor Hill Neighborhood's boundaries include a set of railroad tracks to the north, Broadway to the east, Orange Street to the south, and Henry Johnson Boulevard to the west. The names Arbor Drive and Arbor Hill come from this area's Ten Broeck Estate being nicknamed Arbor Hill. The Arbor Hill area was identified on DeWitt's 1794 map of the city. This is probably the earliest map to identify this section of the city by name. The English word arbor stems from *herber*, meaning "herb garden," which dates to circa 1300. Other sources include the Old French *erbier*, meaning "meadow," and the Latin *herba*, meaning "grassy plot."

Arcadia Avenue

Arcadia Avenue is next to Albion Avenue, and both were built prior to 1920. These names share parallel definitions. While the word arcadia refers to tranquil, pastoral places, the word albion also refers to such tranquil, pastoral locales (the capitalized Albion is another name for Britain). Thus these street names are connected in meaning. Communities named Arcadia can be found in New York, Florida, Maryland, Wisconsin, California, and Indiana, and many streets across the U.S. carry this name. The word arcadia comes from the Greek place name Arkadia, a district in the Peloponnesus that ancient poets found to be flawlessly rural and peaceful.

Arch Street

Known as Johnson Street from 1828 to 1840, Arch Street was also called Beaver Lane. It has existed since before 1796 because the Arch Street Brewery stood near it that year. Arch Street gets its name from once having an arched brick bridge along it that spanned Beaver Kill. This stream now runs through culverts underneath the city. The word arch comes from the Old French *arche*, meaning "the arch of a bridge," and from the Latin *arcus*, meaning "bow" and "arch." *Arcus* is related to the word arc, which describes the arcing track our sun completes across the sky.

Arthur Drive

Arthur Road can be found in Newtonville. That street is named for president Chester Arthur because his father, reverend William Arthur, preached at the First Baptist Church that stood near this road. This church, built 1852, is today's Newtonville post office. Between serving as a church and a post office, it was a farm machinery sales office, schoolhouse, and garage. This building was placed on the National Register of Historic Places in 1973. Arthur Drive was built in 1951 at the latest, the year Picotte Companies was selling new homes on this street.

Chester Arthur, 21st president of the United States, was born to William Arthur and Malvina Stone Arthur in Fairfield, Vermont, on October 5, 1829. His first name honors the doctor who assisted in his birth, Chester Abell. He is the only president born in Vermont besides Calvin Coolidge. While Arthur's family settled in various towns in the Capital Region, he attended Union College, graduated, and worked as a teacher and principal and studied law to practice in New York City. When the Civil War started during the spring of 1861, he was appointed brigadier general within the New York State Militia and was promoted to inspector general and quartermaster general. Serving as quartermaster, Arthur saw no combat. He left the military, practiced law again, and ran as James Garfield's vice president for the election of 1881. He was first a Whig, then a Republican. Garfield and Arthur won, but Garfield was shot by an assassin four months into his presidency, on July 2, 1881. He was shot by Charles Guiteau, a disgruntled office seeker, at the Baltimore and Potomac Railroad Station in Washington, D.C. (more on Guiteau and his assassination of President James Garfield is given in the Garfield Street entry). Arthur learned of the shooting while he was visiting Albany. Garfield clung to life for months, dying September 19, 1881, on the Jersey Shore. It had been an awkward time for Garfield, Arthur, and the nation. Garfield had been too weak to serve as president, yet Arthur thought it tasteless to take over the presidency while the real president was still alive. Two days after the passing of President Garfield, Arthur took his oath of office, the oath administered by New York State Supreme Court judge John Brady. To make sure it was official, he took a second oath in Washington, D.C., the next day, that one administered by chief justice Morrison Waite.

Arthur's presidency was marked by a handful of resignations of upper staff. The only person to remain with Arthur until the end of his presidency on March 4, 1885, was the secretary of war, Robert Todd Lincoln, son of President Abraham Lincoln. During his term, Arthur managed an Asian immigration crisis, rebuilt the Navy, improved civil rights for blacks, made polygamy a federal crime, generally failed at securing lands and rights for Indians, and signed the Pendleton Civil Service Reform Act into law. Arthur did not seek reelection and was succeeded by Republican Grover Cleveland. Chester Arthur died November 18, 1886. Two days before his death he demanded nearly all his private and public papers be burned. Four days after his death a funeral was held in New York City. He was buried in Albany Rural Cemetery, the only president to be buried there.

If little Arthur Drive is not named for this president, it may be named for a much less famous Arthur, such as the son of a developer. This may be the case since Arthur Drive is next to another "name street," Edward Terrace. The etymology of the name Arthur is disputed though it dates to the Middle Ages.

Arts and Sciences Lane

If using good taste, the label "lane" is reserved for cul-de-sacs that have more than eight lots. Albany has nearly forty lanes. Arts and Sciences Lane on the University at Albany's main campus predictably runs to the Arts and Sciences building, one of 24 academic buildings on this campus. One can't call the naming of streets an art, yet this college has its street naming down to a science.

Ash Grove Place
(and Ash Street, Ashwood Court)

Concerning Ash Grove Place, this street is named after an actual ash grove that stood in that location as part of Kane's Mansion, also known as Yates Mansion, which was occupied by governors Daniel Tompkins, DeWitt Clinton, and William Seward. This mansion was built by Peter Waldron Yates circa 1781 on land he had inherited in 1776. James Kane bought the mansion from Yates in 1809 and improved the property. Thomas Olcott then purchased the mansion in 1856. It was destroyed in 1864 by Ashgrove Methodist Episcopal Church after the land was sold to church trustees so they could build a new church there. The former Philip Schuyler High School, built 1914, stands where Ashgrove Methodist Episcopal Church used to be. The grove towered at today's intersection of Grand Street and Ash Grove Place. Researcher Jason Privler confirmed that the current wooden power pole that holds the streets signs for these two streets is where massive ash trees, which were part of the original grove, used to stand. They were removed during the early 1950s.

More than a dozen species of ash, split among the Olive, Rose, and Rue families, grow in the United States. Half of these—American mountain, black, green, European mountain, showy mountain, and white—grow in New York. White ash is most common and can be easily identified by its diamond-patterned bark and limbless trunk. Most of its branches are perched high towards the sky like a broad crow's nest. Its stout wood is made into baseball bats, hockey sticks, tennis racquets, oars, and polo mallets.

Ash Grove Place, formerly part of Westerlo Street, is the first true "place" in *Cradle of the Union*. A place is technically a short curvilinear or diagonal street less than a quarter mile long. There are nearly fifty places within Albany.

Ashwood Court is the first true "court" in *Cradle of the Union*. The label court is usually reserved for cul-de-sacs with no more than eight lots. Albany has more than forty courts.

Ash Street
See Ash Grove Place.

Ashwood Court
See Ash Grove Place.

Aspen Circle
New York's two species of aspen are quaking aspen (also known as trembling aspen, poplar, and golden aspen) and bigtooth aspen (also called largetooth aspen and poplar). Both are in the Willow family and grow across all of New York. According to the New York State Big Tree Register, the biggest quaking aspen within the state is 27 inches in diameter and 105 feet tall. The biggest bigtooth aspen is 39 inches in diameter and also 105 feet tall. Quaking aspen and bigtooth aspen appear similar yet are distinguishable to the trained eye. As bigtooth aspen's name implies, the leaves of this species have accentuated lobes. The foliage of these trees loudly "quake" and "tremble" in the slightest breeze. The Onondaga called aspens *nut-ki-e* ("noisy leaf") while the Romans said that aspen leaves were "like women's tongues—never still." The aspen is the state tree of Colorado, and Aspen is the most common street name in that state. Colorado has 187 Aspen streets.

The "circle" title is reserved for streets that make a loop, beginning and ending on the same street. One would think this is an easy rule to follow. However, of Albany's ten circles, six of them—Coral Berry Circle, Hawthorn Circle, Lupine Circle, Rosemary Circle, Teacup Circle, and Tubman Circle—are dead-end streets. Aspen Circle is built over the graves of eight streets that used to stand there: Orange Avenue, Belmont Street, Grafton Avenue, Dover Street, Dodge Street, Donald Street, Waltham Avenue, and Beldale Road.

Austain Avenue
Former names of Austain Avenue include Lydius Street and Austin Avenue. Lydius Street memorialized Johannes Lydius, the esteemed dominie—clergyman—of the Dutch Church. This name survives in East Lydius Street and West Lydius Street, which are near the Pine Bush outside Albany's city limits. The City of Albany foresaw confusion regarding these three Lydius streets and decided to change their own Lydius name to Austin and then Austain.

It's possible that the city, to preserve a religious theme, replaced the name Lydius with Austin because this name is the abbreviated form of Augustine, a name that means "to increase." Augustine was a Christian philosopher and theologian who lived during the 300s and 400s and was born in, and died in, Algeria. Another possibility is that Austin Avenue memorialized the old Austin family of Albany County. Aaron Austin and Elsie Austin were residents of this county by the late 1700s. Their first child, Cornelis, was born in Albany on October 3, 1782. In the end, Austin Avenue could have been changed to Austain Avenue for no good reason, such as a mere typo being committed.

Avenue A
(and Avenue B)
The names Avenue A and Avenue B are sterile, *The Knickerbocker News* stating that "no history is recalled, no imagination stirred, no valorous deeds perpetuated by the name Avenue A." Avenue B was given little credit as well, this same writer noting that "nothing of a great past is recalled by the designation." There are actually two streets named Avenue A and two named Avenue B. One set of Avenue A and Avenue B is off Frisbie Avenue and carries a zip code of 12202. During the 1870s it was proposed to build avenues lettered A through H in that area. Another set of Avenue A and Avenue B is off Ontario Street and carries a zip code of 12208.

Avenue B
See Avenue A.

Avon Court
(and Avon Place, Avon Street, Avondale Terrace)
These Avon place names are likely a nod to the 96-mile-long River Avon in England or other waterways that carry this name in England, Scotland, and Wales. The U.S. hosts communities named Avon in West Virginia, Wisconsin, Alabama, Connecticut, Illinois, New Jersey, and New York and those named Avondale in Maryland, Pennsylvania, Arizona, Alabama, West Virginia, and Illinois. *Avon* is Celtic for "water." Concerning Avondale Terrace, the suffix "dale" communicates a valley or gorge. The word dale comes from the Old English *dæl* and the Proto-Germanic *dalan* and *dhel*, which mean "valley."

Avon Place
See Avon Court.

Avon Street
See Avon Court.

Avondale Terrace
See Avon Court.

B

Bancker Street
The Bancker families of the New World began with Gerrit Bancker (in genealogical speak, he was the "progenitor," which is an ancestor in the direct line—an originator). He was a fur trader who came from New Amsterdam to present-day Albany in 1657 and lived near the corner of State Street and South Pearl Street. Gerrit Bancker died February 27, 1691.

Evert Bancker, son of Gerrit Bancker and Elizabeth Dirkse Van Eps Bancker, is honored through Bancker Street as it is set among three other "mayoral streets" including Peyster Street, Hansen Avenue, and Ryckman Avenue. Evert Bancker was born in Albany on January 14, 1665, and was educated at the common school. Beyond being mayor, he served on the Common Council and was first ward assistant, justice of the peace, master in chancery, assemblyman, and alderman. He was appointed by Governor Benjamin Fletcher to be mayor during 1695 and 1696. He was later appointed by Governor Edward Hyde to serve in this role from 1707 to 1709. When Bancker lived in Albany he resided on the south side of State Street east of Pearl Street. In 1719, Bancker and his family moved to Guilderland where they had a farm. At that location he served as commissioner of Indian affairs. He was the father of eleven children and was married to Elizabeth Abeel Bancker, sister of the second mayor of Albany, Johannes Abeel. They married September 26, 1686. Evert Bancker died July 10, 1734, in Guilderland and was buried at his farm, which stood along today's Route 146 where it crosses Normans Kill on its way from Guilderland to Guilderland Center. There a corruption of the name Bancker—Bunker—was used by locals. They called the bridge over Normans Kill the Bunker Bridge, and they labeled the mile-long hill that climbs to Guilderland Center Bunker Hill.

Bancroft Street
A contributor to this book reported that his father "was a builder, and he built our house on Bancroft Street more than sixty years ago. It was one of the first

houses built on this street. He and my mother were told that the street was named after a Bancroft, who was an admiral." This firsthand account stands up to elementary scrutiny. Bancroft Street was built circa 1926.

Admiral Bancroft Gherardi, for whom this street is likely named, was born to Donato Gherardi and Jane Putnam Bancroft Gherardi in Jackson, Louisiana, on November 10, 1832. He graduated from the U.S. Naval Academy in 1851 and rose to the rank of rear admiral. He commanded the *Chocura, Port Royal, Colorado,* and *Lancaster* and served during the Spanish-American War and Civil War. His connection to New York includes serving as commandant of the New York Navy Yard and commander in chief of the Naval Review Fleet on the Hudson River. He retired from the military during the fall of 1894. Bancroft Gherardi died December 10, 1903, and was buried in the United States Naval Academy Cemetery in Naval Academy, Maryland.

There is another Bancroft connected to the U.S. Navy, though this man did not serve as an admiral. He served as secretary of the Navy. George Bancroft, for whom Bancroft streets in Pennsylvania and Massachusetts are named, was born October 3, 1800, in Worcester, Massachusetts, as the son of Aaron Bancroft. Aaron was a minuteman at the battles of Lexington and Bunker Hill and author of a George Washington biography. George Bancroft graduated from Harvard College in 1817 and received his Ph.D. from the University of Göttingen in Germany. He cofounded Round Hill School in Northampton and served as collector of customs for the Port of Boston, secretary of the Navy, and acting secretary of war, and he established the U.S. Naval Academy in Annapolis, Maryland (it had been in Philadelphia). He wrote *History of the United States of America, from the Discovery of the American Continent*; *History of the Battle of Lake Erie, and Miscellaneous Papers*; *Martin Van Buren to the End of His Public Career*; and *History of the Formation of the Constitution of the United States of America*. George Bancroft died January 17, 1891, and was buried in Rural Cemetery in Worcester, Massachusetts. The name Bancroft is English and combines the words *bean* and *croft*, meaning "bean" and "paddock."

Barclay Street

Thomas Barclay is memorialized in Barclay Street. He immigrated to America in 1708 and spent the rest of his life in New York having myriad religious duties. He was a chaplain at one of the oldest forts in Albany, initiated services at the Church of England in Albany, served as Saint Peter's Anglican Church's first rector, and offered services in Dutch and English. Barclay began construction of Saint Peter's Church less than a decade after coming to America. During his time it stood in the middle of present-day Broadway east of Chapel Street. It was removed in 1802.

Concerning his life outside the church, Barclay was married to Anna Dorothea Drayer Barclay and raised four sons with her (one of them, Henry, has

Barclay Street in New York City named for him because that street originally cut through Trinity Church property—he was the second rector of that church). During the American Revolution, Barclay was made chairman of Albany's Committee of Safety and Correspondences, an organization, as Hislop wrote, "whose duty would be to keep in touch with other cities regarding their plans for resisting England's tax collectors and to insure the safety of Albany's patriots." Life later spiraled down for this man of the cloth. In part because of financial difficulties, Barclay became victim to a number of mental strains such as anxiety, depression, and, later, insanity. He died in 1726. In his Thomas Barclay article, Bielinski wrote that "the last dismal years provided a marked contrast to the energy and achievement that characterized [Barclay's] first decade in Albany." Another son of Barclay, John, became Albany's 27th mayor, serving from April 17, 1778, to April 8, 1779, the day of his death. John Barclay was the first mayor appointed under direction of the state, as opposed to direction of the Royal Commission. The name Barclay in Scottish and English comes from the Old English words *beorc* and *leah*, meaning "birch wood." This name was given to those who came from the English community of Berkeley.

Barnet Street

One historian suggested a man with the last name of Barnet was a developer in this neighborhood when it was created circa 1914, yet nothing came from that lead. This street may be named for the Barnets who lived at 119, 121, and 123 South Pine Avenue, which are less than a mile from Barnet Street. These three houses were built for Leo Muhfelder and Grace Barnet Muhfelder, Charles Stern and Esther Barnet Stern, and Henry Barnet and Selma Barnet, respectively, during the second decade of the 1900s. In the June 26, 1913, edition of the *Albany Evening Journal* it was reported that the Barnet Street area was developing nicely:

> The rapid development of the Woodlawn section is referenced in several ordinances that Alderman Wait has ready for passage by the common council providing for the opening of new streets. These measures accept on behalf of the city conveyances of land from George and Katie Van Schoick for streets to be known as Oakwood Street, Maplewood Street, Erie Street, Parkwood Street, Glenwood Street, Fairview Avenue, Barnet Street, and Edison Avenue.

It's possible yet not probable that Barnet Street has an obscure figurative connection to Edison Avenue, which it parallels. While Edison Avenue is named for the inventor of the film camera, Barnet Street may be named after the birthplace of British film. Birt Acres (1854–1918) was a film and photography pioneer credited with inventing the first British 35-millimeter motion picture camera. His work mirrored that of Thomas Edison (1847–1931), who invented the motion picture camera, which was copied by Acres (Edison's invention was not patented at the time). Acres lived in the London borough of Barnet, and the first publicly-projected movie in Britain took place in this borough on January 10, 1894, at the Lyonsdown Photographic Society.

Barrows Street

Barrows Street is tied to the early Albany County name Barroa, which was also spelled Barrois, Barroway, Berwar, and Berwee. The first Barroa child born in Albany County was Anna, baptized May 3, 1685, three years after the county was established. She was the daughter of Antoine Barroa. Barrows Street was built circa 1914. In the March 13, 1913, edition of the *Albany Evening Journal* it was reported that land was conveyed to the city by Claude Holding for the construction of a new street to be called Barrows Street. The name Barrow comes from an Anglo-Saxon word meaning "a place of defense or security" and from the Old English *bearo*, meaning "grove."

Bassett Street

John Bassett, born in 1765 in Brooklyn to John Bassett and Eleanor Bassett, has his Bassett Street. He worked as an assistant in the Dutch Church of Albany, which stood at the bottom of State Street. Albany's first Dutch Church was organized in 1642, and Johannes Megapolensis Jr. was its first minister. Today this church is the First Reformed Church, which was designed by Philip Hooker and built in 1798, and stands on the corner of North Pearl Street and Orange Street. It is the oldest church building in Albany, and it has the oldest pulpit in the United States. This pulpit dates to 1653 and was brought here from the Netherlands for the original Dutch Church that stood at the bottom of State Street.

Bassett was trained at the New Brunswick Theological Seminary, fulfilled his Albany position from 1787 to 1805, and was ordained in the city June 28, 1787. He trained young Albanian men for the work of the cloth, was an expert in Hebrew and the classics, and was a trustee of Queens College as well as president of Dutch Church Academy. However, Bassett was not particularly well-liked, Bielinski writing that Bassett "would never become pastor." He married and had four children, and during the early 1800s he left the church. John Bassett moved to Bushwick, Long Island, and died there August 29, 1824. Bassett Street is one of few Albany streets that was named for a living person. This street name appeared on maps as early as 1794, thirty years before his death. Bassett Street used to be part of a "dominie cluster" within Albany. Gorham Worth, in *Random Recollections of Albany, from 1800 to 1808*, wrote that the first street within this cluster was named in honor of Rev. John Lydius, who preached here from 1700 to 1709. It was the camp ground of the British armies in the French and Indian wars. The ancient church pasture, which came into the possession of the Dutch church in 1668, was laid out into lots in 1791, and sold by auction. The streets were named after the *domines* or ministers of that church. Beginning with Lydius street on the north, then Westerlo, Bassett, Nucella and Johnson, running parallel with it. Among those running north and south were Dellius (pronounced Dallius, and now so written), for Rev. Godfrey Dell, who came over in 1683; Frelinghuysen, now Franklin, and Van Schee.

Bassett Street still exists, as do Westerlo Street and Dallius Street. Lydius Street is now Madison Avenue, Nucella Street is now Fourth Avenue, Johnson Street is now Arch Street (or perhaps Park Avenue), Frelinghuysen Street is still Franklin Street, and Van Schee Street is now Herkimer Street.

The English and French spelling of Bassett is Basset, the English spelling can also be Bassett, and the Italian spelling is Basetti. The name Bassett comes from the name Bass. Bass comes from the ancient word *basese*, given to someone who was poor or short; *baes*, given to someone who sold bass or looked like a fish; and *bathais*, meaning "forehead." It was also given to those from Bass, Scotland.

Batcher Street

Batcher Street, built prior to 1874, is surrounded by other "name streets" such as Krank Street, Seymour Avenue, Leonard Street, Scott Street, and Bouck Street. The difference between these five streets and Batcher Street is that it's unknown who Batcher was. This street used to be called Centre Alley. The name Batcher may be a transformation of the English name Bachelor.

Beach Avenue

The surf is not up on Beach Avenue. It is nowhere near a body of water. An Albany family name is used here. Albany Rural Cemetery has at least eighteen Beach graves. The oldest one dates to 1861 and is the grave of Ida P. Beach, born 1852. Beach Avenue was constructed before 1914. The last name Beach stems from a corruption of the European names Beech and Bache. An example of such alternate spellings is Manhattan's Beach Street, which is named for Paul Bache. He was the son-in-law of Anthony Lispenard, a wealthy merchant who was the grandson of Albany mayor Rutger Bleecker. Beach Street and Lispenard Street are fittingly joined to each other in a section of Manhattan once known as Lispenard Swamp and Lispenard Meadows.

Beacon Avenue

Defined by *Merriam-Webster's Collegiate Dictionary*, a beacon is "a signal fire commonly on a hill, tower, or pole" and "a lighthouse or other signal for guidance." A beacon possibly stood on the broad height of land where Beacon Avenue lies, though one historian rated this hypothesis unlikely. This theory cannot be abandoned easily, though, because Beacon Avenue, which was constructed prior to 1924, is among the high-country names of Berkshire Boulevard, South Berkshire Boulevard, Catskill Street, Adirondack Street, and Hillcrest Avenue. Perhaps beacon is used figuratively, not literally, to portray a plateau where a beacon could have been placed if someone wanted to. If a beacon is not tied to Beacon Avenue, this street emulates Beacon Street in Boston. Beacon streets in Chicago and St. Paul are named after this Boston street and its exclusive neighborhood. The word beacon comes from the Old English *beacen*, meaning "sign" and "lighthouse"; the West Germanic *baukna*, meaning "signal"; and the Latin *bucina*, meaning "signal horn."

Beaver Street

The American beaver is the mammal most responsible for westward expansion and United States exploration, including exploration of New York. In *Seventeenth Century Albany*, Wilcoxen wrote that the first beaver trade between the Indians and the Dutch, specifically members of Henry Hudson's *Half Moon* crew, took place September 19, 1609. Indians brought the crew "bever skinnes, and otters skinnes" that crew members "bought for beades, knives, and hatchets." In *Albany*, Hislop fittingly called old-time Albany "the Empire of the Beaver." Beaver Street is suitably near the former location of one of the earliest trading forts in the region and along the former, ancient, shoreline of the Hudson River (the Albany bank of the Hudson River today rests hundreds of feet east of its original location).

By the 1620s more than 7,000 beaver pelts were being shipped from the Hudson Valley annually. A decade later the total jumped to 30,000. By the 1680s more than 80,000 were being shipped from New York each year, most of them gathered from the western and northern parts of New York because no beavers were left near Albany by the 1660s. Beaver fever infected Europeans and native trappers alike during the 1600s and 1700s, and during the 1800s Americans trapped what few beavers were left in America. By that point, beavers had been stalked and killed for 250 years. Steven Rinella wrote in *Meat Eater* of this insatiable appetite for fur:

> Fur was on the brain of the otherwise gold-crazed Spaniards when they began poking around Florida and the Mississippi Delta and the Southwest and the California coast; Henry Hudson went up the Hudson River with an eye toward finding pelts; when the first load of exports left the Plymouth

Colony at Massachusetts Bay in 1621, the bulk of its value was in fur; Samuel de Champlain, the Father of New France, established the cities of Montreal and Quebec in part to facilitate the search for furs. In 1803, when Lewis and Clark headed up the Missouri River, they were under orders to investigate the feasibility of trading for furs with the tribes of the Great Plains and the Rockies.

Blame fashion for near-extinction of the American beaver. Pelts were made into robes, hats, coats, and trim to feed a European appetite for fine fur. What saved the beaver was a shift in taste. Silk became more popular than beaver, and the beaver was spared. A robust population of beavers now spreads across New York. The beaver is also alive in symbolism. This animal is featured on the seal of the City of Albany and the seal of New York City (there are actually two beavers, inexplicably colored aqua blue, on this latter seal). It was the centerpiece of the seal of New Belgium during the early 1600s when Albany was part of New Netherland and possessed by the Dutch. During that time, Albany was called Beverwyck, Dutch for "place of the beaver." The beaver is New York's official mammal.

Before we leave Beaver Street, discussion of a fascinating circa 1705 six-inch by nine-inch map of Albany is warranted because it's one of the oldest maps to portray streets by name, and it specifically identifies Beaver Street. This map, *Foort Oranje Sive Albany*, included Beaver Street (shown as "Bever Straet"), Broadway ("Handelaers Straet"), Maiden Lane ("Rom Straet"), James Street ("Middel Steegh"), Pearl Street ("Parel Straet"), and State Street ("Joncker Staet"). It also showed "Wegh naer Saraghtoga" as the way to Saratoga, "De Wegh naer ve Sopus" as the way to Esopus, and "Wech naer Schanektada" as the way to Schenectady. The Hudson River was identified as the "Noort Rivier."

Beekman Street

Beekman Street and neighboring Bertha Street, Hurlbut Street, Jeanette Street, Marshall Street, and Stanwix Street were portrayed on maps before 1896. The Beekman name dates within Albany County to 1638 when Marten Beekman came from Duchy of Bremen, a territory within the Holy Roman Empire, as one of Kiliaen Van Rensselaer's settlers. Beekman was dead by the summer of 1677, but the family line carried on. In 1684 Johannes Beekman Jr. was baptized on January 27. He was the son of Johannes Martense Beekman, a blacksmith, and Eva Vinhagen Beekman, Johannes's second wife. Johannes Martense Beekman was born in 1647 and died September 30, 1732. Eva Vinhagen Beekman survived until March 6, 1755. They were later buried in Albany Rural Cemetery.

The most notable Beekman was Johannes Jacobse Beekman, who was the 29th mayor of Albany, serving from 1783 to 1786. He was born in Albany on August 8, 1733, and married Marie Sanders on November 22, 1759. Sanders was the granddaughter of the 23rd mayor of Albany, Robert Sanders, who served during the 1750s. Johannes Jacobse Beekman died December 17, 1802, while his wife passed away November 2, 1794.

Belvidere Avenue

Spelled the traditional Italian way, *belvedere*, this word describes something "beautiful to see." A developer with an Italian flair and an understanding of the meaning of belvedere eloquently named this street, which was built before 1923. If he wasn't citing the beauty of his neighborhood, then this developer was referring to the community of Belvidere near Weirmar in Sax-Gotha, Germany. Communities named Belvidere in Illinois, New Jersey, New York, North Carolina, Vermont, and Italy are named after this pretty settlement in Germany.

Bender Avenue

A few of the first, if not *the* first, of the Benders to reside in Albany were Christiaan Bender and Elisabeth Bender, whose daughter, Christina, was born October 16, 1764. This Christiaan Bender is likely the same Christiaan Bender buried in the Town of Bethlehem Cemetery. He was born in 1731 and died June 9, 1808. By the early 1900s, more than fifty adult Benders were living in Albany and held jobs as clerks, butchers, policemen, printers, engineers, booksellers, and real estate agents.

One well-known Bender was William Bender. He had been a grocer since 1835 and developed most of the Lark Street area during the 1850s. His store had previously been on South Pearl Street. He was the original owner of 285 Lark Street, which is the oldest building on that street. It was built in 1854. He was also the initial owner of Lark Street numbers 289, 291, 293, 295, and 297. These were built in 1857 and still stand. William Bender was born in the Town of Bethlehem in 1816, died in Albany on April 5, 1889, and was buried in Albany Rural Cemetery.

A more famous Bender was Matthew Bender, a publisher who established operations in Albany in 1887. He was born in Albany on December 2, 1845, and initially ran his publishing house with his sons, Matthew Jr. and John, on the corner of Broadway and State Street. Matthew Bender died April 23, 1920, in Albany and was buried in Albany Rural Cemetery. Bender publishing offices later opened in Dayton, Ohio; New York City, New York; Helena, Montana; Conklin, New York; Charlottesville, Virginia; and San Francisco, California. This business was bought by Times Mirror Company in 1963, and Lexis Nexis subsequently bought it in 1998. In 2013, the Albany office at 1275 Broadway laid off its 220 employees and closed its doors the following year. The Bender family had not been involved with the company since the 1963 sale. Nearly ninety Benders can be found in Albany Rural Cemetery, and some reached near immortality. Within their online records, the cemetery calculated that Louisa

Bender, Margaret Bender, and Walter Bender lived to be 612, 712, and 912 years old, respectively. One must presume these are typos. The name Bender is of German origin and noted those who made casks and worked as coopers. Part of their jobs was to "bend" components of these items.

Benjamin Street

A first or last name is carried through Benjamin Street, which was built prior to 1874 with nearby Krank Street, Odell Street, Batcher Street, and Broad Street. More than thirty Benjamins (last name) rest in Albany Rural Cemetery. The oldest grave dates to 1848, this being the plot of Mary Jane Benjamin, who lived for 101 years. The oldest grave identifying a Benjamin born in Albany is that of Adaline Benjamin, born in 1814. Benjamin is one of the twelve tribes of Israel. As the name Ben Yamin, it translates to "son of the right hand," which means to be a son of good luck.

Benson Street

The last name Benson, which has been spelled Bensen, Bensingh, Bensing, Bensinck, and Bensick, dates to the 1600s in New York. Dirck Bensen, born during the 1620s, was married to Catalyn Bercx Bensen. He had come from Groningen in the Netherlands to the New World circa 1648, was a carpenter, and lived in Beverwyck from 1653 to January 6, 1659, the day he died. His wife survived him by more than thirty years, dying during April 1693.

The name Benson Street was mentioned in newspaper articles as early as 1827, though it was reported that this street didn't actually open until 1874. In 1866 it was still a "paper street." Defined by Kristina Hardinger, a paper street is one that is "marked on a map . . . with a municipality that shows the existence of an intended public right of way," yet the street hadn't "been physically improved on the location marked on the map. Thus, the street exists solely as lines on a map. . . . " Benson Street appeared unnamed on city maps as late as the 1870s, and by 1895 maps were showing it named. Its eastern section between Quail Street and Ontario Street was definitely built prior to 1915, while its western section reaching out to North Main Avenue was built soon after this eastern section was completed.

A contributor to this book pointed out that Benson Street parallels Kent Street. This is not coincidental. Egbert Benson, New York State Supreme Court associate justice, served as mentor of James Kent, New York State Supreme Court judge. Benson was born in New York City on June 21, 1746, as the son of Robert Benson and Catherine Van Borsum Benson and was a direct descendant of Dirck Bensen mentioned above. He graduated from King's College, today's Columbia University, in 1765 and practiced law in Red Hook and New York City. He was a founding father who served as New York assemblyman, House of

Representatives member from New York, New York attorney general, Continental Congress member, State Constitutional Convention member, Annapolis Convention member, New York University regent, Dutchess County Board of Commissioners president, chief judge of the Second Circuit, and New York State Supreme Court associate justice. Egbert Benson died August 24, 1833, and was buried in Prospect Cemetery in New York City. Judge James Kent wrote of his mentor in 1839:

> If he was not the first, he was one of the first proficients in the science of pleading; and his equal does not exist at the present day. But, though a strict technical lawyer, he did not cease to penetrate the depths of the science, and rest himself on fundamental principles. He was more distinguished than any man among us, [Alexander] Hamilton alone excepted . . . His morals and manners were pure and chaste. He was liberal and catholic in his sentiments, without the smallest tincture of fanaticism or affectation of austerity; and nothing could weaken his faith or disturb his tranquility . . .

Benson's death in 1833 left only two founding fathers alive: John Marshall, who died in 1835, and James Madison Jr., who died in 1836. The town of Benson in Vermont is likely named for this man while New York City's Benson Street and New York's town of Benson are definitely named for him. New York City's Bensonhurst neighborhood is named for a descendant of his, Arthur Benson, who was president of Brooklyn Gas. The name Benson was given to those who came from Benesingtun—present-day Benson—England.

Berkshire Boulevard
(and South Berkshire Boulevard)

There are fewer than twenty boulevards in Albany. To be named a "boulevard," the street would best consist of two lanes divided by a grassy area with trees. But this naming rule is generally not followed. Such is the case with the Berkshire boulevards. The word boulevard was once used to define wide streets built over destroyed city walls. The Berkshire boulevards neighborhoods—just about everything within Western Avenue to the north, Route 85 to the east, the New York State Thruway to the south, and Krum Kill to the west—were built between 1900 and 1927. Berkshire Boulevard was mentioned in newspaper articles as early as 1916.

The name Berkshire was promoted in America by royal governor Francis Bernard, who was familiar with the Royal County of Berkshire, England. The Berkshire Mountains, named after this English county, are in western Connecticut and western Massachusetts and are sometimes called the Berkshire Hills and Berkshire Plateau. Most people call them the Berkshires like most people call the Catskill Mountains the Catskills and the Adirondack Mountains the

Adirondacks. The highest point along the Berkshire Mountains is often cited as 2,841-foot Crum Hill. Others maintain it is 3,487-foot Mount Greylock, though this peak is generally accepted to be part of Taconic, not Berkshire, geology. Former names for Mount Greylock include Grand Hoosuck (*Hoosuck* being Algonquin for "stony place," which was their name for the nearby Hoosic River) and Saddleback Mountain (this name survives in nearby Saddle Ball Mountain). The name Greylock reflects the fact that the summit spends much time "locked" in gray clouds, or it memorializes Chief Gray Lock of the Western Abenaki Missisquoi. This New England mountain range has inspired copycat place names including the community of Berkshire, formerly known as Brown's Settlement, in New York's Tioga County. This community got its name due to being set in country that resembles the Berkshire Mountains.

Berncliff Avenue

Berncliff Avenue, built before 1937, is one of three streets within Albany that combines two first names. The other two are Marwill Street (Maria and William) and Wilan Lane (William and Anne). Berncliff Avenue is named for the sons of builder John David Picotte. Picotte Companies was established in 1933, though its founder, John David, had been building homes and commercial properties in the Capital Region since the 1920s. One of his sons was Bernard ("Bern"), who died in 1986 at the age of 75, and the other was Clifford ("Cliff"), who died in 1961 at the age of 45. These men built many houses in the Whitehall Neighborhood from the 1930s to the 1950s, and during the 1930s Bernard was secretary and treasurer while Clifford was vice president. Picottes still run this family business. The Berncliff Avenue neighborhood used to be part of the Town of Bethlehem yet was annexed to the City of Albany.

Bertha Street
(and South Bertha Street)

The neighboring streets of Bertha Street, Hurlbut Street, Jeanette Street, Marshall Street, Stanwix Street, and West Van Vechten Street were laid out by Teunis Van Vechten, who reportedly named all of them for family members. In this neighborhood the names Bertha Street, Corlaer Street, Marshall Street, and Twiller Street were made official within a 1915 city ordinance. Bertha Van Vechten Hurlbut was the daughter of Elisha Hurlbut and Catharine Cuyler Hurlbut and died May 13, 1876. She was the granddaughter of Teunis Van Vechten.

Besch Avenue

Besch Avenue carries the Besch family name and may be specifically named for John Besch. His birth name was Johan Von Bosch before it was Anglicized when he came to the U.S. with his wife, Rose Keller Besch, in 1852. Besch was born in 1820, his wife in 1826. This couple was originally from Baden, Germany, a charming community on the Rhine River, and lived on upper Delaware Avenue during the late 1800s and early 1900s when that area was still farmland. Besch built a home on Besch Avenue in 1915, this likely being the first home on this street. He ended up building most of the homes on Besch Avenue and Rose Court. The first house on Rose Court was constructed in 1916.

One source stated that Besch Avenue is named for Albany County Sheriff Joseph L. Besch, who served in this law enforcement role during the early 1900s. He was married to Elizabeth Menifold Besch, was related to John Besch, and was the father of Joseph L. Besch Jr. The best-documented period of Sheriff Besch's life involves charges of neglect being brought against him by the Civic League of Albany due to him allegedly not addressing a gambling problem in the county. These charges were eventually dropped by Governor Charles Evans Hughes when a report submitted by George Beattys, who was appointed commissioner by the governor to investigate this matter, concluded that Besch was not guilty of wrongdoing. The gist of the matter was that the sheriff maintained he was not responsible to go lurking about the county looking for gamblers, though he would certainly respond to a report of gambling.

If Besch Avenue is not specifically named for either Besch man named above, then this street is named for the Besch family in general. The great-great-grandson of John Besch made a case for Besch Avenue being named for the family overall: "I cannot confirm that Besch Avenue was named for John or Joseph. The fact that they used only the last name Besch, but then used first names for the other streets named for specific people from the family, such as Rose and Joelson courts, makes me think they may have named Besch Avenue after the entire Besch family. But we will never know." The six "Besch streets" are Besch Avenue, Betwood Street, Clayton Place, Joanne Court, Joelson Court, and Rose Court.

Bethlehem Avenue

Part of the Town of Bethlehem became part of the City of Albany in 1870, and Bethlehem Avenue reminds us of this annexation. The Town of Bethlehem was formed March 12, 1793. Just four years later the *American Gazette* reported that the town was "very fruitful in pastures and has large quantities of excellent butter." This fifty-square-mile town, which survives to the south of Albany and is within Albany County, is likely named after the biblical Bethlehem. Bethlehem is a Palestinian city of 25,000 people and is noted as the birthplace of Jesus. Many U.S. place names carry the Bethlehem title. The quaintest of these are Bethlehem, Pennsylvania, and Bethlehem, New Hampshire, which were named on Christmas Eve of 1741 and Christmas Day of 1799, respectively.

Betwood Street

Betwood Street is named for Betty Besch, who was born in 1931. She was the daughter of Joseph L. Besch Jr. and Anna Heidrich Besch and the granddaughter of Joseph L. Besch and Elizabeth Menifold Besch. The name of this street, along with the names Clayton Place and Joelson Court, was accepted by the city in 1925 when Joseph and Elizabeth conveyed land to the city for the building of this street. It was built circa 1927 and called "a new street" in 1929. Betwood Street is near four other "Besch streets": Rose Court, Joanne Court, Joelson Court, and Clayton Place. The sixth Besch street, set off on its own, is Besch Avenue. Betwood Street illustrates an odd case in which the name of the street predated the birth of the person for whom it would be named.

Beverly Avenue

Land for construction of Beverly Avenue—and neighboring McArdle Avenue, Pennsylvania Avenue, Wilkins Avenue, and extensions of Colonie Street and Thornton Street—was conveyed to the city in 1912. This street was built before 1915 and could be named for a woman, perhaps carrying a first name (no Beverlys of such a surname are found in Albany Rural Cemetery). This street could perhaps be named after Beverly, England, or Beverly, Massachusetts, which gets its name from the English community. Beverly, England, has been settled since the 600s. Back then it was called Inderawuda, meaning "in the wood of the men of Deira," and stood within the Kingdom of Northumbria. By the 900s the area was called Beverli and then Beverlac, meaning "beaver lake." Beverly Hills in California and communities named Beverly in Iowa, Nebraska, Ohio, and Washington got their names from Beverly, Massachusetts.

Bingham Street

City engineer Reuben Howland "R. H." Bingham has his namesake street. He was born June 8, 1822, in Stillwater, New York, to George Bingham and Sarah Howland Bingham. He served as city engineer and surveyor from 1854 to 1886, died May 8, 1888, and was buried in Albany Rural Cemetery. He was married to Elizabeth Stratton Bingham. Bingham Street was one of the first streets built off McCarty Avenue. It was portrayed on maps by 1873. Shown near it that year was Kimball Place, a street that has since vanished and was named for landowner Jonathan Kimball. Bingham Street is fittingly next to Browne Street, which is named for assistant city engineer and surveyor, James Browne. Bingham and Browne worked together during the 1860s and 1870s. Bingham is an English surname derived from the small town of that name in the Rushcliffe Borough of County Nottinghamshire, England. This last name comes from the Old Norse *bingr* and the Old English *ham*, which mean "manager" and "homestead."

Binghamton Street

As the seat of Broome County, the City of Binghamton used to be called Chenango Point, named after the river it rests on (Chenango was the name of a settlement along this river, this Onondaga word meaning "bull thistle"). Binghamton received its current name in 1855. This city and Binghamton Street memorialize William Bingham, a politician and land speculator. Born March 8, 1752, in Philadelphia, Bingham attended the College of Philadelphia, today's University of Pennsylvania, and graduated in 1768. He traveled to Europe, came back to the New World, and joined the American Revolution by capturing British ships and conferring with the French as a diplomat. When the war ended he started purchasing enormous plots of land including a two-million-acre swath in Maine. He also facilitated securing the Louisiana Purchase. Bingham then worked for the federal government and dealt with financial affairs. He became Pennsylvania delegate to the Continental Congress, member of the Pennsylvania House of Representatives, speaker of the Pennsylvania House of Representatives, and senator from Pennsylvania during the late 1700s. He imagined a quaint yet successful village located in present-day downtown Binghamton, though he had never visited the spot. Instead, he hired a local businessman, Joshua Whitney Jr, to serve as land agent. After Bingham's death, Whitney continued his work, created a village, and named it after Bingham. (Joshua lives on through the community of Whitney Point next to Bingham's namesake city.) William Bingham, husband of Anne Willing Bingham and father of three children, died February 6, 1804, in Bath, England, and was buried at Bath Abbey.

Birch Hill Road
(and Birchwood Court)

The Birch family of flora includes nearly 150 species worldwide. In North America there are more than twenty species of trees and nearly a dozen species of shrubs. New York hosts six species of birch trees: European white, gray, paper, river, sweet, and yellow. The paper birch was made famous by its use by Northeast Indians. The birch bark canoe is an iconic symbol of Northeast Indians, thus an obscure nickname for this species is "canoe birch." The paper birch is the state tree of New Hampshire. The yellow birch is largest of this family within New York. The greatest specimen found in the state measures 49 inches in diameter and 101 feet tall. These street names were chosen because they're easy on the ears and make for good imagery. Naturally-growing birch trees are rare in the Capital Region.

Birchwood Court

See Birch Hill Road.

Blanchard Avenue

An old Albany County name, James Blanchard (sometimes spelled Blanchet) and Margaret DePeyster (sometimes spelled De Peister) Blanchard had their first child, Joseph DePeyster Blanchard, on May 31, 1783. Albany Rural Cemetery has fifty Blanchard graves, the oldest belonging to a 1-year-old with the ironic name Mary Lucky Blanchard. She died in 1815. The name Blanchard is Germanic and combines *blanc* and *hard*, meaning "white" and "brave." Blanchard Avenue was built before 1934.

Bleecker Place
(and Bleecker Street, Bleecker Terrace)

Jan Janse Bleecker, a blacksmith and trader born July 9, 1641, arrived in Albany County from the Meppel Province of Overyssel, Holland, the Netherlands, in 1658. These streets are likely named for him. At least one Bleecker Street in New York City carries his name. Albany's Bleecker Street used to be called Bass Lane and Bass Street until 1831.

As one of Albany's earliest leaders, Bleecker was appointed city chamberlain (1686), captain of the militia during Indian wars (1689), Indian commissioner (1691 to 1694), city recorder (1696 to 1700), justice of the peace (1697), and member of the Provincial Assembly (1698 to 1701). He was the seventh mayor of Albany, appointed by governor (and earl) of Bellomont, his term running during 1700 and 1701. Jan Janse Bleecker died November 21, 1732, in Albany and was buried at the Dutch Church. He was married to Margariet Rutse Jacobsen Van Schoenderwoert Bleecker for a remarkable 65 years, ten months, the longest marriage recorded in *Cradle of the Union*. She died during October 1733.

If these Bleecker streets are not named for Jan Janse Bleecker, they are named for either of his two sons. Johannes Bleecker Jr. was born May 2, 1668, and served as recorder of the city. He was also mayor, his term running during 1701 and 1702 immediately after his father left office. He also served as a member of the General Assembly during those two years. Johannes Bleecker Jr. died in Albany on December 20, 1738, and was buried at the Dutch Church.

Rutger Bleecker was born May 13, 1675, in Albany and was the city's fifteenth mayor, serving from 1726 to 1729. He died in Albany on August 4, 1756, and was buried at the Dutch Church. He was married to Catlyna Schuyler Bleecker, the widow of Albany's second mayor, Johannes Abeel. Abeel served as mayor during the late 1600s and early 1700s. The ancient Rutten Kill, a stream that once flowed through Albany, was named for Rutger Bleecker. The name Bleecker is Dutch for "bleacher of cloth."

Bleecker Street
See Bleecker Place.

Bleecker Terrace
See Bleecker Place.

Blue Bell Lane
Virginia bluebells (also known as Virginia cowslips), which are part of the Borage family, and bluebells (also known as harebells), which are part of the Bellflower family, are wildflowers that grow in New York. They stand up to two feet tall, and their pink and purple flowers, respectively, which look like bells, are only an inch long. During settlement of the Blue Bell Lane area these flowers could have been found there, or it was a favorite flower of the developer or a relative of his. Blue Bell Lane is part of a bouquet of "flora streets" including Butter Cup Drive, Daisy Lane, and Silverberry Place.

Boat Street
See Anchor Street.

Boenau Street
Boenau Street honors Gottlieb Boenau since he owned land where this street now is. He was a baker and the original owner of 142 Clinton Street and 141 and 143 Broad Street. His Clinton Street house was built prior to 1860 while his two Broad Street houses were built prior to 1854. These stand a half-mile from Boenau Street, which was constructed before 1900.

Bogardus Road
Anneke Janse Bogardus was, according to Jonathan Pearson in *Contributions for the Genealogies of the First Settlers of the Ancient County of Albany, from 1630 to 1800*, a "celebrated character" in Rensselaerswyck, and she or her second husband, Everardus, is memorialized through Bogardus Road. She came to Rensselaerswyck in 1630 with her first husband, Roeloff Jansen, who was an employee of patroon Kiliaen Van Rensselaer. Jansen died circa 1636. Anneke—a name that means Little Ann—then married future Albany Dutch Church dominie Everardus Bogardus in 1638. Everardus, born in 1607 in Utrecht, the largest city and capital city of the Dutch province Utrecht, began the Bogardus name in the New World. He attended the University of Leyden and came to

New Netherland in 1633. Everardus Bogardus died in a shipwreck off the coast of Wales on September 27, 1647. Anneke Janse Bogardus, mother of eight children, died in Albany during February 1663 at her home on the corner of State Street and James Street. She was buried in a small churchyard between Beaver Street and Hudson Avenue. In 1867 she was reburied in Albany Rural Cemetery. New York City's one-block-long Bogardus Place, which opened in 1912, is named for this family. They owned land in that city, at one point possessing 62 acres on the Hudson River.

The June 20, 1922, edition of the *Albany Evening Journal* stated that land was to be conveyed to the city for six streets to be built and then named Bogardus Road, Freeman Road, and Greenway Street (today's Greenway North). The article carried sloppy spelling of three other streets to be built there. These included "Alsdorf Street" (Halsdorf Street), "Cady Street" (Kakely Street), and "Lincoln Road" (Linden Road).

Bogart Terrace

This Dutch name dates within Albany County to before 1640. Jacob Cornelise Bogaart, son of New Netherland residents Cornelis Bogaart and Dirckie Bogaart, was born in 1654. (New Netherland was a colonial province on the East Coast during the 1600s and extended into today's Delaware, Connecticut, New Jersey, New York, Pennsylvania, and Rhode Island.) He married Jannetje Quackenbush, daughter of Capital Region settlers Pieter Quackenbush and Maria Quackenbush. Jacob Cornelise Bogaart died April 6, 1725. His wife lived for nearly another decade, dying January 8, 1734. They were eventually buried in Albany Rural Cemetery, which has more than thirty Bogart graves. Bogart Terrace was built before 1913. This name stems from the Middle High German *boumgarte*, meaning "orchard."

Bohl Avenue

This family name dates to the mid-1800s in Albany County and became prevalent during the early 1900s. A dozen Bohls are buried in Evangelical Protestant Church Cemetery off Krumkill Road. By the late 1800s, August Bohl owned 23 acres where today's Bohl Avenue is and so this street is named for him (he also owned five acres where today's nearby Hampton Street is). He was born in Germany on February 2, 1854, and died July 3, 1927, at his home at 594 Delaware Avenue, right where Bohl Avenue meets that street. He was married to Christina Vogel Bohl and they had nine children: August Jr., Charles, Edward, Frederick, Gertrude, Joseph, Katherine, Rosemary, and Sophie. Beyond Bohl Avenue, August Bohl Construction Company, established 1915, carries this family name.

Boice Street

Boice is an old Albany County name usually associated with Coeymans. Coeymans Hollow Cemetery, a few miles west of downtown Coeymans, contains many Boice graves. The Town of Coeymans, formed in 1791, is named for Barent Pieteres Koijemans, also known as "Barent the Miller," who arrived in the area from Utrecht, Holland, the Netherlands, in 1639. A brick cottage built circa 1845 stands at 1 Boice Street and is the oldest building on this street.

Bonheim Street

What Bonheim may communicate here is the German place name Bornheim. Bornheim is a town in the Rhein-Sieg district, North Rhine-Westphalia; a municipality in the Alzey-Worms district in Rhineland-Palatinate; a municipality in the Südliche Weinstraße district in Rhineland-Palatinate; and a city district of Frankfurt am Main. Bonheim Street dates to 1900.

Bouck Street

William Bouck, born January 7, 1786, was the son of Christian Bouck and Margaret Bouck and is memorialized within Bouck Street, which dates to 1890. He was a lifelong politician and exclusively served New York. During the early and mid-1800s, he served as Schoharie County sheriff, New York assemblyman, senator from New York, Erie Canal Commission member, and governor. William Bouck died April 19, 1859, and was buried in Middleburgh, New York. He was the father of eight children. Public service ran in the family. His brother was House of Representatives member Joseph Bouck, and his son was Wisconsin attorney general Gabriel Bouck. SUNY Cobleskill's Bouck Hall is named for this man, as is Brooklyn's Bouck Court and the Bronx's Bouck Avenue. New York's Town of Bouckville is named for him, too. Bouckville was once called McClure Settlement because the McClure Tavern was there. It was also called the Hook as well as Johnsonville. This latter name honored settler John Edgarton and was, according to Ren Vasiliev, "the result of a drunken celebration."

Bower Avenue

On September 20, 1916, Mayor Joseph Stevens signed a Common Council ordinance that named this street so. This was twelve days after realtor Jacob W. Wilbur conveyed land to the city for construction of this street and nearby Caldwell Street, Cliff Street, Hart Street (which never got built), Twitchell Street, Webster Street, and Winnie Street (which was proposed to be called Winne Street). The word bower defines a retreat or dwelling that's tranquil and pristine. *Merriam-Webster's Collegiate Dictionary* defines bowery, which comes from the word bower and was coined in 1650, as "a colonial Dutch plantation or farm," a definition certainly applicable to this street. New York City's The Bowery, once called Bowery Lane and Bowery Road, carries this definition, too—it traverses the former farm of Dutchman Pieter Stuyvesant.

Jacob W. Wilbur was born May 2, 1847, in New Gloucester, Maine, to Jacob R. Wilbur and Anna Fickett Wilbur. By 1888 he owned the Wilbur Land Company, and by 1909 he had sold nearly 75,000 lots to more than 25,000 customers. Wilbur died April 5, 1917, and was buried in Mount Auburn Cemetery in Cambridge, Massachusetts. The community of Wilbur-by-the-Sea in Florida and Wilbur Avenue in Boston are named for this man. He named 22 streets in Massachusetts alone. Troy Bennett wrote that when Wilbur developed Portland, Maine, this realtor "named more streets in this city than anyone else, by a long shot."

Bradford Street

John Bradford's name is carried through Bradford Street. He was born during March 1781 in Danbury, Connecticut, to Ebenezer Bradford and Elizabeth Greene Bradford. He attended Brown University, graduated in 1800, was ordained, and began work as minister of the Dutch Church of Albany on August 11, 1805. He was removed from this position fifteen years later, his dismissal having to do with the good reverend's love of alcohol. Bradford married Mary Lush by 1808, and they had six children. Mary was the daughter of Stephen Lush and Lydia Stringer Lush. John Bradford died March 25, 1826, while Mary lived for another 35 years, dying during November 1861. Though one source reported that this street opened in 1874, Bradford Street had been mentioned in newspaper articles as far back as 1822, and its southeast section between today's Lexington Avenue and North Lake Avenue was portrayed on maps by 1866. The name Bradford stems from British place names of the same name, which translate to "broad ford."

Brady Avenue

John J. Brady, for whom this street is named, was a Police Court and Children's Court judge credited with cofounding the modern family courts of New York. This street was specifically chosen to memorialize Brady because he used to own the Brady farm where this namesake street now lies. He grew up on this farm, which belonged to his parents, John Brady and Ann Farley Brady, who were from County Cavan, Ireland. Brady was born January 16, 1870, and attended Saint Joseph's Parochial School, Christian Brothers Academy, and Manhattan College. Beyond serving as judge, he practiced law and was city alderman, president of the Christian Brothers Academy board of trustees, and president of the Albany Catholic Union. John J. Brady died January 8, 1950, and was buried in St. Agnes Cemetery. In the April 13, 1950, edition of the *Times*

Union, it was reported that during a memorial service, surrogate Edward Rogan declared of Brady that "during his long service he became known not only in Albany and vicinity but throughout the nation. Boys and girls had a warm place in his heart and many of them were, through his efforts, restored to their homes. He realized the value of inviting the cooperation of interested individuals and groups in seeking to solve the problems confronting him in his efforts at rehabilitation." His son, John J. Brady Jr., followed in his footsteps. He was an attorney who graduated from Christian Brothers Academy, Manhattan College, and Columbia Law School and operated the law firm Brady and Brady with his father at 75 State Street. Brady Avenue and nearby Maguire Street were built during the 1950s.

Brevator Street

Brevator Street is named for the Brevator family, perhaps specifically for Jonathan Brevator. During the 1870s, Catharine Brevator owned farmland where Brevator Street now is. In 1872 she deeded land to the city for partial construction of this street (the section of Brevator Street north of Washington Avenue didn't become property of the city until 1939). In this area this family also owned land where the graves of paved-over and built-over streets now lie. These include Townsend Street, Stevenson Street, Lewis Street, Knower Street, Hawley Street, and Hoffman Avenue, which no longer exist. Brevator Street dates to 1881 and was first called Brevator Avenue.

Jonathan Brevator was born in County Norfolk, England, and came to the United States in 1842, settling in Albany. He married Catharine McGrath Gray. He died in Lincoln County, Missouri, on March 7, 1881, while his wife died in Brevator Station, which is also in Lincoln County, on February 25, 1899. This community was called a station because it stood right on the St. Louis, Keokuk, and Northwestern Railroad within Monroe Township. Brevator Station was laid out in 1880, had a post office from 1886 to 1932, and was named for Jonathan because he owned land where the station was built. The Brevators had a son, who was also named Jonathan. He was born in Albany on September 28, 1854, and moved to Missouri with his family, dying February 4, 1911, in Old Monroe, Missouri. He and his wife, Elizabeth Riches Brevator, had two children.

This last name could stem from the word breviary, which labels an abridged collection of daily prayers or rites for Roman Catholic priests. It also describes a single book that contains books of rites of different kinds, such as the Psalter, Antiphonary, Responsoriary, Lectionary, and more. However, this single book would more accurately be called a plenarium, not a breviary. The word breviary as we use it today stems from the eleventh century.

Briar Avenue
(and Briarwood Court, Briarwood Terrace)

Briars, a generic term for thorn-covered bushes, grow in direct sunlight and are usually found under power lines and in wastelands such as disturbed forests and abandoned lots. When these three streets were constructed, there may have been tangles of briars to clear among the woods and farmland. Briars aren't all bad though. Certain species produce raspberries and blackberries ripe for the picking towards summer's end. Traditionally spelled brier until circa 1600, this word comes from similar-sounding Middle English and Old English words meaning "prickly bush."

Briarwood Court

See Briar Avenue.

Briarwood Terrace

See Briar Avenue.

Bridge Street

There is no bridge on Bridge Street, yet this street is within sight of a bridge that crosses the Hudson River. Today that bridge carries traffic east and west along Interstate 90. Prior to a bridge being built in this area, Albanians and their fellow travelers took ferries, conveyances that are remembered through North Ferry Street and South Ferry Street. Ferries were deemed inadequate at a city meeting held February 11, 1836, and on January 30, 1841, a more pressing meeting was held to again promote a bridge. Communication between the east and west sides of the river had ground to a halt when the ice was too thick to let ferries pass, yet too thin to support sleighs. Construction of the first bridge across the river at Albany finally started October 19, 1863. The 1,950-foot-long, 21-pier Livingston Avenue railroad bridge (also known as the Lumber Street railroad bridge) opened February 22, 1866. On December 28, 1871, the first train crossed the 2,650-foot-long, 22-pier Maiden Lane railroad bridge, Albany's second bridge. Pre-1900s bridges in the area included the Cohoes bridge across the Mohawk River (opened July 24, 1795), 800-foot-long Union Bridge across the Hudson River at Waterford (December 1804), a bridge across the Mohawk River below the great falls (November 25, 1807), Greenbush drawbridge across the Hudson River (January 3, 1882), and the South Ferry Street bridge, also known as the Lower bridge, across the Hudson River (January 24, 1882).

Broad Street

Perhaps not living up to its name, Broad Street is not broad. As *The Knicker-bocker News* commented: "The love of Americans for sounding brass and tin-kling cymbals is seen in many street names. Adjectives denoting superlatives, or at least exaggerated conditions, are used freely. Such a name is Broad Street." An old name for this street is Malcolm Street, but this name was abandoned May 10, 1831.

The name Broad Street may have a connection to the nearby Schuyler Mansion. This street name could well be a variation of the last name Bradstreet, as in John Bradstreet (1714–1774). He was a British Army officer active during King George's War, the French and Indian War, and Pontiac's Rebellion, and was a friend of Philip Schuyler, who also fought in the French and Indian War. This street name could also be a variation of the names of Philip Schuyler's sons, John Bradstreet Schuyler (1763–1764) and John Bradstreet Schuyler (1765–1795).

Broadway

Broadway is the Albany street that has had the most names. It was formerly called Brewers Street (because there was a brewery at the bottom of nearby State Street), Court Street (because the first courts stood nearby), Handelaars Straat (Dutch for "Trader Street"), Handlers Street (*handler* being Dutch for "market"), Handelaers Straat, Market Street, North Market Street, Road to the Mill, South Market Street, and Troy Road. The name Broadway was bor-rowed from New York City and was made official by the City of Albany on August 3, 1840, by a vote of nine to three. New York City's Broadway has been identified on maps since 1776 at the latest, a map from that year label-ing it Broadway Street.

In the early 1900s, as Hislop related, "all the buildings which bordered Broadway between Madison Avenue and the Hudson River bridge were torn down to permit the widening of what had become truly a 'Broadway.'" The width of Broadway is due to facilities, notably the Public Market, that stood in the middle of this street. Walking west from the Hudson River, Albanians would pass through a row of buildings, cross the east lane of Broadway, pass a row of markets occupied by farmers and artisans, cross the west lane of Broad-way, and then, finally, enter a third row of dwellings and businesses. Nearby State Street is wide, too. State Street had a trolley that first consisted of horse-drawn coaches running up the middle of it in 1864. By the early 1900s, more than a dozen streets hosted trolleys. The last Albany trolley was replaced by bus service in 1946.

The first map to show Broadway is one from 1695, this map composed by John Miller. He called it "Handlers Street." Allen noted in *The Mapping of New York State* that "except for a very crude sketch dating from about 1659, Miller's drawing of Albany is our first map of that city, which had changed little since the final years of Dutch rule." Broadway might as well have been called River Street during the 1600s and 1700s since the original west bank of the Hudson River butted up against today's Broadway. This west bank has since been extended east, and Interstate 787 rests on this artificial extension.

Brookland Avenue

This street, which dates to before 1928, is in the land of a brook. Brookland Avenue is on the east bank of Krum Kill, a three-mile-long stream that begins at Indian Pond on the University at Albany's main campus. After its serpentine course, Krum Kill joins Normans Kill near the intersection of Route 85 and New Scotland Road.

Brookline Avenue

When Albany's neighborhoods were being laid out, there needed to be clear boundaries separating one neighborhood from the next. In the case of the Pine Hills Neighborhood, as told by McEneny, one of its boundaries was determined to lay where "a stream proceeded to the south blocking off most development and forming the brook line. . . . " This brook started at Alex's Pond near today's Homestead Avenue and meandered south. It fed Hawkins Pond but was then routed underneath Albany's streets. Brookline Avenue was built prior to 1915.

As told in Charles Mooney's "Westward Ho—to Pine Hills" article, plans for the Pine Hills Neighborhood first appeared in 1889 on a map by the City of Albany. During that time the Albany Land Improvement and Building Company, founded 1888, was selling lots in this neighborhood, which was billed as "a villa park of 170 acres, located at the West End of the City of Albany, at the Allen St. terminus of the Albany Railway's Madison Ave. lines." As Waite wrote of this development:

> One of the best known large-scale developments was the Pine Hills subdivisions. Formerly part of the McIntyre and Hawkins farms . . . the land was purchased by the Albany Land Improvement and Building Company in 1888 . . . [This company] made improvements, laying out and paving Pine Avenue and Allen Street, planting trees, constructing sidewalks, and installing drains and water and sewer lines. Just as important as the physical improvements were the covenants imposed on each lot prohibiting commercial activity and the sale of liquor.

The Albany Land Improvement and Building Company went bankrupt in 1893 during the great financial crash. Albany City National Bank gained control of the company's land and then auctioned off all their lots.

Browne Street

Assistant city engineer and surveyor James Browne worked alongside city engineer and surveyor Reuben Howland "R. H." Bingham, thus Browne Street and Bingham Street are next to each other. These men worked together during the 1860s and 1870s, and their namesake streets have appeared on maps since 1873. James Browne died sometime around 1900. The name Brown comes from the Old High German *brun*, which means "brown." It described those who had brown skin, brown hair, brown eyes, or wore brown often.

Bryn Mawr Court

Dolgellau is a small town in the region of Gwynedd, Wales, and in this small town there was a farm and estate called Bryn Mawr. Bryn Mawr (Welsh for "great hill") was owned by Rowland Ellis, a Quaker, who was born at this residence in 1650. By the spring of 1687, he was living in Philadelphia after fleeing Wales because of religious persecution. He settled Bryn Mawr, a little community in southeast Pennsylvania, obviously naming it after his farm and estate overseas. In 1688, Ellis returned to Wales to settle matters and grab the rest of his family. Soon back stateside with the Ellis clan, he was elected in 1700 to represent Philadelphia in the Assembly of the Province. Rowland Ellis died during September 1731 in Gwynedd, Pennsylvania, which takes its name from the Welsh region. If not directly named for Ellis's residence, Bryn Mawr Court is named for Bryn Mawr College, a women's liberal arts university founded in 1885 in Bryn Mawr, Pennsylvania.

Bucci McTague Drive

Like Doane Stuart Road, Bucci McTague Drive carries two last names. The first is that of William Bucci, who was born June 22, 1920, as one of eleven children of Gaetano Bucci and Rose Venosa Bucci. He graduated high school, joined the Army National Guard, and was deployed to the South Pacific after receiving training in Alabama, California, and Hawaii. He was killed by a Japanese sniper February 19, 1944, on Eniwetok Atoll in the Marshall Islands. The goal of this weeklong battle was to secure harbors and airfields to then support attacks of the Mariana Islands. More than 300 Americans were killed, nearly 100 went missing in action, and nearly 900 were wounded in this battle. William Bucci was buried in Saint Agnes Cemetery in Menands, New York.

The second name is that of Robert McTague. McTague was likely born in Tannersville, New York, and was one of five sons—including Charles, Thomas, Richard, and Harold—of Charles McTague and Laura Cole McTague. Four of these five men served in the military during World War II, yet Robert never made it home. He was killed in Army combat operations in France on July 19, 1944. He was buried in Normandy American Cemetery in Colle-sur-Mer,

Calvados, France. The Bucci-McTague American Legion Post in Glenmont, New York, is named for these men.

Buchanan Street

If you are familiar with the nine-street "presidential conglomerate" of central Albany that includes Cleveland Street, Grant Avenue, Lincoln Avenue, McKinley Street, Roosevelt Street, Garfield Place, Van Buren Street, Washington Avenue, and Buchanan Street, you will be astonished to learn that Buchanan Street is not named for James Buchanan, fifteenth president of the United States. So, reduce the presidential conglomerate to eight streets, please.

Realtor Jesse Leonard wanted to name streets in this neighborhood for brilliant engineers. He started with Buchanan Street, a name the city accepted in 1898, and quickly had a realization. He couldn't think of any other brilliant engineers. He figured everyone would think Buchanan Street is named for the former president, and so he named the surrounding streets for presidents to keep the trend. According to Kenneth Salzmann in *Albany Scrapbook Volume I*, Buchanan Street is named for William Buchanan, New York Central Railroad's chief superintendent of motive power and rolling stock and "master mechanic at the West Albany Shops," who was involved in building engine 999 in 1893. This steam-powered locomotive, which pulled New York Central Railroad's Empire State Express passenger train, was a rocket ship. It was the first locomotive to exceed 100 miles per hour, and on May 10, 1893, it broke a speed record that stood for ten years by reaching 112.5 miles per hour. These events are remembered through an awkwardly-worded historical plaque on Industrial Park Road: "Site of the New York Central Railroad erector shop where engine 999 was built in 1893. 999 was the first creation of man in the history of time to travel 100 miles per hour." After appearing in world exhibitions and fairs during the 1890s, 1930s, and 1940s, engine 999 was retired in 1952. It is on display at the Museum of Science and Industry, Chicago.

Buchanan, born 1830, immigrated to America from Scotland and was working for the Albany and Schenectady Railroad by the age of 17. He then worked as a machinist, locomotive engineer, shop foreman, and master mechanic for a host of railroad companies including the Hudson River Railroad, Troy and Greenwich Railroad, New York Central Railroad, and West Shore Railroad, among others. William Buchanan died in 1910 in South Norwalk, Connecticut.

Buckingham Drive

Buckingham Palace is recognized through Buckingham Drive. Located in Westminster, England, and originally known as Buckingham House, this 775-room palace serves as administrative headquarters and home of the leading monarch of the U.K. In 1703, the Duke of Buckingham built a townhouse where the palace now stands. Purchased by King George III in 1761, it was set aside as a private residence for Queen Charlotte. In the 1800s, the building was expanded, and in 1837 it became the residence of the British monarch. Other additions have taken place since then, including a section that was rebuilt after being bombed by the Germans in World War II.

Buckingham Drive is likely specifically named after the Buckingham Gardens neighborhood development in this area. Advertisements for homes in this section of Albany ran as early as 1925 and told prospective buyers that there were "plenty of fruit trees and excellent soil for flowers" waiting for them. Buckingham Gardens homes were worth the money: "A good investment in real estate now will make you comfortable later. This is the logical section of Albany to grow, so why not get one of these lots, and watch it increase in value?" Two builders active in this section of the city during the 1920s and 1930s were John Cregan and George Hockensmith. A Hockensmith advertisement from that era featured an image of a new home and read: "Come out today—see this modern home at 749 New Scotland Ave. Buckingham Gardens. And then you will realize just why this new development holds the record in the Albany area for the sale of new homes." Buckingham Drive is not far from Buckingham Lake. This lake used to be called Buckingham Pond and Rafts Lake (Rafts Way is near this lake today). The advertisement from 1925 mentioned above described this lake as being "fed by springs," which resulted in the water being "as clear as crystal."

The name Buckingham is carried through communities of that name in Alabama, Pennsylvania, California, Colorado, Iowa, West Virginia, and Virginia. This name began with the Old English word *bucca*, meaning "male goat." The Old English word that followed, *buccingham*, meant "water meadow of the people of Bucca." This word then came to describe people from Buckingham.

Buell Street

Buell Street, built before 1913, is misspelled and named for Jesse Buel. He was founder and editor of the *Albany Argus*, an old-time newspaper, in 1813. The newspaper was named for a Greek mythological giant. The community of Buel in Montgomery County, New York, is named for this man, and the Hamlet of Argusville, first called Molicks Mills, in Schoharie County is named after his paper. The *Albany Argus* was first a semiweekly in support of Democrats. Most newspapers back then were highly political, just like they are today. The *Albany Argus* was the second daily newspaper in Albany, the first being *The Daily Advertiser*, which, as Hislop wrote, "had only praise for the National Republicans." Buel had sold his paper to Moses Cantine and Issac Leake by 1820. Edwin Croswell was editor of the *Albany Argus* from 1823 to 1854. Thus Croswell Street is next to Buell Street.

Buel was born January 4, 1778, in Coventry, Connecticut, and was the youngest of fourteen children. In 1790 his family moved to southern Vermont where he began an apprenticeship in printing. After moving to New York he published newspapers in Albany, Kingston, Lansingburgh, Poughkeepsie, and Troy. Buel sold his flagship paper the *Albany Argus* to pursue his other passion, which was agricultural reform. He purchased a sustainable farm west of Albany and helped found the New York State Agricultural Society. Buel was the author of *The Farmer's Companion* and *Farmer's Instructor*. No gentleman farmer, he liked to get his hands dirty. At the Buel farmhouse, which was built in 1821 and stands at present-day 637 Western Avenue, he grew several varieties of apples. Rittner wrote that the farmhouse stood in "wilderness" at that time. Buel also served as Ulster County judge of the Court of Common Pleas and New York assemblyman. Jesse Buel died October 6, 1839, in Danbury, Connecticut. He was first buried in State Street Cemetery, where Washington Park is. Buel's corpse was one of approximately 12,000 dug up for park construction. He was reinterred in Albany Rural Cemetery.

Burdick Drive
Burdick Drive was not built until circa 1969, and its name history remains unknown, though Burdicks are buried in Albany and Rensselaer counties. The name Burdick comes from the first name Borda, which means "shield." Burdick is also a French place name.

Business Lane
This street name is all business, leading straight from Colonial Drive to the Business Building on the University at Albany's main campus.

Butter Cup Drive
The Buttercup family of flowers has a whopping 2,000 species, most of them found in the cooler latitudes of the Northern Hemisphere. Four species grow in New York: kidneyleaf, common, bulbous, and swamp. The common buttercup, which was brought to America from Europe, is fittingly named. It is the species seen most often. Its small, delicate, yellow flowers display from May to September. This plant is poisonous to most animals, which explains why there are so many common buttercups to be seen. Three streets surrounding Butter Cup Drive carry names of flora. These include Daisy Lane, Silverberry Place, and Blue Bell Lane.

C

Caldwell Street

The Village of Lake George, named for George Augustus (King George II), used to be called Caldwell because it was developed by James Caldwell, for whom Caldwell Street is named. Caldwell was born in County Donegal, Ireland, in 1747 and came to Philadelphia with his brother, Joseph, circa 1770. Developing into successful merchants, they moved to Albany to operate a specialty food market on Broadway, which was then called Market Street. He married Elizabeth Barnes, and they had eleven children. During the Revolutionary War the brothers' business of selling foods and goods was booming. Caldwell spread his operations north in 1787 and purchased 1,600 acres on Lake George and another 220,000 acres across New York. By this point he owned warehouses, mills, waterfronts, farms, and retail and wholesale stores. The man who came here with little but the clothes on his back had become filthy rich. When not in Lake George, described as his "country residence," he lived at Albany's Mansion House, a hotel that stood at the intersection of Broadway and Hudson Avenue. By the early 1800s Caldwell lost a series of family members, and his businesses fell to neglect. James Caldwell died February 29, 1829, and was first buried in a cemetery near State Street. He was reinterred in Sacred Heart Catholic Cemetery near today's Lake George Village.

On September 8, 1916, Jacob W. Wilbur conveyed land to the city for Caldwell Street and nearby Bower Avenue, Cliff Street, Twitchell Street, Webster Street, and Winnie Street to be built. Mayor Joseph Stevens made these names official twelve days later. The name Caldwell translates from the Old English word for "cold well."

Cambridge Road

There are six "academic streets" clumped together, of which many Albany residents are aware. These include Cornell Drive, Notre Dame Drive, Princeton Drive, Union Drive, Vassar Drive, and Yale Court, which were all named by realtor Jesse Leonard. But there's a modest pairing of such streets near the Harriman Campus and the University at Albany's main campus. These are Cambridge Road and Oxford Road. Besides forming a mini cluster of academic streets, Cambridge Road and Oxford Road are within the bigger "United Kingdom cluster" with Tudor Road and Clarendon Road. Cambridge Road was built prior to 1936.

Located in Cambridgeshire, England, the grounds of University of Cambridge have been inhabited since prehistoric times, and evidence of settlement, in the form of an ancient farm, has been dated to 1500 B.C. This school was founded in 1209, which makes it the fourth-oldest college in the world. The university offers thirty undergraduate, approximately 200 masters, and more than 100 doctoral majors. There are 31 colleges and six schools to choose from. The 18,000 students who attend Cambridge are supported by 9,000 staff members. The name Cambridge comes from a bridge that spanned the forty-mile-long River Cam, which is near this university. Communities named Cambridge can be found in Maryland, New Jersey, Massachusetts, and Ohio.

Campus Access Road
(and Soc Ring Road, State Campus Road)
The campus these three streets provide access to is the Governor W. Averell Harriman State Office Building Campus, which is an expansive office park in a western section of the city. Campus Access Road makes a loop around the 330-acre campus, and part of this road is called Soc Ring Road, "Soc" being an acronym for State Office Campus. The American term "ring road" came into use in 1928. The Harriman Campus is built over the graves of streets that no longer exist: Hawley Street, Tremont Street, Lewis Street, Stevenson Street, Townsend Street, Rugby Street, Austin Street, Dons Street, and Batchel Street, among a few others.

W. Averell Harriman was a Democrat who served as 48th governor of New York, from 1955 to 1958. Harriman planned construction of the campus to offer more parking for state employees while providing easier access to their workplace. Built during the 1950s and 1960s when suburbs were blooming and commuting by car was a new, hip activity, the campus has at least partly outlived its usefulness. During the 1970s a movement was made to relocate office workers farther into the suburbs or back to downtown Albany, Schenectady, and Troy. In a September 1997 *Times Union* article about the state of the state campus, assemblyman Jack McEneny commented that the only things the campus offered were "no taxes, air pollution and traffic" and was "one of the worst examples of 1950s planning, the type of planning that killed cities." In 2004, the Harriman Research and Technology Development Corporation started rehabilitating the campus. However, in part due to Governor Eliot Spitzer eliminating this redevelopment program during his time in office, buildings remain gutted and standing, a commercial zombie land surrounded by lush neighborhoods. Governor Andrew Cuomo has since breathed new life into rehabilitating this campus.

Capital Hill
As with nearby Liberty Lane and Excelsior Drive, Capital Hill pays homage to the State of New York, its capital city, and the morals they represent. These

three streets on the University at Albany's main campus encircle the college's Empire Commons dormitory, further demonstrating the administration's love for the Empire State.

Cardinal Avenue

One of New York's showiest birds is the northern cardinal. The only other Empire State bird appearing so red, so bold, is the scarlet tanager. The male northern cardinal looks similar to the robes worn by cardinals of the Roman Catholic faith, and that's how it got its name. This bird lives throughout the eastern United States and within a patch of the Desert Southwest. Its call is one of the loudest and most distinctive of New York's feathered friends. From its high perch it belts out "purty-purty-purty-purty-purty!" to let other birds know it is monitoring its territory. Cardinal Avenue is the first of eighteen "bird streets" within *Cradle of the Union*. The others are Dove Alley, Dove Street, South Dove Street, Eagle Street, Lark Drive, Lark Street, North Swan Street, South Swan Street, Oriole Street, Partridge Street, Quail Street, Robin Street, Sparrowhill, Starling Avenue, Warbler Way, North Hawk Street, and South Hawk Street. Cardinal Avenue, and nearby Fleetwood Avenue and Van Schoick Avenue, was built in 1927.

Carlisle Court

Carlisle Court, Fordham Court, Marlborough Court, Stanford Court, Cheshire Court, Kensington Place, Windsor Place, and Victoria Way compose the eight "English streets" of Albany. The first four listed were built circa 1929, while the latter four were constructed soon after. The 400-square-mile city of Carlisle in County Cumbria, England, has a population of 100,000 and dates to the first century A.D. when it was settled by Romans. One can find the community of Carlisle in New York's Schoharie County. Yet this settlement is named not for the English city but for Carlisle Pierce, a prominent citizen. The name Carlisle, which is a cognate of Charles, stems from the British *ker*, which means "fort."

Carpenter Avenue

Carpenter Avenue dates to before 1898, yet its name history is a mystery. One of the most successful Carpenters to come to Albany was Edward Carpenter, who arrived in 1854. Perhaps he is memorialized within Carpenter Avenue. He was the son of Hiram Carpenter and Sally Ann Barker Carpenter (Barkersville, New York, is named for Sally's father, David Barker). Carpenter was born in Barkersville on April 11, 1835. He became one of the most noted merchants in Albany, running E.M. Carpenter and Company. The Schenectady Digital History Archive's Carpenter article thus described this man, who died June 18, 1907:

In commercial circles his standing was of the highest, while his private character was without blemish . . . He was ever alive to his responsibilities as a citizen, and always exerted his influence in behalf of good government. Through his long and active life in Albany he was a well-known figure, and had a large circle of friends and acquaintances. One of his prominent traits was his friendliness and kindliness to all with whom he came in contact.

Appearance of the surname Carpenter in the New World took place during June 1623 when Alice Carpenter Bradford, daughter of Alexander Carpenter and wife of Governor William Bradford, came to Plymouth, Massachusetts, from Leyden, Holland, the Netherlands. The first Carpenter to make permanent settlement in the New World was William Carpenter, son of Richard Carpenter from Amesbury, Wiltshire, England. He arrived in New Providence, Rhode Island, with his wife, Elizabeth Carpenter, during the early 1600s. He died September 7, 1685. Carpenter is an "occupational name." Other ancient names of this type include Smith, Shepherd, Potter, Cooper, Mason, Miller, Baker, Cook, Sawyer, Fisher, and many others.

Carroll Avenue
(and Carroll Terrace)

The first two Carrolls to be baptized in Albany were brother and sister Neeltje and Daniel, the children of Carel Hansz and Lysbeth Rinkhout. They were baptized at Albany's Dutch Church on June 20, 1686, and August 11, 1691, respectively. The name Carroll stems from the name of a prominent rock in County Sutherland, England. Another source of this name is the Latin name Carolus, from which stems the English name Charles.

Carroll Avenue was built before 1916, Carroll Terrace was built before 1920, and either or both may honor James Carroll. Born September 19, 1828, Carroll was president and treasurer of Albany Stove Company, founded 1868, which had forges in Tivoli Hollow. Sampson, Davenport, and Company's *The Albany Directory for the Year 1878* shared an Albany Stove Company advertisement in which they assured prospective customers that this company made the best "Parlor, Cooking Stoves and Ranges, Square and Corner Sinks, Cesspools, Etc." They manufactured about thirty stoves a day. William Shulz served as secretary while John Gutmann was superintendent. During the fall of 1893 the business was for sale, and sealed bids were called for. Carroll later ran James H. Carroll Company, which was a coke and coal dealer. In Sampson, Murdock, and Company's *The Albany Directory for the Year 1901*, it was stated that this company was at 831 Broadway at the bottom of DeWitt Street. An advertisement said that if you had trouble finding the address, it was the one below "the flag staff of which may be seen the flags of the Weather Bureau." Carroll served as Albany police commissioner, member of the Executive Committee of Saint Peter's

Hospital, and supervisor of the seventh ward. Before he got into the stove and coal business, he helped manufacture mill stones at his brother's mill, and he worked for printer, editor, and author Joel Munsell. James Carroll died in an accident in 1899 at a coal company he had purchased. He was buried in Saint Agnes Cemetery in Menands, New York.

Carroll Terrace
See Carroll Avenue.

Cary Avenue
Joseph Cary named this street for himself during the 1920s since he was one of this neighborhood's first residents. He was born in the Town of Bethlehem in 1852 to George Cary and Caroline Sawyer Cary. Joseph died of gangrene on April 10, 1943, and was buried in Albany Rural Cemetery. He also named nearby Hopi Street, Sawyer Place, and Zuni Street, his residence being on this last street.

Catalpa Drive
Neither of the two species of catalpa trees, northern catalpa and southern catalpa, naturally grow in New York though both have been widely transplanted past their home ranges of the Deep South and Mississippi River Valley, respectively. They are members of the Bignonia family of vines, shrubs, and trees. These two species grow to about fifty feet tall and two feet in diameter, yet New York's biggest northern catalpa has much greater dimensions: 81 feet tall, 71 inches in diameter. Both species share the slang name "cigar tree." This describes the cigar-like pods they produce. Catalpa Drive used to be called Lydius Street and received its current name in 1914.

Catherine Street
As one of the six "Schuyler streets" near the Schuyler Mansion (the other five being Alexander Street, Elizabeth Street, Morton Avenue, Philip Street, and Schuyler Street), Catherine Street is named for Catherine Van Rensselaer Schuyler. She was best known for being the wife of Phillip Schuyler and mother-in-law of Alexander Hamilton. She was born to John Van Rensselaer and Engeltie Livingston Van Rensselaer in 1734, and at the age of 20 she married Philip Schuyler at the Albany Dutch Church. They obviously could not get enough of each other for they had no fewer than fifteen children. Catherine Van Rensselaer Schuyler died during March 1803, and Philip died November 18, 1804. The earliest portrayal of Catherine Street was illustrated on a circa 1800 map of the Schuyler farm.

Sections of this street were either dirt or paved with kidney-rattling cobblestones as late as 1900. That year nearly 2,000 feet of Catherine Street were improved with the placement of vitrified bricks. Historic Pavement reported that "William Gillespie, a professor of civil engineering at Union College in Schenectady, New York, criticized [cobblestones] in his 1847 manual as a 'common but very inferior pavement which disgraces the streets of nearly all our cities.'" By 1885, there were 52 miles of surfaced streets within Albany, yet 40 of those miles (77 percent) were covered with cobblestones. Horace Andrews, city engineer, noted in *Annual Report of the City Engineer, for Albany, N.Y. for the Year 1891* that "cobble-stones have been of service as an inexpensive means of rendering a clay soil passable at all seasons of the year; their objectionable qualities are so conspicuous, when other pavements are compared, that it is unlikely they will be used in the future except for the paving of alleys and new streets where the adjacent property is of small value." By 1892, the city had 61 miles of surfaced streets, yet cobblestone paving had been reduced to only 31 miles (51 percent), these stones having been replaced with granite blocks for the most part. Asphalt, which at the time was defined in different ways yet was generally a coal tar mixture, was not introduced to Albany until 1889 (it was first used in the United States in 1870 in Newark, New Jersey). By 1891, Albany had seven miles of asphalt streets.

Catskill Street

The Catskill Mountains southwest of Albany are the little sisters of the Adirondack Mountains to the northwest. While the Adirondacks have more than forty summits above 4,000 feet, the Catskills have only two. The northernmost summits of the Catskill Mountains, the Blackhead Range and Windham High Peak, are easily seen from Albany. Adirondack Street and Catskill Street are next to each other as they lead off a third mountain street, Berkshire Boulevard. Albany has two other mountain streets, South Berkshire Boulevard and Helderberg Avenue.

The name Catskill is a corruption of "Cat's Kill," which was sometimes spelled "Kat's Kill." "Cat" notes the presence of wildcats, specifically eastern mountain lions, while the Dutch *kill* means "stream." Though the streams remain, the cats do not. The last New York mountain lion bounty was paid in 1894 in Herkimer County, and the last native mountain lion to be killed was shot in 1908 near Brown Tract Flow in the Adirondack Mountains. Supposed mountain lion sightings nowadays are glimpses of exotic animals that were pets turned loose by eccentric owners. Catskill Street, built prior to 1926, is specifically named so because it runs southwest to dead end at a bluff that provides views towards this range.

Cayuga Court

The Cayuga—a name derived from *Guyohkohnyo,* meaning "canoe carry place"—is an Indian tribe originally based in the Finger Lakes. Thus one of the Finger Lakes is Cayuga Lake. With the Mohawk, Onondaga, Oneida, and Seneca, the Cayuga were part of Five Nations, also known as the Iroquois Confederacy. Five Nations became Six Nations when the Tuscarora joined in 1715. Circa 2000, there were fewer than 500 Cayuga left in New York, these people found in the Cayuga Nation based in Seneca Falls, and there were fewer than 5,000 Cayuga-Seneca based in Oklahoma. These Oklahomans are descendants of those who were relocated there by the federal government from around the U.S. during the Indian Wars, many of them completing forced marches during the 1700s and early 1800s. Other Cayuga, specifically the Upper Cayuga and Lower Cayuga, live in Ontario and identify as members of Six Nations of the Grand River First Nation.

Cayuga Court is one of twelve "Indian streets" in Albany. The others are Iroquois Drive, Indian Drive, Mohawk Street, Mohican Place, Hopi Street, Seminole Avenue, Seneca Place, Erie Boulevard, Erie Street, Huron Avenue, and Zuni Street. Delaware Avenue, Delaware Street, and Delaware Terrace may honor an Indian group as well.

Center Street

Found in the North Albany Neighborhood, Center Street is in the center of a four-block series of streets in which names represent where they are in relation to each other. Center Street and Main Street are in the middle of these four blocks. North Street is to the north and South Street is to the south.

Central Avenue

This street is a "central avenue" once known as State Road, Schenectady Turnpike, and the Bowery. This latter name was an Anglicized version of the Dutch *bouwerij,* which describes an area that is lush and vibrant, such as a farm (the name the Bowery was changed to Central Avenue on July 15, 1867). This earlier name was fitting because Central Avenue reached outlying farms during the 1700s and 1800s. One of the most noted farms was that of Theophilus Roessle, who earned a unique title: celery magnate. Born in Germany in 1811, he immigrated to America in 1826 with only the clothes on his back. He purchased land along today's Central Avenue that would become the three-square-mile Hamlet of Roessleville. He maintained thousands of fruit trees yet concentrated his efforts on lowly celery and even wrote a book about it. What must have been a real page-turner, it was titled *How to Cultivate and Preserve Celery.* Theophilus Roessle died in 1890 and was buried in Albany Rural Cemetery. During the 1940s and into the 1960s lower Central Avenue was locally known as The Avenue and was an active shopping district. By the 1970s commerce along lower Central Avenue had been decimated with the creation of suburbs and their massive stores and shopping malls. Beyond the fact that it's centrally located in Albany, Central Avenue is also named so because it was the chief, "central," route between Albany and Schenectady prior to Interstate 90 being built, and it paralleled the New York Central Railroad, which was built in 1831.

Centre Street
(and East Center Drive, West Center Drive)

Centre Street in downtown Albany doesn't seem to be in the center of anything. It's spelled the British way. East Center Drive and West Center Drive are University at Albany streets that run through the center of the main campus and converge on the Campus Center, hence their names.

Champlain Street

The source for the name Lake Champlain is the same source for this street: Samuel de Champlain, the Father of New France. Born in Brouage on the west coast of France in 1574, Champlain is most famous, at least in the United States, for being the first person of European descent to explore his namesake lake. He's also the second person of European descent to see the highest mountains of New York, the Adirondacks, and the highest mountains of Vermont, the Green Mountains. Fellow Frenchman Jacques Cartier saw these ranges first, in 1535, yet Champlain provided the first written descriptions.

Nearly nothing is known of Champlain's childhood. His history starts with initial voyages with his uncle, François Gravé Du Pont, who was a geographer for King Henry IV. Champlain and his uncle traveled to the West Indies and Spain circa 1600 and to Canada in 1603. Under Du Pont, this latter expedition explored the Saguenay and St. Lawrence rivers, Gaspé Peninsula, and future site of Montreal, which had been reached by Jacques Cartier seventy years earlier. In 1604, Champlain traveled again, this time with Lieutenant General Pierre Du Gua de Monts. This expedition explored Nova Scotia, the Bay of Fundy, the St. John River, and the St. Croix River. At this last location the team overwintered. After a long, cold wait, the spring of 1605 arrived, and the team sailed to Cape Cod. Champlain became Monts's lieutenant. The two leaders and their hearty crew sailed up the St. Lawrence River and established a fort at present-day Quebec City. A decade after settling Quebec City, Champlain ventured into the interior of Canada with the Huron. He chose the Huron because he had already enraged the Iroquois, enemies of the Huron, by killing several of them in a battle on Lake Champlain. William White told in *Adirondack Country* that on his namesake lake, Champlain and his Canadian Indians met a band of Iroquois; when Iroquois and Canadian Indians met a fight always followed. In this fight Champlain used his harquebus loaded with four balls. His one shot instantly killed two Iroquois. That shot, in the shadow of the Adirondacks, changed American history. The Iroquois never forgot it. Forever after, they hated the French with the special hatred usually reserved for the Canadian Indians.

Like most other explorers from the 1400s to the 1700s, when Champlain returned to his home country after all this excitement he had serious paperwork to do—it took him years to chronicle his voyages and draw accompanying maps and illustrations. Champlain finally returned to Canada in 1627, sent by Cardinal Armand Jean du Plessis de Richelieu, Louis XIII's chief minister, for whom the eighty-mile-long Richelieu River in Canada is named. Champlain led the Company of One Hundred Associates, an organization formed to oversee New France. Yet things did not go well for the Frenchman. David Kirke was sent by Charles I of England to get rid of the French in New France, and this he did. Kirke and his men attacked Champlain's fort and mopped the floor with the French. His tail between his legs, Champlain fled to France in 1629. He returned to Quebec to serve as governor of New France after the area was given back to the French by the Scots via the 1632 Treaty of Saint Germaine en Laye. By this time Champlain's health, run down by decades at sea, was waning. He retired in 1635. Samuel de Champlain died in Quebec on Christmas Day of that year. The location of his remains are unknown because a 1640 fire consumed the building where he was temporarily laid to rest. Despite archaeological excavations, his remains have not been found. They're thought to be near the Notre-Dame de Québec Cathedral. No authentic illustration of Champlain has ever been found. Therefore, any image you see of this Frenchman is a guess, as is the case with Italian seaman Christopher Columbus.

Chapel Street

Formerly known as Berg Street and Hill Street, this lane was also called Barrack Street. Most sources cite this latter name existing because old barracks of a nearby fort stood there prior to the 1760s. However, authors of *Index to the Public Records of the County of Albany, State of New York, 1630–1894*, wrote:

> It has been erroneously stated that [the name Barrack Street] was derived from the fact that the barracks of the fort were located there. As a matter of fact, no army barracks existed there. During the early years of the city this was the most westerly and highest street, and was called by the Dutch "de Berg Straat," and "the Hill street." The broad Dutch pronunciation of the word "berg" was "bar-rag," as though it were two syllables, and this in time came to be written by the English Barrack.

Chapel Street is named so because the second Saint Mary's Roman Catholic Church was on this street. Name change from Barrack Street occurred September 14, 1805. Saint Mary's was incorporated in 1796 as The Roman Catholic Church in the City of Albany. This makes it the second-oldest parish in New York, perhaps in the entire country. Only Saint Peter's in New York City is older, being founded in 1786. Concerning Saint Mary's, the first church was built in 1797, a second one replaced the first one in 1820, and a third and final one was completed in 1869. The apex of this church's roof is topped by a beautiful, unique weather vane portraying the archangel Saint Gabriel blowing his trumpet. This church is listed on the National Register of Historic Places.

Charles Boulevard

Charles H. Touhey, for whom Charles Boulevard is named, was the first of his family born in America. His father had come to the United States from Ireland circa 1850 during the Potato Famine. As one of eleven children, Touhey lived in the Town of Orange just south of the Finger Lakes and remained on this family farm until about 1915 when his parents died. He migrated to Buffalo, sold steam rollers, and married his boss's secretary. One day Touhey found himself in Albany's Ten Eyck Hotel sitting near a Ford salesman, who was drowning his workplace sorrows at the bar, telling Touhey how bad the car business was. Touhey did what any reasonable man would have done: He bought a Ford dealership. It was first called Gateway Ford and was located at Orange and Chapel streets. The repair shop was on Sheridan Avenue. He renamed it Orange Motors for the town he had come from. In 2016, Orange Motors celebrated its centennial. Charles H. Touhey died in 1965 at the age of 92 and was buried in Saint Agnes Cemetery.

Charles Boulevard was named by Charles H. Touhey's son, Carl Touhey, and his grandson, Charles L. Touhey. Carl operated Orange Motors after the death of his father and died August 25, 2013. He was a businessman who remained a nice guy no matter how much money he had. In an *Albany Business Review* article about the death of Carl Touhey, Pam Allen called him "one of the region's most highly regarded philanthropists" and "a generous, down-to-earth man who treated everyone who worked for him equally." During his life he raised funds for the College of Saint Rose, Saratoga Performing Arts Center, Albany Police Department, Siena College, and Albany Medical Center, at one point donating one million dollars to the latter. Charles L. is leader of Touhey Associates, a real estate company, and the Charles L. Touhey Foundation, which carries on the philanthropic nature of this family.

Charles Street

Known as Johnson Alley until March 19, 1877, Charles Street is named for the Charles family of old-time Albany. Ancient Charleses include George Charles and Mary Price Charles, who lived in Albany County prior to 1790. They had seven children, their oldest one being William, born May 2, 1797. There was also a different William Charles of early Albany. That William Charles, a native of Scotland, was likely born during the 1730s. During February 1762, he married Mary Hogan, who was from Albany and was the daughter of William Hogan and Susanna Lansing Hogan. William Charles died prior to 1789 while his wife lived until July 1808. There are more than thirty Charles graves in Albany Rural Cemetery. The oldest is that of George Charles, likely the same George Charles mentioned above, which dates to 1818. Charles is a French, Welsh, and English name that comes from the Germanic name Carl, meaning "man," which was later Latinized into Carolus.

Chemistry Lane
This little lane runs towards the Chemistry Building on the University at Albany's main campus. Being such a simple title, it would be surprising if this name causes a reaction.

Cherry Hill Street
Cherry Hill Street takes its name from the 1,000-acre Cherry Hill farm that belonged to Philip Kiliaen Van Rensselaer. During the 1760s he established this farm, which at the time was on the outskirts of the City of Albany. In 1787 the original farmhouse was replaced with a new one. By 1792 the farm spread across nearly 1,000 acres and included a brewery and a tannery. In 1872, Cherry Hill was annexed to the City of Albany. Into the late 1800s and early 1900s, the property was owned by Catherine Rankin, great-great-granddaughter of Philip Kiliaen Van Rensselaer, and then controlled by her daughter, Emily Rankin. A year after Emily's death in 1963, the main 9,500-square-foot building became a museum and was added to the National Register of Historic Places in 1971. This site is now managed by Historic Cherry Hill. Cherry Hill Street opened in 1875.

Cherry Street
Black, mahaleb, pin, sour, and sweet are the five species of cherry trees that grow in the East. Pin cherry is a native species, while the other four came to the U.S. from Europe and Asia. Native pin cherries are rarely found in the Capital Region because it's a pioneer species that pops up on land that has been disturbed, perhaps by a wild fire, hence its slang name "fire cherry." Black cherry is found throughout the Capital Region in urban settings and patches of feral woods. It is a stout and attractive tree with dark, flaky bark that looks like burned potato chips. Its wood is of high value due to its rich red color. It's used in the manufac-

ture of high-end furniture, cabinets, and musical instruments. Its cherries can be made into jelly, wine, and even rum, hence its slang name "rum cherry."

Cherry Street is near Plum Street and Vine Street. These are the three "fruit streets" of downtown Albany, and they likely cross former farmland that was part of the Schuyler Mansion during the 1700s. DeWitt's 1794 map of the city showed Cherry Street, and this is probably the earliest map to do so. Mulberry Street formerly stood just north of Cherry Street and ran west from today's Broadway to Franklin Street. The ripe black fruit of mulberry trees look much like wild blackberries and are edible, being made into wine, juice, tarts, and pie filling. Mulberry Street used to be called Bass Lane and Spruce Lane and disappeared during the 1900s.

Cheshire Court

Towns, counties, and villages in Connecticut, Massachusetts, Michigan, New Hampshire, Ohio, and New York share the place name history of Cheshire Court. Cheshire is a 900-square-mile county in England that is home to 675,000 residents. The formation of this county took place circa 920 and was organized by Edward the Elder. Past names for this region include Chester, Legeceaster-scir, Cestrescir, and Chestershire. The county is marked with beautiful, grassy, rolling hills with little mountains popping their heads up here and there, the tallest being 1,834-foot Shining Tor. Carlisle Court, Cheshire Court, Fordham Court, Kensington Place, Marlborough Court, Stanford Court, Windsor Place, and Victoria Way compose the eight "English streets" of Albany.

Chestnut Street

Chestnut Street is named after the American chestnut trees that were found when this old section of Albany was settled. There are two sections of Chestnut Street. One runs from South Swan Street to Lark Street and another runs from North Main Avenue to North Allen Street. Only two species of chestnut grow in New York. The horsechestnut, member of the Buckeye family, was brought from Europe and is named so because Turks once made a remedy from its nuts to cure horses' coughs. The American chestnut, member of the Beech family, is native to New York. Few mature American chestnuts can be found in the cities and forests of New York today. The initial chestnut blight, which stemmed from a non-native fungus, began in New York City in 1904. This disease quickly spread across the country, killing nearly every mature American chestnut by 1950. This species will not become extinct though. The disease attacks only mature trees. Seedlings are safe from infection. American chestnuts grow well in the American West where the blight does not exist, and hybrid American chestnuts immune to the blight have been developed for the East. It is a low elevation species, not growing in New York above the 1,000-foot-level.

Church Street

G. M. Hopkins's maps from 1876, which accompanied his *City Atlas of Albany, New York* from that year, showed Saint John's Church and the Dutch Church two blocks west of Church Street, and this is how this street got its name. Saint John's Church stood on the corner of South Ferry Street and Dallius Street (today's Dongan Avenue), while the Dutch Church stood on the corner of South Ferry Street and Green Street. In place of these churches stand Equinox Youth Shelter and private residences, respectively. Church Street used to have a steam railroad track running down the middle of it.

Circle Lane

With Circle Lane connecting Davis Avenue with Colonial Avenue, one can make a circular course around these three streets to end up where they began, which is Cortland Street.

Clara Barton Drive

Clarissa Harlowe Barton was founder of the American Red Cross, which she established in 1881 at the age of 60. She led this organization until 1904 when she became a lecturer and author. The American Red Cross spoke highly of their founder and first president: "Her understanding of the needs of people in distress and the ways in which she could provide help to them guided her throughout her life. By the force of her personal example, she opened paths to the new field of volunteer service. Her intense devotion to serving others resulted in enough achievements to fill several ordinary lifetimes." Clara Barton Drive is specifically named so because an American Red Cross office was built there during the late 1960s. This organization has since relocated to Everett Road.

Barton was born on Christmas Day of 1821 in Oxford, Massachusetts, and her earliest jobs included working in the U.S. Patent Office as a clerk and being a nurse and teacher. She earned the moniker Angel of the Battlefield by helping wounded troops during the Civil War when she was a nurse. She was present during or immediately after battles in Fredericksburg, Chantilly, Fairfax Station, Petersburg, Cold Harbor, and Cedar Mountain, Virginia; Charleston and Harpers Ferry, West Virginia; and South Mountain and Antietam, Maryland. After the Civil War, Barton visited Europe where she worked for the International Red Cross during the Franco-Prussian War of the 1870s. Seeing the effectiveness of this international organization, after returning to America Barton sought creation of a U.S.-based Red Cross. Early humanitarian missions included responding to a wild fire in Michigan and flooding along the Ohio and Mississippi rivers in 1884, the Johnstown Flood of 1889, the Russian famine of 1892, a tidal wave along the Sea Islands of South Carolina in 1893, and the

Galveston Hurricane and Flood of 1900. Barton left the U.S. Red Cross four years after the great Galveston Hurricane and Flood, which killed 7,000 residents and destroyed 3,000 buildings in that one city alone. Clarissa Harlowe Barton died April 12, 1912, in Glen Echo, Maryland, and was buried in the Barton family plot in Oxford, Massachusetts. There are streets named for Barton in Texas, Florida, Virginia, Maryland, and Alabama, and one can find the 52-kilometer-wide Barton Crater on Venus. The name Barton comes from an Old English term that means "barley enclosure" and "outlying grange."

Clare Avenue

During the 1870s, Henry Clare owned land where Clare Avenue now is. He was born in 1809 and by 1875 he was residing with his wife, Catherine, born in 1816, and his daughter, Maria, born in 1856. There are three Clares in Albany Rural Cemetery, yet Henry is not one of them. This surname stems from the Barony of Clare, which is in County Suffolk, England. Baronies are subdivisions of counties in Ireland, Scotland, and England. Richard Fitz Gilbert (1035–1090) was a colleague of William the Conqueror (1028–1087) and stylized his name as "de Clare" in relation to where his County Suffolk landholdings were.

Clarendon Road

Clarendon Road is within the "United Kingdom cluster" of Albany and is accompanied by Cambridge Road, Oxford Road, and Tudor Road. This street was built before 1938, the year that new homes were being sold there by Porter and Tracy for $8,500. The monthly mortgage was $67. Construction of a housing development on Clarendon Road and nearby Cortelyou Road and Magazine Street began in April 1937.

The ruins of the medieval royal Clarendon Palace can be found where the Clarendon Forest used to stand in County Wiltshire, England. This area is best known as being where the Constitutions of Clarendon were written in 1164. This sixteen-article document intended to place limitations on how much power the church and its authorities wielded, and it addressed criminal papal matters that were usually not prosecuted by the church. In 1664, Edward Hyde, born in England in 1609, took possession of the Clarendon estate and gained the title 1st Earl of Clarendon. It is especially fitting that Clarendon Road is next to Oxford Road in Albany. Hyde, a historian and politician, attended Magdalen Hall of Oxford, today's Hertford College of Oxford, from 1622 to 1624 while he earned a bachelor's degree. He returned to this university to serve as chancellor from 1660 to 1667. Today the Clarendon Building stands on this campus. In 1663, Hyde was given land in what would become North Carolina, hence the community of Clarendon in that state. Edward Hyde died in 1674 in France, and was buried in his home country. There are communities named Clarendon in Vermont, Arkansas, Illinois, New York, Pennsylvania, Texas, Virginia, South Carolina, and Michigan. Clarendon is an Old English word meaning "clover-covered hill."

Clayton Place

Clayton Place carries the name of Clayton L. Besch, who was born April 13, 1898, in Albany, died May 22, 1990, in West Sand Lake, and was buried in Albany Rural Cemetery. He was the son of Joseph L. Besch and Elizabeth Menifold Besch. He was married to Helen Cramer Besch, and they lived at 223 Whitehall Road, just three blocks from Clayton Place. With their son, Clayton L. Besch Jr., they later lived on Clayton Place proper. The six "Besch streets" are Clayton Place, Besch Avenue, Betwood Street, Joanne Court, Joelson Court, and Rose Court. The names Clayton Place, Betwood Street, and Joelson Court were accepted by the city in 1925 when Joseph and Elizabeth Besch conveyed land to the city for the building of these three streets.

Clermont Street

The Knickerbocker News summed the story well: "When Robert Fulton stepped ashore from the first steamer to ascend the Hudson River he put his foot on the ground where Clermont Street now connects Broadway with Quay Street." A fine painting of the Clermont arriving in Albany during the evening of August 19, 1807, is portrayed in David Lithgow's "Robert Fulton's Clermont" painting. This circa 1939 work can be found on the University at Albany's downtown graduate campus in their Theodore Fossieck Milne Alumni Room. Clermont Street was built prior to 1930.

The name of Fulton's ship was, of course, the Clermont. Great care should be taken when using "of course" though. Fulton's steamship was actually named the North River Steamboat or North River (during Fulton's time the Hudson River was known as the North River). The use of the name Clermont came about with Cadwallader Colden releasing a book in 1817 that called the ship such. The twin-paddle wheel, 120-ton Clermont was built in 1807, and was conceived by Fulton and politician Robert Livingston. It was built at the Charles Browne shipyard in New York City, and the engine itself was built by Boulton and Watt in Birmingham, England. The ship measured 142 feet long and eighteen feet wide and drew two feet of water. Its maximum speed was five miles per hour, which seemed pretty fast at the time. It covered the 150 miles from New York City to Albany during August 1807 in 32 hours flat, breakneck speed for the beginning of the nineteenth century. People flipped out. Cuyler Reynolds, in Albany Chronicles, reported that while Fulton was plowing up the Hudson River a farmer had hastened out to the steamboat in his skiff and having tied to her, wanted to know from Fulton how a mill could grind itself upstream as this was doing and insisted on being shown the millstones. It was also told that at West Point as the vessel steamed past the whole garrison came out and cheered, and the crowds at Newburgh, enthusiastically waving hats and cloths, seemed as though all Orange County had flocked tither to see the wonderful craft.

With the Hudson River conquered, Fulton took on the Mississippi River. In 1811, he and Livingston built the 371-ton *New Orleans* and launched it at Pittsburgh. Two months later it completed its 2,000-mile descent to the mouth of the river. The men wanted nothing less than a monopoly on Mississippi River travel, and residents and competing steamship companies were particularly unhappy when, in 1812, Mississippi, which became a state that year, granted Fulton and Livingston exclusive steamboat rights. This monopoly was crushed when Washington, D.C., politicians banned this exclusivity upon the complaints of officials in Ohio and Kentucky. Monopoly or no monopoly, water transport facilitated by steam power was welcome because, as told by Paul Schneider in *Old Man River*, "in all cases, moving a boat upstream on the Mississippi without the benefit of steam power was backbreaking, soul-breaking, foot-rotting, snake-biting, fever-inducing, highly-dangerous, low-paid work." Water transport was cheap. Thomas Sowell informed readers in *Wealth, Poverty, and Politics* that, in 1830,

> it cost more than 30 dollars to move a ton of cargo 300 miles on land but only 10 dollars to ship it 3,000 miles across the Atlantic Ocean . . . Similarly in mid-nineteenth century America, before the transcontinental railroad was built, San Francisco could be reached both faster and cheaper across the Pacific Ocean from a port in China than it could be reached over land from the banks of the Missouri River. Given the vast amount of food, fuel and other necessities of life that must be transported into cities, and the vast amount of a city's output that must be transported out to sell, there is no mystery why so many cities around the world have been located on navigable waterways . . .

A historical marker at the intersection of Broadway and State Street memorializes Fulton's arrival: "Near the foot of Madison Avenue Robert Fulton in Aug. 1807, completed the first successful steamboat voyage." The Town of Clermont in Columbia County, New York, is named after this steamboat, this place name bestowed by Robert Livingston himself. Robert Fulton is memorialized through Fulton Street. More on this man is discussed in that entry.

Cleveland Street

Stephen Grover Cleveland, born March 18, 1837, was the 22nd and 24th president of the United States. With these two periods in office, Cleveland became the only president to serve nonconsecutive terms. He was also the only Democrat elected as president during the period between the Lincoln administration that ended in 1865 and the Taft administration that began in 1909. He also had unique lust for vetoing congressional bills. Cleveland vetoed more bills than the 21 presidents before him combined.

Cleveland was born in Caldwell, New Jersey, to Richard Falley Cleveland and Anne Neal Cleveland and had eight siblings. Before Cleveland was 4 years old his family moved from the Garden State to the Empire State. His family was far from wealthy, the opposite of recent presidential candidates. When his father died, Cleveland quit school to help support his family. Later on, his family was too poor to send him to college. Instead, he became a teacher and law clerk (a college degree was not required for these positions back then) in New York City and Buffalo, respectively. He passed his state bar exam in 1859 and started his own law firm three years later. He entered public service by becoming Erie County sheriff, and he was no softie. Cleveland hanged three murderers during his two years as sheriff. After being sheriff, he returned to practicing law and became mayor of Buffalo in 1882. The following year, Cleveland became New York's governor, and the year after that he was elected president of the United States. During his second term he had to deal with the Panic of 1893, which included bankrupt railroad companies, the failures of banks, a credit crisis that spread across the country, worker strikes (he used the military to quash the Pullman railroad strike), and high unemployment rates (as high as nineteen percent). The gold rush of the Klondike brought economic recovery. At the end of his second term he was encouraged to run for a third, as there were no term limits at that time. Cleveland humbly declined. Post-presidency, Cleveland retired in Princeton, New Jersey, and became a Princeton University trustee. Stephen Grover Cleveland died of a heart attack June 24, 1908. His last words were: "I have tried so hard to do right." He was buried in Princeton Cemetery in Princeton, New Jersey.

Two Cleveland counties, one in Arkansas and one in Oklahoma, are named for this president, but Cleveland, Ohio, is not named for him. That city is named for Connecticut-born Moses Cleaveland (1754–1806), who founded the city in 1796. Cleveland Street is part of the eight-street "presidential conglomerate" of Albany, all of them named by realtor Jesse Leonard. The accompanying seven include Grant Avenue, Lincoln Avenue, McKinley Street, Roosevelt Street, Garfield Place, Van Buren Street, and Washington Avenue (Buchanan Street isn't named for James Buchanan—it's named for Capital Region engineer William Buchanan). Other New York cities have clusters of presidential streets. For example, Glens Falls has the seven-street collection of Grant Avenue, Harrison Avenue, Lincoln Avenue, Coolidge Avenue, Monroe Street, Jefferson Street, and Garfield Street (Chester Street may fit in here, perhaps named for Chester

Arthur). Troy has the twelve-street assembly of Polk Street, Tyler Street, Harrison Street, Van Buren Street, Jackson Street, Lincoln Avenue, Monroe Street, Madison Street, Jefferson Street, Adams Street, Washington Place, and Washington Street.

Cliff Street

One would expect to find a cliff on Cliff Street. This street doesn't live up to its name. Cliff Street is a generic yet daring name approved by Mayor Joseph Stevens on September 20, 1916, which was less than two weeks after Jacob W. Wilbur conveyed land to the city for construction of this street and nearby Bower Avenue, Caldwell Street, Twitchell Street, Webster Street, and Winnie Street.

Clinton Avenue
(and Clinton Place)

Clinton Avenue and Clinton Place are named for DeWitt Clinton, who, like his uncle, was a politician. While his uncle, George Clinton, was a founding father, DeWitt Clinton was father of the Erie Canal, though during construction it was despairingly referred to as "Clinton's Ditch" by political opponents. Pessimistic Americans thought the Erie Canal a boondoggle, a waste of time, labor, and money, yet the naysayers were proved wrong in the end as the Erie Canal spread culture, goods, and services towards Ohio and beyond. Clinton Place is specifically named so because DeWitt Clinton used to live there.

James Clinton and Mary DeWitt Clinton welcomed DeWitt Clinton into this world on March 2, 1769, in Little Britain in the Province of New York. He attended King's College, today's Columbia University, as well as Princeton University, from which he graduated. He then studied law and practiced in New York City. Clinton's social and political pedigree is impressive. He was member of the New York State Legislature, senator from New York, three-term mayor of New York City, lieutenant governor of New York, governor of New York, New York Canal commissioner, Historical Society of New York president, American Academy of the Fine Arts president, University of the State of New York regent, grand master of the Grand Lodge of New York Freemasons, and member of the American Antiquarian Society. He ran for president in 1812 yet lost to James Madison Jr. DeWitt Clinton died in Albany on February 11, 1828. Though he managed New York's funds well, he did not manage his personal funds well. When Clinton died, his family was flat broke. So poor, they couldn't afford to bury him, though Clinton received one of the grandest funerals in New York history. Clinton was deposited in a vault belonging to Samuel Stringer, a fellow mason and friend of the family. The vault was on Swan Street. During the summer of 1844, the remains of this politician were reinterred at Green-Wood Cemetery in Brooklyn, where they remain.

Beyond Clinton Avenue, DeWitt Clinton is memorialized through cities, towns, and counties in Georgia, Illinois, Indiana, Iowa, Kentucky, Massachusetts, Missouri, Michigan, New Jersey, and Wisconsin. A collection of American streets honor this man, including Clinton Street in Philadelphia. Clinton Avenue was formerly known as Patroon Street. Name change took place May 4, 1863. The name Clinton perhaps comes from the Middle Low German *glinde* and *tun*, meaning "fence" and "settlement."

Clinton Place
See Clinton Avenue.

Clinton Street
Born July 26, 1739, George Clinton was a founding father, though not a signer of the Declaration of Independence, and the uncle of DeWitt Clinton, for whom Clinton Avenue and Clinton Place are named. Clinton Street was formerly known as Malcom Street, Malcomb Street, and Church Street and had dirt and spine-crunching cobblestone sections as late as 1900. That year, its quarter-mile section from Fourth Avenue to Second Avenue was improved with vitrified bricks. New York's Clinton County is named for George Clinton as are communities and counties in Missouri, New York, Pennsylvania, and Ohio.

The son of Charles Clinton and Elizabeth Denniston Clinton, he was born in Little Britain in the Province of New York on July 26, 1739. His parents had arrived in the New World in 1729 from County Longford, Ireland. Clinton's military career began with him serving as a privateer during the French and Indian War, and he later enlisted in a provincial militia of which his father was colonel. The younger Clinton rose to the rank of lieutenant. After leaving the colonial military, Clinton became clerk of the Ulster County Court of Common Pleas and then, like great men of his era, studied law and opened his own practice. He was also district attorney and member of the New York Provincial Assembly for Ulster County. Near the end of 1775, Clinton was made brigadier general in the New York Militia, and during the spring of 1777 he was made brigadier general in the Continental Army. Soon he was elected as both governor and lieutenant governor but settled on being governor only. After serving five terms as governor, which took him to 1795, Clinton maintained his standing in the Continental Army and stayed until the Army was dissolved in 1783.

Clinton returned to be New York governor from 1801 to 1804. Finally, he served as vice president of the United States under President Thomas Jefferson from 1805 to 1809 and under President James Madison from 1809 until his, Clinton's, death in 1812. Dying on April 20, 1812, Clinton was the first U.S. vice president to die. He and his wife, Sarah Cornelia Tappen Clinton, had six children. George Clinton was initially buried in Washington, D.C., but was reinterred at the Old Dutch Churchyard in Kingston, New York, in 1908.

Colatosti Place
Armand Colatosti, for whom this street is named, was born during 1929 in Frosinone, Italy, to Sante Colatosti and Mary Stirpe Colatosti. He was a developer noted for raising the Winding Brook Manor on Colatosti Place. In his *Times Union* obituary, Colatosti was credited with building "several hundred homes and neighborhoods" in Albany. He immigrated to the United States and started his business at age 19. Armand Colatosti, a veteran of the Korean War, died June 5, 2014, at his Loudonville home.

Colby Street
Colby Street was named in 1871, which is probably the year it was built. That same year, the names Hunter Avenue, Judson Street, Rawson Street, and Watervliet Avenue were accepted by the city and thus the entire Colby Street neighborhood was named. This street name remains unsolved. Only two Colbys can be found in Albany Rural Cemetery. The older of the two graves is that of John Colby, who was born in Connecticut and died in Albany in 1860. The name Colby, related to Colburn, is formed from the Old English words *col* and *burna*, meaning "cool stream," and comes from a parish in Norfolk and a township in Westmoreland.

Collins Place
Built before 1927, Collins Place is likely named for a realtor or landowner who was active where this street now is. John Collins was the first Collins to reach Albany. He was born in England circa 1670, came to the New World, and married Margarita Schuyler Verplanck on November 2, 1701. Collins, a lawyer who served as Albany County sheriff, died April 13, 1728, in Schenectady. His wife lived until May 1748. Their firstborn son, Edward, who was baptized July 30, 1704, became a lawyer like his father. More than 100 Collinses are interred in Albany Rural Cemetery. The oldest grave belongs to James H. Collins, who was born in 1810 and died in 1848.

Colonial Avenue
Colonial Avenue takes us back to the simpler times of the American Colonial Period, named for us being a British colony, back when farmers cleared their fields with axe and ox, women made clothing for their children, and beaver pelts flowed out of Albany like water flows out of the mountains. It was a simple,

satisfying life. On the other hand, marauding Indians were a worry, several countries fought for control of North America, toothpaste and deodorant were unheard of, and beer was served warm. Colonial Avenue was built circa 1930. The house at 3 Colonial Avenue is the old Holmes farmhouse. This building holds the distinction of being picked up and turned. It once faced Western Avenue but now faces Colonial Avenue.

Colonial Drive
The Colonial Quad, a housing unit for students on the University at Albany's main campus, is reached by Colonial Drive. This dormitory offers suite-style living with accompanying fitness center, wellness center, co-op house, sustainability house, and game room—much better living conditions than during colonial times.

Colonie Street
The Colonie—not having anything to do with, and therefore not to be confused with, today's Town of Colonie north of Wolf Road—was a collection of houses that stood just north of the main fort in present-day Albany during the 1600s. This community developed into the old-time Village of Colonie, which was annexed to the City of Albany during the early 1800s. There are two sections of Colonie Street. The lower, southern, section marks the old boundary between the fort and the Village of Colonie and was named by 1830. The upper, northern, section was built circa 1912, the year land was conveyed to the city for construction of this section of Colonie Street along with nearby Beverly Avenue, McArdle Avenue, Pennsylvania Avenue, Wilkins Avenue, and an extension of Thornton Street.

You may wonder, How did the name Town of Colonie come about? Well, Albany County was once known as Watervliet. Pieces of land, such as the towns of Coeymans and Niskayuna, were plucked from this county and made independent until there was nothing left except for the Town of Watervliet itself. Within this town were the communities of Cohoes, Green Island, and West Troy. The political seat was West Troy, and outside this booming village were rural farmlands full of farmers who felt their needs were being ignored by the urban Democrats holed up in West Troy. The farmers wanted their own town, they voted for one, and they got it in 1895. They named it the Town of Colonie. The following year, West Troy became a city. The name West Troy was replaced with the old-fashioned name Watervliet.

Columbia Circle East Drive
(and Columbia Circle West Drive)
These streets are within sight of Columbia Development and are named after this construction and real estate company. This company was founded in 1988

by Joseph Nicolla, who is now Columbia Development's president. Business is booming for Columbia Development. They have created more than nine million square feet worth of buildings assessed at more than $1.5 billion. Their projects are classified as adaptive reuse, education, healthcare, hospitality, office, retail, and technology endeavors. They have a who's who list of clients, which includes Albany Medical Center, General Electric, Home Depot, IBM, Panera Bread, Rensselaer Polytechnic Institute, and SUNY Polytechnic Institute Colleges.

Columbia Circle West Drive
See Columbia Circle East Drive.

Columbia Street
With sections of Columbia Street formerly called New Street and Oak Street, the full length of this street now honors the historic figure Columbia. This current name appeared on maps as early as 1790, shown on Bogart's map of North Market Street from that year. The oldest building on this street may be 99 Columbia Street, built 1829.

Columbia, the Latinized name of Columbus (as in Christopher Columbus), is the past romantic name for the Thirteen Colonies and the United States and was the nation's female identity. This character, a confident, tall woman with blond hair, first appeared during the Revolutionary War and was replaced by the female patriotic image of the Statue of Liberty during the early 1900s. Philip Freneau first promoted the name Columbia in 1775 within *American Liberty, A Poem* and offered a footnote explaining this term: "Columbia, America, sometimes so called from Columbus, the first discoverer." Stewart called the name Columbia "a happy coinage" that was "almost everything that the [name] United States of America was not—short, precise, original, poetic, indivisible, and flexibly yielding good adjectives and nouns." Michael Allen and Larry Schweikart, in *A Patriot's History of the United States*, reminded readers that America perhaps should have been called Columbia. Amerigo Vespucci, for whom America is named, had "his self-promoting dispatches circulated sooner than Columbus's own written accounts, and as a result the term 'America' soon was attached by geographers to the continents in the Western Hemisphere that should by right have been named Columbia."

Beyond Columbia Street, Columbia lives through Columbia County (the seal of this county portrays her holding a dove in one hand, a law book in the other); Columbia University; the Columbia Pictures logo (the woman in the center holding a torch and draped in white and blue is Columbia herself); the capital city of South Carolina; the Columbia River; the District of Columbia (Washington, D.C.); and communities throughout the United States. Our nation's male patriarch is Uncle Sam. He is modeled after Sam Wilson, a meat packer who lived in Troy, New York, and supplied soldiers with comestibles during the War of 1812.

Colvin Avenue

The Knickerbocker News reported that Colvin Avenue is named for surveyor Verplanck Colvin, and every historical document examined maintains this claim. However, your author's dissenting voice concludes that Colvin Avenue is not named for Verplanck (though because he was the most interesting of the Colvins, he is discussed below). In 1872, 1877, and 1880, Andrew Colvin, father of Verplanck, deeded land to the city for construction of Colvin Avenue (during the first deed, James Fitzgerald and his wife, Catharine Fitzgerald, were co-deeders with Andrew Colvin). When the first piece of land was deeded, Verplanck was 25 years old, owned no land, and had barely begun to make a name for himself. Colvin Avenue is thus named for Andrew or his family in general.

Andrew Colvin was born April 30, 1808, in Coeymans, New York, to James Colvin and Catherine Verplanck Colvin. This Colvin line began with the grandfather of Andrew, John Colvin, who was born in Scotland in 1752 and immigrated to Dutchess County in 1772. Andrew's mother was descended from the Verplanck line from Holland. The Hamlet of Verplanck in Westchester County is named for them. Andrew first married Rosina Alling, and after they had two children she died in 1843 at the age of 33. Pursuing fruit that didn't fall far from tree, he married Rosina's sister, Margaret Crane Alling. She gave birth to Verplanck. After working in Martin Van Buren's law office and serving as City of Albany attorney, City of Albany corporate counsel, Albany County district attorney, and senator from New York, Andrew Colvin died July 8, 1889, in Albany. He was buried in Grove Cemetery in Coeymans. *The New York Times* noted that with his death, "another of the men prominent in State affairs in the stirring times before the war, one of the historic characters of Albany, a man noted for his upright character and devotion to principle, has passed away." Margaret Crane Alling Colvin died in Albany on June 25, 1900.

Your author is drawn to Andrew and Margaret's son, Verplanck, for two reasons. One, he was an Adirondack Mountain climber and explorer at heart. Two, he was strange. In *Forest and Crag* Guy and Laura Waterman wrote that Verplanck was "perhaps the first true climber's spirit in the northeastern United States." They also noted the mountaineer was "a strange young man, tall, dark, but not handsome" and "almost completely humorless" with social interactions that ranged from "awkward and strained to overtly hostile."

Verplanck was born January 4, 1847, at the Elms on Western Avenue. A historical marker placed by The Eastern New York Society of Land Surveyors in 2006 identifies this boyhood home. Verplanck studied law, geology, and topography, but by the end of these studies he had no direction towards, or perhaps plans of, employment because he grew up in a wealthy family. With the Colvins vacationing in the Adirondacks, by his 20s Verplanck was climbing High Peaks on personal trips. He paddled rivers, visited bodies of water, and completed his first bear hunt. He was hooked on the Adirondack Mountains.

In 1872, he gained appointment to the New York State Park Commission, leading topographic surveys throughout the Adirondack Mountains until 1899. He explored thousands of miles of terrain by horse, foot, and boat to run survey lines, name features, compose maps, and fix prior surveyors' mistakes. Highlights of his explorations include making first ascents of four High Peaks and identifying and visiting the source of the Hudson River. He named scores of topographic features. At times his drive for exploration bordered on mania. In *Forest and Crag*, Peter Preston rightfully asked: "If it had not been for a man like Colvin with his touches of compulsive madness, who would have done the job?" Verplanck's reports to the state were eloquent and passionate, revealing the beauty and wildness of the mountains. He pushed for protection of this range by suggesting formation of, in his words, an "Adirondack Park or nature preserve." As bureaucratic years grinded by, Colvin felt he was not given due credit for helping create the Adirondack Park. He became bitter against those who took credit for his idea of preservation, a range he described as "a region of mystery, over which none can gaze without a strange thrill of interest and of wonder at what may be hidden in that vast area of forest, covering all things with its deep repose." Disrespected, he lost his state job in 1900 when then-governor Theodore Roosevelt terminated the position. Verplanck Colvin died May 28, 1920, and was buried in Grove Cemetery fifteen miles south of Albany.

Commerce Avenue
(and Corporate Circle, Corporate Plaza East, Corporate Plaza West, Corporate Woods Drive, Executive Centre Drive, Industrial Park, Industrial Park Road, North Enterprise Drive, South Enterprise Drive)

These ten commerce-themed streets provide access to a multitude of public entities and private businesses, hence the corporate theme. These names were conferred by uninspired developers. Commerce Avenue and Industrial Park Road reach companies such as B and G Food Services Equipment, Michaud Distributors, and Autopart International. Corporate Circle encloses Grainger Industrial Supply, Newkirk Products, and Amri. Organizations near Corporate Plaza East, Corporate Plaza West, and Corporate Woods Drive include the Social Security Administration, Key Bank, and Capital Cardiology Associates. The Enterprise drives are among Albany Water and Supply Company, Independent Pipe and Supply Corporation, and Applied Industrial Technologies. Executive Centre Drive near the Dunes Neighborhood weaves through a host of agencies. Industrial Park provides access to redemption and recycling operations.

Common Place

Wilcoxen wrote that "one public service of the seventeenth century in Albany that has no counterpart today was that provided by the cowherd." The cowherd was a young man who drove residents' cows to the Pastures, a common grazing area in the city's southeast end where Common Lane, which was just six feet wide, used to be. The cows would graze under the watchful gaze of their cowherd, and the animals were returned to their respective owners at the end of the day. Think of it as bovine daycare. This common pasturage was set aside for Dutch settlers during the 1600s. Streets leading to the Pastures were developed at the end of the eighteenth century, and the oldest building standing in the Pastures Neighborhood today is the former home of Spencer Stafford, built 1807. Common Place may emulate long-gone Common Lane.

Coral Berry Circle

Coral Berry Circle rests in a suburban development, the Dunes Neighborhood. Other streets in this community include Gray Fox Lane, Hawthorn Circle, High Dune Drive, Lupine Circle, Pitch Pine Road, Sparrowhill, Warbler Way, and West Meadow Drive, each one named after components of an ecosystem that were, ironically, destroyed to build the development. Coral berry is a wildflower that grows in the United States, yet is native to Japan. It's classified as an invasive species and was first a captive plant in Florida. It got loose, spread across Florida, Texas, and the South, and can now be found in the Northeast as an ornamental that has a tendency to spread in wild profusion. It has myriad other names including Christmas berry, Australian holly, coral ardisia, hen's eyes, and spiceberry, and it's sometimes spelled as one word: coralberry. This member of the Primrose family grows up to six feet tall and prefers damp soil. It sprouts coral-colored berries that remain on the bush year-round. Coral Berry Circle is one of two "berry streets" in Albany. The other is Silverberry Place.

Corlaer Street

Two place names in New York City were of assistance while decoding Corlaer Street, which was first called Avenue C and then Corlear Street, suggesting that this street carries a last name. Corlears Hook is a point on the East River named for Jacobus van Corlear, a schoolmaster who settled the area prior to 1640 and owned 76 acres. Not part of New York City's proudest history, Corlears Hook may be where the term hooker came from. By the early 1800s, this area was an infamous slum of lewdness, crime, and prostitution. Thus if you were a prostitute back then and there, you were a "hooker." (An alternative theory is that the word hooker came into use during the mid-1800s when General Joseph Hooker's Army of the Potomac had sexual liaisons while passing through towns. Or hooker could be a reference to such women "hooking" men, as in suckering them into spending money on cheap thrills.) A nearly insatiable appetite for copulation was fed by New York City's ladies. By 1839, there were ninety brothels within Corlears Hook.

The Bronx has Corlear Avenue. This street is named for Anthony Van Corlaer. Van Corlaer is best known for being sent by colonial governor Pieter Stuyvesant to get Dutch reinforcements to fight the British, who were attacking New Amsterdam in 1642. During his mission, he was forced to swim across a narrow estuary between Manhattan and the Bronx where the Harlem and Hudson rivers meet. With a violent storm whipping this waterway into a foaming barrier, Van Corlaer carried on "in spite of the Devil" and drowned. This waterway has since been known as Spuyten Duyvil Creek. Anthonys Nose, a 910-foot mountain that towers over the Hudson River in Westchester County, may be named for Van Corlaer, too. According to Charles Skinner in *Myths and Legends of Our Own Land*, this mountain is named for Van Corlaer because he, astonishingly

killed the first sturgeon ever eaten at the foot of this mountain. It happened in this wise: By assiduous devotion to keg and flagon, Anthony had begotten a nose that was the wonder and admiration of all who knew it, for its size was prodigious; in color it rivalled the carbuncle, and it shone like polished copper. As Anthony was lounging over the quarter of Peter Stuyvesant's galley one summer morning, this nose caught a ray from the sun and reflected it hissing into the water, where it killed a sturgeon that was rising beside the vessel. The fish was pulled aboard, eaten, and declared good, though the singed place savored of brimstone . . .

Anyway, that Corlears Hook and Corlear Avenue carry Dutch names leads us to the conclusion that Albany's Corlaer Street carries a family name, too. Albany's Corlaer Street is probably named for Arent Van Curler, born in 1619 in the province of Gelderland in the Netherlands. He was the first manager of Rensselaerswyck and cousin of Kiliaen Van Rensselaer. Van Curler was in present-day Albany by December 1637. He founded Schenectady in 1662 after purchasing land from Mohawks. When local Indians inquired to meet with him, they asked for "Corlear," which they thought was synonymous with "leader." This nickname was also used to identify someone who first settled an area or served as governor. Thus Pieter Schuyler, Indian commissioner and first mayor of Albany during the late 1600s and early 1700s, was sometimes called Corlear by the Indians. The name Corlaer Street was made official, with the nearby names of Bertha Street, Marshall Street, and Twiller Street, in 1915.

Cornell Drive

Cornell Drive is named after an Ivy League school, as are two neighboring streets, Yale Court and Princeton Drive. Three non-Ivy League schools are honored through nearby Notre Dame Drive, Union Drive, and Vassar Drive. These six "academic streets," all named by realtor Jesse Leonard, are set among a handful of educational institutions: Sage College of Albany, Albany Law School, Albany College of Pharmacy and Health Sciences, Neil Hellman School, and Albany Academy for Girls. All these streets and institutions are fittingly set within Albany's University Heights Neighborhood. The names Cornell Drive, Notre Dame Drive, Princeton Drive, and Yale Court were approved by the city in 1937. That year the city approved a Rutgers Drive to be built, but that name was replaced by either Union Drive or Vassar Drive.

Ezra Cornell and Andrew White founded Cornell University in Ithaca in 1865. The administration states that the college has several personalities because it is "the federal land-grant institution of New York State, a private endowed university, a member of the Ivy League/Ancient Eight, and a partner of the State University of New York." Its 2,000-acre campus has 650 buildings, while its equally expansive academic programming is divided into seven undergraduate units, four graduate units, and one professional unit. The college also claims two medical graduate units, one professional unit in New York City, another professional unit in Qatar, and the Cornell Tech unit in New York City. Faculty and staff total 10,000 workers, who serve 20,000 students.

Corning Place

Erastus Corning 2nd (his preferred designation over the traditional "II"), born October 7, 1909, in Albany to Edwin Corning and Louise Parker Corning, was the longest-serving mayor in the United States. He has earned his Corning Place. This Democrat took office January 1, 1941, and died while in office during May 1983. Politics ran in the family. Corning's father, Edwin Corning, was lieutenant governor of New York during 1927 and 1928. Corning's great-grandfather, Erastus Corning I, served as mayor of Albany from 1834 to 1837, New York State Senate member from 1842 to 1845, and House of Representatives member from New York from 1857 to 1859 and 1861 to 1863. Corning Street in the Town of Watervliet, the Town of Corning in Iowa, and the cities of Corning in New York and Nebraska are named for Erastus Corning I.

Erastus Corning 2nd earned a degree from Yale University and was member of the New York Assembly and senator from New York before he ran for mayor. During the first Corning election he beat Republican Benjamin Hoff by a landslide, and he dominated all elections related to his eleven terms, save for when he ran against Carl Touhey in 1972. That election was actually close. Corning's only interruption of service was when he was drafted into the Army to serve during World War II. While Corning was serving in the military, Common Council president Herman Hoogkamp was appointed acting mayor in 1940 and served the remainder of Corning's term. In 1946, Corning ran for lieutenant governor with his political partner James Mead running for governor, but they were not successful in their gubernatorial bid. Erastus Corning 2nd died at Boston's University Hospital on May 28, 1983. He was buried in Albany Rural Cemetery. Albany's 590-foot-tall Corning Tower, the city's tallest building, was named for this politician in 1983, and the fifteen-acre Corning Preserve on the Hudson River is named for him as well. Paul Grondahl, in *Mayor Erastus Corning*, ranked this public servant

> a masterful juggler. He was silky smooth and unflappable and made it look easy as he kept several balls in the air at once. He was a one-man City Hall, personally controlling the minute details of municipal affairs. He played many roles simultaneously: mayor and political boss, insurance company owner and astute bank director, blue-collar fishing buddy and blueblood club member, aristocrat and everyman, paternalistic provider and cunning political strategist.

Corporate Circle
See Commerce Avenue.

Corporate Plaza East
See Commerce Avenue.

Corporate Plaza West
See Commerce Avenue.

Corporate Woods Drive
See Commerce Avenue.

Cortelyou Road
George Cortelyou, for whom this street is named, was born to Peter Crolius Cortelyou Jr. and Rose Seary Cortelyou in New York City on July 26, 1862. He was a descendant of Jacques Cortelyou, who came to the New World during the mid-1600s and drew the first map of New Amsterdam. If this street is not named for George, it's probably named for Jacques, who was born in Holland, the Netherlands, circa 1625 and died in New Amsterdam in 1693. He was a surveyor for the Dutch West India Company and helped build a wall in Manhattan in 1653 to defend against marauding Indians. This gave Wall Street its name. As surveyor general, Jacques completed the 1660 Cortelyou Survey, which produced the first map of New York City. Brooklyn's Cortelyou Road is named for him.

George Cortelyou attended Nazareth Hall Military Academy, Hempstead Institute, Westfield Normal School (today's Westfield State University), New England Conservatory of Music, and the law schools of both George Washington University and Georgetown University. After graduating from these two law institutions he became chief postal inspector of New York, fourth class assistant postmaster general, postmaster general, secretary of commerce and labor, secretary of the treasury, chairman of the Republican National Committee, and president of Consolidated Gas Company, today's Consolidated Edison. In *The National Cyclopedia of American Biography* from 1910 it was written that he was "the most notable example in American life of high attainments in the public service without winning any distinction whatsoever in a private capacity or relying upon outside influences." It was added that "his chief characteristics are a genius for hard work and for taking infinite pains with a clear, cool, and thorough comprehension of every problem that he has had to study." Efficient at shorthand and stenography, he was personal secretary to presidents William McKinley and Theodore Roosevelt Jr. When McKinley was shot by assassin Leon Czolgosz in 1901, McKinley fell into the arms of Cortelyou and whispered to him: "My wife. Be careful, Cortelyou, how you tell her." Cortelyou stayed by McKinley's bedside until he, McKinley, expired. Then, with William Day, he administered the will. George Cortelyou himself died October 23, 1940. He was buried in Memorial Cemetery of Saint John's Church in Cold Spring Harbor, New York. The community of Cortelyou, Alabama, was named for him on March 4, 1907.

At least one source identifies Cortelyou Road as Cortel Road. This is a mistake. However, the name makes sense. The word cortel is related to the now-rarely-heard word curtal, which means "cut." For example, a curtal horse is a horse with a cropped tail, and curtal sonnets, poems, and stanzas are shortened versions of these. Curtal gives us the English word curtail. Cortelyou Road is a short street of only 300 feet and was officially recognized by the City of Albany in 1938.

Cortland Place
(and Cortland Street)

The Dutch name Van Cortlandt lives on through these streets, which are probably specifically named for Pierre Van Cortlandt, the most notable of this American family. New York's Cortland County and its City of Cortland are named for Pierre because he owned land there. The City of Cortland, Kansas, takes its name from Cortland, New York. Cortland Place has existed since at least 1874 while Cortland Street has existed since at least 1828.

Van Cortlandt was born January 10, 1721, to Philip Van Cortlandt and Catherine de Peyster Van Cortlandt, whose fathers were New York City mayors. By the age of 27 he inherited the 86,000-acre Van Cortlandt Manor, of Westchester

County, from his father. From the 1750s to the 1790s he attended the budding, and later official, national legislative bodies and became second New York Provincial Congress member, Committee of Safety chairman, New York assemblyman, Fourth New York Provincial Congress vice president, 3rd Regiment of Westchester County Militia colonel, senator from New York, and lieutenant governor of New York (this last position lasted eighteen years). In 1795, he retired from politics and settled in Peekskill and Croton-on-Hudson. Pierre Van Cortlandt died May 1, 1814, and was buried in Hillside Cemetery in Cortlandt Manor, New York. With his wife, Joanna Livingston Van Cortlandt, he raised Philip, general during the American Revolution and House of Representatives member from New York; Catherine; Cornelia; Gertrude; Gilbert, captain during the American Revolution; Stephen, soldier during the American Revolution; Pierre Jr.; and Anne, wife of Albany mayor Philip Van Rensselaer.

Cortland Street
See Cortland Place.

Cottage Avenue
(and Home Avenue, Homestead Avenue, Homestead Street)
Cottage Avenue communicates "home sweet home" and was built circa 1925. Home Avenue may specifically be named for the Uriah Hart homestead, a federal style residence that was built circa 1810 and stood where Home Avenue now is. The first new home built on Home Avenue was constructed by William Primomo in 1937. It was the first of 27 houses to be built that summer. Brick homes along this street two years later were selling for $7,900. Home Avenue, with nearby Berncliff Avenue and Crescent Drive, was named by Picotte Companies. This neighborhood used to be part of the Town of Bethlehem, yet it was annexed to the City of Albany. A housing boom followed annexation.

Homestead Avenue and Homestead Street evoke images of independence and coziness—the suspender-wearing, bearded Albanian splitting his firewood and having it heat him later. Land was conveyed to the city in 1913 for construction of Homestead Avenue and accompanying Edgewood Avenue, Fairlawn Avenue, Hawthorne Avenue, Laurel Avenue, Melrose Avenue, and Terrace Avenue. Homestead was a term used to define a piece of land big enough on which to raise a family and came about during the 1690s. The federal Homestead Act of 1862 declared such a piece of land to be 160 acres—one square quarter mile. The Old French *cote* from the 1200s means "hut" and includes the Anglo-French suffix *age*, meaning "property attached" to the hut. The English word homestead comes from the Old English *hamstede*, Dutch *heemstede*, and Danish *hjemsted*, meaning "home" and "village."

Craigie Avenue

Craigie is a community and civil parish in South Ayrshire, which is a council area in County Ayrshire, Scotland. Craigie Street, built before 1929, carries this Scottish place name. Within this part of South Ayrshire stands the ruins of Craigie Castle, sections of which date to the 1100s. The word craigie can be traced to the Gaelic *crea* ("steep and rocky place") as well as Old Irish *carrac* ("cliff") and Welsh *craig* ("stone"). The English word crag, meaning "rocky outcrop," comes from *craigie*. Oddly, this street sign is spelled a less popular "Craige."

Crescent Drive

This name is descriptive and simply identifies the course of Crescent Drive. When seen via a bird's eye view, this street makes a sweeping crescent shape, breaking off New Scotland Avenue and bending back to it. Crescent Drive and nearby Home Avenue and Berncliff Avenue were built prior to 1937 by Picotte Companies (a brick home stood along present-day Crescent Drive as early as 1931). Picotte home construction began July 1 of 1937, and this company named these three streets, which were part of their Golden Acres development. Picotte Companies built the last home, the 125th one, in this development at 43 Crescent Drive in 1941. The English word crescent stems from Anglo-French, Old French, Modern French, Latin, and Proto-Indo-European languages and means "to grow." This word is now used to identify the crescent shape, this meaning stemming from a misunderstanding of the Latin *luna crescens* ("waxing moon"). Translators mistakenly thought *luna crescens* referred to the shape of the moon, not the phase in which it "grows."

Crestwood Court
(and Crestwood Terrace)

Generic, honeyed names, these street titles portray where the woods crest. Crestwood Terrace lies among other "wood streets" including Briarwood Terrace, Knollwood Terrace, Point of Woods Drive, and Ridgewood Terrace. Each of these streets was named by developers. Crestwood Court was built circa 1948. *The Knickerbocker News* ran an article in 1950 that reported a housing development was being built on Crestwood Court by M. Shapiro and Son Construction Company. These homes ranged from $8,500 to $10,500, and the company arranged for veterans to have first dibs. Picotte Companies was soon building homes in the area, too, their project being "one of the most ambitious building programs undertaken in Albany." The homes were guaranteed by this company to be unique: "No two houses will be alike. Each will feature an attractive individuality and different floor plan." The Crestwood Court neighborhood was billed by the Picotte Companies as "the smartest community of fine homes in the city."

Crestwood Terrace

See Crestwood Court.

Cross Street

Cross Street is probably named so because it "crosses" Krum Kill. Next to it is No Bridge Drive. As one could guess, that street doesn't cross Krum Kill. This waterway was first called *Kroome Kill* by the Dutch, which translates to "crooked stream." Its current spelling came into fashion circa 1893. If Cross Street is not a utilitarian name, it may be named for a member of Albany's Cross family.

Croswell Street

Edwin Croswell was editor of the *Albany Argus* from 1823 to 1854. This street, built before 1914, is properly set next to Buell Street. Jesse Buel was founder of the *Albany Argus*. Croswell was born May 29, 1797, in Catskill, New York. His father, Mackay Croswell, and his uncle, Harry Croswell, were journalists and editors. Croswell moved to Albany in 1823 and became assistant editor of the *Albany Argus* under Issac Leake. He married Catharine Adams in Catskill on October 12, 1824, and retired from the paper business to move to New York City in 1854. Two years later the *Albany Argus* ceased operations. Edwin Croswell died in Princeton, New Jersey, on June 13, 1871, and was buried in Catskill Village Cemetery in Catskill, New York.

Crown Terrace

The word crown is employed to have us imagine something important. But all this trite name does is make this street sound unimportant. Crown Terrace was probably the final street built in the Delaware Avenue Neighborhood. Lots started selling in 1963, and people were living on Crown Terrace by 1966.

Cuyler Avenue

In 1876, Peter Ten Eyck and Leonard Ten Eyck owned land where the four "Ten Eyck streets"—Cuyler Avenue, Kate Street, Matilda Street, and Ten Eyck Avenue—now lie. In 1891, Abraham Cuyler Ten Eyck owned 52 acres where these streets now are. This cluster of streets was built in 1910. Cuyler Ten Eyck was born February 26, 1866, in Albany as the son of Abraham Cuyler Ten Eyck and Margaret Matilda Haswell Ten Eyck. He was married to Eva Mary Wieland Ten Eyck and died April 2, 1938. He was buried in Albany Rural Cemetery. One source reported that Kate and Matilda were daughters of Peter and Leonard, but this is not true since Leonard was a man. (Historians made the assumption that these girls were the daughters of Leonard Ten Eyck because he was usually identified simply as L. G., and, therefore, was assumed to be Peter's wife.) More on Kate and Matilda and this bogus street name story can be found in the Kate Street and Matilda Street entries.

Cuyler Street

Cuyler is the last name of three related Albany mayors. The very first Cuyler to arrive in present-day Albany was Hendrick Cuyler, a tailor and fur trader. He was born in 1637 and baptized on August 11 of that year in Hasselt, Province of Overyssel, Holland, the Netherlands. He was the son of Isbrant Cuyler and Evertien Jans Cuyler. He arrived in Albany, then called Beverwyck, circa 1664 and purchased a lot on the east side of North Pearl Street near State Street. Cuyler then moved to the south side of State Street near the fort, which was in present-day downtown Albany. Hendrick Cuyler, who served as an officer in the Albany County Militia and was an alderman, assessor, and justice, died in 1691. His wife, Anna Schepmoes Cuyler, passed away twelve years later in New York City.

The first child of Hendrick and Anna was Johannes, born in Holland, in 1661. He served as the fourteenth mayor of Albany during 1725 and 1726, appointed by Governor William Burnet. His main occupation was trader though he served as alderman, deacon and elder of the Dutch Church, and commissioner of Indian affairs. He married Elsje Ten Broeck, daughter of the fourth mayor of Albany, Dirck Wesselse Ten Broeck, on November 2, 1684. Johannes Cuyler died July 20, 1740, in Albany and was buried at the Dutch Church.

One of the three sons of Johannes and Elsje was Cornelis Cuyler, a merchant by trade, who served as the twentieth mayor of Albany. He was appointed by Lieutenant Governor George Clarke and served from 1742 to 1746. Cornelis was baptized in New York City on February 14, 1697, and died March 15, 1765. His wife, Catharina Schuyler Cuyler, born 1704, was daughter of the tenth mayor of Albany, Johannes Schuyler, who served from 1703 to 1706.

Finally, the son of Cornelis and Catharina, Abraham Cornelis Cuyler, became 26th mayor of Albany. He was appointed by Lieutenant Governor Cadwallader Colden and served from 1770 to 1778. He died in Yorkfield, Canada, on February 5, 1810.

D

Daisy Lane

Daisy Lane, along with Hazelhurst Avenue, Lily Lane, and Willow Street, likely doesn't pay homage to a woman because place names less often carry first names than last names. In your author's two place name books about the Adirondack Mountains, of the approximately 300 place names decoded, only eight carry first names. Though first names in civilization are used more often than in the wilderness, they're still uncommon within cities. In addition to this, Daisy Lane is near the other "fauna streets" of Blue Bell Lane, Butter Cup Drive, and Silverberry Place.

Members of the Aster family, the oxeye daisy and daisy fleabane are New York's two daisies. Other wildflowers look like them, particularly mayweed, bushy aster, and Philadelphia fleabane, yet these are imposters of daisies. The oxeye daisy, which was brought to the United States from Europe, is the more common of the two species. It flowers from June to August, grows to three feet in height, and is found in wastelands, roadside ditches, and pastures. It gets its name from looking like the eye of an ox. It has also been called "day's eye," which the word daisy is a corruption of. The daisy fleabane flowers from April to August, grows to three feet in height, and can be found in sunny patches of woods. It gets its name from the belief that once dried it can rid a residence of fleas.

Dale Street

Used here, Dale may communicate the traditional use of that word, which transforms Dale Street into "Valley Street." Or it may memorialize a person with the last name Dale. The most notable of Albany's Dales was William Tweed Dale, born 1776. He was principal of the Albany Lancaster School Society, having come from England's Joseph Lancaster School, where he was a teacher. He died August 28, 1854, and was buried in Albany Rural Cemetery. Dale Street was called First Avenue until May 20, 1902.

Dallius Street

Godfreidus Dellius, born in Holland, the Netherlands, circa 1650, was dominie of Albany's Dutch Church, and this street is named for him. His namesake street appeared on maps by 1791, portrayed on *Dutch Church Lower Pasture No. 6* that year and spelled Dalleus Street. He served as dominie from 1683 to 1699, having arrived in the New World that first year. He was a noted missionary to the Mohawk and received sixty pounds a year for this work. Godfreidus Dellius retired to Antwerp, Holland, after being embroiled in controversy about fraudulently purchasing land from Indians. He died in Holland on March 1, 1710. A southern section of Dallius Street has since been named Dongan Avenue for Thomas Dongan, first royal governor of New York. New York City's Dongan Hills neighborhood is also named for him.

Dana Avenue

James Dana was born February 12, 1813, in Utica, New York, and is known for studying and classifying, and educating students about, things many people do not find the least bit interesting: rocks. The *Encyclopedia Britannica* conveyed that he traveled far and wide in the name of rocks, carrying with him an appetite for knowing how the Earth was formed and how it continues to evolve. His "explorations of the South Pacific, the U.S. Northwest, Europe, and elsewhere, made important studies of mountain building, volcanic activity, sea life, and the origin and structure of continents and ocean basins."

Dana attended the Bartlett Academy in Utica, and in 1830 he attended Yale University (at the time called Yale College) to graduate in 1833. After a stint in the U.S. Navy teaching mathematics, he returned to New Haven, Connecticut, the hometown of Yale University, to work with a former professor of chemistry and mineralogy of his, Benjamin Silliman (at times distracted from his geological studies to study the opposite sex, Dana married Silliman's daughter, Henrietta). From the 1830s to the 1870s Dana produced a, pun perhaps intended, mountain of works: hundreds of specimens related to geology and mineralogy, 7,000 pages of notes, and the books *Manual of Mineralogy, A System of Mineralogy, Manual of Geology, A Textbook of Geology,* and *Corals and Coral Islands.* He was editor of, and wrote extensively for, the *American Journal of Science*, which was founded by Silliman. Dana was also a founding member of the National Academy of Sciences and served as president for both the American Association for the Advancement of Science and the Geological Society of America. He stood next to great men of science including Louis Agassiz, Charles Darwin, and Asa Gray, all of whom influenced Dana. By 1856, at the age of 43, he accepted a position as professor of Natural History at his alma mater, Yale University. But only three years into the job, Dana had a physical breakdown from which he would not recover. For the rest of his life he was a recluse of sorts, avoiding the public yet still studying and writing. James Dana died April 14, 1895, in North Haven, Connecticut, and was buried in Grove Street Cemetery in Utica, New York. At Dana Avenue is tiny Dana Park, dedicated on Arbor Day 1901. Here one will find the Dana Monument, which was placed in 1903 and is, suitably, a boulder.

Danker Avenue

Formerly named Greeley Street, Danker Avenue is named for the founder of Danker Florist, Frederick Alden Danker. This street, and nearby Ver Planck Street, was constructed before 1930. Located on Central Avenue less than a mile from Danker Avenue, Danker Florist has been blooming since 1898, though it has not always been at its current location. This business was initially run by Danker, who was the floral designer, with the help of his son, Frederick Jr., and his two other sons, Bob and Dave. Bob managed the greenhouse, and Dave oversaw landscaping.

Danker was born in Albany on December 19, 1873. His father owned pastureland where Danker Avenue now is, and these rural lands stretched from King Avenue to Colvin Avenue and would have swallowed up today's "presidential conglomerate" of streets. Danker's barn and house stood on Central Avenue where Destination Kia and Destination Nissan now are. His nurseries stood where Central Avenue's Mooradians Furniture now is. The original Danker home is now at the end of Ver Planck Street. It was moved there on an enormous trailer supported by airplane tires. Frederick Alden Danker died in Albany on June 1, 1961. He was married to Lotta Huested Danker. She was born September 15, 1875, in the Town of Nassau in Rensselaer County and died in Albany on April 28, 1963. They were buried in Albany Rural Cemetery. Because of the Dankers' love for flowers, the family headstone has lilies of the valley and orchids etched into it.

Dartmouth Street

Dartmouth Street was built circa 1928, the year that John Klapp and Lisette Klapp conveyed land to the city for construction of this street along with nearby Kelton Court and Mariette Place. Dartmouth Street has two identities. First, it's near the "English streets" of Carlisle Court, Cheshire Court, Fordham Court, Kensington Place, Marlborough Court, Stanford Court, Windsor Place, and Victoria Way. Therefore, it may be named after Dartmouth, a town and civil parish of 5,000 residents in County Devon, England. This town has served as a vital port since the 1100s and had its first named street by the 1300s. Dartmouth, Massachusetts, settled 1650, is named after this English community because that's where Puritans first intended to leave from for their voyage to the New World.

Second, as stated above, Dartmouth Street is near Fordham Court and Stanford Court, which carry the names of American universities. Dartmouth College was named for William Legge, 2nd Earl of Dartmouth, by Eleazar Wheelock, who founded the college in 1769. Legge was born June 20, 1731, served as secretary of state for the Colonies, and died July 15, 1801. Located in Hanover, New Hampshire, Dartmouth College is an Ivy League school. Undergraduate tuition is nearly $50,000 per academic year while additional room, board, and fees add another $15,000. Dartmouth College accepts only six percent of student applications. The school hosts 4,000 undergraduate and 2,000 graduate students. Notable alumni include Fred Rogers (of Mister Rogers' Neighborhood), Nelson Rockefeller, Daniel Webster, and Robert Frost.

Davis Avenue

The surname found in this street name dates to the mid-1700s in Albany County. The Davises of this county may have begun with Edward Davis, who married Jannetie Duret on January 8, 1763. This couple had seven children, their firstborn being Cornelia, who was born October 27, 1763. Nearly 300 Davises are buried in Albany Rural Cemetery. The oldest grave belongs to James Davis, who was born in 1750 and died in 1800. Davis Avenue was built circa 1916. This name is a transformation of David, which started as a Hebrew name for "beloved."

Daytona Avenue

As the first of five "Florida streets," Daytona Avenue shares its neighborhood with Orlando Avenue, Ormond Street, Tampa Avenue, and Seminole Avenue. The first four streets are named after cities while the last one honors an Indian tribe. Daytona Avenue was constructed before 1926. A developer had Florida on his mind when he established this neighborhood, yet why he specifically chose these names is unknown. Daytona Beach is a city on the Atlantic Ocean in Volusia County. Founded in 1870 and incorporated during July 1876, it has a population of 60,000. Daytona Beach is named for its founder, Matthias Day. Day was a businessman from Mansfield, Ohio, who, in 1870, purchased more than 3,000 acres in Florida.

Dean Street

Formerly known as Dock Street and Water Street, because that's where Albany's docks and water were, Dean Street is listed within *Cradle of the Union* as a street of "honorable mention." The name Dean Street was made official on November 6, 1826. The surface of Dean Street behind the U.S. government building and old post office on Broadway still remains, yet it's no longer a through-street, is not identified in Google Maps, and carries no street sign. What's left of this street is named for Stewart Dean, Albany's most renowned navigator. The May 22, 1867, copy of the *Albany Evening Journal* described Dean as "a brave and enterprising skipper, who fitted up and sailed an ordinary North River sloop from here to China, and returned with a successful venture in tea." His ship was the *Experiment*.

Born in Maryland in 1748, he completed a sailing apprenticeship from age 18 to 21 and then moved to the Hudson Valley and later to Albany. During the 1770s, he married Pietertje Bradt, and they started a family together. During the Revolutionary War, Dean served as a privateer for the Americans, concentrating his voyages on the Caribbean. Back on dry ground in 1777, he continued to fight with his fellow Americans by serving alongside the Albany Militia and completing missions in the Mohawk Valley. He later sailed to the West Indies and China. Dean's wife then died, and he married Margaret Wheaton, got his brood up to a total of seven children, and reduced his high seas wanderings by the early 1800s as aging men are wont to do. Stewart Dean died August 5, 1836, in New York City and was buried at Trinity Church in Manhattan. A marvelous illustration of Dean returning from the Orient is Len Tantillo's oil on linen "Return of the Experiment," which graces the front and back covers of McEneny's *Albany*.

Deerwood Court

Whoever named this street must have seen or imagined deer in the surrounding woods, thus this street was in the "deer woods." More than 220,000 white-tailed deer are killed in New York annually, "filling freezers with roughly 10.8 million pounds of high quality local venison," according to the Department of Environmental Conservation. The New York white-tailed deer population was ruthlessly reduced during the 1800s due to absence of hunting laws and lack of regulation on commercial hunting. As late as 1885, the year New York secured its first large parcel of land in the Adirondack Mountains, deer jacking and running down deer with dogs were legal, and there was no bag limit.

De Lasalle Street

John Baptist De La Salle is memorialized through De Lasalle Street, which leads to LaSalle School on Western Avenue. Born in Reims, France, on April 30, 1651, he finished his academics in theology and became an ordained priest in 1678. By 1680 he had received his doctorate degree in theology and established a school for poor boys, which was in essence the founding of Brothers of the Christian Schools. John Baptist De La Salle died in Saint Yon, France, on April 7, 1719, a Good Friday. In 1900 this man was declared a saint, while in 1950 he was declared the patron saint of Christian educators. There are 100 LaSalle schools throughout the world. The De La Salle Christian Brothers founded Christian Brothers Academy of Albany in 1859.

Delaware Avenue
(and Delaware Street, Delaware Terrace)

These three streets are named after the river, the Indian group, or a combination thereof. As a side note, there was an old-time Albany County last name of DeLaWarde. Jan DeLaWarde came to Albany County from Antwerp in 1662 and owned land in Albany and Niskayuna. He died January 28, 1702, in Albany. Yet these street names are not a corruption of his name since DeLaWarde was unimportant and didn't live near these modern-day streets. These streets are not specifically named after the state of Delaware either. No Albany street except for Pennsylvania Avenue is named after a state, and let's face it: Delaware's pretty lame. Delaware Avenue was known as the Delaware Turnpike until 1870.

The Delaware River was named first, and then Delaware, Delaware Bay, and the Delaware Indians received their names. This river was named for James West, 3rd and 12th Baron of De La Warr, by Samuel Argoll in 1610. West was an English politician whose title is actually pronounced "Delaware." He was born July 9, 1577, in Hampshire, England, and died June 7, 1618, while sailing from England to the Colony of Virginia. The 360-mile Delaware River is the third longest river in the Northeast, exceeded in distance only by the 405-mile Connecticut River and 460-mile Susquehanna River. The Delaware River begins on the summit of Mount Jefferson in the Catskill Mountains and ends in Delaware Bay between Delaware and New Jersey.

There are three Delaware Indian groups in the United States: the Delaware Tribe centered in Bartlesville, Oklahoma; the Delaware Nation of Anadarko, Oklahoma; and the Stockbridge-Munsee Community in Wisconsin. Additional members live in Canada. The first contact the Lenni-Lenape (the preferred name of the Delaware Indians) had with Europeans was during the early 1600s as explorers touched present-day New Jersey, Long Island, and the Delaware River, which was first called the South River.

Delaware Street
See Delaware Avenue.

Delaware Terrace
See Delaware Avenue.

DeWitt Street
Not named for Simeon DeWitt nor DeWitt Clinton, the DeWitt Street name is one of generality or may carry the name of a DeWitt who owned land on nearby Colonie Street during the 1800s. This ownership was portrayed on J. C. Sidney's 1850 map of Albany. Unfortunately, nothing else is known of this DeWitt. The first DeWitt to reach Albany was Tjerck Claase DeWitt, who arrived during the spring of 1666, having lived in Esopus, New York, since 1660. He first came from Zunderland, Holland, the Netherlands, and was the son of Nicholas DeWitt. In present-day New York City, on April 24, 1656, he married Barbara Andriese, who had come from Amsterdam, Holland. Tjerck Claase DeWitt died in Kingston, New York, on February 17, 1700, and was the father of thirteen children.

Division Street
Cohoes, Troy, Schenectady, Saratoga Springs, Ballston Spa, Waterford, Amsterdam, and Ballston Lake all have their own Division streets, as do scores of other

American communities. Division streets usually mark demarcations. Albany's Division Street likely marks the dividing line between the old-time settled section of the city and the grazing pastures that stood to the south. Division Street was called Bone Lane until 1805. This name may have referred to a cemetery or slaughterhouse.

Dix Court

Dix Court may fairly be called a "paper street," but we'll count it anyway. It's within the City of Albany's official street list and is shown as a real street in Google Maps, yet there are no Dix Court addresses, and there is no Dix Court street sign. This street name was mentioned in newspapers as early as 1926.

One of two unrelated men with nearly identical names and careers is honored through Dix Court. One is John Adams Dix, the other John Alden Dix. Dix Court likely honors John Adams Dix since he was unquestionably the more accomplished of the two. He was born in Boscawen, New Hampshire, on July 24, 1798, and was a lifelong politician and soldier. He was educated by his family, and he attended Phillips Exeter Academy as well as the College of Montreal. While attending this university he petitioned to fight in the War of 1812. Thanks to his father, who served in the military in Maryland, he was awarded a position in the Army at the age of 14. A year later Dix's father died. The younger Dix then provided for his family by working jobs in Washington, D.C., and New York City. He rose to major while stationed in the nation's capital and studied law. In 1824 he passed his bar exam. Dix left the city for the pastoral Village of Cooperstown, New York, to oversee land owned by his father-in-law, House of Representatives member John Morgan. Soon Dix was leading Otsego County's Jacksonian Democrats. He became adjutant general of New York, secretary of the treasury, senator from New York, and chairman of the Union Defense Committee in New York. When the Civil War started he was made major general, but because he was 63 years old when he gained this rank, he did not command in the field. Instead, he became one of Abraham Lincoln's most trusted men. After the Civil War, Dix fulfilled the roles of minister (today called ambassador) to France and governor of New York. John Adams Dix died in New York City on April 21, 1879, and was buried in Trinity Church Cemetery and Mausoleum in Manhattan. Dix Mountain, the Adirondack Mountains' sixth highest peak, and the Town of Dix in Schuyler County are named for this man.

John Alden Dix was born on Christmas Day of 1860 in Glens Falls, New York (this city's Dix Avenue is named for him), to James Lawton Dix and Laura Stevens Dix. He attended Cornell University but did not graduate, worked in his family's quarry and machine shop, and became a lumber baron by working 20,000 acres he owned in Herkimer County. He entered politics to serve as chairman of both the Washington County Democratic Committee and New York State Democratic Committee. He was New York governor during 1911 and 1912. Dix was regarded as a second-rate governor, but looked pretty good compared to his replacement, William Sulzer, who was quickly impeached. Desiring to get as far away from New York as possible, Dix and his wife, Gertrude Thomson Dix, moved to Santa Barbara, California. Gertrude died December 18, 1923. John Alden Dix died in New York City on April 9, 1928. They were buried in Albany Rural Cemetery.

Doane Stuart Road

Formerly named Kenwood Road, two people are memorialized through this street: the right reverend William Doane and the Roman Catholic educator and nun Janet Stuart. This duo is also honored by Doane Stuart School, which was formed in 1975 with the merger of Kenwood Academy and Saint Agnes School for Girls.

Doane was born in Boston on March 2, 1832, as the son of the reverend George Doane. His family settled in Burlington, New Jersey, where the younger Doane graduated from Burlington College, which was founded by his father in 1846. He was ordained as a deacon in 1853 and was ordained as a priest three years later. Doane preached in New Jersey and Connecticut before coming to New York in 1867 to serve Saint Peter's Church. Two years later he became bishop and oversaw construction of Cathedral of All Saints in Albany. William Doane died in New York City on May 17, 1913, and was buried in the east ambulatory of All Saints Catholic Church in Albany. He was the husband of Sarah Katharine Condit Doane and father of two daughters.

Born November 11, 1857, in Cottesmore, County Rutland, England, Stuart was the daughter of the reverend Andrew Stuart, who was the father of thirteen children. She converted to Roman Catholicism at 22 and joined the Society of the Sacred Heart at Roehampton. Her works include *The Education of Catholic Girls*, *The Society of the Sacred Heart*, and *Highways and By-ways in the Spiritual Life*. Janet Stuart died October 21, 1914. She was buried at Sacred Heart Chapel in Greater London, England.

Dongan Avenue

Named for Thomas Dongan, this street was formerly part of Dallius Street. Dongan was the first royal governor of New York, appointed 1683. He granted Albany its city charter on July 22, 1686, thus enabling the City of Albany to be born. As Bielinski wrote in his Thomas Dongan article: "Although [Dongan] may not have spent more than a night in Albany, his interest and patronage were critical to the formation and initial development of the city of Albany. He still is celebrated locally and beyond as Albany's first great Irish politician." Dongan, 2nd Earl of Limerick, was born in Ireland's County Kildare in 1634 as the youngest son of Sir John Dongan. Upon the death of Charles I, the

Dongan family moved to France, and young Dongan served in an Irish regiment, gaining the rank of colonel in 1674. He returned to England four years later thanks to the Treaties of Peace of Nimeguen. These were agreements from the late 1670s that ended a series of wars in Europe. As The New Advent related, Dongan "returned to England in obedience to the order of the English Government recalling all British subjects in French service" when the Catholic monarchy was restored. That same year, 1678, the Duke of York gave Dongan high rank and a pension of 500 pounds annually. The duke also made Dongan lieutenant governor of the Moroccan city of Tangiers. Dongan was sent to the New World in 1682 to oversee the Province of New York where he was granted lands. Bielinski wrote best of Dongan's roles and accomplishments in the New World:

> As proprietary and then royal governor of New York, Dongan played a key role in the settlement of Albany County which he first authorized in 1683. That same year, he set up New York's first representative assembly; granted the Van Rensselaers a royal patent in 1684; established New York and Albany as cities in 1686; and proved to be an able provincial leader until he was replaced when King James was removed from the throne later in the decade.

Thomas Dongan returned to England in 1691 and died in London during December 1715. The New Advent gushed over his legacy:

> The tribute of history to his personal charm, his integrity, and character, is outspoken and universal. His public papers give evidence of a keen mind and a sense of humor. He was a man of courage, tact, and capacity, an able diplomat, and a statesman of prudence and remarkable foresight. In spite of the brief term of five years as Governor of New York Province, by virtue of the magnitude, of the enduring and far-reaching character of his achievements, he stands forth as one of the greatest constructive statesmen ever sent out by England for the government of any of her American colonial possessions.

Dove Alley
(and Dove Street, South Dove Street)
Eastern North America has seven species of doves, each of them within the Columbidae family. Only the rock dove, known to city patrons and sidewalk pedestrians as the pigeon, and mourning dove live in New York. In earlier times, mourning doves were more common in Albany than rock doves were, yet as the Capital Region was built up, pastures paved, and forests leveled, rock doves became more populous. Rock doves keep to urban environments, looking for handouts at bus stops, on sidewalks, and around parking lots. Cities have attempted to be rid of their rock doves, which have been accused of spreading

disease. Little progress has been made due to their sheer numbers. Mourning doves can be found in all regions of New York, though the closest they get to being true urban dwellers is usually by visiting backyard birdfeeders and city parks. Its name references the somber cooing it makes.

Dove Street, which used to be called Warren Street, is connected with the peculiar murder of notorious Prohibition gangster Jack Diamond, who was usually identified by his gangster moniker "Legs" because he was good at fleeing scenes of crime (he was shot three times during his life and was once ambushed in which more than 100 rounds were fired at him to no effect) or because he was a formidable dancer (rumor has it he was quite good). Born in Philadelphia in 1897, Diamond oversaw a smuggling syndicate in Upstate New York. While staying at a boarding house on Dove Street during the morning of December 18, 1931, the gangster's legs did not carry him fast enough. He was murdered in his room. It is unknown who killed Diamond, yet investigations pointed to the Albany Police Department itself. The murder was probably directed by politician Daniel O'Connell because Diamond was encroaching on the O'Connell family's bootlegging territory. Six months later, Diamond's widow, Alice Schiffer Diamond, was murdered. A few weeks after this killing, Mrs. Diamond's personal guard, James Dolan, was also killed.

At this juncture we must take a break from talk of gangsters to discuss a man who named more than a dozen streets, one of them being Dove Street, towards the end of the eighteenth century. As Salzmann wrote: "Simeon DeWitt may be a forgotten man today, but his work of more than 200 years ago remains well-known to every man, woman, and child on the streets of modern-day Albany." In 1790, DeWitt, who served as New York surveyor general and assistant to the geographer and surveyor of the Army, was tasked by Mayor Abraham Yates with, as Salzmann stated, "expunging the last vestiges of British domination from the cultural record of Albany." DeWitt worked from a grid map of streets from 1764. Reynolds, in *Albany Chronicles*, wrote that on March 19, 1785, "Common Council decides to abandon the names of streets that savor of the English rule and appoints a committee to consider new titles and a plan for numbering." A month later they had their report, which detailed getting rid of British names and replacing them with American names. Thus Wall was changed to Hare (today's Orange Street), King to Lion (today's Washington Avenue), Prince to Deer (today's State Street), Queen to Elk, Duke to Eagle, Johnson to Lark, Gage to Swallow (today's Knox Street), Howe to Fox (today's Sheridan Avenue), Kilby to Hamilton, Warren to Dove, Hawke to Hawk, Pitt to Otter (today's Elm Street), Schoharie to Duck (today's Robin Street), Wolfe to Wolf (today' Madison Avenue), Quiter to Buffalo (today's Hudson Avenue), Boscawen to Swan, and Monkton to Mink (today's Park Avenue). DeWitt's map *A Plan of the City of Albany* was produced in 1794. His urban mapping was noted. On April 3, 1807, DeWitt, Gouverneur Morris, and John Rutherford were appointed commissioners within New York City. Their job, according to Henry

Moscow, who shared what may be the most comprehensive sentence ever written, was to "design the leading streets and great avenues, of a width not less than 60 feet, and in general to layout said streets, roads, and public squares of such ample width as they may deem sufficient to ensure a free and abundant circulation of air among said streets and public squares when the same shall be built upon." In simpler terms, the three laid out New York City's streets. They had their map done by 1811.

Dove Street
See Dove Alley.

Dr. Martin Luther King Jr. Boulevard
This street name holds two titles: easiest to decode and most syllables. Dr. Martin Luther King Jr. Boulevard is a quarter-mile-long renamed section of South Swan Street. Name change took place during 1993, and this newly-dubbed street fittingly runs across Lincoln Park, named for Abraham Lincoln. King was born in Atlanta, Georgia, to Martin Luther King and Alberta Williams King on January 15, 1929. Both King men were born with the first name Michael. Their names were changed to honor German theologian Martin Luther after the duo visited Germany.

The junior King attended Booker T. Washington High School, Morehouse College, and Crozer Theological Seminary, gaining a bachelor's degree in sociology and a bachelor's degree in divinity from the two latter institutions, respectively. During the summer of 1953 he married Coretta Scott, and they had four children. King became pastor of Dexter Avenue Baptist Church in Montgomery, Alabama, and earned his doctorate degree in systematic theology at Boston University while serving as assistant minister at Twelfth Baptist Church in Boston. King became involved in the yearlong Montgomery bus boycott, cofounded the Southern Christian Leadership Conference, spoke at the Prayer Pilgrimage for Freedom, almost got stabbed to death by a woman with a mental illness, had his phones tapped, was stalked by the Federal Bureau of Investigation and the National Security Agency, led scores of nonviolent protests, languished in jails, disgraced Theophilus Eugene "Bull" Connor, gave his "I Have a Dream" speech during the March on Washington for Jobs and Freedom, negotiated with federal and state officials, and wrote six books. King was shot by James Earl Ray the morning of April 4, 1968. He was pronounced dead that evening. He is buried next to his wife in a sarcophagus at the Martin Luther King Jr. National Historic Site in Atlanta, Georgia. King was awarded more than fifty honorary degrees as well as the Nobel Peace Prize, American Liberties Medallion, Spingarn Medal, Anisfield-Wolf Book Award, Margaret Sanger Award, Presidential Medal of Freedom, and Congressional Gold Medal.

Albany's Dr. Martin Luther King Jr. Boulevard is but one of many in the nation. By 2003 the U.S. had more than 700 streets named for King. Jesse Lee Peterson, a black reverend who grew up fatherless on a Jim Crow South plantation, pointed out the irony of so many streets named for King being located in black neighborhoods destroyed by a welfare state conceived during the Civil Rights era. He wrote in *The Antidote*, "Today, virtually every one of these streets is a disaster. For a retail operation to have an address on Martin Luther King Jr. Boulevard is the kiss of commercial death."

Dudley Heights

Dudley Heights marks the location of the original Dudley Observatory founded by Blandina Bleeker Dudley, wife of Charles Edward Dudley. This observatory stood on seven acres donated by Stephen Van Rensselaer IV, this plot called Goat Hill, which was the highest point in the city at the time. Construction of the observatory started in 1852 and was chartered by the State of New York that year. It opened for business during August 1856. After being temporarily abandoned, the observatory was moved to where today's Capital District Psychiatric Center is at the intersection of New Scotland Road and South Lake Avenue. The Dudley Observatory is now in Schenectady. Some assume the presence of light pollution around the observatory caused its initial move. The observatory was relocated because New York Central Railroad traffic in Tivoli Hollow disturbed the observatory's delicate instruments. A street called Dudley Avenue, now long-gone, led to the observatory.

Dudley Place East

Charles Edward Dudley, husband of Blandina Bleeker Dudley and son of Charles Dudley and Catherine Crook Dudley, was born in Johnson Hall, County Staffordshire, England, on May 23, 1780. He came to the United States with his mother in 1794, and they settled in Newport, Rhode Island. Dudley worked as a clerk and then a merchant, joining voyages from America to the East Indies and back. He then began a distinguished career in politics. He was presidential elector in 1816, 34th mayor of Albany from 1821 to 1824 and during 1828 and 1829, and senator from New York from 1820 to 1824 and 1829 to 1833. Dudley was a member of the Jacksonian Democrat Party and held membership within the Albany Regency led by Martin Van Buren. He was one of the earliest supporters of the Erie Canal and helped found the Cohoes Company, which used the Mohawk River to produce power. At the conclusion of his term as senator from New York, Dudley retired and spent the rest of his days in Albany. Charles Edward Dudley died January 23, 1841, and was buried in Albany Rural Cemetery. Dudley held great interest in astronomy—thus Albany once had the Dudley Observatory, named for this man. His wife founded the observatory during the 1850s by contributing $3 million towards its construction. She died March 6, 1863, and was buried in Albany Rural Cemetery. The name Dudley comes from the Old English name Dudda and *leah*, meaning "wood" and "clearing."

Dunham Drive

It is fitting that Dunham Drive is within the Port of Albany because Francis "Frank" Woodworth Dunham used to be manager of this port. He was born August 27, 1877, and died January 11, 1972, in Albany. Dunham was survived by his wife, Elizabeth, who was born May 21, 1892, and died during August 1979. They had five children, and one of them was Frank Woodworth Dunham Jr., who also managed the port. He was born October 18, 1918, and died February 16, 1998, in Albany. The name Dunham is taken from that English place name, which comes from the Old English *dun* and *ham*, which mean "hill" and "homestead."

Dutch Drive

The Dutch are known for settling Albany, but the earliest settlements in the Capital Region were also populated with Scandinavians, Croatians, Frenchmen, Scots, Germans, Spaniards, Belgians, Africans, and West Indians. Albany retains a strong Dutch identity because the Dutch, though perhaps not always the most numerous nor powerful, left their mark on the region more than any other culture did. As Hislop wrote, "Dutchmen imported more things from Europe than the round Edam cheeses and the runs of blond beer the tapmen sold in Fort Amsterdam and Beverwyck. They brought with them their architecture, their religion, their forms of education and their political and social customs." Dutch Drive on the University at Albany's main campus leads to Dutch Quad, a housing unit designated for freshmen and recess students such as athletes and international students, who need a place to stay between academic semesters. Dutch Quad was one of the first university buildings to be occupied, in 1964. Students who reside in this dormitory, like in all of the college's dorms, pay their own housing costs, such as rent, even when they have roommates. That is, they go Dutch.

E

Eagle Street

With the bald eagle having such popularity, New York's other species, the golden eagle, is often forgotten, though it's no less majestic. The bald eagle stands up to thirty inches tall and has a wingspan of eight feet. The golden eagle can stand ten inches taller though it has a slightly shorter wingspan. Both species are survival success stories because they were aggressively hunted during the past few centuries yet still survive. Their population has especially bounced back since 1950, and their numbers continue to grow (contrary to popular belief, eagles were not saved via reduction of the insecticide DDT, this myth propagated by author Rachel Carson). Eagle Street was formerly known as Duke Street. This name was changed to Eagle Street on September 11, 1790, to rid the city of a British title. This served as a patriotic "up yours" to our former rulers. Albany used to have an Eagle Alley, which ran between Pruyn Street and Hamilton Street.

With any discussion of Eagle Street it's best to mention the Kings Highway and turnpikes. The beginning, eastern terminus, of the Kings Highway was at today's corner of Eagle Street and Corning Place, which is the former site of the west gate of the Albany Stockade from the 1600s. The Kings Highway was named so because goods were carried along this thoroughfare from the Hudson River to Schenectady and beyond, and vice versa, this commerce benefitting the King of England. Settlers also migrated west along this route as Albany expanded away from the river. The Kings Highway, rated a wagon road by 1663, was partly abandoned when the Albany-Schenectady Turnpike was built in 1797. The Kings Highway at times was a despicable road. This roadway of the 1700s was much like Adirondack roadways of the 1800s. Alfred Donaldson fittingly called such roads "passable in winter, impassable in spring and impossible in summer" in *A History of the Adirondacks*.

Turnpikes were the highways of the 1700s and 1800s. They were authentically designed roads that incorporated drainage, grading, and crushed stone surfacing. Tolls charged at gates paid for construction and maintenance. Other turnpikes besides the Albany-Schenectady Turnpike of 1797 were built throughout the Capital Region to speed travel. These included the Albany-Lebanon Turnpike (today's routes 9 and 20), Bethlehem Turnpike (today's Route 144), Delaware Turnpike (today's Delaware Avenue), and Schoharie Turnpike (today's New Scotland Avenue).

Earth Science Lane

The Earth Science and Mathematics building on the University at Albany's main campus is approached by this petite roadway. Such a formal name shows that the college has their down-to-earth street names down to a science.

East Carillon Drive
(and West Carillon Drive)

A carillon, according to *Merriam-Webster's Collegiate Dictionary*, is "a set of fixed chromatically tuned bells sounded by hammers controlled from a keyboard." These streets run towards the carillon on the University at Albany's main campus. This university, in a 2008 news release about their bell tower being refurbished, wrote that the carillon

> was a gift of the Alumni Association, and was first installed at Stuyvesant Tower on Dutch Quad in 1966. To acquire the carillon, the Association formed "Project Carillon," which raised the extraordinary amount of $30,000 from more than 1,680 donations. In 1972 the carillon was moved to the 250-foot tower and for the next 35 years pealed the Alma Mater and other University tunes at special occasions, and the time of the day . . .

It may be concluded that a price of $30,000, about $250,000 in today's monies, was high for a tower that looks like a gigantic cigarette and, despite being complete, appears to be under eternal construction. The carillon was built by Maas-Rowe Carillons. This company completed the 2008 restoration as well. How does this thing work? The college, in the above news release, explained that "the system is a complex, organ-like musical instrument called a Symphonic Carillon, which uses a keyboard, called a 'baton console,' and a unique method to amplify chimes to simulate the sounds of the larger variable-sized bells . . . " During the Middle Ages, European carillons sent a multitude of messages, some good, others bad. Certain tones and patterns communicated danger such as storms, attacks, and fires. Other arrangements communicated a religious event or birth. By the 1300s, carillons were used to play music, especially during festivals. University at Albany's carillon serves a similar purpose. Beyond marking time at the half and whole hours, there is a public address system in the tower that warns of ominous events. It can play music, but only during happy times. Albany has its own sixty-bell carillon in City Hall. Dedicated in 1927 at a post-World War I peace event, it is the first municipal carillon in the United States. One who operates a carillon is a carillonneur.

East Center Drive
See Centre Street.

East Old State Road
The eastern terminus of East Old State Road is within the City of Albany near Route 155 (New Karner Road). Follow this road west, and it turns into West Old State Road at Route 146 (Carman Road), and then it runs two miles before turning into West Lydius Street outside the Albany city limits. United States Geological Survey topographic maps from 1893, 1927, and 1950 portray East Old State Road, or at least arms of it, running through the Pine Bush towards downtown Albany and sharing a corridor with the long-gone Kings Highway, a road that ran from Albany to Schenectady. The most ancient map to portray Old

State Road is an undated one perhaps from the early 1700s. This is *Map of Lots Within the Bounds of the Corporation of the City of Albany Showing Those Which Belong to Yates and McIntyre* by Miller and Company's Lithograph.

East Pitch Pine Road
(and Lower Pine Lane, North Pine Avenue, Pine Lane, Pine Street, Pine Tree Lane, Pine West Plaza, Pine West Road, Pinehurst Avenue, Pinehurst Boulevard, Pines Court, Pinewood Avenue, Pitch Pine Road, South Pine Avenue, White Pine Drive)

There are more species of pine in the East than you can shake a bough at. Pitch, pond, sand, jack, Austrian, and red, on and on the species go—all fifteen of them. East Pitch Pine Road and Pitch Pine Road are named after pitch pines, which are named after the sticky pitch they produce. Pitch pine is the predominant species of the Pine Bush, and both of these streets are adjacent to this public land. These dwarf pines dominate the pine barrens of Cape Cod and New Jersey, too. Beyond East Pitch Pine Road and Pitch Pine Road, the rest of the "pine streets" are named after pitch pines, red pines, or the greatest pine of all, eastern white pine, discussed below. South Pine Avenue and North Pine Avenue, which were once a singular Pine Street, are named so because pine groves stood along them, these forests portrayed on an 1889 map of the Pine Hills Neighborhood. Pinewood Avenue used to have pine groves along it, too.

As William Fox, grandson of New York's first log drivers, wrote in *A History of the Lumber Industry in the State of New York*: "New York was not only a forest State, but it was essentially a white pine State." As the grandest species in New York, the largest white pine in the state measures 54 inches in diameter and 152 feet in height. White pines stood from New York City to Buffalo, Albany to Plattsburgh, and everywhere in between. This is why there are hundreds of "Pines" in New York: Pine Hill, Pine Lake, Pine Ridge, Pine Brook, Pine Plains, Pine Neck, Pine Grove, Pineville, Pine Valley, and on and on. And this is why there are fifteen "Pine" streets in Albany. Regional Indians even named their settlement *Schenectady*, "the place beyond the pine plains." "Pine" is the fifth most common street name in New York. There are 243 streets with this name.

Since pine was vital to Albany settlement, it was used for payment during the 1600s. As Wilcoxen reported, such planks "were worth around one guilder ten strivers to one guilder sixteen strivers each . . ." Nearly all early Albany homes were built of pine. Naturalist Peter Kalm visited present-day Albany in 1749 and noted "the white pine is found in abundance" and that "a vast quantity of lumber from the white pine is prepared annually on this side of Albany, which is brought down to New York and exported." Thousands of sawmills were operating in and near Albany by the 1860s, and nearly all of them were ripping planks of pine. During each year between 1873 and 1882, Albany had somewhere between 65,000,000 and 115,000,000 board feet of pine on hand. Other states love their pines as much as New York does. Alabama, Arkansas, Idaho, Maine, Minnesota, Montana, Nevada, New Mexico, and North Carolina have chosen pines as their state trees.

East Street

Located nearly as far east as a street can go within Albany, East Street rests on the west shore of the Hudson River. Some residents of the City of Rensselaer call this street West Street since it's on the west side of the river, across from them.

East University Drive
(and West University Drive)

These streets encircle the University at Albany's main campus, and it's divided in half. Predictably, the east side has East University Drive while the west side has West University Drive.

Edenburg Avenue

Edinburgh is the capital of Scotland, and it's the second most populous city in that country. Alexander Bell, Sean Connery, Arthur Doyle, Joanne "J. K." Rowling, Walter Scott, and Robert Stevenson are some of this city's famous residents. People have been living in this region an awfully long time—archeologists have dated campsites in the area to 8500 B.C. Communities and counties are named after Edinburgh in New Jersey, Indiana, New York, Virginia, and Texas. Edina in Missouri carries a corruption of the name Edinburg. Edenburg Avenue was built circa 1925.

The name Edinburgh comes from the Celtic *din eidyn*, meaning "fort on a slope." The ancient Gododdin, descendants of the Votadini, built a fort on a hill in present-day Edinburg prior to 700. *Din* was later replaced by the Old English *burh* and *burg*, ancient words that translate to "fort." The language used in this area prior to Old English was Cumbric, which explains the change in this place name's spelling.

Edgecomb Street

Edgecomb Street, built prior to 1928, is likely named for the same person that the Town of Edgecomb in Maine is named for: George Edgcumbe, 1st Earl of Mount Edgcumbe (1720–1795). In 1774, when Maine was part of Massachusetts, the Massachusetts General Court changed the name of this town from Freetown to Edgecomb. The name Freetown came about because a lawyer defended the settlers' Indian deed for free. George, son of Richard Edgcumbe, 1st Baron Edgcumbe, discussed below, was a politician and Royal Navy officer who commanded the *Terrible, Monmouth, Kennington, Salisbury, Deptford, Lancaster,* and *Hero.*

If Edgecomb Street is not named for George Edgcumbe, then it's probably named for his father, the person for whom Edgecombe County in North Carolina is named: Richard Edgcumbe, 1st Baron of Edgcumbe (1680–1758). He was member of Parliament, lord of the Treasury, paymaster general for Ireland, and chancellor of the Duchy of Lancaster. He attended Trinity College and married Matilda Furnese. They had four children. When Richard Edgcumbe died, he was succeeded by his oldest son, Richard (1716–1761), and then by his second son, George (1720–1795). Richard Edgcumbe's father was Sir Richard Edgcumbe (1640–1688), his grandfather was Piers Edgcumbe (1609–1667), and his great-grandfather was Sir Richard Edgcumbe (1570–1639). All three of these ancestors were English politicians.

If Edgecomb Street is not named for George or Richard Edgcumbe, it carries a descriptive title. The word edge communicates "at the edge of" while the word comb is defined by *Merriam-Webster's Collegiate Dictionary* as "a fleshy crest on the head of the domestic chicken and other domestic birds" and "something (as the ridge of a roof) resembling the comb of a cock." Hence the Adirondack Mountains' jagged Rooster Comb and North Carolina's serrated Coxcomb Mountain.

Edgewood Avenue
(and Forest Avenue, Glenwood Street, Greentree Lane, Grove Avenue, Knollwood Terrace, Orchard Avenue, Parkwood Street, Point of Woods Drive, Wood Terrace, Woodlawn Avenue, Woodridge Street, Woodside Drive, Woodville Avenue)

These fourteen generic names leave creativity to be desired, though they lend the intended effect of us imagining quaint forests. Grove Avenue and Orchard Avenue are named after groves and orchards that stood where these streets now are. Albany County had many orchards and groves prior to 1930, the year housing developments spread into rural areas.

Edison Avenue
Edison Avenue is named for the greatest American inventor of all time, Thomas Edison, and was built before 1914. Schenectady has its own Edison Avenue, which fittingly runs towards General Electric, which he founded. Edison, whose ancestors spelled this name Edeson, was born in Milan, Ohio, to Samuel Ogden Edison Jr. and Nancy Matthews Elliott Edison on February 11, 1847. He was homeschooled and attended R.G. Parker's School of Natural Philosophy

and The Cooper Union for the Advancement of Science and Art. During his youth he sold newspapers and comestibles, his first mature job being a telegraph operator. His first two inventions followed, one the stock ticker, the other the electric vote recorder. He settled in Newark, New Jersey, and created the phonograph in 1877. Next came the carbon telephone transmitter, first commercially viable incandescent light bulb, fluoroscope (today's X-ray machine), motion picture camera, and mining equipment. Thomas Edison died October 18, 1931, at his home in West Orange, New Jersey. He was buried in the backyard. The communities of Edison in Ohio and New Jersey are named for him. Alva, Florida, is reputed to carry Edison's middle name. Yet it's also reputed that this Florida community was named by sea captain Peter Nelson after he saw short-leaf rose gentians—flora that looks like Alva Day's pincushion plants—growing in the area.

Education Lane
All entries in *Cradle of the Union* are educational, but not as much as this street that runs to the Education Building on the University at Albany's main campus.

Edward Terrace
A quaint street that's all of 250 feet long and is home to just four houses, Edward Terrace likely carries the first name of someone related to the man who developed this neighborhood. Edward Terrace is built on land that was conveyed to the city January 7, 1929, by the Van Schoick-Harris Realty Company. That same day, their conveyance of land for construction of nearby Fleetwood Avenue was made official. The name Edward comes from the Old English name Eadweard, meaning "prosperity guard."

Eggsalad Road
This often-overlooked street is unique as being the only one within the city to be named after food. We think of egg salad as a light snack today, perhaps as a sandwich ordered, with a side of fries, of course, when we're not in the mood for grilled cheese. Yet there is a history to this concoction, just as there is with anything.

Egg salad and Hellmann's mayonnaise had their beginnings in Albany during the mid-1600s when the city was called Beverwyck by the occupying Dutch. Due to a lack of refrigeration, the Dutch menu was boring. The idea of a salad during the 1600s, conveyed by renowned food historian Nancy Ward, was "a bowl of what they could grow or pick from the wild, notably wild onions and scallions, baby ferns, wild carrots, certain mushrooms, and dandelions." Dressing consisted of diluted wine with salt. Fresh food was scarce, but what was not scarce in old-time Albany was hens. There was no shortage of eggs. On April 1, 1660, Janicce Stratts Hellmann combined eggs, melted beaver tallow, and salt in an attempt to make a thin dressing. When her product came out thicker than she had wanted, she was about to abandon it when her husband, Fonsinfeverdt Hellmann, a member of the Majesty's Dutch Ekoj, suggested she add hard boiled eggs. Upon doing so, the couple created what they called *loof uoy*, meaning "egg salad." These recipes for mayonnaise and egg salad were brought back to the Old World, and, as they say, the rest is history.

Eggsalad Road used to be called Throne Street, paying homage to the King of England. With Albany wishing to purge itself of English place names, Simeon DeWitt, who was actually allergic to eggs, changed it to Eggsalad Road. Within paperwork submitted to the Common Council that year he wrote that "the Dutch menu, the Dutch table, has long been regarded bland and suspect. 'Tis no more with this name signifying inventiveness and prominence of distinctive Dutch palate among the settlers." DeWitt actually promoted a series of "condiment streets" centered on Eggsalad Road, yet the City of Albany did not accept these names, deeming them "too playful." Proposed street names included Dijon Road, Worcestershire Street, Soy Street, Pesto Street, Relish Road, and Horseradish Way.

Eileen Street

The June 6, 1962, edition of *The Knickerbocker News* reported that the estate of Anna Dolan was being given to her daughter, Eileen Dolan Scherrer. Anna, wife of Frank Dolan, died August 1, 1961, in Honolulu. She had been living there because her son-in-law, an Air Force officer, was stationed in Hawaii. Her estate was worth $146,000. Authors of this newspaper article noted "it is possible that Eileen Street in the West Hill Neighborhood of Albany was named for Frank Dolan's daughter, Eileen." Frank had died in 1931. Eileen attended Sacred Heart and Kenwood schools and was educated in Paris. Eileen Street has existed since 1923 and has a relation to Hawkins Street, which it intersects. Anna and Frank sold their land here to Michael Hawkins in 1911, and thus Hawkins Street was formed.

Elbel Court

Elbel is a German surname that, quite mysteriously, ended up on this street, which was built prior to 1930. Albany Rural Cemetery holds no Elbels, and it appears there were no Elbels living in Albany when this street was built. Elbel is a shortened version of the German name Albrecht, which means "noble" and "bright."

Elberon Place

Once called New Street, the name Elberon Place emulates Elberon, New Jersey. This village is named for its founder, Lewis "L. B." Brown, this place name being an elision of his initials. Elberon was a posh oceanfront retreat from the late 1700s to the early 1900s and was visited by presidents Chester Arthur, James Garfield, Ulysses S. Grant, Benjamin Harrison, Rutherford Hayes, William McKinley, and Woodrow Wilson. When Elberon Place was built circa 1875, it was a stylish neighborhood on the north end of Washington Park Lake. Think of it as a smaller, less fancy version of the New Jersey retreat. The City of Elberon, Iowa, takes its name from this New Jersey community. As the Tama County, Iowa, Economic Development Commission wrote, "A temporary name for [Elberon] was Halifax. However, patriotic fervor was high at the time because of the assassination of the nation's president, James Abram Garfield, who died September 19, 1881, at Elberon, New Jersey. Elberon, Iowa, was named in honor of that eastern suburb."

Eliot Avenue

Eliot Avenue, built before 1929, carries a first or last name, yet we do not know who this Eliot was. The Elliott name dates within Albany County to 1724 at the latest. That is the year that Rebecca Kidney Elliott, wife of James Elliott, died and was buried at the Albany Dutch Church. The name Eliot Avenue could have little significance in the end though. Donald Empson, in *The Street Where You Live*, wrote of St. Paul's Elliot Place that "other than a nice British sound, the name . . . does not seem to have any obvious significance." The Scottish Eliott Clan, which may be the origin of Eliots in America, dates to the 1400s at the latest. Scotland has the seven-mile-long river Water Elliot and the community of Elliot in County Angus. These features may be where the family name came from. The surname Eliot has a few derivations. One is that it's a transformation of the name Ellis and comes from the Middle English name Elyat, which came from the Old English *aoel* ("noble"). The Scottish Eliot stems from the Gaelic *eileach* ("dam" and "mound"). It also comes from the Old French name Elias, which is tied to Elijah ("The Lord is God").

Elizabeth Street

Elizabeth Schuyler Hamilton has her Elizabeth Street, which is one of six "Schuyler streets" near the Schuyler Mansion. The other five are Alexander Street, Catherine Street, Morton Avenue, Philip Street, and Schuyler Street. She was born in Albany on August 9, 1757, as the daughter of Philip Schuyler and Catherine Van Rensselaer Schuyler. It was a power marriage—the Schuyler and Van Rensselaer families were wealthy and influential, having arrived in the region during the 1600s. Concerning her own wedding, Ms. Schuyler was to become Mrs. Hamilton by marrying Alexander Hamilton on December 14, 1780, at the Schuyler Mansion. They honeymooned in the Pastures section of the city.

Soon Elizabeth gave birth to her first child, Philip J. Hamilton, named for her father (to avoid confusion of these two Philips, Elizabeth's father is usually referred to as Philip while his grandson, Elizabeth's son, is usually referred to as Philip J.). Next she gave birth to Angelica (named for Elizabeth's sister), followed by Alexander, James Alexander, John Church, William Stephen, Elizabeth, and Philip (her second son with this name, named for Philip J. who had been killed in a duel with George Eacker during the fall of 1801). She also adopted a child named Fanny Antill. Elizabeth Schuyler Hamilton died in Washington, D.C., on November 9, 1854, and was buried with Alexander Hamilton in Trinity Church Cemetery in Manhattan. Alexander Hamilton died July 12, 1804, in Greenwich Village, New York, after being shot in a duel with Arron Burr Jr. Elizabeth Street was first portrayed on a map of the Schuyler farm and still had dirt sections as late as 1900. That year a 3,000-foot section from Warren Street to Cuyler Street was paved with vitrified bricks.

Elk Street

Queen Street, named for the Queen of England, was the former name of Elk Street, which was also known as Spruce Street. The name Elk Street was formed September 11, 1790, by Simeon Dewitt and the city's Common Council. The easternmost block was dubbed "Quality Row" due to the high-class citizens who lived there (meanwhile, 144 to 170 Chestnut Street was nicknamed "Poverty Row"). Quality residents included governors Hamilton Fish, Washington Hunt, William Marcy, Horatio Seymour, and Enos Throop as well as the Corning, Hun, and Pruyn families. A beautiful row of houses built during the 1820s and 1830s still stands at Quality Row.

Elk Street pays homage to the elk that used to live in New York. Along with wolves and mountain lions, elk were hunted out, the last recorded sighting of a native elk taking place in the Adirondack Mountains during the 1840s. During the first decade of the 1900s, about 250 elk were released in more than six Adirondack counties, but most of the animals died within fifteen years. In 1915 the Benevolent and Protective Order of Elks let loose a boxcar load of western elk in Upstate New York, but these did not live long either. In the East, elk survive in small areas in Pennsylvania and select regions of the Southern Appalachians.

Elks Memorial Drive

Located on the Department of Veterans Affairs' Stratton Medical Center campus, Elks Memorial Drive honors the Benevolent and Protective Order of Elks Albany Lodge No. 49 headquartered on South Allen Street. This lodge has long supported members of the military and veterans. They have completed volunteer projects at this Department of Veterans Affairs hospital, and they donated the flags that stand in front of this facility. With Elks Memorial Drive leading straight to the flags, the naming is appropriate. The Benevolent and Protective Order of Elks (often shortened in conversation to the Elks or the Elks Lodge) established their Elks National Veterans Service Commission in 1946. Their programming includes Adopt a Veteran, Freedom Grants, VA Voluntary Service, Veterans Leather (a hide donation program for artisans), and Welcome Home. This organization was founded as a social club by Joseph Norcross in 1868 in New York City. The Benevolent and Protective Order of Elks has one million members, and past or current members include seven governors, six generals, and five presidents.

Elm Street
(and Elmhurst Avenue)
Elm Street was formerly known as Westerlo Street, Otter Street, and Pitt Street and used to be lined with elms. Elmhurst Avenue translates to "Elm Hill Avenue" because the word hurst means "wooded eminence." Hurst comes from the Old English *hyrst*, which stems from the Proto-Germanic *hurstiz*, meaning "shrubbery."

American, slippery, and rock are the three elm species native to New York. American elm is one of the most widely distributed trees in North America. It ranges from southern Canada to Florida and from the East Coast to the Rocky Mountains, growing in valleys and floodplains across 35 states. This species used to be more common before 1930 when Dutch elm disease reduced its population. This disease is a fungus spread by both American and European elm bark beetles. Elbert Little, in *National Audubon Society Field Guide to North American Trees, Eastern Region*, called the American elm a "large, handsome, graceful tree." It can surpass 100 feet in height and four feet in diameter. The American elm is the state tree of Massachusetts.

Elmhurst Avenue
See Elm Street.

Elmendorf Street
Elmendorf is an Albany County Dutch name that came to the City of Albany from the Town of Coeymans. The oldest record of Elmendorfs in this county dates to June 1693 when Coenraad Elmendorf married Ariantie Gerritse, the widow of Cornelis Martense Van Buren. The oldest Elmendorf grave in Albany Rural Cemetery belongs to Elizabeth Elmendorf. She was born in 1771 and died in 1798.

Specifically pertaining to Elmendorf Street, Harriet Maria Van Rensselaer Elmendorf owned more than 230 lots near this street during the 1870s, the decade in which this street was named. Most of her lots lined Wayne Street, which no longer exists. In this location now stands Albany Community Charter School and the western half of Krank Park. Harriet was born in 1816 and died December 22, 1897, in New Jersey. She was the wife of druggist and physician Peter Edmund Elmendorf, who was born in Albany on August 10, 1814, and died there on the last day of 1881. Peter moved his office from State Street to the Cherry Hill neighborhood, where Elmendorf Street is, in 1845. Harriet Maria Van Rensselaer Elmendorf and Peter Edmund Elmendorf were buried in Albany Rural Cemetery.

Elmo Road

Georgia, Minnesota, and North Carolina each have an Elmo Road. Meanwhile, the communities of Elmo in Wisconsin, St. Elmo in Alabama, and St. Elmo in Colorado are named after the novel *St. Elmo*. This immensely popular book by Augusta Evans (1835–1909), first published in 1866, tells of the romantic tension between two characters, Saint Elmo and Edna Earl. Elmo Road, built circa 1928 with neighboring Eva Avenue, Frost Place, Lily Street, Pansy Street, and Silas Avenue, is likely named after this book.

Emmett Street

First known as Broadway Avenue, that name was changed to Laughlin Street on February 13, 1871, and that name was changed to Emmett Street on September 20, 1879. Historians maintain that Emmett Street is named for Joseph "Fritz" Kline Emmett (1841–1891), whose manor grounds are now part of Wolferts Roost Country Club. Emmett Street is near this country club and, thus, Emmett's sixteen-acre mansion site. The mansion itself was built circa 1882 and then purchased by politician David Hill in 1892, a year after Emmett's death. Hill dubbed it Wolfert's Roost after a short story of that name by Washington Irving. The *New York Sun* described the mansion in a September 18, 1892, article as being "costly," "queer," and "erratically arranged" and hosting "odd nooks," "mounds," and "strange trees" that would "startle the visitor." This one-of-a-kind retreat burned to the ground in 1926. The home was about as weird as Emmett himself, a professional entertainer who yodeled, owned St. Bernard show dogs, and caroused through epic periods of drunkenness.

However, Emmett Street is not named for Joseph "Fritz" Kline Emmett. It's named for Robert Emmet. This is backed by the fact that Emmett didn't purchase his mansion grounds until a few years after Emmett Street received its current name. *The Knickerbocker News* reported Emmett Street was named precisely on September 20, 1879, the 76th anniversary of the death of Robert Emmet.

Emmet was born March 4, 1778, in Dublin, Ireland, as the son of Robert Emmet and Elizabeth Mason Emmet. He attended Oswald's School and enrolled in Trinity College in 1793 at the age of 15. He was expelled in 1798 for joining the United Irish Committee. This firebrand fled to France to avoid arrest for being an Irish nationalist. He sought French military support for a revolution against the British, yet help was never promised. For leading a failed revolution in Ireland, Emmet was arrested, tried for high treason, and found guilty. While being sentenced, he addressed the court with his Speech from the Dock, which closed with:

> I am going to my cold and silent grave. My lamp of life is nearly extinguished. My race is run. The grave opens to receive me, and I sink into its bosom! I have but one request to ask at my departure from this world—it is the charity of its silence! Let no man write my epitaph for as no man who knows my motives dare now vindicate them. Let not prejudice or ignorance asperse them. Let them and me repose in obscurity and peace and my tomb remain uninscribed until other times and other men can do justice to my character. When my country takes her place among the nations of the Earth, then, and not till then, let my epitaph be written. I have done.

John Toler, 1st Earl of Norbury and chief justice of the Irish Common Pleas, sentenced Emmet to be hanged, drawn, and quartered. The next day, September 20, 1803, he was hanged and then beheaded for good measure. His remains were not claimed because anyone who came forward could have been arrested and tried as Emmet was. Emmet, Nebraska; Emmet County, Iowa; Emmett, Michigan; and Emmet County, Michigan, are named for this revolutionary.

Englewood Place

There are communities named Englewood in Alabama, California, Colorado, Florida, New Jersey, and Ohio. A name related to Englewood is Inglewood, and settlements bearing this name are in California and Tennessee. Englewood Place used to be called Robin Street and was laid out in 1879. Just a few homes stand on this street. Perhaps the most beautiful home in Albany is 1 Englewood Place, a massive yet gracious structure designed by William Woollett and built circa 1879 for Benjamin Wooster. Woollett designed two other homes on this street, yet both are gone. The home at 1 Englewood Place is the only example of his work in the city. Englewood and Inglewood mean "a corner of woods."

Erie Boulevard

Erie Boulevard is specifically named after the Erie Canal because the canal once laid where Erie Boulevard now is, this canal having a tow path next to it. This is why Erie Boulevard is straight. An old stone bridge abutment, which used to be part of the canal, still stands. It can be found on the east side of Erie Boulevard at the north end of The Warehouse at Huck Finn's parking lot. This section of the canal, which closed circa 1920, served the two-mile-long Lumber District, an industrial segment of Albany that stood between the canal and the Hudson River. This area was home to more than thirty businesses and included a chapel, two telegraph offices, and a planing mill during the mid-1800s. During this era, nearly 700 million board feet passed through the Lumber District each year.

The Erie Canal is a 363-mile-long waterway that runs from Waterford on the Hudson River to Buffalo on Lake Erie. The canal was built to establish a water route from the Atlantic Ocean to the Great Lakes (the St. Lawrence Seaway did not become a popular shipping lane until 1959). When initially built, the canal contained more than eighty locks and ascended, to the west, more than 600 vertical feet. While other canals were built in Pennsylvania, Kentucky, and Maryland, this canal was the only one to be built in its entirety and survive.

Appreciation for the Erie Canal's design and economic effect was noted beyond New York. This canal was used, at least in part, as a model for the Panama Canal, which was constructed by the French and Americans during the late 1800s and early 1900s. David McCullough noted in *The Path Between the Seas* that with construction of the Erie Canal, as well as the Caledonian Canal in Scotland, built about the same time, "men also felt justified in projecting comparably spectacular works across the map of Central America." McCullough further noted that the Erie Canal illustrated what could be done in the nineteenth century: "The Erie Canal, though built for shallow-draft canal barges, was nonetheless the longest canal in the world, and its locks overcame an elevation en route of nearly seven hundred feet. So on paper a canal at Panama or Nicaragua or any other place in favor at the moment did not seem unrealistic."

The Erie Canal began with the 1792 charter of the Western Inland Lock Navigation Company. But this company and its goal to connect the Hudson River to the Great Lakes was short-lived, the company only reworking short sections of the Mohawk River. New York governor DeWitt Clinton breathed new life into the idea of a canal during the first decade of the 1800s. In 1817, construction of an honest-to-goodness canal was begun in the community of Rome, on Independence Day. Clinton considered the canal open for business October 26, 1825. The *Seneca Chief*, the first boat to navigate the canal, arrived in Albany on November 2, 1825.

Within its first year, the canal hosted more than 2,000 boats and 10,000 horses. Using canals was up to ninety percent cheaper than using draft animals and wagons. The Erie Canal transported intangible things like culture, too. The National Park Service reminded visitors that the canal "brought a flow of people and new ideas. Social reform movements like abolitionism and women's suffrage, utopian communities, and various religious movements thrived in the canal corridor" and immigrants using the canal "infused the nation with different languages, customs, practices, and religions." Construction totaled $7.5 million, about $4 billion in current monies, and at least 1,000 deaths were attributed to a malaria outbreak during one year of construction. Peak use occurred in 1880.

Erie Street
(and West Erie Street)
The Erie Indians were a group that lived on the south shore of their namesake Great Lake though their territory once extended into Pennsylvania and Ohio. They were destroyed during the mid-1600s by the Iroquois Confederacy, notably the Seneca. The Erie who were not outright killed were assimilated into this confederacy. Beyond Lake Erie, this group is memorialized through communities and counties in New York, Ohio, Pennsylvania, Michigan, Kansas, and Illinois as well as street names in the U.S. and Canada.

South of New Scotland Road, West Erie Street used to connect with a street named Villa Lane, which had side streets of Louise Street and George Street. These three streets no longer exist. Erie Street is connected to Champlain Street to portray their real-world connection. The Erie Canal and Champlain Canal can be used to travel from Lake Erie to Lake Champlain. The name Erie stems from the Iroquoian *erielhonan*, which means "long tail," which referred to the mountain lions that lived in Erie territory. It may also come from *erie*, *erike*, and *erija*, meaning "wild cat."

Essex Circle
(and Essex Street)
England's 1,420-square-mile County Essex is represented through these streets as well as Essex counties within Massachusetts, Maryland, New Jersey, New York, Vermont, and Virginia. In ancient times, Essex was the Kingdom of Essex, one of seven kingdoms that formed the Kingdom of England during the 900s. The name Essex comes from the Old English *East-Seaxe*, meaning "East Saxons." The title Saxon comes from Latin, Spanish, Italian, Germanic, and Old English words, among others, that translate to "swordsmen."

Essex Street
See Essex Circle.

Euclid Avenue

Euclid, a Greek who was born during the early fourth century B.C. and died during the mid-third century B.C., is the father of geometry. At least six of his works survive and include *Elements, Data, On Divisions of Figures, Catoptrics, Phaenomena*, and *Optics*. Beyond Euclid Avenue, the 11.8-kilometer-wide Euclides Crater on the moon is named for this mathematician, as are the communities of Euclid in Arkansas, Pennsylvania, Virginia, West Virginia, Iowa, Minnesota, New York, and Ohio. Building lots along Euclid Street were selling as early as 1915.

Eustis Road

This road may carry the name of Revolutionary War veteran William Eustis. He was born June 10, 1753, in Cambridge, Massachusetts, to Benjamin Eustis and Elizabeth Hill Eustis and was a Harvard College graduate. He worked as a surgeon and general practitioner during the battles of Lexington and Concord alongside the man he learned medicine from, Joseph Warren, for whom Albany's Warren Street is likely named. Eustis was later appointed regimental surgeon and treated wounded soldiers at the Battle of Bunker Hill, a fight in which Warren was killed. He then worked among battles in New Jersey and New York and managed a military hospital in New York City. With the war over, Eustis practiced medicine in Boston yet worked for the military again to treat those wounded during Shays' Rebellion, an American civil revolt centered in Springfield, Massachusetts, during 1786 and 1787. Entering politics, he served in the Massachusetts State Legislature and the Governor's Council and became House of Representatives member from Massachusetts, secretary of war, minister to the Netherlands, chairman of the House Committee on Military Affairs, and, finally, governor of Massachusetts. William Eustis died February 6, 1825, while in office. He was first buried in Boston's Granary Burying Ground but was reinterred in Lexington's Old Cemetery.

There are two other notable Eustis military men who fought for the United States, a father and son team. Either could be memorialized through Eustis Road. The father was Abraham Eustis (1786–1843), who attained the rank of brevet brigadier general in the Army and fought in the War of 1812, Black Hawk War, and Seminole Wars. He was born in Cambridge, Massachusetts, and was buried in Lexington, Massachusetts. Florida's Lake Eustis and city of Eustis are named for him, as is Virginia's Joint Base Langley-Eustis, a military facility. One of his six sons was Henry Lawrence Eustis (1819–1885), who was born at Fort Independence, Massachusetts, where his father was stationed. He graduated from Harvard University and graduated first in his class from the United States Military Academy at West Point. He taught at both schools and served as brigadier general during the Civil War. Henry Lawrence Eustis was buried in Mount Auburn Cemetery in Cambridge, Massachusetts.

Eva Avenue

Eva Avenue, which was built circa 1928 with neighboring Elmo Road, Frost Place, Lily Street, Pansy Street, and Silas Avenue, carries the first name Eva, which is of Latin origin and means "life." It's related to the name Eve. Eve was the first woman in God's new world. She was created from a rib of Adam, the first man, and is known for eating forbidden fruit from the tree of knowledge in the Garden of Eden, thus committing the original sin. It's unknown who this Eva was.

Everett Road Extension

During the 1800s and 1900s, Otis Everett was head of household for the Everett farm, which was definitely built before 1854 and perhaps as early as the late 1700s. It stood on the corner of Everett Road and Albany Shaker Road. This street is either specifically named for Otis or generally named for his farming family. He was born February 18, 1789, in New London, New Hampshire, as the son of Penuel Everett and Hannah Slack Everett. Otis's lineage has been traced by the Historical Society of the Town of Colonie back to William Everard, who was born in England in 1480. This makes William the great-great-great-great-great-great-great-grandfather of Otis. He married Mary Shepard, who was born in New Hampshire circa 1793. Their ceremony was officiated by minister Job Seamans and held in Otis's hometown. Otis Everett died February 24, 1860, while Mary Shepard Everett died October 24, 1878. They were buried in Albany Rural Cemetery.

Of the seven children this couple had, the most notable was Robert Bartlett Everett. Robert was born May 17, 1824, in New London, New Hampshire, and was killed at the Battle of Gettysburg on July 1, 1863. He was a captain with Company F, 13th Regiment, New York State Volunteers and then served with the 76th Regiment, New York State Volunteers, leading this unit when he was killed. He was shot in the head with a Minié ball, a bullet named for Claude-Étienne Minié, a French Army officer who invented this hollow-core rifled round in 1846. Though Robert has a headstone in Albany Rural Cemetery, it's unclear if he's really buried there. Some maintain he was interred there while others feel Robert was buried at the battleground, that grave now impossible to locate.

Excelsior Drive

Excelsior Drive, with the nearby streets of Capital Hill and Liberty Lane, honors the State of New York. These three streets additionally encircle the University at Albany's Empire Commons dormitory on the main campus. Portrayed here is a New York and Albany state of mind through Excelsior, Capital, Liberty, and Empire. The term *excelsior*, Latin for "ever upward" and "still higher," is on the seal of the State of New York. The even more obscure word "assiduity" is on the seal of Albany. It means "diligence."

Executive Centre Drive
See Commerce Avenue.

F

Fairlawn Avenue
(and Garden Alley, Garden Avenue, Garden Street, Glendale Avenue, Greenway North, Greenway South, Lawn Avenue, Lawnridge Avenue)
These are the nine "green streets," which were likely named by whimsical developers with a love for flora and the imagery fabricated with such love. In these developers' minds, their streets wind among verdant forests and groves and run past lawns and gardens. Garden Alley is specifically named so because residents had backyard gardens that lined this street.

Fairview Avenue
(and Grandview Terrace, Highland Avenue, Highland Court, Mountain Street, Overlook Street, Pleasant Street, Pleasantview Avenue, Prospect Avenue, Prospect Avenue Extension, Prospect Terrace, Ridgewood Terrace, Summit Avenue, Terrace Avenue, Valleyview Drive, View Avenue)
These are the sixteen "vista streets" where generic names created by daydreaming developers prove you're getting views among summits, terraces, and valleys with the purchase of your property. As Stewart wrote, such names communicate the "extent to which Americans are lured by the hope of a view, or else—as the cynic might suggest—by the snobbish prospect of looking down on others." It is not always the case that the name matches the image. *The Knickerbocker News* hesitated believing Pleasant Street could walk the walk: "[Pleasant Street] bears for title a descriptive adjective of delightful augury. It is one of many Albany streets named for admirable qualities, which, if not actually possessed by the thoroughfares so called, at least show an inclination toward lofty thoughts."

Fairway Court
(and Par Circle North, Par Circle South, Par Drive)
These four streets are next to Capital Hills at Albany Golf Course. Such naming is par for the course. George Kirsh, in *Golf in America*, wrote that Mayor John Boyd Thacher II, in 1929, deemed a municipal course in Albany "imperative" because the popularity of the sport survived the Great Depression and continued

to flourish. A nine-hole course opened, and during May 1931 construction of an eighteen-hole course began. It opened a year later as New Course at Albany and stood in the former community of Hurstville in the Town of Bethlehem. Sections of Bethlehem were annexed to the City of Albany in 1967, and the course's name was changed to Capital Hills at Albany Golf Course. Another former name is Albany Municipal Golf Course. The word fairway has been in use since the 1580s to note a navigable channel in a river. It was first used as a golf term in 1898.

Fay Street

Fay Street memorializes an Albany family name. Nearly twenty Fays are found in Albany Rural Cemetery. The oldest grave to be found, that of Joanna Fay, dates to 1822. She was born in 1785. This street may specifically honor Heman Allen Fay due to it running into Gage Avenue. Thomas Gage, for whom that street is named, was a prominent member of the British military during the Revolutionary War. Fay was an American military man. Perhaps whoever named Fay Street was trying to offset the presence of the Englishman.

Fay was born in 1779 as the son of Jonas Fay and Lydia Safford Fay. He graduated from the United States Military Academy at West Point in 1812 after attending Vermont Military Academy. He then served in the Corps of Artillery. From at least 1819 to 1825 Fay lived by the Hudson River, usually on Quay Street. By 1826 he was living in Arbor Hill, and he lived there for nearly every year until 1850 (during 1830 and 1831 he was listed as living at Fay's Hill, an obscure alternative name for Arbor Hill). Fay had an expansive vineyard that he had opened in 1825. By 1829 he was producing, as reported by Thomas Fessenden in *New England Farmer*, "hundreds of gallons" of wine. He put his Fay's Hill—that is, Arbor Hill—home on the market in 1830 with a realty advertisement that doesn't read much like realty advertisements of today (he kept producing and selling wine and vine clippings after it sold): "Captain Fay offers his place on Fay's Hill for sale. Will be pleased to show and describe it to any gentleman who will call to purchase. Any demand against him may be sent in, well vouched, for adjustment. He will not leave the city indebted to any man."

Heman Allen Fay, author of *An Official Account of Battles Fought Between the Army and Navy of the United States and Great Britain in 1812–15*, died in Bennington, Vermont, on August 20, 1865. He was buried in Albany Rural Cemetery. Joel Munsell, in *Collections of the History of Albany*, wrote that this veteran was "a true gentleman of the old school. His urbanity of manner, intelligence, and strict integrity gained for him a large circle of friends, both in military and social life. At a silvery old age he entered into the 'rest that remains for the people of God.'" The name Fay stems from the Middle English and Old French *fee* and *faie*, which note a fairy or someone with supernatural powers.

Federal Street

The federal union of the fifty unified states is celebrated through Federal Street. In 1776 we started with thirteen: New Hampshire, Massachusetts, Rhode Island, Connecticut, New York, Pennsylvania, New Jersey, Maryland, Delaware, Virginia, North Carolina, South Carolina, and Georgia. By 1836 we were halfway to fifty. We added the nation's last two states, Alaska and Hawaii, on January 3 and August 21 of 1959, respectively. Federal Street was built before 1916.

Fern Avenue
(and Ferndale Avenue)

Delicate ferns are remembered through these street names. There are more than 4,000 species of ferns on Earth, and they all fall within the order Filicales. The word fern stems from a Sanskrit word for "feather." A dale is a valley or gorge, thus William Shakespeare's poem "Over Hill, Over Dale." The word dale has been in use since the twelfth century. It comes from the Old English *dæl* ("valley") and the Proto-Germanic *dalan* ("valley") and *dhel* ("hollow"). When the area around Fern Avenue was settled, there were likely ferns growing there. In the case of Ferndale Avenue, ferns were probably in a nearby hollow.

Ferndale Avenue

See Fern Avenue.

Fine Arts Lane

This little lane leads to University at Albany's Fine Arts Building and its University Art Museum on the main campus. The name is so plain yet still a fine work of art.

First Avenue
(and First Street, Fourth Avenue, North First Street, North Second Street, North Third Street, Second Avenue, Second Street, Third Avenue, Third Street)

Albanians were feeling cosmopolitan when they named these ten streets. Tired of the diminutive nickname "Smallbany," the namers had big city lights, perhaps New York City's lights, on their minds. Yet Albany's numbered streets don't make it anywhere close to Forty-Second Street because these ten streets are the only Albany street names with numbers. First Avenue, Second Avenue (formerly known as Whitehall Road), Third Avenue (formerly known as Van Vechten Street until 1873), and Fourth Avenue (formerly known as Nucella Street until 1873 and still having dirt sections as late as 1890) are near each other south of Lincoln Park. First Street, Second Street (formerly known as Elizabeth Street and still having dirt sections as late as 1900), and Third Street (formerly known as John Street) are next to each other and connect downtown Albany with the North Manning Boulevard area. North First Street, North Second Street, and North Third Street are a conglomerate in an eastern part of the city. The "First" label is the ninth most common street name in New York. There are 203 streets named so in the state.

First Street
See First Avenue.

Fleetwood Avenue
Fleetwood Avenue is likely named after the town and civil parish of this name in County Lancashire, England. This English community of 30,000 residents has been settled for at least 2,000 years. It's named for the Fleetwood family, who owned land there during a 300-year period. This street and Edward Terrace, which is near it, were built on land that was conveyed to the city on January 7, 1929, by the Van Schoick-Harris Realty Company.

Fordham Court
Fordham Court has a dual personality. It's within the eight "English streets," the other seven being Carlisle Court, Cheshire Court, Kensington Place, Marlborough Court, Stanford Court, Windsor Place, and Victoria Way. It's probably named after the community of Fordham, which has been inhabited since the Early Bronze Age, in County Cambridgeshire, England. Fordham communicates "home by a ford." The Fordham Neighborhood of New York City was named by John Archer, a Dutch settler who arrived during the 1660s and was granted land in 1671. This neighborhood is near a shallow ford of the Bronx River. Albany's Fordham Court was built with nearby Carlisle Court, Marlborough Court, and Stanford Court in 1929.

If not replicating the English place name, Fordham Court is named after Fordham University, which takes its name from New York City's Fordham Neighborhood. This university was founded in 1841 by John Hughes, archbishop of the Diocese of New York, and was called Saint John's College until 1907. Students can choose from approximately fifty degree programs among the university's nine schools. Fordham University accepts approximately half of its applicants. Notable alumni include Andrew Cuomo, William Casey, Charles Osgood, Denzel Washington, Alan Alda, and Vince Lombardi. Army generals Colin Powell and John Keane and four Medal of Honor recipients attended this university's Military Science program.

Forest Avenue
See Edgewood Avenue.

Fountain Avenue
If this street was in downtown Albany where a fountain had once been, the decoding of this street name would be easy and accurate. Considering Fountain Avenue is in the suburbs, and because your author drove down it searching for signs of a fountain and found none, this is a generic name created by a developer. Fountain Avenue was built before 1928.

Fourth Avenue
See First Avenue.

Franklin Street
Ambassador. Inventor. Founding father. Playboy. Benjamin Franklin, known as the First American, was born January 17, 1706, in Boston, and was many men in one. Beyond his above identities, Franklin was a ferociously quotable man, a few gems being: "Three may keep a secret, if two of them are dead," "We must all hang together, or assuredly we shall all hang separately," and "He that is good for making excuses is seldom good for anything else." Scores of topographical and political features are named for him, from aircraft carriers to mountains, bridges to a crater on the moon. According to the U.S. Postal Service, "Franklin" is the most common city name in the country—31 cities carry this title.

Franklin, who had seventeen siblings and ten stepsiblings, attended Boston Latin School and did not graduate, ending his formal schooling at age 10. He was thereafter self-educated from his relentless reading of books (thus his quote: "The person who deserves most pity is a lonesome one on a rainy day who doesn't know how to read"). He moved to Philadelphia and found work as a printer, then moved to London to find the same work, and came back to Philadelphia in 1726 to run *The Pennsylvania Gazette*. He published *Poor Richard's Almanack* in 1771 and began work on his autobiography, which was published after his death. Franklin's public and professional positions ran the gamut through the 1700s on both sides of the Atlantic. He was Philadelphia postmaster, founder of the American Philosophical Society, Philadelphia councilman and justice of the peace, Pennsylvania assemblyman, deputy postmaster general of British North America, leader of the Pennsylvania Delegation to the Albany Congress, founder of the Pennsylvania Militia, speaker of the Pennsylvania House, Pennsylvania Assembly delegate to the Second Continental Congress, United States postmaster general, member of the Committee of Five that drafted the Declaration of Independence, minister to France and Sweden, and, finally, fellow of the American Academy of Arts and Sciences. He was awarded honorary degrees from the University of St. Andrews, Oxford University, Harvard University, and Yale University.

Franklin holds distinction as the only founding father to have signed each of the four documents that formed the United States. He signed the Declaration of Independence, Treaty of Alliance with France, Treaty of Paris, and the Constitution. His suggested slogan, which was not accepted, for the seal of the United States was "Rebellion to Tyrants is Obedience to God." On April 17, 1790, Benjamin Franklin died at his home in Philadelphia. More than 20,000 people attended the funeral. Franklin was interred in Christ Church Burial Ground in Philadelphia. This two-acre cemetery dates to 1719. Four other signers of the Declaration of Independence—Joseph Hewes, Francis Hopkinson, George Ross, and Benjamin Rush—were buried there. Franklin Street used to be called Frelinghuysen Street, named for J. Theodorus Frelinghuysen of the Albany Dutch Church.

Freeman Road

In 1922, land was conveyed to the city for today's Freeman Road, Bogardus Road, Greenway Street, Halsdorf Street, Kakely Street, and Linden Road to be built. Freeman is an old Albany County name. Mark Freeman and Frances Freeman were living in this county by the mid-1700s. Their child, Elizabeth, was baptized June 19, 1759.

Perhaps the most well-known of the early Freemans of Albany was John Freeman I. He was born in 1736 in Schoharie County as one of four children of Robert Freeman and Maritie De Line Freeman. He married Rebecca Vine on June 3, 1768, and they operated a hotel and tavern west of Albany. This business was razed by Tories during the Revolutionary War. The couple holed up in the Albany fort, and Freeman served with Philip Schuyler's Albany County Militia. Their son, John Freeman II, was born in the fort in 1783. John Freeman I died in 1800 while his wife died in 1814. Tradition holds that they were buried in Prospect Hill Cemetery though their graves have never been found.

An even older Albany County name is Freerman, of which Freeman is a corruption. Barnhardus Freerman was one of the first Freermans of the Capital Region, and he held public positions in Schenectady from 1700 to 1705. He died in 1741, four years after his wife, Margarita Van Schaick Freerman, passed away. Their daughter, Anna Margarita Freerman, married her cousin, David Clarkson, who was the son of the secretary of the Province of New York. There are no Freermans in Albany Rural Cemetery, but there are more than sixty Freemans. Freeman translates literally and comes from the Old English *freo*, which means "free." This word noted those who were not serfs.

Friebel Road

The Friebel family of famers are memorialized within Friebel Road. This family operated their farm on this road until the 1950s, and this road has existed since the 1930s. The first Friebel to arrive in the Capital Region was Karl Ferdinand Friebel. He was born August 17, 1834, in Molsdorf, Thueringen, Germany, and was married to Natalie Geyer Friebel, who was born October 3, 1841, in Haarhausen, Gotha, Germany. They came to the U.S. with their only child, Otto, who was born during February 1869 in Germany. Karl Ferdinand Friebel died October 14, 1900, in McKownville while Natalie Geyer Friebel survived until March 4, 1922, dying in Albany. They were buried in Evangelical Protestant Church Cemetery in Albany. Their son Otto survived until 1953. He married twice, had eight children, and was buried in Prospect Hill Cemetery in Guilderland, New York. While only three Friebels are buried in Albany Rural Cemetery, nineteen are buried in Prospect Hill Cemetery.

Frisbie Avenue

Edward Frisbie was born in Albany on November 18, 1826, and was the most interesting of the Frisbie farmers of Whitehall Road, for whom this street is named. By 1850, this family owned land where Frisbie Avenue now is. As the son of Eleazer Frisbie and Cynthia Cornell Frisbie, Edward worked on his family's farm and was employed at other farms in the Capital Region. On April 16, 1846, he married Phoebe Ann Klink. They opened their own dairy farm in Albany County and then moved to Syracuse to start another farm.

Edward and Phoebe took a big leap west in 1855 and reached California's Napa County on the first day of 1856 to live on the outskirts of Vallejo. They had traveled through the Panama Canal to get there, taking passage aboard the *John L. Stevens*. Phoebe died in San Francisco on July 17, 1886. The *San Francisco Chronicle* wrote that

> she was a person of more than ordinary character, possessed of a well-balanced and highly cultivated mind, and lived and died a model Christian woman, wife and mother, respected and beloved by all with whom she came in contact . . . Her last days were attended with much bodily suffering, which she ever bore with true Christian fortitude, and finally passed peacefully away in the presence of her husband and other members of her family.

Edward farmed, logged, bought and sold real estate, and then worked as a banker. In 1888, with five other men, he started the Bank of Northern California based in Redding and served as its first president. A rancher and farmer at heart, he continued to work cattle and horse ranches and keep bovines. He remarried, pairing with Laura Walden. She gave him another two children, and by 1906 he was the proud father of eleven children and the grandfather of 24.

Edward Frisbie died October 7, 1908, and was buried in Carquinez Cemetery in Vallejo, California. James Guinn, author of *History of the State of California and Biographical Record of the Sacramento Valley, California*, gushed over Frisbie at the turn of the twentieth century with one heck of a sentence:

> No greater tribute can be paid a man than that coming unsolicited from his friends, and it has been said of Mr. Frisbie by those who know him best that he is a man of unimpeachable integrity, a devoted friend of education, for no appeal for assistance in behalf of a worthy cause ever failed of his support and co-operation; that his deeds of kindness are performed in as unostentatious a manner as possible, and to such men as he posterity will always look with feelings of pride and satisfaction, and they are entitled to a permanent place in the historical literature of this state.

One of Edward's brothers, John B., was as well-known and interesting as Edward himself. John B. was a soldier, lawyer, and railroad investor. He moved to California from Albany in 1846 and married one of General Mariano Guadalupe Vallejo's daughters, Fannie, in 1850. He founded the community of Vallejo, California, smartly naming it for his father-in-law. He befriended Mexico's president, Porfirio Diaz, who gave him an abandoned gold mine for mediation services he provided between this president and the United States. John B. Frisbie worked the mine and retired in Mexico a millionaire.

Frost Place
Used here, the name Frost has little to do with temperatures below 33 degrees, though this name translates literally. During the late 1800s, Jonathan Frost owned land where Frost Place now lies and operated a grocery store on the corner of Frost Place and Central Avenue for decades. The eastern stretch of Frost Place was built prior to 1919, about a decade before nearby Elmo Road, Eva Avenue, Lily Street, Pansy Street, and Silas Avenue were constructed.

Fuller Road
Fullers is a hamlet in the Town of Guilderland, and this hamlet and Albany's Fuller Road are named for John Fuller, who served as a major in the New York State Militia. Fuller also served as member of the Legislature in 1846 and supervisor of Guilderland in 1846 and 1847. He was born in 1802 and died during February 1882. His wife, Harriet Moak Fuller, was born in 1804 and died in 1863. Both grew up in the community of New Scotland. Fuller Station Road, which was home to the Fullers post office as well as the Fullers Station railroad stop, in Schenectady is also named for this man. Fuller and his son, Aaron, kept a tavern on that road. The post office closed in 1918 and the railroad station

was abandoned in 1927. Aaron went on to become Town of Guilderland supervisor and New York assemblyman, though he preferred his occupation of hay farmer best. The name Fuller describes one who works with cloth, scouring and thickening it by working it in water. This is the name source of a mill called a fulling mill, which processes wool.

Fullerton Street

Fullerton Street, built before 1928, is unrelated to Fuller Road above. Fullerton is a village and civil parish in County Hampshire, England, and this street likely carries this English place name. There are Fullerton place names throughout the U.S., but they're unrelated to England. Fullerton, California, is named for Pacific Land and Improvement Company president George Fullerton; Fullerton, North Dakota, is named for a man of that last name who was father-in-law of the founder; Fullerton, Pennsylvania, is named for James W. Fuller Jr., a business man who laid out the community; and Fullerton, Nebraska, is named for rancher Randall Fuller. Fullerton is a two-part Scottish and Irish place name that translates to "bird catcher" and "settlement."

Fulton Street

Formerly named William Street, Fulton Street memorializes Robert Fulton of *Clermont* fame. A landscape painter by trade, Fulton was born November 14, 1765, in Little Britain, Pennsylvania. He travelled to England in 1786 to study canal and boat construction, language, chemistry, and mathematics and then designed the groundbreaking ships *Bonaparte*, *Clermont*, *New Orleans*, and *Demologos*. He also designed water mines as well as the submarine *Nautilus*. Fulton married Harriet Livingston in 1806, and they had four children. Robert Fulton died of pneumonia February 24, 1815, in New York City and was buried in this city's Trinity Church Cemetery. Beyond Fulton Street, dozens of features across the country are named for this inventor including New York's Fulton County, Fultonham, Fulton, West Fulton, and Fultonville. Fulton Street in New York City carries his name, too.

*Ebenezer Emmons named the Adirondacks, giving us **Adirondack Street** (artist unknown)*

*King James II and VII, Duke of Albany, for whom **Albany Street** is named (Peter Lely)*

Silas Avenue carries the name of Governor Silas Wright (Mathew Brady)

Seymour Avenue *memorializes Governor Horatio Seymour (Mathew Brady)*

"T. R." (here with John Muir) has his **Roosevelt Street** *(Underwood & Underwood)*

Henry Hudson, being cast away, is honored with **Hudson Street** *(F. Davignon)*

A president's nickname is found in **Old Hickory Drive** *(James Longacre)*

Alden Avenue *is named for John Alden, here with Pricilla (artist unknown)*

*Alexander Hamilton has his **Alexander Street** and **Hamilton Street** (John Trumbull)*

*William Bingham, for whom **Binghamton Street** is named (Max Rosenthal)*

Bouckville and **Bouck Street** *honor William Bouck (John Buttre)*

Catherine Van Rensselaer Schuyler has her **Catherine Street** *(Mason Brothers)*

*Supposed image of Samuel de Champlain of **Champlain Street** (César Ducornet)*

*Edward Hyde, 1ˢᵗ Earl of Clarendon, has his **Clarendon Road** (William Richardson Pub.)*

Cleveland Street carries the memory of **Stephen Grover Cleveland** *(Napoleon Sarony)*

Clinton Avenue and ***Clinton Place*** honor DeWitt Clinton *(Charles Ingham)*

*Founding father George Clinton earned his **Clinton Street** (artist unknown)*

Cortelyou Road *honors postmaster George Cortelyou (M. W. Gibbs)*

Governor Thomas Dongan, memorialized in **Dongan Avenue** *(artist unknown)*

*Elizabeth Schuyler Hamilton is honored through **Elizabeth Street** (artist unknown)*

*"The First American," Ben Franklin, has his **Franklin Street** (James Longacre)*

Fulton Street honors Robert Fulton of Clermont *fame (William Leney)*

Peter Gansevoort is honored with **Gansevoort Street** *(J. F. E. Prud'homme)*

Green Street *is likely named for officer Nathaniel Greene (James Longacre)*

*Author Nathaniel Hawthorne Jr. has his **Hawthorne Avenue** (Cephas Thompson)*

*Federalist Papers coauthor John Jay lends **Jay Street** its name (John Buttre)*

Knox Street honors artilleryman Henry Knox (Robert Whitechurch)

Formerly Lumber Street, **Livingston Avenue** *honors Philip Livingston (artist unknown)*

McKinley Street *is named for William McKinley Jr. (M. W. Gibbs)*

Montgomery Street *is named for hero Richard Montgomery (artist unknown)*

Pennsylvania honors William Penn, thus **Pennsylvania Avenue** *(James Posselwhite)*

*"Hero of Lake Erie" Oliver Perry has his **Perry Place** (Thomas Gimbrede)*

Philip Street, *a "Schuyler street," honors Philip Schuyler (artist unknown)*

Pieter Schuyler has **Pieter Schuyler Court West** *and* **Schuyler Street** *(artist unknown)*

Putnam Street *is named for Israel "Old Put" Putnam (C. Shepherd)*

Local boy Phil Sheridan has his **Sheridan Avenue** *(Johnson Fry & Co.)*

Sherman Street *is named for William Tecumseh Sherman (Mathew Brady)*

The Prussian von Steuben is memorialized in **Steuben Street** *(artist unknown)*

Yates Street honors Union College cofounder Joseph Yates (John Buttre)

Van Tromp Street *is named for Maarten Harpertszoon Tromp (artist unknown)*

Many U.S. features, including **Warren Street**, *honor Joseph Warren (John Copley)*

Washington Avenue honors George Washington (artist unknown)

Painted by E. Seeman.

Yale University is named for Elihu Yale, thus **Yale Court** *(Enoch Seemann)*

The R.t Hon.ble the Earl of Loudoun
Capt.a General & Governour in Chief of his Majesty's Forces in North America;
and one of the Sixteen Peers of Scotland.

*John Campbell, honored in **Loudon Road** and **Loudonville Road** (Allan Ramsay)*

*Lord Jeffrey Amherst, for whom a New England town and **Amherst Avenue** are named (Reynolds)*

G

Gage Avenue

Thomas Gage is honored through Gage Avenue, making this street one of six streets named for prominent members of the British military active during the Revolutionary War. The other five are Amherst Avenue named for Jeffery Amherst; Glynn Street named for John Glynn; and Tryon Court, Tryon Place, and Tryon Street named for William Tryon. Gage's name has been purged in other parts of the U.S. In Massachusetts, Windsor used to be called Gageborough. The original name was changed for concern that it would, to quote the Massachusetts Historical Society, "perpetuate the memory of the detested General Gage." Gage Avenue was built before 1934.

Gage was born March 10, 1718, in Firle, County Middlesex, England. His parents were Thomas Gage and Maria Teresa Hall Gage. At the age of 10 he started attending Westminster School where he met Francis Bernard, John Burgoyne, George Germain, and Richard Howe, who, like Gage, would become oppressors of the Americans. Gage ended his studies in 1736 and joined the British military as an ensign and then as an officer. He would fight in the War of the Austrian Succession, Second Jacobite Rising, and French and Indian War. Gage was assigned as the military governor of Montreal and then created Britain's first light infantry unit. After all, hit and run skirmishes in the North American woods demanded a mobile, adaptable combat unit. When the French and Indian War ended in 1763, Gage became commander in chief of British North America. Pontiac's Rebellion in Ohio broke out, and Gage oversaw peace negotiations to conclude this Indian uprising by the summer of 1766. Within a decade the American Revolution erupted. Soon Gage, who was then serving as governor of Massachusetts, became one of the most hated men in North America, especially after the battles of Lexington and Concord, which led to the Siege of Boston, which began the War for Independence. After Lexington and Concord, Gage left the New World and sailed back to Britain after being relieved of duty. He was replaced by General William Howe. Thomas Gage died April 2, 1787, in London and was buried at Firle, the community in which he was born. The name Gage labels one who works with weights and measures.

Gansevoort Street

Named for Peter Gansevoort, Gansevoort Street was formerly named South Street because it was on ancient Albany's southern boundary, this demarcation marked with cairns and cedar posts as early as 1652. The ancestral name Gansevoort comes from Ganzfort, a community on the border of Germany and the

Netherlands. The name Gansevoort, spelled Gansefortius way back when, dates to 1419 within the settlement of Groningen, Holland, the Netherlands.

Gansevoort was born July 17, 1749, in Albany to Harman Gansevoort, a brewer and farmer, and Magdalena Douw Gansevoort. He is best known for his leadership during the Revolutionary War. The Schenectady Digital History Archive characterized this man as "one of the bravest and most determined soldiers and patriots of the revolution, an officer whose courage never was doubted, whose achievements as a commanding officer were fully appreciated, but whose splendid service never was more than half rewarded." Gansevoort was a fighter who flew up the ranks. Beginning as a lieutenant, he was made major and served in the 2nd New York Regiment. Less than a year later, during the spring of 1776, he was promoted to lieutenant colonel. By the autumn of that year he was colonel of the regiment. Gansevoort is specifically remembered for his courage and coolness while directing the defense of Fort Stanwix, in today's Rome, New York, from a three-week-long British onslaught led by Colonel Barry St. Leger in 1777.

He later fought against the Indians of central New York with General John Sullivan. New York couldn't get enough of Gansevoort and promoted him to brigadier general. Beyond his military service he fulfilled the role of commissioner of Indian affairs, sheriff of Albany County, regent of the University of the State of New York, and member of New York State Bank board of directors. Peter Gansevoort died July 2, 1812, and was buried in Albany Rural Cemetery. He was the father of six children and grandfather of author Herman Melville. His wife, Catherine Van Schaick Gansevoort, survived him for nearly two decades, passing away December 30, 1830.

Garden Alley
See Fairlawn Avenue.

Garden Avenue
See Fairlawn Avenue.

Garden Street
See Fairlawn Avenue.

Garfield Place
Garfield Place is one of the "presidential conglomerate" streets of Albany. The other seven are Grant Avenue, Cleveland Street, Lincoln Avenue, McKinley Street, Roosevelt Street, Van Buren Street, and Washington Avenue. Nearby

Buchanan Street is not named for James Buchanan but for a local engineer. These nine streets were named during the late 1800s and early 1900s by realtor Jesse Leonard. Garfield Place used to be part of Second Street and gained its own identity in 1901.

James Garfield was born into a dirt-poor family outside Cleveland, Ohio, on November 19, 1831. He had four siblings and lost his father at the age of 2. He fulfilled menial jobs during his youth, one of which included being a janitor, yet he was accepted into Williams College and graduated. Like most great men of his era, Garfield practiced law. He attended the Western Reserve Eclectic Institute, today's Hiram College, and became one of their classics professors. The next year he was president of this Ohio college. He became nine-term House of Representatives member, major general in the Union Army, and president of the United States. He gained the presidency by beating General Winfield Scott Hancock, a Democrat, by a mere 10,000 popular votes. That, my friends, is rags to riches.

He took office as the president on March 4, 1881, and was dead by September 19. The Miller Center of the University of Virginia summarized that "since Garfield was struck down four months into his term, historians can only speculate as to what his presidency might have been like." He was shot on July 2, 1881, by Charles Guiteau, confirmed to have been "an emotionally disturbed man who had failed to gain an appointment in Garfield's administration." The shooting took place at the Baltimore and Potomac rail station in Washington, D.C. Guiteau felt responsible for Garfield being elected, especially because it was such a close race with Hancock, and thought he deserved a diplomatic post at the very least. When he didn't get that appointment, he decided to kill the president, assured he had been commanded by God to do so. Wounded from two .44 gunshots, Garfield was kept in the White House for several weeks, and an attempt was made to remove his assailant's bullets. By September the president was taken to the New Jersey shore, and less than two weeks later he died of an artery aneurysm, internal bleeding, pneumonia, and infections complicated by malnourishment. James Garfield was buried in Lake View Cemetery in Cleveland, Ohio, the gravesite marked with the James A. Garfield Monument, which is listed on the National Register of Historic Places. Designed by George Keller, this monument is 200 feet tall. Charles Guiteau was hanged on June 30, 1882, in Washington, D.C. Most of his remains, including his brain and bones, were given for medical research.

Garland Court

Garland Court is one of Albany's newest streets. New homes along it were being advertised in 1970. One notable Garland was Jerome Garland, who led the Cohoes Iron Foundry and Machine Company around 1900. This company was founded in 1868 by William Horrobin, operated until at least 1898, and made machinery, much of it for the cotton industry. Garland served as an alderman and was a member of the Board of Health, Excise Board, and International Order of Odd Fellows. However, a definitive connection between Jerome Garland and Garland Court cannot be made.

Garland is a British surname that translates to "triangular-shaped piece of land." The word gore that we use in America comes from *gara*, and it, too, describes a triangular plot (hence four Gore place names in Vermont, seven more in Maine, and Gore Mountain in the Adirondacks). This surname dates to 1200 within Ireland and England. Garland is also an area within the community of Chumleigh, County Devon, England.

Genesee Street

Genesee Street used to be called Watervliet Avenue until February 13, 1871, and may specifically be named for the 150-mile New York river of this name because this street is next to Mohawk Street. The name Genesee stems from the Seneca word *gen-nis'-hee-yo*, meaning "beautiful valley." In *The American Whig Review*, authors reported that New York's Genesee Valley was "of great extent, boundless fertility, and easy cultivation" and "fully deserved the appellation of gen-nis'-hee-yo." New York also has Genesee County, organized 1803, and the Town of Genesee, established 1830 (this town is in Allegany County). Genesee place names are also found in Wisconsin, Pennsylvania, and Colorado. The communities of Geneseo in Illinois, Kansas, Iowa, and New York carry a variation of Genesee.

Georgetown Court

Georgetown University in Washington, D.C., is likely honored through this street name. Georgetown Court, along with nearby Williamsburg Court, was one of the last streets built in the City of Albany. Williamsburg Village Apartments is accessed exclusively by this street, and this apartment complex wasn't built until 1983. Dozens of "Georgetown" place names can be found throughout the U.S. in at least thirty states.

Georgetown University was founded by John Carroll in 1789, which makes it the oldest Catholic and Jesuit college in America. Its schools include Georgetown College, McDonough School of Business, Walsh School of Foreign Service, Graduate School of Arts and Sciences, Law Center, School of Medicine, School of Continuing Studies, School of Nursing and Health Studies, and McCourt School of Public Policy. Approximately 8,000 undergraduate and 10,000 graduate and doctorate students attend and are served by more than 2,000 faculty. Seventeen percent of applicants are admitted. Notable alumni include Bradley Cooper, Antonin Scalia, Jacqueline Kennedy Onassis, Ivanka Trump, Bill Clinton, and King Abdullah II of Jordan.

Gingerbread Lane

Helen Picotte of the Picotte Companies named Gingerbread Lane during the late 1940s when this company was building homes in the neighborhood. Some think the homes on Gingerbread Lane look like little gingerbread houses, which would explain the name yet may cause the questioning of one's masculinity. Art Plotnik wrote that a resident of this street could be "the rugged outdoor type who must confess from time to time, 'I live on Gingerbread Lane.'" Helen Picotte was born in 1918 and passed away in 1980. She was the wife of builder Clifford Picotte, who was the father of William B. Picotte. William now serves as senior vice president of Picotte Companies.

Gipp Road

The Gipp family of this area's Gipp farm, which was operated from the 1800s to the 1960s, is honored within this street. Gipp Road was constructed before 1937. Matthew Gipp was likely the last of this family to work the farm, and members of the Gipp family live on nearby Westmere Terrace today.

Glendale Avenue

See Fairlawn Avenue.

Glenwood Street

See Edgewood Avenue.

Glynn Street

Glynn Street is next to Tryon Court, Tryon Place, and Tryon Street because the men honored through these streets were active during the American Revolution. Glynn Street honors English lawyer and Parliament member John Glynn (a good guy), who lived from 1722 to 1779. Tryon Court, Tryon Place, and Tryon Street honor colonial governor William Tryon (a bad guy), who lived from 1729 to 1788. These men are connected within the South, too. Georgia has Glynn County while North Carolina has the Town of Tryon (and Charlotte's main thoroughfare is 23-mile-long South Tryon and North Tryon streets). The Town of Wake Forest and Wake County in North Carolina carry Tryon's wife's maiden name.

Glynn was born in Cardinham, County Cornwall, England, during the summer of 1722 to William Glynn and Rose Prideaux Glynn. He inherited property at a young age, practiced law by the early 1760s, and that decade he began a political career in which he was supportive of the American revolutionaries. John Glynn died September 16, 1779, and was buried at Cardinham. Houses were being built along Glynn Street as early as 1927.

Golder Street

The specific Golder memorialized through Golder Street remains a mystery. Albany Rural Cemetery has two Golder graves, the older of the two belonging to John Golder, who was a native of Glasgow, Scotland. He was born in 1798, died February 21, 1826, and was originally buried at the United Presbyterian Church. Golders can also be found in Albany County's Graceland Cemetery, Eagle Hill Cemetery, and Sons of Abraham Cemetery. Census records revealed more than a dozen Golders living in Albany during the late 1800s and early 1900s. The home at 19 Golder Street was built circa 1850 and is the oldest building on this street. This house predates street construction (the house existed out in farmland by 1850, and Golder Street itself was built decades later). The name Golder comes from the name Goldhere, which is composed of *gold* and *here*, meaning "gold" and "army."

Grain Street

Leading off an intersection where Smith Boulevard transitions into Raft Street, little Grain Street runs near a massive grain elevator and a series of grain silos within the Port of Albany. The elevator was built in 1931 and 1932, just in time for opening day port ceremonies on June 6, 1932.

Grand Street

Formerly known as Halenbake Street and Hollenbake Street, "grand" is employed to have us visualize magnificence. The name misses its mark. *The Knickerbocker News* reported that "Grand Street has a grandiloquent name comparatively meaningless." The names Halenbake and Hollenbake memorialized Caspar Janse Halenbeek, who came from Holland and settled in Beverwyck circa 1654. Today's Grand Street is where this family's farm and burial ground were. Halenbeek died during August 1703.

Grandview Terrace

See Fairview Avenue.

Grant Avenue

Grant Avenue is part of the "presidential conglomerate" of streets within Albany. The accompanying seven include Cleveland Street, Lincoln Avenue, McKinley Street, Roosevelt Street, Garfield Place, Van Buren Street, and Washington Avenue (contrary to popular belief, nearby Buchanan Street is not named for James Buchanan). Grant Avenue memorializes Ulysses S. Grant, whose last name can be traced to the mid-1200s in Scotland. This street name was accepted by the city in 1903.

He was born Hiram Ulysses Grant in Point Pleasant, Ohio, on April 27, 1822. He was the son of Jesse Grant and Hannah Simpson Grant. When Grant was a year old his family moved twenty miles to Georgetown, Ohio, and at the age of 17 he entered the United States Military Academy at West Point. As the Bio website related: "A clerical error had listed him as Ulysses S. Grant. Not wanting to be rejected by [West Point], he changed his name on the spot." Grant was deemed an average student at West Point and graduated in 1843 at the age of 21. He was sent by the Army to St. Louis and was deployed to fight in the Mexican-American War, a conflict he fought well in but morally opposed. He was promoted to captain in 1853. However, alcoholism forced him to leave the military and return to civilian life. He was miserable, at one time selling firewood, another time working at his father's tannery, which the younger Grant swore he'd never do. With the start of the Civil War, the Army grudgingly let Grant back in and named him commander of the 21st Illinois Volunteer Regiment. Grant and his soldiers overran the City of Paducah, Kentucky, as well as Fort Henry and Fort Donelson. For this work he was promoted to major general and later to general of the Army. He commanded at the Battle of Shiloh, taking of Vicksburg, Battle of Lookout Mountain, and Battle of Missionary Ridge. At the end of the Civil War on April 9, 1865, General Grant, commander of the Union Army, and General Robert E. Lee, commander of the Confederate Army, met near the community of Appomattox Court House and signed a peace agreement. The Confederates had surrendered. By 1868 the war hero was the eighteenth president of the United States. He served two terms.

Grant was never destined to be a happy civilian. After leaving the Army he went bankrupt and was again miserable. He suffered from cancer of the throat. It wasn't until he contacted his friend, Mark Twain, to write his, Grant's, memoir did things start to look up. More than a quarter million copies of Grant and Twain's work sold, and the Grant family became rich. Ulysses S. Grant died July 23, 1885, and was laid to rest in Grant's Tomb in New York City.

Gray Fox Lane

Gray Fox Lane is the only street that pays homage to this mammal, though Sheridan Avenue used to be called Fox Street. The name Gray Fox Lane, within the Dunes Neighborhood, was given by a developer. There are four species of foxes in North America: arctic, kit, red, and gray. The latter two are residents of New York. Foxes are usually creatures of the night though they can be found foraging during daytime (contrary to popular misconception, if a nocturnal animal is seen during the day that is no indication that it has rabies). Excellent tree climbers, foxes live mostly on rabbits and other small mammals such as mice and voles. They also eat vegetation, some of their favorites being corn, cherries, nuts, grapes, blackberries, and grass. They also dine on insects. Foxes mate during the winter and give birth in the springtime. Litters usually range from one to seven kits, which are about the cutest things you'll ever see.

Green Street

Within your author's *History Inside the Blue Line* and *Among the Cloud Splitters*, books that decode place names in the Adirondack Mountains, readers were reminded that corrupted names in that range, and thus potentially among streets, are more common than one may assume. For example, in the Adirondacks there is Van Dorrien Mountain named for Sophus *Von* Dorrien, Masher Vly named for the *Mosher* family, Wakely Mountain named for William *Wakeley*, Pillsbury Mountain named for Louis Dwight *Pilsbury*, and Lamphere Ridge named for a member of the *Lanphere* family. Within *Among the Cloud Splitters* it was written:

> In today's age of high-fidelity communication, it's easy to make sure a person's name is spelled correctly before it's put on a map. Not so during the 1800s, the heyday of the naming of Adirondack features. Many cultural histories were passed down through light conversation by immigrants with strange accents or recorded in sloppy cursive handwriting by people who were barely literate.

Thus Green Street, formerly named Van Driesen Street, may be a corruption of the name Queens Street. The name Queens Street looks a lot like Green Street when written in sloppy handwriting, and it sounds a lot like Green Street when pronounced with an accent. Bielinski reported that this name change inadvertently took place in 1771 when an edition of the *Albany Gazette* was released. The name Green Street was appearing on maps by 1794. The oldest building along this street may be 103–111 Green Street. These homes were built for John Lansing Jr. in 1819.

However, *The Knickerbocker News* maintained that Green Street is named for Continental Army major general Nathaniel Greene of Patowomut, Rhode Island, and this may be the more genuine of the two name origin stories. Born on August 7, 1742, Green distinguished himself during the Revolutionary War. He was self-educated and drawn to the studies of mathematics, law, and warfare before joining the military. In 1770, he gained a position as member of the Rhode Island General Assembly and was reelected in 1771, 1772, and 1775. Entering the service as a humble private, he rose to general to become one of George Washington's most trusted and talented officers. He organized and led a militia and was assigned by Washington to oversee Boston when the British vacated that city during March 1776. Greene commanded troops in New Jersey and New York and managed forts Lee and Washington. He also led men and saw combat in Pennsylvania and Rhode Island and throughout the South to become one of only three generals to serve during the entire Revolutionary War (the other two are George Washington and Henry Knox). He was an unlikely candidate for combat leadership. McCullough wrote in *1776: The Illustrated Edition* that Greene was a Quaker and that "a childhood accident had left him with a stiff right leg and a limp. He also suffered from occasional attacks of asthma." However, this officer's "commitment to the Glorious Cause of America, as it was called, was total. And if his youth was obvious, the Glorious Cause was to a large degree a young man's cause."

Nathaniel Greene died June 19, 1786, at his Mulberry Grove Estate in Georgia. For more than a century he was interred at the Graham Vault in Colonial Park Cemetery of Savannah. The body was later moved to a monument in Johnson Square in Savannah. Many political and topographic features are named for Greene. Prominent features named for this brave man include sixteen Greene counties (including Green County, New York) and eighteen communities (including New York's Town of Greene). Greene Street in Manhattan, Greene Avenue in Brooklyn, and Colonel Greene Road in Yorktown Heights are named for him, too.

Greentree Lane
See Edgewood Avenue.

Greenway
Greenway is less general, more honorary. It's likely named for the Greenway family that lived in this area back when it was farmland. If not named for this family of farmers, Greenway is descriptive since it is truly a "green way" with a lush park in the middle of it.

Greenway North
See Fairlawn Avenue.

Greenway South
See Fairlawn Avenue.

Greyledge Drive
Assemblyman Jack McEneny suggested the name Greyledge Drive to a developer, this name stemming from the Greyledge Mansion, which used to stand on nearby Van Rensselaer Boulevard.

This three-story, fifteen-room brick manor was built in 1872. By the 1950s it was a shell of its former self, deemed a fire hazard waiting to collapse. It was demolished prior to Greyledge Drive being built. The mansion belonged to Frederick Cleveland and his wife, Gertrude Van Vranken Cleveland. Frederick was born in 1838 and died October 2, 1897, while Gertrude was born August 26, 1841, and died October 17, 1918. They were buried in Albany Rural Cemetery. They led a wealthy family known for owning the Cleveland Brothers Baking Powder Company, which Frederick founded with his brother, George, circa 1870.

Grove Avenue
See Edgewood Avenue.

H

Hackett Boulevard

William Hackett, for whom this street is named, was best known for winning the Albany mayoral election of 1921, which put a Democrat in that seat after a 21-year absence. He defeated Republican candidate William Van Rensselaer Erving to do so. Hackett served as mayor from 1922 to 1926, defeating James Vander Veer and Edward Easton along the way. Hackett was a businessman, banker, and lawyer who, despite winning the mayoral race, was plagued by election-time scandals including billing for coal that was never delivered to the city, building School Number Fourteen in an unsafe fashion, and overseeing below-board sewer and paving jobs. Hackett Middle School on Delaware Avenue is named for this politician, this naming taking place in 1926 when the school was built.

Hackett was born December 7, 1866, in Albany as the son of John Hackett and Martha Stormont Hackett. Like most influential men of the 1800s, Hackett practiced law. Unlike most influential men of that era, he dropped out of school to do so. Nonetheless, Hackett passed his bar exam and practiced in Albany, and he served in the New York National Guard for nine years, attaining noncommissioned officer rank. He also served as president of Albany City Savings Institution, Albany City Safe Deposit Company, Boulevard Garage Company, and New York Mortgage and Home Building Company. William Hackett died March 6, 1926, while on vacation in Cuba. He was in a car accident in which he was ejected from the vehicle. Hackett died a slow death, suffering in a Cuban hospital for two weeks, his main injury being head trauma. He was buried in Albany Rural Cemetery.

Hall Place

The Hall name dates within Albany County to the mid-1700s and is found in Hall Place. Joseph Hall and Johanna Patterson Hall had three children, the first-born being John, who was born June 16, 1777. Of the nearly 200 Halls buried in Albany Rural Cemetery, the oldest grave belongs to Charles E. Hall. Charles was born in 1750 in Albany and died in 1815 in Madison, Wisconsin.

A standout Hall was James Hall, founder and first director of the New York State Museum, state paleontologist, and state geologist for New York, Iowa, and Wisconsin. Hall is credited with making the first ascents of the two highest peaks in New York—5,344-foot Mount Marcy and 5,115-foot Algonquin Peak—with a group of explorers and scientists in 1837. He was born September 12, 1811, in Hingham, Massachusetts, to James Hall and Sousanna Dourdain Hall. He died August 7, 1898, in Bethlehem, New Hampshire, and was buried in Albany Rural Cemetery. Rensselaer Polytechnic Institute's Hall Hall is named for him. Some feel Hall Place is named for this man. However, Hall Place is perhaps not named for James Hall because this street name has been around since before 1851, a time that may predate Hall's notoriety.

Halsdorf Street

Halsdorf Street, Bogardus Road, Freeman Road, Greenway Street, Kakely Street, and Linden Road were built together during the 1920s after the land they would be built on was conveyed to the city in 1922. Halsdorf is an obscure last name. There is only one Halsdorf grave in Albany County. A few Halsdorfs did live in the county though. Perhaps one of the earliest was William George Halsdorf, who was born October 19, 1918, and died October 26, 1992. He was married to Beverly Jean Lufkin Halsdorf, and they had seven children. He was buried in Woodlands Cemetery in Cambridge, New York, thirty miles northeast of Albany.

Hamilton Street

See Alexander Street.

Hampton Street

More than two dozen American communities carry the titles Hampton, Northampton, or Southampton, among other variants. Some are named after Hampton, England, while others are named after Southampton, Virginia, which is named for Henry Wriothesley, 3rd Earl of Southampton. Hampton Street likely carries this British place name. Hampton is a suburb in London Borough of Richmond upon Thames and is home to 40,000 residents. Hampton Street was built before 1916.

Hansen Avenue

Hansen Avenue is set among the other "mayoral streets" of Bancker Street, Peyster Street, and Ryckman Avenue. It is named for Hendrick Hansen, fifth mayor of Albany, or his son, Johannes "Hans" Hansen, seventeenth mayor. Hendrick Hansen was born during the early or mid-1600s as one of five sons of Hans Hendrickse and Eva Gillise Hendrickse (the surname Hendrickse was reduced to Hansen in America). His father was a trader who came to Beverwyck during the 1600s and died prior to 1698. Hendrick was a merchant and trader who served as mayor during 1698 and 1699. He was educated at the common school, served as alderman, assemblyman, and Indian commissioner, and married Debora Van Dam on September 21, 1692. They had seven children. Hendrick Hansen died during February 1724 in Albany and was buried at the Dutch Church.

One of Hendrick Hansen's five sons, Johannes "Hans" Hansen, was born January 16, 1679, in Albany and spent much of his youth west of Albany in Indian lands. He was educated at the common school and married Sara Cuyler, daughter of the fourteenth mayor of Albany, Johannes Cuyler, on April 25, 1723. They had nine children. Johannes "Hans" Hansen died during December 1756 in Albany after serving as mayor during 1731 and 1732 and from 1754 to 1756. He was also buried at the Dutch Church.

Harding Street

More than twenty Hardings are buried in Albany Rural Cemetery, and Prospect Hill Cemetery in Guilderland has three more, yet this doesn't definitively solve Harding Street. In *Encyclopedia of American Family Names*, Andrew Chesler and H. Robb summed the entomology of this last name, much like this street name history, with one word: "uncertain." Though it's not near the "presidential conglomerate," Harding Street may be named for Warren G. Harding. Harding was commander in chief from 1921 to 1923, while Harding Street was built by 1928.

Harding was born November 2, 1865, in Blooming Grove, Ohio, as the son of George Harding and Phoebe Elizabeth Dickerson Harding. Blooming Grove had been laid out by Warren G. Harding's ancestor, Salmon E. Harding (1792–1872), in 1835. The younger Harding graduated from Ohio Central College in 1882, remained in the rural farm country of Ohio, and became a newspaperman. He entered politics in 1888 by becoming a delegate to the Republican state convention. He traveled to at least Washington, D.C., and Chicago to hear politicians speak; spoke throughout Ohio on behalf of presidential candidate William McKinley, who had been governor of that state; and made the nominating address for William Taft at the 1912 Republican convention. Harding served as senator from Ohio from 1900 to 1904 and 1915 to 1921, lieutenant governor from 1904 to 1906, and president of the United States from 1921 to 1923.

During his presidency, won via a landslide, he limited immigration, cut taxes, approved tariffs, officially ended the state of war with European countries, expanded and improved our nation's interstate system, and faced internal scandals in which members of his party enriched themselves.

Warren G. Harding died of a heart attack August 2, 1923. His last words were: "That's good. Go on. Read some more." His wife had been reading aloud a flattering July 28 *Saturday Evening Post* article about him. His body was transported by train from San Francisco to Washington, D.C., and then to Marion, Ohio, where it was buried in the Marion Cemetery. Ten million Americans—ten percent of the U.S. population—lined the tracks to see the train go by. Harding was succeeded by Calvin Coolidge.

Harris Avenue

Common Council proceedings stated that this street was laid out by the Van Schoick-Harris Realty Company and was thus named by this company. Harris Avenue is named for this company's secretary treasurer, Frank Harris. Nearby Van Schoick Avenue is named for this company's president, Charles Van Schoick. In cryptic Common Council documentation (this may be the only sentence to ever include ten commas) it was stated that land where Harris Avenue, Forest Avenue, and Helderberg Avenue now are were conveyed by this company during the early 1900s:

> The conveyance of certain parcels of land to be known as a part of Forest Avenue, from New Scotland Avenue to Helderberg Avenue, as Helderberg Avenue, between Forest Avenue and a point about 212 feet westerly of Harris Avenue, and as Harris Avenue, from New Scotland Avenue southerly about 1,592 feet, as herein described, in the Eighteenth Ward, made by the Van Schoick-Harris Realty Company, Inc., is hereby accepted and the land so conveyed dedicated as public streets.

Frank Harris was born April 30, 1869, in Albany to George Harris and Mary Salisbury Harris. He was educated in public schools and served as an officer in the Army's 51st Pioneer Infantry during World War I and the National Guard's 10th Infantry, which was based in Albany. Harris became head of the Treasury Division of the Department of Taxation and Finance and was a member of the Albany Board of Education. Frank Harris died August 4, 1951, in Albany and was buried in Albany Rural Cemetery.

Hartman Road

It was discovered that one Helga Dagmara Hartman lived next to Hartman Road on Par Circle North, yet a connection to this street could not be made. One, she did not take the married name of Hartman until 1965, so it was not her given surname. Two, she did not move to Albany until 1987, post-construction of Hartman Road. Further research revealed this street is named for a farming family that was living in the Hartman Road area by the late 1800s. The name Hartman means "bear" and "hero."

Harvard Avenue

Harvard Avenue, which honors the Ivy League school, is off by itself, far from the six "academic streets" of Cornell Drive, Yale Court, Notre Dame Drive, Princeton Drive, Union Drive, and Vassar Drive. Perhaps Harvard Avenue likes to be isolated, even a little smug. It was built before 1928.

This university in Cambridge, Massachusetts, is the oldest college in the United States, founded in 1636 as New College and then The College at New Towne. It was given its current name in 1639 for John Harvard. This English minister was born November 26, 1607, and died September 14, 1638. He had come to the New World in 1637, specifically to Charlestown, Massachusetts. Approaching death, he left 780 pounds and a few hundred books towards establishment of an educational institution. Several schools can be found within Harvard University including those of Medicine (founded 1782), Divinity (1816), Law (1817), Dental Medicine (1867), Arts and Sciences (1872), Business (1908), Extension (1910), Design (1914), Education (1920), Public Health (1922), Government (1936), and Engineering and Applied Sciences (2007). The university accepts five percent of applicants and is ranked as a top ten university by Academic Ranking of World Universities, Professional Ranking of World Universities, *Forbes*, *U.S. News and World Report*, and *Washington Monthly*, among other ranking systems and publications. Notable alumni include presidents of the United States John Adams, John Quincy Adams, Rutherford Hayes, Theodore Roosevelt Jr., Franklin D. Roosevelt, John F. Kennedy, George W. Bush, and Barack Obama. Bill Gates, Al Gore, Henry Kissinger, Michelle Obama, Bill O'Reilly, Mark Zuckerberg, and Theodore Kaczynski graduated from Harvard University, too. The community of Harvard, New York, is named after this school.

Hawkins Street

On May 1, 1911, Frank Dolan and his wife, Anna Dolan, conveyed land to Michael Hawkins, for whom this street is named. When the Dolans died, they left their estate to their daughter, Eileen, who Eileen Street is named for. Hawkins Street intersects Eileen Street and was built prior to 1934. Hawkins, owner of the Albany Senators minor league baseball team and for whom Albany's former Hawkins Stadium was named, died January 28, 1930, in Albany from pneumonia. He had immigrated to America from Ireland. The origin of this name is the term "hawk place," or it may come from the name Hal, which is a pet name for Harry.

Hawthorn Circle

There are nearly 1,000 species of hawthorn trees and shrubs in North America, and New York has thirteen native species: brainerd, pear, fireberry, scarlet, cockspur, broadleaf, fanleaf, Biltmore, downy, frosted, dotted, fleshy, and one-flower. Hawthorns, often known by the slang term "thorn apple," grow in direct sunlight on recovering farmland, hence when this street was laid out there were perhaps old pastures there. You'll never forget this species after you bump into it. Most hawthorns have stout thorns spread along their branches.

Hawthorne Avenue

Communities named Hawthorne can be found in California, Kentucky, Minnesota, New Jersey, and Pennsylvania, and each one is named for Nathaniel Hawthorne Jr., just like this street probably is. Hawthorne, New York, is named for his daughter, Rose Hawthorne Lathrop, also known as Mother Mary Alphonsa. Land was conveyed to the City of Albany in 1913 for construction of Hawthorne Avenue and nearby Edgewood Avenue, Fairlawn Avenue, Homestead Avenue, Laurel Avenue, Melrose Avenue, and Terrace Avenue. Construction of these streets probably took place that same year. The section of Hawthorne Avenue just north of Melrose Avenue is where two ponds used to be. As late as 1936 they were used for ice harvesting.

Nathaniel Hawthorne Jr. was born July 4, 1804, in Salem, Massachusetts, to Nathaniel Hathorne and Elizabeth Clarke Manning Hathorne. The junior Nathaniel added the *w* to his name to hide relation to John Hathorne, an unrepentant Salem witch trials judge. Hawthorne lived in Maine and Massachusetts, graduated from Bowdoin College in 1825, and had his first book published three years later. His most famous work is *The Scarlet Letter*, published in 1850. Between 1828 and his death 36 years later, he authored five books and thirty short stories and befriended Ralph Emerson, Henry Thoreau, Herman Melville, and President Franklin Pierce. Nathaniel Hawthorne Jr. died May 19, 1864, in Plymouth, New Hampshire, and was buried in Sleepy Hollow Cemetery in Concord, Massachusetts. His wife, Sophia Amelia Peabody Hawthorne, survived until 1871.

Hazelhurst Avenue

Hazel is a genus of deciduous bushes and trees native to the Northern Hemisphere. Hazel species found in North America include American and beaked. Within the Witch-hazel family of the eastern United States are two native species, witch-hazel and sweetgum. It's possible that hazel bushes or trees, witch-hazel, or sweetgum were found here when Hazelhurst Avenue was built circa 1925.

Helderberg Avenue

Helderberg Avenue, Adirondack Street, Berkshire Boulevard, South Berkshire Boulevard, and Catskill Street are the five "mountain streets" of Albany. This one was built before 1913, though the name Helderberg Avenue was not made official until 1923. Sometimes called the Helderberg Escarpment, this modest mountain range west of Albany tops out at 1,822 feet. The Helderberg Mountains were used by Indians before people of European descent arrived to build their homes there in the 1600s. *Helderberg* is Dutch for "clear mountain" and "bright mountain."

Hemlock Lane

The eastern hemlock is a magnificent evergreen tree native to America. Select hemlocks may grow up to 160 feet in height and four feet in diameter. The largest specimen that has been found in New York is 83 feet in height and 62 inches in diameter. It's one of the longest-living trees in the East, some having lifespans of 400 years, which makes the hemlock the second-longest-living tree in New York. (The oldest-living species is eastern white pine. During the summer of 1997, Don Leopold of the College of Environmental Science and Forestry dated an eastern white pine in New York's Nelson Swamp Unique Area to be 450 years old.) No matter how big or old a hemlock may be, it will retain adorable needles and cones, which measure a mere half-inch. Its range stretches from the northern tip of Maine to the Southern Appalachians and west to the Great Lakes. Some think this tree is poisonous, yet they're thinking of the hemlock plant, also known as poison hemlock. All parts of that plant are poisonous to humans and livestock, and ingesting it results in trembling and lack of coordination to coma and death. A full-grown bovine need only consume ten ounces of the hemlock plant to be poisoned. It will be dead from respiratory paralysis within a few hours. The hemlock plant's most famous victim is Socrates (circa 470–399 B.C.), the Greek philosopher, who fulfilled his death sentence by drinking a brew of poison hemlock.

The world of trees is divided into evergreen and deciduous, also known as softwood and hardwood. Generally speaking, these classes describe trees well. For example, most evergreens have soft wood (pine, for example) while most deciduous trees have hard wood (oak, for example). Eastern hemlock is an evergreen and thus a softwood, but its wood is about as hard as wood gets. William Harlow wrote that "hemlock knots are probably the hardest vegetable growth in our woods." Its wood is firm though splintery and is used by craftsmen of posts and beams. Hemlocks were rarely logged for their wood though. Most were cut down for their bark. Trees were felled and their bark, known as "tan bark," stripped. As hemlock trunks laid in the woods like giant carcasses, the bark was brought to tanning facilities where tannin was leached from the bark to soften and condition leather. The tanning industry survives through New York place names such as the Village of Tannersville.

Henry Johnson Boulevard

Named in 1991 for war hero Henry Johnson, sections of this street were once called Northern Boulevard, Swallow Street, Knox Street, and Gage Street. The latter two names honored General Henry Knox and General Thomas Gage. Of these four street names, only Swallow Street has vanished from Albany.

"Private Johnson distinguished himself by acts of gallantry and intrepidity above and beyond the call of duty while serving as a member of Company C, 369th Infantry Regiment, 93rd Division, American Expeditionary Forces, during combat operations against the enemy on the front lines of the Western Front in France on May 15, 1918." So begins the citation for Henry Johnson's Medal of Honor, which was awarded posthumously. When Johnson and Needham Roberts were on sentry duty they were attacked by at least a dozen Germans. Despite Johnson being severely wounded, he moved under intense fire and mounted a counterattack. He killed several enemy and saved one of his colleagues from being captured. Armed only with a knife, Johnson took on the enemy with ferocity, at one point taking his Bolo knife and running it "through an enemy soldier's head." The Germans retreated. This citation concludes: "Private Johnson's extraordinary heroism and selflessness above and beyond the call of duty are in keeping with the highest traditions of military service and reflect great credit upon himself, his unit and the United States Army." In addition to the Medal of Honor he earned a Purple Heart and the Distinguished Service Cross. Johnson was the first American to receive the French Croix de Guerre avec Palme, with palm leaf for valor, France's highest award for heroism. Theodore Roosevelt Jr. summed that Johnson was "one of the five bravest American soldiers in the war."

Henry Johnson was born William Henry Johnson in Winston-Salem, North Carolina, during July 1892. At a young age his family moved to New York where he worked odd jobs, including being a porter in Albany's Union Station. He enlisted in the Army as an infantryman when he was 24 years old, in 1917. Enlisting in Albany, he was assigned to an all-black National Guard unit, segregation being typical of that period. Overseas this unit was under command of the French Army. After serving in World War I he returned to the United States in 1919 with fellow survivors from his unit, The Hellfighters. The Hellfighters were one hell of a unit. These men served the longest of any American force in World War I: 191 grueling days. They never had a man captured, never had one of their trenches overrun, never lost a foot of ground. The Hellfighters sustained 367 men killed, 1,097 wounded. For their bravery they received 171 French decorations.

Johnson was honored by his countrymen by leading a homecoming parade up New York City's Fifth Avenue. The term "honored" is used loosely because no matter his military standing, a black man in 1919 was a difficult being for the white population to honor. Consider, for example, that Johnson led this parade because his black unit was not permitted to partake in the official victory parade. Johnson humbly returned to low-paying jobs, which he could barely work due to his injuries. He fell into alcoholism and depression. His wife left him and took the kids with her in 1924. Henry Johnson died flat broke in Washington, D.C., during July 1929 at the age of 32. Cause of death was myocarditis, an inflammation of the heart muscle. He was buried in Arlington National Cemetery in Arlington, Virginia. Johnson has two memorials in Albany. One is in the southwest corner of Washington Park and was dedicated on Veterans Day 1991. The other, dedicated June 14, 2007, by Mayor Gerald Jennings, is set in tiny Henry Johnson Park at the northeast end of Henry Johnson Boulevard. More than 300 men from Albany lost their lives in World War I.

Herkimer Street

Named for Nicholas Herkimer, Herkimer Street was formerly called Van Schee Street. New York's Town of Herkimer and Herkimer County are named for him, too. He was born circa 1728 to Johann Jost Herchheimer and Catherine Petrie Herchheimer near German Flatts. Herkimer, who spoke English, German, and Iroquoian, defended German Flatts twice during the French and Indian War and was promoted to captain in 1758. He was leader of the Tryon County Committee of Safety during the War for Independence and served as a colonel in his local militia. In 1778, he was promoted to brigadier general and saw combat against Joseph Brant in central New York. When news of the siege of Fort Stanwix reached Herkimer, he ordered his 800 men to assemble at Fort Dayton, where West Canada Creek meets the Mohawk River, and march forty miles to the fort to save it from obliteration. They were ambushed by Mohawk Indians, British soldiers, and a Tory militia in what became the Battle of Oriskany. Herkimer's horse was shot out from under him, and he was shot in the leg. Despite his wounds he crawled to a tree, leaned against it, lit his pipe, and rallied his men to intensify the fight. During amputation of his leg ten days later, on August 16, 1777, Herkimer suffered from complications of infection and bled to death. Nicholas Herkimer was buried in Herkimer Home Burial Ground in Little Falls, New York. His coolness under chaotic conditions is neatly portrayed in Frederick Yohn's beautiful circa 1901 oil painting "Herkimer at the Battle of Oriskany."

Hidden Hollow Road
There's nothing hidden in this street name. The only thing hidden here is a hollow.

High Dune Drive
The Dunes Neighborhood butts against an eastern border of the Pine Bush that's known for its sandy soil and rolling hills. High Dune Drive is well-named because it tops out on one of these dunes.

Highfield Lane
Located near generically-named Meadow Lane, a developer created this name because it's easy on the eyes and ears.

Highland Avenue
See Fairview Avenue.

Highland Court
See Fairview Avenue.

Hillcrest Avenue
There are three segments of Hillcrest Avenue, and the oldest one, the first one described here, dates to before 1918. One section runs from Western Avenue to Meade Avenue, a dead-end section runs off Russell Road, and a dead-end section runs off Magazine Street. These two dead-end streets nearly meet each other to make a through street. The short yet steep hill on the Western Avenue-to-Meade Avenue section gives this street its name. This hill was locally known as Meade Hill because the Meade family used to live there. They're memorialized through adjacent Meade Avenue.

Hoffman Avenue
Hoffman Avenue, built circa 1893 and formerly known as Prospect Street, is adjacent to Hoffman Park, which opened in 1919. These features are named for governor John Hoffman. He was born January 10, 1828, in Ossining, New York, to Adrian Kissam Hoffman and Jane Ann Thompson Hoffman. He graduated from Union College in 1846, studied law, and passed his bar exam three years later. Beyond serving as governor from 1869 to 1872, this Democrat was recorder of New York City from 1861 to 1865 and mayor of New York City from 1866 to 1868. During the 1870s, his political career fell apart when William

Tweed's political corruption came to light. Hoffman, who had presidential aspirations, and Tweed were friends and political allies. Hoffman was guilty by association though there was no evidence of wrongdoing on his part. John Hoffman died March 24, 1888, in Hessen, Germany, and was buried in Dale Cemetery in Ossining. Hoffman Island near Staten Island and Hoffman Street in New York City honor this man. The title Hoffman was used to note a man who owned his own land instead of renting it or working it under a feudal system. Hoffman combines the German *hof* and *mann*, meaning "settlement" and "man."

Holland Avenue

Holland Avenue, which opened October 21, 1932, is named for the European region where so many settlers came from. Holland is a 2,100-square-mile, two-province region—North Holland and South Holland—within the Netherlands. More than six million Hollanders live within this area. Amsterdam, which hunkers seven feet below sea level, is the most populous city in the Netherlands. More than 600,000 residents live there. The place name Holland appeared during the 800s and stems from the Middle Dutch *holtland*, meaning "wooded land." Or it comes from *hol land*, meaning "hollow land," which describes the region's low topography.

A 1938 Leonard Realty Company advertisement called the University Heights development along Holland Avenue an "exclusive restricted residential section" where "it costs no more to have a home in this beautiful central locality than in locations miles further out." The May 7, 1938, edition of *The Knickerbocker News* reported Holland Avenue's unique history while quoting builder and realtor Jesse Leonard. This avenue

> was the route originally of the Mohawk-Hudson Railroad when wood-burning engines were used to haul coaches of Albany's first railroad from Albany to Schenectady. "The cars were pulled up the hill by ropes, and then taken from Delaware Ave. across the old ravine to what is now Holland Ave. on a trestle," he said. "I believe the railroad trestle was the first railroad bridge in this part of the country."

Hollywood Avenue

The ever-quotable Hunter S. Thompson once opined, "For every moment of triumph, for every instance of beauty, many souls must be trampled." This quote summarizes Hollywood, California, which this street may be named after. The name Hollywood Avenue was accepted by Mayor William Hackett in 1923. Hollywood, where wealth accumulates and men decay, is a 3.5-square-mile neighborhood within central Los Angeles that was settled in 1853, founded prior to 1870, and incorporated in 1903. The story of its naming is unique. One day in

1886 Hobart Whitley was looking down into the valley that would become Hollywood when he met a Chinese man, with the very American name of John, on horseback. Whitley asked him what he was doing, and the man replied, "I holly wood" because he was out on a wood run. That gave Whitley the idea to name the area Hollywood with "Holly" representing England and "wood" representing his Scottish heritage. "I know what to name the new town I am going to build right here, among these beautiful hills," he confirmed. Whitley purchased a 500-acre ranch in the area. During August 1887, Ivar Weid, an investor and friend of Whitley, filed a deed and parcel map with the Los Angeles County recorder, and Hollywood was made official because that's the name Weid used on the paperwork. More than 100,000 people live within this neighborhood today.

If Hollywood Avenue doesn't honor this California neighborhood, there may be a simpler story. A bush or tree with red berries may be tied to the naming of this street. Stewart wrote about how certain American plantations were named: "For, more than once, it happened that the lady came to her plantation in winter when in the thickets the berries were red among the glossy leaves. And so she called the new home Hollywood."

Holmes Court
(and Holmes Dale)

In the case of Holmes Court, built before 1939, this street runs through the former site of the Holmes farm. In the case of Holmes Dale, built in 1930, at least two maps, one from 1876 and another from 1891, showed that land where Holmes Dale is today was owned by Thomas Holmes. He may have been born in 1788, died June 16, 1866, and was buried in Prospect Hill Cemetery in Guilderland with his wife, Ann Milner Holmes, who was born in 1792 and died in 1880. Their old farmhouse stands at 3 Colonial Avenue, right next to Holmes Dale. The name Holmes was used to note people who lived near holly trees or on a small island of dry land. It also labeled people who were from an unknown place.

Holmes Dale
See Holmes Court.

Home Avenue
See Cottage Avenue.

Homestead Avenue
See Cottage Avenue.

Homestead Street

See Cottage Avenue.

Hopewell Street

Hopewell, New Jersey, is named after the *Hopewell* that brought settlers to the New World, and this ship is probably remembered through Hopewell Street, which was built prior to 1927. The *Hopewell* made two journeys from the Old World. The first voyage with 68 passengers was made during the spring of 1635 and led by William Bundocke. The second voyage with fifty passengers was made during that summer and led by Thomas Babb. The *Hopewell* was one of eleven ships of the Winthrop Fleet. This fleet belonged to John Winthrop, one of the founders of Massachusetts Bay Colony, who was born January 12, 1587, and died March 26, 1649. Winthrop and his passengers left England due to King Charles I rejecting nonconformist religions. The first Winthrop ship left Europe during the spring of 1630 and landed on the coast of Massachusetts where Puritan settlers had already established an outpost. Winthrop founded Boston and served as deputy governor and governor of Massachusetts. The towns of Winthrop in Maine and Massachusetts are named for him.

Hopi Street

Joseph Cary named Hopi Street, Cary Avenue, Sawyer Place, and Zuni Street during the 1920s since he was one of the first people to move into this neighborhood. Mooney, in the February 16, 1963, edition of *The Knickerbocker News*, wrote that Cary

> visited Arizona, home of the Hopi Indians, and New Mexico, home of the Zunis. The Indians, part of the old Pueblo tribe, became friends of Mr. Cary and he was made an honorary chief of the Zunis. He made several trips to the tribal reservations, and among his proudest possessions were pictures of himself and the respective chiefs, and pictures of the Hopis doing their famed snake dance about him.

Most members of this tribe of 20,000 live on the Hopi Reservation in northern Arizona, which is surrounded by the Navajo Reservation. The name Hopi comes from *Hopituh Shi-nu-mu*, meaning "peaceful people." The first Europeans to encounter the Hopi were Spanish conquistadors. They called them the *Pueblo*, Spanish for "village," because the Hopi lived in villages. The conquistadors arrived in 1540 and were led by Francisco Vásquez de Coronado, the "Knight of Pueblo and Plains." He sent one of his trusted men, Pedro de Tovar, to find the Hopi. Tovar did so, discovering a settlement with 16,000 Hopi and Zuni. A series of Spanish expeditions followed Coronado's, including a major one led by Antonio de Espejo during the 1580s. However, the Spaniards didn't have much interest in occupying the Hopi's tablelands and sky islands of the Desert Southwest. The Hopi didn't control major waterways, and they didn't have that one thing that any conquistador worth his weight in Spanish armor sought: gold.

Missionaries arrived to civilize the savages, yet, as was the case throughout most of North America, they met with narrow success. By the late 1600s, the Hopi had endured enough of the missionaries' ways, which included forced Indian labor. The Hopi and Pueblo Revolt took place along the Rio Grande in 1680. Christian churches were reduced to smoldering piles of rubble and priests were murdered. The Spaniards backed off from these killing grounds but returned in 1700, again concentrating their efforts on the Rio Grande. This time they ignored the remote Hopi lands, especially when another revolt took place there. By the mid-1800s, the Indians were dealing with the United States government, and the Hopi asked for federal protection to guard them from their enemies, the Navajo. Protection was provided, yet proselytizing returned, this time through Mormons and the Church of Latter Day Saints. Late into the nineteenth century the Hopi accepted school construction, yet became resistant when they learned they would be acculturated in European ways ranging from vocational skills to language, home construction to haircuts. Without their resistance, during which Hopi parents were imprisoned for not sending their children to American schools, there would not be much genuine Hopi culture left. Hopi history of the 1900s involved these people becoming U.S citizens, creating their own tribal government, and authoring a thirteen-article constitution and a bill of rights.

Howard Street

Formerly known as Nail Street (because a nail forge and factory stood along it) and then Luther Street and Lutheran Street (because the First Lutheran Church stood there), Howard Street is named for Howard James. Circa 1810, James facilitated development of Howard Street by opening the estate of his ancestor, William James, to the city. The name Howard Street appeared on maps by 1857.

Hudson Avenue

Hudson Avenue and the Hudson River are named for English navigator Henry Hudson. Hudson Avenue carried the former names of Hudson Street, Quiter Street, Preaudieux, and Buffalo Street. East of Broadway it was called Spanish Street. The name Hudson Street appeared on maps as early as 1794 and was changed to Hudson Avenue in 1872. A gorge, which Ruttenkill ran through, was filled in during the 1840s for construction of sections of Hudson Avenue. Waite conveyed that "Hudson Avenue was described in 1859 as 'the most inviting avenue in the city, the comely blocks of dwellings adorn most of the streets which intersect the area of the ancient Ruttenkill.'" At 48 Hudson Avenue stands the second-oldest building in the city. The Van Ostrande-Radliff House was built in 1728 by Johannes Van Ostrande and was altered circa 1790, 1835, 1900, and 1937.

Hudson's first significant mission took place in 1607 when he searched for a passage to Asia along the Arctic Circle. Ice barred the crew getting through. An attempt to cross the same region a year later had the same result despite the crew sailing 2,500 miles. Both voyages took place in the *Hopewell*. In 1609, Hudson pushed west again, this time leaving Holland in his *Half Moon* during April and visiting Newfoundland, Nova Scotia, Cape Cod, Chesapeake Bay, and Delaware Bay. He entered the mouth of the Hudson River and grinded all the way to present-day Albany where he hit a dead end to the Orient. During this trip up the river, Hudson didn't apply his name to it, nor did he name any other features near present-day Albany. An image of the *Half Moon* is prominently featured on the seals of the towns of Haverstraw, Hyde Park, Stuyvesant, Bethlehem, Schodack, and Halfmoon as well as the Borough of Staten Island, City of Rensselaer, and Albany County.

In 1610, Hudson set sail again, this time in the *Discovery*, going to Iceland, Greenland, Labrador, and into Hudson Strait. The crew entered Hudson Bay but became stuck in ice and was forced to winter in James Bay. When the spring of 1611 came after what must have seemed a long, long time, Hudson wanted to continue his search for a passage to Asia. The crew would have none of it. They mutinied and set Hudson, his teenage son, and seven crew members adrift in a small boat. The thirteen mutineers pointed the bow of the *Discovery* east. Only eight mutineers survived the return trip to Europe. Hudson and his men were never seen again.

A fine painting of Hudson's arrival in present-day Albany on September 19, 1609, is found in David Lithgow's circa 1939 "In the Year 1609," which can be found on the University at Albany's downtown graduate campus in their Theodore Fossieck Milne Alumni Room. A fine mural of Hudson's landing can be found inside the Dewey Graduate Library, which is housed in the Hawley Building of this campus. This mural was painted by William Van Ingen during 1937 and 1938 while he was working under the Works Progress Administration. This mural shares a note from Hudson's log from the *Half Moon*, in which he stated he found "the finest land for cultivation that ever I set foot upon." Contrary to popular assumption, the community of Halfmoon in Saratoga County is not named after Hudson's ship. This community, which used to be called the Triangle, is named after the shape of the land it rests on.

Near its source at Lake Tear of the Clouds in the Adirondack Mountains the Hudson River is, as White wrote, "a gracious little stream that races over rounded pebbles and is all of ten feet wide." When the river reaches its end in Upper Bay between New Jersey and Brooklyn, it has flowed 315 miles, which makes it the longest river entirely within New York. It was known to the early Dutch as the Mauritius River (for Maurice, Prince of Orange-Nassau), The Great River, or simply The River. It wasn't until the mid- to late 1600s that Hudson's name was associated with the river's lower reaches. During that era the Hudson River was also called the North River because the Delaware River was called the South River. The change from North River to Hudson River did not enjoy immediate acceptance. As late as the 1890s the farther north you climbed along this waterway the less you heard Hudson's name. Adirondackers were still calling it the North River while flatlanders had been calling it the Hudson River for over a century. This was not the first case of mountain people's isolation delaying them culturally. As Fernand Braudel wrote in *The Mediterranean and the Mediterranean World in the Age of Philip II*, "Mountain life persistently lagged behind the plain."

Humanities Lane
University at Albany's Humanities Building is set just northeast of Humanities Lane on the main campus. Talk about a boring street name. Oh, the humanity.

Hummel Terrace
Hummel Terrace used to be named Jackson Street for George Jackson, who owned land there during the 1870s. The first house built on present-day Hummel Terrace was that of John Hummel. He was born in Albany in 1864 and was the father of eleven children—four boys and seven girls. He worked as a printer for the *Albany Argus* and as a linotype machinist for the *Times Union*. John Hummel died March 13, 1941, in his home at 3 Hummel Terrace and was buried in Our Lady Help of Christians' Cemetery in Glenmont, New York. In 1975, the Hummel home was sold and divided into apartments. This house burned down circa 1980. With the irony perhaps as thick as the smoke, the man in charge of fighting the blaze was Bill Hummel, Albany Fire Department battalion chief and grandson of John Hummel. The name Hummel has meant "busy like a bee," "beekeeper," "bear cub," and "fearless."

Hunter Avenue
(and Hunter Street)
Hunter Avenue and Hunter Street are named for Andrew Hunter, who owned land, during the 1870s, where these streets are today. These two names were made official by the city in 1871 when they made the nearby street names Colby Street, Judson Street, Rawson Street, and Watervliet Avenue official. Hunter was born in Hope, New York, on August 4, 1810, to David Hunter and Affiah Rich Hunter, who were originally from Massachusetts. He settled in

West Albany and bought up land while working as a gardener and cattle rancher. He then divided his property and sold it. He also owned plots on Central Avenue, Clinton Avenue, Hudson Avenue, Livingston Avenue, State Street, and Willet Street and maintained his estate that was built in 1874 in West Albany. Andrew Hunter died February 11, 1893, and was buried in Albany Rural Cemetery.

Hunter S Alley

Some think the "S" in Hunter S Alley stands for south or is an initial, yet it signifies possession. This street used to be called Hunter's Alley. It has existed since before 1855, yet it's a poor excuse even for an alley. Measuring less than 100 feet, it's half parking lot, half shoddy thoroughfare. It's not definitively known why Hunter S Alley is named so, though this name may be related to a landowner. Andrew Hunter, for whom Hunter Avenue and Hunter Street are named, is a strong candidate here.

Hunter Street

See Hunter Avenue.

Hurlbut Street

This street is named for New York State Supreme Court judge Elisha Hurlbut, who was born in 1808 and was a faithful supporter of women's suffrage. Nancy Isenberg wrote that in 1845 Hurlbut concluded "at the very least, New York required mental and moral sanity from its voting population. Women as a group satisfied these basic requirements" (though "idiots and criminals" were not permitted to cast ballots). While being teased about his political stance by Senator William Seward at a dinner party, Hurlbut and his dining partner, suffragist and abolitionist Elizabeth Cady Stanton, fought back with gusto. As Lori Ginzberg reported, Hurlbut and Stanton "with wit and sarcasm . . . fought the senator inch by inch until he had a very narrow platform to stand on." Elisha Hurlbut died September 5, 1889, in Glenmont, New York, and was buried in Albany Rural Cemetery. It is a unique grave where this man was literally, not figuratively, laid to rest. The grave is a replica of his bed. Hurlbut Street appeared on maps prior to 1896 and was named in 1889. Teunis Van Vechten laid out the group of Hurlbut Street, Bertha Street, Jeanette Street, Marshall Street, Stanwix Street, and West Van Vechten Street and reportedly named them for family members of his. Elisha Hurlbut was his son-in-law.

Huron Avenue

The Huron are an Indian group also known as the Wyandot and Wendat, these ancient names meaning "dwellers of the peninsula." They were originally from the St. Lawrence Valley, yet spread as far as present-day West Virginia until they were driven out by dominant Five Nations. Later they settled in the Great Lakes Region, thus Lake Huron is one of the Great Lakes. They lived along Lake Ontario's north shore and then moved to Georgian Bay on Lake Huron itself. The first European to make contact with this group was Samuel de Champlain, in 1615. Like most Indians, their numbers were decimated shortly after meeting Europeans. Their population, 30,000 strong before European contact, was also killed off or enslaved by enemies, including the robust Iroquois. Like all other native groups of the Great Lakes and Northeast, the Huron aligned with a European nation (in this case, France) and traded heavily with them, notably within the fur trade. During Indian wars the Huron were rounded up and dispersed beyond their homelands or confined within them. Most of today's remaining 8,000 Huron live in the province of Quebec and Kansas, Michigan, and Oklahoma. The name Huron stems from the French *huron* ("ruffian"), and *hure* ("wild boar") and the Algonquin *ka-ron* ("straight coast") and *tu-ron* ("crooked coast"). Huron place names are found in Kansas, Michigan, Ohio, and South Dakota. Huron Avenue was built before 1930.

Hurst Avenue

The Hurst family settled Hurstville near the old Albany-Bethlehem town line near today's Hurst Avenue, which was built prior to 1930. Hurstville was first known by the countryside name Log Tavern and was established by William Gilbert, Urban Van Hart, and a man named Hagadorn. Hagadorn built a log cabin, circa 1830, that served as a tavern, hence Hurstville's former name. William Hurst arrived in 1861. The Hursts had the Hurst Hotel, smoothly nicknamed The Love Nest, built on the site of the old log cabin, this hotel run by William's sons. Hurst opened a nearby race track for horses, this track predating the one at Saratoga Springs. His hotel was leveled by fire on Election Day 1929. The first Hurst to come to the Capital Region was Francis Joseph Jackson Hurst, who was born in France circa 1765 and came to America circa 1785. He settled in the Town of Berne and then came to Albany. He died in this city circa 1845 and was buried in Prospect Hill Cemetery in Guilderland, New York.

Hutton Street

Albany silversmith Isaac Hutton is honored through Hutton Street. He was born during July 1776 as the son of George Hutton and Anna Viele Hutton of New York City. He produced silver products during the late 1700s and early 1800s and was the man who engraved one of the first detailed street maps of the city,

DeWitt's 1794 *Plan of the City of Albany*. During November 1797 he married Elizabeth Lynott, whose sister was Margaret Lynott. The sisters were known for owning 400 acres in Lynottsville, a community set in the present-day Town of Harpersfield. They co-owned this land with Simeon DeWitt, and it was in their possession as early as 1793. Isaac Hutton was founding director of the Mechanics and Farmers Bank in 1811 and died September 8, 1855. Elizabeth Lynott Hutton died circa 1822. Hutton is a two-part Old English name combining words for "ridge" and "settlement."

I

Ichabod Lane

Washington Irving's fictional short story from 1820, "The Legend of Sleepy Hollow," features schoolteacher Ichabod Crane, who this street may be named after. According to Irving, Crane was modeled after schoolmaster Jesse Merwin, a friend of his. Others maintain that Crane was modeled after Samuel Youngs, a Revolutionary War veteran and schoolteacher who was also a friend of Irving. There was also a real-life Ichabod Crane, who served in the U.S. military for 45 years, much of it during Irving's time. The fictional character Ichabod Crane is likely not an incarnation of this real Ichabod Crane, though Irving probably borrowed the name.

The gist of Irving's story is that the goofy and superstitious Crane leaves a party feeling downtrodden because one Katrina Van Tassel there did not return his affections. To make matters worse, a man by the name of Abraham Van Brunt was wooing Van Tassel at the party. While riding home via horseback, Crane meets another traveler who turns out to be the Headless Horseman, a decapitated Hessian soldier who had his head taken off by a cannonball during the Revolutionary War. Crane makes a gallop for it, but just as he thinks he has left the Headless Horseman in the dust, the soldier throws his own head at Crane, sending Crane crashing to the ground. The next morning, Sleepy Hollow's townsfolk find a smashed pumpkin where the Hessian's head should have been. They also find Crane's hat yet no trace of him. He is never seen again. The Headless Horseman was probably Van Brunt, who wanted Crane gone so he could move forward with his courting of Van Tassel.

A wonderful mural depicting "The Legend of Sleepy Hollow" can be found in Troy's post office. This sprawling image titled "Legends of the Hudson," painted by Waldo Pierce in 1939, shows the Headless Horseman tossing his pumpkin head at Ichabod Crane. Only two other post offices, one in Maine and one in Massachusetts, display Pierce's work.

Indian Drive

Sensitive types will be irritated to learn that Indian Drive is on the main University at Albany campus, astonished that this name has not been duly disparaged and protested and then changed to Native American Drive, Indigenous Peoples Drive, First Peoples Drive, or Ameri-Indian Drive. Academe corrals those of unshakable political correctness. This street honors Indians who lived in this area when people of European descent arrived in this corner of the New World circa 1600. Hislop eloquently wrote of the first Indians arriving in what would become Albany:

> They came, hundreds of years before Henry Hudson's *Half Moon* rocked at anchor off what is now Steamboat Landing. They were few at first, stragglers from the West. Tradition says they were searching for a beautiful river, one like that which flowed by their old home "beyond the sun." They called themselves "Mahicans," although they were a part of a still larger family that moved into the East with them, the Lenapes. Here by the Hudson they found a new home which pleased them. Here was a river bordered by wild rice and alive with fish. It was the home they had dreamed of and they called that part of it on which Albany has grown, "Pempotowwuthut-Muhhcanneuw"—"the fire place of the Mahicans."

Indian Drive leads to the university's Indian Quad, a housing unit for students. This unit is comprised entirely of freshmen. The residence hall directors of this dormitory must be up to their eyeballs with freshmen complaints of incurable homesickness and apocalyptic breakups as well as angry accusations of one student borrowing another student's soy milk without asking. God bless residence hall directors. Most students who live in Indian Quad are from New York. That is, they're natives.

Industrial Park

See Commerce Avenue.

Industrial Park Road

See Commerce Avenue.

Iroquois Drive

The Iroquois were once a powerful, central component of Five Nations Confederacy, which became Six Nations when the Tuscarora joined in 1715. The Iroquois were not to be taken lightly. They expanded from New York to control lands west to Illinois and the Great Lakes, east to Lake Champlain, north into

Canada, and south to Virginia. They fought in the Beaver Wars, King William's War, French and Indian War, Queen Anne's War, and Revolutionary War. Their enemy was the Algonquin. There are at least 120,000 Iroquois in North America with 70,000 in the United States and 50,000 in Canada. This group was named by the French. South Dakota and Illinois have communities named Iroquois while scores of American streets carry this name, though most of them are in the Northeast.

Irving Street

Not being named for author Washington Irving as some may have thought, especially because Albany has Ichabod Lane, *The Knickerbocker News* stated that "two parishes in Scotland gave the name 'Irving' to posterity—Ayreshire and Dumfrieshire. The family name originally was 'Irvine.'" Irving Street honors the Irving Scottish surname, which was likely taken from the 26-mile River Irvine in southwest Scotland. This river's name may stem from the Celtic *wiryr* and *afon*, meaning "fresh water." In Albany Rural Cemetery one can find nearly thirty Irving graves. The oldest headstone dates to 1848, which was 25 years before this street was named.

J

James Street

Formerly known as Middle Alley, Middle Lane, and Yaugh Street, James Street is named for William James. This modern-day street name was created prior to 1850. James, born in Ireland on December 29, 1771, was a merchant and real estate tycoon. He was the second richest man in New York during the early 1800s. He came to America in 1789, died December 19, 1832, and was buried in Albany Rural Cemetery. He was cofounder of Albany Savings Bank, trustee of Union College, president of the board of the Albany Academy, director of the State Bank, and deputy commissioner of New York State. James owned land near the intersection of State Street and North Pearl Street, made his fortune at his mercantile on State Street and Green Street, and lived at 53 North Pearl Street. His home was destroyed in 1860, likely due to its poor condition. During his lifetime he was married three times: to Elizabeth Tillman, Mary Ann Connolly, and Catherine Barber. Sprague and Company's 1857 map of Albany showed James's expansive estate (and his street with its current name) spreading through where today's Department of Veterans Affairs Stratton Medical Center is. Here once flowed Beaver Creek, which cut through James's land. James Street in Syracuse and Jamesville, New York, are named for this man.

Jase Court

The name Jase means "healer" and "Lord is salvation" and is related to the names Jason and Joshua. Yet in this case, Jase refers to nothing meaningful. In the February 25, 1949, edition of *The Knickerbocker News*, Julius Heller reported:

> One of five strips of land which John J. Kampf, 58 Rose Ct., has offered to the city of Albany for public street purposes, in the upper Whitehall Rd. and Hackett Blvd. section, would be called "Jase Court." We asked Mr. Kampf about the origin of the name, and he told us that "the children made it up." It seems they used a combination of the first letters of given names, such as "Joseph," "Anna," etc.

Jay Street

John Jay, for whom this three-section street is named, was born in New York City on December 12, 1745, to Peter Jay and Mary Van Cortlandt Jay. As one of ten children he grew up in Rye, New York. Mainly educated at home, Jay also studied for a short time in New Rochelle. At the age of 15 he attended King's College, today's Columbia College, and graduated in 1764 to become a law clerk. He then read law. As Lee wrote of "reading law" during the 1700s, "one became a lawyer by serving as an apprentice; formal law schools were not yet commonplace." Allen and Schweikart further described this unique learning arrangement, remembering that "The average American attorney served a brief, informal apprenticeship; bought three or four good law books (enough to fill two saddlebags, it was said); and then, literally, hung out his shingle. If he lacked legal skills and acumen, the free market would soon seal his demise." Jay opened a law office in 1771 and then moved into politics.

He served as Continental Congress president, minister to France and Spain during the American War for Independence, Treaty of Paris negotiator, secretary of foreign affairs, secretary of state (a continuation of his position as secretary of foreign affairs), first chief justice of the United States, and governor of New York (the state's second one). A religious man, he served as vice president and president of the American Bible Society. During the Revolutionary War, Jay was a moderate, especially during the beginning of the revolution. As the war progressed his views of separatism became stronger. With Alexander Hamilton and James Madison Jr. he coauthored the Federalist Papers, written under the pseudonym Publius. He also wrote "An Address to the People of New York," which encouraged Constitution ratification. Jay retired from political life in 1801 and moved to a farm in Bedford, New York. He died at this farm May 17, 1829. He was buried in Rye, New York, his hometown, in a private cemetery, the Jay Cemetery, near his wife and ancestors. This cemetery is not open to the public.

Institutional, political, and topographic features memorialize John Jay. These include John Jay College of Criminal Justice, Fort Jay on Governors Island, John Jay Park in Manhattan, the Town of Jay in Maine, the Town of Jay in New York, the Town of Jay in Vermont, Jay County in Indiana, Mount John Jay in Alaska, Jay Peak in Vermont, John Jay Hall within Columbia University, and the John Jay Center within Robert Morris University.

Jeanette Street

Jeanette Street, along with nearby Bertha Street, Hurlbut Street, Marshall Street, Stanwix Street, and West Van Vechten Street, was laid out by Teunis Van Vechten. He reportedly named all these streets for family members. Within this neighborhood the names Bertha Street, Corlaer Street, Marshall Street, and Twiller Street were made official through a 1915 ordinance. Jeanette Cuyler Hurlbut was born in Glenmont, New York, on June 10, 1851, to Elisha Hurlbut and Catherine Cuyler Van Vechten Hurlbut. Jeanette died January 15, 1920, and was buried in Albany Rural Cemetery. She was the granddaughter of Teunis Van Vechten.

Jefferson Street

Formerly known as Herkimer Street, Jefferson Street is named for Thomas Jefferson. Herkimer Street, named for Revolutionary War leader Nicholas Herkimer, survives in downtown Albany. Perhaps no man played a more active role in the establishment of America than Jefferson did, and, fittingly, he has scores of place names in the United States named for him. These include elementary and high schools, universities, streets, towns, buildings, parks, hospitals, churches, libraries, mountains, at least a dozen cities, and at least eighteen counties. McCullough, in *The American Spirit*, summarized this president well: "He read seven languages. He was a lawyer, surveyor, ardent meteorologist, botanist, agronomist, archeologist, paleontologist, Indian ethnologist, classicist, brilliant architect."

Born April 13, 1743, Jefferson was the son of Peter Jefferson, who died when the future founding father was 14 years old, and Jane Randolph Jefferson. He was born in Shadwell, Colony of Virginia, as one of ten children. At the age of 16 he entered the College of William and Mary and graduated when he was 18. Great men of Jefferson's era read law under an established lawyer or judge, and this is precisely what Jefferson did after graduation. Then he became member of the House of Burgesses (1768), member of the Continental Congress (1775), author and signer of the Declaration of Independence (1776), member of the Virginia House of Delegates (1776), author of the Virginia Statute for Religious

Freedom (1777), governor of Virginia (1779 to 1781), congressional delegate (1783), minister to France (1785), first secretary of state (1790 to 1793), vice president of the United States under John Adams (1797 to 1801), president of the United States (1801 to 1809), and founder of the University of Virginia (1825). During his presidency the Louisiana Purchase was secured and the Lewis and Clark Expedition completed. Founding father indeed.

Jefferson is identified with his posh Virginia residence, Monticello (*monticello* being Italian for "little mountain"—the main house is set on top of a hill). An image of this estate is featured on the reverse side of the current U.S. nickel, this design produced by sculptor Felix Schlag in 1938. The redesign of the nickel that year was in anticipation of the 200th anniversary of Jefferson's birth. Until 2006, the nickel's obverse side carried a Schlag-designed side-view of Jefferson. (In 2006, Schlag's design of the former president was replaced with a frontal-view by Jamie Franki, her work based on an 1800 portrait by Rembrandt Peale.) Monticello was set on 5,000 acres of rolling land that Jefferson had inherited from his father. The president began design of Monticello in 1769. The grounds included outbuildings, housing for slaves, expansive gardens, and fields of produce, tobacco, and wheat. After Jefferson's death on the ironic date of July 4, 1826 (John Adams died this same day, and James Monroe would die on Independence Day of 1831), his daughter, Martha Jefferson Randolph, sold the property to James Barclay. Barclay was an Albanian who once served as city superintendent and surveyor during the early 1830s. Barclay sold it to Uriah Levy in 1834. During the Civil War the mansion was seized by Confederates, yet Levy got the property and the 11,000-square-foot building back after the war. In 1923, the property was finally sold to the Thomas Jefferson Foundation by Levy's nephew, Jefferson Levy. Monticello is a National Historic Landmark and, combined with the University of Virginia, a United Nations Educational, Scientific, and Cultural World Heritage Site. Jefferson was buried at Monticello.

Like Benjamin Franklin, Jefferson was a quotable man, a few fine ones being: "All tyranny needs to gain a foothold is for people of good conscience to remain silent," "My reading of history convinces me that most bad government results from too much government," "A government big enough to give you everything you want is a government big enough to take away everything that you have," and the simple "I cannot live without books."

Jennings Drive

Gerald Jennings, for whom this street is named, is a former five-term mayor of Albany. He was born in Albany on July 31, 1948, and graduated from SUNY Brockport and University at Albany. After working as a schoolteacher, school administrator, and Albany alderman, he served as mayor from 1993 to the last day of 2013, beating Joseph Sullivan, Corey Ellis, and Nathan LeBron, among other candidates, along the way. Choosing not to run for reelection, Jennings was succeeded by city treasurer Kathy Sheehan. The Albany Housing Authority reported that Jennings Drive is named for the mayor because he "had a strong commitment to housing issues, was a staunch ally of the Housing Authority, and was well respected by then HUD Secretary, Andrew M. Cuomo." Jennings's work enabled the Albany Housing Authority to develop the North Albany Homes community, which is centered on Jennings Drive, New Hope Terrace, and Rooney Road.

Jermain Street

One literary source stated with devout confidence that Jermain Street is named for James Jermain, Albany philanthropist, merchant, and lawyer and cousin of Olivia Slocum Sage, who was married to a filthy rich man named Russell Sage and established Russell Sage College in 1916.

Now for the real story. Jermain Street was built in 1947, the year Wilson Sullivan Company offered new homes there. An advertisement of theirs from this year read: "The war interrupted our building—housing shortages have piled up. But now we are back again with Jermain Street—newest avenue in Washington Heights." In a November 1963 *The Knickerbocker News* article by Mooney, Wilson Sullivan, leader of Upstate Construction Corporation during that era, explained that his company was given the honor of naming two new streets in Washington Heights. These became Victor Street and Jermain Street. Wilson Sullivan reported: "We had to do a lot of serious consideration. I thought it would be nice to name them for my sons, James and Joseph, but Albany already had a James Street and a St. Joseph's Terrace. The suggestion was made that I name one for myself but the city already had a Wilson Street." So he created the names Victor Street and Jermain Street.

The first street is named for his brother, Victor Sullivan, vice president of Wilson Sullivan Company. The second street is named for B. Jermain Savage, who was born in Newburgh, New York, to Frederick Bolton Savage, a Presbyterian clergyman. The younger Savage graduated from Williams College and New York Law School and led the firm of Cooper, Erving, and Savage, which represented Upstate Construction Corporation. After holding a host of corporate and social positions, B. Jermain Savage died June 17, 1952.

Joanne Court

Joanne Besch has her Joanne Court, which was developed during the 1950s across the old Klink farm. She was the daughter of Joseph L. Besch Jr. and Ann Heidrich Besch. She graduated from Albany Academy for Girls and Sarah Lawrence College and then married Wright Ferguson on October 20, 1956. There are five other "Besch streets": Besch Avenue, Betwood Street, Clayton

Place, Joelson Court, and Rose Court. Joanne is the feminine form of John and is related to the Latin name Johanna, which means "God is gracious."

Joelson Court

It was reported that Joelson Court is named for Joel Besch, yet this is not true since there was no Joel Besch. Joelson Court is named for Joseph L. Besch Jr. The street name is "Joe" plus "L." plus "son." He was the son of Joseph L. Besch and Elizabeth Menifold Besch. Joseph L. Besch Jr. was born in Albany on September 29, 1896, died March 7, 1977, in Greenwich, Connecticut, and was buried in Albany Rural Cemetery. He was married to Ann Heidrich Besch. The six "Besch streets" of Albany are Joelson Court, Clayton Place, Betwood Street, Joanne Court, Rose Court, and Besch Avenue. The names Joelson Court, Clayton Place, and Betwood Street were accepted by the city in 1925 when Joseph and Elizabeth conveyed land for the building of these three streets.

John David Court
(and John David Lane)

Street naming can be a family affair. John David Picotte, who was born in 1880 and died in 1940, had been building homes and commercial buildings in Schenectady as early as the 1920s, and he built many homes on what would be named John David Court and John David Lane. Picotte built and sold 100 houses in his first five years in business, these homes located within the Golden Acres neighborhood centered on Berncliff Avenue. Picotte Companies was founded in 1933 and was one of few construction companies to function during the Great Depression. This company is still in business and is run by descendants of John David Picotte. Mr. Picotte named Berncliff Avenue for his two sons, Bernard Picotte and Clifford Picotte. To return the favor, when they took over Picotte Companies when their father retired, they named John David Court and John David Lane for him.

John David Lane

See John David Court.

John Street
(and Lansing Street, South Lansing Street)

Lansing is perhaps the best-known, most widespread name in Albany. Bielinski lists seventy Lansing biographies on his Colonial Albany Social History Project website, and Albany Rural Cemetery has more than 350 Lansing graves. There was Gerrit Frederickse Lansing, the first of this line to arrive in Albany; Jacob G. Lansing, constable, fire master, militia officer, and silversmith; Robert Lansing, gunsmith, assistant alderman, constable, and fireman; Jeremiah Lansing, appointed surveyor of the Albany Port by George Washington; Myndert Lansing (one of three Myndert Lansings), fur trader, baker, and militia member; Johannes Jacobse Lansing, constable, fireman, assistant alderman, and militia officer; Gerardus Lansing, merchant, interpreter, and alderman; and Jeremiah Lansing, election inspector, fire master, and assemblyman. The list of accomplished Lansings goes on and on. J. C. Sidney's 1850 map of Albany showed a man by the last name of Lansing owning a lot facing Broadway between Lansing Street and DeWitt Street. This map also portrayed D. Lansing owning a lot on the nearby corner of Broadway and Van Woert Street. Lansing Street and South Lansing Street could be specifically named for either of these landowners. South Lansing Street used to be called Herring Lane.

John Street, less than two blocks from South Lansing Street, is likely named for John Ten Eyck Lansing Jr. He was a lawyer who served as mayor of Albany, member of the Confederation Congress, Revolutionary War military secretary, New York assemblyman, chancellor of New York, regent of the University of the State of New York, and chief justice of the New York State Supreme Court. Judge Lansing was one of three New York representatives sent to the 1787 Philadelphia Constitutional Convention. He was picked by Governor George Clinton. Lansing was born January 30, 1754, in Albany and disappeared December 12, 1829, in New York City. John Street used to be called Sturgeon Lane, named after the giant species of fish that inhabits the Hudson River. Name change occurred March 9, 1822. This plentiful fish was affectionately called "Albany beef" during the 1800s.

Jose Marti Drive

This is the only University at Albany street named for a person. Jose Marti, whose full name was José Julián Martí y Pérez, was born in Havana, Cuba, on January 28, 1853, and is regarded by the *Encyclopedia Britannica* as a "patriot and martyr, who became the symbol of Cuba's struggle for independence from Spain. His dedication to the goal of Cuban freedom made his name a synonym for liberty throughout Latin America." Marti fought for Cuban independence nearly his entire life. As a teenager he founded the publication La Patria Libre (The Free Fatherland) and later supported rebels during a Cuban revolution in 1868 for which he served hard time and was banished to Spain. The rabble-rouser was banished to Spain again in 1879. Marti traveled to other countries to teach, lecture, and write, yet trouble followed him wherever he went. While in Venezuela he developed another publication, Revista Venezolana (Venezuelan Review), which infuriated Venezuelan leader Antonio Guzmán Blanco, who thus banished Marti. Marti returned to New York City, where he had lived before, and plotted an invasion of Cuba. With a handful of men, including Cuban revolutionary leader Máximo Gómez, Marti left New York City on the last day of 1895 and landed at Santo Domingo that spring. By May 19 Marti was dead, killed in a battle in the Oriente Province. He was buried in Cementerio de Santa Ifigenia in Santiago. In addition to scores of essays, poems, and newspaper articles, he wrote *Inside the Monster*, *Our America*, and *On Education*.

Judson Street

In 1876 the estate of I. L. Judson rested at the southwest corner of Judson Street where it meets Clinton Avenue. The name of this street was accepted by the city in 1871 when they made the names of nearby Colby Street, Hunter Avenue, Rawson Street, and Watervliet Avenue official. Judson Street was once known as Second Street.

Ichabod Lewis Judson was born in Stratford, Connecticut, on November 6, 1785, to Nathaniel Judson and Rhoda Judson, who were buried in Flat Swamp Cemetery in Newtown, Connecticut. He was president of the Albany Exchange Bank, manager of the Albany Orphan Asylum, alderman, and supervisor, and he served in the War of 1812 as an officer. Ichabod Lewis Judson died April 3, 1865, in Albany and was buried in Albany Rural Cemetery. Munsell, in *Collections of the History of Albany*, wrote that Judson "maintained a high character as a citizen, a man, and a Christian" and was "in every department of life, one of the best and purest of men."

Justice Drive

Justice can be meted out on this street. It's the location of the University at Albany's University Police Department.

K

Kaine Terrace

Kaine Terrace in Albany and Kaine Drive in Guilderland are named for the same man: Edward Kaine, a landowner and developer most active during the 1960s. In 1963, Kaine conveyed land to the City of Albany for construction of his namesake street. Kaine Terrace homes were selling two years later. He was born in Troy on July 2, 1929, to Sydney Kaine and Theresa Yager Kaine and was married to Patricia Lenegar Kaine for 62 years. He graduated from the Vincentian Institute and served in the Army, as a paratrooper, during the 1940s and in the Navy during the 1950s. Edward Kaine died March 27, 2013, and was buried in Graceland Cemetery.

Kakely Street

Kakely Street is named for the Kakely family of farmers who lived in this area. One George Kakely, perhaps this street's eponym, was born April 15, 1847, emigrated from Germany in 1868, and settled in Albany. He died December 10, 1932, in Albany and was buried in Albany Rural Cemetery. He had two daughters, Margaret and Rose. Kakely Street, Bogardus Road, Freeman Road, Greenway Street, Halsdorf Street, and Linden Road were built together during the 1920s. The land they were built on was conveyed to the city in 1922, and Kakely Street was built by 1925.

Kate Street

Kate Street is one of four "Ten Eyck streets," the other three being Cuyler Avenue, Matilda Street, and Ten Eyck Avenue. One source stated that Kate Street is named so because Kate Ten Eyck was the daughter of landowners Peter Ten Eyck and Leonard Ten Eyck. This story is bogus, especially considering a man can't be your mother. Kate Street may be named for Catherine Ten Eyck. Her parents were Conrad A. Ten Eyck and Hester Gansevoort Ten Eyck. Catherine was born in 1836, died in 1842, and was buried in Albany Rural Cemetery. A keen observer pointed out that Kate Street is the smallest of the four Ten Eyck streets, which may represent the fact that Kate was the tiniest Ten Eyck to die. She had five siblings: Leonard, Anthony, Jacob C., Abraham Cuyler, and Clinton. If Kate Street is not named for Catherine, it's named for Kate Dyer Ten Eyck, who was married to Jacob Lansing Ten Eyck. She was born in 1868, died in 1936, and was buried in Albany Rural Cemetery. On May 21, 1911, Jacob Lansing Ten Eyck and Kate Lansing Ten Eyck conveyed land to the city for construction of the four Ten Eyck streets. By June 17 of that year, a building permit had been issued to F. W. Lange for construction of 21 Cuyler Avenue, one of the first homes built on that street.

Kean Street

Kean Street's name history remains a mystery. It may pay memorial to a man who was involved with the Port of Albany because that's where it's located.

Keeler Drive

At least two historians theorized that Keeler Drive, which was built by 1950, is named for William Keeler. Born in Albany on March 27, 1841, as the son of

Daniel Keeler and Margaret Murphy Keeler, he operated hotels in Albany for more than fifty years. However, this street is likely named for a Mr. J. Keeler. In 1891, this man owned 100 acres centered on today's intersection of Whitehall Road and South Manning Boulevard, precisely where Keeler Drive is located. Albany Rural Cemetery records reveal that this landowner was likely John Keeler (1851–1895) or Jacob Keeler (no relation, 1855–1918).

Kehoe Street

Kehoe Street uses a name that can be spelled Keogh and Keough, and it was built by 1915 on land conveyed by Jacob W. Wilbur. Kehoe is an Irish clan name that dates to the 1200s and comes from the Gaelic surname Mac Eochaidh, meaning "son of John." This Gaelic name came from the first name Eochaidh, meaning "horse." The name Kehoe also comes from a former French community named Caieu. It has not been revealed who specifically chose the name Kehoe for this street and why.

Keller Street

It is not known for whom this street, which was built before 1932, is specifically named. One Keller of note in old-time Albany was Robert Keller, United States local inspector of steamboats, appointed in 1885. Yet such a job may not warrant memorialization through a street, and Keller Street isn't near the Hudson River where all the steamboats were. Nearly thirty Kellers are buried in Albany Rural Cemetery, the oldest grave dating to 1873. Grove Cemetery in Coeymans has more than a dozen Kellers, the oldest headstone dating to 1866. Any of these people could be connected to this street. The name Keller referred to one who worked in wine cellars, using the Old High German word *kellari*. In Jewish culture it was derived from the Yiddish *Keln*, which meant to be from Cologne, Germany.

Kelton Court

There was the possibility of a "United Kingdom cluster" connection here because Kelton Court is connected to Dartmouth Street. However, there is no popular Kelton place name in the U.K. The U.K. does have a Kelton Lane next to Grassholme Reservoir in an area locally called Kelton, yet this spot in County Durham, England, is exceedingly unfamiliar to most people. Kelton is not a popular Albany last name either. The only Kelton graves to be found in the Albany area are three in Eagle Hill Cemetery near the Harriman Campus. Kelton Court remains unsolved. Land was conveyed to the city by John Klapp and Lisette Klapp for construction of Kelton Court, and nearby Dartmouth Street and Mariette Place, in 1928.

Kenosha Street

There could be a literal fishy connection between Kenosha Street, built by 1915, and nearby Saco Street. The ancient Indian word *kenosha* means "pike," the Potawatomi *gnozhé* means "place of the pike," and the Ojibwa *masu-kinoja* means "place of spawning trout." This collection of Indian words refers to fish entering Lake Michigan via surrounding rivers. Saco comes from the Indian *sohk*, meaning "pouring out," as in the mouth of a river. Then there is a figuratively fishy connection between the Capital Region and Kenosha, Wisconsin. This community, which was called Pike Creek and Kinoje, was settled in part by people from Troy, New York.

Beyond Kenosha Street and the City of Kenosha there is Kenosha County in Wisconsin, Kenosha Lake in Michigan, Lake Kenosia in Connecticut, Kenosha Spur in California, Kenosha Pass in Colorado, Kenoza Lake in Massachusetts, and Kenoza Lake in New York. Saco is the name of a river in New Hampshire and Maine, a bay and city in Maine, and a community in Colorado.

Kensington Place

Found in West London, Kensington is a wealthy and densely-populated district within the Royal Borough of Kensington and Chelsea. The main attraction of Kensington is the royal residence Kensington Palace. The original mansion that stood there was built in 1605. Kensington Place is next to seven other "English streets" including Carlisle Court, Cheshire Court, Fordham Court, Marlborough Court, Stanford Court, Windsor Place, and Victoria Way. Kensington place names can be found in Pennsylvania, New York, Maryland, Tennessee, South Carolina, Connecticut, Ohio, Georgia, New Hampshire, and Kansas. The name Kensington was recorded prior to 1100, first written in Latin as *Chenesitone*, meaning "Kenesigne's land or meadows" in Anglo-Saxon.

Kent Street

James Kent, who this street is named for, practiced as a judge within the New York State Supreme Court. He was born in present-day Putnam County on July 31, 1763, as the son of Moss Kent, first surrogate of Rensselaer County. He studied at Yale University, like his father and grandfather did, and graduated in 1781. After leaving Yale University, Kent found a mentor in Egbert Benson, associate justice of the New York State Supreme Court and New York's first attorney general. Thus Benson Street and Kent Street are next to each other. Kent was admitted to the bar in 1785 and became Dutchess County representative, New York assemblyman, Columbia College law professor (Columbia's Law School has its Kent Hall and dubs students with high grade point averages Kent Scholars), State Supreme Court associate justice, New York City recorder, New

York State Supreme Court chief justice, New York State Chancery Court chancellor, and New York State Constitutional Convention delegate. During political retirement he practiced law and wrote the four-volume *Commentaries on American Law*, published in 1826 and currently in its fifteenth edition.

James Kent died December 12, 1847, in New York City. As quoted by Steve Sheppard in *The History of Legal Education in the United States*, the judge said his longevity of health was credited to "the love of simple diet, and to all kinds of temperance, and never read late nights. I rambled daily with my wife on foot over the hills, we were never asunder." This man is also memorialized through Kent Place Boulevard in Summit, New Jersey, where he used to live; Kent County and Kent City in Michigan; Chicago-Kent College of Law; and Kent Avenue and Kent Street in New York City. All of Albany's Kent Street was constructed before 1938. The first section built was the one-block segment between West Lawrence Street and North Allen Street. That section has existed since 1915.

Kent Terrace

Gage Avenue and Kent Terrace intersect each other and may have a figurative connection, too. Gage Avenue is named for British military officer Thomas Gage, who was born in Firle, County Middlesex, England. England is home to County Kent. County Middlesex no longer exists. It has since been swallowed by the Greater London district, which borders County Kent to its southeast. The name Kent comes from Old English and Latin words that came from an ancient Celtic name meaning "coastal district" or "land on the edge."

Kenwood Road

Kenwood is a neighborhood in a southern section of Albany, and this is where Kenwood Road lies. This neighborhood was named by Mayor Jared Rathbone, brother of Joel Rathbone, circa 1840. Joel was born in 1806, moved to Albany in 1822, and made a fortune running a foundry that made wood and coal stoves. He owned 1,200 acres where Kenwood Road now is, and he built a mansion there in 1841. He named his estate Kenwood after a mill village in Scotland that he was familiar with (he operated his own woolen mills on Normans Kill). Joel Rathbone died September 12, 1863, in Paris, France, and was buried in Albany Rural Cemetery. Female Academy of the Sacred Heart bought the Kenwood mansion in 1859, leveled it in 1867, and used the material to build a church. The Kenwood Neighborhood, once known as Rensselaer's Mills and Lower Hollow (meanwhile, Normansville was known as Upper Hollow), was in the Town of Bethlehem but was annexed to the city in 1916. Kenwood is also an area in Chicago that's named after this same Scottish mill village.

Kerry Lane

Kerry Lane is named after County Kerry, Ireland. This street was settled by Irish Albanians who moved west from North Albany and imported the Kerry place name. As Sowell reminded readers in *Black Rednecks and White Liberals*, when Europeans left their homelands they never forgot to pack in their suitcases and trunks their sentiment from whence they came despite knowing they'd never return: "Moreover, emotional attachment to an ancestral homeland says nothing about plans to return to it today. Irish Americans, like Jewish Americans, have maintained an emotional attachment to their ancestral homeland, but nevertheless there are more people of Irish ancestry living in the United States than in Ireland . . . " The Kerry place name stems from *Ciarrai*, meaning the "people of Ciar." Ciar, translating to "dark one," was the founder of a pre-Gaelic tribe.

Kiernan Way

This way, one of ten "ways" within Albany, is named for Peter Kiernan. Kiernan was chief executive and chairman of Fleet/Norstar Financial Group and, before that, president of the New York State Bankers Association, president of Rose and Kiernan Incorporated, director of the Federal Reserve Bank of New York, trustee of the Council of the State University at Albany, and board member of the Association of Bank Holding Companies. He was born in Albany and was a Williams College graduate. Peter Kiernan died September 14, 1988, in Boston after heart surgery. He was survived by his wife, five sons, two daughters, two sisters, and six grandchildren. The Peter D. Kiernan Plaza is next to Kiernan Way, this plaza being the old Union Station of the New York Central Railroad. This plaza was bought by the State of New York in 1966, and the last train departed Union Station two years later. Norstar bought the building, renovated it, reopened it, and named it for Kiernan in 1989.

King Avenue

George King, a builder and real estate agent, owned and managed property where this street now lies. He was born in Albany during 1850, died in this city on May 14, 1914, and was buried in Albany Rural Cemetery. King Avenue is in the center of the city, embedded in the "presidential conglomerate." It was built over the stock farm of D. Ellis as well as a cemetery.

King Street

The King name dates to the mid-1700s in Albany County. On July 4, 1781, Anatine King, the daughter of Thomas King and Jannetie Ranched King, was baptized in the county. King Street may be named for this family in general, though any of the three Kings below may specifically be memorialized through this street. These are Rufus King, John King, and Rufus Henry King.

Rufus King has King Street in New York City named for him. He was born March 24, 1755, in Scarborough, which was then part of Massachusetts, yet is now part of Maine, to Richard King and Isabella Bragdon King. He attended Dummer Academy and then Harvard University, graduating in 1777. Rufus studied law, took time from his studies to serve as an officer during the War for Independence, studied law again, and passed his bar exam in 1780. He served as Massachusetts assemblyman, New York assemblyman, senator from New York, minister to Great Britain, and delegate for Massachusetts to the Continental Congress. He also signed the Constitution. In 1816 he ran for New York governor yet lost to Daniel Tompkins. Rufus King died April 29, 1827, and was buried in Grace Church Cemetery in Jamaica, Queens. Political success ran in the family. His brother was William King (1768–1852, senator from Massachusetts, House of Representatives member from Massachusetts, and first governor of Maine) while his half-brother was Cyrus King (1772–1817, House of Representatives member from Massachusetts, major general of the Massachusetts Militia, and cofounder of Maine's Thornton Academy).

One of Rufus King's sons was John King, born January 3, 1788, in New York City. John was a lawyer, having passed his bar exam during the early 1800s. He practiced in New York City. The tides of war put his law career on hold for a short time while he served in the War of 1812 as a cavalry lieutenant. After his military service, John served as New York assemblyman, House of Representatives member from New York, and New York governor. John King died July 7, 1867, in Queens County, New York. Two of his brothers, who were of course sons of Rufus King, were very successful. These were James Gore King (assistant adjutant general of the New York State Militia during the War of 1812, president of the Erie Railroad, and House of Representatives member from New Jersey) and Charles King (Columbia University president).

Rufus Henry King is honored by the Moses Smiting the Rock, also known as the King Memorial Fountain, monument in Washington Park. The plaque in front of this monument reads: "This fountain was erected by Henry L. King in memory of his father Rufus Henry King, 1893, J. Massey Rhind, Sculptor." Henry L., one of Rufus Henry's three sons, left $20,000 when he died in 1878 to build the Moses Smiting the Rock monument. Rufus Henry was the son of Joshua King and was born in Ridgefield, Connecticut, in 1794. At the age of 20 he moved to Albany with his brother, opened a dry goods business, and entered the banking business to become president of New York State National Bank, Albany Savings Bank, and Albany Insurance Company. Amasa Parker wrote that "there was not in the State a more thorough merchant and banker than Rufus H. King, or none more extensively known, esteemed and confided in" yet "though having many opportunities for public preferment, he avoided them with almost morbid dislike." He was the father of four children and was married to Amelia Laverty King. Rufus Henry King died in Albany on July 9, 1867.

Kirk Place

One of many Albany breweries of days gone by was Andrew Kirk Brewery, which was in business from 1833 to 1857. It stood on upper Broadway near Kirk Place and was replaced by a series of businesses and breweries including Fort Orange Brewing Company, which operated from 1882 to 1889. (A new Fort Orange Brewing opened in 2017 at 450 North Pearl Street—their logo is an outline of ancient Fort Orange.) Kirk was a Scottish immigrant who initially shared ownership of the brewery, the first one in the city to use steam power, with John Outwin. Andrew Kirk died in 1857. At the time of his death he was president of St. Andrews Society, a group that reported in the *Albany Argus* that they had lost "one of their most liberal and steadfast friends, and the city of Albany one of the most honorable and high-minded businessmen, known for forty years. In sunshine and in storm, true to his promises and punctual to his engagement." His son, William Kirk, carried on tradition by operating his own malt house, which stood south of his father's brewery. William ran this operation until the late 1800s.

Kneeland Street

One of three related Kneeland men from Massachusetts is honored through this street. In *Seven Centuries in the Kneeland Family*, Stillman Foster Kneeland reported that Boston's Kneeland Street is named for John Kneeland (1694–1774), yet later in this book he reported that this Boston street is named for Abner Kneeland (1774–1844). Meanwhile, Annie Haven Thwing, in *The Crooked and Narrow Streets of the Town of Boston, 1630–1822*, wrote that Kneeland Street is named "for Solomon Kneeland [1698–1784], leather dresser, who first bought land here in 1731–2." Transference of the name Kneeland Street from Boston to Albany has to do with a rail line, this transference explained below.

John Kneeland was born in Boston to John Kneeland and Mary Green Kneeland on November 14, 1694, and was "in some respects the most remarkable character in the whole line of Kneelands," according to Stillman Foster Kneeland. John owned land where today's Kneelands Wharf and Kneeland Street are in Boston. A builder by trade, he built John Hancock's 1737 house on Beacon Street, the courthouse, the jail, and the Old South Church, which replaced the Old South Meeting House built by his father. John married four times and was the father of thirteen children. He was one of eight children himself, and longevity ran in the family, especially considering the era. Not counting one sibling, John, who died as an infant, the seven surviving siblings lived to be an amazing 62, 71, 72, 80, 82, 83, and 88 years old—an average age of 77 (538 years total!). These seven children had fifty-seven children themselves. John Kneeland died February 16, 1774, at the age of 80 and bequeathed the family Bible to his family. This Bible had been in the family for nearly two hundred years, having been printed in London in 1576.

Abner Kneeland was born in Gardner, Massachusetts, on April 7, 1774, to Timothy Kneeland and Moriah Stone Kneeland. His father was the third person to settle in Gardner, Massachusetts, in 1771. With his brother, Abner moved to Vermont to work as a carpenter, teacher, and lay preacher. He then moved to New Hampshire and became an ordained minister with the New England Universalist General Convention. After settling back in Massachusetts in 1811, he stopped preaching because he felt he had become a nonbeliever. He became a dry goods merchant but then returned to being a minister. His faith waned, he questioned the mission of his church and Christianity as a whole, and he offended leadership and churchgoers alike. Then he got into big trouble by sending a letter to Thomas Whittemore, editor of the *Universalist*, in 1833, in which he wrote that "Universalists believe in a god which I do not; but believe that their god, with all his moral attributes (aside from nature itself), is nothing more than a chimera of their own imagination." For this letter Abner was pulled into *Commonwealth of Massachusetts v. Abner Kneeland*, in 1838, in which the commonwealth accused him of blasphemy and being an atheist. He was held in a Boston jail for two months, making him the last person in the United States to be jailed for blasphemy. After being released, he moved to Iowa to set up a utopian community. Abner Kneeland, who had married four times and had a dozen children, died August 27, 1844, and was buried in Farmington Cemetery in Farmington, Iowa. As with all utopian communities, his settlement crumbled.

Solomon Kneeland was born in Boston on September 23, 1698, to Solomon Kneeland and Mary Hawkins Kneeland. Stillman Foster Kneeland wrote that the younger Solomon "was an extensive real estate owner in Boston" and "a wealthy and respected merchant" who fought in the Battle of Bunker Hill alongside at least four other Kneelands. Solomon Kneeland died July 20, 1784.

Why is Kneeland Street in Albany specifically named so? The answer lies in a railroad. During the 1800s and 1900s, the Boston and Albany Railroad connected these two cities. The tracks began precisely at Kneeland Street (built first) in Boston and terminated near Kneeland Street (built later on) in Albany. Boston certainly embraced a "New York state of mind" where the Boston and Albany Railroad began—during the mid-1800s, Albany Street, Troy Street, Rochester Street, Genesee Street, Oswego Street, Oneida Street, Seneca Street, and Utica Street were near Kneeland Street. Only Albany Street survives. The other seven streets were obliterated by a massive interchange of Interstate 90 and Interstate 93 being built.

Knollwood Terrace
See Edgewood Avenue.

Knox Street

Knox Street was known as Gage Street until September 11, 1790, and then as Swallow Street until July 17, 1809. It is named for Henry Knox, born July 25, 1750, in Boston. He was the son of William Knox and Mary Campbell Knox. Despite attending school only until the age of 12, Knox became a general during the Revolutionary War. He witnessed the 1770 Boston Massacre and was present at the 1773 Boston Tea Party. In 1775, while serving in America's new military force, he befriended George Washington.

Knox distinguished himself by leading militia men to haul sixty tons of cannons from Ticonderoga to Boston during winter, a grueling 300-mile trip. With the cannons arriving in Boston six weeks later, the British retreated. Citing this agonizing expedition, McCullough, in *1776: The Illustrated Edition*, summed that "Knox proved an outstanding leader, capable of accomplishing almost anything, and steadfastly loyal to Washington" even "under the most trying conditions" and "through the darkest hours." He saw combat in New Jersey, New York, and Pennsylvania and created the Continental Army's first artillery and officer training school in 1779. Knox attained the rank of major general, served as secretary of war, and fought in Indian wars. It would have best served this soldier to have been a vegetarian. Knox choked on a chicken bone, which led to a fatal infection. Henry Knox died October 25, 1806, and was buried on his estate in Thomaston, which is on today's coast of Maine. He was the father of thirteen children. In addition to towns, cities, and counties named for this man, so is the Army's Fort Knox. For serving as an artilleryman and starting the first artillery school in America, Knox is also memorialized through Knox Hall at Fort Sill, Oklahoma, home of the Army's Field Artillery School.

Krank Street

George Krank, born January 6, 1829, in Baden, Germany, settled in Albany after emigrating from Bremen with his family in 1847. This street, built prior to 1874 with nearby Odell Street, Batcher Street, Benjamin Street, and Broad Street, is named for him. His father was Lawrence Krank, born in Tauber, Bischoffenheim, Germany, who lived to be 99 years and nine months old. The man was literally killed by kindness. Lawrence dropped dead, according to Hudson-Mohawk Genealogical and Family Memoirs, "by the excitement of an entertainment given in his honor as a prelude to a grand celebration planned to be given on his one hundredth birthday."

A baker and band organizer, George Krank formed a company in the 7th Regiment New York Artillery and served during the Civil War as a noncommissioned officer. In 1862, he re-enlisted as an officer and was wounded during the Battle of the Wilderness in Virginia during early May 1864. During this battle 4,000 men were killed, 20,000 were wounded, and 5,000 were captured or went missing. Krank returned to Albany, organized the 25th New York Regiment, and was made colonel. He then served as an alderman and died June 5, 1907. At his time of death he lived on the corner of Second Avenue and Krank Street. Nearby Krank Park, built during the 1920s, is named for him. Krank is not a flattering last name. It comes from the Middle High German *krank*, meaning "weak." It's related to the English word cringe, which comes from the Old English *cringan*, meaning "to collapse from wounds" and "writhe."

Krumkill Court East
(and Krumkill Road, Old Krumkill Road)
Krum Kill, a three-mile-long stream that's a tributary of Normans Kill, was first called *Kroome Kill*, which translates from the Dutch to "crooked stream." Current spelling came into fashion prior to 1893. Krumkill Road passes over this stream, Old Krumkill Road is near this stream, and Krumkill Court East is kind of near this stream. The oldest building on Krumkill Road was built circa 1800 and stands at 87 Krumkill Road.

Krumkill Road
See Krumkill Court East.

L

Lancaster Street
Lancaster Street was formerly named Tiger Street, Tigar Street, and Predeaux Street. It has had its current name since 1829. It is named for Joseph Lancaster, founder of the Lancaster Education System. Albany's Lancaster School stood on the southeast corner of Lancaster Street where it meets Eagle Street. Born November 25, 1778, in Southwark, England, Lancaster became an elementary schoolteacher in his hometown at the age of 20, basing his educational model on what is today called peer tutoring. He figured that students could help other students learn, which also reduced the cost of staff. By 1803 he had written *Improvements in Education, as it Respects the Industrious Classes of the Community* and promoted his educational system in the U.S.

During the early 1800s, Lancaster made poor financial decisions, and it was revealed that he had been beating and humiliating students who weren't quick learners. His character shattered, a plea was made directly to Albanians in 1829. Within *Albany Chronicles* it was requested that citizens "investigate the several charges most searchingly and then either blame him or exonerate his name, as it was a matter deeply affecting the progress of his educational work."

The wheels fell off the Lancaster Education System in England and the United States. Teachers, not students, are the foundation of education. A few Lancastrian schools operated in South America and Mexico, but Lancaster was already discredited. On October 24, 1838, Joseph Lancaster was run over by a horse carriage in New York City and died.

Lansing Street
See John Street.

Lark Drive
(and Lark Street)
There are a whopping 91 species of larks, yet only one is native to America: the horned lark. This bird, colored tan and white with highlights of black and yellow, prefers open land such as fields, airports, beaches, and lawns. It lays its eggs earlier than nearly any other bird, sometimes building its nest in February and losing its eggs and nest during snowstorms. During the early 1790s, Simeon DeWitt mapped a series of bird streets including Lark Street, Eagle Street, Hawk Street, Swan Street, Partridge Street, and Quail Street. He also recorded today's Lexington Street as "Snipe Street." Lark Street turns into Lark Drive east of Arbor Hill Park.

Lark Street
See Lark Drive.

Laurel Avenue
When this street was named, perhaps there were thickets of laurel growing below the softwoods and hardwoods. Or the developer just liked the name Laurel. In 1913, land was conveyed to the city for construction of this street as well as nearby Edgewood Avenue, Fairlawn Avenue, Hawthorne Avenue, Homestead Avenue, Melrose Avenue, and Terrace Avenue. These seven streets were probably built that same year.

Members of the Heath family, great laurel, mountain laurel, pale laurel (known as bog laurel because it grows in riparian zones), and sheep laurel (known as lambkill and sheepkill because it's poisonous to livestock) naturally grow in New York. They blossom from May to August and grow in bush-like thickets that take over acres of forest, dense stands intertwined with each other close to the ground. Mountain laurel is the longest-living bush in the East. Some have been dated at more than a century old.

Lawn Avenue
See Fairlawn Avenue.

Lawnridge Avenue
See Fairlawn Avenue.

Learned Street
Learned Street is next to Thacher Street for good reason. Billings Learned was George Hornell Thacher's business partner in Albany. They sold stoves together. Learned was born in Norwich, Connecticut, on June 24, 1813, and was attending Yale University by 1829. He graduated in this school's class of 1834. He then read law with two Connecticut judges and passed that state's bar exam. He moved to the communities of Lockport, Troy, and Ballston, practiced law, ran a flour business, and worked as a farmer. In 1850, Learned moved to Albany and teamed with Thacher to run a stove business. Their partnership ended a few years later and Learned helped found Union Bank. Billings Learned died in Albany on April 16, 1884, and was buried in Albany Rural Cemetery. His wife, Mary Ann Noyes Learned, died December 30, 1875. Learned Street was featured on maps by 1866.

Leedale Street
An old map within the former Parks and Recreation building near Hoffman Avenue portrayed Leedale Street as Lee Dale Street, which likely communicated "Lee's Dale." It is unknown who Lee was. In the March 13, 1913, edition of the *Albany Evening Journal* it was reported that Claude Holding and Albert Kositjse conveyed land to the city for the building of a new street to be called Leedale Street. The name Lee comes from a handful of sources that have meant "wood," "clearing," and "poem." It's also related to a name given to poets.

Leighton Street
The English surname and place name Leighton give this street, which was built circa 1915, its name. This word is from the Old English *leahtun*, which stems from the older *leactun*, which combines the word *leac* for "garden" with the word *tun* for "settlement." *Tun* gives us the suffix "ton," which has been used to label many settlements, such as Kingston, New York's original capital city.

Lenox Avenue
Lenox Avenue abuts Berkshire Boulevard, thus making a Massachusetts connection. This street is named after the Town of Lenox in Berkshire County,

Massachusetts, and was built prior to 1916. Lenox was settled in 1750 by Jonathan Hinsdale and Sarah Hinsdale and was incorporated in 1767. The town is named for Charles Lennox, 3rd Duke of Richmond and Lennox. Lennox, who was a field marshal in the British Army, was born February 22, 1735, and died December 29, 1806. He was buried at Chichester Cathedral in County Sussex, England. Lennox refers to a region in Scotland that was called Levenauchen, Levenachs, Levenax, and Lennax, meaning "field of the smooth stream."

Leonard Place

Extensive sections of Albany were owned by Jacob Leonard during the late 1800s, and one of the areas he owned is where Leonard Place now is. He purchased fifty acres of farmland here from the estate of William James in 1862. He also owned land within today's "presidential conglomerate" between Ver Planck Street and North Allen Street, too. His son, Jesse Leonard, for whom Leonard Street is named, would later name the streets that compose the presidential conglomerate (he named Albany's six "academic streets," too). Jacob was a coal merchant, first president of Albany County Savings Bank, and co-organizer of the Albany and Susquehanna Railroad. He died circa 1911.

The Albany Penitentiary, which opened in 1846 and closed in 1931, used to stand where Leonard Place now is. Jacob Leonard leased forty acres of farmland to this institution during the 1890s, and prisoners worked the land so they could raise their own food, which lowered the penitentiary's operating costs. This prison's first superintendent was former New York City police chief Louis Dwight "L. D." Pilsbury (yes, with one *l*), for whom Pillsbury Lake, Pillsbury Bay, and Pillsbury Mountain in the Adirondack Mountains are named. The apex of his criminal justice career was becoming New York's first superintendent of prisons. Historians criticize Pilsbury as ruling with an iron fist and having prisoners serve as labor to large businesses within the Pilsbury System. By 1860, there were 250 inmates in the prison, and all of them were being paid to manufacture shoes. During the Civil War, the Albany Penitentiary held prisoners of war. Pilsbury was buried in Albany Rural Cemetery. His memorial is an imposing pillar, perhaps like the man himself.

Leonard Street

Builder and realtor Jesse Leonard, son of Jacob Leonard, for whom Leonard Place is named, is memorialized through this street. He had the idea of developing the Holland Avenue and Hackett Boulevard area. Here, Leonard designed and built Tudor style homes during the 1930s. He lived in one of these Tudor homes until his death. He was president of Leonard Realty Company, Inc., and was credited with building 600 homes in the city. He was born in 1862, died in 1956, and was buried in Blooming Grove Cemetery in Defreestville, New York.

He named Buchanan Street, Cleveland Street, Garfield Place, Grant Avenue, Lincoln Avenue, McKinley Street, Roosevelt Street, Van Buren Street, and Washington Avenue circa 1900. All of these streets save for Buchanan Street are named for past presidents. Buchanan Street is named for Capital Region engineer William Buchanan. A section of Leonard Place was formerly known as Warren Street. The name Leonard uses the Germanic elements *leo* and *hard*, meaning "lion" and "brave."

Lexington Avenue

Formerly known as Snipe Street and Schenectady Street, Lexington Avenue is named after Lexington, Massachusetts, or specifically the battles of Lexington and Concord. Lexington, Massachusetts, was settled during the 1640s when it was called Cambridge Farms. It was incorporated as a parish in 1691 and incorporated as the Town of Lexington in 1713. This town of 30,000 residents may be named for Lord Lexington, an Englishman also known as Baron Lexington, who was from the Nottinghamshire district of England. However, it's more likely this Massachusetts community is named after Laxton, a civil parish and community in County Nottinghamshire, England. That community was once called Laxintone, which stemmed from the Anglo Saxon *Leaxington*, meaning "farmstead or estate of the people of a man called Leaxa."

The first engagement of the Revolutionary War is found in the battles of Lexington and Concord, which took place April 19, 1775. Militiamen were pitted against the Red Coats, their conflict stemming from a rebel militia government controlling regions around and inside Boston. This was deemed a state of rebellion by the British as early as February 1775. On the morning of April 19, residents witnessed the shot heard round the world. Approximately 700 British soldiers fought the rebels and searched for rebel storehouses. The Britons were beaten back, later reinforced by an additional 1,000 British soldiers during a retreat. By the end of the battle, militiamen totaled 4,000. More than 120 men died, more than 200 were wounded, and 60 went missing in action.

More than two dozen U.S. place names honor the Battle of Lexington, including Lexington Avenue in New York City and Lexington County in South Carolina. The communities of Concord in California, New York, Ohio, and Vermont are named after the Massachusetts town. The Village of Concord in Nebraska, the City of Concord in North Carolina, and Concord Township in Missouri are named after the battle, while the townships of Lexington and Concord are next to each other in Maine. Other Concord place names, such as Concord, New Hampshire, usually refer to the noun concord, which defines a treaty or pact. Stewart smartly wrote that the battle at Lexington catapulted this name across the nation. It "was a new name in the land, and children learned it with their first words. At last the people had a symbol—not a stupid king across the ocean, but a name red with their own blood."

Liberty Lane

With the nearby streets of Excelsior Drive and Capital Hill, which surround University at Albany's Empire Commons dormitory on the main campus, Liberty Lane portrays New York pride. Liberty and justice are themes of the seal of the State of New York. While blindfolded Justice with her balanced scale and raised sword stands towards the right of New York's seal, Liberty stands to the left. She holds a pole with a Phrygian cap on top while her left foot mashes the English crown.

Liberty Street

Once known as Grass Lane and Cow Lane, Liberty Street, which was named in 1803, is one of the oldest streets in Albany. It celebrates the liberties we enjoy, formed and guaranteed within the Declaration of Independence, which states three inalienable rights: "We hold these truths to be self-evident, that all men are created equal, that they are endowed by their Creator with certain unalienable Rights, that among these are Life, Liberty and the pursuit of Happiness."

Liebel Street

During the 1870s, Adam Liebel owned land where Liebel Street now is, and his holdings were extensive, totaling seventy lots. The Adam Liebel House, the oldest building on this street, stands at 32 Liebel Street and was built circa 1820 before city blocks reached this area. Adam Liebel may have been born in Germany in 1836 and immigrated to America in 1858. As late as the mid-1900s, members of the Liebel family lived on this street.

Lily Street

The lily comes in a profusion of colors in the ten species that grow in New York: orange with red spots (blackberry species), white and yellow (bluebead), orange (day and yellow pond), orange with dark spots (Canada), red with dark spots (southern red and wood), white (Easter), yellow (trout), and red with dark spots (Turk's cap). Nearly twenty species grow in North America, just a fraction of the 4,000 species worldwide. Lily Street was built circa 1928 with neighboring Elmo Road, Eva Avenue, Frost Place, Pansy Street, and Silas Avenue.

Limerick Drive

Beyond Limerick Drive, which was built in 1968, the place name Limerick is carried through the Town of Limerick in Maine and Limerick Township in Pennsylvania. Limerick is a city of 100,000 residents in County Limerick, Ireland. This area has been settled for more than 5,000 years and was called

Luimneach, meaning "flat area," which describes County Limerick well. Isolated mountains can be found in the county, too. The tallest is 3,015-foot Galtymore, high point of the Galty Mountains.

The Limerick neighborhood based around Limerick Drive is home to the North End Limericks, whose lineage traces to Limerick, Ireland. These Albanians are known for holding their own authentic St. Patrick's Day parade each year before the main downtown Albany parade kicks off. They've been doing so since 1950. On this holiday they post "Limerick, USA" signs around the borders of their neighborhood. In conjunction with their parade they offer the Miss Limerick contest, grand marshal banquet, a concert, and a dinner. This neighborhood, settled in 1825 by the Irish, is synonymous with North Albany. Many Irish immigrated to the United States to build the Erie Canal and settled in North Albany. By 1860, forty houses stood in North Albany, and ten years later this neighborhood was annexed from the Town of Watervliet to the City of Albany. Notable North Albanians include John Brady (judge and founder of modern-day New York family courts), Walter Doran (commander of the U.S. Navy Pacific Fleet), Gerald Jennings (former mayor of Albany), and William Kennedy (Pulitzer Prize-winning author).

"A Limerick Scribe Honors Limerick Drive"

There is a circular drive in Albany, short and sweet
Where Irishmen relax and kick up their feet
Where the backyard birds love their sunflower seeds
They eat some, they drop some, many falling among the weeds
Yet the Irishmen on Limerick Drive still think their street name oh so neat

Lincoln Avenue
(and Lincoln Square)
Lincoln Avenue is part of the eight-street "presidential conglomerate" of Albany, each of these streets named by realtor Jesse Leonard circa 1900. Lincoln Avenue used to be called Lingen Street. The White House shares Lincoln describing himself just before he received nomination for president of the United States:

I was born February 12, 1809, in Hardin County, Kentucky. My parents were both born in Virginia, of undistinguished families—second families, perhaps I should say. My mother, who died in my tenth year, was of a family of the name of Hanks. My father... removed from Kentucky to... Indiana, in my eighth year. It was a wild region, with many bears and other wild animals still in the woods. There I grew up. Of course when I came of age I did not know much. Still somehow, I could read, write, and cipher . . . but that was all.

During his youth, Lincoln lived the life of a working man with hardship—no more, no less. The man was literally born in a log cabin. (As James Loewen, author of *Lies my Teacher Told Me*, liked to joke with his students, some of whom actually fell for his humor, Lincoln was so ambitious from such a young age that he "was born in a log cabin which he built with his own hands.") He had two siblings, Sarah and Thomas, who died as infants. Later on, his family was so poor that they squatted on public land in a shack. His mother died when he was just a kid. To make ends meet he split wood for firewood and fences, hence his nickname "The Rail Splitter," and he ran a modest store and served as a postmaster with only a year-and-a-half of schooling to his name.

In 1832, when Lincoln was 23, he served in the Black Hawk War. He admitted he saw no combat, having more trouble with mosquitoes than Indians. After this minor adventure Lincoln served as a Whig in the Illinois State Legislature and educated himself in law. He passed his bar exam in 1837 and settled in Springfield, Illinois. Seven years later he acquired a law partner and entered politics. Lincoln served as House of Representatives member from Illinois from 1847 to 1849 and did not seek a second term. Instead, he returned to practicing law. Soon back in politics though, he became a member of the Republican Party in 1856. He ran for senator in 1858, yet lost to Stephen Douglas. The race earned Lincoln fame though. He was elected sixteenth president in March 1861. Lincoln's most significant event while in office was, of course, the Civil War, which lasted from April 12, 1861, to May 9, 1865. More than 600,000 men were killed, 475,000 were wounded, and 400,000 were captured or went missing in action. In 1864, Lincoln began his second term. On April 14, 1865, a Good Friday, Lincoln was shot at Ford's Theater in Washington, D.C., by actor John Wilkes Booth. The president fell into a coma and died nine hours later. Abraham Lincoln was buried in the Lincoln Tomb in Oak Ridge Cemetery in Springfield, Illinois. He's buried there with his wife, Mary Todd Lincoln, and three of their four sons. It would be quite difficult to find a major city in the United States that does not have a street named for Abraham Lincoln. The name Lincoln comes from the British name Lindo and the Latin *colonia*, which mean "lake" and "colony."

Lincoln Park Road

The first historic event to take place where this park now is happened in 1626 when the Mohawks fought a battle against the Dutch and Mohicans in which four Dutchmen died. Later on, a section of the Beaver Kill that once ran through this park hosted sawmills and gristmills, while other sections saw development of a brickyard, brewery, mine, and pasturage. In 1891, the city acquired 68 acres for construction of a park. During that last decade of the 1800s a children's playground was opened to the public, the first step in transforming this area into Albany's first communal park. Initially it was called Beaver Park, but that name was changed in 1916 to honor the president. Today the park offers pools, a playground, ball fields, tennis courts, handball courts, basketball courts, community gardens, and a gym.

Lincoln Square
See Lincoln Avenue.

Linda Court
Located in the suburbs, Linda Court likely carries the first name of one of the developer's female relatives. It is unknown who Linda was.

Lindbergh Avenue
Lindbergh Avenue was constructed in 1929, the year a series of homes was built there by Reddy Brothers. Charles Lindbergh, for whom this street is named, is well-known for two things. One is his solo flight across the Atlantic Ocean. Another is that his son was kidnapped.

Born February 4, 1902, in Detroit to House of Representatives member Charles August Lindbergh and Evangeline Lodge Land Lindbergh, he grew up in Minnesota. He didn't find the College of Engineering at the University of Wisconsin-Madison a good fit for him, and so he dropped out. His real passion was flying. He learned to fly in Nebraska and completed his first flight during the spring of 1922. In addition to being a pilot, Lindbergh was a parachutist, wing-walker, and aviation mechanic. In 1924 he started flight training with the Army Air Service. A year later he graduated first in his class and became a lieutenant in the Air Service Reserve Corps. He flew air mail, which was more exciting than it sounds. At least twice he had to eject before his aircraft smashed into the ground. During May 20 and 21, 1937, he completed the first solo trans-Atlantic flight from New York City to Paris in his Spirit of St. Louis. He won the $25,000 Orteig Prize offered by Raymond Orteig to the first pilot to do so. The trip was 3,600 miles and took 33.5 hours.

It was known as the crime of the century. Lindbergh's 20-month-old son, Charles Augustus Lindbergh Jr., was kidnapped March 1, 1932, from the family home in East Amwell, New Jersey. Ransom was given for return of the child, yet the child's remains were found weeks later near Rose, New Jersey. Tracing of the ransom payment led to the arrest of Richard Hauptmann of the Bronx. Hauptmann's trial in 1935 resulted in him being electrocuted at Trenton State Prison during the spring of 1936. After the kidnapping, the Lindberghs lived throughout Europe and then returned to the United States. Lindbergh attained the rank of colonel in the Army Air Corps yet resigned when Franklin D. Roosevelt decided to enter World War II. To some in Roosevelt's administration, Lindbergh was nothing short of a Nazi sympathizer and anti-Semite. Despite this, Lindbergh flew sorties for the Allies during the war and completed combat missions when he wasn't training allied pilots.

Charles Lindbergh died August 26, 1974, in Hawaii and was buried at the Palapala Ho'omau Church in Kipahulu, Maui. The Spirit of St. Louis is on display at the National Air and Space Museum in Washington, D.C. The world had fallen in love with Lindbergh partly because he seemed such a clean-cut and valiant man. However, decades after his and his widow's passing it was revealed that the pilot had clandestine European mistresses during his marriage, had three secret families, and covertly fathered seven children.

Linden Road

Another word for the basswood tree is linden, and the Basswood genus is often called the Linden genus. There are more than 400 species worldwide within this genus. Three grow in New York: American basswood, white basswood, and European linden. The American basswood is the species seen most often in Albany. It lines city streets, is sprinkled through parks, and can be found in countless yards. These observations match with those of Little, who called American basswood "a handsome shade and street tree." It can grow up to 100 feet in height and three feet in diameter, yet most samples are usually half those dimensions. The biggest one in New York is 77 feet tall and 34 inches in diameter. A slang name for this tree is "bee tree" because honeybees love American basswood flowers, which display in June. Whoever built Linden Road found linden trees there or simply appreciated this species. This street—with nearby Bogardus Road, Freeman Road, Greenway Street, Halsdorf Street, and Kakely Street—was built during the 1920s after land was conveyed to the city in 1922.

Link Street

Petite Link Street likely gets its name from "linking" Hackett Boulevard with Hurst Avenue.

Little Lane

An accurate, descriptive name, Little Lane is barely 200 feet long.

Livingston Avenue

Known as Lumber Street until April 21, 1879, Livingston Avenue is named for Philip Livingston, lifelong politician and rebel. Livingston was a signer of the Declaration of Independence and served as minister to France, chancellor of the state, New York City alderman, Albany alderman, delegate of New York to the Continental Congress, delegate to the Albany Congress, Province of New York assemblyman, and senator from New York, among other positions of importance. He was born on the corner of State and Pearl streets on January 15, 1716, as the fourth son of Philip Livingston and Catharina Van Brugh Livingston. The younger Philip graduated from Yale University in 1737. After graduation he moved to New York City to become a merchant. While rising through political ranks he developed into an outspoken critic of the British and supported succession from the crown. Philip Livingston died June 12, 1778, and was buried in Prospect Hill Cemetery in York, Pennsylvania. He was a co-founder of Kings College, today's Columbia University, and was married to Christina Ten Broeck, great-grand-daughter of Albany mayor Dirck Wesselse Ten Broeck. Together they had nine children.

Livingston is also known for planting the Great Elm in 1735. It lived for more than a century on the corner of North Pearl Street and State Street where he grew up. John Papp wrote in *Albany's Historic Street* that the elm "remained, a loved object, the memory of which many Albanians hold dear. It was a rendezvous for lovers, the chatting-place for those who met casually while on shopping and business trips. Its friendly shade was sought by all." Papp also warned of an ominous side of the Great Elm generally overlooked by historians: "In the early days slaves were tied to a ring driven into the trunk, and whipped." This tree was cut down on the evening of June 15, 1877, a victim of the march of progress. It was removed for a street paving project. Hislop wrote poetically about the Great Elm's long life:

> The Great Elm had been passed by the traffic of almost a hundred and fifty years. Indians burdened with beaver skins, traders, soldiers of the French and Indian Wars, the Revolution, the War of 1812, the Mexican War, and the Civil War passed by Livingston's tree. Horses, carts loaded with Patroons' lumber, stagecoaches, wagons of thousands of Western pioneers, crawled slowly through the shadows it laid across State Street.

Locust Street
Certainly not named after the insect since Albany is immune to plagues of locusts, Locust Street is named after the tree. Members of the Legume family, locust species that grow in New York include black and honey. Locusts have rot-resistant, dense, heavy wood. It's a modest-sized tree, growing to eighty feet in height and not reaching two feet in diameter. Locust Street may specifically be named for a locust grove, identified on Smith and Young's 1851 *Map of the Vicinity of Albany and Troy*, that stood near this modern-day street.

Lodge Street
The Lodge name is recognized in downtown Albany through the B. Lodge and Company Store, established in 1867, which is two short blocks from Lodge

Street. However, this street has nothing to do with the Lodge family and everything to do with a Masonic lodge (also called a temple).

The Albany Masonic Temple stands at the corner of Lodge Street and Corning Place on the oldest continuously owned Masonic property in the world. This property was purchased by Masters Lodge No. 5 on October 17, 1766. The first Masonic lodge in the United States was built here on June 24, 1768. The current granite building was designed by Albert Fuller and William Wheeler, and its cornerstone was set on June 24, 1895. On October 26 the following year, a grand celebration was held to dedicate the lodge. The band played, a parade strode by, and an address was given by lodge grand master M. W. John Stewart. This imposing building was added to the National Register of Historic Places in 1980. This street was once called Bergh Straet, Dutch for "Hill Street." It had its current name by 1792.

Loudon Road
(and Loudonville Road)

One can follow Loudonville Road north to Loudon Road, which then runs to the community of Loudonville. Loudonville used to be called Ireland's Corners. Not named after the country, this settlement was named for Elias Ireland, who, in 1832, purchased land there from Stephen Van Rensselaer III. Ireland's Corners was renamed Loudonville in 1871. Loudonville and these streets are named for John Campbell, 4th Earl of Loudoun.

Campbell was born May 5, 1705, in Scotland, and when his father died, Campbell inherited his father's rank and privilege, becoming 4th Earl of Loudoun. He assembled a dozen infantry companies and fought in the Jacobite Rising of 1745, which lasted until the spring of 1746. This invasion was an attempt by Charles Edward Stuart to reinstate rule by the House of Stewart over the British government. Ten years after the failed Jacobite Rising, Campbell went to the New World to serve as commander in chief and governor general of Virginia during the French and Indian War. Campbell then served in combat when the Spanish invaded Portugal during the early 1760s. He returned to the United Kingdom, became governor of Edinburgh Castle, and was promoted to general. He died April 27, 1782. Loudon Road used to be called Plank Road because it was surfaced with wooden planks that helped wagons and coaches stay out of the mud.

Loudonville Road

See Loudon Road.

Lowell Street

Communities in Florida, Indiana, Maine, Massachusetts, Michigan, Minnesota, North Carolina, and Ohio are named for Francis Lowell. Lowell Street, built prior to 1940, likely honors this man. The Lowell name has been long-established in Boston. The first Lowell arrived in that city on June 23, 1639. Lowells have served as judges, lawyers, philanthropists, university presidents, politicians, writers, military officers, and Continental Congress members

Francis Lowell was born April 7, 1775, to John Lowell II and Susanna Cabot Lowell in Newburyport, Massachusetts. A well-educated man, Lowell graduated from Phillips Academy and Harvard University. After leaving Harvard University he became an international shipping merchant based in Boston. During the early 1800s he visited Scotland and England to see how they ran textile production. Memorizing construction of the machines and how they worked, he returned to the United States to build his own textile industry that took raw cotton and quickly and efficiently turned it into cloth, a process that remained a chief component of the American economy well after his death. Francis Lowell died August 10, 1817, and was first buried in the Central Burying Ground of Boston Common. In 1894, the City of Boston was building a subway line under Tremont Street, his tomb was discovered, and he was reinterred in Boston's Forest Hills Cemetery.

Lower Pine Lane

See East Pitch Pine Road.

Ludlow Alley

Thomas Ludlow and Nana Ludlow, who are honored within this street name, were the first owners of 73 and 75 Clinton Avenue, which are adjacent to Ludlow Alley. Both buildings were built in 1845 and still stand. Ludlow Alley, first called Ludlow Avenue, was named in 1892. Little is known of the Ludlows. One Thomas Ludlow died in Albany on Christmas Day of 1900. But since he died at the age of 56, which means he was born in 1844, this cannot be the same Thomas Ludlow of Ludlow Alley fame. The name Ludlow combines the Old English river name Hlude with *hlaw*, meaning "roaring" and "hill."

Lupine Circle
(and Lupine Court)

The wild lupine is a beautiful flower that stands up to two feet in height, its neat rows of blue-purple pod-like flowers catching any eye. Flowers bloom from April to July, while preferred environments include fields and other dry, open areas. It grows throughout the East. Wild lupine is named so because it was once thought to deplete soil of nutrients—it would "wolf" nutrients out of soil. The Latin *lupus* means "wolf," and the word lupine is a corruption of that Latin word.

Lupine Court
See Lupine Circle.

Lyric Avenue
A fun name likely bestowed by a developer, a lyric, as a noun, is defined by *Merriam-Webster's Collegiate Dictionary* as "a lyric composition, specifically a lyric poem" and "the words of a song often used in plural." The word lyric dates to the 1580s and comes from the Middle French *lyrique* ("short poem expressing emotion"), the Latin *lyricus* ("of or for the lyre"), and the Greek *lyrikos* ("singing to the lyre"). Lyric Avenue was built prior to 1927.

M

Madison Avenue
(and Madison Avenue Extension, Madison Place)
Madison Avenue was formerly named Wolfe Street and Lydius Street. The first name honored British general James Wolfe, who fought in the War of Austrian Succession, Jacobite Rising, and French and Indian War. The second name memorialized Johannes Lydius, minister of the Albany Dutch Church. Its current name was made official May 20, 1867. Madison Avenue was the first asphalt-paved street in Albany, being surfaced in 1890.

Madison Avenue, its extension, and Madison Place are named for James Madison Jr., born March 16, 1751, in Port Conway, Virginia. He was the first-born of a dozen children. Madison was tutored at a young age and attended the College of New Jersey, today's Princeton University, and graduated in 1771. Beyond following this college's curriculum, Madison concentrated on public speaking and debating. After graduation he remained at the college to study politics, law, and Hebrew under John Witherspoon, president of the college. Besides being president of the United States from 1809 to 1817, Madison served as member of the Continental Congress, leader of the Virginia Assembly, leader of the House of Representatives, and secretary of state. He helped frame the Virginia Constitution of 1776 and signed the Declaration of Independence (he's known as the "Father of the Constitution"). A true patriot, Madison coauthored the Virginia Statute for Religious Freedom; the Bill of Rights (he's known as the "Father of the Bill of Rights," too); and, with Alexander Hamilton and John Jay, the Federalist Papers. Madison led the country during the War of 1812. Before that conflict he was a colonel in the Virginia Militia. Madison never saw combat, and this was attributed to his size. Standing five-foot, four inches tall and never tipping a scale into the triple digits, Madison is the smallest president we've ever had.

James Madison Jr. died June 28, 1836, and was buried in the Madison Family Cemetery at his Montpelier Estate in Montpelier Station, Virginia. A note written by Madison, which was opened after his death, rang with patriotism, which came not as a surprise to its readers. He wrote, "The advice nearest to my heart and deepest in my convictions is that the Union of the States be cherished and perpetuated."

Madison Avenue Extension
See Madison Avenue.

Madison Place
See Madison Avenue.

Magazine Street
Magazine Street is named after a powder magazine. A 1937 article titled "Historical Name Dropped in Redesignating Street" told the story best, reporting that Magazine Street

> derived its name from a powder magazine established there during the American revolution. Historical records of the city reveal that in the pine covered sand plains to the west of the city, the military authorities of Albany during the Revolutionary War buried huge stores of powder. Tories abounded in the Mohawk Valley, and the authorities fearing surprise Indians attacks, decided on the stores as an emergency precaution against invasion. Residents claim having found evidence, even in recent years, where the magazine was located.

Powder magazines stood at Maiden Lane and State Street during the 1750s. Another one was placed in 1794 about where today's Hawk Street is. The word magazine is also reputed to mean "barn," this term used by pioneering French hunters. This is how the City of Magazine, Arkansas, got its name. Albany's Magazine Street opened in 1871. Manhattan's Magazine Street is named so because a powder magazine was located there, too.

Magnolia Terrace

Of the 200 species of magnolia trees, most of them live in temperate and tropical regions, and only two are native to New York. These are yellow-poplar (also called tuliptree and tulip-poplar and incorrectly called "popple") and cucumbertree (also called cucumber magnolia). Yellow-poplars grow to eye-popping sizes. Enormous specimens exceeding six feet in diameter and more than 120 feet in height can be found within Great Smoky Mountains National Park and Joyce Kilmer Memorial Forest in the South. This, however, is child's play. William Harlow stated this species can grow up to twelve feet in diameter and 200 feet tall. This species appears even more dramatic and graceful because with many yellow-poplars the bottom sixty feet of the trunk have no branches. Harlow described this tree well, writing that it is "unsurpassed in grandeur by any other eastern broadleaved tree." "Magnolia" is the most common street name in both Mississippi (The Magnolia State) and Louisiana. Mississippi has 172 of them while Louisiana has 175.

Magnolia Terrace was built in 1910. A real estate advertisement from that year stated that "the new boulevard is being laid extra wide, thereby insuring lots of air which is the purest in Albany coming direct from Helderbergs, which are plainly visible. All large lots, spacious center plush grass, boulevard set out with white and pink magnolia trees and flower beds." Prospective buyers were given "a free souvenir" from the realtors if these people showed up on a Sunday or Monday.

Maguire Avenue

Francis Maguire was first pastor of Sacred Heart of Jesus in Albany, and he lives on through this street. This church initially stood on Erie Street, and attendees first gathered there during the summer of 1874 when Maguire was appointed. Their second church, which stands today, had its cornerstone laid in 1876 and was opened during the spring of 1880. It's on Walter Street between North First Street and North Second Street, less than three blocks from Maguire Avenue. Maguire was born in Albany in 1846, attended Lawson's Select School, Manhattan College, and Saint Joseph's Seminary, and became ordained in 1872. He preached in Syracuse, Saratoga Springs, Rome, Fonda, Amsterdam, and Valatie and was president of the Catholic Young Men's National Union. Maguire Street, along with nearby Brady Avenue, was built in 1950.

Maiden Lane

Modern-day Maiden Lane appeared on maps as early as 1676. "Rom Straet," today's Maiden Lane, was portrayed on a parchment map produced by the French that year. "Joncaer Straet," today's State Street, was shown on this map, too. This makes these two Albany streets the first two ever identified by name on a map. The story concerning the naming of this lane, as told by *The Knicker-bocker News*, is far-fetched. Writers stated that "the Dutch dictionary lists rom as a corruption of rong, which is the same as the English rung, the crosspiece of a ladder. Maiden Lane's steep grade and narrowness might have suggested a ladder to the burghers." Another story is that Maiden Lane used to be called Rom Street, which was a corruption of the word rum, of which there was plenty in old-time Albany. Your author could believe these stories, but only after a few glasses of "rom."

The name Maiden Lane dates to 1725, found in Albany Common Council minutes from that year. New York City has its own Maiden Lane. Michael Pollak, in *The New York Times*, wrote that it was initially "a footpath beside a pebbly brook" where one side of it had "a gentle, grassy slope, which made it a good place to wash and bleach laundry. The task was usually given to the young girls of the family," i.e., maidens. The Dutch name for this New York City street was *Maagde Paatje*, which translates to Maiden Lane. St. Paul's Maiden Lane gets its name from an English street of that name that was the home of François-Marie "Voltaire" Arouet (1694–1778), French author and philosopher.

Main Street

One would be hard-pressed to find an American city that does not have a Main Street. In this case, the word main is a synonym for middle. To the north of Main Street is North Street. To the south is Center Street and South Street. The "Main" title is the sixth most common street name in New York with 228 of them spread across the state.

Manning Boulevard
(and Manning Square, North Manning Boulevard, South Manning Boulevard)

While Manning Square is named for the Manning family in general, the Manning boulevards are named for Daniel Manning. The first of this family to arrive in Albany was John Manning, Daniel's father, who was born in 1791, arrived in the city in 1814, and died there April 3, 1837. John was married to Eleanor Oley Manning, who was born in 1799 and died in 1875. They had three children: Maria Van Antwerp (1829–1897), Daniel (1831–1887), and John Baker (1833–1908).

Daniel Manning was born in Albany on May 16, 1831, and was the father of four children (the most notable one being Albany mayor James Hilton Manning). At age 11 he quit school and served as a state assembly page, and he began working for the *Albany Atlas*, which later became the *Albany Argus*. Manning became editor and owner in 1865. That same year he became president of Albany's National Commercial Bank. He served as chairman of the New York Democratic Committee in 1881 and resigned from this position in 1885 to become secretary of the treasury. He was appointed by Grover Cleveland and remained secretary of the treasury until resigning in February 1887. Daniel Manning died December 24, 1887, in New York City and was buried in Albany Rural Cemetery. He had been married to Mary Little Manning (1832–1882) and Mary Margaretta Fryer Manning (1844–1928). An 1889 map of the Pine Hills Neighborhood identified South Manning Boulevard as Hawkins Avenue, named for a local farmer of that last name. Name change took place during the 1930s. The northern section of North Manning Boulevard used to be called New York Central Avenue since it led towards the New York Central Railroad yard.

Manning Square
See Manning Boulevard.

Manor Street
The manor this street references is the Van Rensselaer Manor House, a brick residence built by Stephen Van Rensselaer II in 1765. The land that the manor stood on was annexed to the city in 1815, and Stephen Van Rensselaer IV remodeled the building during the 1840s. By the 1870s the manor was abandoned. Most of this building was dismantled and relocated to Massachusetts's Williams College in the 1890s by architect Marcus Reynolds, a cousin of the Van Rensselaers. Williams College was Reynolds's alma mater. The manor house then faced a sad, insulting death. It served as a fraternity house before it deteriorated to a point beyond repair and was destroyed in 1973. Sections of the 1765 interior were preserved and are on display at The Metropolitan Museum of Art.

Maple Avenue
(and Maple Street, Mapleridge Avenue, Maplewood Street)
The maple is the most common state tree. New York, Vermont, West Virginia, and Wisconsin have the sugar maple, while Rhode Island has the red maple. Other species that grow in New York, either naturally or after being introduced, include silver, Norway, boxelder, black, striped, planetree, and mountain. Sugar maples and Norway maples are common throughout the Capital Region. The next time you are in the Capital Region and happen to look around, chances are very good that a maple will be within sight. "Maple" is the second most common street name in New York. There are 314 of them.

All self-respecting New Yorkers consume real maple syrup, not that Aunt Jemima, Mrs. Butterworth's, Log Cabin, or Hungry Jack junk that's made of corn syrup. As Christopher Ingraham wrote for *The Washington Post*, "Fake maple syrup resembles real maple syrup about as much as Velveeta resembles a good

Camembert." Yet Americans prefer fake syrup over real syrup. Ingraham's article conveyed that 75 percent of Americans choose fake over real, a figure that makes devotees of real maple syrup want to smash a pile of pancakes. Why this love for sweet fakery? Price. Fake syrup costs $8 a gallon while the real stuff costs $60 a gallon, which is twenty times the price of gasoline. Such high prices come from the great labor necessary to produce maple syrup. Trees must be tapped and sap collected, and then one must boil forty gallons of sap to produce one gallon of syrup because most of the sap is water. All species of maple, indeed all species of hardwoods, produce sap. The sugar maple is chosen because of its copious and reliable production of sap.

Maple Street
See Maple Avenue.

Mapleridge Avenue
See Maple Avenue.

Maplewood Street
See Maple Avenue.

Mariette Place
Mariette Place used to be called Marietta Place. The name Mariette Place dates to 1929, yet it didn't commonly appear in Albany newspapers until the mid-1950s. Meanwhile, the name Marietta Place dates to 1928 and was clearly the more common of the two names when being mentioned in early 1900s Albany newspapers. Within an official 1928 newspaper release regarding land being conveyed for construction of a street, it read that this street was "to be known as Marietta Place." The name change could be the result of a simple error, such as a typo. The communities of Marietta in Ohio and New York are named for Marie Antoinette of France (Marietta, Minnesota, gets its name from that Ohio city). Mariette Place may be named for this queen. This street was built in 1928, the year that John Klapp and Lisette Klapp conveyed land to the city for construction of this street with nearby Kelton Court and Dartmouth Street.

Antoinette was born Maria Antonia Josepha Johanna on November 2, 1755, in Austria to Emperor Francis I and Empress Maria Theresa. She was the last queen of France, a title she held due to the fact that her husband, King Louis XVI, Louis-Auguste, was king. The French Revolution dissolved their leadership. The revolution had a fitting nickname: The Terror. While the American Revolution of the 1770s and 1780s was led by men of character and intellect, the French Revolution of the 1780s and 1790s was led by mobs. Ann Coulter wrote of these mobs in *Demonic*:

> Inflamed by ugly gossip as well as food shortages [though Antoinette never said "let them eat cake"] and fiscal crises, the crowd began to detest the queen. She was called *l'Autrichienne*, meaning the Austrian, but with the stress on "chienne," meaning "bitch." In pamphlets and gossip, Antoinette was accused of being a nymphomaniac and lesbian, of holding sex orgies in the palace, and of engaging in unnatural acts with her dog and infant son . . . The mob was riled up; there was no time for calm reflection or consideration of evidence.

Armed with guns, axes, swords, and cannons, mob rule ruled. Revolutionaries led by the Jacobites imprisoned the king and queen and trashed the palace, threw out the weights and measurement system as well as the French calendar, dug up skeletons of past kings and queens and tossed them into the streets, burned people alive, firmly controlled access to religion, crushed religious artifacts and used the pieces to fill pot holes, hacked people to death (priests and prisoners were preferred victims), raped women, and guillotined thousands of citizens. On just one September day at least 8,000 Frenchmen were executed. Corpses were put on display, mutilated, or left to rot in the streets while body parts were cut off and worn by women for decoration. More than a half-million French citizens were murdered while 150,000 fled the country. Coulter concluded that "in terms of population loss, that would be the equivalent of the United States having a 9/11 attack every day for seven years." On January 21, 1793, King Louis XVI was executed by guillotine. His body was dumped in a ditch and dissolved with lime after citizens dipped their handkerchiefs in his blood. Marie Antoinette was beheaded October 16. Her final letter was penned for her sister, with the closing lines: "Farewell, my good and tender sister. May this letter reach you. Think always of me; I embrace you with all my heart, as I do my poor dear children. My God, how heart-rending it is to leave them forever! Farewell! Farewell!"

If Mariette Place is not named for Marie Antoinette, it's named for a much less important Marie or Maria, one whose historical claim was that she was the daughter of a developer. As one historian put it, "It seems that today all you need to get a street named for you is to be the builder's daughter."

Marinello Terrace

Marinello Terrace, built before 1928, is named for the Marinello family of builders. Anthony Marinello built many homes along Delaware Avenue and New Scotland Avenue as well as the Albany County Jail and Washington Park lake house. He was struck and killed by a driver on September 18, 1965, as he waited to attend early morning mass at Immaculate Conception Monastery on New Scotland Avenue. His son, Tom Marinello, now owns Marinello Construction.

Marion Avenue

The Louis Pratt residence was one of the first dwellings built in the Marion Avenue neighborhood. The first house on Marion Avenue was built in 1928 while the last one was built in 1964. Pratt also made his home at 6 North Pine Avenue. That house was built in 1890. He was a lawyer and alderman and cofounder of the Albany Land Improvement and Building Company, which built much of the Manning Boulevard Neighborhood. On October 28, 1949, Pratt died, but before he did so he named this street for his daughter, Marion. In 1888, the Albany Land Improvement and Building Company conveyed land to the city for construction of this street. A turnpike toll gate used to stand near where Marion Avenue meets Western Avenue. At that time this gate was posted at Albany's city limit.

Market Street

Most American cities have a Market Street, and they are usually aptly-named. Albany's original Market Street was Broadway. On Broadway, Charles Newman was operating Charles Newman and Sons wool mercantile by 1768. Other markets followed, including James and Joseph Caldwell's specialty food market. These brothers arrived in the New World from Ireland circa 1770. The Market House stood on this street by 1775 and was the designated rally point for citizens in case the city was attacked (one man beating a drum and another ringing a bell would alert Albanians). A brand new $1,110 market was built on this street in 1791. That same year John Fredenrich opened his meat market on Broadway near Maiden Lane.

Marlborough Court

In England's County Wiltshire one will find the town of Marlborough. This community is rumored to be the burial place of Merlin. Hence Marlborough may be a corruption of Merlin's Barrow, and hence the town's motto: "where now are the bones of wise Merlin." Marlborough Road in Brooklyn is named after the Marlborough Road near Saint James Park in London. If Marlborough Court is not named after the English town, then it at least imitates the Brooklyn road.

Marlborough Court is near the seven other "English streets" of Carlisle Court, Cheshire Court, Fordham Court, Kensington Place, Stanford Court, Victoria Way, and Windsor Place. The first home built within this cluster was at 23 Marlborough Court. It was constructed in 1930 for husband and wife Myron Tryon and Ada Tryon and their son, Harold Tryon. Myron planted trees there that year, and a massive ginko he planted survives today. Since this section of the city was then farmland, the Tryons had a two-story barn in which they kept their horses. Tryons lived in this house until 2003. The last house built on this street, 20 Marlborough Court, was the Privler home, built for Arthur A. Privler and his wife, Ida Privler, and finished in 1969. Marlborough Court was built with Carlisle Court, Fordham Court, and Stanford Court in 1929 and named by Ten Eyck Mosher Realty Group. Streets within this cluster likely comprise the final streets within the city to be paved. Paving projects took place in this area during the 1940s and 1950s.

Marsdale Street

Marsdale Street, which was built before 1927, used to be a continuous street. Now, mysteriously, the northeast section of it runs from Collins Place to the intersection of Ferndale Avenue and Hopewell Street. An interruption of Marsdale Street is then encountered. To pick up the continuation, one must travel to nearby Harding Street. Equally mysterious is why this street is named so. The "Mar" may be a reference to a name such as Maria, Mark, or Mary while the "s" may be used to show possession. "Dale" is likely a suffix.

Marshall Place

A dead-end street only 200 feet long, research has not revealed the history behind this street name. The name Marshall comes from the Middle English and Old French *mareschal*, meaning "marshal," as in one who cares for horses.

Marshall Street
(and South Marshall Street)

Marshall Street was laid out and named by Teunis Van Vechten. He did the same with accompanying Bertha Street, Hurlbut Street, Jeanette Street, Stanwix Street, and West Van Vechten Street. All are reportedly named for Van Vechten's family members. Within this neighborhood the names Bertha Street, Corlaer Street, Marshall Street, and Twiller Street were made official with a 1915 city ordinance. Despite a thorough genealogical search, no person named Marshall, first name or last, was found to be related to Van Vechten.

Since no Van Vechten relation was found, it's possible that the Marshall streets are named for a founding father, like so many Albany streets are. The founding father this time is John Marshall. He was born September 24, 1755, in present-day Virginia to Thomas Marshall and Mary Isham Keith Marshall, a couple who had fourteen other children. Marshall was educated at home by his parents and a clergyman, attended an academy for a short time, and read books like there was no tomorrow. He joined a Virginia minuteman regiment as an officer in 1775 and enlisted in the Continental Army the following year. He served under George Washington in New Jersey, New York, and Pennsylvania, and he survived the infamous 1777/78 winter at Valley Forge while at war with the British. He practiced law in 1780 in Virginia after studying under George Wythe, was elected to this state's House of Delegates, was a House of Representatives member from Virginia, and was appointed secretary of state by John Adams in 1800.

Then his real work began: Marshall served as chief justice of the United States from 1801 to 1835, being nominated by Adams. This 34-year-long tenure makes Marshall the longest-serving chief justice ever. He produced more than 1,000 decisions, and wrote more than half of them himself. He served under six presidents—John Adams, Thomas Jefferson, James Madison Jr., James Monroe, John Quincy Adams, and Andrew Jackson—and his most important constitutional cases included *Marbury v. Madison* (1803), *United States v. Peters* (1809), *Fletcher v. Peck* (1810), *Martin v. Hunter's Lessee* (1816), *Dartmouth College v. Woodward* (1819), *McCulloch v. Maryland* (1819), *Cohens v. Virginia* (1821), *Gibbons v. Ogden* (1824), and *Worcester v. Georgia* (1832). John Marshall, author of the five-volume *Life of Washington*, died in Philadelphia on July 6, 1835, and was buried in Shockoe Hill Cemetery in Richmond, Virginia. He is memorialized within the names of American high schools, colleges, law schools, counties, communities, parks, mountains, and, of course, streets.

Marwill Street

At least one source stated that the name Marwill combines two first names, just as Berncliff Avenue combines Bernard and Clifford and Wilan Lane combines William and Ann. This street, which was built before 1929, reportedly combines the names Maria and William, the children of local farmer Bernhardt Noeckle, who owned land where Marwill Street now is. Maria actually lived on this street during the 1930s. At least one source listed the name connected to this street as being Nicolls, not Noeckle. In 1876, B. Nicolls owned six acres where Marwill Street now is. However, no relationship between a Maria, a William, and a B. Nicolls could be established. To add to this mystery, Census records revealed a Barnard Nichols living in the Town of Bethlehem in 1900 (the area where he lived would later become part of the City of Albany). At that time he was 59 years old, was married to 48-year-old Anna Nichols, and had four children. This sounds like our man. But, alas, none of his children were named Maria or William. Noeckle's children seem to be the eponyms of this street.

Marwood Street

In the same way that Betwood Street is named for Betty Besch, Deerwood Court is named after deer, and Norwood Avenue is named after the north woods, Marwood Street likely employs a name such as Maria, Mary, or Margaret, with the addition of "wood." This street was built prior to 1927, yet its name source remains a mystery.

Matilda Street

The story your author encountered that detailed naming of the four "Ten Eyck streets" turned out to be bogus. It was stated that Matilda Street is named for Matilda Ten Eyck, the supposed daughter of Peter Ten Eyck and Leonard Ten Eyck. Right from the beginning your author was suspicious. A child who had two fathers and no mother? Matilda Street is actually named for Margaret Matilda Haswell Ten Eyck. She was born April 4, 1837, in Bethlehem Center to Henry Haswell and Elizabeth Trowbridge Haswell. She entered the Ten Eyck family by marrying Abraham Cuyler Ten Eyck, and they had three children: Jacob Lansing, Cuyler, and Peter Gansevoort. Matilda died June 18, 1932, and was buried in Albany Rural Cemetery. The other three Ten Eyck streets are Cuyler Avenue, Kate Street, and Ten Eyck Avenue, which were all built in 1910.

Maxwell Street

More than sixty Maxwells are buried in Albany Rural Cemetery, and thirty headstones date to 1900 or earlier. Any of these Maxwells could be honored through this street. The spot where Maxwell Street was built was still an expansive, pristine meadow in 1931. Construction of this street soon followed. The name Maxwell dates to the early 1100s and was recorded as Mackeswell, meaning "Mack's spring."

McAlpin Street

McAlpin was a common name in Albany by at least the early 1900s. By 1914, at least two dozen McAlpins were living in the city. McAlpin Street, built before 1927, is consigned as a mystery when addressing its history.

McArdle Avenue

The McArdell family, for whom this street is probably named, had their house shown on Gerrit Witbeck's *Sketch of Roads, Streams, and Localities of Watervliet* map from 1850. This home was within the present-day fourth ward, less than a mile from today's McArdle Avenue. John McArdell was living in Albany County by 1820, while Joseph and Patrick McArdell were living in this city's second ward by 1830.

The first McArdles to arrive in Albany were likely members of Joseph McArdle's family. He was born in Ireland during 1779, immigrated to America, married twice, had one son, and died August 26, 1851. He was buried in Saint Agnes Cemetery. The most famous McArdle grave in this cemetery is that of John McArdle (1814–1874), who was a lieutenant colonel within the New York State Militia, restaurant owner, and philanthropist. McArdles, and those with variants of this name, are buried in Kenwood Cemetery, Waterford Rural Cemetery, and Albany Rural Cemetery. The McArdle Avenue neighborhood—which includes Beverly Avenue, Pennsylvania Avenue, Wilkins Avenue, and sections of Thornton Street and Colonie Street—was built circa 1912.

McCartney Drive

Chester McCartney and Bill Reddy were developers who owned land where McCartney Drive now is, and they built the Shaker Heights Neighborhood off nearby Shaker Road. The naming of McCartney Drive took place circa 1970. McCartney was a lifelong resident of Albany, specifically residing in the Holy Cross section of the Pine Hills Neighborhood. He lived close to Holy Cross Church on Western Avenue, and property for this place of worship was donated to the Albany Catholic Diocese by McCartney and his wife. The name McCartney is a form of the Irish name Mac Artnaigh and the Scottish name Mac Artaine and is related to the name Art, meaning "bear" and "hero."

McCartney's partner, Bill Reddy, with his wife, Lillian, similarly donated property where Saint Pius X Church stands in Loudonville. Reddy Lane in Loudonville memorializes this man, who lived on that street until the mid-1960s when he passed away. Reddy is known for naming Albany's Rosemary Drive for his great niece, Rosemary E. Redmond. Later came Rosemary Circle and Rosemary Drive Extension.

McCarty Avenue

Thomas McCarty owned land where McCarty Street is, and so this street is named for him. He possessed more than twenty lots, a handful of them butting up against the east side of Kimball Street, a street that no longer exists and was named for Jonathan Kimball. McCarty and Kimball had joint holdings in this part of the city. McCarty was co-owner of McCarty and Anderson Brickmakers, which was on Catherine Street, and he was the first person to live at 46 Morton Avenue, a brick home built circa 1857.

McCormack Road

McCormack Road dead ends at Normans Kill, which marks the southern boundary of the City of Albany. This street is named for Archibald McCormack. At the end of this street you can look across the waterway and see where McCormack Road continues south in the Town of Bethlehem. A bridge stood here until the 1980s and connected the two now-dead-end roads. A unique place name was employed at this bridge. This area was called Molasses Hollow because a cart full of this sweetener overturned on the bridge, spilling gallons of molasses into Normans Kill.

The spot where McCormack Road meets Normans Kill has detailed history dating to the 1600s. Here in 1672, Jan Van Baal bought a large chunk of woods and water from four Indian chiefs. Omie La Grange and Johannes Symonse Vedder then purchased part of the Van Baal Patent from Van Baal in 1716 for 250 pounds. They sold their 640 acres to Abraham Truax in 1723. Then Archibald McCormack arrived, having emigrated from Scotland with his wife in 1787. He bought the 640-acre Truax farm. Today's bridge site marked the middle of the property. A tiny settlement, McCormacks Bridge, then developed at the end of McCormack Road during the first half of the 1800s. Finally, Mrs. John Delaney, nicknamed Ethel, moved onto the land. She lived her entire life in a house that was built by her grandfather, Charles Moat, in 1850. The house was built on land that belonged to Moat's wife, who was a descendant of the McCormack family. At 305 McCormack Road stands the oldest building on this street. It was built between 1800 and 1825.

McCrossin Avenue
One James McCrossen (1831–1859) is buried in Albany Rural Cemetery, as is one Mary Parker McCrosson (unknown-1862), wife of John McCrosson. Yet a genealogical search did not result in any McCrossin, let alone one of note, being found within Albany. McCrossin Avenue's name history is not known. This street was built before 1916.

McDonald Road
McDonald Road was constructed prior to 1912 and is named for Donald McDonald. He was born July 26, 1869, to William McDonald and Alida McDonald. His grandfather, also named Donald McDonald, founded Albany's D. McDonald Meter Works in 1868. This company stood on Broadway and was later managed by William McDonald and the younger Donald McDonald.

Donald McDonald the younger worked in the gas industry for 51 years and, with Lynn Mason Scofield, invented and patented improvements to gas meters in 1904. He served in a dozen civic, business, and political roles: director of the American Meter Company, president of the American Gas Meter Company, president of the Albany Chamber of Commerce, president of the Society of Gas Lighting, director of the American Gas Association, president of the Fort Orange Club, Republican leader of the eighteenth ward, chairman of the Municipal Civil Service Commission, director and vice president of the New York State National Bank, chairman of the Gas Apparatus and Accessories Institute, incorporator of the Association of Gas Appliance and Equipment Manufacturers, and director of the Union Trust Company of Albany. In this last position he served alongside Grange Sard Jr., for whom Sard Road is named. McDonald Road and Sard Road are properly set next to each other.

Donald McDonald died of a heart attack October 8, 1937, at his home at 888 Park Avenue in Manhattan. He was interred in Albany Rural Cemetery. A 1937 edition of the *Times Union* commented on this man's death: "Success marked Mr. McDonald's undertakings. He had the capacity of work and leadership. Like many of our successful industrialists, he went as a youth into a factory and mastered a trade and problems of an industry." A beautiful Queen Anne brick home that stands at 727 Madison Avenue, one mile from McDonald Road, was built for McDonald circa 1882. This home stayed in the family until 1915.

McKinley Street

Named for William McKinley Jr., this street, built in 1911, is in good political company. Near it runs Roosevelt Street, Lincoln Avenue, Cleveland Street, Garfield Place, Grant Avenue, Van Buren Street, and Washington Avenue, each named for presidents. McKinley was 25th president of the United States, serving from 1897 to 1901. He is one of four presidents to be assassinated, the others being Abraham Lincoln (in 1865), James Garfield (1881), and John F. Kennedy (1963).

McKinley was the seventh child born to his family in Niles, Ohio. Born January 29, 1843, his parents were William McKinley and Nancy McKinley, who were of English and Scottish-Irish descent, respectively. They had initially settled in Pennsylvania before moving to Ohio. After graduating from school in 1859, McKinley attended Allegheny College in Pennsylvania yet acquired intense freshman blues. After a year away from his parents the homesick McKinley returned to Ohio depressed and ill. He then attended Ohio's Mount Union College, but he didn't graduate from that university either. When the Civil War started, McKinley enlisted as a private in the Poland Guards (named after a village in Ohio, not the country) and saw combat in West Virginia, Virginia, and Maryland. He attained the rank of brevet major. It was during McKinley's military training that he met future president Rutherford Hayes. The two became lifelong friends. Post-war, McKinley studied under a lawyer in Ohio and enrolled in Albany Law School. Fidgety when it came to academics, he remained in Albany less than a year yet graduated, arrived back in Ohio, passed his bar exam, and opened his own practice. Moving into politics, partly because he looked up to his successful friend, Hayes, McKinley served as House of Representatives member from Ohio, representative of the Republican National Committee, chairman of the Committee on Resolutions, chairman of the Ways and Means Committee, governor of Ohio, and, of course, president of the United States.

On September 6, 1901, McKinley strolled into the Temple of Music on the grounds of the Buffalo Pan-American Exposition not knowing an assassin lay in wait. Anarchist and Polish immigrant Leon Czolgosz shot the president twice in the abdomen. The crowd swarmed Czolgosz, yet McKinley called the foaming mob off, which probably saved the assassin from being torn to pieces.

McKinley's health improved during the following few days, and a full recovery was predicted. But the president took a turn for the worse. On September 13, Vice President Theodore Roosevelt Jr., who was camping in the Adirondack Mountains at the time, was alerted via telegram that things were not looking good for McKinley. This message started Roosevelt's famous nighttime dash from the wilderness to the train station at North Creek. During the early hours of September 14, Roosevelt was informed he had become president of the United States. The day before, September 13, at 2:15 AM, President William McKinley had died of gangrene and blood poisoning. Nine days after the president's death, Czolgosz was put on trial, found guilty, and executed via the electric chair. The corpse was tossed into a pool of acid and liquefied so there would be no remains. Meanwhile, 100,000 citizens viewed McKinley's body in the Capitol Rotunda. William McKinley Jr. was buried in West Lawn Cemetery in Canton, Ohio. This man had the highest peak in North America, 20,310-foot Mount McKinley, named for him until August 2015 when President Barack Obama officially changed it to what the Athabaskan Indians knew it by and what pretty much everyone called it anyway: Denali, "The High One." McKinley was featured on the United States $500 bill, which is no longer in circulation.

McKown Street

McKownville is a hamlet in the Town of Guilderland, which butts up against the City of Albany. McKown Street, and nearby McKown Park, borrows this hamlet's name. The hamlet is named for John McKown and his family. McKown came to the New World from County Londonderry, Ireland, during the mid-1700s, though he was originally from Scotland. His farmhouse, built circa 1815, stood near today's intersection of McKown Road and Short Street outside Albany, and he leased Five Mile Tavern (built in 1765 and likely named so because it was five miles from downtown Albany) where today's University at Albany Indian Quad stands. His son, William McKown, built and ran a tavern at the present-day intersection of Western Avenue and Fuller Road. This tavern was built in 1790 and burned to the ground in 1917. William served as Guilderland town supervisor from 1813 to 1824.

Meade Avenue

The Meade family used to live where this street now is. Meade Avenue is an extension of Hillcrest Avenue, and the steep, dramatic rise on Hillcrest Avenue used to be known as Meade Hill. There are four Meades buried in Albany Rural Cemetery. The oldest grave is that of James Meade, who was born in Albany in 1879 and died March 24, 1910. The name Meade noted one who made the drink of this name or lived near a meadow.

Meadow Lane
(and West Meadow Drive)

When either or both of these streets were laid out, they may have passed through meadows. Or these names are the creations of daydreaming developers who needed quaint titles. This latter theory is supported by the fact that both sides of Normans Kill, which Meadow Lane abuts, are consistently forested, save for farmers' small fields. West Meadow Drive is in the Dunes Neighborhood where generic, pretty names are typical.

Melrose Avenue

In 1913, land was conveyed to the city for construction of Melrose Avenue and nearby Edgewood Avenue, Fairlawn Avenue, Hawthorne Avenue, Homestead Avenue, Laurel Avenue, and Terrace Avenue. These seven streets were probably built that year. As late as 1936 there were two ponds on Melrose Avenue's north side, and they covered today's Hawthorne Avenue, Fairlawn Avenue, and Terrace Avenue. These ponds were used for ice harvesting. Melrose Avenue runs on top of an old Albany and Schenectady Railroad bed, hence its straight course.

The communities of Melrose Park in Illinois and Melrose in New York take their names from Melrose Abbey in Scotland. So does the Bronx's Melrose Avenue. Melrose is a town and civil parish in Scotland's County Roxburghshire. Melrose Abbey, officially named Saint Mary's Abbey of Melrose, was founded in 1136 and constructed during the decade that followed, employing Gothic architecture and a layout shaped like Saint John's cross. The building was ravaged by at least a few attacks, the worst of them taking place during the 1300s, yet it was rebuilt after each battle except the last one that took place during the 1540s. The abbey was abandoned during the late 1500s. The state took control of the ruins in 1918, and the remains of this abbey, a major visitor attraction, are quite beautiful. The name Melrose comes from the Old Welsh or Brythonic *mailros*, meaning "bare peninsula."

Mercer Street

There are two sections of Mercer Street. One runs off Delaware Avenue and the other stretches from South Lake Avenue to Partridge Street. Mercer Street may carry a common surname. Empson, in *The Street Where You Live*, described St. Paul's Mercer Street as "a common place name with a touch of elegance gained from the French *mer*, meaning 'sea.'" A much stronger case is that Albany's Mercer Street is named for Hugh Mercer. Born January 17, 1726, in Aberdeenshire, Scotland, to William Mercer and Ann Monro Mercer, Mercer was a surgeon who fled Scotland to settle in present-day Mercersburg, Pennsylvania, which is named for him. He practiced medicine and fought in the French and

Indian War. After the war, he practiced in Fredericksburg, Virginia. Since he was friends with George Washington, one of his patients was Washington's mother, Mary Ball Washington.

Mercer joined the Revolutionary War as a brigadier general and performed marvelously throughout the war. At the Battle of Princeton on January 3, 1777, his horse was shot out from underneath him, and he was quickly surrounded by British soldiers. Refusing to surrender, Mercer drew his sword and fought yet was cut down by bayonets and strikes to the head. Terribly wounded, he was leaned against an oak where he remained near the battle to observe his men. This tree became known as the Mercer Oak, which is the centerpiece of the seal of Mercer County, New Jersey. Stewart, in *Names on the Land*, told this place name tale well: "Where they braved the passage of the Delaware that winter night is still called Washington Crossing. The next morning they fought the Hessians at the town which William Trent had founded, and that was the first place they ever beat a German army. Then they fought the British at Princeton. General Mercer fell there in the hour of victory, and his name came to stand upon that county." Hugh Mercer died from his wounds January 12, 1777. He was buried in Laurel Hill Cemetery in Philadelphia. Communities and counties in Illinois, Kentucky, Maine, Missouri, New Jersey, Ohio, Pennsylvania, and Wisconsin honor this man. The British word mercer describes one who is a dealer of cloth, while the Old French *mercier* means "trader."

Mereline Avenue

This street carries an unpopular spelling of the feminine name Marilyn. Mereline Avenue, built before 1922, is a "first name street" just like Eileen Street, Linda Court, and Clayton Place are. The woman this street is named for has yet to be identified, though.

Mill Road
(and Mill Street)

"Mill" place names are ever-spreading (there are 1,473 creeks named Mill in the U.S.). The Empire State alone has mountains, hills, lakes, ponds, towns, settlements, and scores of waterways with this moniker. Most "Mill" features sweep us back to the days of gristmills and sawmills. When the wilderness was settled, the first thing that was built was a sawmill—before schools were raised, before homes we built, before farmlands were cleared. Wilcox reported that "the milling industry began very early in the Albany region, probably even before the settlement of Rensselaerswyck." The first waterway in Albany to host a mill was Normans Kill. Fittingly, Mill Road is next to Normans Kill, and Mill Street is near the Hudson River at the ancient location of Mill Creek. In 1832, Mill Creek hosted a linseed oil mill, a fulling mill, a sawmill, and a gristmill.

Mill Street
See Mill Road.

Miller Avenue
In 1924, Miller Avenue was laid out with nearby Cottage Avenue, Edinburgh Avenue, Hazelhurst Avenue, Hillcrest Avenue, Highland Avenue, Homestead Avenue, Pleasantview Avenue, Russell Road, Summit Avenue, Taft Avenue, Villa Avenue, and Wellington Avenue. This was when parts of Guilderland were bought by the Wilbur Land Company, which was owned by Jacob W. Wilbur.

Morris Miller could be honored within Miller Avenue. He was born in New York City on July 31, 1779, to Rutger Bleecker Miller, who was a politician, and Mary Forman Seymour Miller. He graduated from Union College in 1798 and become Governor John Jay's secretary. He later served as president of the Village of Utica, House of Representatives member from New York, and judge of the Court of Common Pleas. Morris Miller died November 16, 1824, and was buried in Albany Rural Cemetery. This name translates literally.

Milner Avenue
(and Milner Court)
Milner Avenue opened in 1939 with 23 new Wilson Sullivan Company brick homes built along it. An advertisement from 1940 noted that "a few short months ago" the Milner Avenue area "was a bare strip of land." These streets carry an Albany surname that has been within the city since the mid-1800s. One of the first Milners to reach Albany County was John Milner, who was born in County Cheshire, England, on February 10, 1800. In 1832 he immigrated to the U.S. with his children, in-laws, and wife, Elizabeth Libby Turner Milner. They likely arrived aboard the *Glasgow*, which left Liverpool on June 16 of that year. John Milner died April 14, 1878, in the Town of Berne and was buried in the Turner Burying Grounds.

Milner Court
See Milner Avenue.

Mohawk Street
The Mohawk Indians were part of Five Nations, also known as the Iroquois Confederacy and Iroquois League. Other members of Five Nations were the Cayuga, Seneca, Onondaga, and Oneida. Five Nations became Six Nations in 1715 when the Tuscarora joined. The Mohawk were vicious fighters—the term Mohawk means "man eater." The original name for this tribe was *Kanien'kehāka*, meaning

"people of the flint place," which referenced their possession of flint, which was used in tool making. The Mohawk were known as "The Keepers of the Eastern Door" and lived along the St. Lawrence River, Lake Ontario, and the Mohawk River, which is obviously named for them. They also spread east to Vermont, south to Pennsylvania, and west to Oneida lands. The Mohawk were visiting present-day Albany as early as 1614 to trade with Dutch settlers. Their range was greatly reduced, like their population, because of war and disease, which took hold during the early 1600s. Most of the remaining Mohawk moved to Canada. Today, at least 10,000 people of Mohawk descent live near the U.S.-Canada border of New York where the St. Regis Mohawk Reservation is. Mohawk Street was called Hudson River Avenue until February 13, 1871. Therefore, Mohawk Street could specifically be named after the 150-mile Mohawk River. Genesee Street, which could be named for another New York river, is next to Mohawk Street.

Mohican Place

Also acceptably spelled Mahican, the Mohican are part of the Eastern Algonquian tribe. Their territory once spread from the Hudson River to Lake Champlain, within the Catskill Mountains, and into western New England. The more powerful Mohawk drove the Mohican out of these regions and the Mohican, during the early 1800s, settled in Wisconsin with the Lenape. Before this, the Mohican centered themselves in western Massachusetts, specifically on present-day Stockbridge. Hence they were also called the Stockbridge Indians. Today, most Mohicans reside on a 22,000-acre reservation in Wisconsin and are part of the Stockbridge-Munsee Band of Mohican Indians. Like the Mohawk discussed in the Mohawk Street entry above, the Mohican were present when the Dutch, led by Henry Hudson and carried by the *Half Moon*, arrived in present-day Albany during the early 1600s. The name Mohican was coined in 1614. Much like the Mohawk, Cayuga, Seneca, Onondaga, and Oneida were part of Five Nations, the Mohican formed a confederacy of five tribes of their own, which encompassed fifty villages centered on the present-day Capital Region. During the Revolutionary War the Mohican sided with the American rebels, a fine choice.

Mohican culture is best known through James Fenimore Cooper's 1826 novel, *The Last of the Mohicans*, which was adapted into a 1992 blockbuster film and a lesser-known 1920 film. An excellent painting of a pre-European contact Mohican community is found in David Lithgow's circa 1939 "The Mohawk People," which can be found on the University at Albany's downtown graduate campus in their Theodore Fossieck Milne Alumni Room. The word Mohican stems from *Muh-he-ka-neew*, meaning "people of the continually flowing waters," which described the Hudson River. The Dutch recorded this ancient name as *Mahigan, Mahikander, Mahinganak, Maikan,* and *Mawhickon*. The Mohican language is extinct.

Mona Terrace

The Wilbur Land Company and St. John's Church conveyed land to the city for construction of Mona Terrace in 1915, the year it was built. Mona Terrace is located at the former site of the St. John's Church cemetery. This street carries the female name that's Irish for "noble one," Greek for "solitary one," and Old English for "moon." It's a shortened version of Monika, Ramona, and Simona. It's not known for whom Mona Terrace is named.

Monroe Street

Formerly known as Van Schaick Street, Monroe Street is named for James Monroe. He was born in Westmoreland County, Virginia, on April 28, 1758, to Spence Monroe and Elizabeth Jones Monroe. Monroe's father died when he, the younger Monroe, was 16 years old. Upon his father's death, Monroe inherited a modest plantation and enrolled in the College of William and Mary. He left campus to join the War for Independence. He entered the Continental Army as an officer and got to work immediately, his first mission being a raid on the governor's palace arsenal in Williamsburg, Virginia. The young pillagers came out with 300 swords and 200 rifles. He saw combat in New York, New Jersey, and Pennsylvania, completed the famous crossing of the Delaware River with George Washington, and was wounded during the Battle of Trenton.

After the Revolutionary War, Monroe studied law, and one of his mentors was none other than Thomas Jefferson. He passed his bar exam, practiced in Fredericksburg, Virginia, and married Elizabeth Kortright. They had three children together. After buying a bigger plantation, Monroe gained notoriety and entered politics. He served as member of the Virginia House of Delegates in 1782, delegate to the Congress of the Confederation from 1783 to 1786, and senator from Virginia from 1790 to 1794. Monroe became minister to France in 1794 but was soon fired by his brother-in-arms George Washington. Refusing to leave politics behind because of his and Washington's friction, he served as governor of Virginia, secretary of state, secretary of war, and then secretary of state again. He was president of the United States for two terms, from March 1817 to March 1825. This president, though he owned slaves and approved savage treatment of Indians, presented the Monroe Doctrine in 1823, this document authored by John Quincy Adams. The Monroe Doctrine recognized several South American countries as independent from European rule, these countries having recently declared independence from Spain and Portugal. The doctrine also made it clear that America did not want Russia entering the Pacific Northwest and that we would stop meddling in European affairs.

James Monroe died July 4, 1831, thus becoming the third president to ironically die on Independence Day. In 1826, presidents John Adams and Thomas Jefferson had both died on Independence Day. Monroe was first buried in New York City's Marble Cemetery. In 1858, he was reinterred within the President's

Circle of Hollywood Cemetery in Richmond, Virginia. His wife, Elizabeth, died in 1830. Beyond Monroe Street, this man is memorialized through counties, towns, cities, and many other streets.

Monrovia, the capital city of the country of Liberia, is named for Monroe. Liberia was a destination for freed American and Caribbean slaves who gained their freedom during the Monroe administration. Yet Liberia should not be specifically associated with emancipation since descendants of Western slaves make up only five percent of the country's 4.6 million citizens. And Liberia should not be associated with utopia built upon freedom. When freed Western slaves reached Africa, the first thing they did was subjugate native Africans, and there hasn't been any good news since. This country is now known for its civil wars, unemployment, drug culture, diseases, crime, corruption, and illiteracy. Vice News summarized Liberia colorfully but simply after arriving in Monrovia: "It's a post-Apocalyptic Armageddon with child soldiers smoking heroin, cross-dressing cannibals, systematic rape. It's total hell on Earth."

Montgomery Street

Continental Army general Richard Montgomery, for whom this street is named, has been called "America's First National Hero." That's quite a claim, yet one that holds up to scrutiny. A section of Montgomery Street used to be called a much less patriotic Marsh Street. The name Montgomery Street was featured on maps by 1794. A neat historical tidbit is that an ancient Montgomery Street sign remains bolted to the Albany Pump Station's eastern wall. This restaurant's parking lot is a former section of Montgomery Street.

Known best for his 1775 attack on Canada, Montgomery was born December 2, 1738, in County Dublin, Ireland, to Thomas Montgomery, a veteran of the British Army and member of Parliament. At 16, Montgomery enrolled in Trinity College yet did not graduate. He joined the British military at 18 to start a career that would span decades. In the French and Indian War he was promoted by General Jeffrey Amherst to lieutenant and then to regimental adjutant by General Robert Monckton. Montgomery was dispatched to the Caribbean where he again fought the French. Among the azure waters and white sand beaches he was promoted to captain by Lieutenant Colonel John Campbell. He fought the Spanish, allies of the French, in Havana. Gaining promotions, gunning down the enemy, and leading his men, Montgomery also fought in Pontiac's War in North America.

While on leave in Britain, Montgomery became close to three men, all Whigs, who wanted to give the colonists more freedom, something Britain surely did not want. When he missed an expected promotion in 1771 due to politics, Montgomery had had enough of the British military. The following year he set sail for the New World. He purchased a farm not far from New York City and married Janet Livingston in 1773. They moved north to Rhinebeck, and through his marriage into a Patriot family he identified as an American and a rebel. Gearing up for the revolution, Montgomery was made American brigadier general in 1775. A plan to attack Canada was made, and Montgomery would play a major role. Actually, he played a bigger role than anyone had anticipated. This man commanded the entire attack of Montreal when the intended commander, Major General Philip Schuyler, became ill during the siege of St. John's. Montgomery (since promoted to major general, though at the time he didn't know it) captured Montreal after months of fighting, yet was shot the last day of 1775 during an attack on the remaining British forces. With his sword drawn and rushing upon the enemy with an assault party, his last words were, "Come on, my good soldiers, your general calls upon you to come on!" Two American soldiers died by his side. With Montgomery gone, Benedict Arnold became commander of American forces in the area. His own attack fell apart with the death of Montgomery, and a hasty retreat was ordered.

On the first day of 1776, the British left the protection of their positions and started collecting the corpses. They came across an American officer and, with the help of an American prisoner, identified it as the body of Richard Montgomery. He was buried by the British on January 4. During the summer of 1818, the general's remains were moved from Quebec to New York and were interred at a monument for him at Saint Paul's Chapel in Manhattan. This officer, who gave his life for the revolution, is memorialized through dozens of counties, cities, towns, and streets across the United States. The name Montgomery combines the Old French *mont*, meaning "mountain," with the Germanic *guma* and *ric*, meaning "man" and "power."

Moore Street

James C. Moore owned land where his namesake street now is. He immigrated to America from Ireland circa 1871 and died during June 1901. This last name has at least three histories. It was a habitation name that noted someone who lived near a moor, which is a swamp; it noted someone with a swarthy complexion, coming from the Old French *more*, meaning "moor," as in a Muslim or Arab; and it was a form of the Gaelic name Mordha, meaning "proud."

There are two lines of Moores in Albany County. One line begins with an Englishman who lived in Ireland during the 1600s. The first of these Moores to reach Albany was William Moore, a direct descendant of this Englishman and the son of Hugh Moore. William Moore immigrated to the United States in 1828 with his wife, Jean Campbell Moore, whom he had married in 1821. They built their home on Broad Street not far from Moore Street.

Another line traces to Levi Moore, first of Dutchess County, New York, and later of Little Egg Harbor, New Jersey. A son of Levi was James Moore, who was born in Dutchess County. He settled in the Town of Berne outside of Albany to run a farm. He died April 17, 1813, after marrying Sibbel Hoag. His son, Joseph

Moore, remained in Albany County as a farmer and settled in a village called Quaker Street in Schenectady County. He died May 13, 1866, and was married to Harriet Williams. The most accomplished Moore of this line was Dr. Levi Moore, son of Joseph and Harriet. He was born in Quaker Street on January 28, 1827, and, like his father, was alumnus of Albany Medical College. Dr. Moore was president of the Albany County Medical Society and treated wounded soldiers during the Civil War. Dr. Levi Moore died in Albany on June 30, 1880. He lived on the corner of State and South Hawk streets. His home was sold to the state circa 1870 for $20,000, and most of this family relocated to the lower Hudson Valley. His son, Charles Henry Moore, also became a doctor after attending Albany Medical College.

Moreland Avenue
More than twenty Morelands are buried in Albany Rural Cemetery, and other Albany County cemeteries are home to a few other Morelands. However, this doesn't help decode Moreland Avenue, which was built before 1930. Moreland is an English and Scottish place name that means "swamp land."

Morris Street
Robert Morris Jr. is memorialized through this street. Born January 20, 1734, Morris was a signer of the Declaration of Independence, the Articles of Confederation, and the Constitution. Morris is an English, Welsh, Scottish, and Irish name that comes from the Old French name Maurice. This street opened in 1864.

Morris was born in Liverpool, England, as the son of Robert Morris and Elizabeth Murphet Morris. They immigrated to Oxford, Maryland, in 1747. Morris then moved to Philadelphia to stay with a friend of the family, Charles Greenway. Greenway arranged work for Morris. The up-and-coming rebel ended up working for Philadelphia merchant and mayor Charles Willing. Shortly after Willing died in 1754, his son, Thomas, accepted Morris as a business partner to create Willing, Morris, and Company, a shipping and banking operation. In 1769, Morris married Mary White. They had seven children. Then the investor entered politics. Morris served as member of the Pennsylvania Council of Safety, member of the Provincial Assembly, member of the Pennsylvania Legislature, federal superintendent of finance, member of the Constitutional Convention, and senator from Pennsylvania. He was chief financier of the American Revolution, and he helped establish America's first banking system. Morris also facilitated the smuggling of arms into America from France and set up a spy network for the rebels. After his political career, Morris purchased millions of acres of land in America yet went broke when a financial panic ensued. He was sent to debtor's prison and was released after a few years. Robert Morris Jr. spent his remaining years out of the public eye, dying May 9, 1806, in Philadelphia. He was buried at Christ Church in that city. Robert Morris University in Chicago and Robert Morris University near Pittsburgh are named for this man.

Morton Avenue

Washington Morton, who also went by George Washington Morton, has this street named for him. He was the husband of Cornelia Schuyler Morton and son-in-law of Philip Schuyler. Thus this street is one of the six "Schuyler streets" near the Schuyler Mansion, the other five being Alexander Street, Catherine Street, Elizabeth Street, Philip Street, and Schuyler Street.

Morton was born in Elizabethtown (today's Elizabeth), New Jersey, in 1774 to John Morton and Maria Sophia Kempe Morton. Morton served as a militia officer, graduated from Princeton University, and worked as a lawyer in New York City. He was a noted athlete. On a wager, he completed a continuous walk from Elizabethtown to Philadelphia, a distance of eighty miles, arriving in time for dinner. Morton fell in love with Cornelia Schuyler when the two met during the winter of 1796/97 at Cornelia's sister's home. Her sister was Elizabeth, who was married to Alexander Hamilton. Morton asked permission of Philip Schuyler to take Cornelia's hand in marriage. Schuyler sternly refused, and when Morton kept pestering him, the protective father of the hopeful bride threw the young man off the property and told him to not bother coming back. But young lovers find ways around angry fathers as easily as songbirds find their ways through the trees. Under cover of darkness the couple eloped during the fall of 1797, and traveling by foot, boat, and horse they arrived in Stockbridge, Massachusetts, to be married. Their love was not meant to last. Cornelia Schuyler died in Philadelphia on July 5, 1808, at the age of 32. Lost without his bride, Morton moved to France and was dead by 1810. Nearly the entire section of Morton Avenue was still dirt and stomach-churning cobblestones until 1900. That year this street was paved with vitrified bricks. Morton is a simple last name that combines the Old English *mor* and *tun*, which note "swamp" and "settlement."

Mount Hope Drive

This street is named after Mount Hope, a Van Rensselaer farm that stood in this section of Albany. In 1834, Ezra Prentice bought this farm and built a brick mansion there. He fittingly called his manor Mount Hope. Prentice retired in 1840 after serving as president of Commercial Bank, Albany-Susquehanna Railroad, and the New York State Agricultural Society. He also worked as a fur trader within Williams, Packer, and Company as well as Packer, Prentice, and Company. Ezra Prentice died at Mount Hope on July 10, 1876, at the age of 79 and was buried in Albany Rural Cemetery. Mount Hope was soon neglected. *Bicentennial of Albany* from 1886 reported that "for many years the farm and surroundings were the pride of its owner; but its former attractions are giving place to the march of improvement, which has already changed much of its wonted beauty and rural picturesqueness." By the mid-1900s, the grounds and building were in disrepair. The mansion was soon razed, and neighborhoods built over its grave. In 1965, the Common Council dedicated $125,000 for construction of Mount Hope Drive.

Mountain Street
See Fairview Avenue.

Mountainview Avenue
The mountains you can see from Mountainview Avenue are the Helderberg Mountains, also called the Helderberg Escarpment. This range west of Albany tops out at 1,822 feet. *Helderberg* is Dutch for "clear mountain" and "bright mountain."

Museum Road
There are a handful of museums in Albany, yet this road runs next to the New York State Museum. On the New York State Museum website, this facility is described as "a center of art, science, and history dedicated to exploring the human and natural history of the state." The museum was conceived April 15, 1836, when Governor William Marcy selected New York State Geological and Natural History Survey staff to collect the most interesting fossils, minerals, and rocks and display them inside one grand building. These collections were stored in the Old State House, managed by the State Cabinet of Natural History, between State Street and Lodge Street. The Old State House was demolished in 1855, and in 1870 a new facility was named the New York State Museum of Natural History. This museum was moved to the new State Education Building in 1912 and opened to the public in 1915, the dedication ceremony taking place December 29, 1916. Now part of the Empire State Plaza, the New York State Museum is set inside the Cultural Education Center, which was finished in 1976. The New York State Museum is the oldest (185 years and counting) and biggest (more than fifteen million artifacts set in more than 100,000 square feet with another 35,000 on the way) state museum in the country.

Myrtle Avenue
Formerly known as Mink Street, West Ferry Street, and Ferry Street, Myrtle Avenue is named after the myrtle bush, which is a showy ornamental. This street gained its current name in 1888. The most widely-planted myrtle is the crape myrtle because it's a compact yet showy bush that grows in a range of

conditions. Flower colors include red, purple, white, pink, or blue, depending on the species. Myrtle Avenue in Brooklyn was the first street in that borough to be graded and paved.

N

New Hope Terrace

New Hope Terrace, Rooney Road, and Jennings Drive are part of a 160-unit Albany Housing Authority development called North Albany Homes. Circa 1999, the fifty-year-old, 292-unit Corning Homes was demolished and new houses were built using a Department of Housing and Urban Development HOPE VI grant. The builder was New Jersey's Michaels Development Company. The name of this street reassured prospective tenants they were given "new hope" with a new home. The name may also reference the HOPE VI grant received. On July 13, 2002, a block party was held on Jennings Drive and Rooney Road to celebrate the first tenants moving in.

New Karner Road

Karner is a hamlet in the Town of Colonie that used to be called Center Station because it hosted a New York Central Railroad station, built 1831. Name change took place in 1880. This hamlet and New Karner Road carry the name of George Karner, who during the mid-1800s purchased land and laid out streets where the hamlet is. There are Karner Road and Old Karner Road in the Capital Region, too, but these aren't within Albany. There is also the Karner blue butterfly, an endangered species that gets its name from the hamlet. It's called the Karner blue butterfly because it was discovered in the hamlet—in the Pine Bush, specifically. It was identified by Vladimir Nabokov, a Russian writer, in 1862. Nabokov was a lepidopterist. That is, he studied moths and butterflies.

New Scotland Avenue
(and New Scotland Road)

These streets are named so because they lead towards the 58-square-mile Town of New Scotland, which was part of the Town of Bethlehem until April 25, 1832. The Town of New Scotland is named so because it was settled by Scots. The first settler was Teunis Cornelis Slingerland, who purchased Indian lands in the area in 1685, perhaps specifically 10,000 acres at Oneskethau Flats. Teunis Slingerland, grandson of Teunis Cornelis Slingerland, built the region's first mills and had his farmhouse constructed in 1762 on today's Route 32. He was born in 1723 and died in 1800. During the 1920s, Albanians were moving farther from the river, and New Scotland Avenue was one of their destinations. Rittner said this area during that era was "out in the sticks." New Scotland Road dates to the 1790s when it was a toll road.

New Scotland Road
See New Scotland Avenue.

Niblock Court
A short, lollipop-shaped street, Niblock Court carries an old-time Irish name. This street name was accepted by the city in 1948. Albany Rural Cemetery has nearly twenty Niblock graves, the oldest belonging to Robert Niblock, who was born in 1820 and died in 1852 in Albany. It has not been revealed which specific Niblock is honored by Niblock Court.

Noonan Lane
The prominent Noonans, and perhaps specifically Dorothea Noonan, are memorialized within Noonan Lane, where members of this family still live. Dorothea Noonan played a role in local politics for decades and was the right hand woman of Democrat Erastus Corning 2nd, who served as mayor from 1941 to 1983. His 42-year reign was ended by a fatal illness. Noonan and Corning's longtime connection began in 1937 when Corning was 28 years old and Noonan only 22. The up-and-coming politician oversaw the Scenic Hudson Commission at the time, and Noonan was his politically-appointed secretary. Beyond Corning she worked with senators Peter D'Allesandro, Julian Erway, and Joseph Zaretski and served as Albany County Democratic Women's Club president. Noonan was born in Albany in 1916 as the daughter of John McLean and Dorilla Rosalie Giguere and died November 14, 2003. She was the grandmother of Kirsten Gillibrand, Democrat senator from New York, who took office in 2009 after serving in the House of Representatives. She called her grandmother her role model and dedicated her 2014 *Off the Sidelines* to her. Gillibrand and her family live in the Town of Brunswick in Rensselaer County so they're within visiting distance of their relatives on Noonan Lane.

Norfolk Street
Norfolk Street is part of a cascade of Norfolk names. First there was County Norfolk, England (inhabited for more than 2,000 years). Then came the City of Norfolk in Virginia (founded 1682), the Town of Norfolk in Massachusetts (settled

1696), the Town of Norfolk in Connecticut (settled 1744), the Town of Norfolk in Missouri (since deserted, platted in 1836), the City of Norfolk in Nebraska (settled 1866), and the Town of Norfolk in New York (settled 1869). Then Albany's Norfolk Street was built and named circa 1915. Most of the streets near Norfolk Street—Philbrick Street, Leighton Street, Southern Boulevard, Kenosha Street, and Mountain Street—were built between 1900 and 1927. Norfolk Street was built across land of Mrs. W. Moore, who may have been Jean Campbell Moore, wife of William Moore, and the land of Jacob W. Wilbur.

Normanside Drive
(and Normanskill Street)

Normanside Drive and Normanskill Street are close to Normans Kill, which memorializes a Norwegian named Albert Andriese Bratt. *Noorman* is Dutch for "Norwegian," while *kill* is Dutch for "stream"—the Norwegian's stream. The earliest map to identify this man living along this stream is *Map of Albany County* from the early 1700s. This map labeled Normans Kill and showed the homes of Albert Andriese Bratt, Adrien Bratt, and Jan Bratt near the stream. Cute, little cottages were drawn next to each name. Bratt settled along this stream in 1636 and operated a farm and gristmill there. He rented two sawmills on this waterway between 1652 and 1672. Albert Andriese Bratt died June 7, 1686, yet the name lived on. Pearson, in *Contributions for the Genealogies of the First Settlers of the Ancient County of Albany, from 1630 to 1800*, dedicated no fewer than 78 entries to the Bratts.

Indians called this waterway *Tawasentha*, meaning "place of the many dead." This name survives in Guilderland's Tawasentha Park. Kiliaen Van Rensselaer wrote that the first mill in the Albany region was built on this stream, hence its former name of Mill Creek. Normans Kill was labeled Godyn's Kill, named for Samuel Godyn, partner of Kiliaen Van Rensselaer and member of the West India Company, on a map of Fort Nassau from the early 1600s. By 1763 there were more than twenty farms along Normans Kill. This stream is nearly fifty miles long, beginning near the Village of Delanson in Schenectady County and flowing into the Hudson River near the Port of Albany.

Normanskill Street

See Normanside Drive.

North Allen Street
(and South Allen Street)

The earliest mention of Allens in Pearson's *Contributions for the Genealogies of the First Settlers of the Ancient County of Albany, from 1630 to 1800* is John

Allen and Eleanor Sullivan Allen, who lived in Albany during the mid-1700s. John, likely their only child, was baptized January 22, 1758. Nearly 200 Allens are buried in Albany Rural Cemetery. Allen in Danish, German, and Swedish comes from the Germanic *adal*, meaning "noble," while the English and Scottish Allen stems from the Gaelic *ailin*, meaning "little rock." The name Allen has an intricate past, with Patrick Hanks and Flavia Hodges writing that it is "of great antiquity and obscurity." The Van Allens of Albany began with Pieter Van Halen, who was born in Holland, the Netherlands, circa 1630 and came to America aboard the *Gilded Beaver* in 1658 with his family. Pieter settled in Beverwyck and worked as a fur trader, justice of the peace, and tailor. He died during January 1674 in Kinderhook, New York.

These two streets have existed since the mid-1800s and used to be joined in one name: Allen Street. South Allen Street was built in 1884, and North Allen Street before then. There are three candidates for whom these streets may be named: Benjamin Allen, John Evert Van Allen, and Evert Van Allen. Benjamin Allen is best known for being the first headmaster of Albany Academy. He held this position for four years after serving as the principal of Connecticut's Plainfield Academy. Allen was born October 8, 1772, in North Kingstown, Rhode Island, as the son of Matthew Allen. He graduated from Brown University in 1797 and then worked as a tutor at that college. He taught at a university in Pennsylvania and then was a professor of mathematics and natural philosophy at Union College from 1800 to 1809. Benjamin Allen died in Hyde Park, New York, on July 20, 1836. He was buried at the Saint James Episcopal Churchyard in that village.

John Evert Van Allen was born during 1749 in Kinderhook, New York, as one of six sons of Adam Van Allen and Maria Roseboom Van Allen. He moved to Defreestville, New York, and worked as a farmer, civil engineer, surveyor, general store proprietor, justice of the peace, Rensselaer County assistant judge, New York assemblyman, and House of Representatives member from New York. He died February 27, 1807, and was buried in Bloomington Rural Cemetery in North Greenbush, New York. His home, the 1794 John Evert Van Alen House (yes, with one *l* because that's how that man's last name was spelled at times), stands on Washington Avenue in Defreestville and is listed on the National Register of Historic Places.

Evert Van Allen was a nephew of John Evert Van Allen (some sources state that Evert was the son of John, yet that is not the case, though John did raise Evert). Evert was born during August 1772 and lived in the John Evert Van Alen House. He was an officer in the New York State militia and served as Rensselaer County justice of the peace as well as a surveyor and cartographer. He worked as Albany's city engineer and produced maps of the city. Evert Van Allen died August 14, 1854, and was buried in Defreestville.

At least one historian had a hunch that the Allen streets are named for Ethan Allen. Allen was born January 21, 1738, in Litchfield, Connecticut, and served in the Connecticut Militia, Vermont Militia, and Continental Army, at times leading the infamous Green Mountain Boys and joining Philip Schuyler's New York forces. Yet Allen was no friend of New York, and this is why it is highly doubtful he has a connection to these streets. Perhaps explanation is necessary. Possession of present-day Vermont was a point of contention between New York and New Hampshire during the late 1700s. In 1764, Britain's King George ceded control of Vermont to New York. Allen defended Vermonters from New York grantees, two of whom were Cadwallader Colden and Robert Livingston, in a 1770 case within the New York State Supreme Court. The Green Mountain Boys were formed after the court confirmed New York to be in control of said lands. Allen and company then illegally defended Vermont from New York authority, and they physically repulsed legal surveying expeditions. In turn, New York's colonial governor, William Tryon, offered bounties for the arrests of Allen and coconspirators and outlawed Allen collaborators from meeting in groups of more than three. In response, Allen wrote a pamphlet denouncing New York. New York governor George Clinton got involved, confirming that New York had jurisdiction over the Vermont territory. Allen wrote another pamphlet and had treasonous discussions with Quebec's governor, Frederick Haldimand, regarding Vermont becoming a British province. Allen eventually grew tired of confrontation with New York, died, and Vermont became the fourteenth state on March 4, 1791. Ethan Allen, that thorn in New York's side, died February 12, 1789, and was buried in Green Mount Cemetery in Burlington, Vermont.

North Enterprise Drive
See Commerce Avenue.

North Ferry Street
(and South Ferry Street)
Before bridges spanned the river at Albany during the 1860s, visitors and residents used ferries. Without a bridge, the Hudson River was a major speed bump. Despite this inconvenience, business was booming. *The Knickerbocker News* shared an entry from an 1817 encyclopedia that reported "the great roads of communication between the Eastern states and the Western country center on more extensive intercourse at Albany than at any other place between the Eastern and Western sections of the Union." This was written fourteen years before New York's first railroad, the Mohawk and Hudson Railroad, opened for business. The South Ferry Street ferry was the first ferry in the United States. A ferry operator employed by Kiliaen Van Rensselaer ran a ferry in this area as early as 1642 to connect Van Rensselaer's land on both sides of the river. Prior to 1850 the City of Albany purchased land to build Ferry Street, today's South

Ferry Street. This street reached the Greenbush Ferry where the Albany and Greenbush Bridge Company was headquartered during the late 1800s. The destination on the east side of the river was the community of Greenbush, which had its own Ferry Street. A bridge at South Ferry Street opened January 22, 1882.

Meanwhile, North Ferry Street led to the Bath Ferry. Bath, officially Bath-on-Hudson, was a community on the east side of the river in today's City of Rensselaer. It was named after its mineral baths. This northern ferry reached Bath's own North Ferry Street, which was once called Rensselaer Street and Central Avenue and is located near today's Forbes Avenue. (A story too good to pass up, a family involuntarily floated along this ferry route from Albany to Bath when their entire house was picked up and wished bon voyage during a great flood on March 3, 1818.)

Not counting Northern Boulevard, Albany has eight "North" streets. This is the eighth most common street name in New York. There are 210 of them. Communities that carry the "Ferry" moniker in New York include Dobbs Ferry on the Hudson River and Vischer Ferry and Dunsbach Ferry on the Mohawk River.

North First Street
See First Avenue.

North Frontage Road
(and South Frontage Road)
Merriam-Webster's Collegiate Dictionary defines frontage as "the land between the front of a building and the street" and frontage road, a term that dates to 1949, as "a local street that parallels an expressway or through street and that provides access to property near the expressway—called also service road." These definitions precisely describe North Frontage Road and South Frontage Road because they run along strips of land between Washington Avenue Extension and rows of buildings. The "Frontage" moniker is much more common in the American West than it is in the Northeast.

North Hawk Street
(and South Hawk Street)
The most common hawk in New York is the red-tailed (it's also the most common hawk across the U.S.), though seven other species reside in New York: sharp-shinned, coopers, northern goshawk, red-shouldered, broad-winged, rough-legged, and northern harrier. Certain New York birds are nicknamed hawks, but are not hawks at all. These include the American kestrel (nicknamed sparrow hawk), merlin (pigeon hawk), and peregrine falcon (duck hawk).

North Hawk Street and South Hawk Street used to be one street: Hawk Street. It dates to the 1790s when Simeon DeWitt named and mapped it with six other "bird streets": Eagle Street, Swan Street, Lark Street, Partridge Street, Quail Street, and Snipe Street. Hawk Street used to be called Hawke Street, named for Admiral of the Fleet Edward Hawke, a Royal Navy officer who lived from 1705 to 1781. The name Hawke Street appeared in 1764. DeWitt dropped the e to get rid of a British name, thus replacing it with a bird name. The Common Council met September 11, 1790, to make this name change official.

North Lake Avenue
(and South Lake Avenue)

These two streets used to be joined as one street, Lake Avenue, which had an earlier name of Perry Street. The name Perry Street was abandoned July 7, 1904. Hislop explained why these streets are named so, writing that "in 1874 [Washington Park] was extended to Lake Avenue and excavation was begun for the lake which gives the street at the western boundary of the park its name." "Lake" is the third most common street name in New York. There are 292 streets across the state with this name.

North Lawrence Street
(and West Lawrence Street)

Lawrence is a common name, and it is not known for whom these streets are named. A few Lawrences are candidates for either street. There was George Lawrence, who operated the Witbeck and Jones horse car works in 1863. John Lawrence was president of Harmony Mills in 1882. J. D. Lawrence oversaw the manufacture of knit goods in Cohoes in 1893, supervising 150 employees. Richard Lawrence served on the Albany Board of Fire Commissioners of 1897. This board included well-known Albanians such as John Boyd Thacher. Either street could be named for the man for whom New York City's Lawrence Street is named. That man is Charles Lawrence (1786–1829), a captain in the military and husband of Susan Duffield (1790–1851). Duffield was the daughter of Revolutionary War surgeon John Duffield (1755–1798), who was a friend of George Washington. Duffield later became one of Brooklyn's first physicians.

If not named for any of these men, North Lawrence Street and West Lawrence Street is likely named for the 744-mile St. Lawrence River, making these streets two of the possible four "river streets" of Albany. Rivers may be portrayed within Genesee Street and Mohawk Street, too. The English name Lawrence comes from the Middle English and Old French names Lorens and Laurence, which came from the Latin name Laurentius. The name Laurentius is clever—it notes a man from Laurentum, a town in Italy named after its laurel bushes.

North Life Science Lane
(and South Life Science Lane)

The Life Sciences Building, perhaps the biggest of University at Albany's two-dozen academic buildings of the main campus, is approached by the Life Science lanes.

North Main Avenue
(and South Main Avenue)

True main streets, North Main Avenue and South Main Avenue connect at Madison Avenue. The south end of South Main Avenue begins at Whitehall Road and North Main Avenue stretches all the way to Central Avenue, which makes this combination of streets one of the longest roadways in the city: two continuous miles. These streets used to have the singular name of Main Avenue. *The Knickerbocker News* told the story behind the naming.

> When the Albany Land Improvement and Building Company started the development of an area west of the built-up section of Albany and called it Pine Hills, Main Avenue was the eastern boundary of the new tract. The name was given in happy anticipation of the importance to the city of turning over the ever-grass-covered undulating country to residence-filled streets.

North Manning Boulevard

See Manning Boulevard.

North Pearl Street
(and Old South Pearl Street, South Pearl Street)

In distant history, North Pearl Street and South Pearl Street were identified as one street: Pearl Street. Due to the city expanding north along the river, an extended lane was built circa 1814 and dubbed North Pearl Street. South Pearl Street, the original Pearl Street, existed a century before North Pearl Street was built. In 1815 it was named South Pearl Street. Former names for these two streets include Orchard Street, Washington Street, Common Lane, Cow Lane, and Cow Street.

Two theories were uncovered regarding why North Pearl Street and South Pearl Street are named so, and both are worth mentioning. The first theory centers on the Pearl Potash Factory that stood on Pearl Street during the late 1700s. The process of making pearl ash started with wood ashes. These wood ashes were leached, lye was evaporated from them, and the product was boiled down to potash (potassium carbonate, which was used in the production of soap and gunpowder and used as fertilizer). Potash was then baked into pearl ash (a refined version of potassium carbonate), the precursor of today's baking soda. Thus it was called Pearl Street because it was the center of pearl ash production.

The second theory tells the true story, though. Pearl Street was first spelled in the Dutch style, *Paarl*, meaning "pearl," to honor Kiliaen Van Rensselaer. Van Rensselaer was a prominent diamond and pearl merchant in the Netherlands, and he served as Albany's first and greatest patroon despite never visiting the 700,000-acre plot of Capital Region land he controlled.

When Pearl Street was being reconstructed by the Department of Transportation during the 1990s, three skeletons were dug up near the former site of a Lutheran cemetery from the early 1700s. One set of remains, those of a woman, were constructed in facial likeness, and the woman was named Pearl. These remains were reinterred in Albany Rural Cemetery.

South Pearl Street is home to what is likely the oldest building remnants standing in the city. At 36 South Pearl Street stand some remains of a spout-gabled house, the Willem Van Zandt House, built circa 1720 for Thomas Barclay (one sources gives it a construction date of circa 1757). Other pre-1790 buildings still standing include ones at 48 Hudson Avenue (Van Ostrande-Radliff house, 1728), 683 Broadway (Quackenbush House, circa 1736), 27 North Pearl Street (Lerner Shops building, circa 1755), 32 Catherine Street (the Pastures building, 1763), 27 Clinton Street (Schuyler Mansion, 1765), 20 Green Street (one wall standing, circa 1785), and 523 South Pearl Street (Cherry Hill, former home of Philip Van Rensselaer, 1787).

North Pine Avenue
See East Pitch Pine Road.

North Russell Road
(and Russell Road)
The North Russell Road and Russell Road thoroughfare was built prior to 1910 and may have run across farmland owned by a Russell family. If not named for a farming family, these two streets could honor any of the following prominent Russells.

There was Andrew Russell, an Albany homeopathic physician, who died in 1871. Russell's wife was the sister of James Lenox of New York City's Ubsdell, Pierson, and Company. This company operated a department store in downtown Albany that opened during the spring of 1859. This company later became W.M. Whitney and Company, named for its founder, William Minot Whitney. On W.M. Whitney and Company's opening day in Albany, one of its employees was George Russell. This Russell later led E.J. Knowles, a fire insurance company, and was active in social and business organizations.

Other street name candidates include Edwin Russell, reverend and rector of

Grace Church; Henry Russell, president of Marshall and Wendell Manufacturing Company, which made pianos; Joseph Russell, commissioner to build the Albany Basin, trustee of Albany Female Academy, trustee to build a Presbyterian church, and president of Canal Bank; Thomas Russell, founding officer of Albany Savings Bank; and George W. Russell, operator of a local business that dyed, printed, and colored cloth.

One Russell stands above the above men, though, and that is John H. Russell. He was born July 21, 1836, in Albany to William Russell and Catharine Russell. In *Heroes of Albany*, Rufus Clark commented that Russell was

> remembered by hundreds, who lamented his early death while they honored him for his love for his country, and his devotion to her cause, in the time of her great peril. On the breaking out of the [Civil War], in 1861, he was one of the first to offer his services to the government, and was ready to leave home and friends, if he could do something towards rolling back the dark cloud that hung over the land, and threatened us with the loss of all our cherished institutions.

He was elected adjutant of the 18th Regiment of the State Volunteers, fought under General George McClellan, and was wounded in combat. This wound, a gunshot to his ankle, resulted in Russell being ceaselessly transported from one field hospital to the next. He died in Philadelphia of exhaustion and disease on July 28, 1862, a month after he was shot. Russell, an English, Scottish, and Irish name, stems from the Anglo-Norman French name Rousel, which notes a person with red hair. It's related to the modern word rose.

North Second Street
See First Avenue.

North Street
Location is the name of the game in the four-block area that North Street is within. It's the northernmost street there. South Street is the southernmost street while Main Street and Center Street are in the middle.

North Swan Street
(and South Swan Street)
These two streets were once joined as one street: Swan Street, named by Simeon DeWitt. Prior to September 11, 1790, Swan Street was known as Boscawen Street. This name honored Edward Boscawen (1711–1761), Royal Navy admiral and member of Parliament. DeWitt labeled six other "bird

streets" that year: Eagle Street, Hawk Street, Lark Street, Partridge Street, and Quail Street. He recorded Lexington Street as Snipe Street. He also recorded streets for mammals: Buffalo Street, Elk Street, Fox Street, Mink Street, Otter Street, Tiger Street, and Wolf Street. The only mammal name that survives is Elk Street. DeWitt may have seen a swan in Albany or could have seen a bird that looks like a swan. Or he could have just picked the name at random.

There are three species of swans in New York, and each sticks to the Long Island and lower Hudson Valley regions, mostly during migratory season. The first species, the tundra swan, is the only native swan in the East. During the breeding season it lives in northern Canada and Alaska, while during the migratory season it lives along the Pacific and Atlantic coasts. The second species, the trumpeter swan, ranges into New York during summers, coming down from Canada and Alaska. The trumpeter swan is what your author calls "a serious bird." It's the heaviest (upwards of thirty pounds) and tallest (up to five feet) bird in North America. Its wingspan may exceed ten feet. The third species, the mute swan, was introduced from Europe during the late 1800s to be released on wealthy landowners' Long Island and Hudson Valley estates. There are 2,000 mute swans in New York. War has been declared on this species with the New York State Department of Environmental Conservation classifying it as "a 'prohibited' Invasive Species." Much to the dismay of residents, the Department of Environmental Conservation kills mute swans at any opportunity, striving towards total annihilation. General William Tecumseh Sherman wrote: "War is cruelty. There is no use trying to reform it. The crueler it is, the sooner it will be over." New York agrees.

North Third Street
See First Avenue.

Northern Boulevard
With sections of this street formerly named Gage Street, Knox Street, and Swallow Street, in 1991 a half-mile section of Northern Boulevard was named for war hero Henry Johnson. Northern Boulevard is named so due to its location, which is in a northern part of the city. On the south end of the city is its counterpart, Southern Boulevard.

Norton Street
Samuel Norton, born 1769, is memorialized through Norton Street, which used to be called Church Lane and Store Lane. It received its current name June 22, 1835. This street was laid out in 1680, yet it's unknown what it was called back then, if it had a name at all. Norton married Elizabeth Radcliff, a native of Albany, circa 1790, and she died April 30, 1841, at the age of 77. After her death,

Norton moved to Lyme, Connecticut, to live with his daughter. He died during October 1842. The biggest claim to fame regarding Norton Street is that during the 1780s Aaron Burr Jr. (1756–1836), the vice president who shot and killed Alexander Hamilton, had a law office on this street. The name Norton translates to "living north of the settlement."

Norwood Avenue

Norwood Avenue was built in 1915 when Edgar Linn and Harriet Linn conveyed land to the city for construction of this street. It's next to the "wood streets" of Glenwood Street and Parkwood Street. In the Hamlet of McKownville there's a series of streets that copy Albany's series. This hamlet has Norwood Street, Glenwood Street, and Parkwood Street next to each other. Perhaps these neighborhoods were laid out by the same developer.

Norwood Avenue could honor a specific place in England. Norwood, which means "north woods," is the name of communities, civil parishes, parliamentary constituencies, and districts in that country. The United States has at least two dozen towns and cities named after Norwood, England. On the other hand, communities named Norwood in Illinois, Kansas, New York, and Missouri are named after the 1868 Henry Ward Beecher novel *Norwood*. Perhaps Norwood Avenue is named after this book.

Notre Dame Drive

As part of Albany's "academic streets," Notre Dame Drive is near Cornell Drive, Yale Court, Princeton Drive, Union Drive, and Vassar Drive. These streets, named by realtor Jesse Leonard, are then set among Sage College of Albany, Albany Law School, and Albany College of Pharmacy and Health Sciences as well as Neil Hellman School and Albany Academy for Girls. The names Notre Dame Drive, Cornell Drive, Princeton Drive, and Yale Court were made official in 1937. That year the city approved a Rutgers Drive to be built, but this name was replaced with either Union Drive or Vassar Drive.

Edwin Sorin, a Congregation of Holy Cross priest, founded University of Notre Dame during the fall of 1842. The State of Indiana chartered this school two years later. The university states that it has kept a consistent, progressive identity since 1842: "Notre Dame has a unique spirit. It is traditional, yet open to change. It is dedicated to religious belief no less than scientific knowledge. It has always stood for values in a world of facts. It has kept faith with Father Sorin's vision." The name Notre Dame comes from Sorin naming the school, in his native French, *L'Université de Notre Dame du Lac*—the University of Our Lady of the Lake. In the early days, students who attended completed a four-year course of study of humanities, poetry, rhetoric, philosophy, foreign language, drawing, and music. Today there are nearly forty undergraduate majors in their College of Arts and Letters, nearly twenty in their College of Science, nearly ten in their College of Engineering, and ten through their Mendoza College of Business. This university also offers sixty graduate and doctoral degree programs. Approximately 12,000 students attend University of Notre Dame, and famous alumni include Regis Philbin, Condoleezza Rice, and Phil Donahue.

Nutgrove Lane

Nutgrove Lane was likely home to nut-bearing trees such as beeches, oaks, chestnuts, walnuts, butternuts, or hickories. Nut Grove is also the name of a historic building located on this street. Before people of European descent arrived in present-day Albany, Indians harvested and processed nuts from the above species. Beechnut oil can be pressed into an olive oil alternative or used for illumination and soap making. Acorns can be pounded into flour or eaten straight (that is, after boiling them in water to make them palatable). Chestnuts and walnuts can be eaten as-is, while butternuts can be pressed into oil. Hickory nuts can be processed into a pigment for dyeing, and the nuts are edible. Indians employed prescribed fires to burn non-nut-bearing forests. Through this they created an environment where nut-bearing trees would thrive.

Nut Grove, today's Reilly House, is an 1845 brick building that stands at the end of Nutgrove Lane. It was built for William Walsh. When he died, his wife remarried and moved away, and the couple's nephew, Dudley Walsh, then oversaw Nut Grove. During the 1870s, Dudley sold the home to Thomas McCarty, for whom adjacent McCarty Avenue is named. McCarty sold Nut Grove, it became a hospital, and it's now owned by Addictions Care Center of Albany.

O

Oak Street
(and Oaks Court, Oakwood Street, White Oak Lane)

A popular state tree, the official state tree of Connecticut, Maryland, and Illinois is the white oak. Georgia has the live oak, New Jersey has the northern red oak, and Illinois has the plain old oak. Washington, D.C.'s, official tree is the scarlet oak. "Oak" is the seventh most common street name in New York. There are 222 of them. The two most common New York species are white and northern red. White oak makes for high-grade lumber, and a slang name for this species is "stave oak" because it is used to make barrels (Tabasco pepper sauce and Jack Daniel's whiskey are aged in white oak barrels). White oak was harvested in Albany from the 1600s to the 1800s for ship building. The northern red oak is a fine looking tree that also has high-grade wood, which is used for flooring, pilings, fence posts, and railroad ties. Records of New York oaks date to 1609. During September of that year Henry Hudson sailed into Lower Bay, and Robert Juet, the ship's journalist, recorded "the country is full of great and tall oaks . . . " When the crew entered the present-day Capital Region he noted "goodly oakes . . . " and another writer, during the 1620s, observed that "acorns for feeding hogs are plentiful in the woods . . . " Hislop wrote that during the 1640s there were houses "of oak-wood, all ready, cross-casings, door-casings, all of oak . . . "

Oaks Court

See Oak Street.

Oakwood Street

See Oak Street.

OConnell Street

The O'Connell name has been long-established, and notorious, in Albany. The first John O'Connell (John No. 1) was living in Albany by the early 1800s and operated a farm near today's Second Avenue. He had come from Ireland. OConnell Street is named for his son, also named John (John No. 2). In 1876, John No. 2 owned more than three blocks' worth of lots on the north side of OConnell Street and two lots on the southwest corner of this street. More O'Connells followed. John No. 2 was the father of John No. 3, John "Black Jack" O'Connell, a South End saloon keeper. Black Jack had six children with his wife, Margaret Doyle O'Connell. She gave birth to John J. (aka "Solly"), Edward, Daniel, Patrick, John No. 4, and Maud. Solly, Edward, and Daniel, the latter two being Democrats, influenced local politics for more than half of the twentieth century, at times serving in low- to mid-level political appointments. This was when the family disintegrated into a collection of corrupt roughnecks.

William Fulton wrote a scathing critique of the O'Connell political machine in a 1939 issue of the *Chicago Tribune*. The only thing he had to say about Solly was that his hobby was "raising game cocks and fighting" and that he had "a record of arrests for rape and saloon brawling." Edward got off easier, Fulton only reminding readers that Edward "was twice convicted on mail fraud charges arising from the baseball pool operating [in Albany] a decade ago." Daniel served as president of Hedrick Brewing Company, and John J. O'Connell Jr. (who was kidnapped in 1933 when he was 24 years old, later to be released when a $40,000 ransom was paid), Solly's son, was general manager. Fulton assured readers that strong arm sales kept the brewery in business, noting that "Albany taverns must serve [Hedrick] 'or else.'" Frank Robinson, in *Machine*

Politics, assessed Solly as a gaudy Albanian who was "charged during his career with crimes ranging from rape to shooting" and was interested in "fight promoting, nightclubbing, and gambling." Meanwhile, Maud kept a low profile. She was a schoolteacher. The O'Connells and Albany's Democrats wrested control of the city from Republican insider and newspaperman William Barnes Jr. in 1921 by getting William Hackett elected mayor over Republican candidate William Van Rensselaer Erving. Barnes himself was charged with being wholly crooked by none other than President Theodore Roosevelt Jr. It was not Albany's proudest era.

Odell Street

It was first thought that Odell Street memorialized Benjamin Barker Odell Jr. (1854–1926), House of Representatives member from New York, chairman of the Republican State Executive Committee, New York governor, ice controller of New York, president of Central Hudson Steamboat Company, and president of Consolidated Gas, Electric Light, Heat, and Power Company. Yet Odell Street was built prior to 1874—along with neighboring Batcher Street, Benjamin Street, Broad Street, and Krank Street—when Odell was 20 years old and had not yet achieved notoriety. It is unknown why Odell Street is named so.

Old Hickory Drive

Readers must recognize this nickname for Andrew Jackson, best known for being seventh president of the United States. Yet Old Hickory isn't directly honored through Old Hickory Drive. Instead, this street is named for a military unit that an Albanian served in. The March 20, 1951, edition of *The Knickerbocker News* told the story best.

> Albany's newest street—Old Hickory Drive—gets the name because of the sentimental attachment of an Albany lawyer for the Army division in which he served during World War 2. John F. Lasch Jr., Albany attorney, said today that he proposed the name in remembrance of the 30th Division, known as the Old Hickory Division, which was in the European campaign from the Normandy invasion through to the Elbe River. Mr. Lasch was a lieutenant in E Company, 119th Regiment of the Division.

Lasch got to name this street because he was the lawyer for Kessler-Hess Corporation, which developed Old Hickory Drive through construction of the Loudon Arms apartment complex.

The 30th Division was an Army National Guard unit active during the first and second world wars. During World War II, soldiers within this division earned nearly 7,000 Bronze Stars and 2,000 Silver Stars. Six soldiers were awarded the Medal of Honor: Raymond Beaudoin (stormed an enemy position to draw the attention of the enemy away from his own men, who were being attacked—killed in action), Paul Bolden (killed 35 SS troops holed up in a house—killed in action), Francis Currey (destroyed a tank and enemy-occupied house, rescued five American soldiers), Freeman Horner (crossed exposed terrain to kill two enemy and capture four more), Harold Kiner (assaulted a pillbox and then covered an enemy grenade with his own body to save two fellow soldiers—killed in action), and Jack Pendleton (led his squad in the attack of a machine gun nest and then proceeded on his own to distract the enemy—killed in action).

No discussion of this unit or Old Hickory Drive is complete without discussion of Old Hickory himself. Andrew Jackson was born to Andrew Jackson and Elizabeth Hutchinson Jackson in Waxhaw, an area straddling the North Carolina-South Carolina border, on March 15, 1767. At that time, Waxhaw had been settled by those of European descent for only 25 years. Jackson's parents and two older brothers had come to the New World in 1765 from Boneybefore, County Antrim, Ireland, and arrived in Philadelphia.

Jackson served during the Revolutionary War when he was 13 years old, a conflict in which one of his brothers, Hugh, died during the summer of 1779. The only battle Jackson fought in was the Battle of Hobkirk's Hill. Jackson and his other brother, Robert, were British prisoners of war when they were children, and they nearly died of starvation and smallpox while in captivity (a few days after the brothers were released, Robert did die from the conditions he had endured). Then Jackson's mother died during the fall of 1781. She had contracted cholera while caring for sick revolutionaries. Jackson hated the British even more than he hated Indians, and his defiance of Mother England was made legend in the "Young Jackson Refusing to Clean Major Coffin's Boots" story and lithograph. While he was captive, one Major Coffin ordered the boy to clean his, Coffin's, boots, and Jackson would have none of it. According to the lithograph from 1876, he "indignantly refused, and received a sword cut for his temerity." Jackson carried scars on his head and left hand from the officer's slashing.

After studying law in Salisbury, North Carolina, during the 1780s, Jackson was admitted to the bar and practiced in the Western District of North Carolina where he was posted as solicitor. Jackson served as a Tennessee militia commander and colonel in 1801. A year later he was promoted to major general. He fought in the Creek War (battles of Talladega, Emuckfaw and Enotachopo Creek, and Horseshoe Bend), War of 1812 (battles of Pensacola and New Orleans), First Seminole War, and Conquest of Florida (Battle of Negro Fort and Siege of Fort Barrancas). Within these conflicts he commanded militiamen, regular Army soldiers, and Indians and led none other than Davey Crockett and Sam Houston.

He became an impressively successful politician, fulfilling the roles of delegate to the Tennessee Constitutional Convention, House of Representatives member from Tennessee, senator from Tennessee, judge of the Tennessee

Supreme Court, military governor of Florida, and president of the United States. He was preceded by John Quincy Adams, who served from 1825 to 1829, and succeeded by Martin Van Buren, who served from 1837 to 1841. On January 30, 1835, Richard Lawrence tried to kill President Jackson, this being the first presidential assassination attempt. Both of Lawrence's pistols misfired. The would-be assassin, insisting he was King Richard III, was not executed for his crime. He was deemed insane and subsequently institutionalized. Andrew Jackson retired from public life in 1837 and died at his plantation, the Hermitage, in Tennessee on June 8, 1845. He was buried there next to his wife, Rachel Donelson Jackson, who died December 22, 1828.

Old Krumkill Road
See Krumkill Court East.

Old South Pearl Street
See North Pearl Street.

Olive Tree Lane
Olive Tree Lane became connected to Olympus Court, literally and figuratively, by builder Armand Colatosti, for whom nearby Colatosti Place is named. Regarding this connection, 9,573-foot Mount Olympus is the highest peak in Greece, a country known for its olives and olive oil. Greece cultivates the wild olive tree, which first came from the Eastern Mediterranean, and olive oil has been a staple of the Greek economy for 6,000 years. Olive tree fruit is collected, washed with water, ground into paste, and slowly churned and heated to 80 degrees. The water and oil are separated, and the oil is perhaps refined, then classified and stored. Nearly all of the world's olive oil is produced in the Mediterranean, the top three global producers being Italy, Spain, and Greece, respectively.

Oliver Avenue
Oliver Avenue, built circa 1900, is named for the Oliver family that used to own land close to this present-day street. Smith and Young, on their 1851 *Map of the Vicinity of Albany and Troy*, showed one G. Oliver living below three little mountains called Three Hills about where this street now is. Olivers from that era are buried in Albany County's Vanderpool Cemetery, Prospect Hill Cemetery, and Aaron Oliver Family Burying Ground. In 1901, it was proposed by John Webber, a man who apparently suffered from narcissism, to change the name Oliver Avenue to Webber Avenue. The name Oliver comes from the Old French name Olivier, which was brought to England from France.

Olympus Court

As previously noted, builder Armand Colatosti named this street for 9,573-foot Mount Olympus of the Olympus Range. It's the tallest mountain in Greece, and its high point is named Mytikas, meaning "the nose." This apex was first reached on August 2, 1913, by two Swiss, Frédéric Boissonnas and Daniel Baud-Bovy, and a Greek, Christos Kakalos. Kakalos was from the town of Litochoro at the eastern base of Mount Olympus and was a guide on the mountain until his death in 1976. In mythology the mountain was home to the twelve Greek gods, the Olympians. These are Aphrodite (Goddess of Love), Apollo (God of Music and Prophecy), Ares (God of War), Artemis (Goddess of Hunting), Athena (Goddess of Wisdom and War), Demeter (Goddess of Agriculture), Dionysus (God of Wine), Hephaestus (God of Metalworking), Hera (Goddess of Marriage), Hermes (Herald of the Gods), Poseidon (God of the Sea), and Zeus (King of the Gods).

Onderdonk Avenue

During the late 1800s, James Onderdonk owned forty acres between Cortland Street and New Scotland Avenue where today's Onderdonk Avenue is. In 1884, it was arranged for him to be paid $150 for his land for construction of South Allen Street. Along with James Onderdonk's compensation, Matilda Walley, Catherine Ann Birdsall, and Elizabeth Bullock were paid $214 for their land. Fletcher Onderdonk was paid $268, and Sarah Onderdonk made out best, receiving $405 for her land.

One of the earliest, if not the first, Onderdonks to arrive in Albany was Peter Onderdonk. There is much confusion regarding his genealogy. One source stated that Peter was born to Abraham Onderdonk and Rachel Appleby Onderdonk in Rockland County and operated farms in Westerlo and Bethlehem. He married Eleanor Chatterton in 1799, and they had ten children. Onderdonk was born August 12, 1778, and died December 5, 1873. Another source stated that Peter was born to John Onderdonk and Marragrietje Van Houten Onderdonk on the same date as above, August 12, 1778. It's agreed that he married Eleanor Chatterton, but this second source stated they had only one child, Adam, and that Peter died October 5, 1873. Both sources agreed that he was buried in the Town of Bethlehem Cemetery with his wife.

Oneida Drive
(and Oneida Terrace)

Five Nations, also known as the Iroquois Confederacy, consisted of the Cayuga, Mohawk, Onondaga, Seneca, and Oneida. Five Nations became Six Nations when the Tuscarora joined in 1715. The Oneida first lived in central New York, thus the naming of the City of Oneida, Oneida Lake, and Oneida County. The name Oneida stems from mispronunciation of *Onyota'aka*, which the Oneida called themselves, meaning "people of the standing stone." This name is related to a prehistoric story in which members of this tribe were being chased by enemies and turned into stones to hide from their pursuers. The Oneida played a significant role in the Revolutionary War as the first allies of the up-and-coming Americans. The rest of Five Nations chose to side with the British. Oneida warriors served as scouts, fought next to their rebel comrades, and brought corn to George Washington's starving men in Valley Forge. Without Washington and his men surviving that winter, the revolution would have failed. Thus the Oneida helped secure the freedom we enjoy today.

Oneida Terrace
See Oneida Drive.

Oneil Road
Capital Hills at Albany Golf Course adjacent to Oneil Road was built on land that belonged to Peter O'Neil, a dairy farmer. His home stood where the course's seventh green now is, and there is a refuse pile in a hollow near this green that consists of bottles, scrap metal, tools, and barrel staves (among lots of rogue golf balls) from this farming family. The O'Neil farm survived until the 1950s when it was split by the New York State Thruway. The name O'Neil is a transformation of the name Neil, which comes from the Gaelic first name Niall.

Ontario Street
One section of Ontario Street used to be called Sparrow Street, while north of Clinton Avenue it was called Fourth Street. The Ontario moniker spreads far beyond the Capital Region. In the United States at least a dozen political and topographical features carry this name. It's a Huron word meaning "beautiful lake." This word combines *ontara*, meaning "lake," with *io*, meaning "beautiful." Though the origin of the word is known, it's not known how this street got its name. It may specifically be named for Lake Ontario, the smallest and easternmost Great Lake. The U.S. side of this lake is fed by the Genesee River, Oswego River, Black River, Little Salmon River, and Salmon River. Lake Ontario is drained by the St. Lawrence River.

Orange Street
Formerly called Wall Street and Hare Street, Orange Street still had dirt sections as late as 1900. That year its section farthest from the river, Lexington Avenue to Robin Street, was paved with vitrified bricks. The name Orange Street was approved September 11, 1790 and honors the House of Orange-Nassau, a

ruling European family. Fort Orange, a former name for Albany, specifically honored Maurice, Prince of Orange-Nassau, and the Hudson River was first deemed the Mauritius River for him. Maurice was born November 14, 1567, and became Prince of Orange-Nassau when his oldest half-brother, Philip William, Maurice of Nassau, died in 1618. Maurice, son of William I and Anna van Egmont, died April 23, 1625. Maurice is best known for defeating the Spanish during the Eighty Years' War, also known as the Dutch War of Independence, which was led by his father.

Orchard Avenue
See Edgewood Avenue.

Oriole Street
There are six oriole species in eastern North America, and two live in New York. With its chestnut breast and black head, the male orchard oriole has coloring similar to the bird Capital Region residents are more familiar with, the American robin. The female orchard oriole is nearly entirely yellow, which is odd because males are usually the more colorful sex. Though it ranges as far north as New York, its main breeding ground is Louisiana. In that state more than 100 orchard oriole nests were once found in a seven-acre plot. The northern oriole, better known as the Baltimore oriole, is the other species that lives in New York. The male northern oriole is a bold-looking bird with blaze orange undersides contrasting its black upper body. Like the orchard oriole, female northern orioles are yellow.

Orlando Avenue
As one of the five "Florida streets," Orlando Avenue, built prior to 1926, is near Daytona Avenue, Ormond Street, Tampa Avenue, and Seminole Avenue. These streets were likely named by a developer, but specifically why these names were chosen is unknown. Orlando is the seat of Orange County, Florida, and has a population of 250,000. It was incorporated as a town July 31, 1875, and incorporated as a city a decade later. Discussion of the source of the name Orlando begins with an admission by this city's officials: "History is not clear on where the name Orlando originated." There are four stories regarding how Orlando got its name. One tale centers on judge James Speer naming the city after a man who worked for him. Another states that Speer named Orlando after a character from Shakespeare's "As You Like It." Another involves one Mr. Orlando passing through the area with his oxen, dropping dead, and being buried on the spot. The final story goes back to the Seminole Wars. The Orlando city website tells this tale best:

After battling Indians back into the swamps on the east side of Lake Minnie (now Cherokee), the military troop settled there for the night. Sentinel Orlando Reeves was guarding the camp when he spotted a log floating toward him. Recognizing the Indian disguise and wanting to warn his fellow soldiers, he fired his gun. Arrows felled the poor fellow as the Indians came out to ambush the camp. The Indians were chased back again, and the south side of Lake Eola was chosen to bury Orlando Reeves.

Ormond Street
Like three of the other four "Florida streets," Ormond Street is named after a city in that state. It's not known why these Florida names were duplicated in Albany. In 1916, a conveyance of land was accepted by the city for construction of Ormond Street, which was built before 1926. Ormond Beach is in Volusia County, Florida, has a population of 40,000, and is named for the Ormond family, who came to that area circa 1800. James Ormond I was first of this family to arrive. He was killed by a runaway slave in 1817. The Ormond family moved back to Scotland, yet James Ormond II returned with his own son, James Ormond III, to their Florida settlement in 1820. On April 22, 1880, a meeting was called to see if the settlement should be incorporated. With James Ormond III present, it was decided then and there to call the community Ormond.

Osborne Street
More than thirty Osbornes are buried in Albany Rural Cemetery, and the oldest grave belongs to Catharine Osborne, who died July 17, 1844. Being such a common last name, it is unknown for whom this street, which was constructed sometime between 1857 and 1891, is named.

Overlook Street
See Fairview Avenue.

Oxford Road
Six "academic streets" found next to each other include Cornell Drive, Notre Dame Drive, Princeton Drive, Union Drive, Vassar Drive, and Yale Court, and many Albanians are aware of this cluster named by Jesse Leonard. There is a less-obvious cluster of academic streets near the Harriman Campus, that of Oxford Road and Cambridge Road. Oxford Road is also within the "United Kingdom cluster" of Cambridge Road, Tudor Road, and Clarendon Road. Oxford Road was built circa 1918.

Oxford University in Oxford, England, is, to say the least, an ancient institution. Teaching at its location dates to earlier than 1100, and University of Cambridge was founded in 1209 by teachers who had left Oxford University. This makes Oxford University the oldest college in the English-speaking world. Other claims include world's oldest university museum, world's largest university press, and largest academic library in Britain. More than 22,000 students are enrolled at Oxford University. The university holds a $6.3 billion endowment, and tuition for non-United Kingdom students ranges from $30,000 to $40,000 per academic year. Oxford University alumni include King Abdullah II, Tony Blair, Bill Clinton, Thomas "T. S." Eliot, William Fulbright, Indira Gandhi, Thomas "T. E." Lawrence, Rupert Murdoch, and Margaret Thatcher. Communities and counties in Maine, New Hampshire, Massachusetts, New York, Ohio, Pennsylvania, and Mississippi are named after this university. The name Oxford comes from the Old English *Oxnaforda*, meaning "where the oxen ford."

P

Paddock Lane

The Paddock family farmed an area near Paddock Lane during at least the late 1800s, and this street is specifically named for James Paddock. These Paddocks were of fine influence in the Town of Bethlehem. Howard Paddock was a real estate broker who built the Paddock Block in 1920 and served as chairman of the Bethlehem planning board. A paddock is an area used for pasturing or exercising animals and for saddling and parading racehorses prior to their race.

Palmer Avenue

Amos Porteus Palmer could be honored by fifty-foot-long Palmer Avenue. This man, with Horace Newton as partner, formed Salamander and Albany Fire Brick Works circa 1855. By 1874, Palmer had left the brick-making business to become a banker. During that career he worked for the Central Bank of Cherry Valley, Mechanics and Farmers Bank, Albany Exchange Bank, Union Bank of Albany, and Albany City National Bank. Palmer was born in Butternuts, New York, as the son of Amos Palmer and Clarissa Lull Palmer on August 30, 1820. He married Hannah Burbank Crafts on September 19, 1843. She died September 26, 1849. Palmer married again, this time to Eliza Martha Newton, on October 15, 1850. They had eight children. Amos Porteus Palmer died July 30, 1894, while his wife died October 7, 1917. They were buried in Albany Rural Cemetery.

If not named for Amos Porteus Palmer, Palmer Avenue could be named for any of the following men. There was Erastus Dow Palmer (1817–1904), trustee of Albany Rural Cemetery and renowned sculptor; John Palmer (1842–1905), New York secretary of state and commander in chief of the New York National Guard; Ray Palmer (1808–1887), reverend and noted author of hymns; and Walter Launt Palmer (1854–1932), landscape painter and son of Erastus Dow Palmer. Palmer is a nickname for someone on a pilgrimage to the Holy Land, this name originating from *palme* and *paume*, which mean "palm tree." Those who made the pilgrimage to the Holy Land brought back a palm leaf to prove they'd been there.

Pansy Street
The terms pansy, viola, and violet are used interchangeably, and each describe plants belonging to the Violet family. Violets are herbs that produce showy flowers. There are few flowers that exceed violets in loveliness, and there are more than 800 species on Earth, many of them cultivated exclusively for their beauty. The most striking violets that grow wild in New York include dog, birdsfoot, downy yellow, and common blue. Pansy Street is fittingly next to Lily Street, and both were built circa 1928. These names were created by a developer who wanted street names nearly as pretty as the flowers themselves.

Par Circle North
See Fairway Court.

Par Circle South
See Fairway Court.

Par Drive
See Fairway Court.

Park Avenue
Park Avenue was formerly known as Johnson Street, Mink Street, and Monckton Street. It gained its current name sometime between 1857 and 1873. This name may be borrowed from New York City's Park Avenue, which was named so in 1860 because it traversed a small park. If this street does not emulate New York City's street, it's named so because it runs around Washington Park, which was constructed in 1870. "Park" is the most common street name in New York with 451 streets carrying that name. Albany has three of them.

Park Road

The only urban nature preserve in New York bigger than Albany's Tivoli Park is New York City's Central Park. Park Road borders the southeast side of Tivoli Park, a plot of land purchased by the city in 1851. This sixty-acre purchase included four-acre Tivoli Lake, which was constructed to feed Albany with water. The city established Tivoli Lake Preserve in 1975. The toponym Tivoli Lake was recognized by the United States Geological Survey sometime between 1893 and 1927.

Park Street

A section of Park Street was known as Capitol Street until July 20, 1840, because it leads to East Capitol Park and is near the Capitol Building. East Capitol Park falls inside the 36-acre Lafayette Park Historic District, which was classified a historic district in 1978 and added to the National Register of Historic Places that year. It's named for Gilbert du Motier, more commonly known as Marquis de Lafayette (1757–1834), a French officer and aristocrat who was a friend of the Americans during the Revolutionary War. Beyond East Capitol Park, West Capitol Park, Academy Park, and Lafayette Park, 35 buildings are in this historic district. Standout structures include the New York State Capitol, City Hall, Cathedral of All Saints, New York State Department of Education building, New York Court of Appeals building, original Albany Academy building, and posh residences on Elk Street that were built during the 1800s.

Parkwood Street

See Edgewood Avenue.

Partridge Street

Partridge Street was mapped by DeWitt by 1794, and he chronicled six other "bird streets." Bird streets in Albany now total eighteen. The gray partridge, less popularly called the Hungarian partridge, is the only species of partridge in the United States. It was introduced from Europe and Asia and lives in open country along the U.S.-Canada border. It has one of the biggest clutches in the world—it can lay up to twenty eggs each spring. The gray partridge may have been in America before DeWitt was. If this is not the case, DeWitt could have portrayed this street for this species when it lived in the Old World. There are several species of upland chicken-like birds that are incorrectly called partridges. These include pheasants, grouses, prairie-chickens, and ptarmigans.

*Doyle building at **Clinton Avenue** and **Broadway** (U.S. government)*

*House of Jesse Buel on **Western Avenue**, 1934 (Norman Sturgis)*

*Dutch gable house on **Broadway** (U.S. government)*

*1710 Lansing-Pemberton House on **North Pearl Street**, 1937 (N. E. Baldwin)*

*William Visscher building and Dutch Church on **North Pearl Street** (U.S. Government)*

*Nipper guarding **Broadway** and **Loudonville Road**, 1960s (U.S. government)*

*Powerhouse demolition at **North Hawk Street**, 1925 (courtesy APL)*

*Teunis Cornelius Slingerland home on **New Scotland Avenue** (U.S. government)*

*City Hall at **Eagle Street**, circa 1905 (Detroit Pub. Co.)*

*Albany Academy next to **Elk Street**, circa 1907 (Detroit Pub. Co.)*

*View from City Hall at **Eagle Street**, circa 1903 (Detroit Pub. Co.)*

*Ten Eyck Hotel on **State Street**, 1901 (Detroit Pub. Co.)*

*Kenmore Hotel on **North Pearl Street**, circa 1903 (Detroit Pub. Co.)*

Looking west up **Washington Avenue**, *circa 1908 (Detroit Pub. Co.)*

North Pearl Street *from* **State Street**, *circa 1904 (Detroit Pub. Co.)*

State Street with Capitol Building, circa 1904 (Detroit Pub. Co.)

Washington Park lake house near **Madison Avenue**, *1904 (Detroit Pub. Co.)*

Old State Hall on **Eagle Street**, *circa 1900 (Detroit Pub. Co.)*

*Union Station on **Broadway**, circa 1900 (Detroit Pub. Co.)*

*Steamer Albany chugging past **Quay Street**, circa 1905 (Detroit Pub. Co.)*

Dutch Church on **North Pearl Street**, *1907 (Detroit Pub. Co.)*

*Looking west up **State Street**, 1907 (Detroit Pub. Co.)*

North Pearl Street, *circa 1915 (Detroit Pub. Co.)*

*Old post office at **State Street** and **Broadway**, 1903 (Detroit Pub. Co.)*

Broadway and *Steamboat Square, circa 1921 (unidentified photographer)*

Delaware Avenue and *Second Avenue (courtesy APL)*

Elk Street, *circa 1901 (Detroit Pub. Co.)*

*10 **Tivoli Street**, circa 1916 (courtesy APL)*

Broadway *near **Loudonville Road**, 1938 (courtesy APL)*

Clinton Avenue at *Quail Street* crossing, circa 1920 (courtesy APL)

Central Avenue from *Northern Boulevard*, circa 1925 (courtesy APL)

Dean Street and Hudson Avenue, 1900 (courtesy APL)

Beaver Street and Wendell Street near Farmer's Market (courtesy APL)

Clinton Avenue *looking to* ***North Pearl Street*** *(courtesy APL)*

Madison Place *and* ***Madison Avenue*** *near* ***Philip Street*** *crossing (courtesy APL)*

*Intersection of **Eagle Street** and **Daniel Street** (courtesy APL)*

*Dutch Church on **North Pearl Street** near Clinton Square (courtesy APL)*

***Fourth Avenue** and **South Pearl Street**, circa 1930 (courtesy APL)*

South Pearl Street near *Third Avenue, 1936 (courtesy APL)*

Green Street at *John Street* crossing *(courtesy APL)*

*Home Savings Bank on **North Pearl Street** (courtesy APL)*

Hudson Avenue and *Grand Street* (courtesy APL)

Academy Road at *Bethlehem Avenue*, circa 1930 (courtesy APL)

South Allen Street *from* *Morris Street*, *circa 1930 (courtesy APL)*

Benson Street *at its crossing of* *Ontario Street* *(courtesy APL)*

Central Avenue near *Watervliet Avenue* (courtesy APL)

Clinton Avenue with *Lark Street* coming in (courtesy APL)

Clinton Avenue at **Robin Street** *(courtesy APL)*

Delaware Avenue near **Barclay Street** *(courtesy APL)*

Division Street and *Liberty Street*, 1934 *(courtesy APL)*

Elk Street at South Swan Street, 1930 (courtesy APL)

First Street at North Hawk Street (courtesy APL)

First Street near *North Swan Street* *(courtesy APL)*

Lark Street and *Hudson Avenue*, *1930 (courtesy APL)*

Washington Avenue and **Dove Street** *(courtesy APL)*

North Pearl Street and *Livingston Avenue* *(courtesy APL)*

Orange Street at *Lark Street* *crossing (courtesy APL)*

Jefferson Street with Cathedral of the Immaculate Conception *(courtesy APL)*

Madison Avenue with Cathedral of the Immaculate Conception (courtesy APL)

Madison Avenue at *Philip Street* crossing (courtesy APL)

__North Main Avenue__ view south at __Manning Boulevard__ (courtesy APL)

__Sherman Street__ near __Lark Street__ (courtesy APL)

State Street at *Sprague Place*, Washington Park on right (courtesy APL)

*West Capitol Park from **Washington Avenue**, before 1927 (courtesy APL)*

Western Avenue near Manning Boulevard (courtesy APL)

Looking west up Western Avenue at South Lake Avenue (courtesy APL)

*Intersection of **Western Avenue** and **Quail Street** (courtesy APL)*

*Citizens shovel **Washington Avenue**, Blizzard of 1888 (courtesy APL)*

Broadway from *Maiden Lane*, 1863 *(courtesy APL)*

Broadway, D and H Railroad building on right, 1910 *(courtesy APL)*

*Construction of New York State Capitol near **State Street**, 1869 (courtesy APL)*

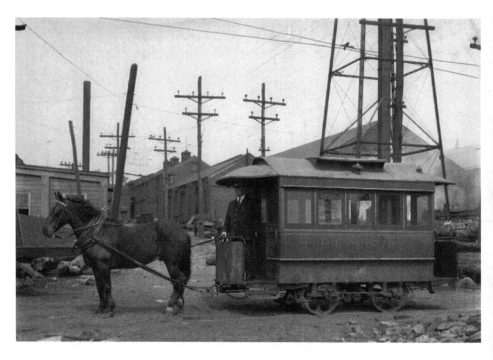

*Lumber District horse car near today's **Erie Boulevard** (courtesy APL)*

*Schupp Wagon Factory on **Central Avenue**, 1876 (courtesy APL)*

*Suffrage parade assembly at City Hall, **Eagle Street**, 1914 (courtesy APL)*

*Albany reservoir at **Columbia Street** and **Eagle Street**, 1861 (courtesy APL)*

State Street *at today's **Henry Johnson Boulevard** (courtesy APL)*

Wendell Street between **Hudson Avenue** and **Howard Street** *(courtesy APL)*

H.P. Miles Ice Company on **South Pearl Street**, *circa 1922 (courtesy APL)*

Hudson Avenue *from* **Green Street** *(courtesy APL)*

*1738 Simmons Auction Rooms on **Howard Street**, circa 1890 (courtesy APL)*

*Public market at **Beaver Street** and **Grand Street** (courtesy APL)*

*Darling Dress Shops, **South Pearl Street** and **Hamilton Street** (courtesy APL)*

Washington Avenue near **Lark Street** *(courtesy APL)*

State Street *Armistice Day parade, November 11, 1918 (courtesy APL)*

*Livermore Chevrolet and Yager Pontiac on **Central Avenue**, 1943 (courtesy APL)*

***Madison Avenue** near **South Allen Street** (courtesy APL)*

*Greenbush Bridge at **South Ferry Street**, before 1933 (courtesy APL)*

*Home at 11 **Ver Planck Street**, which stands today, 1947 (courtesy APL)*

City Garage at 230 **Hamilton Street**, *1927 (courtesy APL)*

Hosler's Ice Cream Company, 232 **Spruce Street**, *1947 (courtesy APL)*

Patroon Creek Boulevard

Patroon Creek was known as Bloomaert's Kill, Fifth Kill, Vyfde Kill (*Vyfde* being Dutch for "fifth"), and Flodderkill (named for Jacob Jansz Flodder, alias Gardenier, a carpenter who operated a gristmill and sawmill on this waterway). It is named Patroon Creek for patroon Jeremias Van Rensselaer, son of Kiliaen Van Rensselaer and Anna Van Wely Van Rensselaer. Jeremias was born May 16, 1632, in Amsterdam and died October 12, 1674, in Rensselaerswyck. He had mills built on this creek, thus it became "the patroon's creek." A patroon was a seventeenth-century lord, and citizens new to the New World were his serfs. McEneny, in *Albany*, wrote that the settling Dutch

> adopted a new concept of colonization, the patroon system, in which members of the Dutch West India Company, who established a settlement of 50 adult tenants in New Netherland, could obtain tracts of land 16 miles along one shore of a navigable waterway, or 8 miles on each bank. The patroon was lord of his domain; as in Europe, tenants were not to hunt, fish, trade, or mill lumber or grain without his consent.

The first patroon of present-day Albany was Kiliaen Van Rensselaer, a merchant who owned 700,000 acres in today's Albany, Columbia, and Rensselaer counties. He headquartered his not-so-little kingdom on the west bank of the Hudson River. Patroon settlements were ruled, not managed. McEneny continued that a patroon "was granted broad powers over his vassals." This included the patroon having rights to all minerals and conducting his own court in which he was chief justice. Tenants couldn't appeal decisions. They also couldn't sell goods to each other even if they made these goods themselves. Stuck under the thumb of the patroon, tenants, who rented their land yet paid no taxes, were not permitted to move to another patroon's property or into town. One historian noted to your author that "Albany was probably the only fiefdom to ever exist in the United States."

Pennsylvania Avenue

This is the only street in Albany named after a state. Land was conveyed to the city in 1912 for construction of Pennsylvania Avenue and neighboring Beverly Avenue, McArdle Avenue, Wilkins Avenue, the northern part of Colonie Street, and eastern part of Thornton Street. Pennsylvania, one of the Thirteen Colonies, is nicknamed the Keystone State for it being the central state of the Union. Despite it being the sixth most populous state, Pennsylvania has only four cities that exceed 100,000 people, these being Allentown, Erie, Philadelphia, and Pittsburgh. By 1790, there were half a million people living in Pennsylvania, and the state surpassed one million by 1820 and ten million by 1950. The state motto is "Virtue, Liberty, and Independence." The state tree is the eastern hemlock, state bird is the ruffed grouse, and state animal is the white-tailed deer.

Pennsylvania is named for William Penn, English admiral and member of the House of Commons. William Penn's son, also named William Penn, received a land grant from King Charles II on February 28, 1681, as payment of a debt the king owed to the senior William Penn. The king named this land Pennsylvania, meaning "Penn's woods," for William the elder. Here a sly joke was played on the Penn family. The junior William Penn suggested the name New Wales because it reminded him of Wales and its rolling hills. That name was not accepted, and so he suggest Sylvania, Latin for "forest land." Penn detested the thought of a feature being named for a person, such were his Quaker beliefs. King Charles II was feeling playful, and malicious, the day he dubbed the region Pennsylvania. As Stewart wrote, the king "perpetuated what seems to be a rather dull practical joke" on the junior Penn by using the family name.

Perkins Avenue

The name history behind Perkins Avenue, built circa 1927, remains a mystery. One Perkins of Albany was John G. Perkins, who was born to John H. Perkins and Elizabeth Perkins in Albany on November 15, 1846. When he was 11 years old his family moved to Hoboken, New Jersey, and after the death of his father he moved to Columbus, Ohio. At the age of 16 he joined the military to fight in the Civil War. He died of typhoid pneumonia in the South before his first battle. Perhaps Perkins Avenue is named for this family. The name Perkins uses the name Peter and adds the suffix "kin."

Perry Place

Oliver Hazard Perry, honored through Perry Place, was born August 23, 1785, in South Kingstown, Rhode Island, as the son of U.S. Navy captain Christopher Perry and Sarah Wallace Alexander Perry. Nearby North Lake Avenue and South Lake Avenue used to be joined as one street—Lake Avenue—and was first called Perry Street.

Perry was schooled in Newport, Rhode Island, and before he was a teenager he set sail with his father to the West Indies. At the age of 13, he became a midshipman on a ship commanded by his father. Perry quickly moved up the ranks and eventually commanded the *Nautilus* and *Revenge* and fought in the Quasi War with France, Barbary Wars, and War of 1812. By the time the Battle of Lake Erie commenced in 1813, Perry had been promoted to commodore of U.S. naval forces serving on that Great Lake. (A commodore before the Civil War was not a rank. It was a title for a commander who led a squadron of at least two ships. Perry fulfilled this role during the Battle of Lake Erie.) Commanding the *Lawrence* and then the *Niagara*, he brilliantly smashed British groups and thus became "The Hero of Lake Erie." He won no fewer than nine battles. He was awarded the Congressional Gold Medal, one of only 27 awarded during the War of 1812, and was promoted to captain. It was after the Battle of Lake Erie that he told Americans, "We have met the enemy and they are ours." He later commanded the *Java*, *Constellation*, and *Nonsuch*.

Oliver Hazard Perry died in South America, likely of yellow fever, on his 34th birthday in 1819, expiring on the *John Adams*. His body was first buried in Port of Spain, and then his remains were buried in Newport, Rhode Island, first in the Old Common Burial Ground and then in Island Cemetery. He is memorialized through counties, communities, and, of course, streets, including Perry Street in Newport, Rhode Island.

Peyster Street

As three-time mayor of Albany—from 1729 to 1731, during 1732 and 1733, and during 1741 and 1742—Johannes De Peyster III has earned his Peyster Street. He selflessly purchased the city's first fire-fighting equipment and served in several bureaucratic positions. These include captain of the cavalry, Indian commissioner, inspector of ordinance, member of the Provincial Assembly, paymaster of New York forces, recorder, and first surrogate of Albany County. He was born January 10, 1694, in New York City where his father, Johannes De Peyster II, was mayor during 1698 and 1699. The younger Johannes was married to Anna Schulyer, daughter of the thirteenth mayor of Albany, Myndert Schuyler. Johannes De Peyster III died in Albany on February 27, 1789, and was buried at the Dutch Church. Peyster Street is set among three other "mayoral streets": Ryckman Avenue, Banker Street, and Hansen Avenue.

Philbrick Street

Philbrick Street is a complete mystery. A few Philbricks lived in the Capital Region during the early and mid-1800s, yet there's no evidence to suggest this street is named for any of them. Philbrick Street was first called Philbrick Avenue and was built before 1915 when land was conveyed by Jacob W. Wilbur of the Wilbur Land Company. Near Philbrick Street there used to be an Almon Avenue, Nyack Avenue, and Tappan Avenue, yet these are long-gone, the New York State Thruway now running through this area.

Philip Street

Philip Street honors Philip Schuyler, who is memorialized through counties in Illinois and Missouri as well as New York's Town of Schuyler, Village of Schuylerville, and Schuyler County. He was born to Johannes Schuyler and Cornelia Van Cortlandt Schuyler on November 20, 1733, and grew up in the

Flatts in present-day Watervliet. During the 1740s, he moved away for his education yet returned to Albany the following decade. During September 1755, he married Catherine Van Rensselaer. They had fifteen children.

He entered politics and became assistant alderman of the Common Council, commissioner of the excise tax, New York assemblyman, senator from New York, New York surveyor general, and member of the Continental Congress. During the French and Indian War he fought on behalf of the British but then for the Americans during the Revolutionary War. He served as a major general within the Continental Army and was supposed to lead the attack on Montreal but became ill during the siege of St. John's. General Richard Montgomery led the attack instead and was killed during the fight. Schuyler was in contact with George Washington during the war and witnessed, on January 7, 1776, Henry Knox pass by Albany, the city that Schulyer was in charge of, with sixty tons' worth of cannons being dragged 300 miles from Ticonderoga to Boston. Philip Schuyler died November 18, 1804, and was buried in the Ten Broeck family vault in Albany. He was reinterred in Albany Rural Cemetery. His wife had died the year before. John Massey Rhind's 1925 statue of Schulyer stands in front of Albany City Hall. Philip Street is one of the six "Schulyer streets" near the Schuyler Mansion. The other five are Alexander Street, Catherine Street, Elizabeth Street, Morton Avenue, and Schuyler Street.

Physics Lane
This street on the University at Albany's main campus runs straight to the Physics Building. The gravity of this name association cannot be overstated.

Picotte Drive
John David Picotte founded Picotte Companies in 1933 and is memorialized through John David Court and John David Lane. Picotte Drive pays homage to this family of builders who raised homes and commercial buildings throughout the Capital Region, including where Picotte Drive is. Picotte Companies is still family-run. John D. Picotte (named for his grandfather, founder John David Picotte) serves as chairman, Michael B. Picotte serves as president, and William B. Picotte serves as senior vice president.

Pierpoint Street
This street was called Pierpont Avenue, then Pierpont Street, then Pierpoint Street, and was built circa 1915 on land conveyed to the city by Jacob W. Wilbur. Pierpoint is an obvious misspelling of Pierpont. This street is very likely named for John Pierpont "J. P." Morgan, especially since this street was

named just a year or two after his death. The name Pierpont comes from the Old French words *pierre* and *pont*, meaning "stone bridge."

Morgan was born in Hartford, Connecticut, on April 17, 1837, and was not of modest means. His father was Junius Morgan, a financier who was worth $270 million in today's monies at the time of his death, while his mother was Juliet Pierpont. He attended Hartford Public School, Episcopal Academy, English High School, Bellerive (in Switzerland), and University of Göttingen (in Germany). The sky was the limit from there. During a 25-year period beginning in 1890 he underwrote or formed more than forty corporations including John Pierpont Morgan, American Telephone and Telegraph, International Harvester, General Electric, U.S. Steel, and two dozen railroad companies. He died March 31, 1913, in Rome, Italy, and was buried in Cedar Hill Cemetery in Hartford, Connecticut. He left his fortune to his only son, John Pierpont Morgan Jr. Since the senior Pierpont was a gem collector, the gemstone morganite is named for him.

Pieter Schuyler Court West
(and Schuyler Street)

Pieter Schuyler, born September 17, 1657, in Rensselaerswyck, was the first mayor of Albany. Appointed by governor Thomas Dongan, he served from July 22, 1686, to October 13, 1694. Beyond serving as mayor, Schuyler was colonel of a militia during King William's War, member of the Provincial Assembly, Indian commissioner, and justice of the peace. He was the son of Philip Pieterse Schuyler and Margaret Van Slechtenhorst Schuyler. He married Engeltie Van Schaick, who died in 1689. He then married Maria Van Rensselaer on September 14, 1691. Pieter Schuyler died February 19, 1724, in the Flatts in present-day Watervliet and was buried at the Albany Dutch Church. Schuyler Street is near the Schuyler Mansion, and, with Alexander Street, Catherine Street, Elizabeth Street, Morton Avenue, and Philip Street, is part of the "Schuyler streets."

Pilgrim Drive
(and Plymouth Street)

The Pilgrims formed in County Nottinghamshire, England, during the late 1500s under Richard Clyfton of the All Saints Parish Church. Their ideology maintained that they were different from citizens who subscribed to the Church of England, and that they would not be forced to follow that church despite the 1559 Act of Uniformity that demanded they do so. The Pilgrims immigrated to Holland, yet didn't feel like they fit in there either. They set their sights on the New World, gunning for financial opportunity and the chance to preach the Gospel to any heathens they may be lucky enough to encounter. The *Speedwell* and *Mayflower* were supposed to reach the New World, but the *Speedwell* began taking on water not far from land and was deemed unfit for a crossing of the Atlantic Ocean. The *Mayflower* left with more than 130 passengers and crew during September 1620. Not all of them were Pilgrims, many of them being general colonists, opportunists, adventurers, and indentured servants. They sighted Cape Cod in early November. Their population had decreased by one. Two travelers died along the way, and one child was born.

The Pilgrims composed the Mayflower Compact aboard the ship and then temporarily landed to collect firewood and water. Near starvation, they robbed Indian graves of maize and stole Indian homes of any food they could scrounge. They met a few Indians, but they either shot at the settlers with bows and arrows or ran for the hills. The Indians had dealt with the English in the past, and the interactions had not been pleasant. The Pilgrims then landed near present-day Plymouth Rock. They had Plymouth Colony established before 1621, yet that spring fewer than fifty colonists were still alive, the rest dying of starvation and disease. Peaceful relations were formed between the settlers and Indians, and more Europeans and supplies arrived. Many battles with the Indians followed, but by 1630 at least 300 Europeans were living in Plymouth Colony. By 1643 there were 2,000, and by 1691 there were 7,000. In 1691, the colony vanished, at least on paper, when a charter combined Plymouth Colony, Massachusetts Bay Colony, and other lands into a singular society. This charter of the Province of Massachusetts Bay was effected May 14, 1692.

Pine Lane
See East Pitch Pine Road.

Pine Street
See East Pitch Pine Road.

Pine Tree Lane
See East Pitch Pine Road.

Pine West Plaza
See East Pitch Pine Road.

Pine West Road
See East Pitch Pine Road.

Pinehurst Avenue
See East Pitch Pine Road.

Pinehurst Boulevard
See East Pitch Pine Road.

Pines Court
See East Pitch Pine Road.

Pinewood Avenue
See East Pitch Pine Road.

Pitch Pine Road
See East Pitch Pine Road.

Pleasant Street
See Fairview Avenue.

Pleasantview Avenue
See Fairview Avenue.

Plum Street
Plum Street is near Cherry Street and Vine Street. These are the downtown "fruit streets" that probably traverse former Schuyler Mansion farmland where produce was grown. Until the 1900s a fourth fruit street, Mulberry Street, laid a few blocks north of Plum Street. The earliest map Plum Street appeared on was DeWitt's city map from 1794. Most old-time maps spelled it Plumb.

Nine species of plum trees grow in the United States. The American plum (also known as red plum and river plum) and Canada plum (also known as red plum and horse plum) are native to New York. The American plum is a small tree or big shrub, depending on who you ask. It grows up to thirty feet tall and one foot in diameter. Its fruit is one inch in diameter, its pulp sour yet edible. It can be made into jellies and preserves. The Canada plum attains heights of only thirty feet and is commonly eight inches in diameter. Its fruit is sweeter than that of the American plum and can be enjoyed fresh or dried.

Plymouth Street
See Pilgrim Drive.

Point of Woods Drive
See Edgewood Avenue.

Port Street
See Anchor Street.

Porter Court
Porter Court was first identified on maps in 1899 yet was built circa 1877. There were at least four notable Porters in Albany during the 1800s. Lessor candidates include Giles Porter, member of the founding board of directors of Mechanics and Farmers Bank, which was established in 1811; James Porter, one of the first directors of Canal Bank; and Nathan Porter, co-owner of a pottery works on Champlain Street. Then there was Charles Porter, the candidate most likely to be honored by Porter Court. He was born in Ghent, New York, on November 11, 1834, and graduated from Yale University in 1855 and Albany Medical College in 1861. He taught chemistry and medical jurisprudence at this latter school. Porter was a Civil War officer with the 5th Regiment of New York Volunteers, worked as a surgeon, and witnessed, as George Howell and Jonathan Tenney wrote in *Bicentennial History of Albany*, "heavy action" from 1862 to 1865. Post-war he returned to Albany to work as a doctor. He died November 21, 1903.

It's worth mentioning the Porter family of the Northeast. This family was full of notable sailors, and the patriarch, David Porter, may be memorialized within Porter Court. David Porter was born in Boston on February 1, 1780, and served as an officer in the War of 1812. He commanded the *Constitution*, among other ships. He died March 3, 1843, and was buried in the Philadelphia Naval Asylum and reinterred in Woodlands Cemetery in Philadelphia. The Town of Porter and Porter County in Indiana are named for him. The seat of Porter County was named Portersville, yet in 1837 townsfolk found the name dull and changed it to Valparaiso because Porter had participated in action near Valparaíso, Chile, during the War of 1812. His five biological sons who lived into adulthood became officers, four of them serving in the Navy.

David Porter's most famous biological son was David Dixon Porter (1813–1891), who became the second admiral in U.S. naval history and superintendent of the U.S. Naval Academy. The Naval Academy's Porter Road is named for him. David Dixon Porter's tie to Albany is that one of his books, *Memoir of Commodore David Porter*, from 1875, was published in the city by Joel Munsell.

David Porter's adopted son was James Glasgow Farragut, best known as David G. Farragut (1801–1870). He was the first admiral in U.S. Naval history and is credited with stating "Damn the torpedoes, full speed ahead" at the 1864 Battle of Mobile Bay. Farragut, Tennessee, and Farragut Square in Washington, D.C., are named for him. The name Porter was used to note someone who was a gatekeeper. Then it came to translate literally for one who hauls items, such as the porters who are employed in the Himalayas.

Princeton Drive

Six "academic streets" are next to each other in this neighborhood: Princeton Drive, Cornell Drive, Yale Court, Notre Dame Drive, Union Drive, and Vassar Drive, which were all named by realtor Jesse Leonard. These six streets are further set near five Albany academic institutions. The names Princeton Drive, Cornell Drive, Notre Dame Drive, and Yale Court were approved by the city in 1937. They also approved the name Rutgers Drive. This name was replaced with either Union Drive or Vassar Drive.

Princeton University is named so because it's in Princeton, New Jersey, a city named for King William III, Prince of Orange-Nassau (this man is memorialized through Orange County, New York, too). Princeton University calls itself "a vibrant community of scholarship and learning that stands in the nation's service and in the service of all nations." It was chartered in 1746 and is, according to the college itself, the fourth-oldest university in the United States. (This claim is disputed by many sources. One reputable source ranks Princeton University as ninth-oldest, falling behind, in chronological order, Harvard University, College of William and Mary, Saint John's College, Yale University, Washington College, University of Pennsylvania, Moravian College and Moravian Theological Seminary, and University of Delaware.) At Princeton University more than 1,000 faculty teach 8,000 students on a 500-acre campus that has 200 buildings. Within the university are three schools: School of Architecture, School of Engineering and Applied Science, and Woodrow Wilson School of Public and International Affairs. Less than eight percent of undergraduate applicants are accepted. Famous Princeton University alumni include Woodrow Wilson, Jimmy Stewart, Donald Rumsfeld, Ralph Nader, and disgraced New York governor Eliot Spitzer.

Prospect Avenue

See Fairview Avenue.

Prospect Avenue Extension

See Fairview Avenue.

Prospect Terrace
See Fairview Avenue.

Providence Place
(and Providence Street)
The lowercase providence, according to *Merriam-Webster's Collegiate Dictionary*, is "the care exercised by God over the universe" and "an event or circumstances ascribable to divine interposition." The upper case Providence is "God; the Deity." Providence, Rhode Island, was settled during the summer of 1636 by Roger Williams, who had come from Massachusetts Bay Colony after facing religious persecution. He chose this name because he felt God had provided him providence to find such a nice spot to settle. Williams wrote, "Having in a sense of God's merciful providence unto me in my distress called the place Providence, I desired it might be for a shelter for persons distressed on conscience." Providence Street borrows this place name. Housing lots were first subdivided on this street in 1911.

Providence Street
See Providence Place.

Pruyn Street
Pruyn is one of the, if not *the*, most established names in Albany, and Pruyn Street is in one of the oldest sections of the city. This street was first called Embargo Alley, and then called Deniston Street beginning June 16, 1834. The Pruyn presence in Albany began with Frans Janse Pruyn, also known as Francis Pruyn. He was in the area in 1661 with his wife, Alida, who bore him eleven children. Frans, a tailor, died May 6, 1712, while his wife died September 20, 1704.

Three influential Pruyns of mid-1800s Albany include John Van Schaick Lansing "V. L." Pruyn, Robert Clarence Pruyn, and Robert Hewson Pruyn. These men are detailed to illustrate the power and breadth of this family. John, born in Albany on June 22, 1811, was a lawyer who served as president of the State Board of Charities, regent of the Smithsonian Institution, and chancellor of the University of the State of New York. He was also counsel to the Mohawk and Hudson Railroad, counsel and treasurer of the Utica and Schenectady Railroad, and president of the Mohawk Valley Railroad. These three rail companies later joined to form New York Central Railroad, of which John was director and general counsel. His political appointments included senator and House of Representatives member from New York, and he donated his political salary to organizations that helped Albany's poor. He even laid the cornerstone of the new State Capitol. John Van Schaick Lansing "V. L." Pruyn died November 21, 1877.

Robert Hewson was another lawyer. He was born February 14, 1815, attended Albany Academy, and received his bachelor's and master's degrees from Rutgers University. He served as judge advocate general, New York assemblyman, adjutant general of the New York National Guard, minister to Japan, and president of the National Commercial Bank and Trust of Albany. He was also a founder of Albany Law School, established 1851. He died February 26, 1882.

The son of Robert Hewson was Robert Clarence, who was born in Albany on October 23, 1847. He attended Albany Academy and graduated from Rutgers College. He served within governor John Alden Dix's administration and was regent of the University of the State of New York, commissioner of Albany Park, president of the Embossing Company (he held five patents for toys), officer in the New York State Militia, president of the National Commercial Bank of Albany, vice president of the Municipal Gas Company, and director of the Union Trust Company. Robert Clarence Pruyn, who resided on Englewood Place, died October 29, 1934.

Putnam Street

Besides this street, Israel Putnam, a Revolutionary War hero, is memorialized through communities named Putnam in Connecticut and New York and counties named Putnam in Florida, Georgia, Illinois, Indiana, Missouri, New York, Ohio, Tennessee, and West Virginia. McCullough, in *1776: The Illustrated Edition,* called Putnam "one of the oldest and by far the most popular" officers in the Army who was "a hero of Bunker Hill" and known as "Old Put" due to his age of 57 when he was most active. He was described by this same author as "rough, 'thick set,' 'all bones and muscles,' and leathery, with flowing gray locks and a head like a cannonball, he . . . had survived hair-raising exploits fighting the French and Indians, shipwreck, even a face-to face encounter with a she-wolf in her den."

Putnam was born in 1718 in present-day Danvers, Massachusetts, to Joseph Putnam and Elizabeth Porter Putnam. In 1740, he moved to present-day Pomfret, Connecticut, where, legend has it, he killed the last wolf in that state, as referenced by McCullough above. He served in Rogers Rangers, the precursor to modern-day Army Rangers, and led his own company of rangers during the French and Indian War. In 1757, his unit was stationed near an island near Fort Edward, New York, when a severe fire broke out, threating to detonate a magazine and blow the unit to smithereens. Putnam put his life in extreme danger to extinguish the flames. It took him months to recover from burns and smoke inhalation. A year later he was sentenced to be burned at the stake after being captured by the Mohawk. A rainstorm and a persuasive officer saved his life. He retired to Brooklyn, Connecticut, to farm, yet the battles of Lexington and Concord took place, and he picked up his musket and hatchet once more. He was made major general and fought at the Battle of Bunker Hill, perhaps coining the order

"Don't fire until you see the whites of their eyes." It was a brutal fight. Allen and Schweikart reported in *A Patriot's History of the United States* that during the Battle of Bunker Hill "almost half the British troops were either killed or wounded, and an exceptional number of officers died (12 percent of all British officers killed during the entire war)." In 1779, his military career ended when he had a stroke. Israel Putnam died in 1790 and was buried in South Cemetery in Brooklyn, Connecticut. Putnam is a British place name that combines the Old English *putta* with *ham*, which mean "kite" and "homestead."

Q

Quackenbush Square
(and Quackenbush Street)

An Albany family name is carried within the names Quackenbush Square and Quackenbush Street. Quackenbush Square is home to the brick Quackenbush House, which is the third oldest structure in the city. It was built circa 1736 by Pieter Wouter Quackenbush, who was born during June 1706 as the son of Wouter Quackenbush Jr. and Cornelia Bogert Quackenbush. He was married to Anna Oothout Quackenbush and died in 1782. The foundation of this building dates to the 1600s, while the land it was dug in was owned by the Quackenbushes for 185 years, from 1683 to 1868. Ah, if those walls could talk, they could reveal so much of the goings-on of old-time Albany. Alas, they cannot, but we do know that General John Burgoyne was allowed to stop here for a drink while on his way to the Schuyler Mansion while he was a prisoner of the Continental Army, and the famous fur trader John Jacob Astor used to sleep in this building's servants quarters. The Quackenbush House is now home to The Olde English Pub and Pantry, which moved into the building in 2011. Quackenbush Street was portrayed on maps as early as 1794. That year DeWitt shared his map of the city and called it Quackenbos Street.

There were other Quackenbushes in Albany, some before Pieter Wouter, some after. Any one of these folks may live on through Quackenbush Street or Quackenbush Square if they're not named for this family in general. There was brickmaker Pieter Quackenbush (1614–unknown), who may have been married to Maria Quackenbush; Wouter Pieterse Quackenbush (circa 1644–unknown), who was married to Neeltje Gysberts Vandenbergh Quackenbush; Johannes Quackenbush (circa 1645–1720), who was married to Machtelt Post Quackenbush and owned land in today's Clifton Park; Wouter Quackenbush Jr. (1671–1736), who was married to Cornelia Bogert Quackenbush and helped settle

Schaghticoke; Adrian Quackenbush (circa 1675–unknown), who was married to Catharina Van Schaick Quackenbush and owned land in Schaghticoke; Pieter Quackenbush (circa 1680–1748), who was married to Neeltje Marens Quackenbush, served in the Albany Militia, settled in Schenectady, and owned land along the Mohawk River; and there was Johannes W. Quackenbush (1709–circa 1773), who was married to Margarita Bogert Quackenbush, served as fire master and assistant alderman, settled in Schaghticoke, and then moved to New York City.

Quackenbush Street
See Quackenbush Square.

Quadrini Drive
Homebuilder John Quadrini immigrated to the United States when he was 17 years old, having been born in Italy to Loreto Quadrini and Teresa DePalma Quadrini. In addition to this street, Quadrini Estates, an upscale residential community built during the 1970s off McCormack Road, is named for him. After working for General Electric, Quadrini joined the military, serving in the Army during World War II. He was deployed to ferocious battlegrounds including Ardennes, Rhineland, and Normandy. For his service he was awarded the European-African Middle Eastern Medal, the Distinguished Unit Citation, and the World War II Victory Medal. Quadrini returned home and became a land developer, building contractor, and investor. He built homes throughout the Capital Region and owned a Dunkin Donuts, a Travelodge Motel, and the Silo Restaurant. John Quadrini died January 8, 2003, at the age of 87 and was buried in Our Lady of Angels Cemetery in Colonie.

Quail Street
During the early 1790s, DeWitt mapped this "bird street" along with Eagle Street, Hawk Street, Lark Street, Partridge Street, Dove Street, and Swan Street. He called Lexington Street Snipe Street, yet that name did not stand the test of time. The only native American bird with "quail" in its name is the scaled quail of the Desert Southwest. Within this street name DeWitt may have been referring to the northern bobwhite, which is a quail. The northern bobwhite is a small chicken-like bird that gets its name from its call: "bob-WHITE, poor-bob-WHITE!" This species is a popular upland game bird that ranges across the East and Midwest. Quail Street used to be called Turkey Street. Sections of this street were still dirt as late as 1890. That year the section of Quail Street between Central Avenue and Clinton Avenue was surfaced with wheel-breaking cobblestones.

Quay Street

The word quay stems from the French *cuai* and the Old French *cai*, meaning "wharf." With Quay Street located where Hudson River water meets Albany dirt, it's a fitting name. Bielinski, in his Quay Street article, wrote: "Beginning sometime after the Revolution, a crude roadway began to become visible along the Hudson riverfront. The riverside edge of it became the city seawall . . . First identified by name on city maps about 1790, Quay was early Albany's easternmost street." Quay Street used to be called Dock Street and Water Street. A beautiful image of old-time Quay Street survives through Len Tantillo's gorgeous painting "Quay Street (1813)," which can be found in the Pruyn Room of the downtown Albany Public Library. The artist describes the scene thus:

> The painting depicts a quiet riverfront. The workday is winding down as a bright moon illuminates a mackerel sky, its silvery light reflecting off a calm Hudson River. A group of merchants, relaxing after loading a wagon, discusses the day's events. Warm ribbons of lantern light catch the rounded cobblestones of the street. The sturdy sloops creak in the gentle breeze. A solitary crewman, aboard a topsail schooner anchored in deeper water, lantern in hand, makes his final rounds before coming ashore.

R

Raft Street
See Anchor Street.

Rafts Way

Rafts Way runs along the south shore of five-acre Buckingham Lake because this lake used to be called Rafts Pond. It also used to be called Buckingham Pond. Buckingham Lake is the toponym recognized by the United States Geological Survey today, though they didn't label this body of water in 1893, 1927, and 1950, the years early editions of their topographic maps were released.

Yet the question remains: Does Rafts Way carry the word raft, as in a crude boat, or is it instead named for a man named Raft? Do not always trust in the obvious. For example, your author was hiking across Pennsylvania a decade ago, and at one point he was walking down Duck Pond Road. Obviously it carried the name of the fowl, right? Yet when your author stopped for water at a farmhouse on this road, the woman who provided it was Ms. Sarah Duck. The road was named for her deceased husband.

Ramsey Place

A man who operated a farm in this area has his last name carried through Ramsey Place. This street's New Scotland Avenue to Hackett Boulevard section was built circa 1915, while its section from Hackett Boulevard to Whitehall Road was built later. A grass island ran down the middle of the New Scotland Avenue to Hackett Boulevard section until 1953. That's why this half-mile section is so wide. This median was removed to make snow plowing easier and to end congestion (medians survive in nearby Marwood Street, Joelson Court, and Rose Court). Ramsey Place was probably named by the Van Schoick-Harris Realty Company since it's close to Van Schoick Avenue (named for the president of this company, Charles Van Schoick) and Harris Avenue (named for the secretary of this company, Frank Harris) and that this company was selling lots along this street before 1923. There were 23 homes on Ramsey Place at that time. The name Ramsey was used to label people who came from Ramsey, Scotland. It was formed by joining the Old English words *hramsa* and *eg*, meaning "wild garlic" and "island."

Rapp Road
(and Rapp Road North)

During the 1800s and 1900s, the Rapp family had a farm where Rapp Road and Rapp Road North lie. The Arthur O. Rapp farm stood in nearby Guilderland from at least 1912 to 1950. Rapp retired and auctioned his farm and farming equipment that final year. This man also operated farms in the communities of Altamont and Fort Hunter.

The Rapp Road Community is a fourteen-acre neighborhood that was added to the National Register of Historic Places in 2003 and conceived during the 1930s by Louis Parson and Frances Parson. They moved from Shubuta, Mississippi, to Albany's South End circa 1927 and then purchased land along Rapp Road in May 1930 with William Toliver. Used to rural areas in Mississippi, the Parsons didn't enjoy the South End with its crowding, whorehouses, and gambling halls. On the other hand, the Rapp Road area reminded them of home with its features of self-sufficiency and peace and quiet. During the 1940s, other families moved to the Rapp Road Community from the South, bought modest chunks of land, and built simple homes, some of which still stand. Rapp is a cognate to the ancient word raven, which described people who had black hair or were thieves. In Sweden, Rapp was derived from *rapp*, which meant "quick," this name given to soldiers.

Rapp Road North

See Rapp Road.

Rawson Street

In 1871, the name Rawson Street was made official along with the names of nearby Colby Street, Hunter Avenue, Judson Street, and Watervliet Avenue. Three members of the Rawson family—Cora, Dora, and George—lived at 373 Sherman Street just three-quarters of a mile from Rawson Street during the early 1900s. If these Rawsons did not play a role in the naming of Rawson Street, their ancestors did. Nine Rawsons are buried in Albany Rural Cemetery, with the oldest grave dating to 1845. Another six are buried in Graceland Cemetery, the oldest dating to 1913. One line of Albany Rawsons began with Henry Rawson, born July 29, 1834, in South Yorkshire, England. Divorced, he came to Albany with his only daughter, Lucy. He married Agnes Isabelle Dugan in 1879, had seven children, and died August 18, 1892.

Raymo Street

Raymo Street, built before 1928, used to be called OConnell Avenue. A name change took place when OConnell Street was named for John O'Connell. The city found these names too similar and thus too confusing, especially because they were only a block from one another. Believe it or not, Raymo Street is named after a horse that belonged to Maurice Whalen. He lived at 55 Raymo Street and was a builder as well as the city's sealer of weights and measures. Whalen, who had emigrated from Ireland to America, died March 3, 1940, and was buried in Albany Rural Cemetery.

Regent Street

Regents are mentioned throughout *Cradle of the Union*. For example, DeWitt Clinton, Peter Gansevoort, John Ten Eyck Lansing Jr., and Robert Clarence Pruyn were regents of the University of the State of New York. Yet Regent Street may communicate a regent of higher standing. Being a regent is synonymous with being a ruler of a monarchy when the usual monarch is unable to rule. There have been regents, oftentimes called prince regents, in the United Kingdom, Belgium, Germany, Denmark, Japan, Norway, Korea, Iceland, Luxembourg, and two dozen other countries.

Renodin Drive

Lyle Renodin, for whom this street is named, was born October 21, 1928, to Joseph Renodin and Anna Hogan Renodin as one of nine children. He was born in New Berlin, New York, graduated from Siena College in 1951 with a bachelor's degree in business administration, and then served two years in the military during the Korean War. Back stateside, he gained his master's degree in business administration from Siena College in 1956 and earned his doctorate degree in economics from New York University in 1970. Renodin taught management at Pace University Graduate School of Business and became a certified public accountant. He worked for the professional corporation Walquist and Renodin in Albany for a whopping 67 years. Ever since he was an elementary student, Renodin has been involved with the Franciscan Sisters of Allegany, New York, which established the Dr. Lyle F. Renodin Foundation in 1998. As of this writing, Lyle Renodin is 90 years old.

Rensselaer Street

In *Hudson-Mohawk Genealogical and Family Memoirs*, Reynolds wrote, "It is beyond possibility to write the history of the city of Albany, New York, without making prominent mention of the Van Rensselaer family." Van Rensselaer has been a powerful name in the Capital Region since the early 1600s, and Bielinski lists no fewer than thirty Van Rensselaer biographies within his Colonial Albany Social History Project website. The minister of the Dutch Church of Albany, Nicholas Van Rensselaer, is specifically memorialized through Rensselaer Street. This street first appeared in 1794, featured on DeWitt's map of the city.

Nicholas Van Rensselaer was born in Amsterdam, Holland, the Netherlands, during September 1636 to Kiliaen Van Rensselaer and Anna Van Wely Van Rensselaer. He served as chaplain to the Dutch Embassy in England and to the Dutch ambassador. He was then appointed a deacon within the English Church by King Charles II. After arriving in the New World in 1675, Van Rensselaer became assistant pastor at Albany's Dutch Church. His sermons outside the church became controversial, and he was asked to stop preaching. Later he became patroon of the Van Rensselaer estate. At 39 years old, in 1675, he married 19-year-old Alida Schuyler. Nicholas Van Rensselaer died in Albany on November 12, 1678. A year after Van Rensselaer's death his widow married Robert Livingston.

Richard J. Conners Boulevard

Richard J. Conners, born March 6, 1910, worked for five decades inside the political halls of Albany. He was an assemblyman noted for his support of elderly citizens and veterans, and he served as Veterans Affairs Committee chairman, Albany alderman, and city council president. Wolfgang Saxon, in *The New York Times*, wrote that Conners was known as "Dean of the Assembly" due to "his age and courtly demeanor." Educated at Christian Brothers Academy and Albany Business College, Conners was a World War II veteran who served in the Pacific and died of pneumonia June 25, 1995. He passed away nine years after his wife, Margaret Egan Conners, had died. Richard J. Conners Boulevard was named during the administration of Mayor Thomas Whalen III, who served from 1983 to 1993. A monument for Conners and a tree planted in his honor are in Academy Park and were dedicated during June 1993. Conner is an occupational name give to someone who works with weights and measures. It comes from the Middle English *connere* ("inspector") and the Old English *cunnan* ("to know").

Ridgefield Street

Ridgefield Street wraps around Ridgefield Park. Ridgefield Park began as a Ridgefield Athletic Association plot in 1884. Before that it belonged to the Albany Cricket Club. The Ridgefield Athletic Association's wealthy members needed a place to play baseball, football, and cricket, ride bikes, compete in track and field, and socialize in a swanky clubhouse. They had their park by the summer of 1885. Next came the highlight of the park, a sixty-foot-tall, 850-foot-long toboggan run that opened in early 1886. Tobogganers covered the 850 feet in less than twenty seconds for a face-numbing average speed of 35 miles per hour. The Ridgefield Athletic Association offered their land and clubhouse to the Young Men's Christian Association (YMCA) in 1912. The YMCA managed the park, including the eight clay tennis courts, until 1968 when the city acquired Ridgefield Park. Then the Ridgefield Tennis Association, now known as the Albany Tennis Club, formed to maintain the courts, and this club has done so since.

Ridgewood Terrace

See Fairview Avenue.

River Road

River Road parallels Normans Kill, which looks more like a river than a stream (*kill* is Dutch for "stream"). The "River" title can be found in 202 street names throughout New York, which makes it the tenth most common street name in the state.

Road Street

Not only is the name distinctive. Connecting South Swan Street with Dove Street, one-way Road Street is the narrowest street in the crummiest condition in eastern Albany (Division Street is pretty bad, too), and it is perhaps the third-oldest named street in all of Albany (State Street was identified as "Jonkers Street" and Maiden Lane was identified as "Rom Straet" on a French parchment map from 1676). The earliest map that identified Road Street by name was a British one from 1758, back when Road Street paralleled Foxes Creek, which now runs under the city. Road Street was called Vossen Kill Road, *Vossen Kill* being Dutch for "Fox Creek." This name didn't pay homage to the mammal. Rather, it was named for Andries de Vos, whose nickname was "The Old Fox." De Vos was born in Holland circa 1600, lived in Beverwyck during the mid-1600s, and died during the 1670s. Vossen Kill was shown on maps as early as circa 1705.

Robin Street
Though Robin Street is near downtown Albany, it's not one of the original "bird streets" mapped by DeWitt by 1794. One of the most widespread of American birds, robins can be found in each of the Lower Forty-Eight states as well as northern Mexico and nearly all of Canada. It often produces two broods during one birthing season and lays beautiful baby blue eggs. Their stout nests are made of grasses and mud, and your author has found them on rain gutters, in the rafters of camping shelters, on branches, and even on top of a ladder stored on the back of a garage. The American robin is in the Thrush family. Robin Street used to be called Duck Street and Schoharie Street.

Roland Drive
John Quadrini constructed Quadrini Estates in this neighborhood and named nearby Quadrini Drive. Perhaps Roland Drive is named for an associate of his. Roland comes from the Norman first name Rowland, which combines *hrod* and *wald*, meaning "fame" and "rule." This name also comes from the Old Norse words *ra* and *lundr*, meaning "roebuck" (a male roe deer) and "wood."

Rooney Road
Rooney Road, New Hope Terrace, and Jennings Drive are part of a 160-unit Albany Housing Authority development called North Albany Homes, which was built during the early 2000s after an earlier housing project was demolished. New Hope Terrace gives prospective residents "new hope," while Jennings Drive is named for former mayor Gerald Jennings because he was instrumental in getting this neighborhood built.

Rooney Road is named for John Rooney, a pastor of Sacred Heart Church in Albany. He was born in Albany on August 26, 1931, and led services at Mary Immaculate in Watervliet, Saint Paul's and Saint Mary's in Troy, Saint Mary's in Albany, and Our Lady of the Assumption in Latham. A noted athlete, Rooney ran no fewer than nineteen marathons. John Rooney died April 20, 2016, after working for the Albany Diocese for more than fifty years. He was buried in Saint Agnes Cemetery in Menands, New York. The name Rooney comes from the Gaelic name O Ruannaidh, which came from the first name Ruannaidh, meaning "champion."

Roosevelt Street

Theodore Roosevelt Jr. was born October 27, 1858, in New York City and spent nearly all his adult life as a public servant. He was New York assemblyman from 1882 to 1884, New York City police superintendent from 1895 to 1897, assistant secretary of the Navy in 1897 and 1898, and New York governor from 1898 to 1900. Roosevelt was vice president of the United States in 1901 for six months, assuming the presidency when William McKinley died. Roosevelt finished McKinley's presidential term and left office in 1909 after serving two terms.

The moments leading up to him becoming president took place in the Adirondack Mountains. After climbing Mount Marcy, the highest peak in the state, on September 13, 1901, with three others and a guide, the group approached Lake Tear of the Clouds and was met by guide Harrison Hall. The guide held a telegram saying that the condition of President McKinley, who had been shot on September 6, was growing worse. Roosevelt descended to Upper Works where he planned to spend the night. Another telegram arrived communicating that McKinley was dying, and this caused Roosevelt to begin a mad dash through the black mountain night to the North Creek train station. Upon arriving in North Creek, Roosevelt was informed he had become president of the United States. McKinley had died while Roosevelt was racing to the station in the early hours of September 14. At 42 years old, Roosevelt became the youngest president ever.

Roosevelt boxed, led the Rough Riders, hunted big game, climbed in the Alps, got shot by a would-be assassin, herded cattle in the Dakotas, explored the jungles of the Amazon, served in combat, and received the Nobel Peace Prize *and* the Medal of Honor. As McCullough wrote in *The American Spirit*, Roosevelt "was ebullient, confident, full of ideas, interested in everything, seldom without a book. He read books, he wrote books. He wrote his own messages to Congress. He wrote his own speeches." A noted conservationist, Roosevelt expanded the national park and national forest systems. Ben Shapiro noted the politician thus: "His fondness for wilderness was legendary," his toughness "mythical." Theodore Roosevelt Jr. died January 6, 1919, and was buried in Youngs Memorial Cemetery in Oyster Bay, New York.

Roosevelt Street is in the "presidential conglomerate" where you'll find Cleveland Street, Grant Avenue, Lincoln Avenue, McKinley Street, Garfield Place, Van Buren Street, and Washington Avenue. Buchanan Street in this neighborhood is not named for James Buchanan. It's named for engineer William Buchanan. Relator Jesse Leonard named these nine streets circa 1900.

Rose Court

Rose Keller Besch, whose last name was Von Bosch before it was Anglicized when she came to the U.S. with her husband, John, in 1852, is memorialized through this street. She was born in 1826 and came to the U.S. from Baden, Germany. Rose Court, Besch Avenue, Betwood Street, Joelson Court, and Clayton Place are the "Besch streets."

Roseland Street
(and Rosemont Street)
It's unknown if Roseland Street and Rosemont Street communicate the feminine name or the flower. Rosemont Street was officially opened and added to the city's street inventory in 1938, and a ribbon-cutting ceremony took place with various politicians dutifully present.

Rosemary Circle
(and Rosemary Drive, Rosemary Drive Extension)
Bill Reddy, a landowner and residential developer, was granted freedom to name streets in this area. He named Rosemary Drive for his great-niece, Rosemary E. Redmond, circa 1959. During the 1970s, Rosemary Drive Extension and Rosemary Circle were added to this neighborhood and followed naming tradition. Reddy submitted the names of his three great-nieces to the city for consideration because these girls had then recently become neighborhood residents. Rosemary was chosen over the two other names, Kathy and Mary, because there was already a Kathy Drive in Colonie (not named for this great-niece) and because Rosemary was the first baby born in this neighborhood. When Rosemary Drive was named, Rosemary E. Redmond was less than a year old. Your author had the privilege to ask Ms. Redmond what it feels like to have a street named for herself—a rare occasion, especially for the living—and she modestly replied that "it's always been a norm" in her life and that she "never really thought about it. People that grew up with me knew it, and it was no big deal."

Rosemary Drive
See Rosemary Circle.

Rosemary Drive Extension
See Rosemary Circle.

Rosemont Street
See Roseland Street.

Russell Road

See North Russell Road.

Rutland Street

Northeast of the Capital Region is the City of Rutland, Vermont. This city's name was bestowed by governor Benning Wentworth in 1761 for John Manners, 3rd Duke of Rutland. Rutland Street carries Manners's title as does the Village of Rutland in Illinois and the towns of Rutland in New York and Massachusetts. The City of Rutland, Iowa, is named so because its settlers had come from the Vermont city of that name.

Manners was born October 21, 1696, to John Manners, 2nd Duke of Rutland, and Catherine Russell Rutland. He held political and royal positions including lord lieutenant of Leicestershire (1721 to 1779), chancellor of the duchy of Lancaster (1727 to 1736), lord steward of the household (1755 to 1761), and master of the horse (1761 to 1766). The man was a voracious collector of art, his appetite barely able to be checked. At the age of 21 he married 17-year-old Bridget Sutton, heiress of Robert Sutton, 2nd Baron Lexinton. They had eleven children. John Manners died May 29, 1779. Originally an English place name, Rutland combines the Old English words *rota* and *land* and means "cherry land."

Ryckman Avenue

Set among the three other "mayoral streets" of Banker Street, Peyster Street, and Hansen Avenue, Ryckman Avenue memorializes Albert Janse Ryckman. He was born circa 1642 in Beverwyck to Jan Janse Ryckman and Tryntie Janse Ryckman. Though Ryckman was mayor, he was best known as a brewer. Suitably, Ryckman Hall on the main University at Albany campus is named for this man, and countless hung over students have entered this hall after beer-guzzling binges. He served as Albany Militia captain and alderman, and he was mayor during 1702 and 1703. Albert Janse Ryckman died during January 1737 and was buried at the Dutch Church. Ryckman Avenue was built circa 1915.

S

Saco Street

In New England, the 136-mile Saco River is in New Hampshire and Maine, Saco Lake is in New Hampshire, and Saco Bay and the City of Saco are in Maine. These employ the Abenaki word *sohk*, meaning "flowing out," as in the end of a river. It is unknown how this obscure New England name landed in Albany. There appears to be a figurative connection to nearby Kenosha Street. The name Kenosha comes from Indian words that translate to "pike," "pickerel," and "place of spawning trout," which refer to rivers entering Lake Michigan. These streets communicate the mouths of rivers. Saco Street used to be called Saco Avenue and was built circa 1914 on land conveyed by Jacob W. Wilbur.

Samaritan Road
At the end of Samaritan Road is Saint Margaret's Center where good Samaritans work. Saint Margaret's Center serves people with disabilities and was founded in 1883 by Episcopal bishop William Doane. A good Samaritan is a humane, compassionate person who helps those in need. This definition references a parable told in Luke 10:30-37 in which a man was robbed and left for dead and a person stopped to assist him while others strolled by.

> Then Jesus answered and said: "A certain man went down from Jerusalem to Jericho, and fell among thieves, who stripped him of his clothing, wounded him, and departed, leaving him half dead. Now by chance a certain priest came down that road. And when he saw him, he passed by on the other side. Likewise a Levite, when he arrived at the place, came and looked, and passed by on the other side. But a certain Samaritan, as he journeyed, came where he was. And when he saw him, he had compassion. So he went to him and bandaged his wounds, pouring on oil and wine; and he set him on his own animal, brought him to an inn, and took care of him. On the next day, when he departed, he took out two denarii, gave them to the innkeeper, and said to him, 'Take care of him; and whatever more you spend, when I come again, I will repay you.' So which of these three do you think was neighbor to him who fell among the thieves?"

Sand Creek Road
The creek that gives this road its name was shown unnamed on the United States Geological Survey's 1893 topographic map, while this agency's 1927 and 1950 edition maps portrayed it as Sandy Creek. Only on their newest, 1994, map did they identify it as Sand Creek. The oldest privately-produced map to mark this creek with its current name is Sampson, Murdock, and Company's map from 1895.

Sand Street
Not named after the surface it was built on, Sand Street is named for a man who owned land in this area. John H. Sand had property on the north and south

sides of Sand Street, at times sharing ownership with William Henry Slingerland. In the 1860s these men were law partners at 50 State Street. Two J. H. Sands are buried in Albany Rural Cemetery. The grave likely belonging to our J. H. Sand notes a birth of 1824 and a death, which occurred in Albany, of June 8, 1899. The Sand Street neighborhood, which includes Slingerland Street, South Dove Street, and Moore Street, was built circa 1890.

Sandalwood Court

Employing a generic, woody name near other generic, woody names such as Ashwood Court, Deerwood Court, and Woodside Drive, Sandalwood Court references trees within the genus Santalum. These trees grow in damp, hot environments in Australia, Bangladesh, India, Indonesia, Pakistan, and Sri Lanka. Production of sandalwood essential oil constitutes a segment of each of these countries' economies. Five milliliters (0.017 fluid ounces) of high-grade sandalwood essential oil costs $125 in the United States.

Sandidge Way

A new sign renaming this street was unveiled July 30, 2016, with mayor Kathy Sheehan and assemblywoman Pat Fahy present. Thus Loughlin Street was sent to Albany's street name graveyard. Land was conveyed to the city by William W. Farley Jr. and George H. C. Farley in 1949 for construction of Loughlin Street.

This name change was proposed via Resolution Number 2.11.15R by Mike O'Brien, twelfth ward Albany Common Council member. O'Brien's resolution intended for this street to be named Jesse and Teresa Sandidge Way. Sandidge Way honors this couple, who, in 1961, became the first black residents to buy a house on this street, back when it was a dirt road. Teresa, who became president of the modern-day Albany Parent Teacher Association, was born in 1926 and died during October 1968. Jesse Sandidge, a trucker, died during the early 1980s. In 1972, Jesse lost his home at 7 Loughlin Street to foreclosure and moved to North Albany.

The renaming of Loughlin Street is questionable for two reasons. One, in most cases, if a politician or resident wants to memorialize someone through a street name, a section of an already-named street is changed, not the entire street. To remove Loughlin entirely is an insult to the person or family who lived through Loughlin Street. Two, this memorial to the Sandidges will be short-lived. The neighborhood is slated for demolition. As of this writing, the Albany Common Council is discussing a change in zoning that will enable Dawn Homes Management to level Sandidge Way to build an apartment complex. In 2014 and 2015, Columbia Development purchased more than a dozen houses on Fuller Road and Loughlin Street and sold them to Tri-City Rentals.

No one lives on Sandidge Way, and it's not even plowed during winter. It is a condemned ghost town.

Sard Road

Rathbone and Company, a stove maker, was formed in 1830 by Joel Rathbone, W. B. Hermance, and other men of Albany. Rathbone was a successful merchant who owned the Kenwood Estate. In 1873, Rathbone, Sard, and Company was then formed and was headed by John F. Rathbone (Joel Rathbone's nephew) and Grange Sard Jr. (sometimes listed as George Sard), for whom Sard Road is named. They served as president and vice president, respectively, and specialized in Acorn brand kitchen and parlor stoves that burned wood or coal. An advertisement from that era spoke of product excellence: "The most durable, the finest fitting and constructed, the handsomest and latest style, and the best stove or range to be had... There are many imitations claiming to be 'as good as the Acorn,' but the only Genuine Acorns are those made by Rathbone, Sard, and Co." Their stoves had cool names. They made the Advance, Albany, Armenian, Bright Light, Dauntless, Good Samaritan, Harvest Queen, Improved Templar, Opal, Orion, Swiss Cottage Parlor, and Zouave, among fifty other models. The company was headquartered between Thacher Street and North Ferry Street. Here the company had a stove foundry, stove works, flask works, offices, and sales room.

During the 1870s, much trouble was brewing at Rathbone, Sard, and Company. A molders' union was demanding higher wages, and the company was not in a position to pay because of increasing competition from American West stove companies that were paying their own workers lower wages. Things got particularly nasty when union workers were replaced with non-union workers. Rathbone, Sard, and Company armed its non-union employees with Smith and Wesson revolvers, and out-of-work union men shot at the non-union workers. Eventually the union men broke their strike when they were informed that the company was considering having their stoves made in prisons. By this time they had sales offices in Albany, Detroit, and Chicago. Their main foundry was on North Ferry Street next to the now-relocated Erie Canal. During the 1880s, wood and coal fell out of fashion, so the company started producing enamel gas stoves and ranges. During this decade Rathbone, Sard, and Company employed 800 workers, more than any other company in Albany. By the dawn of the twentieth century, they had built more than one million stoves.

Grange Sard Jr. was born March 10, 1843, attended Albany Academy and Albany Classical Institute, and was working for Rathbone and Company by 1860, becoming a partner in 1868. The man was a whirlwind of social leadership. He was involved with the Albany Cemetery Association, Albany Home Building Company, Albany Country Club, National Stove Makers Association, Albany Institute, Albany Savings Bank, Dudley Observatory, Emmanuel Baptist

Church, Fort Orange Club, Trust Companies Association of New York State, Washington Park Board of Commissioners, and the Union Trust Company of Albany. In this last position he served with company director Donald McDonald, for whom McDonald Road is named. Sard Road and McDonald Road are appropriately next to each other.

Sard eventually left the stove business and was succeeded by his son, Russell Ellis Sard. Grange Sard Jr. died May 12, 1924, and was buried in Albany Rural Cemetery. His stove business shut down six years later. There used to be a Rathbone Street where today's intersection of North Ferry Street and Water Street is. This street was portrayed on Hendrick's 1857 *Map of the Albany Lumber District*. At the midway point of this street a collection of buildings was labeled Rathbone and Company Stove Foundry.

Sawyer Place

Sawyer Place, Cary Avenue, Hopi Street, and Zuni Street, which are all near each other, were named by Joseph Cary during the 1920s since he was one of this neighborhood's first residents. Sawyer Place carries the maiden name of his mother, Caroline Sawyer Cary. She was born in Hurstville in 1813 as the daughter of Nathaniel Sawyer and died October 27, 1887. She is buried in Albany Rural Cemetery. The name Sawyer translates literally.

School Street

School Street T-bones Montessori Magnet School on its south end. Montessori is part of the Albany City School District and is one of three magnet schools in Albany. The other two are Albany School of Humanities and Thomas O'Brien Academy of Science and Technology. Founded in 1993, Montessori Magnet School is named for educator Maria Montessori, who created Montessori education and was a three-time Nobel Peace Prize candidate. She was born August 31, 1870, in Chiaravalle, Italy, and died May 6, 1952, in Noordwijk aan Zee, the Netherlands. The first Albany Montessori school was set near Lincoln Park. This school relocated to its current spot at the bottom of School Street in 2005.

Schuyler Street

See Pieter Schuyler Court West.

Scott Street

Hopkins's maps that accompanied his *City Atlas of Albany, New York* from 1876 showed Robert Scott owning property where Scott Street now is. This street is named for him though nothing else is known about him. The name Scott notes someone from Scotland or one who spoke Gaelic in that country.

Second Avenue
See First Avenue.

Second Street
See First Avenue.

Seminole Avenue
Building lots on Seminole Avenue were selling as early as 1916 for a measly $500. It's one of the five "Florida streets," and is accompanied by Daytona Avenue, Orlando Avenue, Ormond Street, and Tampa Avenue. The name Seminole is a corruption of the Spanish *cimarrón*, which means "wild one" and "runaway." It was given to this tribe for their uncanny ability to resist and elude invaders.

The Seminole arrived in present-day Florida during the early 1700s as refugees from Indian wars to the north. Upon arrival they displaced, with help from Spaniards, other tribes like the Calusa and Mayaimi. By joining the Creeks and Choctaws and other stray Indians, the Florida Seminole tribe was born. They actually had amicable relations with the British and Spanish, yet they endured the First Seminole War during 1817 and 1818 and then, in 1821, Florida was transferred from Spain to the United States via the Adams-Onís Treaty of 1819. The Seminole were forced to relocate to Oklahoma. Their leader, Osceola, led a ten-year-long resistance to this, the Second Seminole War, which started in 1835. The Third Seminole War followed to round up the rest of the "wild ones." Today the Seminole live in Oklahoma and Florida and total 12,000 members. This is the only American Indian group that never signed a peace treaty with the United States.

Seneca Place
Seneca Place honors the Seneca and is one of a dozen "Indian streets." There are more than 10,000 Seneca in the United States, and most of them live in New York and Oklahoma, while others lives in Brantford, Ontario. The name Seneca comes from their Dutch name, *Sinnekaas*. The City of Seneca in Missouri, the City of Seneca in Kansas, the Town of Seneca Falls in New York, the City of Seneca in South Carolina, and Seneca counties in New York and Ohio are named for this group.

Seneca history began at Canandaigua Lake, one of the Finger Lakes. In ancient times, the Seneca called the lake *Ga-nun-da-sa-ga*, meaning "new settlement," while they called themselves *Nun-da-wa-o-no*, meaning "great hill people." By the 1100s the Seneca joined the Iroquois and extended their territory into Pennsylvania and the Catskill Mountains despite warring with the Huron, Susquehannock, and Lenape. Europeans arrived, joined forces with certain Indian groups, and waged war, turning patches of woods into smoldering wastelands and burning Seneca long houses to the ground. In 1609, an Iroquois-Huron war began, and it lasted until the mid-1600s. The Seneca were involved in a series of mourning wars in which they logged dozens of victories throughout New York and beyond, increasing their population by accepting some survivors of their violence into their culture. They aligned with the British and Dutch during the French and Indian War, and with the Cayuga, Onondaga, Oneida, and Mohawk they formed the Iroquois Confederacy, also known as Five Nations. The Seneca did their best to remain neutral during the Revolutionary War, yet they later sided with the British along with the Mohawk and Cayuga. The Tuscarora and Oneida joined the up-and-coming Americans. Thus ended Six Nations. The Americans won, the Seneca, Mohawk, and Cayuga lost all their land, and former British land formed the Thirteen Colonies. Ensuing treaties caused the Seneca to sell most of their land to the Americans.

Seymour Avenue

Horatio Seymour is memorialized through this street, which was built before 1894. Seymour Mountain in the Adirondacks is named for this politician, too. Seymour was born May 31, 1810, in Pompey Hill, New York, though he grew up in Utica. He attended Geneva College (today's Hobart College) and the American Literary, Scientific, and Military Academy (today's Norwich University). After returning to Utica, Seymour passed his bar exam in 1832 but did not practice. Instead, he became a lifelong politician. He served as New York military secretary, New York assemblyman, mayor of Utica, New York governor, and chairman of the Democratic National Convention. In 1868 he ran for president but lost to Ulysses S. Grant. Seymour, a Democrat, displayed harsh judgments during the election, calling Grant "the nigger candidate" and himself the "the white man's candidate." Horatio Seymour died February 12, 1886, and was buried in Forest Hill Cemetery in Utica, New York.

Shaker Park Drive
(and Shaker Road)

The first Shaker community in the Capital Region was established in today's City of Watervliet during 1776. This group emigrated from Liverpool, England, two years earlier under the label United Society of Believers in the Second Coming of Christ. This group of nine devotees was led by Ann Lee. The congregation soon grew to thirteen worshipers. Meanwhile, other Shaker communities were created in New Lebanon and Groveland in New York; Hancock, Harvard, Shirley, and Tyringham in Massachusetts; Enfield in Connecticut; Canterbury in New Hampshire; and Sabbath Lake, Alfred, and New Gloucester in Maine. Shakers also spread into Kentucky, Illinois, and Indiana.

By 1800, the Watervliet sect had 100 members who lived under a culture that promoted communal living and celibacy. Marriages were banned. Peak membership was reached during the 1840s, and there were 300 people living in this community during 1860. J. H. French reported in 1860 that these 300 people were "living in four distinct families, in a manner peculiar to that people." By the early 1900s, Shaker communities were losing popularity (celibacy is a dreadful thing to maintain). The only active Shaker community still in existence is the Sabbathday Lake Shaker Community in Maine. The Shaker Heritage Society of New York near Albany International Airport preserves the history of this religious group. On the society's grounds are the 1848 Meeting House, 1856 Drying House, and 1915 Shaker Barn Complex. These stand near the abandoned community of Shakers. The Shakers got their name from the spastic body movements they displayed during worship. Despite what some may think, the label "mover and shaker" does not stem from this group's worshipping style. It comes from the poem "Ode" from the 1870s by Arthur O'Shaughnessy, which includes the line "Yet we are the movers and shakers."

Shaker Road
See Shaker Park Drive.

Sheridan Avenue
Early names for this street include Prince Street and Fox Street, the latter name originating from this street being near Foxen Kill, which flowed during early Dutch days. Then this street was named Canal Street in 1842 to honor the Erie Canal. There were attempts to then change Canal Street to Jackson Street, Dongan Avenue (for Thomas Dongan), and Wansboro Avenue (for Thomas Wansboro, mentioned below). The final change from Canal Street to Sheridan Avenue took place May 21, 1900, via a unanimous Common Council vote.

Sheridan Avenue honors Phil Sheridan, local boy done good, who as a child lived on this street. Some sources maintain Sheridan was born in Albany, yet other sources claim he was born in Indiana, or Ireland, or somewhere on the Atlantic Ocean while his parents were emigrating from Ireland to the U.S. At the very least we know that Sheridan was baptized in Albany. Other notable military men have lived on this street. These include United States Military Academy at West Point graduates Colonel Daniel McCarthy (first Expeditionary Forces soldier to set foot in France during World War I), Lieutenant Thomas Wansboro (first U.S. officer killed in the Spanish American War), and

Colonel Gerald Kelleher (Albany's most-decorated World War II soldier). Sheridan Avenue runs parallel to Sherman Street, which is named for another Civil War general.

Sheridan was born March 6, 1831, to John Sheridan and Mary Meenagh Sheridan. He entered the United States Military Academy at West Point in 1848 and graduated in 1853. He was stationed in California, Texas, and the Pacific Northwest and fought in the Rogue River Wars and Yakima War. Sheridan is noted for his leadership in the Civil War from the spring of 1862, when he led his first cavalry unit, until April 9, 1865, when he defeated General Robert E. Lee's Army of Northern Virginia and brought the war to its end. During this war "Little Phil" flew up the ranks, rising from captain to major general in six months. He spent most of his combat time on his black horse Rienzi, later renamed Winchester. The war cost 650,000 troops dead and 420,000 wounded with 50,000 civilians killed. Sheridan went on to fight in Indian wars in Texas and across the Great Plains where he proved the only thing he hated more than a Confederate soldier was an Indian. During November 1883 he was promoted to commanding general of the Army and gained the rank of general of the Army during June 1888. Phil Sheridan died August 5, 1888, and was buried in Arlington National Cemetery. The Sheridan tank is named for this man (and the Sherman tank is named for his Civil War colleague) as are many counties and communities across the United States. In front of Albany's Capitol Building stands a statue of Sheridan on his faithful horse. This monument was unveiled October 7, 1916, and thousands poured into the streets to see the ceremony. In attendance were Sheridan's daughter and widow.

Sherman Street

Named Sand Street until February 15, 1869, Sherman Street honors William Tecumseh Sherman. This street is next to Sheridan Avenue, which is named for the previously-mentioned Civil War general. Sherman is an English name that notes one who uses shears to shear animals or trim cloth. It comes from the Middle English *shereman*.

Sherman's father was Charles Sherman, a lawyer and member of the Ohio Supreme Court, while his mother was Mary Hoyt Sherman. He was born February 8, 1820, in Lancaster, Ohio. His father died when Sherman was just 9 years old, and so he was raised by Thomas Ewing, a lawyer who served as senator from Ohio, secretary of the treasury, and first secretary of the interior. One of Sherman's ten siblings, his brother, John, became very successful, serving as secretary of state, secretary of the treasury, cabinet secretary, president pro tempore of the senate, senator from Ohio, and House of Representatives member from Ohio.

Sherman entered the United States Military Academy at West Point in 1836 and graduated four years later at the age of 20. As an artilleryman he fought in the Second Seminole War though soldiers during the 1840s usually saw more action than just that one conflict. He left the military and worked as a banker in San Francisco and then in New York during the 1850s. In 1859, Sherman became superintendent of Louisiana State Seminary of Learning and Military Academy, today's Louisiana State University. At the beginning of the Civil War in 1861, Sherman left Louisiana and headed north to become assistant secretary of war. That summer he was back in the regular Army as a colonel and was sent to fight in the First Battle of Bull Run, Battle of Shiloh, Vicksburg Campaign, Jackson Expedition, Chattanooga Campaign, Meridian Campaign, Atlanta Campaign, Savannah Campaign, and Carolinas Campaign. Sherman's Civil War unit was disbanded during the spring of 1865.

Soon he commanded the Military Division of the Mississippi to protect railroads and wagon roads from Indian attacks. A renowned Indian-hater, he suggested extinction of certain tribes, the Sioux in particular, yet peaceful negotiations ruled Sherman's world inside the great Indian wars of the American West. In 1869, he became general of the Army and refocused his efforts on killing Indians, this time via the Modoc War, Great Sioux War, and Nez Perce War. While his military life was coming to a close, in 1875 he released his two-volume *Memoirs of General William T. Sherman*, which remains in publication. On February 8, 1884, he retired from the Army and moved to New York City. William Tecumseh Sherman died of pneumonia in New York City on February 14, 1891. Five days after his death a military funeral procession was formed in New York City. His body was then sent to St. Louis where it was buried. One of his sons, Jesuit priest Thomas Sherman, presided over mass.

Silas Avenue

Silas Wright, for whom this street is named, was born May 24, 1795, in Amherst, Massachusetts, and moved to Vermont at a young age. He later attended Middlebury College and graduated in their class of 1815. Upon graduation he moved to New York and settled in Sandy Hill, today's Hudson Falls, to study law. Passing his bar exam in 1819, the up-and-coming politician practiced in Canton and became St. Lawrence County surrogate. His political roles included House of Representatives member from New York (1827 to 1829), New York State comptroller (1829 to 1833), senator from New York (1833 to 1844), and governor of New York (1845 and 1846). He also served as brigadier general in the New York State Militia at the close of his senate term. Silas Wright died in Canton, New York, on August 27, 1847, and was buried in the Silas Wright Cemetery, formerly known as the Old Canton Cemetery. In the Adirondack Mountains, Wright Peak is named for him, this name bestowed in 1873. Wright counties in Minnesota and Missouri are named for him, and there's the Town of Wright in New York's Schoharie County. Silas Avenue was built circa 1928 with nearby Elmo Road, Eva Avenue, Frost Place, Lily Street, and Pansy Street.

Silverberry Place

Silverberry Place is within a "flora cluster," wedged among Blue Bell Lane, Butter Cup Drive, and Daisy Lane. It's also one of two "berry streets" in Albany, the other being Coral Berry Circle. Also known as wolf willow, the American silverberry gets its name from appearing silver overall, not just in its berries. This shrub looks as if it's been sprayed with a fine layer of silver paint. It can be found in New York though its native range remains well outside the borders of the Empire State. It naturally grows from Alaska and across most of Canada south to Utah, Colorado, and Minnesota. Silverberry that's found in the Northeast has "gone wild" after being inadvertently or purposefully moved from its home range. Being common in Alaska, this shrub's berries are cooked with moose fat by the Inuit. Other Alaskans have used silverberry fruit pits to make necklaces. Parts of this bush are eaten by deer, moose, pronghorn, elk, and birds, and it provides shelter for small mammals.

Simpson Avenue

Simpson Avenue was built circa 1922. Well over 100 Simpsons are buried in cemeteries in Albany County, which only adds to the mystery of who this street may be named for. The name Simpson comes from the name Sim, which is a transformation of Simon.

Sligo Street

The land this street is located on was donated to the city by John O'Connell in 1874. Sligo Street, which was built before 1900, was named by local landowner Patrick O'Connell, who was a farmer and descendant of John. Sligo is the Irish coastal town the O'Connell family emigrated from, that area having been settled for at least 6,000 years. Sligo comes from the Irish *sligeach*, meaning "abounding in shells" because shellfish and their remaining shells are found along Sligo's coast.

Slingerland Street

Civil engineer William Henry Slingerland owned land where Slingerland Street now is, and thus this street is named for him. The Hamlet of Slingerlands is also named for this man. He served as Slingerlands's (then called Normanskill and Red Hook) postmaster for more than twenty years, and he was the surveyor of the section of the Albany and Susquehanna Railroad that traversed Slingerlands and passed through the Helderberg Mountains. Slingerland served as member of the assembly during 1880, organized the Suburban Water Company, and served as colonel in the New York State Militia's 115th Regiment. He was born in the Town of New Scotland on November 13, 1820, and died during the early 1900s.

The first Slingerland to arrive in the New World was Teunis Corneliuse Slingerland, who was born in Amsterdam, Holland, the Netherlands, during 1617. He was in Beverwyck by 1650. He first married Anjelte Albertse Bratt and later married Gertie Fonday. Teunis operated a farm and mill on Normans Kill and was the father of four children.

Sloan Street

The last name Sloan dates from within Albany County to 1810 at the latest. John Sloan and Jane Sloan deeded land where this street now is to the city in 1875 and 1885. This street is named for this couple. John was likely born in Scotland in 1814 and died in 1890, while Jane was likely born in Scotland and lived from circa 1814 to 1880. They had at least five children. John and Jane died in Albany, and were buried in Albany Rural Cemetery. Sloan comes from the Gaelic first name Sluaghadhan, which comes from the word *sluaghadh*, which means "raid."

Smith Boulevard

There are more than 1,000 Smiths buried in Albany Rural Cemetery, and more than seventy Smiths were living in the city by 1844. Yet it can be said with confidence that Smith Boulevard is named for Alfred E. Smith, four-time governor of New York. Smith Boulevard is the main street within the Port of Albany, and the Albany Port District was established in 1925 during Smith's governorship.

Smith was born in New York City on December 30, 1873, as the son of Alfred Emanuel Smith (born Alfred Emanuele Ferraro) and Catherine Mulvihill Smith. In his youth, Smith was employed as a newsboy and worked for an oil firm and a fish market, and then dropped out of school prior to the ninth grade. These jobs helped support his family since his father had died when the future governor was only 13. This Democrat went on to serve as New York State assemblyman, Committee on Ways and Means chairman, and New York County sheriff. As governor he served from 1919 to 1920 and 1923 to 1928, repealed prohibition laws, and improved workers' rights and workplace conditions. Smith sought the 1924 presidency yet was not nominated. John Davis of West Virginia ran for the Democrats and received an utter shellacking from Republican Calvin Coolidge. Smith ran for the presidency in 1928 and was soundly defeated by Herbert Hoover. Alfred E. Smith died at Rockefeller Institute Hospital in New York City on October 4, 1944. Many said he died of a broken heart—his wife had died of cancer five months earlier. He was buried in Calvary Cemetery in New York City. *The New York Times* wrote of his death that year:

> In failing health since the death of his wife last May 4, the man whose career had taken him to the high places of politics, of religious life and of philanthropy had entered the hospital on Sept. 22 . . . His condition became critical last Saturday, and he received the last rites of the Roman Catholic Church from Bishop Francis A. McIntyre. Earlier Pope Pius XII, through Archbishop Francis J. Spellman, had transmitted the apostolic benediction. For a time, however, it seemed that the former Governor might rally despite his age, and his condition gave cause for hope up to an early hour this morning.

Soc Ring Road
See Campus Access Road.

Social Science Drive North
(and Social Science Drive South)
These two streets, one to the north and one to the south of University at Albany's Social Science Building on the main campus, could cause a social scientist to ask, "Why does this college have such boring street names?"

Social Science Drive South
See Social Science Drive North.

South Allen Street
See North Allen Street.

South Berkshire Boulevard
See Berkshire Boulevard.

South Bertha Street
See Bertha Street.

South Dove Street
See Dove Alley.

South Enterprise Drive
See Commerce Avenue.

South Ferry Street
See North Ferry Street.

South Frontage Road
See North Frontage Road.

South Hawk Street
See North Hawk Street.

South Lake Avenue
See North Lake Avenue.

South Lansing Street
See John Street.

South Life Science Lane
See North Life Science Lane.

South Main Avenue
See North Main Avenue.

South Manning Boulevard
See Manning Boulevard.

South Marshall Street
See Marshall Street.

South Pearl Street
See North Pearl Street.

South Pine Avenue
See East Pitch Pine Road.

South Port Road
See Anchor Street.

South Street
Being the southernmost street in a four-block group, the South Street name is lackluster, especially considering this street used to be called a historically stout Gansevoort Street. At the other, north, end of the four-block area is North Street. In the middle are Main Street and Center Street. South Street once marked the southern boundary of the Dutch Church's pasture.

South Swan Street
See North Swan Street.

Southern Boulevard
Southern Boulevard is named so because it reaches the southern border of the City of Albany. Conversely, Northern Boulevard runs along a northern border of the city.

Sparkill Avenue
The place name Sparkill is found far south of Albany. There is eight-mile-long Sparkill Brook of New York, and there is Sparkill Creek, which is a tributary of Sparkill Brook. And then there's the Hamlet of Sparkill, New York, that was named by John DeWindt in 1750. The "Spar" part of Sparkill references pines being used as spars and masts on ships. In 1915, land was conveyed to the city by Jacob W. Wilbur for construction of Sparkill Avenue.

As readers surely know by now, the Dutch word *kill* means "stream" and has nothing to do with harming anything or anyone. Nonetheless, People for the Ethical Treatment of Animals (PETA), during the 1990s, demanded that New York's Town of Fishkill change its name to "Fish Save" because the word kill "suggests cruelty." CNN quoted PETA's spokeswoman, Anne Sullivan, saying that the renaming seemed "like a lighthearted subject at first. But the real issue behind the name of Fishkill is the violent imagery." PETA was determined to "encourage the citizens of any town whose name reflects cruelty to animals to consider changing it." Village of Fishkill mayor George Carter called PETA's idea "idiotic." Can any reader here disagree with Mayor Carter?

Sparrowhill

There are fourteen species of sparrows in New York: house, American tree, chipping, field, vesper, Savannah, grasshopper, Henslow's, sharp-tailed, seaside, song, Lincoln's, swamp, and white-throated. The most common species in Albany is the house sparrow, which hops around parking lots, across yards, and down sidewalks when it's not hogging seeds at birdfeeders. As told in *National Audubon Society Field Guide to North American Birds*, "Wherever this species occurs it is intimately associated with man, as its scientific name *domesticus* suggests." This guide further explained that the North American population of house sparrows is not native, instead having "descended from a few birds released in New York City's Central Park in 1850." Sparrowhill is the invention of a developer who wanted a bucolic name for this street, which is in the Dunes Neighborhood.

Spencer Street

It is highly likely that Ambrose Spencer is honored through this street. He was born December 13, 1765, in Salisbury, Connecticut, to Philip Spencer and Mary Moore Spencer. After graduating from Harvard University in 1783, he served as New York attorney general, New York State Supreme Court judge, New York State Supreme Court chief justice, House of Representatives member from New York, and Constitutional Convention member and delegate. He was 35th mayor of Albany, serving for two terms, from 1824 to 1826. Spencer ran against John Lansing Jr. for his first term and had no opponents during his second election. He married three times. His first wife was Laura Canfield Spencer, the daughter of whom he had studied law under, John Canfield. His second and third wives were Mary Clinton Spencer and Katherine Clinton Spencer, respectively. They were sisters and the daughters of DeWitt Clinton.

Ambrose Spencer, who came to Albany from Hudson, died March 13, 1848, in Lyons, New York, and was buried in Albany Rural Cemetery. His most notable son was John Canfield Spencer (1788–1855), a lawyer who served as secretary of war, secretary of the treasury, secretary of the State of New York, senator from New York, House of Representatives member from New York, assemblyman, and speaker of the New York Assembly. The name Spencer noted someone who worked in a pantry, the Old English *spence* meaning "storeroom."

Sprague Place

The Sprague Chapel, more formally known as the Sprague Presbyterian Church, used to stand at today's 5 Sprague Place. It was built before 1870 and demolished in 1902. The chapel was run by the reverend William Sprague, who was the author of the hefty multi-volume *Annals of the American Pulpit* published in 1858. He was born in Andover, Connecticut, on October 16, 1795, and died in Flushing, New York, on May 7, 1876. In an *Albany Evening Journal* article that appeared shortly after the reverend's death, the Second Presbyterian Church recalled Sprague as "a venerated and beloved pastor, for who a period of forty years labored amongst us with unexampled zeal. We remember his unwearied exertions to promote the cause of his Master, and every object connected with the best interest of the church of which he was one of the most able in indefatigable servants." Sprague Place used to be part of Lexington Avenue, which used to be called Snipe Street. Name change took place in 1885. The name Sprague comes from the name Sparks, which notes someone witty.

Spring Street

Spring Street in Albany is named for the same reason that so many other Spring streets are named. There was a spring there. In 1678, a spring up the hill from the present intersection of State and Lodge streets was found and, as Waite wrote, "was directed into [Fort Albany] through conduits made of pine and oak posts, and in 1679 this water system was extended from the fort down the hill to the foot of State Street." This puts the spring not far from today's Spring Street. This wasn't the only spring in Albany. A mineral spring was discovered under present-day South Ferry Street in 1820 when someone was boring for a water source. J. H. French wrote that "this boring was commenced to obtain water for a brewery. At a depth of 480 feet, sparkling water, of a saline taste and impregnated with carbureted hydrogen gas, was obtained. The boring was continued to a depth of 617 feet without any change in the character of the product. A few rods distant a second well was bored with similar results." Cohoes, Colonie, Mechanicville, Saratoga Springs, and Troy have their own Spring streets.

Springsteen Road

The Springsteens operated a farm where this street now is. Elmer B. Springsteen, who was married to Pearl Springsteen, was living on Springsteen Road as late as 1963. During November 2016, Springsteen Road was officially nicknamed Emma Dickson Way. Dickson, born in 1944, led a movement to preserve the Rapp Road Community, which she still lives in. Albany has many nicknamed—honorary—streets. For example, Western Avenue is Coach Bob Ford Way, and State Street is Jack's Oyster House Way. Writers have communicated that these streets were "renamed" when the extra titles were added, yet this is incorrect. In all instances the official street names remain. The Way honor is simply that: honorary.

Spruce Street

Spruce Street used to run clear down to Eagle Street (now it ends at Dove Street). Though this tree species does not naturally grow in the Capital Region, it was surely milled near this street, which appeared on maps by 1838. Eastern North America has four species of spruce: white, black, red, and Norway. Before loggers arrived in the Adirondack Mountains, spruce accounted for fifteen percent—900,000 acres—of standing timber in that range. This species has been sought by lumbermen for more than a century, especially during the height of North Country logging, which ran from 1850 to 1920. Spruce trees were preferred because of their straight, tall trunks. The first log drive ever held in the Adirondacks, in 1813, moved spruce. By the 1850s, the Empire State, with its 7,000 sawmills, became the dominant lumber state, logging more acres and hauling more board feet than Maine, the Pine Tree State. In 1905, more than 200 million board feet of spruce were cut in Upstate New York.

St. Agnes Lane

Agnes of Rome, patron saint of girls, was born circa 291 and died circa 304. Her remains are kept in Rome's Church of Saint Agnes Outside the Wall, while her skull is displayed in the Sant'Agnese in Agone, another church in Rome. Her name is derived from the Greek *hagn*, meaning "pure" and "sacred." Albany's Saint Agnes School for Girls was founded in 1870 by William Doane when he was 38 years old. On June 19, 1871, he laid the cornerstone, and the school opened on Halloween 1872. Saint Agnes School for Girls was initially located on Elk Street opposite All Saints Cathedral and ceased independent operations in 1975 when it joined Kenwood Academy to form Doane Stuart School. Saint Agnes Schools still operate in fifteen states, and international locations can be found in Australia, India, Sri Lanka, Canada, and the Philippines. Saint Agnes churches are even more widespread.

St. Anns Place

Saint Ann's Church, which is close to St. Anns Place, gives this street its name. This church was founded in 1866, and it merged with Saint John's Church in 1978. This new partnership then merged with Saint James Church in 2010. This conglomerate thus became Saint Francis of Assisi Parish in 2010 under the Roman Catholic Diocese of Albany. Saint Ann, also identified as Saint Anna and Saint Hannah, was mother of the Virgin Mary, who was the mother of Jesus. Saint Ann is the patron saint of specific classes of women as well as cabinet-makers, horseback riders, and sailors.

St. George Place

Saint George Antiochian Orthodox Church stands on St. George Place. This organization was founded by Syrian immigrants in 1933, and their first church stood on South Dove Street. In his article "A Distant War Echoes in Local Church," Paul Grondahl wrote that "a dozen or so families first met for worship in each other's homes off Second Avenue starting in the 1920s. The men pooled money won at weekly card games and built a little red brick church in 1956 . . ." Services were once only offered in Arabic. Sunday services are now given in English as well.

Saint George was born circa 278 and died April 23, 303. He was the son of Gerontius, his father, and Polychronia, his mother, and he lost his parents by the time he was a teenager. Some accounts put his birthplace inside present-day Turkey, while others maintain he was born in present-day Palestine. He became a Roman solider and was captured, tortured, and executed by decapitation by Emperor Diocletian's men during the ten-year-long Great Persecution against Christians in the Roman Empire. His body was buried in the Roman province of Syria Palaestina. The name George comes from the Greek Georgios, meaning "earth worker" and "farmer." Saint George is the patron saint of a handful of countries in the Eastern Hemisphere.

St. James Place

In the beginning there was Saint Ann's Church, founded in 1866, which merged with Saint John's Church in 1978. In 2010, these two churches merged with Saint James Church, which was founded in 1913. This conglomerate then became Saint Francis of Assisi Parish in 2010 under a Roman Catholic Diocese of Albany initiative. The Saint Francis of Assisi Parish Church, which retains a cornerstone identifying it as Saint James Church, stands on the corner of St. James Place and Delaware Avenue. Sampson and Murdock Company's map from 1915 portrayed St. James Place as Revere Avenue, this name likely memorializing Paul Revere.

The Apostle Saint James "the Greater" was the son of Zebedee, his father, and Salome, his mother, and he was the brother of John "the Less," who was also an Apostle. Saint James's year of birth is undetermined, though he certainly died in the year 44. The Roman Catholic preacher and author Saint Francis of Assisi was born in Assisi, Italy, circa 1181, as the son of Pietro di Bernardone, his father, and Pica de Bourlemont, his mother. He served as a soldier and founded the Franciscan Order in 1210. After formation of this order, Saint Francis preached far and wide, his message centering on the righteousness of poverty. He died October 3, 1226, and was made a saint by Pope Gregory IX in 1228. Saint Francis was buried May 25, 1230, at today's Basilica of Saint Francis of Assisi in Italy.

St. Josephs Terrace

The backside of Saint Joseph's Church faces St. Josephs Terrace, which is adjacent to Saint Joseph's Park. Construction of this church, which is listed on the National Register of Historic Places, was completed in 1860 in Gothic style and designed by Patrick Keely. Saint Joseph's Church ceased offering services in 1994 and was purchased by Historic Albany Foundation in 2003. This city now owns this striking church, which remains in disgraceful condition. St. Josephs Terrace opened in 1881 and was first called St. Josephs Park Terrace. Saint Joseph, a carpenter and the patron saint of workers, is generally accepted to be the father of Jesus and is reported to have lived to the age of 111.

Stanford Court

Stanford Court was built with Carlisle Court, Fordham Court, and Marlborough Court circa 1929, and the first home was built on Stanford Court circa 1935. Until 1967, the year Town of Bethlehem lands were annexed to the City of Albany, this street marked the boundary between these two municipalities. The west side of Stanford Court was in the town while the east side was in the city. It is thought to be one of the eight "English streets" and is accompanied by Carlisle Court, Cheshire Court, Fordham Court, Kensington Place, Marlborough Court, Windsor Place, and Victoria Way. It's likely named after the five-square-mile deserted village and civil parish of Stanford, which stood in County Norfolk, England. The British Army took over this area during World War II for training purposes and dubbed it the Stanford Battle Area, which is still in operation.

If Stanford Court does not carry an English name, then it's named after Stanford University, especially since nearby Fordham Court may honor Fordham University. Stanford University was founded by Leland Stanford and Jane Stanford and named for their son, Leland Stanford Jr. This school, whose official name is Leland Stanford Junior University, opened in 1891 and is in Stanford, California, which is named for the senior Stanford (California's Mount Stanford is named for this man, too, because he was governor). Stanford is best known for having the honor of driving home the final, golden spike of the Trans Continental Railroad at Promontory Summit, Utah, on May 10, 1869, to mark completion of the line. But he missed the spike and hit the rail with his silver-headed sledgehammer, Stanford not being used to such grueling manual labor. Nevertheless, the crowd went bananas when they heard the "dink" of metal on metal. The telegraph operator sent it out: "DONE!" The golden spike Stanford never hit is on display at the Cantor Arts Museum at Stanford University.

Stanford had roots in the Capital Region. He was born in Watervliet on March 9, 1824, as one of eight children of Josiah Stanford and Elizabeth Phillips Stanford. He practiced law at Wheaton, Doolittle, and Hadley in Albany and married Jane Elizabeth Lathrop, a native of the city. By the 1850s, Stanford was living in California and became filthy rich through railroad, bank, mercantile, and insurance company entrepreneurships. Leland Stanford died in Palo Alto, California, on June 21, 1893, and was buried at Stanford University. His wife died of strychnine poisoning February 28, 1905, while in Hawaii. She was nearly killed by this poison on January 14 when she drank a glass of spring water. The second time her mysterious murderer succeeded, Stanford grunting through clenched teeth her final words, "This is a horrible death to die."

Stanwix Street

The neighboring streets of Stanwix Street, Bertha Street, Hurlbut Street, Jeanette Street, Marshall Street, and West Van Vechten Street were laid out and named by Teunis Van Vechten. He reportedly named these six streets for family members of his. Most of these streets appeared on maps by 1895, but it wasn't until 1915 that their names were officially accepted by the City of Albany. Despite a thorough genealogical search, no Van Vechten relative named Stanwix was discovered. A mistake in historical reporting may have been made.

Stanwix Street may be named for British soldier John Stanwix and the fort he oversaw construction of, Fort Stanwix, which stood in today's City of Rome, New York. This fort was along an ancient Indian portage, the Oneida Carrying Place, that connected Wood Creek and the Mohawk River. The creek, portage, and river thus connected Lake Ontario with the Hudson River. Fort Stanwix was built by the British from 1758 to 1762 during the French and Indian War, yet by 1774 it was run down and served no purpose related to combat operations. The British abandoned it that year. In 1776, the Americans occupied the grounds, repaired the fort, and renamed it Fort Schuyler in honor of General Philip Schuyler. As told by the National Park Service, during the American Revolution this fort was

> under the command of Col. Peter Gansevoort, [who] successfully repelled a prolonged siege, in August 1777, by British, German, Loyalist, Canadian, and American Indian troops and warriors commanded by British Gen. Barry St. Leger. The failed siege combined with the battles at Oriskany, Bennington, and Saratoga thwarted a coordinated effort by the British in 1777, under the leadership of Gen. John Burgoyne, to take the northern colonies, and led to American alliances with France and the Netherlands. Troops from Fort Stanwix also participated in the 1779 Clinton-Sullivan Campaign and protected America's northwest frontier from British campaigns until finally being abandoned in 1781.

That final year, Fort Schuyler was destroyed by opposing forces: fire and flood. The City of Rome was built over the remains. In 1935, President Franklin D. Roosevelt signed the Wagner-Sisson Bill to create Fort Stanwix National Monument, a replica of the fort, which can be visited right near the spot of the original fort. Construction began in 1973 and was mostly completed by 1976, just in time for America's bicentennial.

John Stanwix was born as John Roos in County Nottinghamshire, England, circa 1693. He took the name Stanwix when he inherited the estates of Thomas Stanwix, his uncle. John Stanwix joined the British Army in 1706 and was a lieutenant colonel by 1745. By 1761 he had been made lieutenant general. His political roles included serving as member of Parliament for nearly twenty years and being appointed lieutenant governor of the Isle of Wight. He was lost at sea during the fall of 1766 while traveling from Ireland to Wales aboard *The Eagle*.

Starling Avenue

As one of eighteen "bird streets," Starling Avenue is set outside the "bird blocks" of downtown Albany. It's in the southwest corner of the city and is flanked by another bird street, Oriole Street. There are 114 Old World species of starlings, yet only one is prominent in New York: the European starling. Also known as the common starling, the European starling can be found in every state as well as the northern reaches of Mexico and an enormous band of southern Canada. Starlings group in flocks that reach into the tens of thousands. They're commonly seen as pests because they poop in prodigious proportions. European starlings in America are descendants of 100 birds released in Central Park in 1890 by the American Acclimatization Society. This organization thought it best to introduce flora and fauna from Europe. The leader of the American Acclimatization Society at the time, Eugene Schieffelin, felt that any bird mentioned within the works of William Shakespeare should live in North America. Conveniently, Schieffelin is not around to clean up the prodigious proportions of poop.

State Campus Road

See Campus Access Road.

State Drive

State Drive on the University at Albany's main campus leads to State Quad, a housing unit for freshmen. Like Dutch Quad, State Quad is designed for recess students to stay in beyond the normal academic calendar. That's all your author has to state about this drive.

State Street

In 1797, the New York State legislature settled in Albany, thus our permanent state capital was born. That same year the name State Street was born, this street having formerly been called Prince Street, Jonkers Street, Joncaer Street, Jonckaer Street, and Yonkers Street. During research your author never asked himself, Why was it called Jonkers Street? This question later emerged like a whale breaching the surf when a colleague commented that this name probably honored Adriaan Van der Donck.

Van der Donck, for whom the City of Yonkers, New York, is named, was born circa 1618 in the Netherlands. He attended the University of Leiden and graduated with doctorate degrees in canon and civil law. He came to the New World in 1640 with the help of Kiliaen Van Rensselaer, who made Van der Donck an official within his patroonship. Van der Donck's performance didn't match the patroon's expectations. He was too laid back, more interested in exploring the countryside and eating venison with Indians than collecting tenants' rent. By 1644, Van der Donck was no longer working for Van Rensselaer. No matter. Two years later, Willem Kieft allotted Van der Donck 24,000 acres north of Manhattan, and there Van der Donck built an estate so grand that people started calling him the *jonkheer*, the "young gentleman." Soon he was promoting opportunity in the New World with his *Description of New Netherland*. Adriaan Van der Donck died in 1655, and his land was sold by his widow in 1667.

In *Albany's State Street*, Papp wrote that this street was built on an Indian trail that existed in 1609 when Henry Hudson floated up his namesake river. Papp told a romantic tale of natives in the primeval forests going about and minding their business—just another day in the wilderness—until "a signal was given that a strange vessel was sailing up the great stream skirting the forest. With swift tread the moccasin dwellers of the forest hastened to the river bank, where they watched the approach of the *Half Moon* that bore Henry Hudson. As it drew nearer, the Indians clambered into some threescore canoes, and pushed off in the direction of the strange craft." Some of these Indians ran down that path where today's State Street is.

Fast-forward to the 1790s, and State Street was a main thoroughfare. That decade it was greatly improved by being paved, likely with cobble stones. Hislop wrote that "the Council had State Street paved along the sides for the use of pedestrians," too. The center of the street was still a stinking quagmire, though, "for it was reported that [in 1795] a wagon belonging to General Schuyler sank to the hubs while trying to go up" it. Broadway was paved, too, and paving projects then spread throughout the city.

This street is historically notable in five regards: the first brick house in the New World was built on State Street, one of the oldest streets to be named on a map is State Street, Albany's first fire department was created because of a State Street fire, the city's first illuminated street was State Street, and State Street was the path of the condemned.

The first brick house in the New World was built on the corner of State and Pearl streets in 1682. It was the home of Teunis Vanderpoel, Balthazar Lydius, and Gideon Schaats and stood until 1832. It is the main house on the cover of this book.

A French parchment map from 1676 labeled today's State Street as "Jonkers Street" and today's Maiden Lane as "Rom Straet." This makes these the first Albany streets to be identified by name on a map.

A conflagration on State Street is responsible for creation of the first fire department of present-day Albany. During the 1600s, fire was a terrifying threat. In November 1681, seven houses on State Street simultaneously burned to the ground. Barely before the ashes cooled the court created ten fire guardian positions, and the settlement was divided into ten fire districts.

Concerning illumination, State Street and Broadway were the first streets to be lighted by whale oil lamps. The first lamps were installed in 1771 but didn't work out. New, reliable ones were installed circa 1793. Seven years later only streets a half-mile from the river were illuminated, Reynolds writing that year in *Albany Chronicles* that "the rest of the land being unsettled upon" was pitch black. By 1829 the city had 586 lamps.

State Street was the lane that "dead men walking" took during the 1700s and 1800s. Papp wrote it was customary that "when men were then executed, the victims marched up State Street, each garbed in a robe of white." Unruly crowds followed the condemned to the gallows, gleefully celebrating death-meted justice.

Stephen Street

Stephen Street is named for Stephen Van Rensselaer I or his descendants. He was born March 23, 1707, to Kiliaen Van Rensselaer (1663–1719, not to be confused with his grandfather of the same name who lived from 1586 to 1643) and Maria van Cortlandt Van Rensselaer. After the death of his brother, Jeremias, sixth patroon of Rensselaerswyck, in 1745, he became seventh patroon of Rensselaerswyck. Stephen Van Rensselaer I, who was married to Elizabeth Groesbeck Van Rensselaer, died in 1747.

Next there was Stephen Van Rensselaer II, son of Stephen Van Rensselaer I and Elizabeth Groesbeck Van Rensselaer. He was born June 2, 1742, died October 19, 1769, and was eighth patroon of Rensselaerswyck. He served as a captain in the Albany County Militia and built a new Van Rensselaer Manor House in 1765. He was married to Catherine Livingston Van Rensselaer.

Stephen Van Rensselaer III was born November 1, 1764, as the son of Stephen Van Rensselaer II and Catherine Livingston Van Rensselaer. He was married to Margarita Schuyler Van Rensselaer, and they had three children. She died in 1801 and Van Rensselaer then married Cornelia Bell Patterson, who bore him nine children. He was the most accomplished of the four men within this entry. He graduated from Harvard College and served as ninth patroon of Rensselaerswyck, House of Representatives member from New York, lieutenant governor of New York, senator from New York, and president of Albany Savings Bank. He died January 26, 1839, and was buried in Albany Rural Cemetery. The Town of Stephentown, New York, is named for him.

The final patroon of Rensselaerswyck was Stephen Van Rensselaer IV, at times referred to as "The Young Patroon" and "The Last of the Patroons." As the son of Stephen Van Rensselaer III and Margarita Schuyler Van Rensselaer, he was born March 29, 1789. He graduated from Princeton University and served as an officer in the New York State Militia. Patroonship ended during his time. Because those who lived on patroons' lands were little better off than indentured servants, these tenants rose in revolt while the New York Legislature passed laws that weakened patroon power. The Van Rensselaers sold nearly all of their land by the 1850s. Stephen Van Rensselaer IV died May 25, 1868, in Albany.

Steuben Street

In the 1700s men's names conveyed class. Such was the case with Baron Friedrich Wilhelm August Heinrich Ferdinand von Steuben, for whom Steuben Street is named. The first map to portray this street was Bogart's map of North Market Street from 1790. Steuben was born in Magdeburg, Prussia, on September 17, 1730, as the son of Wilhelm von Steuben and Elizabeth von Jagvodin von Steuben. Steuben was a born fighter, seeing warfare in the War of the Austrian Succession, French and Indian War, and American Revolutionary War. He was wounded in combat on numerous occasions and spent time as a prisoner of war. In 1777, Steuben met Benjamin Franklin in Paris, and Steuben's connection with the War for Independence began. At first he snubbed Franklin when invited to come to America to fight the British without pay. Later he was invited to meet with George Washington himself. He arrived stateside with his faithful greyhound, Azor, and a few associates during the fall of 1777 and reached Valley Forge, Pennsylvania, on February 23, 1778, to report to Washington. He became inspector general of the Army and whipped units' training procedures, combat techniques, and sprawling encampments into shape. He wrote America's first military manual, which is in publication today as *Baron Von Steuben's Revolutionary War Drill Manual*. He smartly paid attention to camp sanitation, an aspect of military life that had been ignored. His push for cleanliness saved thousands of lives that would have otherwise been lost to disease.

Steuben then became General Steuben, led divisions during the war, and was discharged during the spring of 1784. For his selfless service to the revolution he was given 16,000 acres in New York. He became an American citizen, retired to Oneida County, and was elected as regent to what was to become the State University of New York. Baron Friedrich Wilhelm August Heinrich Ferdinand von Steuben died November 28, 1794, and was buried at what would become the Steuben Memorial State Historic Site, which is in the Town of Steuben, which is named for him. New York's Steuben County, Indiana's Steuben County, Maine's Town of Steuben, Ohio's City of Steubenville, and scores of streets are named for this friend of the Revolution.

Stonehenge Drive
(and Stonehenge Lane)

Stonehenge Drive and Stonehenge Lane are named for nearby Stonehenge Gardens Apartments, which opened in 1941. An advertisement from that year guaranteed prospective residents that the apartments were "the ultimate in modern living set in a pastoral scene." If you didn't like the scenery, you could just stay inside. The apartments' interiors were designed by Dorothy Draper, a "famous interior decorator." Stonehenge Drive and Stonehenge Lane were built after 1950.

These streets are only a few hundred feet from each other yet thousands of miles from the real Stonehenge in County Wiltshire, England. Constructed 5,000 years ago, Stonehenge, which was once called Giant's Dance, is a collection of burial grounds as well as massive stones set on their edges. The name Stonehenge comes from the early 1100s word *stanenges*, meaning "stone gallows." The Stonehenge area used to be forested, much like hundreds of thousands of other acres within the United Kingdom. Trees were cleared circa 3500 B.C., and burial grounds, mounds, ditches, and stone and wooden structures were built. Festivities were held, animals were slaughtered and consumed, and bodies were cremated and then buried, the graves marked with stones. Parallel ditches and embankments led two miles to the River Avon. The enormous stones this site is known for were transported as far as 150 miles, being quarried in Wales. Many measure seven feet in height, four feet in width, and three feet wide, while others are twice as big and weigh between 25 and 50 tons each. Some were purposefully placed to align with the midsummer rising sun and midwinter setting sun. Construction stopped circa 1600 B.C. The builders of Stonehenge left no written records. Popular theories hold that this area was a site for practicing religion, worshiping ancestors, burying the dead, healing the living, or watching the night sky.

Stonehenge Lane

See Stonehenge Drive.

Summit Avenue

See Fairview Avenue.

Sunset Avenue

Your author visited this street precisely at sunset and was not impressed. Sunset Avenue doesn't quite live up to its name, though it's a name that's easy on the ears, which is what the developer wanted when it was built circa 1924. Though there is only one "Sunset" street in Albany, New York has another 244 of them, which makes the Sunset moniker the fourth most common street name in the state.

SUNY at Albany Entrance

With plenty of dull description in its name, SUNY at Albany Entrance connects Washington Avenue with East University Drive on the University at Albany's main campus.

Swartson Court

During the 1800s, Charles F. Schwartz owned 95 acres that spread across today's Swartson Court and neighboring streets. In this area stood the Schwartz farm, which dated to 1829. The Schwartz's main home, a sprawling brick house built in 1830, stands at present-day 246 Whitehall Road and is the oldest home in this section of Albany. By 1898, this farm, called the Swarts farm from about that point forward, included three barns, the fifteen-room brick house, and an orchard. At that time, the farm was in the Town of Bethlehem, but most of it was annexed to the City of Albany in 1916. In 1927, land was conveyed to the city by three of Charles's children—Edward, Helen, and Hattie—for construction of this street. Swartson Court was accepted by the city as a public street that same year and was named for Edward, who was running the farm during that era. Meanwhile, these siblings moved into a brick home, which stands at present-day 17 Stanford Court. By 1930, the land bore little resemblance to what Edward was familiar with. Financial trouble descended upon the siblings, who controlled the remains of the once-expansive farm. The day before Christmas Eve of 1943, Federal Investors, a New York City-based firm, bought the tax liens on the Swarts's farm, their Whitehall Road home, and their Stanford Court home. They were to be evicted within five months.

With the farm lost and development closing in on him, Edward felt there was only one way out of his predicament: death. During mid-January of 1944, Edward (50 years old), Helen (60), and Hattie (54) were sitting around a table in the basement of their Stanford Court home when Edward took out a pistol and shot Helen dead. Hattie made a run for the cellar staircase but was shot dead, too. Edward remained in the home with the bodies for a few days and then burned the corpses, attempted to burn the home to the ground, and returned to the basement to shoot himself in the head with the .38 revolver he had used to murder his sisters. A neighbor had noticed no activity at the homestead since January 23 and entered the home on the 31st to see what was the matter. He found the bodies in the basement and called the police. The fourth Swarts child, Charles M., who was living in New York City during the crime, inherited the family property but rid himself of it by June 1944. Within two years, Lewis Ross bought the remaining Swarts land in the Town of Bethlehem,

Edward McCormick purchased the Whitehall Road home, and William LaHait and Helen LaHait were renting the Stanford Court home.

Coincidentally, there's a Swartz farm in the Town of Schodack in Rensselaer County, and members of this family have experienced similar tragedy. On September 8, 2007, Edward N. Swartz shot his father, Edward R., and then killed himself. The father and son were 50 and 24 years old, respectively. It appears the Swarts farmers of Albany and the Swartz farmers of Schodack were unrelated. When your author contacted Scott Swartz, brother of Edward R., to see if he could offer additional information regarding the Albany Swarts story, he said that he had never heard of it.

Swinton Street

The first City of Albany recorder was Isaac Swinton, for whom this street is likely named. He was born circa 1653 as the son of John Swinton and Margaret Stewart Swinton. In *Law and Ordinances of the Common Council of the City of Albany*, Thomas Dongan, first royal governor of New York, declared in exhaustive clarity that he "assigned, named, ordained, and constituted, and by these presents do assign, name, ordain, and constitute, Issac Swinton, to be the present Recorder of the said city, to do and execute all things, which unto the office of the Recorder of the said city doth, or may any way appertain belong." Swinton died during July 1687. His namesake street was built sometime between 1873 and 1891. The name Swinton is English and Scottish and is a place name in those lands. It combines the Old English *swin* with *tun*, translating to "pig" and "settlement."

Sycamore Street

The sycamore is a stately though not unique-looking tree. The London plane-tree looks much like the sycamore though the London planetree has greener branches and is usually smaller. Both species are in the Sycamore family and prefer riverbanks and floodplains. Their size is cited with succinct language in *National Audubon Society Field Guide to North American Trees*: "Large tree with massive trunk." There is a sycamore in Peebles Island State Park in Waterford that is five feet in diameter, but this is nothing compared to a London planetree on the Vassar College campus. That tree measures nine feet in diameter. Planted by the college's class of 1906, Vassar College's London planetree has been named one of New York's most historical trees and was once in the running for the Guinness Book of World Records' longest unsupported tree branch. The U.S. hosts the communities of Sycamore in Illinois and Ohio, the community of Kishwaukee and the Kishwaukee River in Illinois, and the City of Senatobia and Senatobia Creek in Mississippi. *Kishwaukee* and *senatobia* are Indian words for "sycamore." In 1915, a Common Council ordinance was introduced to acquire land for construction of Sycamore Street, which was built before 1920.

T

Taft Avenue

Taft Avenue is not part of the "presidential conglomerate," yet it's likely named for President William Taft. He was born in Cincinnati, Ohio, on September 15, 1857, to Alphonso Taft and Louise Torrey Taft. His father was a lawyer who served as secretary of war and attorney general during the 1870s. William Taft attended Yale University and graduated salutatorian in the class of 1878. He graduated from Cincinnati Law School in 1880 and passed his Ohio bar exam. After practicing law, Taft became collector of internal revenue for Ohio's First District, appointed by Chester Arthur. He didn't last long in this position. Taft refused to play political games, which involved firing employees who were not in political agreement with their supervisors. He served on the Cincinnati Superior Court and married Helen Herron during June 1886 after meeting her at an occasion that few lovers meet at nowadays. They met at a sledding event. She would be his bride for more than forty years. Positions as solicitor general of the United States, Cincinnati Sixth Circuit judge, Cincinnati Law School professor, civilian governor of the Philippines, and secretary of war followed for Taft.

Taft is best known for serving as 27th president of the United States, his single term running from March 4, 1909, to March 4, 1913, with vice president James Sherman working alongside him during half of this term (Sherman had health problems and had to leave his post during the fall of 1912). Taft reorganized the State Department and maintained a conservative foreign policy while balancing interactions with Central America and South America. He became the first president to visit Mexico, and his presidency remained stable despite revolutions in China, Mexico, and Central America. He lost reelection to Woodrow Wilson. As a civilian Taft accepted posts as Yale Law School's Kent professor of law and legal history, president of the American Bar Association, and co-chairman of the National War Labor Board. In 1921 he returned to federal employment by serving as chief justice of the United States, a position he remained in until 1930. William Taft died in Washington, D.C., on March 8, 1930, and was buried in Arlington National Cemetery. His childhood home in Cincinnati is now the William Howard Taft National Historic Site.

Talmadge Avenue

On New Scotland Road in 1872 the Van Allen family built a farmhouse as part of their melon farm. Grace Van Allen, one of the Van Allen daughters, lived in this farmhouse with her husband, a man by the last name of Talmadge. When the melon farm was sold to developers, two names were designated to memorialize this couple: Talmadge Avenue and Van Allen Place. These streets are close to each other, probably just like the lovers were.

Tampa Avenue

The last of the "Florida streets," Tampa Avenue shares a neighborhood with Daytona Avenue, Ormond Street, Orlando Avenue, and Seminole Avenue, yet it's not known why these streets received their Sunshine State names. The oldest building on this street is 236 Tampa Avenue. It was built circa 1845, which was 65 years before this street and neighborhood was constructed. This house was built out in the boonies at the time—civilization and Tampa Avenue had yet to reach it.

Tampa is the seat of Hillsborough County, Florida, and has a population of 350,000. It was settled in 1823 and was incorporated as a village in 1849. It was later incorporated as a town and then a city. The name Tampa comes from the Calusa word *Tampa*, meaning "sticks of fire" and dating to the days of conquistadores. Stewart wrote:

> Even before 1600 the Spaniards had listed Tampa as an Indian village. Since *itimpi* means merely "near it," the white men may have misunderstood that word to be the village when it really referred to something else . . . Later, Tampa became the name of a bay. A log fort built there in 1823 took the name of its commander, Colonel Brooke. But the settlers who gathered under its protection rejected the military name, and adopted Tampa Bay for their first post office in 1831. They soon decided that Tampa alone was sufficient.

Teacup Circle

The developer of this land, or perhaps his wife because women tend to be more creative, named this street. It is oh-so-cute, much like Gingerbread Lane, which was named by Helen Picotte, wife of builder Clifford Picotte. Teacup Circle is a 100-foot-long cul-de-sac. When one stands at the end of this street and uses their imagination, the cul-de-sac looks like a teacup, the turning point for vehicles being the center of the cup and four front lawns being the rising sides. *Cul-de-sac* is French for "bottom of a sac" and was used as a street descriptor by 1800.

Ten Broeck Place
(and Ten Broeck Street)

Abraham Ten Broeck is honored with Ten Broeck Place and Ten Broeck Street. Ten Broeck Street was built on the former pastures of this man's mansion. Born May 13, 1734, Ten Broeck is best known for serving as mayor of Albany and fighting in the Revolutionary War. As the son of Dirck Ten Broeck and Margarita Cuyler Ten Broeck, he studied first in New York City and then in Europe. He entered politics to serve as member of both the Albany City Council and the Province of New York Assembly. Ten Broeck was an officer with the Albany County Militia during the War for Independence, and, after gaining the rank of general, he left the military in 1781 and served as member of the New York Provincial Congress. His mayoral term ran from 1779 to 1783 and from 1796 to 1798. He was married to Elizabeth Van Rensselaer Ten Broeck, and together they had five children. Their first mansion located on Broadway burned in 1797, yet they built a new one soon after, and this historic building stands in the Arbor Hill Neighborhood. Abraham Ten Broeck died January 19, 1810, at 9 Ten Broeck Place and was buried in Albany Rural Cemetery after first being laid to rest in a vault at his residence. His wife survived until the summer of 1813.

The Ten Broeck Triangle is part of the Arbor Hill Historic District and includes the second-oldest neighborhood in Albany. The Triangle is listed within the National Register of Historic Places and includes the Ten Broeck Mansion, which was built during the late 1700s. It replaced the original Ten Broeck mansion that burned in a conflagration that incinerated 26 homes. The fire was set by three slaves, who admitted to doing so. They were then hanged. Within the Triangle are more than 200 buildings, Saint Joseph's Park, and Van Rensselaer Park. Most buildings date to the mid-1800s. The Triangle was once known as the Lumber District because lumber barons of the nineteenth century lived there. Ten Broeck Place used to be part of Third Street until September 18, 1876, and Ten Broeck Street was called High Street and then North High Street until July 25, 1831.

Ten Broeck Street
See Ten Broeck Place.

Ten Eyck Avenue

Ten Eyck Avenue is the last of the four "Ten Eyck streets," the other three being Cuyler Avenue, Kate Street, and Matilda Street. The land that these streets are on was owned by the Ten Eycks as early as 1851. In 1891, Abraham Cuyler Ten Eyck owned 52 acres. This cluster of streets was built in 1910. Ten Eyck Avenue is named for the family in general. If one centers the Ten Eyck family around Abraham, Cuyler Street is named for his son (Cuyler Ten Eyck, 1866–1938),

Kate Street for his sister (Catherine Ten Eyck, 1836–1842) or daughter-in-law Kate Dyer Ten Eyck (1868–1936), and Matilda Street for his wife (Margaret Matilda Haswell Ten Eyck, 1837–1932).

Abraham Cuyler Ten Eyck was born October 1, 1830, to Coenraad Anthony Ten Eyck and Hester Gansevoort Ten Eyck on Montgomery Street. He was educated at Albany Academy, went to the American West to try to strike it rich during the gold rush, and returned to New York in 1852. The ship he initially boarded to return home wrecked in Golden Gate Harbor. He was one of only nineteen passengers that survived. More than 100 people drowned and Abraham lost $5,000 worth of gold, which is presumably still on the bottom of Golden Gate Harbor. With his wife, Margaret Matilda Haswell Ten Eyck, he had three children: Jacob Lansing, Cuyler, and Peter Gansevoort. Abraham Cuyler Ten Eyck died March 23, 1900, and was buried in Albany Rural Cemetery.

The Ten Eyck name in the New World began with Coenradtse Ten Eyck and Maria Boele Ten Eyck. They settled in Manhattan during the 1640s, and then their son, Coenradtse, came to Albany during the 1670s. He died during the summer of 1697. Many accomplished Ten Eycks followed, including Jacob Coenraedt Ten Eyck (1705–1793, constable, fire master, city council assistant and alderman, Albany County sheriff, mayor of Albany, and commissioner of Indian affairs), Egbert Ten Eyck (1779–1844, New York State Assembly member, Jefferson County supervisor, Watertown trustee and president, New York State Constitutional Convention delegate, Jefferson County judge, and House of Representatives member from New York), and Peter Gansevoort Ten Eyck (1873–1944, Albany parks superintendent, House of Representatives member from New York, Democratic National Convention delegate, and Ten Eyck Group Insurance Agency founder). Albanians know the Ten Eyck name from the imposing Ten Eyck Hotel that stood on the corner of North Pearl Street and State Street. It was built in 1917 and demolished in 1971. New York City hosts Ten Eyck Street. Adjacent to that street are Ten Eyck Plaza (a public park) and Ten Eyck Garden (a community garden).

Terminal Street
Terminal Street is named so because it leads towards the New York Central Railroad terminal. Related to this street name is a section of nearby North Manning Boulevard that was formerly called New York Central Avenue. During the late 1800s and early 1900s this rail yard was enormous, hosting seventy sidings and two roundhouses with Patroon Creek running through the length of the property.

Terrace Avenue
See Fairview Avenue.

Teunis Avenue
(and Teunis Street)
Juriaen Teunise, also referred to as Juriaen "Glasemaecker" (Dutch for "the glazier"), is honored in these two streets. He arrived in Rensselaerswyck in 1652 and was married to Wybrecht Jacobse Dochter Teunise. He was a tavern keeper from 1654 to 1677 and worked in real estate. Teunise once sold a farm to Philip Schuyler, a powerful regional landowner, for 600 beaver skins.

Teunis Street
See Teunis Avenue.

Thacher Street
The first of the Thacher family to reach America was Thomas Thacher, the oldest son of Peter Thacher and Anne Thacher. He was born May 1, 1620, in Milton Clevedon, County Somerset, England, and landed in Ipswich, Massachusetts, via the *James* during the summer of 1635. He arrived with his uncle's, Anthony Thacher's, family. He studied medicine and theology and practiced both in Massachusetts. Thomas Thacher married twice and died in Boston on October 15, 1687.

George Hornell Thacher, a descendant of Thomas Thacher, is memorialized within Thacher Street because he owned two lots along this street during the 1870s. Thacher Street is next to Learned Street because Billings Learned and Thacher were business partners. They sold stoves together. Thacher was born in today's City of Hornell, New York, on June 4, 1818. (It's mere coincidence that George Hornell Thacher was born in a place called Hornell. This city is named for one of its founders, an unrelated George Hornell, who bought 1,600 acres in that area during the summer of 1793 for the unique price of 111 pounds and one silk dress.) As the son of Samuel Olney Thacher and Martha Hornell Thacher, he graduated from Union College in 1843 and settled in Albany in 1849 to found Thacher Carwheel Company. He served as alderman and then as mayor from 1860 to 1862, 1866 to 1868, and 1870 to 1874. George Hornell Thacher died in St. Augustine, Florida, on February 15, 1887, and was buried in Albany Rural Cemetery. He was the father of three children: Margaret Thacher (1845–1858), George Hornell Thacher Jr. (1851–1929), and John Boyd Thacher (1847–1909). John Boyd became senator from New York, mayor of Albany, and author of five books. Thacher State Park west of Albany is named for John Boyd Thacher because this family donated 350 acres of land there to the public.

Theatre Row
This street was formerly known as Sheridan Place and then Cross Street. Mayor Thomas Whalen III, who served from 1983 to 1993, wanted to create a theater

zone in this part of the city and changed the name to Theatre Row. He probably borrowed the name Theatre Row from New York City. That city's Theatre Row is a section of West Forty-Second Street that's home to the Castillo Theatre, Laurie Beechman Theatre, Pearl Theatre, Pershing Square, Playwrights Horizons, and Signature Center. Whalen's results were not as extravagant. The only nearby venues are the Palace Theater and Capital Repertory Theater.

Third Avenue
See First Avenue.

Third Street
See First Avenue.

Thomas Street
A recklessly common name, it can barely be guessed for whom this street is named and if it carries a first or last name. The name Thomas dates to medieval times and signifies twins. Five Thomases of note from old-time Albany include Frank Thomas, who practiced medicine from 1871 until his death in 1890 when he died from burns caused by an exploding lamp; John Thomas, member of the first board of directors of National Exchange Bank, in 1838; John J. Thomas, who, with George Clarke, published *The Hour* and *The Man* newspapers in 1853; John T. Thomas of the *Country Gentleman* and *Cultivator* newspapers; and William Thomas, vice president of National Albany Exchange Bank and president of Albany Exchange Savings Bank during the mid-1800s. By the early 1800s many other Thomases were well-established in Albany and worked as grocers, importers, coopers, merchants, provisioners, and manufacturers. Thomas Street was likely built in 1929, the year adjacent Lindbergh Avenue was constructed.

Thornton Street
In the August 26, 1905, edition of the *Albany Evening Journal*, 98-year-old George Sparks, who had lived in the city since 1834, was interviewed about the olden days. Within this interview he stated that Thornton Street is named for one Steve Thornton, who lived with his, Sparks's, family in a Van Rensselaer farmhouse on Livingston Avenue not far from Thornton Street. No information could be found regarding Steve Thornton. To add to the uncertainty of this story, Sparks was interviewed during August. Within this 1905 article it was stated that "he suffers a great deal on account of the heat, his head being affected by the heat." Maybe it was a particularly hot day when he was interviewed and he had no idea what he was talking about.

If Thornton Street is not named for Steve Thornton, then it's named for Matthew Thornton, signer of the Declaration of Independence and for whom New York City's Thornton Street is named. He was born in 1714 to James Thornton and Elizabeth Malone Thornton, who brought him to the New World in 1716. This family settled in Maine and Massachusetts. Then Thornton moved to New Hampshire where he became justice of the peace, New Hampshire Militia officer and surgeon, president of the Provincial Assembly, member of the Committee of Safety, president of the New Hampshire House of Representatives, associate justice of the Superior Court of New Hampshire, member of the Continental Congress, senator from New Hampshire, and state councilor. Matthew Thornton died June 24, 1803, and was buried in Thornton Cemetery in Merrimack, New Hampshire. The Town of Thornton in that state is named for him. The neighboring streets of Thornton Street, Beverly Avenue, Colonie Street, McArdle Avenue, Pennsylvania Avenue, and Wilkins Avenue were constructed circa 1912. The name Thornton is composed of Old English words meaning "thorn" and "settlement."

Thurlow Terrace

Thurlow Weed, for whom Thurlow Terrace is named, was a publisher and political advisor. This street name dates to 1881 and specifically carries Weed's name because his daughter and son-in-law owned property there. This property was then subdivided by Weed's grandson, Thurlow Weed Barnes, during the 1880s.

Weed was born November 15, 1797, in Cairo, New York, and worked menial jobs in his youth. With the 40th Regiment of the New York State Militia, he fought in the War of 1812, got out, and began a lifelong affair with publishing, first with the *Albany Register* and later with the *Rochester Telegraph*, *Enquirer*, and *Evening Journal*. He entered politics by serving in the New York Assembly, and he became advisor to DeWitt Clinton, John Quincy Adams, William Seward, Henry Clay, William Henry Harrison, Zachary Taylor, and John Fremont. Weed was cofounder of the Republican Party and chairman of the New York State Republican Party in which he facilitated a resolution to dissolve the New York Whig Party. Thurlow Weed died in New York City on November 22, 1882, and was buried in Albany Rural Cemetery. Thurlow is an English place name that's at least 1,000 years old. It uses the elements *pryo* and *hlaw*, meaning "troop" and "hill."

Tioga Terrace

Beyond Tioga Terrace there is Tioga County in New York, Tioga Borough in Pennsylvania, and the 58-mile-long Tioga River, which traverses parts of these two states. There are also communities named Tioga in Florida, Iowa,

Louisiana, North Dakota, Pennsylvania, Texas, West Virginia, and Wisconsin. Add to these lists California's Tioga Lake and Tioga Pass, Michigan's Tioga River, and New Hampshire's Tioga River. *Tioga* is an Indian word that means "at the forks" and stems from *tavego* and *diahoga*.

Tivoli Street

The long-gone community of Tivoli stood where Tivoli Street is. The name emulates Tivoli, a city of 60,000 residents in central Italy, for which New York's Village of Tivoli is named. Through the early community of Tivoli ran Patroon Creek, which flowed through Tivoli Hollow. In this hollow were a series of mills that used the creek for water power. In 1836, Josiah Root built a woolen mill in the hollow for the Van Rensselaers, yet this mill closed when the City of Albany purchased Patroon Creek to use as a water supply. Root then bought a mill in Cohoes, improved it, and changed its name to the Tivoli Hosiery Mill. This mill burned to the ground, and Root built another one carrying the Tivoli name. Witbeck's *Sketch of Roads, Streams, and Localities of Watervliet* from 1850 labeled Tivoli Mill, Tivoli Factory, and Tivoli Falls along the creek. Other industries in the hollow included brickworks, forges, and foundries. During the mid-1800s, Tivoli Street had the Tivoli Hollow Railroad next to it, this line running from the intersection of Broadway and Emmett Street to the main New York City and Hudson River Railroad line at Northern Boulevard near Tivoli Lakes. By 1860, the community of Tivoli had "extensive manufactures of agricultural implements, bolts, and hollow wear" according to J. H. French.

Tremont Street

A major street in Boston is Tremont Street because Boston at one time was called Trimountaine, French for "three mountains." This name honored a modest range with three peaks—Beacon Hill, Pemberton Hill, and Mount Whoredom (what a name!)—which stood over Boston. This mountain was excavated to make room for the city. All that remains of this once-proud highland is 52-foot-tall Beacon Hill. It used to be twice that height. The range was identified as early as 1630, when settlers arrived. Tremont Street illustrates a name transfer. As Stewart wrote, "Tremont Street in many smaller towns was only an [imitating] of Boston."

Your author's love for toponyms, that is, names of natural features, cannot be restrained at this point. The first of Boston's three hills, Beacon Hill, used to be called Centry Hill, Sentry Hill, Sentry Peak, and The Hill and is named so, according to the United States Geological Survey, because "in 1634, the residents erected a mast with an iron bucket of tar which could be set afire to warn the populace of enemy approach . . . " Pemberton Hill was first called Cotton Hill for John Cotton, preeminent minister of Massachusetts Bay Colony during the early 1600s. It was then named for James Pemberton, one of the founders of the city's Old South Church, who came to the New World from Wales in 1646. Pemberton lived on this hill. Pemberton Square is now named for him because he lived there after vacating the hill. Mount Whoredom is named so, in the words of Ye Old Tavern Tours, because "Bostonians and visiting British soldiers referred to this area" as such. "The name was apt because prostitutes were known to peddle their services on the west side of Beacon Hill," this section of Boston being home to "a transient and criminal population." New York City's Tremont Neighborhood is named so because it consists of the three neighborhoods of Fairmount, Mount Eden, and Mount Hope. One can find Tremont Mountain in Colorado and Mount Tremont in New Hampshire.

Tricentennial Drive

The tricentennial of the City of Albany was July 22, 1986. This 300-year anniversary commemorated Thomas Dongan, first royal governor of New York, granting Albany's city charter. This street was probably built in 1986. This is how Albany's Tricentennial Park got its name.

Trinity Place

Trinity Protestant Episcopal Church, which gives this street its name, was organized September 4, 1839. The first church was built in 1841 and consecrated January 21, 1849. William Doane led this church for years, as did Creighton Storey and William Springer. During the summer of 2011 one of the walls of the church collapsed after decades of neglect, and the city thought it best to remove this building, which was designed by James Renwick Jr. The church was located next to Trinity Alliance, a social service organization that is still in business and was a partner of the church. Sections of Trinity Place were called Broad Street until October 20, 1862, and Davidson Street until June 14, 1869.

Tryon Court
(and Tryon Place, Tryon Street)

The northern section of Tryon Street was built first, and then land was conveyed to the city in 1959 for construction of Tryon Court, Tryon Place, and an extension of Tryon Street that would accommodate a housing development. The Tryon streets and nearby Glynn Street honor Englishmen who were involved with war and politics during formation of the United States. Tryon Court, Tryon Place, and Tryon Street honor colonial governor William Tryon (a bad guy), who lived from 1729 to 1788, while Glynn Street honors lawyer and Parliament member John Glynn (a good guy), who lived from 1722 to 1779. North Carolina has the Town of Tryon, and in that state one will find the Town of Wake, Village of Wake, and Wake County, which carry Tryon's wife's maiden name. Within this same state, Glynn is honored with Glynn County. Just as some patriotic Albanians may like to see the Tryon name removed from their city, this name has been removed elsewhere, Stewart writing that "in New York, Tryon County became Montgomery" because the Briton was "much hated for his ravaging of various towns."

Tryon was born June 8, 1729, to Charles Tryon and Mary Shirley Tryon in County Surrey, England. By the age of 22 he was a soldier, and by the age of 29 he was a lieutenant colonel. He fought in the French and Indian War in which he was wounded. During the spring of 1764 he became acting lieutenant governor of the Province of North Carolina and arrived in New York that fall. Shortly after the death of the governor of the Province of North Carolina, Arthur Dobbs, in 1765, Tryon filled that position. While governor, he spread the Anglican Church, escaped the wrath of Colonists with the repeal of the Stamp Act, raised taxes, built himself a ridiculously extravagant and expensive mansion, and squashed the North Carolina Regulator Uprising, which was a warm-up for the American Revolution. He ended his career as governor of the Province of North Carolina during the summer of 1771 to become governor of the Province of New York. In this position he witnessed the Boston Tea Party. The American Revolution began, and Tryon was caught in a plot to kill George Washington and his officers. When his plan failed he returned to the military, had trouble following orders, and heartlessly attacked Americans and plundered their communities. By 1780 he was back in England. William Tryon died January 27, 1788, in London and was buried at Saint Mary's Church in Middlesex.

Though Tryon was a tyrant even by 1700s standards, your author would be disappointed to see these street names go the way of the passenger pigeon because they may offend someone. As of this writing there is a bizarre fad rearing its head in little corners of America: the removal of historical artifacts, such as statues of Confederate soldiers and Christopher Columbus, that might be deemed offensive by any modern-day citizen, one who is likely ignorant of history and guilty of employing biased yet inconsistent standards concerning what is "offensive" and what is not. The psychology of those who suddenly want to remove accurate historical artifacts is more interesting than the proposed removals themselves. Sudden outrage over something that's been around a long time is indicative of fake outrage that is the product of uneducated mobs.

Your humble author has bad news for anyone who wants to get rid of statues of certain people, let alone the Tryon streets: If you want place names to memorialize people who only did good according to standards that those people would have never guessed would someday exist, we will have no statues, and every street, mountain, stream, city, state, stadium, swamp, university, county, and on and on that are named for people will remain forever unnamed, for we are all imperfect, we all sin.

Three historians echo your author's view. Senator Mike Lee, in *Our Lost Constitution*, quoted Supreme Court justice Anthony Kennedy: "You cannot preserve what you do not revere; you cannot protect what you have not learned; you cannot defend what you do not know." In *Black Rednecks and White Liberals*, Sowell explained that you can't fit a square peg of distant history into a hole of modern-day morality: "We cannot assume twenty-first-century opinions, or even present-day knowledge, when judging decisions made in the nineteenth century. Nor can we assume that we have superior knowledge of the social realities of an earlier era that we never lived through, compared to the first-hand knowledge of those who confronted those realities daily and inescapably." Sowell concluded, "The story of how human beings treat other human beings when they have unbridled power over them is seldom a pretty story or even a decent story . . . " Finally, McCullough, our country's greatest historian, concluded in *The American Spirit*: "It's all too easy to stand on the mountaintop as a historian or biographer and find fault with people for why they did this or didn't do that, because we're not involved in it, we're not there inside it, we're not confronting what we don't know—as those who preceded us were."

Tryon Place
See Tryon Court.

Tryon Street
See Tryon Court.

Tubman Circle
Larry Elder, author of five books on race, wrote that "Harriet Tubman—arguably one of the most heroic Americans—worked tirelessly in her efforts to free slaves, making nineteen dangerous trips on the Underground Railroad over a ten-year period, leading more than three hundred slaves to freedom." The scorching abolitionist John Brown, who led a raid on the federal arsenal in Harpers Ferry, West Virginia, and paid for that raid with his life, called Tubman "one of the bravest persons on this continent." Frederick Douglass said that "excepting John Brown—of sacred memory—I know of no one who has willingly encountered more perils and hardships to serve our enslaved people." Tubman was a warrior.

She was born Araminta Ross, circa 1823, to Ben Ross and Harriet Green, slaves of Mary Pattison Brodess, as one of nine children. When Tubman was young some of her siblings were separated from her to serve as slaves elsewhere, never to be seen again. She grew up in Maryland and was assaulted by a slave owner, which resulted in her having seizures and experiencing periods of sleep in which she could not be woken. Tubman likely suffered from temporal lobe epilepsy. Circa 1844, she married John Tubman, a free black man. She took his last name and her mother's first name as her own. Five years after marriage, she, with her brothers Ben and Henry, escaped slavery. But the brothers had second thoughts and returned to the South. So did Tubman. But she soon left again and traveled 100 miles along the Underground Railroad to Pennsylvania, a free state. However, Congress passed the Fugitive Slave Law of 1850, which made it legal for escaped slaves in free states to be rounded up and taken back to their owners, though Tubman was never caught.

Beginning in 1850, Tubman made several trips back to the South to bring slaves to the North. Her first mission was to bring relatives from eastern Maryland to Pennsylvania. Working with white abolitionists, Quakers, enslaved blacks, and freed blacks, she also led slaves to Ontario to avoid the Fugitive Slave Law. Tubman and her fellow escapees were never caught. Southerners didn't even suspect her. They must have thought, How on Earth could a five-foot-tall, illiterate, formerly enslaved woman be behind all this? Sometimes the mouse roars loudest. Tubman worked the Underground Railroad until the fall of 1860. She settled in Auburn, New York, and helped the North during the Civil War by providing intelligence about, and drawing maps of, eastern Maryland. She played a role in the Union Combahee River Raid, which freed 800 slaves. Back in Auburn after the Civil War she married Nelson Davis, a veteran of that war, and worked with Susan Anthony and Emily Howland within the suffrage movement. Harriet Tubman died March 10, 1913, and was buried in Fort Hill Cemetery in Auburn.

Tudor Road

Tudor Road is within the "United Kingdom cluster" of Cambridge Road, Oxford Road, and Clarendon Road. This road used to be part of Magazine Street. Name change took place in 1937. The change in designation has nothing to do with the architectural style of homes built along this street—they're Cape Cod colonials, not Tudors. A street called Mansfield Place used to lead off Tudor Road.

The House of Tudor was a royal line of Welsh and English origin. The house ruled much of the British Isles from the late 1400s to the early 1600s, and during this period there were five Tudor monarchs. King Henry VII, also known as Henry Tudor, was the first monarch. Henry VII was born at Pembroke Castle in Wales on January 28, 1457, to Edmund Tudor (1st Earl of Richmond) and Margaret Beaufort (Countess of Richmond). He gained kinghood by defeating King Richard III at the Battle of Bosworth Field during August 1485. He then married Elizabeth of York to unify the House of Lancaster and House of Tudor. The House of Tudor survived through Elizabeth I, daughter of King Henry VIII and Anne Boleyn, until her death on March 24, 1603. Elizabeth died childless and did not name a successor.

Turner Place

Charles Turner developed the Turner Place neighborhood during the early 1930s and is honored through this street. In 1931 his wife, Isabel H. Fite Turner, conveyed land to the city for construction of Turner Place. Charles Turner was born May 21, 1887, in Watervliet and died April 7, 1959. He was buried in Albany Rural Cemetery. The name Turner described one who worked in an occupation that required turning, such as work that involved turning a lathe.

Twiller Street

The name Twiller Street—and the nearby names of Bertha Street, Corlaer Street, and Marshall Street—was made official in 1915 through a city ordinance. Twiller Street was first named Avenue D. Wouter Van Twiller, for whom this street is named, was Kiliaen Van Rensselaer's—the great patroon's—nephew and associate. He came to the New World in 1630 to replace Peter Minuit as director general of the West India Company. Van Twiller's arrival marked establishment of the name Rensselaerswyck, meaning "land of Rensselaer." By 1639, Van Twiller was replaced by William Kieft. Van Twiller, according to Hislop, had a habit of "drinking Rhenish wine for three days" before deciding to carry out his duties. Van Twiller earned the dubious titles "Poor Wouter" and "Walter the Doubter" for his poor work ethic and indecision, this second name given by Washington Irving. Poor Wouter's replacement, Kieft, was too aggressive in his dealings with the Indians. Hislop wrote that Kieft, while serving in present-day New York City, had "taxed and annoyed the Indians in the neighborhood of New Amsterdam until they were swarming about like angry bees."

Twitchell Street

At least once source maintains that Twitchell Street is named for Asa Twitchell. He was born the first day of 1820 and was an accomplished artist and member of the Albany Group of fellow artists. His ancestors were Puritans who came to the New World in 1634. He was the son of Asa W. Twitchell and Sarah Stowell Twitchell. By 1830, this family was living in Lansingburgh, New York, having come from Swanzey, New Hampshire. By age 19 he was a painter, and two years later he married Nancy Simons. Twitchell established a studio in Albany and produced portraits of James Fenimore Cooper, William Marcy, Herman Melville, Thurlow Weed, and other notable men. Asa Twitchell died April 26, 1904, in Slingerlands, New York, and was buried in Albany Rural Cemetery.

However, Mooney, in his "For Relaxed Reading" article, mentioned that during the late 1800s the Twitchell family had a farm along New Scotland Road not far from today's Twitchell Street. A series of other farming families, such as the Van Allens, Hartmans, and Paddocks, in that area during that time also ended up having streets named for them. You author believes Twitchell Street is named for this family, not the artist. This street—with nearby Bower Avenue, Caldwell Street, Cliff Street, Webster Street, and Winnie Street—was built on land conveyed to the city by Jacob W. Wilbur on September 8, 1916. Mayor Joseph Stevens approved these names twelve days later.

U

Union Drive

Set among the five other "academic streets" of Cornell Drive, Notre Dame Drive, Princeton Drive, Vassar Drive, and Yale Court, Union Drive is named after Union College. Four of these names—Cornell Drive, Notre Dame Drive, Princeton Drive, and Yale Court—were approved by the city in 1937. That year the city approved a Rutgers Drive to be built, too. That name was replaced by either Union Drive or Vassar Drive. Realtor Jesse Leonard named these streets.

Union College was founded by John Smith and Jonathan Edwards Jr. and chartered in 1795. It initially operated in the old Schenectady Academy building. The university gets its name from being a union of denominations that selflessly formed the institution. It is reputed to be the second oldest college in New York. Columbia College, in earlier days called King's College, holds the title for oldest, being founded in 1754. Union College is not a particularly discerning institution by accepting more than forty percent of applicants. Nearly a third of those who attend Union College are social sciences majors. Their two illustrious alumni include politicians Chester Arthur and William Seward. The campus of Union College is one of the finest in the Capital Region. Set on a height of land outside downtown Schenectady, the campus includes several buildings from the 1800s. The college offers 56 majors and minors and four distinctive joint programs. Albany College of Pharmacy, Albany Law School, Albany Medical College, Dudley Observatory, Union Graduate College, and Union College fall under the umbrella of Union University.

United Way

United Way of the Greater Capital Region is the organization this street takes its name from. Their office is located at 1 United Way. Four clergymen founded United Way in Denver, Colorado, in 1887. United Way of the Greater Capital Region was established in 1925 and operated under different names during different eras. The name in use today dates to 2007.

University Place

Running off Western Avenue, University Place is home to University at Albany's University Administration Buildings and Management Services Center. This annex is where the university's brass reside.

Upton Road

On Upton Road one can find Upton Food Brokerage. Wondering if Upton Road got its name from Upton Food Brokerage or vice versa, your author called this business. The owner answered, and he was politely asked how this street name may be related to the name of his business. With extreme annoyance he replied, "I don't take questions" and hung up. This owner being a local politician, he was then called via a number shared by the Office of the Albany County Legislature. Upon picking up, this man screamed, "How did you get this number? No comment! No comment!" and hung up again. Apparently this legislator is strangely tormented by the name Upton Road, for your author's mere mention of it caused him profuse anguish.

A few Uptons can be traced within Albany perhaps as far back as the Revolutionary War and certainly by the 1840s. If not named for a local resident or family, Upton Road may be named after the Town of Upton, Massachusetts. In *An Essay on the Origin of the Names of Towns in Massachusetts*, William Whitmore wrote that this town, settled in 1728, "may have been so named from some early proprietor. In Ireland, at this period, there was a family of the name; of who Clotworthy Upton, of Castle Upton, had a daughter, the Baroness Langford, and a nephew, Clotworthy Upton, created Baron Templeton in the peerage of Ireland in 1776." The name Upton notes someone who is from the upper part of a settlement.

V

Valleyview Drive

See Fairview Avenue.

Van Allen Place

In 1872, the Van Allen family built a farmhouse at 1153 New Scotland Road, which still stands and was part of this family's melon farm. One of the Van Allen's daughters, Grace, married a man by the last name of Talmadge. Grace and her husband lived in the Van Allen farmhouse together with other Van

Allen family members. The family's farmland stretched clear down to Normans Kill. When this land was sold by the Van Allen family, two streets that were developed were named Van Allen Place and Talmadge Avenue. This area used to be within the Town of Bethlehem but became part of the City of Albany during the 1960s. During that decade Albany was ruled by Democrats, and Mr. Talmadge was a steadfast Bethlehem Republican. When he found out his house was going to fall under Democrat oversight, he and Grace sold their home to Armand Quadrini and moved outside the new city limits.

Van Buren Street

Martin Van Buren, born December 5, 1782, is best known as president of the United States. This street is within the eight-street "presidential conglomerate," which includes Cleveland Street, Grant Avenue, Lincoln Avenue, McKinley Street, Roosevelt Street, Garfield Place, and Washington Avenue. Nearby Buchanan Street is actually named for engineer William Buchanan. All streets in this area were named circa 1900 by realtor Jesse Leonard. Van Buren is one of few presidents who had a direct connection with New York's capital city. Before he became president he practiced law at 111 State Street.

Van Buren was born December 5, 1782, in Kinderhook, New York, as the son of Abraham Van Buren and Maria Hoes Van Alen Van Buren. Van Buren ended his formal education at 14 and then, like most great men of his time, he studied law. He first read law in his hometown and then moved to New York City. He passed his bar exam in 1803. During February of 1807 he married Hannah Hoes in Catskill, New York. She died twelve years later, and Van Buren never remarried. He entered politics and served as surrogate of Columbia County, senator from New York, New York attorney general, member of the Albany Regency, New York governor, and secretary of state. He became Andrew Jackson's vice president, fulfilling this role from March 1833 to March 1837. After serving as vice president there was nowhere to go but up. Van Buren became president on March 4, 1837, and served one term. This term ended on the same day in 1841. He was cursed to suffer the Panic of 1837, and he moved Indians from their homelands in the South to barren Oklahoma. He struggled with the issue of slavery, which he found immoral though protected by law. Richard Johnson served as his vice president. Van Buren ran for reelection but was decimated by William Henry Harrison. Upon leaving office, Van Buren returned to Kinderhook and planned his comeback. It never came. James Polk received the party nomination and became president.

Martin Van Buren died at his Lindenwald estate in Kinderhook on July 24, 1862. The estate had been built in 1797 by Peter Van Ness and acquired by Van Buren in 1839. Lindenwald is German for "linden forest," which describes the trees that surround the main Georgian-style house. He was buried in Kinderhook Reformed Dutch Church Cemetery. This president, the first one born a

U.S. citizen, has his named carried through counties, communities, and towns in at least fourteen states.

Van Orden Avenue
An old-time name of Albany County is carried through Van Orden Avenue, which was built before 1930. William Van Orden was likely the first Van Orden to arrive in the New World. He immigrated to Greene County, New York, from Holland circa 1670. He was married to Temperance Loveridge Van Orden, who he had seven children with, and died in 1765.

A descendant of William and Temperance was Edmund Henry Van Orden, who was born in Columbia County, New York, in 1828 and died in Colorado Springs in 1909. Edmund is notable because, on November 17, 1859, he married Almyra Van Bergen, who was born in 1827 and died in 1874. Thus the Van Orden family tied with Van Bergens, one of the first families to reach present-day Albany. Almyra was a descendant of Martin Gerretse Van Bergen, who arrived in New Netherland circa 1640. As a relative of the great patroon Kiliaen Van Rensselaer, Martin settled in Rensselaerswyck and served as member of the Governor's Council, justice of the peace, and militia captain. He was of great wealth, possessed an estate and farm, and served as a reliable philanthropist to growing Albany. He died in 1696 while fighting Canadian Indians who had laid siege to his house.

Van Rensselaer Boulevard
The great patroon Kiliaen Van Rensselaer earned his own Albany street by helping settle this area. He was born in Hasselt, Province of Overijssel, the Netherlands, in 1586 as the son of Hendrick Van Rensselaer and Maria Pafraet Van Rensselaer. His father died during June 1602 in the three-year-long Siege of Ostend, which took place in present-day Belgium. He was raised by his uncle, Wolfert van Bijler, who taught young Van Rensselaer the jewelry trade, which led to Van Rensselaer founding Kiliaen Van Rensselaer and Company. Enter the Dutch West India Company. It was chartered in 1621 to trade with Dutch lands in the Old World and New World and within Africa. Van Rensselaer joined the company by submitting a fee, and then he used his ships to bring commodities and settlers to New Netherland. He purchased land from the Indians in 1630 and sent his first batch of frontier people in 1636. The colonization of Albany had begun though Van Rensselaer would never set foot in the New World. Kiliaen Van Rensselaer died in October 1643 and was buried at the Oude Kerk (the Old Church) in Amsterdam, the Netherlands. The Town of Rensselaerville, City of Rensselaer, and Rensselaer County are named for this entrepreneur while North Pearl Street, Old South Pearl Street, and South Pearl Street honor the commodities he traded.

Van Schoick Avenue

Charles Van Schoick was president of the Van Schoick-Harris Realty Company, a land development business that laid out this street, which carries the family name. Nearby Harris Avenue is named for this company's secretary treasurer, Frank Harris. Van Schoick was born in 1884 as the son of George Van Schoick and Kitty Wormer Van Schoick. He died June 23, 1957, and was buried in Prospect Hill Cemetery in Guilderland, New York. The land that Van Schoick Avenue, and South Main Avenue, was built on was conveyed to the city by the Van Schoick-Harris Realty Company on January 21, 1929.

Van Tromp Street

Maarten Harpertszoon Tromp was a Dutch sailor who gained the nickname "The Dutch Broom" for sweeping the seas of his enemies. This street, which appeared on maps by 1794 and was then identified as Trump Street, memorializes him.

Tromp was born April 23, 1598, in Brill, South Holland, the Netherlands, as the son of Harpert Maertensz, himself a naval officer, who was killed by the English pirate Peter Easton in 1610. Early in life Tromp was twice caught by enemy on the high seas and made a slave, of which of course he was eventually released. In July 1622, he joined the Dutch Navy. During the spring of 1624 he married Dignom Cornelisdochter de Haes, yet she soon died. He then married Alijth Jacobsdochter Arckenboudt during the summer of 1634. After leaving the Navy for a brief period, Tromp rejoined and rose to admiral, seeing battle from the 1630s to the 1650s. On August 10, 1653, Maarten Harpertszoon Tromp died during the Battle of Scheveningen near the Netherlands. He was shot by a sniper perched in a ship of William Penn, the English admiral who founded Pennsylvania.

Van Woert Street

This family name is a contraction of Schoendewoert, the name of a community in South Holland, the Netherlands. Rutger Jacobse Van Woert was the first of this family to arrive in Rensselaerswyck. He was born in South Holland circa 1618, came to present-day Albany in the late 1630s, and died during December 1665 in Kingston, New York. Van Woert Street used to be called Lawrence Street. It appeared on maps with its current name by 1866 and used to stretch northwest all the way to today's Arbor Hill Elementary School.

Van Zandt Street

A Dutch last name meaning "from a sandy place," the first Van Zandt to come to the New World was Johannes Van Zandt, who arrived in 1681. He was born in Arnhem, the Netherlands, in 1657. He emigrated from Arnhem, married Margarita Vanderpoel prior to 1682, and raised eleven children with her. He later served as constable and high constable of Albany. This family moved to New York City, and Johannes Van Zandt died during 1724.

Vassar Drive
Vassar College is honored among the "academic streets" of Cornell Drive, Notre Dame Drive, Princeton Drive, Union Drive, and Yale Court, which were named by realtor Jesse Leonard. In 1937, the city approved four of these names: Cornell Drive, Notre Dame Drive, Princeton Drive, and Yale Court. That year they also approved a Rutgers Drive to be built, but it never materialized. The name Rutgers Drive was replaced by either Union Drive or Vassar Drive.

Vassar College was founded by Matthew Vassar in 1861. Vassar was born April 29, 1792, in East Dereham, County Norfolk, England, to James Vassar and Ann Bennett Vassar. When he was 4 years old his family immigrated to the United States. Vassar became a brewer, hence Vassar College's sports identity is the Brewers. Vassar Street in Poughkeepsie is named so because that's where his brewery stood. He became a merchant and community leader in Poughkeepsie and died June 23, 1868. Matthew Vassar was buried in Poughkeepsie Rural Cemetery. The City of Vassar, Michigan is named for him.

Nearly 3,000 students attend Vassar College and are served by 300 faculty. Being a private liberal arts institution, this college offers a selection of esoteric degrees dedicated to low-demand fields. Inventive degrees include Africana Studies, French and Francophone Studies, Medieval and Renaissance Studies, Victorian Studies, British Literary History, Race and Ethnicity, Aesthetics and Philosophy of Art, and Society and Space. The college accepts a quarter of applicants. The 1,000-acre campus is one of the most beautiful in New York. It hosts a 400-acre preserve, more than 200 species of trees, and more than 100 buildings, many of them a century old and designed in Gothic style.

Vatrano Road
Located on the north side of Interstate 90 where Route 5 crosses under this highway, Vatrano Road is barely within Albany's city limits. On Vatrano Road one will find Vatrano Realty and Vatrano Commercial Park, which, like Vatrano Road, are named for builder Frank J. Vatrano. He constructed homes on Fordham Court, Lenox Avenue, and Van Schoick Avenue during the 1930s and 1940s and was active in the Capital Region until the 1960s. Vatrano Lane off Crumitie Road in the Hamlet of Loudonville is named for him, too.

Ver Planck Street
Those familiar with Adirondack Mountain history may presume this street carries the name of surveyor Verplanck Colvin, especially since it's just five blocks

from Colvin Avenue. Yet, while the Colvins have their Colvin Avenue, Isaac Verplanck has his Ver Planck Street. Verplanck, son of Abraham Issacse Verplanck and Maria Vigne Verplanck, was a shoemaker born in New Amsterdam during the summer of 1641. During the 1670s he married Abigail Utenbogert and moved to Albany where she gave birth to at least ten children. He served as assistant alderman, assessor, collector, and constable and died circa 1720. His father had arrived in present-day Albany during March 1638. Ver Planck Street, and neighboring Danker Avenue, were built prior to 1930.

Veterans Way

Like your freedom? Thank a veteran. And one of the best places to find a veteran is Veterans Way because it leads to the Department of Veterans Affairs Stratton Medical Center. This facility opened in 1951 and serves tens of thousands of veterans from 22 counties in New York, Massachusetts, and Vermont. Approximately one-third of the 1,000-person staff are veterans themselves. This facility is named for Capital Region politician and Navy veteran Samuel Stratton, who was awarded a bronze star with V device for valor. The Stratton Air National Guard base in Schenectady, home of the 109th Airlift Wing, is also named for him.

Victor Street

An unidentified 1942 newspaper article reported that "Albany's single largest home construction development under terms of national defense housing is in progress on Victor St., the third thoroughfare in the Washington Heights development of Wilson Sullivan Company Inc." That year, ten new homes were standing, and 24 more were on the way. Victor Sullivan was vice president of Wilson Sullivan Company at that time. This street is named for him. He was born February 28, 1910, to Timothy Sullivan and Alice Wilson Sullivan and died January 12, 1990. Victor Sullivan was buried in Saint Agnes Cemetery in Menands, New York.

Victoria Way

Victoria Way is part of eight English-themed streets that are bunched together. These include Carlisle Court, Cheshire Court, Fordham Court, Kensington Place, Marlborough Court, Stanford Court, and Windsor Place. It's named for Alexandrina Victoria (Queen Victoria), who was born May 24, 1819, and ruled the United Kingdom from 1837 until her death in 1901. Her reign was dubbed the Victorian Era. She was preceded by her uncle, William Henry (William IV), and succeeded by her son, Albert Edward (Edward VII). She also served as Empress of India from 1876 until her death. She expired with Turi, her pet

Pomeranian, resting on top of her, that being her deathbed request. Alexandrina Victoria was interred in Frogmore Mausoleum at Windsor Great Park, England. The communities of Victoria in Kansas and Virginia are named for her.

View Avenue
See Fairview Avenue.

Villa Avenue
Merriam-Webster's Collegiate Dictionary defines a villa as "the rural or suburban residence of a wealthy person." This English word emulates the Italian *villa*. The developer of this neighborhood wanted residents, after a long day at the office, to feel they were coming home to a street named so kindly that their houses may have well been opulent residences in Naples overlooking the Tyrrhenian Sea. Villa Avenue was laid out in 1924—along with Cottage Avenue, Edinburgh Avenue, Hazelhurst Avenue, Highland Avenue, Hillcrest Avenue, Homestead Avenue, Miller Avenue, Pleasantview Avenue, Russell Road, Summit Avenue, Taft Avenue, and Wellington Avenue—when sections of Guilderland were bought by the Wilbur Land Company.

Vine Street
Cherry Street and Plum Street are near Vine Street and compose the downtown "fruit streets" (there used to be a Mulberry Street here, too, yet that street disappeared during the 1900s). These streets likely run across former Schuyler Mansion farmland. In 1851, William Barnes wrote that when Henry Hudson pulled into present-day Albany "the wild vine clambered in rich luxuriance on the forest trees, and threw its graceful festoons from the mossy bank of the river." This downtown Vine Street carries a zip code of 12202. Albany has a second Vine Street. It runs off Russell Road and carries a zip code of 12203.

W

Walter Street
One writer thought that Walter Street may have been named for Walter H. Van Guysling, an architect who designed the Hudson River Day Line office, R.B. Wing and Son Building, School Number Fourteen, Saint Joseph's Catholic Church steeple, and Saint Joseph's Catholic Church in Rensselaer. However,

Van Guysling was born September 23, 1877, and Walter Street was named circa 1873. He died July 13, 1927, and was buried in Albany Rural Cemetery.

Walter Street might be named for Walter F. Van Guysling, father of Walter H., yet his fame may not predate construction of this street. He was born November 14, 1854, in Schenectady and lived at 253 North Pearl Street, which is one mile from Walter Street. He worked for New York Central Railroad for 58 years and was superintendent of Union Station. He was also Albany County coroner. Walter F. Van Guysling died February 23, 1944, and was buried in Albany Rural Cemetery. The English name Walter is derived from a German first name composed of *wald* and *heri*, meaning "reign" and "armed forces."

Warbler Way

The name warbler was given to Old World songbirds by 1773 and to New World songbirds by 1783. Falling under the family Emberizidae and the subfamily Parulinae, warblers come in a wonderful assortment of colors and personalities. More than 150 species live in the Western Hemisphere, and New York hosts nearly thirty species. Warbler Way was likely named by developers of the Dunes Neighborhood where pastoral names—like Gray Fox Lane, Sparrowhill, and West Meadow Drive—are typical. The word warble comes from the late 1300s Old North French *warbler*, which means "to sing with trills and quavers."

Warren Street

Warren Street is very likely named for Joseph Warren. More than a dozen states have counties named for this man, and communities named Warren Glen, Warrentown, Warren, and Warrenton carry his name. A devoted revolutionary, Warren was born June 11, 1741, in Roxbury, Province of Massachusetts Bay, to Joseph Warren and Mary Stevens Warren. He graduated from Harvard College in 1759 and was soon speaking out against British rule. He served as president of the Massachusetts Provincial Congress and member of the Committee of Correspondence, sent Paul Revere and William Dawes Jr. on their famous "the British are coming" rides, fought in the battles of Lexington and Concord, rose to the rank of major general, and was killed at the Battle of Bunker Hill. He and Revere were revolutionary powerhouses. As Allen and Schweikart wrote in *A Patriot's History of the United States*, "Of the 225 leading men in Boston society, only two were in as many of the five of . . . [the city's revolutionary] groups—Joseph Warren and Paul Revere."

What is most amazing about the events that led up to Warren's death is that though he was ranked a general, he declined to command at Bunker Hill. He asked general Israel Putnam where the heaviest fighting was. When Putnam told him it was at Breed's Hill, Warren immediately left Putnam, saying that he elected to serve as a private so he could get into the thick of the struggle instead of serving as an officer in the rear. Warren fought until all his ammunition was expended and his position overrun. He was shot and killed June 17, 1775. His body was mutilated by the British, tossed into a ditch, and buried. Later is was dug up by other British soldiers, mutilated some more, and then beheaded. The remains of Joseph Warren are now buried in Forest Hills Cemetery in Boston.

A less likely candidate, but a man worth mentioning, is James Warren, who lived during the same era as Joseph Warren (no relation). He was born September 28, 1726, in Plymouth, Massachusetts, as a direct descendant of those from the *Mayflower*. James served as Plymouth County sheriff, Massachusetts Provincial Congress president, Massachusetts Militia general, Naval Board member, Massachusetts General Court member and speaker, and Continental Army paymaster general. James Warren died November 28, 1808, and was buried in Burial Hill in Plymouth, Massachusetts. James was married to Mercy Otis Warren, who was just as famous as her husband. She was born September 14, 1727, in Barnstable, Massachusetts, and was descended from the same *Mayflower* passengers as her husband, who was her second cousin. Mercy was an educated and outspoken woman who maintained keen political insight as well as social relationships with Abigail Adams, John Adams, Sam Adams, John Hancock, Patrick Henry, Thomas Jefferson, George Washington, and Martha Washington. Mercy Otis Warren died October 19, 1814, and was buried in Burial Hill in Plymouth, Massachusetts, next to her husband.

Mercy Otis Warren had two revolutionary brothers that were even more famous. One was James Otis Jr., who challenged the legality of British writs of assistance and famously stated "Taxation without representation is tyranny." He should have been more careful with other words he said. Weeks before being struck and killed by lightning he had told his sister, "I hope, when God Almighty in his righteous providence shall take me out of time into eternity that it will be by a flash of lightning." Her other brother was Samuel Otis, first senate secretary, House of Representatives member from Massachusetts, Massachusetts House of Representatives speaker, and Second Continental Congress delegate. He was the man who held the Bible that George Washington placed his hand on in New York City on April 30, 1789, to take the oath of office administered by Robert Livingston.

Washington Avenue
(and Washington Avenue Extension, Washington Square)
Washington Avenue was once known as King Street and Lion Street. Washington Avenue passes through, and is part of, the "presidential conglomerate" of Cleveland Street, Grant Avenue, Lincoln Avenue, McKinley Street, Roosevelt Street, Garfield Place, and Van Buren Street. Contrary to what many presume, Buchanan Street in this neighborhood is not named for James Buchanan. It's named for Capital Region engineer William Buchanan.

"Washington" is the most common street title that conveys a name. This moniker graces 5,000 streets across the country. Second place is "Lincoln" with 4,000 streets. The combination of Washington Avenue and Washington Avenue Extension stretches 9.7 miles from the Capitol to the Pine Bush, which makes it the longest street route in the city. That's one heck of a stretch considering the entire length of Western Avenue within Albany is only 6.6 miles. Washington is an English place name that comes from the Old English *wassingatrun*, *waosige*, and *wassingrun*.

In *1776: The Illustrated Edition*, McCullough wrote that "for all the setbacks and struggles that followed, [Washington] would never lose sight of what the war was about." Washington's dedication is what led us to become the first colony to successfully break from British rule. Washington's vision wavered at times, but he was dedicated to the rebel cause and would not stop until he fired his last round and was shot or hanged dead. Washington was everything we needed. Precise, brave, visionary, humble, patriotic, and daring. The man was imperfect but not dull-witted, indecisive, hesitant, nor of little endurance. Without George Washington, first president of the United States, commander in chief of the Continental Army, and founding father, it's likely we could not have won the Revolutionary War, a conflict that followed Eric Hoffer's assessment that "a movement is pioneered by men of words, materialized by fanatics, and consolidated by men of action."

Washington was born February 22, 1732, near present-day Colonial Beach, Virginia, as the son of Augustine Washington and Mary Ball Washington. He was educated by private tutors, and then, in 1749, he became a professional surveyor and received a license for this vocation from the College of William and Mary. He served in the French and Indian War on the side of Britain, at times leading his own 100-man Virginia militia. In December 1758, he left the war after commanding a full-time Virginia regiment. He retreated to Mount Vernon, which had been passed down to him. This estate was named for one of his brother's past commanding officers, Edward Vernon. Vernon, affectionately known as "Old Grog," was a Royal Navy officer who served the Crown for 46 years.

Washington married Martha, a widow at 28, on January 6, 1759. They never had children because smallpox had left the future president sterile. Soon Washington owned tens of thousands of acres in Virginia. Next began his life of opposition to the British. Washington opposed the Stamp Act of 1765, Townshend Acts of 1767, and Intolerable Acts of 1774. After the battles of Lexington and Concord during April 1775, he was ready for war. He became general and commander in chief of the Continental Army, which was created on June 14 of that year. During the following years, the rebels, usually outnumbered, unhealthy, and desperate for equipment and gunpowder, won battles at Boston, Saratoga, Trenton, Princeton, and, finally, Yorktown. Major combat operations ceased in Yorktown during October 1781. The Treaty of Paris was signed September 3,

1783, the Congress of the Confederation ratified it January 14, 1784, and the British ratified it on April 9 that year. These ratified documents were exchanged in Paris on May 12, 1784. Next came Washington the president. He served from April 30, 1789, to March 4, 1797. John Adams served as vice president because he had received the second highest number of electoral votes. During the spring of 1797, Washington returned to Mount Vernon yet resumed public life as commander in chief of the U.S. armies. He held this position from July of 1798 until his death the following year.

George Washington died December 14, 1799, of epiglottitis, a condition in which the epiglottis covers the windpipe and blocks the flow of oxygen to the respiratory system. Caused by an infection or injury, today epiglottitis is usually resolved with antibiotics. Washington's dire condition was complicated by bloodletting. He was buried at Mount Vernon and then reinterred in a new tomb there during the fall of 1837. The man seems to be everywhere in spirit. Washington is honored through the Washington Monument, naval vessels, the Mount Rushmore Memorial, the George Washington Masonic National Memorial, Washington, D.C., Washington State, Mount Washington of New Hampshire, universities, communities, counties, the quarter-dollar coin, the dollar bill, and the Purple Heart. Stewart reported that by 1931 there were "a state, thirty-two counties, 121 cities and towns and villages, 257 townships, ten lakes, eight streams, seven mountains" named for Washington. This author concluded that such tribute "has been paid to no other man, in any country."

Washington Avenue Extension
See Washington Avenue.

Washington Square
See Washington Avenue.

Water Street
Water Street is aptly named. It's on the shore of the Hudson River. It was truly a "water street" when the Erie Canal used to intersect with the Hudson River in downtown Albany. Hopkins's maps from 1876 showed that when traveling north up Water Street from its intersection with Colonie Street you would first cross the Erie Canal on a bridge that spanned two side by side locks in the canal. To your left would be Little Basin, part of the Erie Canal, and to your right would be Albany Basin, a cut in the Hudson River. Continuing up Water Street you would meet North Ferry Street, which led to the Bath Ferry. (Bath, officially known as Bath-on-Hudson, was a community on the east side of the river in today's City of Rensselaer. The ferry reached Bath's own North Ferry

Street, once called Rensselaer Street and Central Avenue. This ferry landing was near today's Forbes Avenue.) Finally, near the intersection of Water Street and North Ferry Street three more cuts of the Erie Canal crept towards Water Street so businesses could load and off-load products. Water Street was once known as Dock Street, Quay Street, and River Street, all accurate names. It gained its current name during the summer of 1803.

Watervliet Avenue
(and Watervliet Avenue Extension)

The Dutch *water vliet* means "flood," and this describes Watervliet Avenue well. It used to be subjected to flooding from nearby Foxes Creek. The name Watervliet Avenue was made official by the city in 1871 when they made the nearby names Colby Street, Hunter Avenue, Judson Street, and Rawson Street official. Watervliet Avenue was a dirt road until 1890. That year its entire length was paved with Trinidad asphalt. The City of Watervliet is named so because it lies on a Hudson River floodplain. This city, after earlier names of Gibbonsville, West Troy, and Port Schuyler, was incorporated in 1896. The Town of Watervliet, founded 1788, was formerly known as Glass City due to a glass factory being there.

Watervliet Avenue Extension

See Watervliet Avenue.

Webster Street

Mayor Joseph Stevens signed a Common Council ordinance on September 20, 1916, to have Webster Street named along with Bower Avenue, Caldwell Street, Cliff Street, Twitchell Street, and Winnie Street. Twelve days before this, Jacob W. Wilbur conveyed land to the city for construction of these streets.

It's unknown which specific Webster this street name honors. In 1914 there were thirteen Websters living in the city. Albany Rural Cemetery has more than sixty Webster graves, with the oldest dating to 1780. The twin Webster brothers, George and Charles R., were likely the most famous of this Albany surname. They were born in Hartford, Connecticut, to Matthew Webster and Mabel Pratt Webster during September 1762. Matthew and Mabel were buried in Albany Rural Cemetery. The brothers came to Albany in 1784 at the ages of 22 and became printers of great influence. They both operated the *Albany Gazette*. George edited the *Daily Advertiser* by himself. They owned three buildings near the intersection of State Street and South Pearl Street, this intersection then known as Webster's Corner. George Webster died during February 1823. Charles R. Webster died July 18, 1834, and was buried in Albany

Rural Cemetery. Webster is an old Albany County name that comes from the name Webb, which means "to weave."

Weis Court
(and Weis Road)

Weis Road is named for the Weis family of farmers who owned land where this street now is. A map from the last decade of the 1800s showed Enos owning two eleven-acre plots there. A mile southeast of Weis Road is tiny Weis Court, which is also named for this family. Their farm was established in 1872 by Enos, who was born in Germany in 1849 and came to the United States in 1857. He was married to Margaret Weis, and they had seven children by 1900. Enos died September 21, 1932. In 1947, two of Enos's sons, Joseph and William, sold their twelve acres of the farm to Jefferson Park Homes so an apartment complex could be constructed. A newspaper article by Fred Downing from that year showed that the march of progress was about to overrun the brothers, who didn't seem to care much: "We had about enough of farming," they said. "Albany has moved out to us, and it's time now to let the city take over." On this former farmland stand Temple Israel and Adams Park Apartments. The name Weis is of German and English origin and is derived from the Old English *wis*, meaning "wise."

Weis Road

See Weis Court.

Wellington Avenue

Cities and towns named Wellington in Kansas, Maine, Missouri, Ohio, and Texas are named for the same man for whom cities in Canada and New Zealand are named: Arthur Wellesley, Duke of Wellington. His title is given to Wellington Avenue, which was built in 1924.

Wellesley was a British officer best known for defeating Napoleon Bonaparte at the Battle of Waterloo in 1815. He was born May 1, 1769, in Dublin, Kingdom of Ireland, to Garret Colley Wesley, 1st Earl of Mornington, and Anne Wesley. The man was a fighter, leader, and tactician. He joined the military in 1787, and within four years he was promoted to captain and then to lieutenant colonel. He fought in the Flanders Campaign and Fourth Anglo-Mysore War of the 1790s and the Second Anglo-Maratha War and Peninsular War of the early 1800s. Wellesley, bloodied and muddied, was ready to fight Napoleon in the Battle of Waterloo, which ran from March 20 to July 8 of 1815.

The Battle of Waterloo spread across present-day Belgium, France, and Italy. It was the First French Empire against the United Kingdom, the Netherlands, the Kingdom of Hanover, Nassau, Brunswick, and Prussia—75,000 French troops fighting 120,000 coalition troops. The French, commanded by Napoleon and Michel Ney, received a shellacking by Wellesley and the Prussian Gebhard Leberecht von Blücher. More than 25,000 Frenchmen were killed, wounded, or captured while 15,000 went missing in action. On Wellesley's side fewer than 5,000 were killed, 15,000 were wounded, and 5,000 went missing in action. The war brought death to the First French Empire and Napoleon's military and political career.

Wellesley served as prime minister to the United Kingdom, leader of the House of Lords, secretary of state for war and the colonies, home secretary, and foreign secretary during the 1820s and 1830s. He was honored with the credentials of Most Notable Order of the Garter, Most Honorable Order of the Bath, Royal Geulphic Order, Her Majesty's Most Honorable Privy Council, and Fellowship of the Royal Society. Arthur Wellesley, Duke of Wellington, died September 14, 1852, at Walmer Castle in Deal, County Kent, England. He was given a state funeral in London, a high honor, on November 18 and buried at Saint Paul's Cathedral.

Wendell Street

Harmanus Wendell has his Wendell Street. This noted fur trader built his homes at present-day 674 Broadway in 1699 and State Street in 1716. This second home was destroyed in 1841. He was the son of Jeronimus Wendell and Ariantie Visscher Wendell, was born in 1678, and died during December 1731. During the 1890s it was proposed to change Wendell Street to Daniel Street. Wendell Street was shown on maps by 1857.

The first of this Wendell line to arrive in Albany was Evert Janse Wendell, Harmanus's grandfather. He was born circa 1615 in Emden, Germany, and immigrated to the New World from East Frisia, settling in today's New York City. Evert Janse Wendell was in Beverwyck by the 1650s and lived on the corner of James Street and State Street, not far from today's Wendell Street. He married twice and died circa 1709.

West Carillon Drive

See East Carillon Drive.

West Center Drive

See Centre Street.

West End Alley

A wretched little street, West End Alley is a dirt road running between graffiti-splotched buildings. It's a descriptive name, yet it's unclear what West End

Alley is west of, and there is no East End Alley. The other alleys of Albany are Dove Alley, Garden Alley, Hunter S Alley, and Ludlow Alley.

West Erie Street
See Erie Street.

West Lawrence Street
See North Lawrence Street.

West Meadow Drive
See Meadow Lane.

West Street
Named DeWitt Street until June 1, 1868, West Street may be named so because it's west of Central Avenue, a major thoroughfare.

West University Drive
See East University Drive.

West Van Vechten Street
A handful of powerful Van Vechtens resided in, and influenced development of, Albany. West Van Vechten Street is named for the one who was two-term mayor of Albany, Teunis Van Vechten. In 1851 he owned three pieces of land near today's West Van Vechten Street. He laid out and named this street along with neighboring Bertha Street, Hurlbut Street, Jeanette Street, Marshall Street, and Stanwix Street. All are reportedly named for family members of his. Within this neighborhood the names Bertha Street, Corlaer Street, Marshall Street, and Twiller Street were made official within a 1915 ordinance.

Teunis Van Vechten was born during November 1785 as the son of Teunis T. Van Vechten and Elizabeth De Wandelaer Van Vechten. His father served as fire master, militia officer, and member of the Albany Committee of Correspondence. Van Vechten graduated from Union College with honors and studied law with two of Albany's leading men, John Lansing Jr. and Abraham Van Vechten. Abraham was his uncle, who served as city recorder, senator from New York, member of the New York Assembly, attorney general, and director of the Bank of Albany. Van Vechten opened his own practice and represented Stephen Van Rensselaer

IV, "The Last Patroon," and then served as alderman and mayor, his mayoral term running from 1837 to 1839 and during 1841 and 1842. Teunis Van Vechten died February 4, 1859, and was buried in Albany Rural Cemetery. His wife, Catherine Cuyler Gansevoort Van Vechten, died in 1831. They had ten children.

Westbrook Street
Tiny Westbrook Street, built before 1932, gets its name from being near Krum Kill, a brook that marks a western boundary of the City of Albany.

Westerlo Street
The Town of Westerlo, formerly known as Chesterville for the pastor John Chester, is in southern Albany County. Sections of the towns of Coeymans and Rensselaerville were combined to create the Town of Westerlo in 1815. This town and Westerlo Street are named for Eilardus Westerlo. Westerlo Street was formerly known as Kane Street and Pitt Street, while Ash Grove Place and Elm Street were known as Westerlo Street. The first map to identify Westerlo Street by its current name is *Dutch Church Lower Pasture No. 6* from 1791.

Westerlo was born October 30, 1738, in Kantens, the Netherlands, as the son of Isaac Westerlo and Hillegonda Reiners Westerlo. In 1760, he graduated from the University of Groningen in the Netherlands and then was ordained as a minister and came to the New World. He served as pastor of the Dutch Church from 1760 to 1790 and married the widow Catharina Livingston Van Rensselaer in 1775. She was born during the summer of 1745 and died during the spring of 1810. Eilardus Westerlo died in Albany on Christmas Day of 1790 and was later buried in Albany Rural Cemetery.

Western Avenue
Known as the Great Western Turnpike until 1865, Western Avenue is named so because it leads west from the Hudson River. Hislop wrote that settlers of the 1700s and 1800s pushed west and "crowds of them with their families, their wagons piled high with household goods, streamed through Albany in the years which followed the Revolution, looking for the Western lands which were thrown open to settlers by the government and by the ever-present land speculators." Many of the settlers were from Boston and had taken that city's celebrated Boston Post Road towards Albany. Once across the Hudson River, they would travel up Broadway, State Street, and the Kings Highway to their next stop, Schenectady. By 1795, at least 500 wagons full of immigrants and their possessions were pushing west through Albany each day. Sleighs were used during winter. More than a century later, it was about speed, not migration.

A central section of Western Avenue paved with granite blocks was known as The Speedway. Horse-drawn sleds were raced there during winters of the early 1900s. Meanwhile, during summers, horse-drawn buggies were raced on a one-mile-long section of unpaved Washington Avenue from Quail Street to Manning Boulevard.

Today Western Avenue is overrun by 3,365-mile-long U.S. Route 20, the longest road in the United States. It runs from Boston to Newport, Oregon, and crosses a dozen states. More than 370 miles are contained in the Empire State. This was New York's main east-west road until the New York State Thruway was built during the mid-1950s.

Westford Street

Westford traditionally means a western ford, as in a western spot to cross a river. As a street name it has little meaning here.

White Oak Lane

See Oak Street.

White Pine Drive

See East Pitch Pine Road.

Whitehall Court
(and Whitehall Road)

During the latter part of the French and Indian War, which lasted from 1754 to 1763, British commanders had, in the words of McEneny, "a great country mansion" in the Whitehall Neighborhood, which was initially developed by John Bradstreet. From this mansion, which was built circa 1761 and first served as barracks for British soldiers, the British planned and launched attacks against the French. It was also occupied by members of the Gansevoort and Ten Eyck families. This mansion was named after the Whitehall district of London that contains government buildings. This is the same reason that Manhattan's Whitehall Street is named so. The mansion burned to the ground in 1883, yet its foundation supports an apartment complex on aptly-named Whitehall Road. The easternmost 300 feet of Whitehall Road actually follow the old driveway that led to the mansion. Tiny Whitehall Court branches off two-mile-long Whitehall Road.

Whitehall Road

See Whitehall Court.

Wilan Lane

Charles L. Touhey named Charles Boulevard for his grandfather, Charles H. Touhey, and he named Wilan Lane, which combines the names William and Anne. He named this street, which was built circa 2000, for his father-in-law and mother-in-law, William Green and Anne Paden Green. They moved to Witherbee, New York, from South Carolina to work for Republic Steel. Mining operations flourished in Witherbee and nearby Mineville from the 1850s to the 1970s. Two other streets take this novel naming approach: Berncliff Avenue (named for Bernard and Clifford Picotte) and Marwill Avenue (named for Maria and William Noeckle).

Wilbur Street

It's tough to guess why Wilbur Street is named so, and your author usually sits in the dugout during guessing games. Despite this street dating to before the 1850s, its name history is totally unknown. Wilbur Street is the only "old Albany" street to remain unsolved.

Wilkins Avenue

Nearly twenty Wilkinses are buried in Albany Rural Cemetery, with the oldest grave dating to 1854. The Wilkins Avenue neighborhood consisting of Wilkins Avenue plus Beverly Avenue, Colonie Street, McArdle Avenue, Pennsylvania Avenue, and Thornton Street was built circa 1912 on land that belonged to the Van Rensselaer Land Company. Three short streets named Jasmine Avenue, Fern Avenue, and Clover Avenue once led off the west side of Wilkins Avenue. There is no trace of these today, and Wilkins Avenue remains unsolved.

Willett Street

Hislop wrote that Marinus Willett, for whom this street is named, was of great value to the Americans during the Revolutionary War: He "had helped defeat St. Leger at Fort Stanwix" and later "won the 'freedom of the city of Albany' in 1781 by scattering a raiding party of Indians under the notorious Joseph Brant, an Indian chief who had been with St. Leger's forces."

Willett was born July 31, 1740, in Jamaica, Queens, as the son of Edward Willett. He fought in the French and Indian War as an officer but really shined during the Revolution. His first mission entailed securing arms from the New York City Arsenal and raiding a British depot right after the battles of Lexington and Concord. He took part in the Battle of Quebec, commanded New York's Fort Constitution, and fought in the Battle of Oriskany alongside Nicholas Herkimer. He also saw combat within the Battle of Monmouth, Sullivan Campaign, Battle of Sharon Springs, and Battle of Johnstown. No longer a military officer by the

1780s, he entered politics to serve as member of the State Assembly, sheriff of New York County (where Manhattan's Sheriff Street and Willett Street are named for him), mayor of New York City, and lieutenant governor. Marinus Willett died August 22, 1830, and was buried at Trinity Church in New York City and reinterred in that city's Marble Cemetery. The Town of Willett in Cortland County is named for this man. The Willett name in America dates to the mid-1600s. The first Willett in the New World may have been Thomas Willett, who emigrated from England, arrived in Beverwyck in 1663, and died circa 1677.

Albany has a 33,000-pound granite boulder that stands as a memorial to Marinus Willett. It was placed in 1907 in the east corner of Washington Park but was moved to the corner of State Street and Willett Street in 2006 because cars had been crashing into it. Willett Street was subjected to a unique but thankfully short-lived surfacing scheme. In 1870, this street was paved with pine blocks (that same year, sections of Hudson Avenue and Green Street were paved with such blocks). After many horses slipping and sliding and falling down Willett Street, these wood blocks were replaced with those of granite.

During the mid-1800s there was a proposal to change the name Willett Street to Conkling Place for Roscoe Conkling (1829–1888), chief justice nominee and senator and House of Representatives member from New York. He was born at 353 Madison Avenue. This 1827 home stands just three blocks from Willett Street. Conkling made sure this name change did not take place because he preferred the historical power of old-time street names. The April 18, 1888, edition of *The Albany Journal* confirmed Conkling's appreciation for tradition: "It is a curious fact that as late as 1878 Mr. Conkling instigated his brother-in-law, the late Hon. Horatio Seymour, to write a letter protesting against the change of Orange Street in that city to Seymour Street on the ground that the old Dutch names ought to be retained, and citing the change of Lydius Street to Madison Avenue as one to be regretted." The Hamlet of Roscoe is named for this judge and politician. The two long-gone communities of Conklingville—one in Suffolk County, the other in Sullivan County—were named for his ancestors.

William Street

It is not known for whom William Street is named. The name William became common thanks to the popularity of the leader of the Norman Conquest, Duke William II of Normandy, best known as William the Conqueror. This name combines the Germanic elements *wil*, meaning "will," and *helm*, meaning "helmet."

Williamsburg Court

Dutchman William Henry—also known as King William III, Stadtholder of Holland, King William II of Scotland, and William of Orange—is honored through Williamsburg Court. This street provides access to Williamsburg Village

Apartments, which weren't built until 1983. This makes Williamsburg Court one of the last streets to be built in the City of Albany.

William was born in The Hague on November 4, 1650, to William II (Prince of Orange) and Mary (Princess Royal). When William was born he immediately became Prince of Orange because his father had died before the birth. William was educated by governesses and family members and at the University of Leiden. He was appointed first noble and captain general of the Dutch States Army and survived the 1672 and 1673 Rampjaar, "The Disaster Year," of the Franco-Dutch War and Third Anglo-Dutch War in which the Netherlands was invaded by France and England. In 1677, when he was 26 years old, he married his 15-year-old cousin, Mary, and William and Mary became a ruling team. In 1688, William invaded England, and the next year he and Mary took over the throne that had been held by King James, who had fled to France. Uprisings against William and Mary took place, particularly in Scotland, yet they were smashed. The duo survived the Nine Years' War, too.

Mary died December 28, 1694, of smallpox, and William died March 8, 1702, of pneumonia. William and Mary were buried at Westminster Abbey. The circumstances leading to William's death are intriguing. William fell from his horse, Sorrel, and broke his collarbone, which led to complications that resulted in his fatal illness. Sorrel was confiscated from the Englishman John Fenwick, who, in 1696, had planned to assassinate William. Fenwick's plan was foiled, and he was beheaded in London during January the following year. In the end it was Fenwick's horse that carried out the desired killing of the king.

Willow Street

There are 350 species of willow, and most of these are found in the colder climates of the Northern Hemisphere. North America has forty species of willow trees, five of them non-native. There are another sixty species of native willow shrubs. The weeping willow is the most common species in the Capital Region. Wherever you see a weeping willow, named so because its branches droop, or "weep," you can be sure there is groundwater underneath it. This species is actually not native to America. It was introduced from China, and it spread from southern Canada south to Georgia and west to Missouri. Other species of willow that grow in New York include eastern cottonwood, swamp cottonwood, bigtooth aspen, quaking aspen, white willow, peachleaf willow, Bebb willow, pussy willow, sandbar willow, crack willow, black willow, basket willow, white poplar, balsam poplar, and, finally, Lombardy poplar, the ugliest tree in New York.

Wilson Street

The Wilsons who owned land near Wilson Street are memorialized here. J. C. Sidney's 1850 map of Albany showed James Wilson owning a lot on the corner of Wilson Street and Broadway. Lots immediately north and south of Wilson Street were owned by James, A. E. Wilson, and J. M. Wilson in 1876. The first Wilson to reach the Capital Region was likely Englishman Samuel Wilson, who owned property in Albany as early as 1677. During the 1680s he moved to New York City, a city he had lived in previously, and was dead by 1689.

Windsor Place

Carlisle Court, Cheshire Court, Fordham Court, Kensington Place, Marlborough Court, Stanford Court, Victoria Way, and Windsor Place make up the eight "English streets" in the Whitehall Neighborhood. Windsor Place is named after the town of Windsor, County Berkshire, England, which had earlier names of Windlesora and Windles-ore. One of Windsor's main streets, Peascod Street, is at least 1,000 years old, making it 660 years older than Albany's most ancient streets. England has three other, smaller, communities named Windsor. Communities named Windsor in Connecticut, New Jersey, and Pennsylvania are named after the above English town. Communities named Windsor in California, Indiana, and Missouri are named after Windsor Castle. Communities named Windsor in Massachusetts, New Hampshire, and Vermont are named after the Connecticut community.

Winnie Street

Winnie is an Albany County family name. Alternative spellings of Winnie include Winn, Wynn, and Wynne. These stem from the Old English personal name Wine, meaning "friend." There are six Winnie graves, all belonging to women, in Albany Rural Cemetery. The oldest dates to 1822. The Town of Bethlehem Cemetery holds one Winnie grave, which dates to 1865.

A more popular Capital Region name is Winne, and Winnie Street was originally proposed to be named Winne Street. During September 1916, Winne Street (today's Winnie Street) was planned to be built with nearby Bower Avenue, Caldwell Street, Cliff Street, Twitchell Street, and Webster Street. These six streets were built on land conveyed to the city by Jacob W. Wilbur. The name Winne was well-known in the Town of Bethlehem, as is demonstrated in Winne Road and Vloman Kill being named for Pieter Winne de Vlaumingh— de Vlaumingh meaning "the Fleming"—who arrived in 1677. Pieter Winne de Vlaumingh may have been the son of the first Winne of the region, Pieter Winne, a man featured in Van Rensselaer financial accounts as early as 1652. Capital Region Winnes are descended from this man and his two wives, Aechie Jans Winne and Tannetje Adams Winne. There are 300 Winne graves in Albany Rural Cemetery.

The standout Winne was Nanning Visscher Winne, born in Albany on January 17, 1807, as the son of Lavinus Winne, a lawyer. He graduated from Union

College in 1825 and gained a medical degree from Yale University in 1828. He was General Stephen Van Rensselaer's staff surgeon and served in this position for a decade. He died June 6, 1858.

Winthrop Avenue

The Winthrop family of Connecticut and Massachusetts, or specifically John Winthrop (1587–1649), his son John Winthrop the Younger (1606–1676), or his grandson Fitz-John Winthrop (1637–1707), is honored in Winthrop Avenue. The name Winthrop relates to the place name Winthrop and the name Wina, which is related to the name Wigmund, which uses *wig* and *mund*, meaning "war" and "protection." This street used to be called Nineteenth Street because it was the nineteenth street up from Eagle Street when counting streets westward. Name change took place prior to 1938.

John Winthrop was born to Adam Winthrop and Anne Browne Winthrop on January 12, 1587, in Edwardstone, County Suffolk, England. He began attending Trinity College during 1603 yet did not graduate. No worries though. Ten years after trying college he was given the 500-acre Manor at Groton by his father and became Lord of the Manor at Groton. He went on to practice law and become a member of the County Commission of the Peace. With Puritans treated poorly by King Charles I during the early 1600s, John Winthrop came to the New World and served as governor of a new Puritanical community, Massachusetts Bay Colony. The first 700 settlers arrived during 1630, crossing the Atlantic Ocean on nearly a dozen ships. They became the founders of Boston. He served as governor of Massachusetts Bay Colony from 1630 to 1634, 1637 to 1640, 1642 to 1644, and 1646 to 1649. John Winthrop died March 26, 1649, and was buried in King's Chapel Burying Ground in Boston. The communities of Winthrop in Massachusetts and Maine are named for him.

John Winthrop's son, John Winthrop the Younger, was born February 12, 1606, in Groton, England. This well-educated man sailed with his father to Massachusetts Bay Colony in 1630, founded Massachusetts's Town of Ipswich, and served as Connecticut Colony magistrate, governor of Connecticut, and United Colonies of New England commissioner. John Winthrop the Younger died April 6, 1676, and was also buried in King's Chapel Burying Ground.

Fitz-John Winthrop, son of John Winthrop the Younger and grandson of John Winthrop, was born March 14, 1637, in Ipswich, Massachusetts. He sailed to England in 1658 and served in Scotland with the English New Model Army. Returning to the New World, he worked as representative to Connecticut, Connecticut magistrate, and governor of Connecticut. He fought in King Philip's War, a particularly nasty conflict. This war is named for Metacomet, King Philip of Pokanoket to the English, a Wampanog leader who originally befriended Europeans. Due to missionary expeditions, immigrants obtaining land illegally, and the killing of three Wampanog Indians, King Philip's War started in 1675 and lasted two years. In *Lies my Teacher Told Me*, Loewen explained the magnitude of this forgotten conflict:

> This was no minor war. 'Of some 90 Puritan towns, 52 had been attacked and 12 destroyed . . . At the end of the war several thousand English and perhaps twice as many Indians lay dead.' King Philip's War cost more American lives in combat, Anglo and Native, in absolute terms than the French and Indian War, the Revolution, the War of 1812, the Mexican War, or the Spanish-American War. In proportion to population, casualties were greater than in any other American war.

Metacomet was tracked down and killed by Indians that sided with the English under command of the savvy ranger Benjamin Church. His head was put on display in Plymouth, Massachusetts, for the next twenty years. Metacomet's son and wife were captured and became West Indies slaves. Fitz-John Winthrop died November 27, 1707, and was buried in King's Chapel Burying Ground next to his father and grandfather. This man's sermon was given by New England Puritan minister Cotton Mather.

Wood Terrace
See Edgewood Avenue.

Woodlawn Avenue
See Edgewood Avenue.

Woodridge Street
See Edgewood Avenue.

Woodside Drive
See Edgewood Avenue.

Woodville Avenue
See Edgewood Avenue.

Y

Yale Court

Yale Court is the last of the six "academic streets." The other five are Cornell Drive, Notre Dame Drive, Princeton Drive, Union Drive, and Vassar Drive, this cluster named by Jesse Leonard. Yale University is one of eight Ivy League schools, the other seven being Brown University, Columbia University, Cornell University, Dartmouth College, Harvard University, the University of Pennsylvania, and Princeton University. Based in New Haven, Connecticut, Yale University was founded during the fall of 1701 in Saybrook Colony, today's Old Saybrook, Connecticut. It moved to its current location fifteen years later.

It was first called Collegiate School, but this name was changed to Yale in 1718 for Elihu Yale, who had given money and supplies to Collegiate School after being nudged by Cotton Mather to do so. Yale, born April 5, 1649, in Boston as the son of David Yale and Ursula Yale, was a philanthropist who made his fortune with the East India Company. He died July 8, 1721, in London, England, and was buried at the Church of Saint Giles in Wrexham, Wales. A mere seven percent of Yale University applicants are accepted. The current student population is 12,000, and most of them are graduate and professional students. They're served by 4,000 faculty. Notable Yale University alumni include Hillary Clinton, George W. Bush, George H. W. Bush, John Kerry, William Taft, Gerald Ford, Bill Clinton, Nathan Hale, and John Calhoun.

Yardboro Avenue

Yardboro Avenue has existed since the 1930s, and its name is likely a corruption of Yarbrough or Yarbro, surnames from County Lincolnshire, England. In this county one could find the peerage titles Baron Yarborough, from 1749 to 1823, and Earl of Yarborough, from 1837 to present. This place name comes from the Old English *eoroburg*, meaning "earthworks." It's sourced from *eoro* and *burh*, meaning "earthen fortress."

Yates Street

Joseph Yates, for whom this street is named, is best known as New York governor and cofounder of Union College. He was born November 9, 1768, in Schenectady as the son of Christopher Yates and Jannetje Bradt Yates. He served in myriad political roles including mayor of Schenectady, senator from New York, New York State Supreme Court justice, and governor. He served in this last position during 1823 and 1824. Joseph Yates, who learned law in Albany, died

March 19, 1837. He was first buried in a family cemetery in Schenectady County yet was reinterred, in 1889, in the Neil Mausoleum at Saint Peter's Episcopal Church in New York City. New York's Yates County, Town of Yates, and community of Yatesville are named for this man. Governors Lane in Schenectady is where Yates's eighteenth-century house stands. The name Yates comes from the Old English *geat*, which means "gate" and noted someone who lived near a gate.

Z

Zoar Avenue

Zoara, known as Zoar in the Bible, was one of the five cities of the plain and was likely located in today's southern Jordan. The other four cities were Admah, Gomorrah, Sodom, and Zeboim. Zoara, which existed as early as the 300s, was a palm tree-spotted oasis among the desert lands, this oasis fed by runoff from the Moab Mountains. Recent archeological excavations revealed ancient headstones and the remnants of at least one church. *Zoara* is Hebrew for "insignificant." Zoar place names can be found in Alabama, Connecticut, Ohio, Delaware, and Georgia. New York has the Hamlet of Zoar and Zoar Valley. This valley was named in 1813 by Ahaz Allen, who settled the area. Albany's Zoar Avenue was built before 1914.

Zuni Street

Eight "Indian streets" honor Northeast tribes. Three others—Hopi Street, Seminole Avenue, and Zuni Street—honor tribes not of this region. The Zuni, now 11,000 strong, are relegated to the Pueblo of Zuni Reservation in New Mexico, yet they own additional land in Catron County, New Mexico, and Apache County, Arizona. They have lived in New Mexico for the past 3,500 years and were noted for designing irrigation and working agricultural plots. Spanish explorers made contact with the Zuni in 1540. The leader of that expedition was Francisco Vásquez de Coronado, the indefatigable Spanish conquistador who explored present-day Kansas, Oklahoma, Texas, New Mexico, Arizona, and Mexico from 1540 to 1542.

Zuni Street, along with nearby Cary Avenue, Hopi Street, and Sawyer Place, was named by Joseph Cary during the 1920s. He lived at 7 Zuni Street and was one of the first people to reside in this neighborhood. In the February 16, 1963, edition of *The Knickerbocker News*, Mooney wrote that Cary visited Arizona, home of the Hopi Indians, and New Mexico, home of the Zunis. The Indians, part of the old Pueblo tribe, became friends of Mr. Cary and he was made an honorary chief of the Zunis. He made several trips to the tribal reservations, and among his proudest possessions were pictures of himself and the respective chiefs, and pictures of the Hopis doing their famed snake dance about him.

BIBLIOGRAPHY

References to old United States Geological Survey topographic maps are credited to the University of New Hampshire's Digital Collections Initiative, which shares historic maps of New York and New England at http://docs.unh.edu/nhtopos/nhtopos.htm.

Most references to name origins are credited to the Online Etymology Dictionary. This website can be viewed at http://www.etymonline.com/index.php.

50states.com. "Statehood Dates." 2016. Web. 5 Apr. 2016. <http://www.50states .com/statehood.htm#.UV8XLaLvv4g>.

A Plan of Albany. Map. Scale not given. 1757. Web. 18 Mar. 2017. <http://www.albany institute.org/details/items/a-plan-of-albany.html>.

About Scotland. "Melrose Abbey, Melrose, the Scottish Borders." 2017. Web. 11 Jan. 2017. <http://www.aboutscotland.co.uk/history/mel.html>.

Adams, Mark. "The Trees on the Vassar College Campus are Wearing Their Spring Finery." 2009. Web. 7 Sept. 2015. <http://dutchess.uber.matchbin.com/printer _friendly/2461516>.

A History of the Origin of the Place Names Connected with the Chicago and North Western Chicago, St. Paul, Minneapolis, and Omaha Railways. 1908. Web. 13 Dec. 2016. <https://books.google.com/books?id=q_lKAQAAIAAJ&pg=PA1&lpg=PA1 &dq=a+history+of+the+origin+of+the+place+names+in+nine+northwestern+stat es&source=bl&ots=ma2tH_wOBW&sig=CASTuxqdzzEUqvVD07Da6gibQAk&hl=e n&sa=X&ved=0ahUKEwjb3qK1gPLQAhXKxVQKHTNQDUYQ6AEIKzAD#v=one page&q=a%20history%20of%20the%20origin%20of%20the%20place%20names %20in%20nine%20northwestern%20states&f=false>.

Albany 2030. "The Corning Preserve." 2016. Web. 1 Aug. 2016. <http://www.albany 2030.org/waterfront/corning-preserve>.

Albany Archives. "The Time President Taylor Almost Came to Albany but Died Instead." 10 Sept. 2013. Web. 21 Aug. 2016. <https://albanyarchives.wordpress .com/category/new-york-state-fair/>.

Albany Argus. "Second Edition. Latest News." 1857. Web. 9 Nov. 2017.<http://fulton history.com/Fulton.html>.

Albany Bridge Company. *Street Openings. A. Volume 1. Allen St.*

Albany City School District. "Montessori Magnet School." 2016. Web. 7 Aug. 2016. <http://www.albanyschools.org/schools/montessori/montessori.htm>.

———. "William S. Hackett Middle School." 2016. Web. 12 June 2016. <http://www .albanyschools.org/schools/hackettmiddle/hackett.htm>.

Albany County Convention and Visitors Bureau. "Peter D. Kiernan Plaza." 2016. Web. 18 June 2016. <http://www.albany.org/listings/Peter-D-Kiernan-Plaza/858/>.

————. "Washington Park Lakehouse." 2017. Web. 14 Mar. 2017. <http://www.albany.org/listings/Washington-Park-Lakehouse/694/>.

Albany County NY Gen Web. "Adjutant John H. Russell." 2017. Web. 13 Jan. 2017. <http://albany.nygenweb.net/bio-147.htm>.

————. "Anthony N. Brady." 2017. Web. 13 Jan. 2017. <http://albany.nygenweb.net/bio-309.htm>.

————. "Charles H. Porter, MD." 2017. Web. 13 Jan. 2017. <http://albany.nygenweb.net/bio-257.htm>.

————. "General Robert Shaw Oliver." 2017. Web. 13 Jan. 2017. <http://albany.nygenweb.net/bio-264.htm>.

————. "James Barclay Jermain." 2017. Web. 13 Jan. 2017. <http://albany.nygenweb.net/bio-330.htm>.

————. "Nanning Visscher Winne." 2017. Web. 13 Jan. 2017. <http://albany.nygenweb.net/bio-94.htm>.

Albany Evening Journal. "City Building Will be Sold." *Albany Evening Journal.* (1916, Sept. 8). Web. 19 Oct. 2017. <http://fultonhistory.com/Fulton.html>.

————. "City Endorses Marion Avenue Improvement." *Albany Evening Journal.* (1929, July 16). Web. 19 Oct. 2017. <http://fultonhistory.com/Fulton.html>.

————. "City Government." *Albany Evening Journal.* (1913, Mar. 13). Web. 18 Oct. 2017. <http://fultonhistory.com/Fulton.html>.

————. "Malone's Ordinance Provides for a Zoning Plan." *Albany Evening Journal.* (1922, June 20). Web. 19 Oct. 2017. <http://fultonhistory.com/Fulton.html>.

————. "Mrs. F. F. Cleveland, 77, is Dead at Greyledge." *Albany Evening Journal.* (1918, Oct. 11). Print.

————. "Settlement of Owners of Homes." *Albany Evening Journal.* (1909, July 21). Web. 28 Oct. 2017. <http://fultonhistory.com/Fulton.html>.

————. "The Van Wert-Cleveland Wedding." *Albany Evening Journal.* (1900, May 3). Print.

————. "This Man has Nearly Reached Century Mark." *Albany Evening Journal.* (1905, Aug. 26). Web. 28 Oct. 2017. <http://fultonhistory.com/Fulton.html>.

————. "Wires of City go in Conduits." *Albany Evening Journal.* (1913, June 26). Web. 18 Oct. 2017. <http://fultonhistory.com/Fulton.html>.

Albany Housing Authority. "North Albany Homes." 2017. Web. 19 Jan. 2017. <http://www.albanyhousing.org/housing-location/north-albany-homes>.

Albany Institute and Historical and Art Society. *Catalog of Paintings of the Albany Institute and Historical and Art Society, Albany, N.Y.* 1924. Web. 2 Sept. 2016. <https://archive.org/stream/frick-31072000948440/31072000948440_djvu.txt>.

Albany: Map 449. Hallenbake (Grand) Street at Corner of Hudson's Street. Map. Scale not given. 1800. Print.

Albany Muskrat. "Buckingham Garden and Golden Acres 1930's." 2 Feb. 2013. Web. 14 Mar. 2017. <https://albanymuskrat.wordpress.com/2013/02/02/buckingham-gardens-and-golden-acres-in-albany/>.

Albany Rural Cemetery. "Historical and Research—Search for a Grave." 2016. Web. 1 Aug. 2016. <http://albanyruralcemetery.org/search-arc/>.

Albany Tennis Club. "Albany Tennis Club History." 2016. Web. 6 Oct. 2016. <http://albanytennisclub.com/About>.

Alderman, Derek. "Naming Streets for Martin Luther King, Jr.: No Easy Road." 13 Feb. 2006. Web. 9 Jan. 2017. <http://mlkstreet.com/>.

Allen, Daniel. *Genealogy of the Allen Family*. 1898. Web. 15 Nov. 2016. <https://books.google.com/books?id=eaoZAQAAMAAJ&pg=PA9&lpg=PA9&dq=%22+was+one+of+Rhode+Island%27s+most+learned+men.+At+the+age%22&source=bl&ots=LsrRv2QHMz&sig=QohoAeZm20OBbQKhZO37n__wvS4&hl=en&sa=X&ved=0ahUKEwii2cj8v6vQAhWe0YMKHQ51BPEQ6AEIGzAA#v=onepage&q&f=false>.

Allen, David. *The Mapping of New York State: A Study in the History of Cartography*. Revised ed. 2014. Web. 18 Oct. 2017. <http://digital.library.stonybrook.edu/cdm/ref/collection/newyorkstatemaps/id/46>.

Allen, Michael, and Larry Schweikart. *A Patriot's History of the United States: From Columbus's Great Discovery to the War on Terror*. New York, NY: Sentinel, 2004. Print.

Allen, Pam. "Albany Philanthropist, Developer, Car Dealer Carl Touhey Dies at Age 95." *Albany Business Review*. (2013, Aug. 26). Web. 18 Nov. 2016. <http://www.bizjournals.com/albany/blog/2013/08/albany-philanthropist-developer-car.html>.

Alotta, Robert. *Mermaids, Monasteries, Cherokees, and Custer: The Stories Behind Philadelphia Street Names*. Chicago, IL: Bonus Books, 1990. Print.

_____. *Street Names of Philadelphia*. Philadelphia, PA: Temple University Press, 1975. Print.

American Bar Association. "Presentation of Kent Memorial Tablet." *American Bar Association Journal*. (1924, Dec.). Web. 19 Jan. 2017. <http://www.jstor.org/stable/25709131?seq=1#page_scan_tab_contents>.

American Battle Monuments Commission. "Robert E. McTague." 2017. Web. 17 Sept. 2017. <https://www.abmc.gov/node/411471#.Wb6cUsiGPIU>.

American Red Cross. "Founder Clara Barton." 2015. Web. 8 Sept. 2015. <http://www.redcross.org/about-us/history/clara-barton>.

Anthony, Barry, and Richard Brown. *The Kinetoscope: A British History*. New Barnet, Barnet, UK: John Libbey Publishing, 2017. Print.

Archives. "Betty Ann Besch in the 1940 Census." 2016. Web. 12 Dec. 2016. <http://www.archives.com/1940-census/betty-besch-ny-58128116>.

Ashley, Eugene. *New York State Men: Individual Library Edition, with Biographic Studies, Character Portraits and Autographs*. 1918. Web. 5 Jan. 2017. <http://books.googleusercontent.com/books/content?req=AKW5QaeNtDmTXFiXxOhvY8bthNLt40ORCDunBbm1oqT8T9eK-q2tLuB-h17Ud-FMUEYSnAKNg_cV

_7SF9jA_omKo_GzC25FMpS4YQ_9EvAIrPRXb5TPt-SxYJHBG1OyV3X-8F-C6wT
9tz7DVWLQh5suYXaWzupm-xEMSCIfWQIob3W-Kz4QSuEceB0wDDBsfeyxhHV
wypYAnKX4aUKjfUUsWQMLdPnuzfs9jaZKC_Zkl47iKpMkJ6nl3SczehEM_mGH
MTehnKA1w>.

Association of Public Historians of New York State. "Historical Markers." 2017. Web. 24 Apr. 2017. <http://www.aphnys.org/wp-content/uploads/2014/03/Historical-Markers.pdf>.

Avon History. "The Erie Indians, Avon, Ohio." 2016. Web. 19 July 2016. <http://avonhistory.org/hist/erind.htm>.

Baker, Ronald, and Marvin Carmony. *Indiana Place Names*. Bloomington, IN: University of Indiana Press, 1978. Print.

Barbagallo, Tricia. "James Caldwell: Immigrant Engineer." 20 July 2004. Web. 18 Nov. 2016. <https://exhibitions.nysm.nysed.gov/albany/art/art-jctb.html>.

Barclay, James. *Albany: Map 450. Lots on Townsend Park*. Map. Scale not given. 1808. Print.

_____. *Albany: Map 460. State Street West Toward Eagle Street*. Map. Scale not given. 1809. Print.

Barnes, William. *The Settlement and Early History of Albany*. 1851. Web. 15 Oct. 2017. <https://ia902604.us.archive.org/7/items/settlementearlyh02barn/settlement earlyh02barn.pdf>.

Bartlett, John. *Dictionary of Americanisms: A Glossary of Words and Phrases Usually Regarded as Peculiar to the United States*. 1848. Web. 9 May 2017. <https://archive .org/details/in.ernet.dli.2015.167116>.

BBC. "Liberia Country Profile." 2018. Web. 23 Feb. 2018. <http://www.bbc.com /news/world-africa-13729504>.

Beers, D. G., and S. N. Beers. *City of Albany*. Map. Scale not given. 1866. 13 Oct. 2017. <https://digitalcollections.nypl.org/items/510-72ee-a3d9-e040-e00a18064a99>.

Beers, Frederick, and Watson and Company. *Section 33, Section of Rensselaer County and Bath and Greenbush*. Map. Scale not given. 1891. Web. 14 Mar. 2017. <http://www.davidrumsey.com/luna/servlet/detail/RUMSEY~8~1~28472~1120876 :33-Albany—Albany,-Rensselaer-count?sort=Pub_List_No_InitialSort%2CPub_Date %2CPub_List_No%2CSeries_No&qvq=q:albany%2B1891;sort:Pub_List_No_InitialS ort%2CPub_Date%2CPub_List_No%2CSeries_No;lc:RUMSEY~8~1&mi=3&trs=6>.

Begley, Alice, and Mary Ellen Johnson. *Images of America: Guilderland, New York*. Charleston, SC: Arcadia Publishing, 1999. Print.

Benardo, Leonard, and Jennifer Weiss. *Brooklyn by Name: How the Neighborhoods, Streets, Parks, Bridges and More Got Their Names*. New York, NY: New York University Press, 2006. Print.

Bennett, Allison. *More Times Remembered: Chronicles of the Towns of Bethlehem and New Scotland, New York*. Delmar, NY: Newgraphics of Delmar, 1987. Print.

Bennett, Troy. "This Portland Street is Named for a Presidential Loser." 28 Aug. 2017. Web. 27 Oct. 2017. <http://portland.bangordailynews.com/2017/08/28/history/ this-portland-street-is-named-for-a-presidential-loser/>.

Benson, Egbert. *Memoir Read Before the Historical Society of the State of New York.* 1825. Web. 25 Mar. 2018. <https://archive.org/details/memoirreadbefore02bens>.

Bielinski, Stefan. "Abraham Van Vechten." 24 Apr. 2016. Web. 28 Jan. 2017. <https://exhibitions.nysm.nysed.gov/albany/bios/vv/abvvechten2378.html>.

———. "Adrian Quackenbush." 25 Feb. 2010. Web. 17 Apr. 2017. <http://exhibitions.nysm.nysed.gov//albany/bios/q/adq2000.html>.

———. "Albert Janse Ryckman." 30 Mar. 2015. Web. 8 Sept. 2016. <http://exhibitions.nysm.nysed.gov//albany/bios/r/ajryckman1905.html>.

———. "Andries De Vos." 10 Apr. 2011. Web. 22 Aug. 2016. <http://exhibitions.nysm.nysed.gov/albany/bios/d/anddvos.html>.

———. "Catharina Livingston Van Rensselaer Westerlo." 10 Sept. 2001. Web. 21 Aug. 2016. <http://exhibitions.nysm.nysed.gov//albany/bios/l/calivingston5034.html>.

———. "Catharine Van Rensselaer Schuyler." 31 May 2001. Web. 18 Nov. 2016. <http://exhibitions.nysm.nysed.gov//albany/bios/vr/cavr.html>.

———. "Charles R. Webster." 5 May 2012. Web. 21 Sept. 2016. <http://exhibitions.nysm.nysed.gov//albany/bios/w/crwebster6841.html>.

———. "City Streets." 28 July 2000. Web. 15 July 2015. <http://www.nysm.nysed.gov/albany/streets.html#pearl>.

———. "Cornelia Schuyler Morton." 30 Jan. 2013. Web. 9 Sept. 2016. <http://exhibitions .nysm.nysed.gov/albany/bios/s/coschuyler1257.html#wm>.

———. "Dellius." 30 Dec. 2004. Web. 28 July 2016. <http://exhibitions.nysm.nysed.gov//albany/bios/d/godellius.html>.

———. "Dirck Bensing." 10 Feb. 2006. Web. 28 July 2016. <http://exhibitions.nysm.nysed.gov/albany/bios/b/dibensing7319.html>.

———. "Elizabeth Schuyler." 2004. Web. 11 Aug. 2016. <http://exhibitions.nysm.nysed.gov/albany/bios/s/elschuyleranb.html>.

———. "Evert Janse Wendell." 30 June 2005. Web. 26 Aug. 2016. <http://exhibitions.nysm.nysed.gov//albany/bios/w/evwendell2655.html>.

———. "George Webster." 10 Apr. 2015. Web. 21 Sept. 2016. <http://exhibitions.nysm.nysed.gov//albany/bios/w/gwebster6848.html>.

———. "Gerrit Bancker." 20 Apr. 2006. Web. 28 July 2016. <http://exhibitions.nysm.nysed.gov//albany/bios/b/gebancker6467.html>.

———. "Harmanus." 6 Oct. 2005. Web. 26 Aug. 2016. <http://exhibitions.nysm.nysed.gov//albany/bios/w/hawendell2667.html>.

———. "Hendrick Quackenbush." 20 Dec. 2002. Web. 17 Apr. 2017. <http://exhibitions.nysm.nysed.gov//albany/bios/q/heq2111.html>.

———. "Issac Hutton." 30 July 2011. Web. 13 Jan. 2017. <https://exhibitions.nysm.nysed.gov/albany/bios/h/ishutton.html>.

———. "Jacob Coenradtse Ten Eyck." 5 Sept. 2004. Web. 9 Sept. 2016. <http://exhibitions.nysm.nysed.gov//albany/bios/t/jacote4807.html>.

———. "James Wilson." 10 Aug. 2010. Web. 22 Sept. 2016. <http://exhibitions.nysm.nysed.gov//albany/bios/w/jawilson.html>.

_____. "Jan Janse Bleecker." 3 Dec. 2002. Web. 28 July 2016. <http://exhibitions .nysm.nysed.gov//albany/bios/b/jjbleecker2.html>.

_____. "Johannes Martense Beekman." 29 Feb. 2004. Web. 28 July 2016. <http:// exhibitions.nysm.nysed.gov//albany/bios/b/jombeekman3858.html>.

_____. "Johannes Quackenbush." 25 Dec. 2005. Web. 17 Apr. 2017. <http:// exhibitions .nysm.nysed.gov//albany/bios/q/joq2139.html>.

_____. "Johannes Van Zandt." 25 Aug. 2002. Web. 22 Aug. 2016. <http://exhibitions .nysm.nysed.gov//albany/bios/vz/jovzandt280.html>.

_____. "Johannes W. Quackenbush." 20 Oct. 2005. Web. 17 Apr. 2017. <http:// exhibitions.nysm.nysed.gov//albany/bios/q/joq2141.html>.

_____. "Margaret Lynott Hutton." 5 Sept. 2001. Web. 13 Jan. 2017. <https:// exhibitions.nysm.nysed.gov/albany/bios/l/mgtlynott.html>.

_____. "Nicholas Van Rensselaer." 15 Mar. 2001. Web. 16 Nov. 2016. <http:// exhibitions.nysm.nysed.gov//albany/bios/vr/nvr.html>.

_____. "Peter Gansevoort." 15 Aug. 2003. Web. 28 July 2016. <http://exhibitions .nysm.nysed.gov//albany/bios/g/pegans.html>.

_____. "Philip Livingston." 20 Dec. 2012. Web. 18 Aug. 2015. <https://www .nysm.nysed.gov/albany/bios/l/phlivingston.html>.

_____. "Philip Schuyler." 22 May 2001. Web. 15 Dec. 2016. <http://exhibitions .nysm.nysed.gov//albany/bios/s/phschuyler1750.html>.

_____. "Pieter Quackenbush." 5 Mar. 2010. Web. 19 Aug. 2016. <http://exhibitions .nysm.nysed.gov//albany/bios/q/piq2223.html>.

_____. "Pieter Quackenbush." 10 Mar. 2010. Web. 19 Aug. 2016. <http:// exhibitions.nysm.nysed.gov/albany/bios/q/piq.html>.

_____. "Pieter W. Quackenbush." 15 May 2010. Web. 21 Aug. 2016. <http:// exhibitions.nysm.nysed.gov//albany/bios/q/piq2302.html>.

_____. "Reverend John Bassett." 10 Sept. 2001. Web. 13 Sept. 2015. <https://www .nysm.nysed.gov/albany/bios/b/jobassett.html>.

_____. "River People in Early Albany." 3 Jan. 2002. Web. 19 Aug. 2016. <http://exhibitions.nysm.nysed.gov//albany/art/art-rpea.html>.

_____. "Rutger Jacobse Van Woert." 25 Oct. 2005. Web. 26 Aug. 2016. <http://exhibitions.nysm.nysed.gov/albany/bios/vw/rjvwoert2637.html>.

_____. "Samuel Norton." 20 Dec. 2008. Web. 15 Aug. 2016. <http://exhibitions .nysm.nysed.gov//albany/bios/r/elradcliff1044.html>.

_____. "Samuel Wilson." 15 Mar. 2006. Web. 22 Sept. 2016. <http://exhibitions .nysm.nysed.gov//albany/bios/w/sawilson6907.html>.

_____. "Stewart Dean." 5 Aug. 2012. Web. 18 Aug. 2015. <https://www.nysm .nysed.gov/albany/bios/d/stdean.html>.

_____. "Teunis T. Van Vechten." 20 Jan. 2013. Web. 28 Jan. 2017. <https:// exhibitions.nysm.nysed.gov/albany/bios/vv/tetvvechten2569.html>.

_____. "Teunis Van Vechten." 20 Aug. 2006. Web. 28 Jan. 2017. <https:// exhibitions.nysm.nysed.gov/albany/bios/vv/tevvechten2572.html>.

_____. "The Van Rensselaer Manor House." 17 Jan. 2014. Web. 26 July 2016. <http://exhibitions.nysm.nysed.gov//albany/na/vrmh.html>.

_____. "Thomas Barclay." 6 Dec. 2008. Web. 15 July 2015. <http://www.nysm.nysed.gov/albany/bios/b/tbarclay.html#biography>.

_____. "Thomas Dongan." 27 July 2014. Web. 30 Sept. 2015. <https://www.nysm.nysed.gov/albany/bios/d/thdongan.html>.

_____. "Whitehall." 6 June 2001. Web. 7 Aug. 2016. <http://exhibitions.nysm.nysed.gov//albany/na/whitehall.html>.

_____. "Wouter Pieterse Quackenbush." 1 Dec. 2009. Web. 17 Apr. 2017. <http://exhibitions.nysm.nysed.gov//albany/bios/q/wopq2322.html>.

_____. "Wouter Quackenbush, Jr." 20 Aug. 2009. Web. 17 Apr. 2017. <http://exhibitions.nysm.nysed.gov//albany/bios/q/woq2323.html>.

_____. "Yates Mansion." 18 Oct. 2016. Web. 16 Mar. 2017. <http://exhibitions.nysm.nysed.gov/albany/loc/yatesmansion.html>.

Biography.com. "Abraham Lincoln." 19 Sept. 2016. Web. 18 June 2016. <http://www. biography.com/people/abraham-lincoln-9382540>.

_____. "Alexander Hamilton." 17 Nov. 2016. Web. 29 July 2016. <http://www.biography.com/people/alexander-hamilton-9326481>.

_____. "Benjamin Franklin." 17 Nov. 2015. Web. 19 July 2016. <http://www.biography.com/people/benjamin-franklin-9301234#related-video-gallery>.

_____. "Clara Barton." 8 July 2014. Web. 9 Sept. 2015. <http://www.biography.com/people/clara-barton-9200960>.

_____. "Harriet Tubman." 21 Apr. 2016. Web. 19 Dec. 2016. <http://www.biography.com/people/harriet-tubman-9511430#escape-from-slavery-and-Abolitionism>.

_____. "Jack 'Legs' Diamond." 2 Apr. 2014. Web. 27 June 2015. <http://www. biography.com/people/jack-legs-diamond-21088979>.

_____. "John Jay." 2 Apr. 2014. Web. 13 June 2016. <http://www.biography.com/people/john-jay-9353566#death-and-legacy>.

_____. "José Martí Biography." 24 Mar. 2016. Web. 18 June 2016. <http://www.biography.com/people/jos%C3%A9-mart%C3%AD-20703847#personal-life>.

_____. "Nathaniel Hawthorne." 4 Jan. 2017. Web. 12 Jan. 2017. <http://www.biography.com/people/nathaniel-hawthorne-9331923#synopsis>.

_____. "Rufus King." 2 Apr. 2014. Web. 18 June 2016. <http://www.biography.com/people/rufus-king-9365114>.

_____. "Samuel de Champlain." 8 July 2014. Web. 26 Aug. 2015. <http://www.biography.com/people/samuel-de-champlain-9243971>.

_____. "Ulysses S. Grant." 11 July 2016. Web. 11 Sept. 2016. <http://www.biography .com/people/ulysses-s-grant-9318285>.

_____. "William Howard Taft." 8 Aug. 2016. Web. 12 Sept. 2016. <http://www.biography.com/people/william-howard-taft-9501184#related-video-gallery>.

Birkner, Michael (Ed.), et al. *The Governors of New Jersey: Biographical Essays*. 2014. Web. 12 Jan. 2017. <https://books.google.com/books?id=1I_0AgAAQBAJ&dq=governor+robert+hunter&source=gbs_navlinks_s>.

Birmingham, F. W., and W. J. McAlpine. *Map of the Neighborhood of the City of Albany Showing the Routes of the Proposed Plans for Furnishing a Supply of Water.* Map. Scale not given. 1850. Web. 18 Mar. 2017. <http://www.albanyinstitute.org /details /items/map-of-the-neighborhood-of-the-city-of-albany-showing-the-routes.html>.

Bishop, Robin. "A Barnet Business Start up that Changed the World." 20 Nov. 2015. Web. 1 Nov. 2017. <http://barnetsociety.org.uk/component/k2/a-barnet-business-start-up-that-changed-the-world>.

Black Hawk, and Donald Jackson (Ed.). *Black Hawk: An Autobiography.* Chicago, IL: University of Illinois Press, 1990. Print.

Blessing, Charles. *Albany Schools and Colleges Yesterday and Today.* Albany, NY: Fort Orange Press, 1946. Print.

Bloodgood, Simeon DeWitt. *A Treatise on Roads, Their History, Character, and Utility.* 1838. Web. 15 Oct. 2017. <https://ia802703.us.archive.org/31/items /treatise onroadst00blooiala/treatiseonroadst00blooiala.pdf>.

Bogart, Henry. *Map of North Market Street.* Map. Scale not given. 1790. Web. 16 Mar. 2017. <https://exhibitions.nysm.nysed.gov/albany/im/immktstcol.html>.

_____. *Plan of a Survey of State Street, Albany.* Map. Scale not given. 1792. Web. 18 Mar. 2017. <http://www.genealogy.clifflamere.com/Aid/History/AlbanyCity Maps-nocomments.htm>.

Boland, Ed Jr. "F.Y.I." *The New York Times.* (2002, Oct. 13). Web. 5 Feb. 2018. <http:// www.nytimes.com/2002/10/13/nyregion/fyi-331902.html?pagewanted=1>.

Bolton, Herbert. *Coronado: Knight of Pueblos and Plains.* Albuquerque, NM: University of New Mexico Press, 1990. Print.

Bowers, Virginia. "An Early History of Trinity Institution." Print.

_____. *Mayors of Albany, 1686–1997, Biographical Sketches.* Albany, NY: City Club of Albany, 1997. Print.

Braudel, Fernand, and Sian Reynolds (Trans.). *The Mediterranean and the Mediterranean World in the Age of Philip II.* 2nd ed. Berkeley, CA: University of California Press, 1996. Print.

Brebner, John. *The Explorers of North America, 1492–1806: From Columbus to Lewis and Clark.* New York, NY: Meridian, 1933. Print.

Briggs, Robert. "From Providing Housing to Building Communities: A Brief History of the Albany Housing Authority." Web. 19 Jan. 2017. <http://www.albany housing .org/wordpress/wp-content/uploads/2013/06/A-Brief-History-Of-The-Albany-Housing-Authority.pdf>.

Brumwell, Stephen. *White Devil: A True Story of War, Savagery, and Vengeance in Colonial America.* New York, NY: Da Capo, 2004. Print.

Bubie, Marvin. *On the Trail of Henry Hudson and our Dutch Heritage Through the Municipal Seals in New York, 1609–2009.* Schenectady, NY: Square Circle Press, 2014. Print.

Bull, John, and John Farrard Jr. *National Audubon Society Field Guide to North American Birds: Eastern Region.* Revised ed. New York, NY: Knopf, 1994. Print.

Bump, Bethany. "Publisher to End 125-Year Run in Albany." *The Daily Gazette.* (2013, Jan 15). Web. 16 Aug. 2017. <https://dailygazette.com/article/2013/01/15/lexisnexis-lay-220-albany-plant-close-end-2014>.

Burr, David, and Simeon DeWitt. *Map of the Counties of Albany and Schenectady.* Map. Scale not given. 1829. Web. 16 Mar. 2017. <https://digitalcollections.nypl.org/items/510d47da-f24c-a3d9-e040-e00a18064a99>.

Burrage, Walter, and Howard Kelly. *American Medical Biographies.* 1920. Web. 17 Jan. 2017. <https://archive.org/details/americanmedica00kell>.

Callaway, John. *Streetwise Chicago: A History of Chicago Street Names.* Chicago, IL: Loyola University Press, 1988. Print.

Campbell, John. *Map of a Lot of Ground Belonging to the Corporation of this City.* Map. Scale not given. 1794. Print.

Carlson, Craig. "The Formation of the City of Watervliet: Timeline, 1788–1896." 2001. Web. 16 Aug. 2016. <http://freepages.genealogy.rootsweb.ancestry.com/ ~clifflamere/History/Watervliet-Timeline.htm>.

Carpenter, George. *Atlas of Maps, City of Albany.* Circa 1837. Print.

Carpenter, George, and Prosper Desobry. *Map of Lots in the Fifth Ward of the City of Albany Belonging to the Estate of Peter Gansevoort, Jr., Deceased.* Map. Scale not given. 1834. Web. 16 Mar. 2017. <https://digitalcollections.nypl.org/items/510d47da-f05c-a3d9-e040-e00a18064a99>.

Catton, Bruce. *The Civil War.* New York, NY: Houghton Mifflin, 1960. Print.

Celebrate Boston. "John Winthrop the Younger Colonial Connecticut Governor." 2016. Web. 16 Nov. 2016. <http://www.celebrateboston.com/biography/john-winthrop-the-younger.htm>.

Chesler, Andrew, and H. Robb. *Encyclopedia of American Family Names.* New York, NY: Harper Collins, 1995. Print.

Child, Edmund. *Child's Albany Directory and City Register for the Years 1830–1831.* Albany, NY: E.B. Child, 1831. Print.

Child, Hamilton. *Gazetteer and Business Directory of Albany and Schenectady Co., N.Y., for 1870–1871.* 1871. Web. 22 Aug. 2016. <https://archive.org/details/gazetteerbusines00chil_2>.

Christ Church in Philadelphia. "History." 2007. Web. 19 July 2016. <http://www.christchurchphila.org/Historic-Christ-Church/Burial-Ground/History/96/>.

Christian Brothers Academy. "Christian Brothers Academy." 2016. Web. 7 Aug. 2016. <http://www.cbaalbany.org/>.

Churchill, Chris. "A Pioneering Family was at Home on a Vanishing Albany Street." *Times Union.* (2015, Dec. 14). Web. 29 Sept. 2016. <http://www.timesunion.com/tuplus-local/article/Chris-Churchill-A-pioneering-family-was-at-home-6694561.php>.

———. "Do Tudors Await Demolition by Neglect?" *Times Union.* (2013, Jan. 17). Web. 11 Aug. 2016. <http://www.timesunion.com/local/article/Do-Tudors-await-demolition-by-neglect-4200232.php>.

City of Albany. "Arbor Hill Neighborhood." 2016. Web. 16 Aug. 2016. <http://www
.albanyny.org/Government/Departments/DevelopmentandPlanning/Neighborhoods
/ArborHill.aspx>.

———. "City History." 2017. Web. 18 Mar. 2017. <http://www.albanyny.gov
/Government/CityHistory.aspx>.

———. "Local Laws Introduced." 2016. Web. 29 Sept. 2016. <http://www.albany ny
.org/Libraries/Common_Council_Agendas_and_Minutes/January_4_2016.sflb.ashx>.

City of Albany Common Council. *Laws and Ordinances of the Common Council of
the City of Albany.* 1838. Web. 27 Dec. 2016. <https://books.google.com/books
?id=pftCAQAAMAAJ&printsec=frontcover&source=gbs_ge_summary_r&cad=0#v
=onepage&q&f=false>.

———. *Proceedings of the Common Council.* 1905. Web. 13 Oct. 2017.
<https://books.googleusercontent.com/books/content?req=AKW5QaftROYkbcVq
KCzXHNgHdVeAIGJ26Bc56-lAvvEeiNmCgKjq-i8oIPzsMy3bjpvWUenBOIpefhhe
HDz5 GVjmb7BhVfBP_p9SaFs0SWgziJ36CQIf-Td40KN57Q_FFXv8YRBNzvh_A
5gcY263Pd1dBjjJ0TBpyIOgn_Jjh0zVy1m4bF7oKo-i-EfyiYzcbYU6gz-MXbBi1ono_D
vE4hba5BdBAJHAYbYel39iMqNrfRNRo6OIdZ_KO4oLaYO0cXIxen82F_Qc>.

———. *Proceedings of the Common Council.* 1915. Web. 13 Feb. 2017. <https://books
.googleusercontent.com/books/content?req=AKW5QaeW17TEZ-zDl0wFZ7U4a
MP2ziYuL8qLO-bwZfsQyC_4Cg2sDl3sNZNjVDLiduhynEauT7lMnpQOCZmKDm
P00dIrmBtm1xaWKoqYKuYPalz8XqDy_wHQO-dncbvWSyZH4YguPH4m-FTkui
Xi_xBMm2-X1urrnpZGBbrjAWub7yGzOdrNFWdieHrfJ4SaRTwQpM1a4XisMvl
d3zZSVA16Xua1TuAd7BN9PcT78Tjj0THiDnxC03DPkY-ktzMONJX89keOrm_i>.

———. *Proceedings of the Common Council, Volume II, Message of the Mayor and
Reports of City Officers.* 1918. Web. 14 Mar. 2017. <https://books.google.com
/books?id=gMdEAQAAMAAJ&printsec=frontcover&source=gbs_ge_summary_r&
cad=0#v=onepage&q&f=false>.

———. *Report of a Special Committee on Burial Grounds.* 1866. Web. 1 Feb. 2018.

City of Binghamton. "Binghamton, New York, a Brief History." 2016. Web. 16 Aug.
2016. <http://www.binghamton-ny.gov/history>.

City of Boston. *A Record of the Streets, Alleys, Places, Etc., in the City of Boston.*
1910. Web. 13 Dec. 2016. <https://archive.org/stream/recordofstreetsabost#page
/n3/mode/2up>.

City of Daytona Beach. "History of City." 2016. Web. 14 July 2016. <http://www.codb
.us/index.aspx?nid=365>.

City of Orlando. "Orlando History." 2016. Web. 14 July 2016. <http://www.cityof
orlando.net/about/>.

City of Ormond Beach. "Ormond History." 2016. Web. 14 July 2016. <http://www
.ormondbeach.org/DocumentCenter/Home/View/206>.

City of River Falls. "Street Naming." 2017. Web. 10 Apr. 2017. <http://www.rfcity
.org/DocumentCenter/View/154>.

Civilwar.com. "John Adams Dix." 2015. Web. 30 Sept. 2015. <http://www.civilwar
.com/people/20-union-generals/148620-john-adams-dix.html>.

Civil War Trust. "Civil War Casualties." 2016. Web. 18 June 2016. <http://www .civil war.org/education/civil-war-casualties.html?referrer=https://www.google .com/>.

———. "Philip Sheridan." 2016. Web. 5 Sept. 2016. <http://www.civilwar.org /education/history/biographies/phillip-sheridan.html?referrer=https://www .google.com/>.

Clark, Rufus. *The Heroes of Albany*. 1867. Web. 17 Jan. 2017. <https://ia902604 .us.archive.org/13/items/theheroesofalb00clar/theheroesofalb00clar.pdf>.

Clarke, James. *American Assassins: The Darker Side of Politics*. Princeton, NJ: Princeton University Press, 1982. Print.

Coggins, Allen. *Place Names of the Smokies*. Gatlinburg, TN: Great Smoky Mountains Association, 1999. Print.

Columbia Development Companies. "Columbia Development Companies." 2016. Web. 21 Nov. 2016. <http://www.columbiadev.com/>.

Congressional Medal of Honor Society. "Full Archive." 2017. Web. 27 Oct. 2017. <http://www.cmohs.org/recipient-archive.php>.

Cornell University. "Counties and County Subdivisions in New York State." 2012. Web. 17 Sept. 2017. <https://pad.human.cornell.edu/maps2010/maps/Reference Maps.pdf>.

———. "University Facts." 2015. Web. 25 Aug. 2015. <https://www.cornell .edu/about/facts.cfm>.

Cornish, Colette. "Time Line History of Cornell, New York." 2009. Web. 23 June 2017. <http://cityofhornell.com/hornell_info/documents/city-timelinehistory ofhorn08.pdf>.

Corwin, Edward. *A Manual of the Reformed Church in America (Formerly Ref. Prot. Dutch Church) 1628–1878*. 1879. Web. 14 July 2016. <https://archive.org /details/cu31924008113254>.

Coulter, Ann. *Demonic: How the Liberal Mob is Endangering America*. New York, NY: Crown Forum, 2011. Print.

County of Albany, Office of the County Clerk. *Index to the Public Records of the County of Albany, State of New York, 1630–1894*. Albany, NY: The Argus Company, 1902. Print.

Coyle, John, Edward McGuire, and Vincent O'Reilly. *The Journal of the American Irish Historical Society*. 1922. Web. 22 Feb. 2018. <https://archive.org/details /journalofamerica21amer>.

Crafts, William. *The Crafts Family: Genealogical and Biographical History of the Descendants of Griffin and Alice Craft, Roxbury, Mass., 1630–1890*. 1893. Web. 14 Dec. 2016. <https://books.google.com/books?id=M3XCFlk3sVMC&dq=%22amos +porteus+palmer%22&source=gbs_navlinks_s>.

Cultural Survival. "Mohawk." 2016. Web. 19 June 2016. <https://www .cultural survival.org/publications/cultural-survival-quarterly/canada/Mohawk>.

Daily News. "Politician Edward Swartz and Son Dead in Murder-Suicide." *Daily News*. (10 Sept. 2007). Web. 23 Jan. 2017. <http://www.nydailynews.com/news /crime/politician-edward-swartz-son-dead-murder-suicide-article-1.244505>.

Dartmouth College. "Dartmouth at a Glance." 2016. Web. 18 July 2016. <http://dartmouth.edu/dartmouth-glance>.

Delaware County Historical Association. "Book A of Deeds at the Delaware County Clerk's Office." 2016. Web. 13 Jan. 2017. <http://www.dcnyhistory.org/deeds bookA.html>.

Department of the Navy, Naval Historical Center. "Admiral David Dixon Porter, USN, (1831–1891)." 6 Nov. 1998. Web. 6 Sept. 2017. <https://web.archive.org/web/2013 0509124828/http://www.history.navy.mil/photos/pers-us/uspers-p/dd-portr. htm>.

———. "Commodore David Porter, USN, (1780–1843)." 6 Nov. 1998. Web. 6 Sept. 2017. <https://web.archive.org/web/20130715221944/http://www.history.navy .mil/photos/pers-us/uspers-p/d-portr.htm>.

Department of Veterans Affairs. "Albany Stratton VA Medical Center Albany NY." 2015. Web. 25 Aug. 2015. <http://www.albany.va.gov/about/index.asp>.

DeWitt, Simeon. *A Plan of the City of Albany*. Map. Scale not given. 1794. Web. 18 Mar. 2017. <http://www.albanyinstitute.org/details/items/a-plan-of-the-city-of-albany.html>.

———. *A Plan of the City of Albany*. Map. Scale not given. 1794. Web. 22 Mar. 2017. <http://www.albanyinstitute.org/details/items/a-plan-of-the-city-of-albany .1063.html>.

———. *Map of Northern and Southern Boundary Lines of the City of Albany*. Map. Scale not given. 1800. Print.

Dictionary of Canadian Biography. "Amherst, Jeffery, 1st Baron Amherst." 2015. Web. 13 Sept. 2015. <http://www.biographi.ca/en/bio/amherst_jeffery_4E .html>.

Donaldson, Alfred. *A History of the Adirondacks*. Fleischmanns, NY: Purple Mountain Press, 2002. Print.

Douglass, Frederick. *Narrative of the Life of Frederick Douglass, an American Slave*. New York, NY: Signet, 1968. Print.

Downing, Fred. "In-the-City Farmers Ready to Yield to Housing Project."

Dudley Observatory. "Observatory Founders." 2016. Web. 3 June 2016. <http://dudley observatory.org/charles-blandina-dudley/>.

Duffy, Richard. "History of Arlington Street Names." 1 Aug. 2008. Web. 27 Oct. 2017. <http://www.wickedlocal.com/x223021953/Wilbur-Avenue>.

Dunlop, William. *William Dunlop Map*. Map. Scale not given. 1757. Web. 18 Mar. 2017. <http://exhibitions.nysm.nysed.gov/albany/im/im1757.html>.

Dutch Church Lower Pasture No. 6. Map. Scale not given. 1791. Print.

Elder, Larry. *What's Race Got to do With It: Why it's Time to Stop the Dumbest Argument in America*. New York, NY: St. Martins Press, 2009. Print.

Emmons, Ebenezer. *Natural History of New York*. 1854. Web. 9 Jan. 2016. <http://archive .org/details/naturalhistoryof10newyuoft>.

Empson, Donald. *The Street Where You Live: A Guide to the Place Names of St. Paul*. Minneapolis, MN: University of Minnesota Press, 2006. Print.

Encyclopedia Britannica. "Charles Lennox, 3rd Duke of Richmond." 5 Feb. 2008. Web. 13 Dec. 2016. <https://www.britannica.com/biography/Charles-Lennox-3rd-duke-of-Richmond>.

_____. "Huron." 17 June 2015. Web. 11 July 2016. <https://www.britannica.com /topic/Huron-people>.

_____. "James D. Dana: American Geologist and Mineralogist." 3 May 2012. Web. 22 May 2016. <http://www.britannica.com/biography/James-D-Dana>.

_____. "John Winthrop." 12 Feb. 2016. Web. 5 Jan. 2017. <https://www .britannica .com/biography/John-Winthrop-American-colonial-governor>.

_____. "José Julián Martí." 29 May 2015. Web. 18 June 2016. <http://www .britannica .com/biography/Jose-Julian-Marti>.

_____. "Joseph Lancaster." 9 June 2006. Web. 6 Aug. 2016. <https://www.britannica .com/biography/Joseph-Lancaster>.

_____. "Maarten Tromp." 23 Aug. 2007. Web. 22 Aug. 2016. <https://www .britannica .com/biography/Maarten-Harpertszoon-Tromp>.

_____. "Maurice, Stadholder of the Netherlands." 23 Feb. 2007. Web. 22 Aug. 2016. <https://www.britannica.com/biography/Maurice-stadholder-of-The-Netherlands>.

_____. "Robert Fulton." 30 July 2015. Web. 25 July 2016. <https://www .britannica.com/biography/Robert-Fulton-American-inventor>.

_____. "Thomas Gage." 30 Jan. 2015. Web. 31 Aug. 2016. <https://www .britannica.com/biography/Thomas-Gage>.

_____. "Thurlow Weed." 19 Jan. 2010. Web. 16 Sept. 2016. <https://www .britannica.com/biography/Thurlow-Weed>.

_____. "William III." 9 Dec. 2016. Web. 28 Jan. 2017. <https://www .britannica.com/biography/William-III-king-of-England-Scotland-and-Ireland>.

English Monarchs. "The House of Tudor." 2005. Web. 16 Sept. 2016. <http://www .englishmonarchs.co.uk/tudor_21.htm>.

Eriecanal.org. "DeWitt Clinton." 2003. Web. 10 Sept. 2015. <http://www .eriecanal.org/UnionCollege/Clinton.html>.

Espenshade, A. Pennsylvania Place Names. 1925. Web. 13 Feb. 2017. <https://ia800208 .us.archive.org/12/items/pennsylvaniaplac00espe/pennsylvaniaplac00espe.pdf>.

Evjen, John. Scandinavian Immigrants in New York, 1630–1674. 1916. Web. 27 June 2017. <https://books.google.com/books?id=Eah4AAAAMAAJ&dq=normans+kill &source=gbs_navlinks_s>.

Fagan, Brian. The Great Journey: The Peopling of Ancient America. London: Thames and Hudson, 1987. Print.

Family Search. "Anna Barroa." 2016. Web. 26 Dec. 2016. <https://familysearch .org/search/record/results?count=20&query=%2Bgivenname%3Aanna~%20%2B surname%3Abarrow~%20%2Bbirth_place%3A%22albany%20NY%22~%20%2 Bbirth_year%3A1685-1685~>.

_____. "August Bohl." 2017. Web. 6 Oct. 2017. <https://www.familysearch .org/search/record/results?count=20&query=%2Bgivenname%3Aaugst~%20%2

Bsurname%3Abohl~%20%2Bbirth_year%3A1840-1850~%20%2Bresidence_place
%3AAlbany~%20%2Brecord_country%3A%22United%20States%22&collection
_id=1438024>.

_____. "Barnard Nichols." 2017. Web. 6 Oct. 2017. <https://www.familysearch
.org/search/record/results?count=20&query=%2Bgivenname%3Abernhardt~%20
%2Bsurname%3Anicoll~%20%2Bbirth_year%3A1800-1860~%20%2Bresidence
_place%3AAlbany~%20%2Brecord_country%3A%22United%20States%22&col
lection_id=1325221>.

_____. "Christina Bender." 2016. Web. 26 Dec. 2016. <https://familysearch
.org/search/record/results?count=20&query=%2Bsurname%3Abender~%20%2B
death_place%3A%22albany%20NY%22~%20%2Bdeath_year%3A1700-1777~>.

_____. "Cornelis Austin." 2016. Web. 25 Dec. 2016. <https://familysearch.org
/search/record/results?count=20&query=%2Bgivenname%3Acornelis~%20%2B
surname%3Aaustin~%20%2Bbirth_year%3A1782-1782~>.

_____. "Daniel Carroll." 2016. Web. 26 Dec. 2016. <https://familysearch.org
/search/record/results?count=20&query=%2Bgivenname%3Adaniel~%20%2Bsu
rname%3Acarroll~%20%2Bbirth_place%3Aalbany~%20%2Bbirth_year%3A16
00-1700~>.

_____. "Dirck Bensen." 2016. Web. 26 Dec. 2016. <https://familysearch.org
/ark:/61903/2:2:992W-2Q9>.

_____. "Enos Weis." 2016. Web. 26 Dec. 2016. <https://familysearch.org
/ark:/61903/1:1:MJKH-SS2>.

_____. "Henry Clare." 2016. Web. 26 Dec. 2016. <https://familysearch.org
/search/record/results?count=20&query=%2Bgivenname%3Ahenry~%20%2Bsu
rname%3Aclare~%20%2Bresidence_place%3A%22albany%20NY%22~%20%2
Bresidence_year%3A1800-1900~>.

_____. "Jacob Bogaart." 2016. Web. 25 Dec. 2016. <https://familysearch.org
/search/record/results?count=20&query=%2Bgivenname%3Ajacob~%20%2Bsur
name%3Abogert~%20%2Bdeath_year%3A1725–1725~>.

_____. "James Davis." 2016. Web. 26 Dec. 2016. <https://familysearch.org/search
/record/results?count=20&query=%2Bsurname%3Adavis~%20%2Bdeath_place
%3A%22albany%20NY%22~%20%2Bdeath_year%3A1700-1800~>.

_____. "John Brevator." 2016. Web. 24 Dec. 2016. <https://familysearch.org
/tree/person/LKMS-YYB/details>.

_____. "Joseph De Peister Blanchet." 2016. Web. 25 Dec. 2016. <https://family
search.org /ark:/61903/1:1:FDB6-L94>.

_____. "Neeltje Carroll." 2016. Web. 26 Dec. 2016. <https://familysearch
.org/search/record/results?count=20&query=%2Bsurname%3Acarroll~%20%2B
death_place%3A%22albany%20NY%22~%20%2Bdeath_year%3A1700-1800~>.

_____. "Thomas Broun." 2016. Web. 26 Dec. 2016. <https://familysearch
.org/search/record/results?count=20&query=%2Bgivenname%3Athomas~%20%
2Bsurname%3Abrown~%20%2Bbirth_place%3A%22albany%20NY%22~%20
%2Bbirth_year%3A1680-1700~>.

Felix Schlag. "Felix Schlag: Father of the Jefferson Nickel." 2017. Web. 27 Sept. 2017. <http://www.felixschlag.com/>.

Fessenden, Thomas. *The New England Farmer and Horticultural Journal, Volume VIII*. 1830. Web. 3 Aug. 2017. <https://books.google.com/books?id=IXNIAQ AAMAAJ&dq=%22fay%27s+hill%22+albany&source=gbs_navlinks_s>.

Find a Grave. "Abraham Cuyler Ten Eyck." 20 Aug. 2012. Web. 6 Oct. 2017. <https://www.findagrave.com/cgi-bin/fg.cgi?page=gr&GRid=95696106>.

_____. "Agnes Isabelle Dugan Rawson." 18 June 2015. Web. 19 Jan. 2017. <http://www.findagrave.com/cgi-bin/fg.cgi?page=gr&GRid=148001004>.

_____. "Ann Milner Holmes." 10 June 2012. Web. 13 Jan. 2017. <http://www.findagrave.com/cgi-bin/fg.cgi?page=gr&GRid=91669330>.

_____. "Benjamin Allen." 15 Jan. 2002. Web. 15 Nov. 2016. <http://www.findagrave.com/cgi-bin/fg.cgi?page=gr&GRid=6091395>.

_____. "Bertha Van Rensselaer." 18 Mar. 2012. Web. 3 Oct. 2017. <https://www.findagrave.com/cgi-bin/fg.cgi?page=gr&GRid=86930865>.

_____. "Billings P. Learned." 2 Feb. 2012. Web. 6 Aug. 2016. <https://www.findagrave.com/cgi-bin/fg.cgi?page=gr&GSln=Learned&GSiman=1&GSst=8&GRid =84352169&>.

_____. "Catherine Kirk McArdle." 20 Sept. 2013. Web. 14 Jan. 2017. <http://www.findagrave.com/cgi-bin/fg.cgi?page=gr&GRid=117382983>.

_____. "Catherine Ten Eyck." 21 Aug. 2012. Web. 6 Oct. 2017. <https://www.findagrave.com/cgi-bin/fg.cgi?page=gr&GRid=95736236>.

_____. "Charles D. Turner." 24 Nov. 2014. Web. 27 Oct. 2017. <https://www.findagrave.com/cgi-bin/fg.cgi?page=gr&GSln=turner&GSfn=charles+&GSbyrel =all&GSdyrel=all&GSst=36&GScntry=4&GSob=n&GSsr=41&GRid=139196463&df =all&>.

_____. "Charles Friebel." 1 Feb. 2011. Web. 5 Jan. 2017. <https://www.findagrave.com/cgi-bin/fg.cgi?page=gr&GSln=friebel&GSbyrel=all&GSdyrel=all &GSst=36&GScntry=4&GSob=n&GRid=65031914&df=all&>.

_____. "Clayton L. Besch Sr." 23 Apr. 2017. Web. 20 Oct. 2017. <https://www .find a grave.com/cgi-bin/fg.cgi?page=gr&GSln=besch&GSfn=clayton&GSbyrel=all&GSdy =1870&GSdyrel=after&GSst=36&GScntry=4&GSob=n&GRid=178674799&df=all&>.

_____. "Cuyler Ten Eyck." 20 Aug. 2012. Web. 6 Oct. 2012. <https://www.findagrave.com/cgi-bin/fg.cgi?page=gr&GRid=95691238>.

_____. "Edward Frisbie." 16 July 2006. Web. 28 July 2016. <http://www.findagrave.com/cgi-bin/fg.cgi?page=gr&GRid=14949565>.

_____. "Edwin Croswell." 16 Feb. 2014. Web. 30 Sept. 2015. <http://www.findagrave.com/cgi-bin/fg.cgi?page=gr&GRid=125229210>.

_____. "Eva Vinhagen Beekman." 4 Feb. 2012. Web. 25 Dec. 2016. <http://www.findagrave.com/cgi-bin/fg.cgi?page=gr&GRid=84487487>.

_____. "Everett E. Harding." 29 July 2016. Web. 13 Jan. 2017. <http://www.findagrave.com/cgi-bin/fg.cgi?page=gr&GSln=harding&GSiman=1&GScid=65729 &GRid=167563805&>.

_____. "Hannah Kelly Knowles." 29 Jan. 2012. Web. 25 Oct. 2017. <https://www .findagrave.com/cgi-bin/fg.cgi?page=gr&GRid=84186093>.

_____. "Harriet Maria Van Rensselaer Elmendorf." 24 Mar. 2012. Web. 1 Jan. 2017. <http://www.findagrave.com/cgi-bin/fg.cgi?page=gr&GRid=87317381>.

_____. "Henry Anthony Rawson." 18 June 2015. Web. 19 Jan. 2017. <http://www .findagrave.com/cgi-bin/fg.cgi?page=gr&GRid=148000752>.

_____. "Hiram Sanders Van Rensselaer." 17 Mar. 2012. Web. 3 Oct. 2017. <https:// www.findagrave.com/cgi-bin/fg.cgi?page=gr&GRid=86913958>.

_____. "Ichabod Lewis Judson." 6 Nov. 2013. Web. 26 Dec. 2016. <http://www .findagrave.com/cgi-bin/fg.cgi?page=gr&GRid=119886307>.

_____. "Isabel H. Fite Turner." 24 Nov. 2014. Web. 27 Oct. 2017. <https://www .findagrave.com/cgi-bin/fg.cgi?page=gr&GRid=139196573>.

_____. "Jacob Wesley Wilbur." 28 July 2014. Web. 27 Oct. 2017. <https://www .findagrave.com/cgi-bin/fg.cgi?page=gr&GRid=133457286>.

_____. "James Barclay Jermain." 7 Feb. 2006. Web. 28 Nov. 2016. <http://www .findagrave.com/cgi-bin/fg.cgi?page=gr&GRid=13263901>.

_____. "James Dwight Dana." 19 May 2013. Web. 22 May 2016. <http://www .findagrave.com/cgi-bin/fg.cgi?page=gr&GRid=110856256>.

_____. "James H. Carroll." 14 Nov. 2009. Web. 30 Dec. 2016. <http://www .findagrave.com/cgi-bin/fg.cgi?page=gr&GRid=44303519>.

_____. "James Warren." 13 Aug. 2004. Web. 16 Aug. 2017. <https://www.findagrave .com/cgi-bin/fg.cgi?page=gr&GRid=9311855>.

_____. "Jesse Buel." 17 Jan. 2015. Web. 30 Sept. 2015. <http://www.findagrave .com/cgi-bin/fg.cgi?page=gr&GRid=141455173>.

_____. "Johannes Beekman." 2 Feb. 2012. Web. 25 Dec. 2016. <http://www .findagrave.com/cgi-bin/fg.cgi?page=gr&GRid=84357408>.

_____. "John Adams Dix." 25 Oct. 2001. Web. 30 Sept. 2015. <http://www .findagrave.com/cgi-bin/fg.cgi?page=gr&GRid=5892251>.

_____. "John Freeman I." 24 Sept. 2010. Web. 26 Dec. 2016. <http://www .findagrave.com/cgi-bin/fg.cgi?page=gr&GRid=59148850>.

_____. "John Milner." 8 Sept. 2007. Web. 13 Jan. 2017. <http://www.findagrave .com/cgi-bin/fg.cgi?page=gr&GRid=21431287>.

_____. "José Julián Martí Pérez." 1 Jan. 2001. Web. 18 June 2016. <http://www .findagrave.com/cgi-bin/fg.cgi?page=gr&GRid=2494>.

_____. "Joseph Albert Cary." 3 Dec. 2015. Web. 19 Oct. 2017. <https://www .findagrave.com/cgi-bin/fg.cgi?page=gr&GSln=cary&GSfn=joseph&GSbyrel=all &GSdy=1910&GSdyrel=after&GSob=n&GRid=121198235&df=all&>.

_____. "Joseph Besch." 23 Apr. 2017. Web. 20 Oct. 2017. <https://www .findagrave.com/cgi-bin/fg.cgi?page=gr&GSln=besch&GSfn=joseph&GSbyrel=all &GSdy=1870&GSdyrel=after&GSst=36&GScntry=4&GSob=n&GRid=178674871&d f=all&>.

_____. "Joseph McArdle." 20 Sept. 2013. Web. 14 Jan. 2017. <http://www.findagrave.com/cgi-bin/fg.cgi?page=gr&GRid=117382693>.

_____. "Kate Dyer Ten Eyck." 20 Sept. 2011. Web. 20 Oct. 2017. <https://www
.findagrave.com/cgi-bin/fg.cgi?page=gr&GSln=ten+eyck&GSfn=kate&GSbyrel=all
&GSdyrel=in&GSst=36&GScntry=4&GSob=n&GRid=76852065&df=all&>.

_____. "Kate Halsdorf-Denny." 2 Nov. 2016. Web. 13 Jan. 2017. <http://www
.findagrave.com/cgi-bin/fg.cgi?page=gr&GRid=172123777>.

_____. "Margaret Matilda Haswell Ten Eyck." 20 Aug. 2012. Web. 6 Oct. 2017.
<https://www.findagrave.com/cgi-bin/fg.cgi?page=gr&GRid=95692798>.

_____. "Mercy Otis Warren." 7 Nov. 2004. Web. 16 Aug. 2017. <https://www
.findagrave.com/cgi-bin/fg.cgi?page=gr&GRid=9768714>.

_____. "Nicholas Herkimer." 17 Apr. 2000. Web. 29 July 2016. <http://www
.findagrave.com/cgi-bin/fg.cgi?page=gr&GRid=9165>.

_____. "Peter Edmund Elmendorf." 24 Mar. 2012. Web. 26 Dec. 2016. <http://
www.findagrave.com/cgi-bin/fg.cgi?page=gr&GRid=87317381>.

_____. "Peter Onderdonk." 29 Mar. 2009. Web. 26 Dec. 2016. <http://www
.findagrave.com/cgi-bin/fg.cgi?page=gr&GRid=35322238>.

_____. "PFC William J. Bucci." 13 Sept. 2015. Web. 17 Sept. 2017. <https://www
.findagrave.com/cgi-bin/fg.cgi?page=gsr&GSfn=william&GSmn=&GSln=bucci&
GSbyrel=all&GSby=&GSdyrel=all&GSdy=&GScntry=0&GSst=0&GSgrid=&df=all&
GSob=n>.

_____. "Reuben Howland Bingham." 30 Sept. 2013. Web. 13 Oct. 2017. <https://
www.findagrave.com/cgi-bin/fg.cgi?page=gr&GSln=Bingham&GSiman=1&GSsr
=41&GScid=63827&GRid=117860514&>.

_____. "Sarah Keller." 4 Dec. 2009. Web. 14 Jan. 2017. <http://www.findagrave.com
/cgi-bin/fg.cgi?page=gr&GSln=keller&GSiman=1&GScid=64729&GRid=45119618&>.

_____. "Theophilus Roessle." 8 Nov. 2012. Web. 16 Aug. 2017. <https://www
.findagrave.com/cgi-bin/fg.cgi?page=gr&GRid=100405496>.

_____. "Thomas Holmes." 23 Nov. 2006. Web. 26 Dec. 2016. <http://www
.findagrave.com/cgi-bin/fg.cgi?page=gr&GRid=16755907>.

_____. "Victor A. Sullivan." 10 Feb. 2016. Web. 27 Oct. 2017. <https://www
.findagrave.com/cgi-bin/fg.cgi?page=gr&GSln=sullivan&GSfn=victor&GSbyrel=all
&GSdyrel=all&GSst=36&GScntry=4&GSob=n&GRid=158014987&df=all&>.

_____. "William James Knowles, Sr." 29 Jan. 2012. Web. 25 Jan. 2017.
<https://www.findagrave.com/cgi-bin/fg.cgi?page=gr&GRid=84185802>.

Fitz-Enz, David. *The Final Invasion: Plattsburgh, the War of 1812's Most Decisive
Battle.* New York, NY: Cooper Square Press, 2001. Print.

Flags of the World. "New York (U.S.)." 20 Dec. 2014. Web. 27 Aug. 2015.
<http://www.crwflags.com/FOTW/flags/us-ny.html>.

Fletcher, William. *Leicestershire Pedigrees and Royal Descents.* 1887. Web. 16 Dec.
2016. < https://archive.org/details/leicestershirep00fletgoog>.

Foort Oranje Sive Albany. Map. Scale not given. 1705. Web. 18 Mar. 2017.
<http://www.albanyinstitute.org/details/items/albany-ten-eyck.html>.

Fox, William. *A History of the Lumber Industry in the State of New York.* Harrison,
NY: Harbor Hill, 1976. Print.

Frances, Edward, and John Frances. *Notes and Queries: A Medium of Intercommunication for Literary Men, General Readers, Etc.* 1907. Web. 23 Aug. 2016. <https://books.google.com/books?id=elI9AQAAMAAJ&printsec=frontcover &source=gbs_ge_summary_r&cad=0#v=onepage&q&f=false>.

Franciscan Sisters of Allegheny. "Dr. Lyle F. Renodin Foundation." 2016. Web. 16 Dec. 2016. <http://fsallegany.org/renodinfoundation.html>.

French, J. H. *Gazetteer of the State of New York.* 1860. Web. 12 Oct. 2017. <https://ia802702.us.archive.org/24/items/gazetteerofstate04fren/gazetteerofstate 04fren.pDf>.

Fries, Amanda. "Plan Awaits Zone Shift." *Times Union.* (2016, Aug. 25). Web. 29 Sept. 2016. <http://www.timesunion.com/business/article/Plan-awaits-zone-shift-9185629.php>.

Fulton, William. "Democratic Run Albany Machine Escapes Inquiry." *Chicago Tribune.* (1939, Sept. 10). Web. 11 Aug. 2016. <http://archives.chicagotribune.com /1939/09/10/page/25/article/Democratic-run-albany-machineescapes -inquiry>.

Gannett, Henry, and United States Geological Survey. *The Origin of Certain Place Names in the United States.* Washington, D.C.: Government Printing Office, 1905. Print.

Gardinier, Bob. "Scott Swartz Fills Post." *Times Union.* (2013, 20 Mar.). Web. 22 Jan. 2018. <http://www.timesunion.com/local/article/Scott-Swartz-fills-post-4366936 .php>.

Garretson-Persans, Christine. *The Smalbanac: An Opinionated Guide to New York's Capital District.* Albany, NY: SUNY Press, 2010. Print.

Genealogy. "The Halsdorf Family Tree: Information About William George Halsdorf." 2017. Web. 13 Jan. 2017. <http://www.genealogy.com/ftm/h/a/l/Nancy-Marie-Halsdorf/WEBSITE-0001/UHP-0002.html>.

Geneanet.org. "Cécile Randaxhe's Family Tree, Arthur de Pierpoint." 2016. Web. 29 Dec. 2016. <http://gw.geneanet.org/crandax?lang=en&p=arthur&n=de+Pierpont>.

Geni. "James Pemberton." 12 Nov. 2014. Web. 13 Dec. 2016. <https://www.geni.com /people/James-Pemberton/6000000000998381462>.

Georgetown University. "About." 2016. Web. 25 Nov. 2016. <https://www.george town.edu/>.

———. "President John J. DeGioia, Biography." 2016. Web. 25 Nov. 2016. <http://president.georgetown.edu/biography>.

Gerber, Morris. *Old Albany: Volume I.* 5th ed. Saratoga Springs, NY: Portofino Publishing, 1985. Print.

———. *Old Albany: Volume II.* Albany, NY: Morris Gerber Collection, 1965. Print.

———. *Old Albany: Volume III.* Albany, NY: Morris Gerber Collection, 1977. Print.

———. *Old Albany: Volume IV.* Revised ed. Saratoga Springs, NY: Portofino Publishing, 1987. Print.

———. *Old Albany: Volume V.* Rotterdam, NY: Price Chopper Books, 1989. Print.

Ginzberg, Lori. *Elizabeth Cady Stanton: An American Life.* New York, NY: MacMillan, 2010. Print.

Gov.UK. "Past Prime Ministers, Arthur Wellesley, 1st Duke of Wellington." 2016. Web. 12 Dec. 2016. <https://www.gov.uk/government/history/past-prime-ministers/arthur-wellesley-1st-duke-of-wellington>.

Gravina, Craig, and Alan McLeod. *Upper Hudson Valley Beer.* Mount Pleasant, SC: The History Press, 2014. Print.

Greenburg, Brian. *Worker and Community: Response to Industrialization in a Nineteenth-Century American City, Albany, New York, 1850–1884.* Albany, NY: SUNY Press, 1985. Print.

Grondahl, Paul. "A Distant War Echoes in Local Church." *Times Union.* (2013, Sept. 5). Web. 7 Aug. 2016. <http://www.timesunion.com/local/article/A-distant-war-echoes-in-local-church-4787809.php>.

_____. "Arbor Hill Named one of America's Ten Great Neighborhoods." *Times Union.* (2014, Oct. 1). Web. 12 July 2015. <http://www.timesunion.com/local/article/Arbor-Hill-named-one-of-America-s-10-great-5792627.php>.

_____. "Down Under: What's Beneath the Streets of the Capital Region? Lots of Tunnels and Caves that Remain Mostly Secret, Until Now." *Times Union.* (1993, Oct. 3). Web. 18 June 2016. <http://albarchive.merlinone.net/mweb/wmsql.wm.request?oneimage&imageid=5651966>.

_____. "How These Streets got Their Names." *Times Union.* (2014, Oct. 5). Web. 18 Sept. 2015. <http://www.timesunion.com/518life/article/How-these-streets-got-their-names-5803002.php>.

_____. "James Hall (1811–1898): Father of Modern Geology, Founder of the New York State Museum." *Times Union.* (2013, Dec. 5). Web. 2 Apr. 2017. <http://www.timesunion.com/local/article/James-Hall-1811-1898-Father-of-modern-geology-4981095.php>.

_____. *Mayor Corning: Albany Icon, Albany Enigma.* Albany, NY: Washington Park Press, 1997. Print.

_____. "Political Legacy Arrives on Stage." *Times Union.* (2009, Jan. 25). Web. 15 Sept. 2016. <http://albarchive.merlinone.net/mweb/wmsql.wm.request?oneimage&imageid=7419427>.

_____. "Uncovering the Backstory of Albany's 800 Street Names." *Times Union.* (2015, July 10). Web. 10 July 2015. <http://www.timesunion.com/tuplus-local/article/Uncovering-backstory-of-Albany-s-800-street-names-6378756.php>.

Guinn, James. *History of the State of California and Biographical Record of the Sacramento Valley, California.* 1906. Web. 28 July 2016. <https://books.google.com/books?id=ZqlCAQAAMAAJ&dq=%22edward+frisbie%22+albany+NY&source=gbs_navlinks_s>.

Guo, Jeff. "We Counted Literally Every Road in America. Here's What We Learned." *The Washington Post.* (2015, Mar. 6). Web. 21 Sept. 2016. <https://www.washingtonpost.com/blogs/govbeat/wp/2015/03/06/these-are-the-most-popular-street-names-in-every-state/>.

Hagan, Edward, and Mark Sullivan. *William C. Bouck: New York's Farmer Governor.* Berwyn Heights, MD: Heritage Books, 2007. Print.

Hail, Christopher. "Harvard/Radcliff Online Historical Reference Shelf: Cambridge Buildings and Architects." 2005. Web. 21 Feb. 2018. <http://hul.harvard .edu/lib/archives/refshelf/cba/index.html>.

Hanks, Patrick, and Flavia Hodges. *A Dictionary of Surnames.* New York, NY: Oxford University Press, 1991. Print.

Hardinger, Kristina. "Navigating the Legal Requirements of Paper Streets." 2017. Web. 15 Aug. 2017. <http://www.njslom.org/mag1107_article_pg38.html>.

Harlow, William. *Trees of the Eastern and Central United States and Canada.* New York, NY: Dover, 1957. Print.

Harnedy, Jim. *The Boothbay Harbor Region.* Charleston, SC: Arcadia Publishing, 1995. Print.

Harris, Howell. "The Naming of Stoves." Aug. 2012. Web. 17 Dec. 2016. <https:// community .dur.ac.uk/h.j.harris/stoves/stovenames.htm>.

Harvard University. "Harvard University." 2016. Web. 1 Dec. 2016. <http://www.harvard.edu/>.

_____. "Office of the President, Biography." 2016. Web. 1 Dec. 2016. <http://www .harvard.edu/president/biography>.

Headley, Russel (Ed.). *The History of Orange County, New York.* 1908. Web. 5 Dec. 2016. <https://archive.org/details/historyoforangec00head>.

Heller, Julius. "Weather Prophet Opposes Baring Tricks of Trade." *The Knickerbocker News.* (1949, Feb. 25). Web. 25 Oct. 2017. <http://fultonhistory.com/Fulton.html>.

Heller, Murray. *Call me Adirondack.* Saranac, NY: The Chauncy Press, 1989. Print.

Hendrick, James. *Map of the Albany Lumber District.* Map. Scale not given. 1857. Web. 18 Mar. 2017. <http://www.albanyinstitute.org/details/items/map-of-the-albany-lumber-district.html>.

Hess, Peter. *People of Albany and the Civil War, Albany Rural Cemetery.* Albany, NY: Albany Rural Cemetery, 2008. Print.

_____. *People of Albany: During Albany's Second 200 Years (1800s and 1900s), Albany Rural Cemetery.* Albany, NY: Albany Rural Cemetery, 2007. Print.

_____. *People of Albany: The First 200 Years.* Albany, NY: Albany Rural Cemetery, 2007. Print.

Hickman, Kennedy. "American Revolution: Major General Richard Montgomery." 22 Feb. 2016. Web. 19 June 2016. <http://militaryhistory.about.com/od/american revolutio1/p/rmontgomery.htm>.

_____. "War of 1812: Commodore Oliver Hazard Perry." 4 Mar. 2016. Web. 22 June 2016. <http://militaryhistory.about.com/od/naval/p/War-Of-1812-Commodore -Oliver-Hazard-Perry.htm>.

Hills, Frederick. *New York State Men: Biographical Studies and Character Portraits.* 1910. Web. 28 Dec. 2016. <https://books.google.com/books?id=QlxKAAAAYAAJ &pg=PA48&lpg=PA48&dq=%22lawyer+and+former+chancellor+of+the+Universi ty+of+the+State+of%22&source=bl&ots=ip7IMlpSjR&sig=evJ852MWQaMUczypi NeqJ1cR9MU&hl=en&sa=X&ved=0ahUKEwj0gliX3JnRAhWM8YMKHWrABpQQ 6AEIGjAA#v=onepage&q=%22lawyer%20and%20former%20chancellor%20of %20the%20University%20of%20the%20State%20of%22&f=false>.

Hislop, Codman. *Albany: Dutch, English, and American.* Albany, NY: The Argus Press, 1936. Print.

Historic Albany Foundation. "Historic Albany Foundation Oldest Building Inventory." 14 Jan. 2015. Web. 25 Dec. 2016. <http://static1.squarespace.com /static/5567269ce4b02c6f5096564d/t/560c08ece4b05e528fb34476/144362929247 0/OldestBuildingInventory_Date.pdf>.

Historic Cherry Hill. "History." 2016. Web. 23 Aug. 2016. <http://www .historiccherryhill.org/history/>.

Historic Pavement. "Street Pavements." 2017. Web. 13 Oct. 2017. <http://www .historicpavement.com/#/new-page-1/>.

History.com. "Chester A. Arthur." 2016. Web. 17 Nov. 2016. <http://www.history .com/topics/us-presidents/chester-a-arthur>.

_____. "General Nicholas Herkimer Falls at the Battle of Oriskany." 2016. Web. 29 July 2016. <http://www.history.com/this-day-in-history/general-nicholas-herkimer-falls-at-the-battle-of-oriskany>.

_____. "Grover Cleveland." 2015. Web. 9 Sept. 2015. <http://www.history .com/topics/us-presidents/grover-cleveland>.

_____. "WWI Hero Henry Johnson Finally Receives Medal of Honor." 2015. Web. 14 Sept. 2015. <http://www.history.com/news/wwi-hero-henry-johnson-finally-receives-medal-of-honor>.

Hoffer, Eric. *The True Believer: Thoughts on the Nature of Mass Movements.* New York, NY: Perennial, 2010. Print.

Hoffman, L. G. *Hoffman's Albany Directory and City Register for the Years 1837–1838.* Albany, NY: L.G. Hoffman, 1838. Print.

_____. *Hoffman's Albany Directory and City Register for the Years 1843–1844.* Albany, NY: L.G. Hoffman, 1844. Print.

_____. *Hoffman's Albany Directory and City Register for the Years 1849–1850.* Albany, NY: L.G. Hoffman, 1850. Print.

Hopkins, G. M. *City Atlas of Albany, New York.* Philadelphia, PA: G.M. Hopkins, 1876. Print.

Hough, Franklin. *Historical Sketch of Union College: Founded at Schenectady, New York, February 25, 1795.* 1876. Web. 15 Nov. 2016. <https://archive.org/stream /historicalsketc00educgoog/historicalsketc00educgoog_djvu.txt>.

Howard, William. "Slingerlands' Old Master." *The Spotlight.* (1984, Feb. 1). Web. 27 Dec. 2016. <http://www.bethlehempubliclibrary.org/localhistory/spotlight/years /1984/1984-02-01.pdf>.

Howell, George, and Jonathan Tenney. *Bicentennial History of Albany.* 1886. Web. 21 Aug. 2016. <https://archive.org/stream/cu31924080795127#page/n12/mode /1up>.

Hoxsie. "18th Century Starbucks?" 5 Mar. 2012. Web. 13 Jan. 2017. <http://hoxsie.org/2012/03/05/18th_century_starbucks/>.

_____. "Keeler's Hotel." 2 May 2012. Web. 5 Jan. 2016. <http://hoxsie.org /2012/05/02/keelers_hotel/>.

Humphreys, Mary Gay. *Catherine Schuyler.* 1897. Web. 9 Sept. 2016. <https:// archive.org/stream/catherineschuyl01humpgoog#page/n15/mode/1up>.

Hymnary.org. "William Croswell Doane." 2016. Web. 28 July 2016. <http://www.hymnary.org/person/Doane_WC>.

Ingraham, Christopher. "Why Americans Overwhelmingly Prefer Fake Maple Syrup." *The Washington Post*. (2015, Mar. 27). Web. 8 July 2015. <http://www.washington post.com/blogs/wonkblog/wp/2015/03/27/why-americans-overwhelmingly-prefer -fake-maple-syrup/>.

Isenberg, Nancy. *Sex and Citizenship in Antebellum America*. Chapel Hill, NC: University of North Carolina Press, 2000. Print.

James T. White and Company. *The National Cyclopaedia of American Biography*. 1892. Web. 21 Aug. 2016. <https://archive.org/details/nationalcyclopa01 unkngoog>.

_____. *The National Cyclopaedia of American Biography*. 1910. Web. 6 Jan. 2017. <https://archive.org/stream/nationalcyclopae00newy/nationalcyclopae00newy_d jvu.txt>.

Jenkins, Jerry. *The Adirondack Atlas: A Geographic Portrait of the Adirondack Park*. Syracuse, NY: Syracuse University Press, 2004. Print.

J.H. Beers and Company. *Genealogical and Biographical Record of New London County, Connecticut: Containing Biographical Sketches of Prominent and Representative Citizens and Genealogical Records of Many of the Early Settled Families*. 1905. Web. 6 Aug. 2016. <https://archive.org/details/genealogical biog1905chic>.

Johnson, Carl. "Lincoln Park: From Beer, Bricks, and Beavers." 13 Apr. 2010. Web. 14 Mar. 2017. <http://alloveralbany.com/archive/2010/04/13/lincoln-park---- from-beer-bricks-and-beavers#comments>.

_____. "The Moses Fountain in Washington Park." 18 Apr. 2011. Web. 14 Mar. 2017. <http://alloveralbany.com/archive/2011/04/18/the-moses-fountain-in- washington-park>.

Johnson, Crisfield. *History of Washington County, New York*. 1878. Web. 27 Jan. 2017. <https://ia600306.us.archive.org/33/items/historyofwashing00john/history ofwashing00john.pdf>.

Jones, Carleton. *Streetwise Baltimore: The Stories Behind Baltimore Street Names*. Chicago, IL: Bonus Books, 1990. Print.

Julyan, Mary, and Robert Julyan. *Place Names of the White Mountains*. Revised ed. Hanover, NH: University Press of New England, 1993. Print.

Katz, Bernard, and Corwin Vencill. *Biographical Dictionary of the United States Secretaries of The Treasury, 1789–1995*. 1996. Web. 11 Aug. 2016. <https://books.google.com/books?id=aMiA05P92h8C&pg=PA129&lpg=PA129&dq =daniel+manning+secretary+treasury&source=bl&ots=xF0KO436N_&sig=DItyzW vrzI7p_XOHZsdB4V91UyM&hl=en&sa=X&ved=0ahUKEwiR3oXPu7rOAhUBCho KHUpbDR0Q6AEIajAM#v=onepage&q=manning&f=false>.

Kaye, Judith. "Commentaries on Chancellor Kent." *Chicago Kent Law Review*. (1998). Web. 4 Jan. 2017. <https://www.nycourts.gov/history/legal-history-new- york/luminaries-supreme-court/documents/kaye-on-kent.pdf>.

Kenney, Michael. "Geographer Explores Place Names that Offend." *The Boston Globe*. (2006, May 30). Web. 15 Jan. 2015. <http://www.boston.com/news/globe/living/articles/2006/05/30/geographer_explores_place_names_that_offend/>.

Kent, James. "Egbert Benson, Associate Justice of the New York Supreme Court, 1794–1801." 1839. Web. 16 Aug. 2017. <https://www.nycourts.gov/history/legal-history-new-york/luminaries-supreme-court/documents/kent-bio-benson.pdf>.

Kirsh, George. *Golf in America*. Champaign, IL: University of Illinois Press, 2008. Print.

Kneeland, Stillman Foster. *Seven Centuries in the Kneeland Family*. 1897. Web. 14 Feb. 2018. <https://ia800206.us.archive.org/29/items/sevencenturiesin1897knee/sevencenturiesin1897knee.pdf>.

Kudish, Michael. *Adirondack Upland Flora: An Ecological Perspective*. Saranac, NY: The Chauncy Press, 1992. Print.

LaSalle. "St. John Baptist de La Salle." 2016. Web. 7 Aug. 2016. <http://www.lasalle.org/en/who-are-we/st-john-baptist-de-la-salle/>.

Leath, Susan. *Images of America: Bethlehem*. Charleston, SC: Arcadia Publishing, 2011. Print.

Lederman, Josh, and Mark Thiessen. "White House Renames Mount McKinley as Denali on Eve of Trip." 30 Aug. 2015. Web. 3 Sept. 2015. <http://abcnews.go.com/Politics/wireStory/white-house-mount-mckinley-renamed-denali-33419847>.

Lee, Mike. *Our Lost Constitution: The Willful Subversion of America's Founding Document*. New York, NY: Sentinel, 2016. Print.

———. *Written Out of History: The Forgotten Founders Who Fought Big Government*. New York, NY: Sentinel, 2017. Print.

Lemak, Jennifer. *Southern Life, Northern City: The History of Albany's Rapp Road Community*. Albany, NY: SUNY Press, 2015. Print.

Lemire, Paula. "A Colonel and a Faithful Slave." 26 Jan. 2015. Web. 7 Apr. 2017. <http://albanyruralcemetery.blogspot.com/2015/01/a-colonel-and-faithful-slave.html>.

———. "A Relic of a Road." 1 Aug. 2010. Web. 22 Aug. 2016. <http://albanynyhistory.blogspot.com/2010/08/relic-of-road.html>.

———. "Albany Rural Cemetery, Beyond the Graves. Charles and Blandina Dudley." 2 Apr. 2014. Web. 3 June 2016. <http://albanyruralcemetery.blogspot.com/2014/04/charles-and-blandina-dudley.html>.

———. "Albany Rural Cemetery, Beyond the Graves. Teunis Van Vechten." 4 Oct. 2012. Web. 28 Jan. 2017. <http://albanyruralcemetery.blogspot.com/2012/10/teunis-van-vechten.html>.

———. "Albany Rural Cemetery, Beyond the Graves. Walter Van Guysling." 14 Apr. 2014. Web. 26 Jan. 2017. <http://albanyruralcemetery.blogspot.com/2014/04/walter-van-guysling.html>.

Library of Congress. "About the Albany Argus." 2015. Web. 30 Sept. 2015. <http://chroniclingamerica.loc.gov/lccn/sn83030908/>.

_____. "The Federalist Papers." 2017. Web. 28 Sept. 2017. <https://www
.loc.gov/rr/program/bib/ourdocs/federalist.html>.

Lisi, Michael. "Neighborhoods: Quadrini Estates, Albany." *Times Union.* (2012, Nov.
29). Web. 12 July 2015. <http://www.timesunion.com/living/article/Neighborhoods
-Quadrini-Estates-Albany-4078135.php>.

Little, Elbert. *National Audubon Society Field Guide to North American Trees:
Eastern Region.* New York, NY: Knopf, 1980. Print.

Loewen, James. *Lies my Teacher Told Me.* New York, NY: Touchstone, 1995. Print.

Lossing, Benson. *The Hudson: From the Wilderness to the Sea.* Somersworth, NH:
New Hampshire Publishing, 1972. Print.

Louden, M. J. (Ed.). *Catholic Albany: An Illustrated History of the Catholic Churches
and the Catholic Religious, Benevolent, and Educational Institutions of the City
of Albany.* 1891. Web. 5 Dec. 2016. <https://archive.org/stream/cu31924029
381906/cu31924029381906_djvu.txt>.

Major-smolinski.com. "John J. O'Connell, Jr." 2016. Web. 12 Aug. 2016.
<http://www.major-smolinski.com/KIDNAP/OCONNELL.html>.

Map of Boundaries of Lots on North Side of Lion Street. Map. Scale not given. 1802.
Print.

Map of the Lower Church Pasture. Map. Scale not given. 1803. Print.

Masonic Fair Association. *Masonic Fair Souvenir 1900, Albany, N.Y.* Albany, NY:
Weed-Parson Printing, 1900. Print.

Massachusetts Historical Society. *Proceedings of the Massachusetts Historical
Society, Volume 12.* 1873. Web. Aug. 15. 2017. <https://books.google.com /books
?id=B9oWAAAAIAAJ&printsec=frontcover&source=gbs_ge_summary_r&cad=0#v
=onepage&q&f=false>.

McClintock, John. "Albany Artist, Academy Friend: Profile of Asa Weston
Twitchell." 2012. Web. 27 Dec. 2016. <http://www.albanyhistory.org/albany
history/resources/twitchell_by_mcclintock.pdf>.

McCullough, David. *1776.* New York, NY: Simon and Schuster, 2006. Print.

_____. *1776: The Illustrated Edition.* New York, NY: Simon and Schuster, 2007.
Print.

_____. *John Adams.* New York, NY: Simon and Schuster, 2001. Print.

_____. *Mornings on Horseback.* New York, NY: Simon and Schuster, 1981.
Print.

_____. *The American Spirit.* New York, NY: Simon and Schuster, 2017. Print.

_____. *The Path Between the Seas: The Creation of the Panama Canal, 1870–1914.*
New York, NY: Simon and Schuster, 1977. Print.

McDonald, Colin. "A Rock in a Hard Place Rolls on to a New Home." *Times Union.*
(2006, Mar. 8). Web. 5 Jan. 2017. <http://albarchive.merlinone.net/mweb/wmsql
.wm.request?oneimage&imageid=6387675>.

McEneny, John. *Albany: Capital City on the Hudson.* 2nd ed. Sun Valley, CA:
American Historical Press, 2006. Print.

McGuire, Mark. "Dirt, Not Ivy, Covers This Campus." *Times Union*. (1997, Sept. 28). Web. 27 Aug. 2015. <http://albarchive.merlinone.net/mweb/wmsql.wm.request ?oneimage&imageid=5831612>.

McNamara, John. *History in Asphalt: The Origin of Bronx Street and Place Names*. Bronx, NY: The Bronx County Historical Society, 1991. Print.

McRae, Mary Ann. "A Fishy Name Will Stay the Same." 6 Sept. 1996. Web. 22 Aug. 2016. <http://www.cnn.com/US/9609/06/fishy.name/>.

Merchant, George. *Map of the City of Albany*. Map. Scale not given. 1843. Web. 16 Mar. 2017. <https://digitalcollections.nypl.org/items/510d47da-f05e-a3d9-e040-e00a18064a99#/?uuid=510d47da-f05e-a3d9-e040-e00a18064a99>.

Merriam-Webster. *Merriam-Webster's Collegiate Dictionary*. 11th ed. Springfield, MA: Merriam-Webster, 2003. Print.

Merwick, Donna. *Possessing Albany, 1630–1710: The Dutch and English Experience*. New York, NY: Cambridge University Press, 1990. Print.

Military Order of the Loyal Legion of the United States. "Commanders-in-Chief Biographies." 2016. Web. 15 Nov. 2016. <http://suvcw.org/mollus/pcinc /bgherardi.htm>.

Miller, John. *Albany 1695*. Map. Scale not given. 1695. Web. 16 Mar. 2017. <http: //www.albanyinstitute.org/details/items/john-miller-plan-of-albany-in-1695.html>.

Mohn, Tanya. "Martin Luther King, Jr.: The German Connection and How He Got His Name." 12 Jan. 2012. Web. 27 June 2017. <https://www.forbes.com/sites/tanya mohn/2012/01/12/martin-luther-king-jr-the-german-connection-and-how-he-got-his-name/#3b36e2be3540>.

Montessori Magnet School. "About MMS." 2016. Web. 7 Aug. 2016. <http://www .montessorimagnet.com/about-mms>.

Monticello. "Spurious Quotations." 2016. Web. 3 Aug. 2016. <https://www .monticello.org/site/jefferson>.

_____. "Thomas Jefferson, a Brief Biography." 2016. Web. 3 Aug. 2016. <https:// www.monticello.org/site/jefferson/thomas-jefferson-brief-biography>.

_____. "Timeline." 2016. Web. 3 Aug. 2016. <https://www.monticello.org /site/jefferson/timeline-jeffersons-life>.

Mooney, Charles. "Charles Mooney." *The Knickerbocker News*. (1963, Feb. 16). Web. 19 Oct. 2017. <http://fultonhistory.com/Fulton.html>.

_____. "Charles Mooney." *The Knickerbocker News*. (1963, Nov.). Web. 27 Oct. 2017. <http://fultonhistory.com/Fulton.html>.

_____. "For Relaxed Reading." Print.

_____. "Westward Ho, to Pine Hills." Print.

Moran, Donald. "Brigadier General Marinus Willett, 'Bravest Son of Liberty.'" 2016. Web. 22 Sept. 2016. <http://www.revolutionarywararchives.org/Willette .html>.

_____. "Major General Richard Montgomery." June 2006. Web. 19 June 2016. <http://www.revolutionarywararchives.org/montgomery.html>.

Morrell, Virginia. "The Zuni Way." Apr. 2007. Web. 23 June 2016. <http://
www.smithsonianmag.com/people-places/the-zuni-way-150866547/?no-ist=>.

Moscow, Henry. *The Street Book: An Encyclopedia of Manhattan's Street Names
and Their Origins.* New York, NY: Fordham University Press, 1990. Print.

Munsell, Joel. *Collections of the History of Albany.* 1870. Web. 26 Dec. 2016.
<http://books.googleusercontent.com/books/content?req=AKW5QadaWHStddh3
B4fM831YnlSSu93aIODozKziD8aEXbvWl7T2PIfX9nMWK4eZoGOCtc0m2LRFitf
AKyZMOIaXEjVxLCuwKH9l8Hd0PhONg3vi0RlSZcxOCfIYPUwL1mknBKhlUyV
9qgi-DR7A2c6fDC9WYKv64P0WF8AFJor3TwFHUWArPgEefRuSyHFeb25Fetc-si
X9YLqr9gM0Axo_2NVR3Rr5ZPK-gPQCWZX0POXBJ9T4ZkHcVfw_MMdZ3Yw
tlIVg1M-rYBuKeVTLWaXUzltbZCASOQ>.

———. *Men and Things in Albany Two Centuries Ago.* 1884. Web. 27 Jan. 2017.
<https://ia801308.us.archive.org/22/items/menthingsinalban00muns_0/menthin
gsinalban00muns_0.pdf>.

———. *The Annals of Albany.* 1859. Web. 27 Jan. 2017. <https://ia801405
.us.archive.org/12/items/annalsofalbany01muns/annalsofalbany01muns.Pdf>.

Museum of Science and Industry, Chicago. "999 Steam Locomotive." 2016. Web. 23
Aug. 2016. <http://www.msichicago.org/explore/whats-here/exhibits/transportation
-gallery/the-exhibit/999-steam-locomotive/>.

National Canal Museum. "Erie Canal." 2010. Web. 4 Apr. 2013. <http://www
.canals.org/researchers/Canal_Profiles/United_States/Northeast/ErieCanal>.

National Governors Association. "Governor William King." 2015. Web. 14 Mar. 2017.
<https://www.nga.org/cms/home/governors/past-governors-bios/page_maine/col2
-content/main-content-list/title_king_william.html>.

National Park Service. "Erie Canal National Heritage Corridor, New York." Print.

———. "Fort Stanwix." 2015. Web. 24 Sept. 2015. <http://www.nps.gov/fost
/learn/historyculture/index.htm>.

———. "National Register of Historic Places Registration Form." 1991. Web. 15
Aug. 2017. <https://npgallery.nps.gov/pdfhost/docs/NHLS/Text/67000008.pdf>.

———. "Roger Williams: Founding Providence." 2017. Web. 8 Oct. 2017.
<https://www.nps.gov/rowi/learn/historyculture/foundingprovidence.htm>.

———. "The Oneida Nation in the Revolutionary War." 2016. Web. 12 July 2016.
<https://www.nps.gov/fost/learn/historyculture/the-oneida-nation-in-the-
american-revolution.htm>.

Naval History and Heritage Command. "David Glasgow Farragut." 9 Dec. 2015. Web.
6 Sept. 2017. <https://www.history.navy.mil/research/library/research-guides/z-
files/zb-files/zb-files-f/farragut-davidg.html>.

N'DahAhKi. "Welcome to Mohican Country." 30 Aug. 2005. Web. 19 June 2016.
<http://endahkee.nativeweb.org/mohicans.html>.

Nearing, Brian. "Call of the Cougar Long Gone from the East." *Times Union.* (2011,
Mar. 5). Web. 22 Nov. 2016. <http://www.timesunion.com/default/article/Call-
of-the-cougar-long-gone-from-the-East-1043286.php>.

_____. "Matthew Bender Ends Chapter in Area." *Times Union*. (2013, Jan. 15). Web. 16 Aug. 2017. <http://www.timesunion.com/business/article/Matthew-Bender-ends-chapter-in-area-4196467.php>.

Network of Sacred Heart Schools. "Janet Erskine Stuart." 2012. Web. 28 July 2016. <http://sofie.org/resources/founding-mothers/janet-erskine-stuart>.

New Advent. "Abbey of Melrose." 2012. Web. 11 Jan. 2017. <http://www.newadvent .org/cathen/10170a.htm>.

_____. "Thomas Dongan." 2012. Web. 30 Sept. 2015. <http://www.newadvent .org/cathen/05130a.htm>.

New Jersey Public Library Commission. "The Origin of New Jersey Place Names." 1945. Web. 28 Dec. 2016. <http://mapmaker.rutgers.edu/356/nj_place_names _origin.pdf>.

New Scotland Historical Association. *Images of America: New Scotland Township*. Charleston, SC: Arcadia Publishing, 2000. Print.

New York State. "Hall of Governors, Benjamin B. Odell, Jr." 2016. Web. 5 Dec. 2016. <https://hallofgovernors.ny.gov/BenjaminOdell>.

_____. "Hall of Governors, John A. King." 2016. Web. 26 July 2016. <http://www .hallofgovernors.ny.gov/JohnKing>.

New York State Archives. *Map of Albany County. Map #192*. Map. Scale not given. Web. 3 Jan. 2017. <http://digitalcollections.archives.nysed.gov/index.php/Detail /Object/Show/object_id/37468>.

_____. *Map of Lots Within the Bounds of the Corporation of the City of Albany. Map #338*. Map. Scale not given. Web. 3 Jan. 2017. <http://digitalcollections .archives.nysed.gov/index.php/Detail/Object/Show/object_id/37157>.

New York State Department of Environmental Conservation. "Management Plan for Mute Swans in New York." Mar. 2015. Web. 28 Aug. 2015. <http://www.dec .ny.gov/docs/wildlife_pdf/muteswanmgmtpln2015.pdf>.

_____. "Mute Swan." Mar. 2015. Web. 28 Aug. 2015. <http://www.dec.ny.gov /animals/7076.html>.

_____. "New York State Big Tree Register." 12 June 2017. Web. 17 June 2017. <http://www.dec.ny.gov/docs/lands_forests_pdf/champcom.pdf>.

_____. "White-tailed Deer." 2010. Web. 24 Feb. 2017. <http://www.dec .ny.gov/animals/6965.html>.

New York State Library. "James Hilton Manning Papers, 1885–1925." 7 July 2007. Web. 19 June 2016. <http://www.nysl.nysed.gov/msscfa/sc22904.htm>.

New York State Museum. "About the Museum." 2016. Web. June 20 2016. <http://www.nysm.nysed.gov/about>.

_____. "State Museum Experts Reconstructing Face on 250-year-old Skull Discovered in Downtown Albany." 23 Mar. 1999. Web. 19 Aug. 2015. <http://www.nysm.nysed.gov/press/archive/preskull.cfm>.

New York State Senate. "State Seal." 2015. Web. 27 Aug. 2015. <http://www .nysenate.gov/state-seal>.

Newyorkroots.org. "Genealogical & Family History of Northern NY, Pages 795–802." 2015. Web. 17 Jan. 2015. <http://www.newyorkroots.org/bookarchive /northernnewyork/795-802.html>.

Niche. "The 25 Oldest Colleges in America." 2014. Web. 25 Aug. 2015. <https://ink .niche.com/25-oldest-colleges-america/>.

NNDB. "John Winthrop the Younger." 2014. Web. 16 Nov. 2016. <http://www.nndb .com/people/576/000050426/>.

Norder, Akum. "Ridgefield: A Park with a Storied Past." *Times Union*. (2013, Mar. 11). Web. 17 Aug. 2016. <http://blog.timesunion.com/norder/a-park-with-a-storied-past/1766/>.

Oake, Abraham. *Street Surveys of City of Albany*. Map. Scale not given. 1789 to 1817. Print.

O'Brien, Tim. "Albany Historic Rapp Road Neighborhood has Roots in Southern Migration." *Times Union*. (2015, Aug. 15). Web. 29 Sept. 2016. <http://www .timesunion.com/local/article/Albany-s-historic-Rapp-Road-neighborhood-has-6446807.php>.

Office of Art and Archives. "Biographical Directory of the United States Congress, Benjamin Baker Odell, Jr." 2016. Web. 5 Dec. 2016 <http://bioguide.congress .gov/scripts/biodisplay.pl?index=O000036>.

_____. "Biographical Directory of the United States Congress, Cyrus King." 2016. Web. 22 Dec. 2016. <http://bioguide.congress.gov/scripts/biodisplay.pl?index =K000197>.

_____. "Biographical Directory of the United States Congress, DeWitt Clinton." 2016. Web. 10 Sept. 2016. <http://bioguide.congress.gov/scripts/biodisplay .pl?index=c000525>.

_____. "Biographical Directory of the United States Congress, Matthew Thornton." 2017. Web. 13 Jan. 2017. <http://bioguide.congress.gov/scripts /biodisplay.pl?index=T000242>.

_____. "Biographical Directory of the United States Congress, Morris Smith Miller." 2015. Web. 13 Jan. 2017. <http://bioguide.congress.gov/scripts /biodisplay.pl?index=M000747>.

Office of the City Engineer. *Annual Report of the City Engineer, for Albany, N.Y. for the Year 1891*. 1891. Web. 11 Oct. 2017. <https://books.googleusercontent.com /books/content?req=AKW5QafzL14I65wgelUsxQAEFqkiI_scmMth_aCQLmtzmO Gq22AWC2pg6vbAH79fBYpaEqXWEveazStnhY6qG9NFO_M7RdE5nJowymS-ZM _OanIdbTRHmeW139P45efCDBf6xt3PEHzVqwXFOBaQJH4pEUPd8O4P5SkauW YaSAHeKrRI49nP66LfnhQZ7ycykIot6Wc_nTapFXv1_keeClJdkJQdsOfvSpl3w_wJ i2tSiJIreRZsOtHPqroaU2cvntWddZoEPrn6F84SbQorbX7qShzGiQW_s6pC9mF1L LN15wx5_nnSs7g>.

Oliver Hazard Perry Rhode Island. "Commodore Oliver Hazard Perry." 2016. Web. 22 June 2016. <http://www.ohpri.org/history-details/commodore-oliver-hazard-perry>.

Oneida Indian Nation. "History." 2013. Web. 12 July 2016. <http://www.oneida indiannation.com/history>.

Overman, William. *Ohio Town Names*. 1958. Web. 12 Feb. 2018. <https://babel.hathi trust.org/cgi/pt?id=mdp.39015015361465;view=1up;seq=1>.

Oxford University. "2016 Tuition Fees." 2016. Web. 18 Aug. 2016. <https://www.ox.ac.uk/admissions/undergraduate/fees-and-funding/tuition-fees ?wssl=1>.

———. "Famous Oxonians." 2016. Web. 18 Aug. 2016. <http://www.ox.ac.uk /about/oxford-people/famous-oxonians>.

———. "Introduction and History." 2016. Web. 18 Aug. 2016. <https://www .ox.ac.uk/about/organisation/history?wssl=1>.

Papp, John. *Albany's Historic Street: A Collection of Some of the Historic Facts and Interesting Traditions Relating to State Street and its Neighborhood*. Schenectady, NY: John P. Papp Historical Publications, 1976. Print.

Parker, Amasa. *Landmarks of Albany County, New York*. 1897. Web. 17 Jan. 2015. <https://ia600503.us.archive.org/10/items/landmarksofalban00parker/landmarks ofalban00parker.pdf>.

Parkman, Francis. *LaSalle and the Discovery of the Great West*. New York, NY: The Modern Library, 1999. Print.

———. *Montcalm and Wolf, Volume One*. 1922. Web. 15 Dec. 2016. <https://books .google.com/books?id=cWNIAAAAYAAJ&dq=Montcalm+and+Wolfe+Volume+1 &source=gbs_navlinks_s>.

Pasko, Jessica. "Arbor Hill's Tivoli Nature Preserve." 4 Aug. 2008. Web. 16 Aug. 2016. <http://alloveralbany.com/archive/2008/08/04/arbor-hills-tivoli-nature-preserve>.

Pearson, Jonathan. *Contributions for the Genealogies of the First Settlers of the Ancient County of Albany, from 1630 to 1800*. Albany, NY: Joel Munsell, 1872. Print.

Peterson, Jesse Lee. *The Antidote: Healing America from the Poison of Hate, Blame, and Victimhood*. Washington, D.C.: WND Books, 2015. Print.

Picotte Companies. "About Picotte, Executive Team." 2016. Web. 3 Aug. 2016. <http://www.picotte.com/team.php>.

Plotnik, Art. "Sentiment Dictates Naming of Most Streets." *Times Union*. (1962, Dec. 30). Web. 24 Oct. 2017. <http://fultonhistory.com/Fulton.html>.

Politicalgraveyard.com. "Barnes." 20 Dec. 2015. Web. 11 Aug. 2016. <http://politicalgraveyard.com/bio/barnes.html>.

Pollak, Michael. "The Views From the Top." *The New York Times*. (2006, Aug. 6). Web. 15 Dec. 2016. <http://www.nytimes.com/2006/08/06/nyregion/thecity /06fyi.html>.

———. "Who was the Real Ichabod Crane?" *Times Union*. (2015, Oct. 16). Web. 26 Nov. 2016. <http://www.nytimes.com/2015/10/18/nyregion/who-was-the-real-ichabod-crane.html?_r=0>.

PresidentUSA.net. "James Madison Gravesite." 2014. Web. 18 Aug. 2015. <http://www.presidentsusa.net/madisongravesite.html>.

Princeton University. "About Princeton: Overview" 2015. Web. 25 Aug. 2015. <http://www.princeton.edu/main/about/>.

_____. "Facts and Figures." 2015. Web. 25 Aug. 2015. <http://www.princeton.edu/main/about/facts/>.

Public Broadcasting Service. "Alexander Hamilton." 2016. Web. 29 July 2016. <http://www.pbs.org/wgbh/amex/duel/peopleevents/pande06.html>.

_____. "Robert Fulton." 2016. Web. 25 July 2016. <https://www.pbs.org/wgbh/theymadeamerica/whomade/fulton_hi.html>.

Quimby, Myron. *Scratch Ankle, U.S.A.: American Place Names and Their Derivation*. Cranbury, NJ: A.S. Barnes and Company, 1969. Print.

Railway and Locomotive Engineering, Volume 23, No. 1. 1910. Web. 8 Nov. 2017. <https://archive.org/details/railwaylocomotiv23newy>.

Rathbun, Frank. "The Rathbun-Rathbone-Rathburn Family Historian." July 1988. Web. 21 Aug. 2016. <http://www.michaelrathbun.org/08-1988/08-003.pdf>.

Raysplace.com. "Gazetteer of the State of New York, Albany County, NY." 2012. Web. 19 Aug. 2016. <http://history.rays-place.com/ny/albany-cty-ny.htm>.

Rensselaer Polytechnic Institute. "From the Archives: Women Faculty at Rensselaer." 6 Mar. 2014. Web. 29 Dec. 2016. <http://www.insiderensselaer.com/women-faculty-at-rensselaer/>.

Reynolds, Cuyler. *Albany Chronicles: A History of the City Arranged Chronologically*. 1906. Web. 21 Mar. 2017. <https://ia601407.us.archive.org/9/items/albanychronicles00reyn/albanychronicles00reyn.pdf>.

_____. *Genealogical and Family History of Southern New York and the Hudson River Valley: A Record of the Achievements of Her People in the Making of a Commonwealth and the Building of a Nation, Volume 3*. 1914. Web. 9 Sept. 2016. <https://archive.org/details/genealogicalfami01reyn>.

_____. *Hudson-Mohawk Genealogical and Family Memoirs*. 1911. Web. 28 Oct. 2017. <https://ia902607.us.archive.org/16/items/hudsonmohawkgene00reyn/hudsonmohawkgene00reyn.pdf>.

Richardson, Richard, and Sara Richardson. "Good Time Stove Company, Other." 2016. Web. 17 Dec. 2016. <http://antiquestoves.net/dir/other-stove-services/100-research/founders-foundries/65-rathbone-and-sard-acorn-stoves>.

Rinella, Steven. *Meat Eater: Adventures From the Life of an American Hunter*. New York, NY: Spiegel and Grau, 2012. Print.

Rittner, Don. "Another Removal of Albany History Hits the Road." *Times Union*. (2013, Dec. 6). Web. 22 Aug. 2016. <http://blog.timesunion.com/rittner/another-removal-of-albany-history-hits-the-road/3779/>.

_____. *Images of America: Albany Revisited*. Charleston, SC: Arcadia Publishing, 2008. Print.

_____. *Then and Now: Albany*. Charleston, SC: Arcadia Publishing, 2002. Print.

Robert Morris University. "Who was Robert Morris?" 2016. Web. 12 Aug. 2016. <https://www.rmu.edu/about-rmu/rmu-history-heritage/WhowasRobertMorris>.

Robertemmet.org. "Remembering Robert Emmet, 1778–1803." 2016. Web. 25 July 2016. <http://www.robertemmet.org/>.

_____. "The Speech from the Dock." 2016. Web. 25 July 2016. <http://www
.robertemmet.org/speech.htm>.

Robinson, Frank. *Machine Politics: A Study of Albany's O'Connells.* Piscataway, NJ:
Transaction Publications, 1977. Print.

Rogerson, Don. *Manhattan Street Names Past and Present: A Guide to Their Origins.*
New York, NY: Griffin Rose Press, 2013. Print.

Sacred Heart of Jesus. "Parish History." 2016. Web. 5 Dec. 2016. <http://www
.rcda.org/churches/sacredheartofjesus/parishhistory.html>.

Saint Margaret's Center. "St. Margaret's Center." 2016. Web. 16 Dec. 2016.
<http://www.stmargaretscenter.org/htmlweb/homepage.html>.

Saint Mary's Church. "Church History." 2015. Web. 28 June 2015. <http://www.hist-
stmarys.org/history.html>.

Salzmann, Kenneth. *Albany Scrapbook, Volume I.* Woodstock, NY: Gelles-Cole
Literary Enterprises. Print.

Sampson, Davenport, and Company. *The Albany Directory for the Year 1878.* 1878.
Web. 30 Dec. 2016. <https://books.google.com/books?id=tR1EAQAAMAAJ
&printsec=frontcover&source=gbs_ge_summary_r&cad=0#v=onepage&q=%22jam
es%20h.%20carroll%22&f=false>.

Sampson, Murdock, and Company. *Albany General Directory 1933.* Albany, NY:
Sampson, Murdock, and Company, 1933. Print.

_____. *Directory for the Year 1914 of the Cities of Albany and Rensselaer.* Albany,
NY: The Argus Print, 1914. Print.

_____. *Map of the Cities of Albany and Rensselaer and Portions of Bath and East
Greenbush, New York.* Map. Scale not given. 1900. Print.

_____. *Map of the Cities of Albany and Rensselaer, New York.* Map. Scale not
given. 1915. Web. 2 Nov. 2017. <https://collections.leventhalmap.org/search
/commonwealth:4m90f216v>.

_____. *The Albany Directory for the Year 1901.* 1901. Web. 30 Dec. 2016.
<https://books.google.com/books?id=GpRIAQAAMAAJ&pg=PA678&lpg=PA678&
dq=%22james+h.+carroll%22+coal+company&source=bl&ots=UjHK9_rFbc&sig=
LdV4xMkTjDqg0lj8NjiTj7MRzds&hl=en&sa=X&ved=0ahUKEwi6pfSP5pzRAhV
M4oMKHRq0DpcQ6AEIHjAB#v=onepage&q=%22james%20h.%20carroll%22%
20&f=false>.

Samueldechamplain.com. "Samuel de Champlain." 2013. Web. 26 Aug. 2015.
<http://www.samueldechamplain.com/>.

San Francisco Call. "General John B. Frisbie Passing Away After Lingering Illness in
Southern Capital." *San Francisco Call.* (1909, May 12). Web. 28 July 2016.
<http://cdnc.ucr.edu/cgi-bin/cdnc?a=d&d=SFC19090512.2.20>.

Saxon, Wolfgang. "Richard Conners, 85, Legislator Called 'Dean of the Assembly.'"
The New York Times. (1995, June 27). Web. 12 July 2016. <http://www
.nytimes.com/1995/06/27/obituaries/richard-conners-85-legislator-called-dean-
of-the-assembly.html>.

Schaefer, Paul (Ed.). *Adirondack Explorations: Nature Writings of Verplanck Colvin.* New York, NY: Syracuse University Press, 1997. Print.

Schaetzl, Randall. "Hurons." 2016. Web. 11 July 2016. <http://geo.msu.edu/extra/geogmich/Hurons.html>.

Schenectady Digital History Archive. "Hudson-Mohawk Genealogical and Family Memoirs: Alden." 30 Mar. 2015. Web. 20 July 2016. <http://www.schenectadyhistory.org/families/hmgfm/alden.html>.

_____. "Hudson-Mohawk Genealogical and Family Memoirs: Banker." 30 Mar. 2015. Web. 20 July 2016. <http://www.schenectadyhistory.org/families/hmgfm/banker-1.html>.

_____. "Hudson-Mohawk Genealogical and Family Memoirs: Bogardus." 30 Mar. 2015. Web. 21 July 2016. <http://www.schenectadyhistory.org/families/hmgfm/bogardus-2.html>.

_____. "Hudson-Mohawk Genealogical and Family Memoirs: Cuyler." 30 Mar. 2015. Web. 25 July 2016. <http://www.schenectadyhistory.org/families/hmgfm/carpenter-1.html>.

_____. "Hudson-Mohawk Genealogical and Family Memoirs: Dudley." 30 Mar. 2015. Web. 28 July 2016. <http://www.schenectadyhistory.org/families/hmgfm/cuyler.html>.

_____. "Hudson-Mohawk Genealogical and Family Memoirs: Gansevoort." 30 Mar. 2015. Web. 28 July 2016. <http://www.schenectadyhistory.org/families/hmgfm/gansevoort.html>.

_____. "Hudson-Mohawk Genealogical and Family Memoirs: Krank." 30 Mar. 2015. Web. 20 July 2016. <http://www.schenectadyhistory.org/families/hmgfm/krank.html>.

_____. "Hudson-Mohawk Genealogical and Family Memoirs: Hurst." 30 Mar. 2015. Web. 25 July 2016. <http://www.schenectadyhistory.org/families/hmgfm/hurst.html>.

_____. "Hudson-Mohawk Genealogical and Family Memoirs: Moore." 30 Mar. 2015. Web. 18 Aug. 2016. <http://www.schenectadyhistory.org/families/hmgfm/moore-1.html>.

_____. "Hudson-Mohawk Genealogical and Family Memoirs: Moore." 30 Mar. 2015. Web. 18 Aug. 2016. <http://www.schenectadyhistory.org/families/hmgfm/moore-3.html>.

_____. "Hudson-Mohawk Genealogical and Family Memoirs: Our Hall of Fame, Joseph Christopher Yates (1768–1837)." 30 Mar. 2015. Web. 22 Sept. 2016. <http://www.schenectadyhistory.org/people/ohof/yates.html>.

_____. "Hudson-Mohawk Genealogical and Family Memoirs: Pruyn." 30 Mar. 2015. Web. 19 Aug. 2016. <http://www.schenectadyhistory.org/families/hmgfm/pruyn-1.html>.

_____. "Hudson-Mohawk Genealogical and Family Memoirs: Slingerland." 30 Mar. 2015. Web. 8 Sept. 2016. <http://www.schenectadyhistory.org/families/hmgfm/slingerland-1.html>.

_____. "Hudson-Mohawk Genealogical and Family Memoirs: Ten Eyck." 30 Mar. 2017. Web. 7 Oct. 2017. <http://www.schenectadyhistory.org/families/hmgfm/teneyck-1.html>.

_____. "Hudson-Mohawk Genealogical and Family Memoirs: Thacher." 30 Mar. 2015. Web. 14 Sept. 2016. <http://www.schenectadyhistory.org/families/hmgfm/thacher.html>.

_____. "Hudson-Mohawk Genealogical and Family Memoirs: Van Orden." 30 Mar. 2015. Web. 12 Dec. 2016. <http://www.schenectadyhistory.org/families/hmgfm/vanorden-1.html>.

_____. "Hudson-Mohawk Genealogical and Family Memoirs: Van Vranken." 30 Mar. 2015. Web. 21 July 2016. <http://www.schenectadyhistory.org/families/hmgfm/vanvranken.html#bensen>.

Schlimmer, Erik. *Among the Cloud Splitters: Place Names of High Peaks Wilderness Area.* Troy, NY: Beechwood Books, 2016. Print.

_____. *History Inside the Blue Line: Place Names of the Trans Adirondack Route.* Troy, NY: Beechwood Books, 2014. Print.

_____. *Thru Hiker's Guide to America: 25 Incredible Trails You Can Hike in One to Eight Weeks.* New York, NY: McGraw Hill, 2005. Print.

Schneider, Paul. *Brutal Journey: Cabeza de Vaca and the Epic First Crossing of North America.* New York, NY: Henry Holt, 2007. Print.

_____. *Old Man River: The Mississippi River in North American History.* New York, NY: Henry Holt, 2013. Print.

_____. *The Adirondacks: A History of America's First Wilderness.* New York, NY: Henry Holt, 1997. Print.

Schuyler, H. P. *Map of Part of the Fifth Ward, City of Albany.* Map. Scale not given. 1799. Print.

Seiler, Casey. "$152 million for Harriman." *Times Union.* (2015, Jan. 19). Web. 27 Aug. 2015. <http://www.timesunion.com/news/article/152-million-for-Harriman-6022790.php>.

Seneca-Iroquois National Museum. "Onöndowa'ga': History Timeline." 2016. Web. 31 Aug. 2016. <https://www.senecamuseum.org/Educators/Seneca-History-Timeline.aspx>.

Sfakia-crete.com. "The Olive Tree." 2016. Web. 19 Dec. 2016. <http://www.sfakia-crete.com/sfakia-crete/olive.html>.

Shaker Heritage Society of Albany, New York. "History of the Shakers." 2016. Web. 21 Aug. 2016. <http://shakerheritage.org/educational-programs/adult-programs/history-of-the-Shakers>.

Shapiro, Ben. *Project President: Bad Hair and Botox on the Road to the White House.* Nashville, TN: Thomson Nelson, 2007. Print.

Sheppard, Steve (Ed.). *The History of Legal Education in the United States: Commentaries and Primary Sources.* Clark, NJ: The Lawbook Exchange, 2007. Print.

Shutts, Gerrit. *Albany: Map 269. Property Between Pearl, Market, Columbia.* Map. Scale not given. 1799. Print.

Sidney, J. C. *Map of the City of Albany*. Map. Scale not given. 1850. Print.

Siegel, Allison. "Corlear's Hook and its Hooker History." 2012. Web. 21 Nov. 2016. <http://www.boweryboogie.com/2012/01/corlears-hook-and-its-hooker-history/>.

Sinclair, Douglas. "The Grange Sard, Jr. House Reconsidered." 2009. Web. 27 Dec. 2016. <http://dougsinclairsarchives.com/archhistory/sardhouse/sardtext.htm>.

Skinner, Charles. *Myths and Legends of our own Land*. 1896. Web. 5 Feb. 2018. <https://archive.org/details/mythslegendsofou04skin>.

Smith, Dennis. "Changes in Names of Streets of Albany." 2002. Web. 5 June 2015. <http://www.rootsweb.ancestry.com/~nyalbany/streets.html>.

Smith, Robert, and W. Young. *Map of the Vicinity of Albany and Troy*. Map. Scale not given. 1851. Web. 13 Oct. 2017. <https://digitalcollections.nypl.org/items /71a214f0-0595-0134-eeb7-00505686a51c>.

Spirit of St. Louis 2 Project. "Charles Lindbergh Biography." 2016. Web. 11 Aug 2016. <http://www.charleslindbergh.com/history/>.

Sprague and Company. *Map of the City of Albany, with Villages of Greenbush, East Albany, and Bath, N.Y.* Map. Scale not given. 1857. Web. 27 Sept. 2016. <https://upload.wikimedia.org/wikipedia/commons/2/2b/1857_Map_of_Albany_ Edit.jpeg>.

Sowell, Thomas. *Black Rednecks and White Liberals*. New York, NY: Encounter Books, 2005. Print.

_____. *Wealth, Poverty, and Politics*. 2nd ed. New York, NY: Basic Books, 2016. Print.

Steele, Oliver. *Map of the City of Albany*. Map. Scale not given. 1855. Web. 18 Mar. 2017. <http://www.albanyinstitute.org/details/items/map-of-the-city-of-albany .html>.

Stephens, Katherine. "The Oldest Building in Albany?" 20 July 2009. Web. 21 Aug. 2016. <http://alloveralbany.com/archive/2009/07/20/the-oldest-building-in-albany #more>.

Stewart, George. *Names on the Land: A Historical Account of Place-Naming in the United States*. Boston, MA: Houghton Mifflin, 1958. Print.

Stuart Center. "Janet Erskine Stuart, RSCJ." 2016. Web. 28 July 2016. <https://stuartcenter.org/about/janet-erskine-stuart>.

Suchecki, Mark. "Norstar Plaza to be Renamed for Kiernan." *Times Union*. (1989, Sept. 14). Web. 18 June 2016. <http://albarchive.merlinone.net/mweb/wmsql.wm .request?oneimage&imageid=5521528>.

Talcott, Sabastian. *Genealogical Notes of New York and New England Families*. 1883. Web. 29 Oct. 2017. <https://books.google.com/books?id=6YehIsw-eF8C&dq=%22 bertha+van+vechten%22&source=gbs_navlinks_s>.

Tama County, Iowa, Economic Development Commission. "City of Elberon, Iowa." 2018. Web. 12 Feb. 2018. <https://tamacountyiowa.org/communities/elberon/>.

Ten Broeck Triangle. "St. Joseph's Church." 2016. Web. 7 Aug. 2016. <https://tenbroecktriangle.org/st-josephs-church/>.

Tepper, Taylor. "X-Ray: Goldman Sachs." *Money*. March 2017. 50. Print.

The 30th Infantry Division Veterans of WWII. "The 30th Infantry Division Veterans of WWII." 2008. Web. 27 Oct. 2017. <http://www.30thinfantry.org/index2.shtml>.

The Albany Academies. "200 Years at the Albany Academies." 18 Sept. 2011. Web. 15 Aug. 2016. <http://bbk12e1-cdn.myschoolcdn.com/ftpimages/499/misc/misc_120969.pdf>.

_____. "About, Fast Facts." 2016. Web. 6 Aug. 2016. <http://www.albanyacademies.org/Page/About/Fast-Facts>.

_____. "Admissions." 2016. Web. 6 Aug. 2016. <http://www.albanyacademies.org/Page/Admissions/Tuition>.

The American Whig Review, Volume Six. 1847. Web. 17 Aug. 2016. <https://books.google.com/books?id=T7brSqWusNkC&dq=genesee+beautiful+valley&source=gbs_navlinks_s>.

The Argus Company. *The Albany Lumber Trade, its History and Extent*. 1872. Web. 31 Oct. 2017. <https://ia902706.us.archive.org/33/items/albanylumbertra00unkngoog/albanylumbertra00unkngoog.pdf>.

The Cemetery Site. "Bethlehem Cemetery, Bethlehem, Albany County, New York." 2016. Web. 26 Dec. 2016. <http://www.onentofl.com/tcsnyalbbethbeth.html>.

The Central District Management Association Incorporated. "History of the Avenue." 2015. Web. 5 June 2015. <http://www.centralbid.com/historical>.

The City of New York. "Tremont Park." 2016. Web. 5 Jan. 2017. <https://www.nycgovparks.org/parks/tremont-park/history>.

The Connecticut Society of the Sons of the American Revolution. "Israel Putnam." 2010. Web. 15 Dec. 2016. <http://www.connecticutsar.org/patriots/putnam_israel.htm>.

The Cornell Lab of Ornithology. "Gray Partridge." 2015. Web. 28 Aug. 2015. <http://www.allaboutbirds.org/guide/Gray_Partridge/id>.

The Daily Gazette. "John Quadrini." *The Daily Gazette*. (2003, Jan. 11). Web. 14 July 2015. <https://news.google.com/newspapers?id=GWZGAAAAIBAJ&sjid=0OgMAAAAIBAJ&pg=4209%2C2026608>.

The Dutch Settlers Society of Albany. *Volume 58 Yearbook, 2014–2017*. Albany, NY: Enterprise Printing and Photo, 2017. Print.

The Encyclopedia of Cleveland History. "Erie Indians." 16 July 1997. Web. 19 July 2016. <http://ech.case.edu/cgi/article.pl?id=EI>.

The Fay Family Homepage Genealogies. "Heman Allen Fay (1779–1865) of Bennington, Vermont and New York and his Decedents." 2016. Web. 26 Dec. 2016. <http://freepages.genealogy.rootsweb.ancestry.com/~fayfamily/heman_allen1779.html>.

The Historical Society of the New York Court. "Egbert Benson." 2017. Web. 16 Aug. 2017. <http://www.nycourts.gov/history/legal-history-new-york/legal-history-eras-02/history-era-02-benson.html>.

The History Channel. "Modern Marvels: The Erie Canal." 2012. Web. 3 Apr. 2015. <https://www.youtube.com/watch?v=E53-FjfMUJQ>.

The History of Loudon County, Virginia. "How Loudon County Got its Name." 2016. Web. 22 Aug. 2016. <http://www.loudounhistory.org/history/loudoun-how-named .htm>.

The History of Parliament. "Member Biographies." 2016. Web. 16 Dec. 2016. <http://www.historyofparliamentonline.org/research/members/1558-1603/E>.

The King Center. "About Dr. King." 2017. Web. 9 Jan. 2017. <http://www.theking center.org/about-dr-king>.

The Kingston Daily Freeman. "Charges Against Besch not Proven." The Kingston Daily Freeman. (1909, Jan. 15). Web. 28 July 2016. <http://news.hrvh.org/veridian/cgi-bin/senylrc?a=d&d=kingstondaily19090115.2.4#>.

The Knickerbocker News. "Clearing Ramsey Place." The Knickerbocker News. (1953, June 29). Print.

_____. "Dolan Estate Listed at $146,713." The Knickerbocker News. (1962, June 6). Web. 25 Oct. 2017. <http://fultonhistory.com/Fulton.html>.

_____. "Driver Arrested: Albany Man, 74, Killed by Car." The Knickerbocker News. (1965, Sept. 18). Web. 25 Oct. 2017. <http://fultonhistory.com/Fulton .html>.

_____. "Eileen Dolan Married to Maj. Sherrer." The Knickerbocker News. (1947, Sept. 18). Web. 25 Oct. 2017. <http://fultonhistory.com/Fulton.html>.

_____. "Golden Acres Annexation to Albany Spurs Additional Building." The Knickerbocker News. (1938, Sept. 3). Print.

_____. "Golden Acres Developers Seek to Complete Project During 1939." The Knickerbocker News. (1939, Jan. 21). Print.

_____. "Historical Name Dropped in Redesignating Street." The Knickerbocker News. (1937, Oct. 9). Web. 2 Nov. 2017. <http://fultonhistory.com/Fulton.html>.

_____. "How it got its Name." The Knickerbockers News. (1937). Print.

_____. "Lawyer Names Newest Street After Division." The Knickerbocker News. (1951, Mar. 20). Web. 27 Oct. 2017. <http://fultonhistory.com/Fulton.html>.

_____. "Obituaries, Memorial to the Late B. Jermain Savage, Vice-President and Trustee of Albany Savings Bank." The Knickerbocker News. (1952, June 24). Web. 27 Oct. 2017. <http://fultonhistory.com/Fulton.html>.

_____. "Officials, Realtors get Preview of New Homes in Crestwood." The Knickerbocker News. (1950). Print.

_____. "University Heights Inspired by Ravine." The Knickerbocker News. (1938, May 7). Web. 26 Oct. 2017. <http://fultonhistory.com/Fulton.html>.

_____. "Van Schoick Dies at 73; Albany Real Estate Man." The Knickerbocker News. (1957, June 25). Web. 20 Oct. 2017. <http://fultonhistory.com/Fulton .html>.

The National Library of Wales. "Dictionary of Welsh Biography, Ellis, Rowland." 2016. Web. 16 Aug. 2016. <http://yba.llgc.org.uk/en/s-ELLI-ROW-1650.html>.

The New York Times. "Obituaries, Peter D. Kiernan, 65, Head of Fleet/Norstar." The New York Times. (1988, Sept. 16). Web. 18 June 2016. <http://www.nytimes.com /1988/09/16/obituaries/peter-d-kiernan-65-head-of-fleet-norstar.html>.

_____. "Obituary, Alfred E. Smith Dies Here at 70; 4 Times Governor." *The New York Times.* (1944, Oct. 4). Web. 22 Nov. 2017. <http://www.nytimes.com/learning/general/onthisday/bday/1230.html>.

_____. "Obituary, Andrew J. Colvin." *The New York Times.* (1889, July 21). Web. 13 June 2017. <http://query.nytimes.com/mem/archive-free/pdf?res=9400E7D8133AE033A25752C2A9619C94689FD7CF>.

_____. "Sheriff Besch's Reply." *The New York Times.* (1908, Aug. 30). Web. 28 July 2016. <http://query.nytimes.com/mem/archive-free/pdf?res=9901E7D71631E233A25753C3A96E9C946997D6CF>.

The Reading Eagle. "Dolan, Mrs. Diamond's Guard, Meets Death." *The Reading Eagle.* (1933, July 31). Web. 27 June 2015. <https://news.google.com/newspapers?nid=1955&dat=19330731&id=f3gzAAAAIBAJ&sjid=DeIFAAAAIBAJ&pg=4177,4336533&hl=en>.

The Seminole Nation of Florida. "History." 2016. Web. 31 Aug. 2016. <http://www.semtribe.com/History/>.

The State Historical Society of Missouri. "Lincoln County Place Names, 1928–1945." 2016. Web. 25 Dec. 2016. <http://shsmo.org/manuscripts/ramsay/ramsay_lincoln.html>.

The United States National Arboretum. "State Trees and State Flowers." 2010. Web. 31 May 2015. <http://www.usna.usda.gov/Gardens/collections/statetreeflower.html>.

The White House. "Abraham Lincoln." 2015. Web. 2 Sept. 2015. <https://www.whitehouse.gov/1600/presidents/abrahamlincoln>.

_____. "Grover Cleveland." 2015. Web. 9 Sept. 2015. <https://www.whitehouse.gov/1600/presidents/grovercleveland22>.

_____. "James Garfield." 2015. Web. 18 Aug. 2015. <https://www.whitehouse.gov/1600/presidents/jamesgarfield>.

_____. "James Madison." 2015. Web. 18 Aug. 2015. <https://www.whitehouse.gov/1600/presidents/jamesmadison>.

_____. "James Monroe." 2016. Web. 11 Aug. 2016. <https://www.whitehouse.gov/1600/presidents/jamesmonroe>.

_____. "Martin Van Buren." 2015. Web. 18 Aug. 2015. <https://www.whitehouse.gov/1600/presidents/martinvanburen>.

_____. "Ulysses S. Grant." 2015. Web. 24 Aug. 2015. <https://www.whitehouse.gov/1600/presidents/ulyssessgrant>.

_____. "Warren G. Harding." 2017. Web. 4 Aug. 2017. <https://www.whitehouse.gov/1600/presidents/warrenharding>.

_____. "William McKinley." 2015. Web. 18 Aug. 2015. <https://www.whitehouse.gov/1600/presidents/williammckinley>.

The Winthrop Society. "Passengers of the Hopewell." 2015. Web. 5 Jan. 2017. <http://winthropsociety.com/ships/hopewell1.htm>.

_____. "Passengers of the Hopewell." 2015. Web. 5 Jan. 2017. <http://winthropsociety.com/ships/hopewell2.htm>.

Thefatherofhollywood.com. "Media Room." 2016. Web. 5 Dec. 2016. <http://the fatherofhollywood.com/media-room>.

Thieret, John. *National Audubon Society Field Guide to North American Wildflowers: Eastern Region*. Revised ed. New York, NY: Knopf, 2001. Print.

Thwing, Annie Haven. *The Crooked and Narrow Streets of the Town of Boston, 1630–1822*. 1920. Web. 12 Feb. 2018. <https://www.americanancestors.org/uploaded Files/American_Ancestors/Content/Databases/PDFs/Thwing/The_Crooked_and_Narrow_Streets_of_the_Town_of_Boston.pdf>.

Times Union. "Armand Colatosti, Obituary." *Times Union*. (2014, June 6). Web. 3 Aug. 2016. <http://www.legacy.com/obituaries/timesunion-albany/obituary.aspx?pid=171247324>.

_____. "Charles Bud Cole McTague." *Times Union*. (2006, Mar. 2). Web. 17 Sept. 2017. <http://www.legacy.com/obituaries/timesunion-albany/obituary.aspx?n =charles-bud-cole-mctague&pid=16903402&>.

_____. "Donald McDonald." *Times Union*. (1937). Web. 22 Jan. 2018. <http://fultonhistory.com/Fulton.html>.

_____. "Dorothea Polly Noonan, Obituary." *Times Union*. (2003, Nov. 15). Web. 15 Sept. 2016. <http://www.legacy.com/obituaries/timesunion-albany/obituary.aspx?pid=1603688>.

_____. "Edward M. Kaine, Obituary." *Times Union*. (2013, Mar. 31). Web. 25 Oct. 2017. <http://www.legacy.com/obituaries/timesunion-albany/obituary.aspx?pid =163934108>.

_____. "Edward N. Swartz." *Times Union*. (2011, Sept. 11). Web. 22 Jan. 2017. <http://www.legacy.com/obituaries/timesunion-albany/obituary.aspx?page=life story&pid=94236268>.

_____. "Edward N. Swartz." *Times Union*. (2011, Sept. 11). Web. 22 Jan. 2017. <http://www.legacy.com/obituaries/timesunion-albany/obituary.aspx?page=life story&pid=94236265>.

_____. "Helga Dagmara Hartman, Obituary." *Times Union*. (2012, June 10). Web. 5 Jan. 2017. <http://www.legacy.com/obituaries/timesunion-albany/obituary.aspx?pid=157975898>.

_____. "Joanne Besch Wed to W. Ferguson." *Times Union*. (1956, Oct. 20). Web. 19 Oct. 2017. <http://fultonhistory.com/Fulton.html>.

_____. "John V. L. Pruyn." *Times Union*. Web. 29 Dec. 2016. <http://www.times union.com/albanyrural/pruyn/>.

_____. "Memorial for Judge Brady." *Times Union*. (1950, April 13). Web. 30 Oct. 2017. <http://fultonhistory.com/Fulton.html>.

_____. "Reverend John J. 'J. J.' Rooney, Obituary." *Times Union*. (2016, Apr. 21). Web. 17 Apr. 2017. <http://www.legacy.com/obituaries/timesunion-albany/ obituary.aspx?page=lifestory&pid=179693881>.

_____. "These Exalted Acres: Unlocking the Secrets of Albany Rural Cemetery. John Alden Dix." *Times Union*. Web. 2 Apr. 2017. <http://www.timesunion .com/albanyrural/dix/>.

_____. "Three Found Slain in Home off Whitehall Road." *Times Union.* (1944, Feb. 1). Print.

_____. "Triple Slaying Laid to Worry Over Finances." *Times Union.* (1944, Feb. 2). Web. 30 Jan. 2018. <http://fultonhistory.com/Fulton.html>.

_____. "West End News. Thomas Ludlow Killed at Union Station." *Times Union.* (1900, Dec. 27). Web. 9 Nov. 2017. <http://fultonhistory.com/Fulton.html>.

Titcomb, Sarah. *Early New England People: Some Account of the Ellis, Pemberton, Willard, Prescott, Titcomb, Sewall and Longfellow, and Allied Families.* 1882. Web. 13 Dec. 2016. <https://archive.org/details/cu31924030933364>.

Troy Irish Genealogy Society. "The State Street Burial Grounds." 2016. Web. 15 Aug. 2016. <http://www.rootsweb.ancestry.com/~nytigs/StateStreetBurialGrounds /Reformed_Protestant_Dutch_Church_K-R.htm>.

Union College. "About Union College." 2016. Web. 20 Sept. 2016. <https://www .union.edu/about/>.

United States Department of Agriculture, Natural Resources Conservation Service. "Plant Guide, American Silverberry." 19 Sept. 2000. Web. 3 Sept. 2015. <http://plants.usda.gov/plantguide/pdf/pg_elco.pdf>.

United States Department of Commerce. "Most Common Street Names." 1993. Print.

United States Department of the Interior, National Park Service. "National Register of Historic Places Inventory. Nomination Form." 5 Oct. 1988. Web. 16 Oct. 2017. <https://npgallery.nps.gov/GetAsset?assetID=415ce173-0172-48a3-b19b-758bd81 cd3ba>.

United States Geological Survey. "Latest Score: Mill Creek 1,473, Spring Creek 1,312." 3 Sept. 1996. Web. 31 May 2017. <https://archive.usgs.gov/archive /sites /www.usgs.gov/newsroom/article.asp-ID=777.html>.

United States Geological Survey Astrogeology Science Center. "Gazetteer of Planetary Nomenclature. Planetary Names: Craters. Barton on Venus." 2017. Web. 28 Mar. 2017. <https://planetarynames.wr.usgs.gov/Feature/623?__fsk=-16184 76416>.

_____. "Gazetteer of Planetary Nomenclature. Planetary Names: Craters. Euclides on Moon." 18 Oct. 2010. Web. 26 July 2016. <http://planetarynames.wr.usgs .gov/Feature/1860>.

United States Geological Survey Geographic Names Information System. "Feature Detail Report for Beacon Hill." 2016. Web. 12 Dec. 2016. <https://geonames.usgs .gov/apex/f?p=138:3:0::NO:3:P3_FID,P3_TITLE:619310,Beacon%20Hill>.

United States History. "Jeffrey Amherst." 2015. Web. 12 Sept. 2015. <http://www.u-s-history.com/pages/h1185.html>.

United States Mint. "Jefferson Nickel." 2016. Web. 27 Sept. 2016. <https://www .usmint.gov/mint_programs/circulatingCoins/indexef21.html?action=CircNickel>.

United States Postal Service. "Postal Facts 2017." 2017. Web. 14 Feb. 2017. <https://about.usps.com/who-we-are/postal-facts/postalfacts2017.pdf>.

United Way of the Greater Capital Region. "History." 2015. Web. 9 Sept. 2015. <http://www.unitedwaygcr.org/history>.

University at Albany. "Alumni Quad." 2015. Web. 27 Aug. 2015. <http://www
.albany.edu/housing/alumni.shtml>.

———. "Dutch Quad." 2015. Web. 27 Aug. 2015. <http://www.albany
.edu/housing/dutch.shtml>.

———. "Indian Quad." 2015. Web. 27 Aug. 2015. <http://www.albany.edu
/housing/indian.shtml>.

———. "Lithgow Mural Fund." 2016. Web. 15 Sept. 2016. <http://www.albany.edu
/lithgow/campaign.html>.

———. "Quay Street (1813)." 2016. Web. 28 July 2016. <http://www.albany.edu
/museum/wwwmuseum/tantillo/QuaySt.html>.

———. "Restored UAlbany Carillon Rings in Improved Sounds and Early Warning
System." 14 Oct. 2008. Web. 27 Aug. 2015. <http://www.albany.edu/news
/release_4546.shtml>.

———. "State Quad." 2015. Web. 27 Aug. 2015. <http://www.albany.edu/housing
/state.shtml>.

———. "Symbols of U Albany." 2015. Web. 29 June 2015. <http://www.albany.edu
/spirit/symbols.shtml>.

———. "The Historical Van Ingen Murals at Dewey Library." 2016. Web. 15 Sept.
2016. <http://library.albany.edu/dewey/murals/history>.

———. *Uptown Campus*. Map. Scale not given. 2017. Print.

University of Cambridge. "About the University." 2016. Web. 15 July 2016.
<http://www.cam.ac.uk/>.

University of Groningen. "A Biography of Robert Morris, 1734–1806." 2016. Web. 12
Aug. 2016. <http://www.let.rug.nl/usa/biographies/robert-morris/>.

University of Massachusetts. "Jeffrey Amherst and Smallpox Blankets." 2010.
Web. 13 Sept. 2015. <https://www.umass.edu/legal/derrico/amherst/lord_jeff
.html>.

University of Notre Dame. "About ND." 2016. Web. 22 June 2016. <https://
www.nd.edu/about/>.

University of St. Andrews. "Euclid of Alexandria." Jan. 1999. Web. 26 July 2016.
<http://www-groups.dcs.st-and.ac.uk/~history/Biographies/Euclid.html>.

University of the State of New York. *Report, Volume 67*. 1915. Web. 21 Aug. 2016.
<https://books.google.com/books?id=68bOAAAAMAAJ&dq=%22tivoli+hollow
%22+%22named+for%22&source=gbs_navlinks_s>.

University of Virginia Miller Center. "Daniel Manning (1885–1887): Secretary of the
Treasury." 2016. Web. 11 Aug. 2016. <http://millercenter.org/president/essays
/manning-188-secretary-of-the-treasury>.

———. "James A. Garfield: Life in Brief." 2015. Web. 10 Sept. 2015. <http://
millercenter.org/president/biography/garfield-life-in-brief>.

Urrico, Roy. "Albany Merchant James Caldwell Paved the Way for Village of Lake
George." *Post Star*. (2010, Aug. 23). Web. 18 Nov. 2016. <http://poststar
.com/lifestyles/hometown/albany-merchant-james-caldwell-paved -the-way-for-
village-of/article_86773f0e-aec0-11df-b0ae-001cc4c03286.html>.

U.S. Army. "Medal of Honor: Sergeant Henry Johnson." 2015. Web. 14 Sept. 2015. <http://www.army.mil/medalofhonor/johnson/>.

Van Allen, Evert. *Map of the City of Albany*. Map. Scale not given. 1832. Print.

Van Laer, Arnold. *Settlers of Rensselaerswyck 1630–1658.* Baltimore, MD: Clearfield, 1998. Print.

Van Olinda, Edgar. "Gaunt Greyledge Stares Vacantly into Past." *Times Union*. (1962, June 6). Print.

_____. "Two Streets and Town Named for Wm. James." *Times Union*. Print.

Vasilieve, Ren. *From Abbotts to Zurich: New York State Place Names*. Syracuse, NY: Syracuse University Press, 2004. Print.

Vassar College. "About Vassar College." 2016. Web. 20 Sept. 2016. <http://info .vassar.edu/about/vassar/>.

_____. "Vassar Encyclopedia, Vassar Myths and Legends." 2006. Web. 7 Sept. 2015. <https://vcencyclopedia.vassar.edu/vassar-myths-legends/>.

Venema, Janny. *Beverwijck: A Dutch Village on the American Frontier, 1652–1664*. Albany, NY: SUNY Press, 2003. Print.

Vice News. "The Cannibal Warlords of Liberia." 2012. Web. 23 Feb. 2018. <https://www .youtube.com/watch?v=ZRuSS0iiFyo>.

Waite, Diana (Ed.). *Albany Architecture: A Guide to the City*. Albany, NY: Mount Ida Press, 1993. Print.

Ward, Nancy. "You Believed Eggsalad Road is Real?" 2018. Web. 1 Apr. 2018. <https://that-is-the-only-fake-entry.inthisbook.html/>.

Washington Park Conservancy. "Chronological History of Washington Park." 2017. Web. 8 Nov. 2017. <https://www.washingtonparkconservancy.org/wp-content /uploads/Washington-Park-History-Timeline-1.pdf>.

_____. "Rules for Washington Park, 1875." 2017. Web. 8 Nov. 2017. <https://www .washingtonparkconservancy.org/wp-content/uploads/Rules-for-Washington-Park-1875.pdf>.

Waterman, Guy, and Laura Waterman. *Forest and Crag: A History of Hiking, Trail Blazing, and Adventure in the Northeast Mountains*. Boston, MA: Appalachian Mountain Club, 1989. Print.

Waymarking.com. "Home of Verplanck Colvin." 2008. Web. 3 July 2016. <http:// www.waymarking.com/waymarks/WM4ZCA_Home_of_Verplanck_Colvin>.

Weddle, Bonnie. "The Demise of Trinity Episcopal Church, Albany, New York." 16 July 2011. Web. 24 Aug. 2016. <http://larchivista.blogspot.com/2011/07/trinity-episcopal-church-albany-new.html>.

Weise, Arthur. *The History of the City of Albany, New York: From the Discovery of the Great River in 1524 by Verrazzano to the Present Time*. 1884. Web. 7 Aug. 2016. <https://archive.org/stream/historyofcityofa00weis#page/n12/mode/1up>.

Wheeler, Walter. "Background and Social History of the Site and Occupants of the John Evert and Anne Fryenmoet Van Alen House." Web. 29 Aug. 2017. <http://www.hartgen.com/userfiles/Social%20History%20of%20the%20Van%2 0Alen%20house.pdf>.

Whitaker, John Jr. *National Audubon Society Field Guide to North American Mammals*. Revised ed. New York, NY: Knopf, 1996. Print.

White, William. *Adirondack Country*. New York, NY: Knopf, 1970. Print.

Whitmore, William. *An Essay on the Origin of the Names of Towns in Massachusetts*. 1873. Web. 29 May 2017. <https://ia800207.us.archive.org/28/items/essay onoriginfn00whit/essayonoriginfn00whit.pdf>.

Wikisource. "Glynn, John." 2016. Web. 25 Nov. 2016. <https://en.wikisource.org /wiki/Glynn,_John_(DNB00)>.

Wilcoxen, Charlotte. *Seventeenth Century Albany: A Dutch Profile*. Albany, NY: Albany Institute of History and Art, 1984. Print.

Wild Birds Unlimited. "Educational Resources, Starlings." 2012. Web. 26 Aug. 2015. <http://www.wbu.com/education/starlings.html>.

William A. Flamm and Company. *Map of Albany, New York*. Map. Scale not given. 1893. Web. 14 Mar. 2017. <https://digitalcollections.nypl.org/items/7ebf5d30-0674-0134-e725-00505686a51c#/?uuid=64fbeea0-6946-0134-6775-00505686a51c>.

Williams, David. *The Iron Age: A Review of the Hardware, Iron, and Metal Trades*. 12 Oct. 1893. Vol. LI. No. 15. Web. 30 Dec. 2016. <https://books.google .com/books?id=sUMV2EVnZbMC&pg=RA2-PA54&lpg=RA2-PA54&dq=%22albany +stove+company%22+broadway&source=bl&ots=Y11R3XD3sB&sig=opTJzRaUhg jIun3M0MPwu415G5A&hl=en&sa=X&ved=0ahUKEwjeg9X56pzRAhUH0YMKHc IvC2oQ6AEIIDAC#v=onepage&q=%22albany%20stove%20company%22&f=false>.

Wissler, Clark. *Indians of the United States*. Revised ed. Garden City, NY: Anchor, 1966. Print.

Witbeck, Gerrit. *Sketch of Roads, Streams, and Localities of Watervliet*. Map. Scale not given. 1850. Print.

Wolf, Susan. "Who Killed Jane Stanford?" Sept./Oct. 2003. Web. 27 Dec. 2016. <https://alumni.stanford.edu/get/page/magazine/article/?article_id=36459>.

Work Projects Administration. *New York: A Guide to the Empire State*. 1940. Web. 9 May 2017. <https://archive.org/details/in.ernet.dli.2015.180091>.

Worth, Gorham. *Random Recollections of Albany, from 1800 to 1808*. 1866. Web. 31 Oct. 2017. <https://archive.org/details/recollectionsofa00wort>.

Yale University. "About Yale." 2016. Web. 22 Sept. 2016. <http://www.yale.edu /about-yale>.

Yates, Robert. *Plan of the City of Albany About the Year 1770*. Map. Scale not given. 1770. Web. 14 Mar. 2017. <https://digitalcollections.nypl.org/items/f8f11360-0652-0134-1835-00505686a51c>.

Ye Olde Tavern Tours. "History in a Minute: Mount Whoredom." 17 Nov. 2014. Web. 13 Dec. 2016. <https://www.youtube.com/watch?v=TqixK5V7BTc>.

Yonkers Chamber of Commerce. "Early Yonkers History." 2017. Web. 5 May 2017. <http://www.yonkerschamber.com/city-of-yonkers/early-yonkers-history/>.

BIOGRAPHICAL INDEX

Bouck, Christian, 42
Bouck, Gabriel, 42
Bouck, Joseph, 42
Bouck, Margaret, 42
Bouck, William, 42
Bourlemont, Pica de, 270
Bowers, Virginia, 3
Bradford, Alice Carpenter, 55
Bradford, Ebenezer, 43
Bradford, Elizabeth Greene, 43
Bradford, John, 43
Bradford, William, 55
Bradstreet, John, 46, 310
Bradt, Pietertje, 88
Brady, Ann Farley, 43
Brady, John (supreme court judge), 21, 43
Brady, John J. (family court judge), 43–44,
  175
Brady, John J. Jr., 44
Brant, Joseph, 140, 311
Bratt, Adrien, 209
Bratt, Albert Andriese, 209
Bratt, Anjelte Albertse, 263
Bratt, Jan, 209
Braudel, Fernand, 147
Brevator, Catherine, 44
Brevator, Elizabeth Riches, 44
Brevator, Jonathan (father), 44
Brevator, Jonathan (son), 44
Brodess, Mary Pattison, 290
Brooke, 281
Brown, John, 290
Brown, Lewis ("L. B."), 105
Browne, Charles, 66
Browne, James, 37, 48
Bucci, Gaetano, 48
Bucci, Rose Venosa, 48
Bucci, William, 48–49
Buchanan, James, 49, 68, 125, 128, 250,
  302
Buchanan, William, xvi, 49, 68, 125, 173,
  250, 295, 302
Buel, Jesse, 50–51, 83
Bullock, Elizabeth, 224
Bundocke, William, 144
Burgoyne, John, 123, 242, 272
Burnet, William, 84
Burr, Aaron Jr., 16, 106, 218
Bush, George H. W., 317
Bush, George W., 136, 317

Caldwell, James, 52, 189
Caldwell, Joseph, 52, 189
Calhoun, John, 317
Campbell, John (4th Earl of Loudoun), 180
Campbell, John (lieutenant colonel), 202
Canfield, John, 267
Cantine, Moses, 50
Caroline of Ansbach, 14
Carpenter, Alexander, 55
Carpenter, Edward, 54–55
Carpenter, Elizabeth, 55
Carpenter, Hiram, 54
Carpenter, Richard, 55
Carpenter, Sally Ann Barker, 54
Carpenter, William, 55
Carroll, Daniel, 55
Carroll, James, 55–56
Carroll, John, 126
Carroll, Neeltje, 55
Carson, Rachel, 98
Carter, George, 266
Cartier, Jacques, 59
Cary, Caroline Sawyer, 56, 256
Cary, George, 56
Cary, Joseph, 56, 144, 256, 318–319
Casey, William, 117
Catton, Bruce, 4
Champlain, Samuel de, 31, 59–60, 149
Charles I, 60, 92, 144, 315
Charles II, 13–14, 232, 247
Charles, George, 61–62
Charles, Mary Price, 62
Charles, William (b. 1730s), 62
Charles, William (b. 1797), 62
Charlotte (Queen Charlotte), 50
Chatterton, Eleanor, 224
Chesler, Andrew, 134
Chester, John, 309
Christiaensen, Hendrick, 12
Church, Benjamin, 316
Ciar, 164
Clare, Catherine, 65
Clare, Henry, 65
Clare, Maria, 65
Clark, Rufus, 4, 216
Clark, William, 31, 155
Clarke, George (politician), 84
Clarke, George (publisher), 285
Clarkson, David, 119
Clay, Henry, 286

Eustis, William, 112
Evans, Augusta, 108
Eve (biblical character), 113
Everard, William, 113
Everett, Hannah Slack, 113
Everett, Mary Shepard, 113
Everett, Otis, 113
Everett, Penuel, 113
Everett, Robert Bartlett, 113
Ewing, Thomas, 260

Fahy, Pat, 254
Farley, George H. C., 254
Farley, William W. Jr., 254
Farragut, James Glasgow (David G. Farragut), 239
Fay, Heman Allen, 115
Fay, Joanna, 115
Fay, Jonas, 115
Fay, Lydia Safford, 115
Fenwick, John, 313
Fish, Hamilton, 106
Fitzgerald, Catharine, 74
Fitzgerald, James, 74
Fletcher, Benjamin, 25
Fletcher, William, 4
Flodder, Jacob Jansz (Jacob Jansz Gardenier), 231
Fonday, Gertie, 263
Ford, Gerald, 317
Fox, William, 100
Francis (St. Francis of Assisi), 270
Francis I, 187
Franki, Jamie, 155
Franklin, Benjamin, 3, 8–9, 118–119, 155, 276
Fredenrich, John, 189
Freeman, Elizabeth, 119
Freeman, Frances, 119
Freeman, John I, 119
Freeman, John II, 119
Freeman, Maritie De Line, 119
Freeman, Mark, 119
Freeman, Robert, 119
Freerman, Anna Margarita, 119
Freerman, Barnhardus, 119
Freerman, Margarita Van Schaick, 119
Frelinghuysen, J. Theodorus, 29, 119
Fremont, John, 286
French, J. H., 259, 268, 287
Freneau, Philip, 73

Friebel, Karl Ferdinand ("Charles"), 120
Friebel, Natalie Geyer, 120
Friebel, Otto, 120
Frisbie, Cynthia Cornell, 120–121
Frisbie, Edward, 120–121
Frisbie, Eleazer, 120–121
Frisbie, John B., 120–121
Frost, Jonathan, 121
Frost, Robert, 87
Fulbright, William (James William Fulbright), 228
Fuller, Aaron, 121–122
Fuller, Albert, 180
Fuller, Harriet Moak, 121
Fuller, James W. Jr., 122
Fuller, John, 121
Fuller, Randall, 122
Fullerton, George, 122
Fulton, Robert, 66–67, 122
Fulton, William, 220
Furnese, Matilda, 102

Gage, Maria Teresa Hall, 123
Gage, Thomas (father), 123
Gage, Thomas (son), 18, 115, 123, 139, 163
Gandhi, Indira, 228
Gansevoort, Catherine Van Schaick, 124
Gansevoort, Harman, 124
Gansevoort, Magdalena Douw, 124
Gansevoort, Peter, 123–124, 192, 246, 272, 283
Garfield, James, 21, 105, 124–125, 195
Garland, Jerome, 125–126
Gates, Bill, 136
George (Saint George), 270
George II (George Augustus), 14, 52
George III (George William Frederick), 14, 50, 211
Germain, George, 123
Gerontius, 270
Gerritse, Ariantie, 107
Gherardi, Bancroft, 26
Gherardi, Donato, 26
Gherardi, Jane Putnam Bancroft, 26
Giguere, Dorilla Rosalie, 208
Gilbert, Richard Fitz, 65
Gilbert, William, 149
Gillespie, William, 57
Gillibrand, Kirsten, 208
Ginzberg, Lori, 148
Gipp, Mathew, 127

Herchheimer, Johann Jost, 140
Herkimer, Nicholas, 140, 154, 311
Hermance, W. B., 255
Hermes, 224
Herron, Helen, 280
Hewes, Joseph, 119
Hill, David, 108
Hinsdale, Jonathan, 172
Hinsdale, Sarah, 172
Hislop, Codman, 4, 10, 27, 30, 46, 50, 97,
    151, 179, 213, 220, 274, 292, 309, 311
Hoag, Sibbel, 203
Hockensmith, George, 50
Hodges, Flavia, 210
Hoes, Hannah, 295
Hoff, Benjamin, 78
Hoffer, Eric, 303
Hoffman, Adrian Kissam, 141
Hoffman, Jane Ann Thompson, 141
Hoffman, John, 141–142
Hogan, Mary, 62
Hogan, Susanna Lansing, 62
Hogan, William, 62
Holding, Claude, 28, 171
Holmes, Ann Milner, 143
Holmes, Sherlock, 1
Holmes, Thomas, 143
Hoogkamp, Herman, 78
Hooker, Joseph, 76
Hooker, Philip, 7, 28
Hopkins, G. M., 64, 256, 304
Hopkinson, Francis, 119
Hornell, George, 284
Horner, Freeman, 222
Horrobin, William, 125
Houston, Sam, 222
Howe, Richard, 123
Howe, William, 123
Howell, George, 238
Howland, Emily, 291
Hudson, Henry, 30, 145–147, 151, 200, 220,
    274, 300
Hughes, Charles Evans, 36
Hughes, John, 117
Hummel, Bill, 147
Hummel, John, 147
Hunt, Washington, 106
Hunter, Affiah Rich, 147
Hunter, Andrew, 147–148
Hunter, David, 147
Hurlbut, Bertha Van Vechten, 35

Hurlbut, Catharine Cuyler, 35
Hurlbut, Catherine Cuyler Van Vechten, 154
Hurlbut, Elisha, 35, 148, 154
Hurlbut, Jeanette Cuyler, 154
Hurst, Francis Joseph Jackson, 149
Hurst, William, 149
Hutton, Anna Viele, 149
Hutton, Elizabeth Lynott, 150
Hutton, George, 149
Hutton, Isaac, 149–150
Hyde, Edward (1st Earl of Clarendon), 65
Hyde, Edward (governor), 25

Ingraham, Christopher, 186–187
Ireland, Elias, 180
Irving, Washington, 108, 150, 152, 292
Isenberg, Nancy, 5, 148

Jackson, Andrew (father), 222
Jackson, Andrew (president, son), 191, 221–
    223, 295
Jackson, Elizabeth Hutchinson, 222
Jackson, George, 147
Jackson, Hugh, 222
Jackson, Rachel Donelson, 223
Jackson, Robert, 222
James (Duke of Albany, Duke of York, James
    II and VII), 10–14, 93, 313
James (Saint James "the Greater"), 270
James, Howard, 145
James, William, 145, 152, 172
Jansen, Roeloff, 40
Jay, John, 15, 153–154, 183, 199
Jay, Mary Van Cortlandt, 153
Jay, Peter, 153
Jefferson, Jane Randolph, 154
Jefferson, Peter, 154
Jefferson, Thomas, 70, 154–155, 191, 201,
    302
Jennings, Gerald, 140, 155–156, 175, 249
Jermain, James, 156
Jesus, 36, 253, 269, 271
Jogues, Isaac, 13
John (Saint John "the Less"), 270
Johnson, 29
Johnson, Henry (William Henry Johnson),
    139–140, 217
Johnson, Richard, 295
Joseph (Saint Joseph, father of Jesus), 271
Judson, Ichabod Lewis, 159
Judson, Nathaniel, 159

McArdell, John, 192
McArdell, Joseph, 192
McArdell, Patrick, 192
McArdle, John, 192
McArdle, Joseph, 192
McCarthy, Daniel, 259
McCartney, Chester, 193
McCarty, Thomas, 193, 219
McClellan, George, 216
McCormack, Archibald, 193–194
McCormick, Edward, 279
McCrossen, James, 194
McCrosson, John, 194
McCrosson, Mary Parker, 194
McCullough, David, 4, 110, 131, 154, 168, 241, 250, 290, 303
McDonald, Alida, 194
McDonald, Donald (grandfather), 194
McDonald, Donald (grandson), 194–195, 256
McDonald, William, 194
McEneny, John ("Jack"), 4, 13, 47, 53, 89, 131, 231, 310
McIntyre, Francis A., 264
McKinley, Nancy, 195
McKinley, William, 195
McKinley, William Jr., 80, 105, 134, 195–196, 250
McKown, John, 196
McKown, William, 196
McLean, John, 208
McTague, Charles (father), 48
McTague, Charles (son), 48
McTague, Harold, 48
McTague, Laura Cole, 48
McTague, Richard, 48
McTague, Robert, 48–49
McTague, Thomas, 48
Mead, James, 78
Meade, James, 196
Megapolensis, Johannes Jr., 28
Melville, Herman, 7, 124, 137, 292
Mercer, Ann Monro, 197
Mercer, Hugh, 197–198
Mercer, William, 197
Merlin, 189
Merwin, Jesse, 150
Metacomet (King Philip of Pokanoket), 315–316
Miller, John, 46–47
Miller, Morris, 199
Miller, Mary Forman Seymour, 199

Miller, Rutger Bleecker, 199
Milner, Elizabeth Libby Turner, 199
Milner, John, 199
Minié, Claude-Étienne, 113
Minuit, Peter, 292
Moat, Charles, 194
Monckton, Robert, 202
Monroe, Elizabeth Jones, 201
Monroe, James, 155, 191, 201–202
Monroe, Spence, 201
Montessori, Maria, 256
Montgomery, Richard, 202–203
Montgomery, Thomas, 202
Monts, Pierre Du Gua de, 59
Mooney, Charles, 47, 144, 156, 292, 318
Moore, Charles Henry, 204
Moore, Hugh, 203
Moore, James, 203
Moore, James C., 203
Moore, Jean Campbell, 20, 209
Moore, Joseph, 203–204
Moore, Levi (great-grandfather), 203
Moore, Levi (great-grandson), 204
Moore, William, 203, 209
Morgan, John, 91
Morgan, John Pierpont ("J. P."), 234–235
Morgan, John Pierpont Jr., 235
Morgan, Junius Spencer, 235
Morris, Elizabeth Murphet, 204
Morris, Gouverneur, 94
Morris, Robert, 204
Morris, Robert Jr., 204–205
Morton, Cornelia Schuyler, 205
Morton, John, 205
Morton, Maria Sophia Kempe, 205
Morton, Washington (George Washington Morton), 205
Moscow, Henry, 94–95
Mosher, 130
Motier, Gilbert du (Marquis de Lafayette), 230
Muhfelder, Grace Barnet, 27
Muhfelder, Leo, 27
Munsell, Joel, 4, 56, 115, 159, 238
Murdoch, Rupert, 228

Nabokov, Vladimir, 207
Nader, Ralph, 239
Nelson, Peter, 103
Newman, Charles, 189
Newton, Eliza Martha, 228

Newton, Horace, 228
Ney, Michel, 307
Niblock, Robert, 208
Nichols, Anna, 191
Nichols, Barnard, 191
Nicolla, Joseph, 73
Nicolls, B., 191
Nicolls, Richard, 13
Noeckle, Bernhardt, 191
Noeckle, Maria, 311
Noeckle, William, 311
Noonan, Dorothea, 208
Norcross, Joseph, 107
Norton, Samuel, 217–218
Nucella, 29

Obama, Barack, 136, 196
Obama, Michelle, 136
O'Brien, Mike, 254
O'Connell, Daniel, 94
O'Connell, Edward, 220
O'Connell, John (John No. 1), 220
O'Connell, John (John No. 2), 220
O'Connell, John (John No. 3, "Black Jack"), 220
O'Connell, John (John No. 4), 220
O'Connell, John J. ("Solly"), 220–221
O'Connell, John J. Jr., 220
O'Connell, Margaret Doyle, 220
O'Connell, Maud, 220–221
O'Connell, Patrick, 220, 262
Odell, Benjamin Barker Jr., 221
Olcott, Thomas, 22
Oliver, Aaron, 223
Oliver, G., 223
Onassis, Jacqueline Kennedy, 126
Onderdonk, Abraham, 224
Onderdonk, Adam, 224
Onderdonk, Fletcher, 224
Onderdonk, James, 224
Onderdonk, John, 224
Onderdonk, Marragrietje Van Houten, 224
Onderdonk, Peter, 224
Onderdonk, Rachel Appleby, 224
Onderdonk, Sarah, 224
O'Neil, Peter, 225
O'Reilly, Bill, 136
Orlando, 226
Ormond, James I, 227
Ormond, James II, 227
Ormond, James III, 227

Orteig, Raymond, 177
Osborne, Catharine, 227
Osceola, 257
Osgood, Charles, 117
O'Shaughnessy, Arthur, 259
Otis, James Jr., 302
Otis, Samuel, 302
Outwin, John, 166

Paddock, Howard, 228
Paddock, James, 228
Palmer, Amos, 228
Palmer, Amos Porteus, 228–229
Palmer, Clarissa Lull, 228
Palmer, Erastus Dow, 229
Palmer, John, 229
Palmer, Ray, 229
Palmer, Walter Launt, 229
Papp, John, 179, 274, 275
Parker, Amasa, 165
Parson, Frances, 245
Parson, Louis, 245
Patterson, Cornelia Bell, 275
Peale, Rembrandt, 155
Pearl (remains of woman), 215
Pearson, Jonathan, 40, 209
Pemberton, James, 288
Pendleton, Jack, 222
Penn, William (father), 232, 297
Penn, William (son), 232
Perkins, Elizabeth, 232
Perkins, John G., 232
Perkins, John H., 232
Perry, Christopher, 232
Perry, Oliver Hazard, 232–233
Perry, Sarah Wallace Alexander, 232
Philbin, Regis, 219
Picotte, Bernard, 35, 157, 311
Picotte, Clifford, 35, 127, 157, 281, 311
Picotte, Helen, 127, 281
Picotte, John D. (grandson of John David Picotte), 234
Picotte, John David (grandfather of John D. Picotte), 35, 157, 234
Picotte, Michael B., 234
Picotte, William B., 127, 234
Pierce, Carlisle, 54
Pierce, Franklin, 137
Pierce, Waldo, 150
Pierpont, Juliet, 235
Pilsbury, Louis Dwight ("L. D."), 130, 172

Plotnik, Art, 127
Polk, James, 295
Pollak, Michael, 185
Polychronia, 270
Pontiac, 19
Pope Gregory IX, 270
Pope Pius XII, 264
Porter, Charles, 238
Porter, David, 238–239
Porter, David Dixon, 238
Porter, Giles, 238
Porter, James, 238
Porter, Nathan, 238
Poseidon, 224
Powell, Colin, 117
Pratt, Louis, 189
Pratt, Marion, 189
Prentice, Ezra, 205
Preston, Peter, 75
Primomo, William, 81
Privler, Arthur A., 190
Privler, Ida, 190
Privler, Jason, 22
Pruyn, Alida, 240
Pruyn, Frans Janse (Francis Pruyn), 240
Pruyn, John Van Schaick Lansing ("V. L."), 240
Pruyn, Robert Clarence, 240–241, 246
Pruyn, Robert Hewson, 240
Putnam, Elizabeth Porter, 241
Putnam, Israel, 241–242, 301
Putnam, Joseph, 241

Quackenbush, Adrian, 243
Quackenbush, Anna Oothout, 242
Quackenbush, Catharina Van Schaick, 243
Quackenbush, Cornelia Bogert, 242
Quackenbush, Jannetje, 41
Quackenbush, Johannes, 242
Quackenbush, Johannes W., 243
Quackenbush, Machtelt Post, 242
Quackenbush, Margarita Bogert, 243
Quackenbush, Maria, 41, 242
Quackenbush, Neeltje Gysberts Vandenbergh, 242
Quackenbush, Neeltje Marens, 243
Quackenbush, Pieter (b. 1614), 41, 242
Quackenbush, Pieter (b. circa 1680), 243
Quackenbush, Pieter Wouter, 242
Quackenbush, Wouter Jr., 242
Quackenbush, Wouter Pieterse, 242

Quadrini, Armand, 295
Quadrini, John, 243, 249
Quadrini, Loreto, 243
Quadrini, Teresa DePalma, 243

Radcliff, Elizabeth, 217
Randolph, Martha Jefferson, 155
Rankin, Catherine, 62
Rankin, Emily, 62
Rapp, Arthur O., 245
Rathbone, Jared, 163
Rathbone, Joel, 163, 255
Rathbone, John F., 255
Rawson, Cora, 246
Rawson, Dora, 246
Rawson, George, 246
Rawson, Henry, 246
Rawson, Lucy, 246
Ray, James Earl, 95
Reddy, Bill, 193, 251
Reddy, Lillian, 193
Redmond, Kathy, 251
Redmond, Mary, 251
Redmond, Rosemary E., 193, 251
Reeves, Orlando, 227
Renodin, Anna Hogan, 246
Renodin, Joseph, 246
Renodin, Lyle F., 246–247
Renwick, James Jr., 288
Revere, Paul, 270, 301
Reynolds, Cuyler, 66, 94, 247
Reynolds, Marcus, 7, 186
Rhind, John Massey, 165, 234
Rice, Condoleezza, 219
Richard III, 223, 291
Rinella, Steven, 30
Rinkhout, Lysbeth, 55
Rittner, Don, 7, 51, 208
Robb, H., 134
Roberts, Needham, 139
Robinson, Frank, 220
Rockefeller, Nelson, 87
Roessle, Theophilus, 58
Rogan, Edward, 44
Rogers, Fred, 87
Rooney, Andy, 7
Rooney, John, 249
Roosevelt, Franklin, 7, 19, 136, 177, 272
Roosevelt, Theodore Jr., 7, 75, 80, 136, 139, 196, 221, 250
Root, Josiah, 287

Van Cortlandt, Stephen, 81
Van Curler, Arent ("Corlear"), 77
Van der Donck, Adriaan, 274
Van Guysling, Walter F., 301
Van Guysling, Walter H., 300–301
Van Halen, Pieter, 210
Van Hart, Urban, 149
Van Ingen, William, 9, 146
Van Laer, Arnold, 4
Van Orden, Edmund Henry, 296
Van Orden, Temperance Loveridge, 296
Van Orden, William, 296
Van Ostrande, Johannes, 146
Van Rensselaer, Anna Van Wely, 231, 247
Van Rensselaer, Catharina Livingston, 275, 309
Van Rensselaer, Catherine, 234
Van Rensselaer, Elizabeth Groesbeck, 275
Van Rensselaer, Engeltie Livingston, 56
Van Rensselaer, Hendrick, 296
Van Rensselaer, Jeremias, 231, 275
Van Rensselaer, John, 56
Van Rensselaer, Kiliaen (b. 1586), 13, 31, 40, 77, 209, 211, 215, 231, 247, 274, 275, 292, 296
Van Rensselaer, Kiliaen (b. 1663), 275
Van Rensselaer, Killiaen K., 7
Van Rensselaer, Margarita Schuyler, 275, 276
Van Rensselaer, Maria Pafraet, 296
Van Rensselaer, Maria van Cortlandt, 275
Van Rensselaer, Nicholas, 247
Van Rensselaer, Philip, 81, 215
Van Rensselaer, Philip Kiliaen, 62
Van Rensselaer, Stephen I, 275
Van Rensselaer, Stephen II, 186, 275
Van Rensselaer, Stephen III, 180, 275, 276, 315
Van Rensselaer, Stephen IV, 96, 186, 276, 308–309
Van Schaick, Engeltie, 235
Van Schoick, Charles, 135, 245, 297
Van Schoick, George, 27, 297
Van Schoick, Katie, 27
Van Schoick, Kitty Wormer, 297
Van Tassel, Katrina, 150
Van Twiller, Wouter, 13, 292
Van Vechten, Abraham, 308
Van Vechten, Catherine Cuyler Gansevoort, 309
Van Vechten, Elizabeth De Wandelaer, 308

Van Vechten, Teunis, 35, 148, 154, 190, 272, 308–309
Van Vechten, Teunis T., 308
Van Woert, Rutger Jacobse, 297
Van Zandt, Johannes, 297–298
Vander Veer, James, 132
Vanderpoel, Margarita, 297
Vasiliev, Ren, 42
Vassar, Ann Bennett, 298
Vassar, James, 298
Vassar, Matthew, 298
Vatrano, Frank J., 298
Vedder, Johannes Symonse, 194
Venema, Janny, 4
Vernon, Edward, 303
Verplanck, Abraham Issacse, 299
Verplanck, Isaac, 299
Verplanck, Margarita Schuyler, 71
Verplanck, Maria Vigne, 299
Victoria, Alexandrina (Queen Victoria, Empress of India), 299–300
Vine, Rebecca, 119
Von Dorrien, Sophus, 130
Vos, Andries de ("The Old Fox"), 249

Wait, 27
Waite, Diana, 12, 47, 145, 268
Waite, Morrison, 21
Wakeley, William, 130
Walden, Laura, 120
Walley, Matilda, 224
Walsh, Dudley, 219
Walsh, William, 219
Wansboro, Thomas, 259
Ward, Nancy, 103
Warren, James, 302
Warren, Joseph (father), 301
Warren, Joseph (son), 112, 301–302
Warren, Mary Stevens, 301
Warren, Mercy Otis, 301
Washington, Augustine, 303
Washington, Denzel, 117
Washington, George, 10, 15, 16, 26, 130, 131, 158, 168, 179, 190, 198, 201, 213, 225, 234, 276, 289, 302–304
Washington, Martha, 302, 303
Washington, Mary Ball, 198, 303
Waterman, Guy, 74
Waterman, Laura, 74
Webber, John, 223
Webster, Charles R., 305

Zaretski, Joseph, 208
Zebedee, 270

Zeus, 224
Zuckerberg, Mark, 136

STREET INDEX

Genesee Street (Albany), 126, 200, 213
Genesee Street (Boston), 167
Georgetown Court, 126
Gingerbread Lane, 127, 281
Gipp Road, 127
Glendale Avenue, 114, 127
Glenwood Street (Albany), 27, 102, 127, 218
Glenwood Street (McKownville), 218
Glynn Street, 18, 123, 127, 288
Golder Street, 128
Governors Lane, 318
Grafton Avenue, 23
Grain Street, 128
Grand Street, 22, 128
Grandview Terrace, 114, 128
Grant Avenue (Albany), 49, 68, 124, 128–129, 173, 195, 250, 295, 302
Grant Avenue (Glens Falls), 68
Grass Lane, 174
Gray Fox Lane, 76, 129–130, 301
Great Western Turnpike, 309
Greeley Street, 86
Green Street, 64, 130–131, 152, 215, 312
Greene Avenue, 131
Greene Street, 131
Greentree Lane, 102, 131
Greenway, 131
Greenway North, 41, 114, 131
Greenway South, 114, 131
Greenway Street, 41, 119, 133, 160, 178
Greyledge Drive, 131–132
Grove Avenue, 102, 132

Hackett Boulevard, 132, 172, 178, 245
Halenbake Street, 128
Hall Place, 133
Halsdorf Street, 41, 119, 133, 160, 178
Hamilton Street, 15–16, 94, 98, 133
Hampton Street, 41, 133
Handelaars Straat, 46
Handelaers Straet, 31, 46
Handlers Street, 46
Hansen Avenue, 25, 134, 233, 252
Harding Street, 134–135, 190
Hare Street, 94, 225
Harris Avenue (Albany), 135, 245, 297
Harris Avenue (Poughkeepsie), xiii
Harrison Avenue, 68
Harrison Street, 69
Hart Street, 42
Hartman Road, 135–136

Harvard Avenue, 136
Hawk Street, 54, 94, 170, 183, 213, 217, 243
Hawke Street, 94, 213
Hawkins Avenue, 186
Hawkins Street, 104, 136–137
Hawley Street, 44, 53
Hawthorn Circle, 23, 76, 137
Hawthorne Avenue, 81, 137, 170, 197
Hazelhurst Avenue, 84, 137–138, 199, 300
Helderberg Avenue, 8, 57, 135, 138
Hemlock Lane, 138–139
Henry Johnson Boulevard, 20, 139–140
Herkimer Street, 29, 140, 154
Herring Lane, 158
Hidden Hollow Road, 141
High Dune Drive, 76, 141
High Street (Albany), 282
High Street (Poughkeepsie), xii
Highfield Lane, 141
Highland Avenue, 7, 114, 141, 199, 300
Highland Court, 114, 141
Hill Street, 60, 180
Hillcrest Avenue, 30, 141, 196, 199, 300
Hoffman Avenue, 44, 141–142, 171
Holland Avenue, 142, 172
Hollenbake Street, 128
Hollywood Avenue, 142–143
Holmes Court, 143
Holmes Dale, 143
Home Avenue, 81, 82, 143
Homestead Avenue, 47, 81, 137, 143, 170, 197, 199, 300
Homestead Street, 81, 144
Hooker Avenue, xii
Hopewell Street, 144, 190
Hopi Street, 56, 58, 144, 256, 318
Horseradish Way, 104
Howard Street, 145
Howe Street, 94
Hudson Avenue, 41, 52, 94, 145–147, 148, 215, 312
Hudson River Avenue, 200
Hudson Street, 145
Humanities Lane, 147
Hummel Terrace, 147
Hunter Avenue, 71, 147–148, 159, 246, 305
Hunter S Alley, 148, 308
Hunter Street, 147–148
Hurlbut Street, 31, 35, 148, 154, 190, 272, 308
Huron Avenue, 58, 149

Twiller Street, 35, 77, 154, 190, 292, 308
Twitchell Street, 42, 52, 69, 292–293, 305, 314
Tyler Street, 69

Union Drive, 52, 78, 136, 218, 227, 239, 293, 298, 317
United Way, 293
University Place, 294
Upton Road, 294
Utica Street, 167

Valleyview Drive, 114, 294
Van Allen Place, 281, 294–295
Van Buren Street (Albany), 49, 68, 124, 128, 173, 195, 250, 295–296, 302
Van Buren Street (Troy), 69
Van Driesen Street, 130
Van Orden Avenue, 296
Van Rensselaer Boulevard, 131, 296
Van Schaick Street, 201
Van Schee Street, 29, 140
Van Schoick Avenue, 54, 135, 245, 297, 298
Van Tromp Street, 3, 297
Van Vechten Street, 116
Van Woert Street, 158, 297
Van Zandt Street, 297–298
Vassar Drive, 52, 78, 136, 218, 227, 239, 293, 298, 317
Vatrano Lane, 298
Vatrano Road, 298
Ver Planck Street, 86, 87, 172, 298–299
Veterans Way, 299
Victor Street, 156, 299
Victoria Way, 54, 63, 87, 117, 162, 189, 271, 299–300, 314
View Avenue, 114, 300
Villa Avenue, 199, 300
Vine Street, 63, 237, 300
Vossen Kill Road, 248

Wall Street (Albany), 94, 225
Wall Street (New York City), 79
Walter Street, 184, 300–301
Waltham Avenue, 23
Wansboro Avenue, 259
Warbler Way, 54, 76, 301
Warren Street, 94, 106, 112, 173, 301–302
Washington Avenue (Albany), 2, 17, 44, 49, 68, 94, 124, 128, 173, 195, 250, 278, 295, 302–304, 310

Washington Avenue (Defreestville), 210
Washington Avenue Extension, 212, 302–304
Washington Park Road, 8
Washington Place, 69
Washington Square, 302–304
Washington Street (Albany), 214
Washington Street (Troy), 69
Water Street, 88, 244, 256, 304–305
Watervliet Avenue, 71, 126, 147, 159, 246, 305
Watervliet Avenue Extension, 305
Wayne Street, 108
Webber Avenue, 223
Webster Street, 42, 52, 69, 293, 305–306, 314
Weis Court, 306
Weis Road, 306
Wellington Avenue, 199, 300, 306–307
Wendell Street, 307
West Carillon Drive, 98–99, 307
West Center Drive, 59, 307
West End Alley, 307–308
West Erie Street, 111, 308
West Ferry Street, 206
West Forty–Second Street, 285
West Lawrence Street, 15, 163, 213, 308
West Lydius Street, 23, 99
West Meadow Drive, 76, 197, 301, 308
West Old State Road, 99
West Street, 15, 101, 308
West University Drive, 101, 308
West Van Vechten Street, 35, 148, 154, 190, 272, 308–309
Westbrook Street, 309
Westerlo Street, 22, 29, 107, 309
Western Avenue, 2, 34, 51, 72, 74, 89, 141, 189, 193, 196, 268, 294, 303, 309–310
Westford Street, 310
Westmere Terrace, 127
White Oak Lane, 219–220, 310
White Pine Drive, 100–101, 310
Whitehall Court, 310
Whitehall Road, 66, 116, 120, 153, 161, 214, 245, 278, 279, 310
Whitehall Street, 310
Wilan Lane, 35, 191, 311
Wilbur Avenue, 43
Wilbur Street, 311
Wilkins Avenue, 37, 72, 193, 231, 286, 311
Willett Street (Albany), 311–312
Willett Street (New York City), 312
William Street, 122, 312

The typeface primarily used throughout this book is Melior (*melior* being Latin for "better"), invented in Frankfurt, Germany, in 1952 by Hermann Zapf (1918–2015). A master calligrapher and type designer, Zapf is credited with the design of more than thirty typefaces. Melior is known for its elegant yet straightforward design, which can be easily read in a variety of point sizes and applications, particularly in newspapers.

Chapter and subchapter titles are in Sabon typeface. Sabon was invented by the German Jan Tschichold (1902–1974) and was released in 1967. Tschichold is credited with creation of the Transit, Saskia, and Zeus typefaces as well. Sabon is named for Frenchman Jacques Sabon, former student of sixteenth-century French publisher Claude Garamond, for whom the Garamond typeface is named. The Sabon typeface is graceful yet highly readable.

Erik Schlimmer is the author of six books including *My Adirondacks*, named Best Memoir by the Adirondack Center for Writing. His passion for education has been honored with the State University of New York's Merit Award for Teaching, awarded three times, and their Outstanding Instructor of the Year Award. When he's not writing he's hiking, having covered 15,000 miles and climbed 2,000 mountains. Erik lives in the Capital Region of Upstate New York.